Second Edition

Write Time, Write Place

PARAGRAPHS AND ESSAYS

Mimi Markus

Broward College

Boston · Columbus · Indianapolis · New York · San Francisco · Upper Saddle River
Amsterdam · Cape Town · Dubai · London · Madrid · Milan · Munich · Paris · Montreal · Toronto
Delhi · Mexico City · São Paulo · Sydney · Hong Kong · Seoul · Singapore · Taipei · Tokyo

Executive Editor: Matthew Wright
Senior Development Editor: Marion Castellucci
Director of Marketing: Roxanne McCarley
Senior Supplements Editor: Donna Campion
Senior Media Producer: Sara Gordus
Content Specialist: Erin Jenkins
Production/Project Manager: Eric Jorgensen
Project Coordination and Text Design: Electronic Publishing Services Inc., NYC
Electronic Page Makeup: Laserwords Pvt. Ltd.
Senior Cover Design Manager: John Callahan
Cover Designer: John Callahan
Cover Image: © Adrianna Williams/Corbis
Senior Manufacturing Buyer: Roy L. Pickering, Jr.
Printer/Binder: Courier/Kendallville
Cover Printer: Lehigh-Phoenix Color/Hagerstown

Credits and acknowledgments borrowed from other sources and reproduced, with permission, in this textbook appear on the appropriate page within text or on page 599.

10 9 8 7 6 5 4 3 2—V011—16 15 14

Student ISBN 10:   0-321-90850-3

ISBN 13: 978-0-321-90850-6

ALC ISBN 10:   0-321-90848-1

ISBN 13: 978-0-321-90848-3

www.pearsonhighered.com

Contents

A Message to Students

The founder of McDonald's, Roy Kroc, once said that "The two most important requirements for major success are: first, being in the right place at the right time, and second, doing something about it." "Being in the right place at the right time" means to be in a position or place where something good may happen. Some people call it luck. For example, suppose the psychology course you want to take is full, but when you check again you find that someone has dropped the course and you are able to register for it. You were in the right place at the right time.

The title of this book, *Write Time, Write Place,* is a play on these words. As you read this text, know that this is the right time to learn to write at the college level. The right place is the space where learning happens—in a classroom, online, in a discussion group, or at a lecture. It is also a place in your mind where you learn, think about, and analyze ideas and prepare to share them with others in your college community. You are in the right place at the right time.

But being in the right place at the right time is, according to Ray Kroc, only the first requirement for major success. The second part is "doing something about it." That means using *Write Time, Write Place* to learn and practice the most important skill associated with college success, **writing.** This text will prepare you for the writing assignments you will encounter in your college courses. It will help you to write well-developed paragraphs and essays using correct grammar and punctuation. It will also give you the opportunity to read material from college courses such as psychology, sociology, criminal justice, and business.

So, you are at the right place, and it's the right time. Now it's up to you to take advantage of this opportunity and achieve "major success" in your college career.

MIMI MARKUS

Preface

How do you prepare your students for the demands of the writing and reading assignments they will encounter in their college-level courses? This is the question I struggled with when choosing developmental writing textbooks and creating syllabi. Is teaching them basic writing, grammar, punctuation, and mechanics skills enough?

Through my experience teaching writing as part of a learning community team, I learned that this was not enough. Of the four classes students were taking, only one was a college-level course, music appreciation. Students soon realized that this course required more effort than they expected; for example, they had trouble understanding the textbook and were overwhelmed by the number of new terms they had to learn. Writing assignments were challenging, too. I seized the opportunity to help students by integrating the material from the music appreciation course into class discussions, reading, and writing assignments.

Through this experience, I realized that developmental writing students needed to be exposed to college-level reading material from a variety of college disciplines *as early as possible*. It was this experience that inspired me to write the *Write Time, Write Place* series. *Write Time, Write Place* uses textbook excerpts from across the disciplines to provide an academic context for instruction, exercises, and writing activities. These excerpts show students how academic writing is organized, give them practice reading and responding to college-level material, increase their general knowledge, and perhaps create an interest in enrolling in courses they might not have considered. In addition, the text enhances student learning through a structured step-by-step approach to the writing process, graphic organizers for planning writing, abundant writing opportunities, and simple, straightforward grammar instruction.

However, a textbook can only do so much. It is up to us as instructors to bring the concepts and content to life in ways that will be meaningful to our students. *Write Time, Write Place* is a flexible resource that supports a variety of instructional techniques to engage students and promote effective learning and understanding.

What's New in the Second Edition?

Deeper MyWritingLab Integration New to this edition, resources and assessment designed specifically for *Write Time, Write Place* are in MyWritingLab along with the etext and all the diagnostic, practice, and assessment resources of MyWritingLab. Students can use MyWritingLab to access media resources, practice, and assessment for each chapter of *Write Time, Write Place*. When they see this logo **MyWritingLab™** in the text, students have the option of completing the activity online right in MyWritingLab. Practice assessments will flow to the instructor gradebook in MyWritingLab, reducing grading time and allowing instructors to focus attention on students who may need extra help and practice.

- All QuickWrites and many Writing Assignments can be completed in MyWritingLab, giving students access to a wide range of customizable instruction, practice, and assessment.
- All the blank graphic organizers in the text also appear in MyWritingLab in interactive form. Students can develop their paragraphs and essays using the graphic organizers as planning tools.

A New Chapter, "Correcting Sentence Errors" Sentence errors are among the most common and most serious errors that student writers make. A new chapter shows students how to identify and correct fragments, run-ons, and comma splices. A variety of exercises helps students apply what they have learned (Ch. 21).

A New Reader-Response Activity In each of the writing chapters and after each reading in the end-of-book readings section, a new activity called Reader Response gives students an opportunity to practice both reading and writing by responding to a textbook passage, essay, article, or student writing.

New Coverage of Writing a Summary-Response Essay The first edition's coverage of writing a summary essay has been expanded to include writing a response as well. Students are shown how to summarize a selection and also how to write about their reactions to it. Besides learning how to connect a text to themselves, they learn to connect text-to-text and text-to-world (Ch. 16). Expanded instruction on identifying and correcting plagiarism helps students avoid this problem in their own summaries.

New and Redesigned Graphic Organizers In the writing chapters, several new graphic organizers along with others that have been redesigned help students break down the writing process into manageable steps. Students benefit from making decisions about how to plan and organize details for paragraphs and essays. New examples of students using the essay organizers have been added. In the end-of-book reading selections, organizers assist in processing information, improving reading comprehension, and reading to learn.

New High-interest Readings The paragraphs and essays in the instructional chapters and the end-of-book readings enhance the text's emphasis on academic writing. More than half of the end-of-book readings, which pair a textbook passage with an essay or article on the same topic in an academic discipline, have been replaced with readings on topics such as being single, the science of attraction, and the mind-body connection.

Features of *Write Time, Write Place*

Write Time, Write Place includes all the elements that students and instructors need to succeed in today's writing classroom (and beyond).

Write Time, Write Place and *MyWritingLab* Provide a Framework for Learning

Learning Objectives Students learn better when they have a clear understanding of what they are expected to master. Learning objectives at the beginning of each chapter give students an overview of what they will accomplish by working through the chapter. To provide further guidance, each objective is keyed to a section of the chapter.

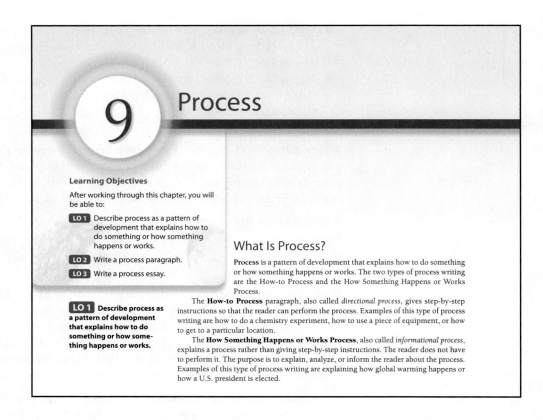

9 Process

Learning Objectives

After working through this chapter, you will be able to:

LO 1 Describe process as a pattern of development that explains how to do something or how something happens or works.

LO 2 Write a process paragraph.

LO 3 Write a process essay.

LO 1 **Describe process as a pattern of development that explains how to do something or how something happens or works.**

What Is Process?

Process is a pattern of development that explains how to do something or how something happens or works. The two types of process writing are the How-to Process and the How Something Happens or Works Process.

The **How-to Process** paragraph, also called *directional process*, gives step-by-step instructions so that the reader can perform the process. Examples of this type of process writing are how to do a chemistry experiment, how to use a piece of equipment, or how to get to a particular location.

The **How Something Happens or Works Process**, also called *informational process*, explains a process rather than giving step-by-step instructions. The reader does not have to perform it. The purpose is to explain, analyze, or inform the reader about the process. Examples of this type of process writing are explaining how global warming happens or how a U.S. president is elected.

MyWritingLab™

Complete this activity at mywritinglab.com

Practice and Assessment Each chapter's activities and practices are designed to test whether students have achieved the chapter's objectives. Students can complete many of the text's exercises online in MyWritingLab. They can also write and submit their paragraphs and essays online.

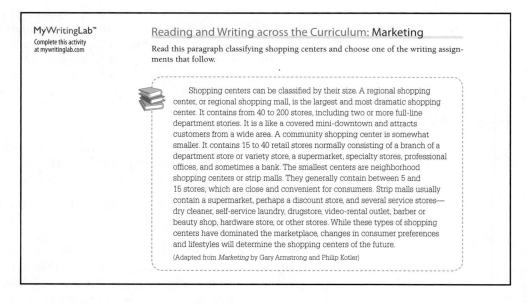

MyWritingLab™

Complete this activity at mywritinglab.com

Reading and Writing across the Curriculum: Marketing

Read this paragraph classifying shopping centers and choose one of the writing assignments that follow.

Shopping centers can be classified by their size. A regional shopping center, or regional shopping mall, is the largest and most dramatic shopping center. It contains from 40 to 200 stores, including two or more full-line department stories. It is a like a covered mini-downtown and attracts customers from a wide area. A community shopping center is somewhat smaller. It contains 15 to 40 retail stores normally consisting of a branch of a department store or variety store, a supermarket, specialty stores, professional offices, and sometimes a bank. The smallest centers are neighborhood shopping centers or strip malls. They generally contain between 5 and 15 stores, which are close and convenient for consumers. Strip malls usually contain a supermarket, perhaps a discount store, and several service stores— dry cleaner, self-service laundry, drugstore, video-rental outlet, barber or beauty shop, hardware store, or other stores. While these types of shopping centers have dominated the marketplace, changes in consumer preferences and lifestyles will determine the shopping centers of the future.

(Adapted from *Marketing* by Gary Armstrong and Philip Kotler)

MyWritingLab™

Use the interactive graphic organizer at mywritinglab.com

Graphic Organizers As a complement to the step-by-step instruction, numerous graphic organizers provide visual tools for students to use in prewriting and planning their paragraphs and essays. Interactive versions of the graphic organizers are also available in MyWritingLab so students can plan and develop their writing online.

Classification Essay Graphic Organizer

MyWritingLab™
Use the interactive graphic
organizer at mywritinglab.com

Introduction

Lead-in:

Bridge:

Thesis Statement:

Body Paragraphs

Body Paragraph 1

Topic Sentence for Group 1:

Description:

   Details:

Body Paragraph 2

Topic Sentence for Group 2:

Description:

   Details:

Body Paragraph 3

Topic Sentence for Group 3:

Description:

   Details:

Conclusion

Effective Closing Technique:

Concluding Statement:

MyWritingLab™

MyWritingLab's Additional Resources What makes MyWritingLab so effective?

- **Diagnostic Testing:** MyWritingLab's diagnostic test comprehensively assesses students' skills in grammar. Students can be given an individualized learning path based on the diagnostic's results, identifying the areas where they most need help. These areas can be added to the *Write Time, Write Place* module for additional study and practice.
- **Progressive Learning:** The heart of MyWritingLab is the progressive learning that takes place as students complete the Recall, Apply, and Write exercises within each topic. Students move from literal comprehension (Recall) to critical understanding (Apply) to the ability to demonstrate a skill in their own writing (Write). This progression of critical thinking, not available in any other online resource, enables students to truly master the skills and concepts they need to become successful writers.

- **Online Gradebook:** All student work in MyWritingLab is captured in the Online Gradebook. Students can monitor their own progress through reports explaining their scores on the exercises in the course. Instructors can see which topics their students have mastered and access other detailed reports, such as class summaries, that track the development of their entire class and display useful details on each student's progress.
- **eText:** The *Write Time, Write Place: Paragraphs and Essays* eText is accessed through MyWritingLab. Students now have the eText at their fingertips while completing the various exercises and activities within MyWritingLab. Students can highlight important material in the eText and add notes to any section for reflection and/or study throughout the semester.

Write Time, Write Place Sets the Stage for College Success

An Introductory Chapter on College Writing The expectations of college professors and the nature of college assignments are introduced in Chapter 1, "Writing in College," along with the importance of writing in Standard Written English. A discussion of appropriate language choices help students understand the need to adjust their written language for college assignments. These fundamentals are carried through in the rest of the text's instruction.

---

4 CHAPTER 1 Writing in College

College Writing Assignments

LO 2 Choose the appropriate form of written English for different types of writing assignments.

You can expect to have many different kinds of writing assignments in college, not only in your English composition classes but in your other classes, too. These writing assignments have specific purposes and can be divided into two general groups: informal and formal. In all assignments, you will be expected to use Standard Written English.

Informal Writing Assignments

Some writing assignments in college will be informal. These assignments are generally short, require less planning, and may be done in class or for homework. For instance, in your English course, your teacher may ask you to keep a journal or blog, review other students' writing, or participate in an electronic discussion. In other classes, informal writing assignments may include response papers, reading notes, interviews, or scenarios.

The following chart summarizes some of the types of informal writing assignments you may be asked to complete.

English Success Tip: Paragraph Length

Many students want to be told the exact number of sentences that a paragraph should have. Requiring a specific number of sentences, a percentage of a page, or a word count does not address the purpose of a paragraph: to make a point and support it fully.

A paragraph of two or three sentences is likely to be too short and does not give enough support. On the other hand, a paragraph can be too long. This can happen when the topic is too broad, when the writer offers too many details, or the writer repeats details.

A successful paragraph will be the right length when it supports a narrowed topic with adequate and relevant details.

English Success Tips
Chapters 1-17 conclude with suggestions for improving students' study skills, mastery of English, and their performance in English courses. Topics include guidelines for emailing instructors, manuscript formatting, use of spell-check software, writing improvement logs, learning journals, and portfolios.

Write Time, Write Place Provides Academic Models of Writing

To expose students to college writing and subject matter, many paragraph- and passage-length examples from textbooks are provided to illustrate the patterns of development. In addition, textbook excerpts are used as writing prompts and in grammar practices. The use of authentic college materials provides contextual basic skills instruction.

The Oxbow captures the Catskill Mountains scene after the storm by presenting themes of light and dark. In the left side of the painting, Cole depicts the wilderness. The two trees at the left have been blasted by lightning. The forest is dense and frightening, and a thunderstorm rolls across the mountainous landscape. This wild scene contrasts dramatically with the civilized valley floor on the right. Here, bathed in serene sunlight, are cultivated fields, hillsides cleared of timber, and farmhouses from whose chimneys rise gentle plumes of smoke. The Connecticut River itself flows in a giant arc that reinforces the tranquility of the scene. Cole's umbrella juts out across the river from the rock at the right. Just below it, to the left, is Cole himself, now at work at his easel. The furious forces of nature have moved on, and the artist captures the scene just as civilization would tame the wild.

(Adapted from *A World of Art* by Henry M. Sayre)

Write Time, Write Place Provides Many Opportunities to Practice and Write

Engaging and Various Writing Prompts Today's students need a variety of topics to write about. Although many enjoy writing about themselves, personal writing does not appeal to everyone, particularly those who are uncomfortable sharing their lives, whether for cultural or confidentiality reasons. Thus, in addition to providing suggestions for personal writing, *Write Time, Write Place* provides a variety of writing options:

- **QuickWrites** encourage spontaneous writing in response to a question or topic.
- **Paragraph Practices** provide step-by-step guidance for students for prewriting, planning, drafting, revising, and editing their own paragraphs.
- **Reading and Writing across the Curriculum** has students read a textbook paragraph and then write in response.
- **Comment on a Contemporary Issue** offers topical prompts for persuasive writing.
- **Write about an Image** offers interesting photographs and other visuals as subjects for writing.
- **Writing Paragraphs and Essays** prompts provide general and academic topic suggestions for writing.

Abundant and Varied Grammar Exercises Today's students need a variety of ways to practice new skills. To address the wide range of basic skills knowledge and learning styles, *Write Time, Write Place* offers different types of exercises for grammar, sentence skills, and punctuation. While identification and drills are useful at the beginning stages of learning, students need opportunities to make connections between the rules of Standard Written English and their application in students' own writing. Therefore, this text goes beyond drills, using continuous discourses, editing in context, sentence combining, and original sentence generation. *Write Time, Write Place* emphasizes sentence building rather than error avoidance. There are several types of exercises:

- **Practices and Activities** help students apply what they have just learned.
- **Help Desks** ask students to edit or improve the work of others.
- **Group Activities** promote collaborative learning and writing.
- **Writing Assignments** ask students to practice a grammar or sentence skill through original writing.

Developmental Writing Resources

Book-Specific Ancillary Material

Annotated Instructor's Edition for Write Time, Write Place: Paragraphs and Essays, 1/e (ISBN 0-321-90855-4). The Annotated Instructor's Edition for Write Time, Write Place includes general teaching tips, guidance on tailoring instruction for English language learners, and answers to the exercises, all on page for ease of reference.

Instructor's Manual/Test Bank for Write Time, Write Place: Paragraphs and Essays, 1/e (ISBN 0-321-90852-X). Prepared by Caroline Seefchak, Edison State College, and Mimi Markus, and available online in the Instructors Resource Center, the Instructor's Manual/Test Bank offers additional material to help instructors meet their course objectives. The manual follows the learning objectives established in the text, offers information on teaching developmental college students, includes material for quizzes, and provides graphic organizers in support of the various writing types and genres outlined in the text.

PowerPoint Presentation for Write Time, Write Place, 2/e (ISBN 0-321-90851-1). A chapter-by-chapter set of slides is available to adopters for download from the Instructor Resource Center.

Answer Key for Write Time, Write Place, 2/e (ISBN 0-321-95920-5). The Answer Key contains the solutions to the exercises in the student edition of the text. Available for download from the Instructor Resource Center.

Additional Instructor Resources

The Pearson Writing Package Pearson is pleased to offer a variety of support materials to help make teaching writing easier for teachers and to help students excel in their coursework. Many of our student supplements are available free or at a greatly reduced price when packaged with *Write Time, Write Place: Paragraphs and Essays*. Visit www.pearsonhighereducation.com, contact your local Pearson sales representative, or review a detailed listing of the full supplements package in the *Instructor's Resource Manual* for more information.

Acknowledgments

Writing *Write Time, Write Place* has been a journey and the fulfillment of a dream, which would not have been possible without the many people who have helped, supported, and inspired me.

In particular, I appreciate the comments and suggestions offered by instructors who served as reviewers at various stages of the text's development:

Susan Achziger, Community College of Aurora; Gloria Bennett, Gainesville State College; Mary Anne Bernal, San Antonio College; Amy Boltrushek, Richland College; Janice Brantley, University of Arkansas at Pine Bluff; Chris Burdett, Georgia

Perimeter College; Juan F. Calle, Broward College; April Carothers, Linn-Benton Community College; Christopher L. Costello, Reading Area Community College; Kate Cross, Phoenix College; Deborah Davis, Richland College; Marjorie Dernaika, Southwest Tennessee Community College; Kristin Marie Distel, Ashland University; Rebecca Ferguson, Springfield College; Deborah Fuller, Bunker Hill Community College; Anthony C. Gargano, Long Beach City College; Alexandros Goudas, Darton College; Angela Lucas Green, Troy University; Bill W. Hall, St. Petersburg College; Jane Hasting, Cleveland State Community College; Matthew Horton, Gainesville State College; Mary Jenson, Hawkeye Community College; Cheryta Jones, Southwest Tennessee Community College; Laura Kingston, South Seattle Community College; James M. Landers, Community College of Philadelphia; Maria Garcia Landry, Palm Beach State College; Marilyn Lancaster, Tarrant County College, South; Angie Lazarus, Bevill State Community College (Sumiton); Shannon Lerro, Terra Community College; Gina Mackenzie, Community College of Philadelphia; Peter M. Marcoux, El Camino College; Erin T. Martz, Northern Virginia Community College; James S. May, Valencia Community College; Judy McKenzie, Lane Community College; Patricia A. Meadows, University of Arkansas at Pine Bluff; Terry Meyer, Terra Community College; Catherine Moran, Bristol County Community College; Erin Nelson, Blinn College; Brit Osgood-Treston, Riverside Community College; Eldo Ostaitile, Volunteer State Community College; Irene M. Pace, Camden County College; Marcus Patton, Sacramento City College; Linda Paule, Terra Community College; Kelly Pietrucha, Camden County College; Paula Porter, Keiser University; Ashford University; Sharon Rinkiewicz, Broward College (Central); Rebecca Samberg, Housatonic Community College; Desmond Sawyerr, Hillsborough Community College; Marcea Seible, Hawkeye Community College; Jeffrey Simmons, University of Maryland; Carmen Simpson, St. Petersburg College; Allyson Smith, North Georgia Tech College; Elizabeth Smith, State College of Florida—Sarasota, Manatee; Helen M. Smith (Higbee), Kentucky State University; John Stasinopoulos, College of DuPage; Trisha Travers, Penn State University (Abington); Christine M. Tutlewski, University of Wisconsin-Parkside; Arnold Wood Jr., Florida State College at Jacksonville

I got helpful, specific feedback on the manuscript from my developmental English students:

Imtieas (Adrian) Amirbaksh; Valerie Bailey; Sevin Barnes; Tiffany Brown; Tori Brown; Desiree Carter; Joseph Chen; Jackie Cineus; Joshua Cummings; Tationa Freeman; Lenz Lamisere; Kenneth Lang; Michelle McGriff; Melissa Mendez; Dashka Milus; Urzule Renosa; William Runde; Dennis Su; Jemara Smith; George Vazquez; Natasha D. Wallace; Kia White; Justin Wright

I also benefited greatly from the contributions of Sally Gearhart, English as a Second Language specialist, who reviewed the manuscript, prepared the English Language Learner Tips, and offered suggestions that helped strengthen the instruction for English language learners.

I am grateful to my Pearson team who supported me throughout the process of bringing this book to life. I appreciate executive editor Matt Wright's belief in the concept for *Write Time, Write Place* and his support for its publication and revision. Matt's knowledge of the changes occurring in the developmental English field and the needs of students and instructors across the United States have strengthened this book's features. Most importantly, I am indebted to Marion Castellucci, development editor, who with her expertise and knowledge of the field, skillfully guided me chapter by chapter. Her calm, steady demeanor and gentle nudging not only kept me on track, but also sustained me.

I also owe a debt of gratitude to the text's production team. Project editor Carrie Fox guided me through each stage of the production process, and copy editor Julie Hotchkiss checked the manuscript for clarity, consistency, and accuracy.

Many of my students deserve gratitude for their role in creating this text. First, I'm grateful to those who willingly gave me permission to use their paragraphs and essays as models and for activities; they are helping other students realize that they, too, can become effective writers. Finally, I thank all of my students who over the years have been and continue to be my greatest teachers.

MIMI MARKUS

Writing the College Paragraph and Essay

PART 1

1 Writing in College

Learning Objectives

After working through this chapter, you will be able to:

LO 1 Explain language choices for college writing.

LO 2 Choose the appropriate form of written English for different types of writing assignments.

LO 3 Describe the stages of the writing process.

Now that you are a college student, you will have to write many different kinds of papers in your courses to show what you know and how you think. For example, you may have to write essays and research papers in English class, lab reports in science class, and progress reports in a business course.

When you write at the college level, your instructors expect you to use **Standard Written English.** Standard Written English is the form of written English that is widely accepted as correct in education, publishing, government, science, and business. Standard Written English has some similarities with spoken English. However, it has its own set of rules for sentence and paragraph structure, word choice, punctuation, grammar, and spelling. You have probably learned many of these rules as you progressed through school before entering college. Your college textbooks use Standard Written English as in this example from an anthropology textbook. (**Anthropology** is the study of differences and similarities, both biological and cultural, in human populations.)

Most of us have come to depend on writing for so many things that it is hard to imagine a world without it. Yet humans spent most of their history on earth without written language and many, if not most, important human achievements happened before written language. This is not to say that writing is not important. Far more information and far more literature can be preserved for a longer period of time with a writing system. As more and more accumulated knowledge is written and stored in books, journals, and databases, attainment of literacy in those written languages will be increasingly critical to success.

(Adapted from *Anthropology* by Carol R. Ember, Melvin Ember, and Peter N. Peregrine)

Knowing how to use Standard Written English will help you succeed in college, get a job, and advance in the workplace. In fact, many employers consider writing ability an essential skill for hiring and for promotion. With the fast pace of electronic communications, the need for clear and correct writing is more important than ever before.

Language Choices for College Writing

LO 1 Explain language choices for college writing.

As a beginning college writer, you may not realize that writing the same way you talk, chat, or text message, is not appropriate for most college writing assignments.

Most spoken English is conversational. When you talk with someone, you use simple, conversational words and expressions, contractions, sounds, slang (informal expressions), and even nonstandard forms. Here is an example of one person talking to a friend:

> Well, I can't take you to school 'cause, like, I have to leave real early in the morning to make up a test, and, you know, like sometimes we have to rush because you always take like soooo long to get ready anyways. Call me, 'kay? Cool. Gotta go.

Style Reminder. To learn more about effective word choice for college writing, see Chapter 31.

In contrast, when you write for a college audience, which includes your instructor and other students, you are expected to write in a more formal style. This means that you should avoid all conversational word choices and slang. In addition, many instructors prefer that you avoid contractions. Instead of *she's, we'd, don't,* use *she is, we would, do not.* Also, avoid *you* unless you are writing instructions or directions.

ACTIVITY 1.1 Listing Popular Slang Terms

Working in small groups of two to three students, make a list of some of popular slang terms and their meanings.

ACTIVITY 1.2 Creating an Informal Word List

Create a list of words, symbols, and expressions that you use in informal emails and text messages. Next to each one, give the meaning. Show how the word is used in a sentence. Then, share your list with the other groups in your class.

ACTIVITY 1.3 Using Standard Written English Words and Expressions

Find the conversational words and expressions in these sentences. Then revise each sentence by replacing those words and expressions with Standard Written English.

1. A very dumb driving distraction for guys is hot girls.

_____

2. On Friday night, I like to hang out with my friends.

_____

3. Boy, was I wrong.

_____

4. I wasn't the best of singers, but I took a shot at it.

_____

5. Well, yes, getting my hair and nails done makes me feel happy.

_____

College Writing Assignments

LO 2 Choose the appropriate form of written English for different types of writing assignments.

You can expect to have many different kinds of writing assignments in college, not only in your English composition classes but in your other classes, too. These writing assignments have specific purposes and can be divided into two general groups: informal and formal. In all assignments, you will be expected to use Standard Written English.

Informal Writing Assignments

Some writing assignments in college will be informal. These assignments are generally short, require less planning, and may be done in class or for homework. For instance, in your English course, your teacher may ask you to keep a journal or blog, review other students' writing, or participate in an electronic discussion. In other classes, informal writing assignments may include response papers, reading notes, interviews, or scenarios.

The following chart summarizes some of the types of informal writing assignments you may be asked to complete.

Informal College Writing Assignments	
Type	**Description**
Personal journal	Write about daily events, thoughts about personal beliefs or goals, assess real-life situations
Learning journal	React to readings, lectures, instructors' questions, prepare for tests, summarize information, observe your own learning process
QuickWrite	Respond to an instructor's question about concepts presented in a class or write to get ideas
Scenario	Apply knowledge and creativity to respond to an imaginary situation
Blog	Publish your thoughts on a blogging website for personal or class electronic discussions
Field notes	Write about what occurred during observation
Course notes	Take notes on important points given in class or from the textbook and outside readings

 ACTIVITY

1.4   **Using a Learning Journal**

Practice writing a learning journal entry by answering this question: What is the most important thing you learned from your English class discussion or lesson from Chapter 1 of this textbook?

Formal Writing Assignments

Most of your writing assignments in college will be formal and challenging. Your current English course is preparing you to do the different types of writing assignments through practice with writing the college-level paragraph, essay, and summary, and by reviewing grammar, punctuation, and mechanics.

As you take required courses for your major and optional courses (electives), you will learn the vocabulary, the content, and the style of writing needed to communicate in those subjects through your instructor's lectures, the textbook, and outside readings. The following chart summarizes a few of the types of formal writing assignments you may encounter in college.

Formal College Writing Assignments	
Type	**Description**
Summary	Select and present the most important points in a reading
Review	Summarize, analyze, and evaluate a book, article, film, or other work
Review of the literature in a particular field	Summarize and compare published information and research in a subject area
Argument	Take a position on an issue, present evidence to support your position, answer any opposing points of view, and convince your reader
Lab report	Write about a scientific experiment, describing the methods used, the results, and their significance
Proposal for research	Identify a topic to research, and develop a plan and method for researching it
Research paper	Read and select evidence from the writing of experts to support your topic through analysis or argument

ACTIVITY

1.5

Investigating Formal Writing for a Course

Talk to an instructor at your school who teaches a college-level course in a field you are interested in to find out what types of formal writing assignments he or she gives. First, with your class or in small groups, create a list of questions to ask the instructor, such as the types of papers assigned, the average length, and the required research, if any. After collecting your information, give a brief oral report to the class or write a paragraph about what you found.

The Writing Process

LO 3 **Describe the stages of the writing process.**

Writing at the college level is challenging. It requires a conscious effort and lots of practice. Knowing how to use the writing process will help you manage any writing assignment.

Researchers who study the way people write have discovered that most writers go through a similar process. The **writing process** consists of stages that writers use to compose: prewriting, organizing and drafting, revising, and proofreading and editing. The graphic below gives you an overview of these stages.

Stages of the Writing Process

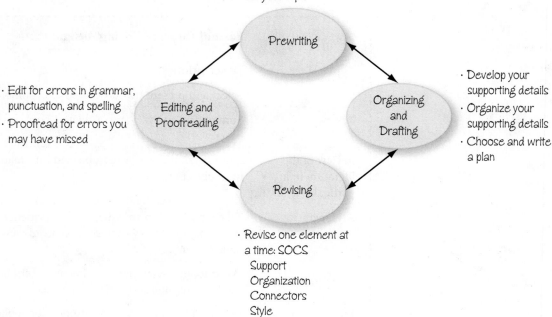

· Understand your topic, purpose, audience, and point of view
· Develop ideas for your topic
· Narrow your topic

· Develop your supporting details
· Organize your supporting details
· Choose and write a plan

· Edit for errors in grammar, punctuation, and spelling
· Proofread for errors you may have missed

· Revise one element at a time: SOCS
  Support
  Organization
  Connectors
  Style

The writing process is not a formula with steps that must be followed in order. Writers tend to switch back and forth through the various stages of the process. By learning about and practicing each stage in the process, you will discover what works best for you.

MyWritingLab™
Complete this activity at mywritinglab.com

QuickWrite

Take a moment and write about the process you use when you write.

Writing Assignments

Help Desk

Chris wrote the following email and sent it to his teacher. Notice his use of English. Answer the questions that follow the email.

| Send | Save Now | Discard | Draft autosaved at 2:30 PM (1 minute ago) |

To: Prof Markus

Add Cc | Add Bcc

Subject: i am going to miss class today

Attach a file

B *I* U F· T· T T ☺ ⊕ ≣ ≣ ≣ ≣ ❝ ≣ ≣ ≣ I **Check Spelling** ▼
« Plain Text

Hello Teacher, i'm one of your students but i missed monday day one.
Honest mistake, I left the dentists around 11am rushed to class and
i went to the wrong class (Honest mistake) i thought i had reading class
first all because of rushing. I went to your classroom after reading but
know one was there. I know im two days late but don't take my
actions the wrong way please. I probably missed alot for the first day,
i was wondering if you can send me some paper work or tell me
what i need for the next class.
Thankyou so much. Chris.

| Send | Save Now | Discard | Draft autosaved at 2:30 PM (1 minute ago) |

1. Has Chris considered his audience? What advice would you give him?

_____

_____

_____

2. Rewrite the email.

_____

_____

_____

_____

Reading and Writing across the Curriculum: Anthropology

Spanglish is a combination of English and Spanish. Spanglish is an example of **codeswitching**, the use of more than one language in a conversation.

 Codeswitching involves a great deal of knowledge of two or more languages and an awareness of what is considered appropriate or inappropriate in a community. For example, in the Puerto Rican community in New York City, codeswitching within the same sentence seems to be common in speech among friends, but if a stranger who looks like a Spanish speaker approaches, the language will shift entirely to Spanish.

(From *Anthropology* by Carol R. Ember, Melvin Ember, and Peter N. Peregrine)

What codeswitching do you do? Observe yourself and others in conversation over a period of several days. You can include text messaging and instant messaging as a form of conversation. Write down whom you spoke to, the situation, and the type of language you used. What did you notice?

Write a paragraph explaining how you change your word choice and speaking style depending on your situation. Use the examples that you noted from your own observations.

MyWritingLab™
Complete this activity
at mywritinglab.com

Comment on a Contemporary Issue

Many educators and parents are concerned that text messaging is hurting students' language skills. Others believe that it is actually increasing reading and writing skills. What do you think? Write a paragraph explaining your point of view.

English Success Tip: You Are What You Email: Guidelines for Emailing Your Instructor

Over the course of a semester, you may need to email your instructor. The informal style of emails and text messages you write to friends and family may not be appropriate in an email to the instructor. For example, Chris's email on page 7 shows how *not* to write an email to your instructor.

To give your instructor a good impression of you, keep the following guidelines in mind when emailing:

- **Subject line.** Write a specific subject including your course number, title, and meeting time.
- **Salutation.** Begin with the instructor's name as written on your syllabus, such as "Hi Professor Benjamin."
- **Body of email.** Identify yourself as a student in your instructor's class, and then present your problem or concern in an organized way. Be respectful and polite; do not use offensive language. Use proper spelling, grammar, and punctuation. Avoid abbreviations and emoticons if your professor does not like them.
- **Conclusion.** End with a sentence of appreciation, such as "I appreciate your time." Write your first and last name.

Finally, think about your reason for emailing. Use email for important issues; otherwise, wait to see your instructor in class.

2 Prewriting the Paragraph

Learning Objectives

After working through this chapter, you will be able to:

LO 1 Explain what an academic paragraph is and describe its three parts.

LO 2 Use prewriting strategies to explore a topic.

LO 3 Narrow your topic before writing.

LO 4 Write an effective topic sentence.

What Is an Academic Paragraph?

The **academic paragraph** is a unit of writing with an organized group of sentences that logically develop one main point. The academic paragraph has a distinct appearance and specific parts.

---

1 in. top margin

McLemore 1

Desiree McLemore

Professor Markus

English 25

March 13, 2014

Brown Skin and an Accent

½ in.

Because I have brown-colored skin and a Spanish accent, I have been **stereotyped.** For example, some people think that all people from Latin America have the same personality. When I was working for Company X, one of my regional managers called me "firecracker." I was a little surprised about this term, and I asked her why she called me that name. She told me that I had a bad temper and that bad tempers were common in Latin people. I explained to her that I always speak out when I do not agree with something, just like the other employees. My personality has nothing to do with my country of origin. Because of her belief, I had problems getting a promotion. Everybody in the company thought that I had a bad temper until they got to know me and realized that I was just like everyone else.

1 in. left and right margins

to stereotype
to have an often unfair and untrue belief about people or things from a certain group

Double-space

LO 1 Explain what an academic paragraph is and describe its three parts.

Parts of the Academic Paragraph

The academic paragraph has three parts:

1. **Topic Sentence** The topic sentence states the narrowed topic and the point the writer will prove.
2. **Supporting Details** The supporting details make up the body of the paragraph. Supporting details contain the specific information that the writer uses to explain, prove, describe, or analyze the point stated in the topic sentence.
3. **Concluding Sentence** The concluding sentence draws the paragraph to a close.

The following is an example showing the parts of an academic paragraph:

Topic sentence

Supporting details

Concluding sentence

> **Different people can actually taste the same food very differently, depending on their "taster" status. One-third of all Americans are "super-tasters," people who are extra-sensitive to the taste of food, especially bitterness. Super-tasters seem to have a particularly strong ability to taste bitterness in certain foods such as broccoli, coffee, grapefruit juice, green tea, spinach, and alcoholic beverages. They have more food dislikes, and are more likely to ask for sauce and dressings on the side. Another one-third are in an average range, dubbed "tasters." Moderately sensitive tasters tend to think about food in the most positive way of all three groups; chefs are most likely to be moderate tasters. The final group, the "non-tasters," have less-than-average taste sensitivity. Non-tasters are the most likely to prefer food that is intensely sweet. Women are more likely to be super-tasters, as are Asians and Africans. Knowing a person's taster status can help him or her decide which foods to choose or avoid.**
>
> (Adapted from *Food and Nutrition for You* by Suzanne Weixel and Faithe Wempen)

ACTIVITY 2.1 Identifying the Parts of the Paragraph

Identify the three parts of student Sang-Don Lee's paragraph. Underline the topic sentence once, and the concluding sentence twice. Then circle three main supporting details.

As a native speaker of Korean, learning English has been difficult. First of all, the Korean language does not have prepositions and articles. Therefore, I have no idea what they mean in sentences. For example, during my first English class, the teacher said she was looking for me. I visited her office and asked her, "Why were you looking at me?" The teacher said, "I was not looking at you. I was looking for you, Don." She then explained the difference between "look for" and "look at." My face turned red as a beet, and I felt sorry because it was impolite. Also, the Korean language has characters, not an alphabet. English sounds f, p, r, v, x, and z do not exist. Often, people do not understand my pronunciation. For example, when I took a vision test for my driver's license, I could not pronounce the Z sound correctly. I told the officer I could not make that sound, but I drew the letter for him. He said, "Follow me! Z." That was how I learned the Z sound. Another problem is that English idioms are confusing. To illustrate, when I went to a restroom, my friend said, "Hey, Don, your fly is open!" I asked, "What! Is a fly open?" I did not understand. I thought he meant the fly as an insect. After I found out what he meant, I felt a bit ashamed. Learning English continues to be difficult, but I am improving.

Prewriting

LO 2 **Use prewriting strategies to explore a topic.**

When you get your paragraph assignment, you need to understand what you are being asked to write about, who will read what you write, and what your purpose is for writing.

Understand Your Topic

Your instructor may assign a topic, give you a list of topics to choose from, or ask you to choose your own. The **topic** is the subject you have been asked to write about.

The topic can be assigned in the form of a question, a phrase, or several sentences.

Question	What are some money-saving ideas for college students?
Phrase	Money-Saving Ideas for College Students
Several Sentences	With rising costs of college tuition and living expenses, students do not have a lot of money. This makes managing money a challenge. To save money, students need to become aware of how they spend money every day. Write a paragraph about some ways students can save money.

Read your assigned topic carefully to be sure that you understand it. Look up any words you do not know. If you are not sure how to approach the subject, ask your instructor for some guidance. If you are asked to pick your own topic, find something that is interesting to you and relevant to your studies or your life.

ACTIVITY   **Asking Questions about a Topic**

2.2   Assume that you were assigned the topic Money-Saving Ideas for College Students on a Budget, but you have some questions about it. Write your questions.

Understand Your Purpose

The **purpose** is your reason for writing. Assignments have different purposes. For example, you may be asked to explain how something works, tell a story, give examples, or compare two things. In Part 2 of this textbook, you will be learning about the different purposes for writing and the patterns for organizing your writing.

Understand Your Audience

The **audience** is the person or group who will read your writing. Knowing your audience helps you decide what to say and how to say it. In your English class, most of the time you will be writing for your instructor and your classmates. When planning your writing, think about connecting with your readers by answering these questions:

- What does my audience already know about my topic?
- How can I organize my writing so that my audience will understand what I write?
- What do I want my audience to think of me?

 ACTIVITY   **Learning about Your Audience**

2.3   Try this activity to learn more about your audience: your teacher and the students in your class. On a small piece of paper or a 3" × 5" card, write four things that the people in your class do not know about you. Do not write your name on the paper or card. Form groups of four or five people. Choose one person to conduct the activity. That person will read one item on the card at a time to see if anyone in the group can guess who is being described. If no one can guess, then the person will self-identify.

Understand Your Point of View

Point of view is the approach you use: first, second, or third person. The following chart explains the three points of view:

Point of View		
Person	**Pronoun**	**When to Use**
First person	I, we	When writing about a personal experience or using a personal experience as a supporting detail
Second person	you	When giving directions or instructions
Third person	he, she, it, they	When writing about an object, idea, or someone other than yourself

You will write many academic assignments in third person; however, there are some writing situations in which other points of view can be used.

Prewrite to Develop Ideas for Your Topic

To get ideas for your topic, use a prewriting technique. **Prewriting** helps you think of ideas. You actively work with the topic until you feel comfortable enough to write about it.

The most commonly used prewriting techniques are questioning, freewriting, concept mapping, listing, and brainstorming.

Questioning   **Questioning** is the process of asking questions about your topic and answering them. You can write your own list of questions and answers or use the set of six questions journalists use: Who? What? Where? When? Why? How?

Here is Jessica's list of questions and answers for our topic Money-Saving Ideas for College Students on a Budget:

Jessica's Questioning

Who needs to save money?   Most college students today

What is the problem?   Students buy stuff without thinking about what they're doing, spend too much money going out, on food, or shopping, charge every little thing on their credit card and run up bills, go over their talk minutes or texting limits, having to have the latest trend in clothing and hair styles, get nails done

Where can students save money?   Discount and dollar stores, online, work, sale days, student discounts

When can students save money?   Weekends by not hanging out with people who spend a lot, picking cheaper things to do when going out, going to an early movie, buying cheaper food at a restaurant, not driving around burning gasoline

How can students save money?   Don't run up credit card bills, don't eat out so much, buy used books, get a cheaper cell phone plan, don't buy expensive coffee drinks or smoothies, go to clubs on ladies' night, buy bottled drinks and bring them along, make my own healthy snacks

---

 ACTIVITY

Practicing Questioning

2.4   Try the questioning prewriting strategy by answering the journalist's six questions about one of these topics or a topic of your own.

sports	jobs	music
studying	fashion	online communication

Freewriting **Freewriting** is a method that involves writing about any thoughts you have about a topic for five to fifteen minutes without stopping. You don't have to think about organizing ideas or making mistakes. If you get stuck, write about how you are feeling at that moment. Just keep writing. Soon the thoughts that distracted you will be gone, and you will be able to focus on the topic again.

The following freewrite shows how one student responded to the topic Money-Saving Ideas for College Students on a Budget:

Berenise's Freewrite

I have a lot of money problems. My family has always been poor. I am the first person in my family to go to college and everyone is proud of me but I have to work to help out the family expenses. So I have a job, I don't like it but I have to do it. After I give some money from my paycheck to my mother, I keep the rest for myself. I like to go out with my friends like go dancing. But lots of times I have to say no I can't go because then I won't have enough money to pay for things like my phone. I got so upset last month because my cell got cut off. I didn't have enough money to pay my bill which was really expensive from talking to and texting my boyfriend.

After reading her freewrite, Berenise realized that she wanted to focus her writing on ways she can manage her money.

ACTIVITY **Freewriting**

2.5 Freewrite for five to fifteen minutes on one of these topics or on a topic of your own.

an activity you enjoy   your career goals   money

After reading your freewrite, choose ideas you would like to develop.

Concept Mapping **Concept mapping** is a technique for placing ideas in a visual form. Concept maps help you picture your ideas and see the relationships among them. Some writers refer to this method as clustering, bubbling, or mind mapping. To make a concept map, follow these steps.

1. Write your subject in a circle in the center of a blank piece of paper.
2. Think of details and examples that relate to the subject (subtopics), and put them in circles around your center circle (your subject).
3. Draw lines from the center to each of the outer circles.
4. Continue to add more branches to your map as you think of ideas and examples that relate to each subtopic.

Here is an example of a student's concept map on Money-Saving Ideas for Students on a Budget. In his first attempt, Davon came up with five subtopics.

Davon's Concept Map

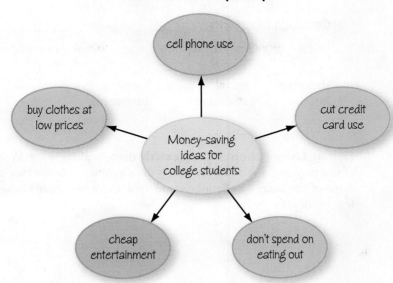

Then, he added specific examples to each of the subtopics.

Davon's Revised Concept Map

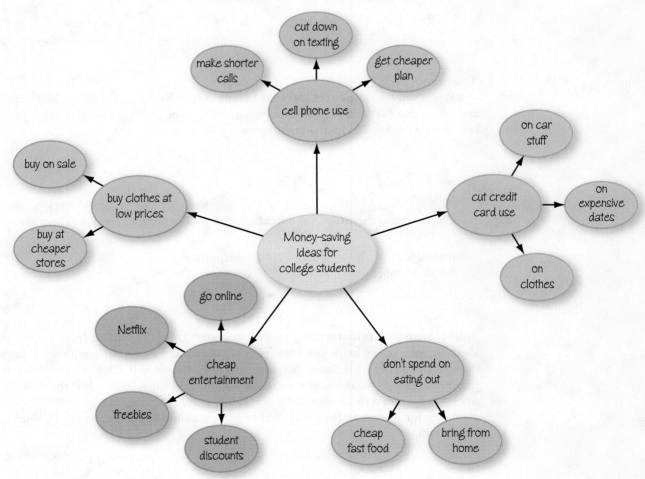

ACTIVITY 2.6   Concept Mapping

Using your own paper, prepare a concept map about one of these or your own topic:

shopping	travel	friends
Internet	restaurants	advertising

Listing   **Listing** involves doing exactly that—making a list. Write your topic at the top of the page and list of all the words details, and examples that come to mind. Here are some of the ideas that Ermilie came up with for the topic Money-Saving Ideas for College Students on a Budget.

Ermilie's List

stop buying expensive drinks	free activities on campus
borrow textbook or buy used	shop at discount stores
take public transportation	get haircuts at cheaper salons
get financial aid	email instead of calling long distance
share music and DVDs	buy less makeup
no vending machine food	pay bills on time

When you have run out of ideas, take a look at your list for ideas that can be grouped and others that can be taken out. Ermilie noticed that she could group some of her ideas into categories: books, entertainment, personal items, and phone.

ACTIVITY 2.7   Listing

Choose one of these topics and write a list on your own paper or on the computer.

traditions	food	transportation
family members	stress	computers

Brainstorming   **Brainstorming** is an interactive group technique for thinking of ideas. Brainstorming helps you share your ideas and find new ideas you may not have thought of on your own. Small groups of two to five work well. Choose one person to record the group's ideas about a topic. As each person suggests an idea, the recorder writes it down in a list. Instead of a list, you can use a concept map or other graphic organizer for recording the ideas. Ten to fifteen minutes is usually enough time to brainstorm.

ACTIVITY

Brainstorming

2.8   Form a group of two to five people. Together, choose one of the topics from the following list or a topic of your own. Ask one member to record the ideas, and then brainstorm together for ten to fifteen minutes.

peer pressure	teachers	special events
success	credit cards	new products

Now, look over the list for ideas that can be grouped together for development into a paragraph or essay. Then, discuss the advantages of brainstorming a topic with a small group.

QuickWrite

Explain which prewriting strategy works best for you.

Narrow Your Topic

LO 3 Narrow your topic before writing.

After prewriting on your topic, review all of your ideas. The topic should be narrow enough so that you can support your point in one paragraph.

In her list on the topic Money-Saving Ideas for College Students, Ermilie thought of items like books, entertainment, personal items, and phone. After looking at her list, she realized that she wanted to write about the ways students could save money as illustrated in the following diagram:

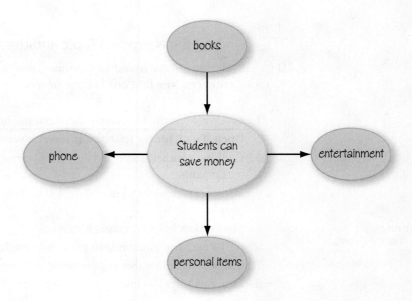

ACTIVITY   Narrowing a General Topic

2.9   Practice narrowing a general topic.

1. restaurants _____

2. fitness _____

3. an academic subject _____

4. relationships _____

5. clothing styles _____

Write the Topic Sentence

LO 4 **Write an effective topic sentence.**

Once you have narrowed your topic, you can write a topic sentence for your paragraph. The **topic sentence** controls the content of the paragraph. The topic sentence has two important parts:

1. It states your **narrowed topic**.
2. It states the point you will prove.

> **Online shopping** has several advantages.
> **Some energy drinks** contain harmful ingredients.
> **The neighbors on my street** have annoying habits.
> **Hurricane Sandy** taught me how to live without electricity.

Here is the topic sentence Ermilie wrote for Money-Saving Ideas for College Students.

> **College students** can save money by making economical choices.

ACTIVITY   Finding the Narrowed Topic and the Main Point

2.10   Underline the narrowed subject once, and the main point twice, in the following topic sentences. The first one is done for you.

1. Last week's tornado severely damaged the homes on my street.
2. Uncle Tai's Chinese Restaurant serves a variety of traditional Chinese dishes.
3. Cooking competition television shows present unusual challenges for the participants.
4. My customer service job at Target is helping me learn how to interact with people.
5. **Meditation** helps to manage stress.
6. LA Fitness has membership plans for people of all ages.
7. Quick weight loss diet supplements can have dangerous side effects.
8. New cars offer the latest technology.

meditation the act of giving your attention to only one thing, either as a religious activity or as a way of becoming calm and relaxed

Characteristics of a Good Topic Sentence

To better understand the elements that make a good topic sentence, let's look at some topic sentences written by students for the prewriting example topic Money-Saving Ideas for College Students.

1. The topic sentence makes one point.

   Poor—Makes more than one point: College students can save money by cutting back on unnecessary spending and setting long-term financial goals.

   Trying to support two topics will cause the paragraph to lose its focus.

   Poor—Makes an incomplete point: Making a budget to save money.

   This is not a complete sentence. The reader does not know who should make a budget.

   Good—Makes one point: College students can save money by cutting back on unnecessary spending.

2. The topic sentence states the point specifically.

   Poor—Does not state point specifically: As a college student, saving money is good.

   A word that is not specific may be misunderstood. The word *good* merely tells the reader that you like or do not like something.

   Poor—Announces the topic: I am going to discuss ways that college students can save money.

   Avoid announcing what you will do: "I plan to explain," "My paper is going to be about," "This paper describes," "I am writing my paper on."

   Poor—Asks a question: Can college students save money?

   A topic sentence written as a direct statement makes the point clearly.

   Good—States point specifically: College students can save money by spending less on entertainment.

3. The topic sentence is limited enough to be developed in a single paragraph.

   Poor—Too narrow: College students can save money by cutting out expensive coffee drinks.

   This main point leaves little to explain after you tell the reader how much you spend on gourmet coffee each day.

   Poor—Too broad: College students all over the world have poor spending habits.

   This main point is too big for one paragraph.

   Good—Limited: College students can save money by setting up a budget.

4. The topic sentence can be proved.

   Poor—Is a fact: Fifty percent of all college students get financial aid to pay tuition.

   This statement is a fact and does not need additional proof.

   Better—Can be proved: College students can save money by limiting spending on personal items.

   This statement can be supported by examples.

> **TIPS** | **Writing Good Topic Sentences**
>
> Here are some tips for writing good, concise topic sentences.
>
> 1. Make one point about your narrowed topic.
> 2. State the point specifically.
> 3. Limit the point enough so it can be developed in a single paragraph.
> 4. Choose a point that can be proved.

 ACTIVITY   Evaluating and Revising Topic Sentences

2.11   Identify the problems in the topic sentences below. Then revise them. If the sentence is good, write **G.**

1. In this paper, I am going to explain my opinion about the ways to avoid identity theft.

   _____

   _____

2. Moving to the United States by myself.

   _____

   _____

3. What are the benefits of hybrid cars?

   _____

   _____

4. The science museum is a great place to visit.

   _____

   _____

5. Students can be easily distracted in computer classrooms.

   _____

   _____

ACTIVITY   Writing Your Own Topic Sentence

2.12   Write your own topic sentence based on one of your prewrites in this chapter. Underline the narrowed topic once and the main point twice.

Writing Assignments

Help Desk

One of your classmates, Valery, is an English language learner. She attended high school for two years in the United States. Now as a college student, she is not confident about her written English skills. Her grades on grammar tests are very good, but her grades on written assignments are barely passing. Valery has trouble understanding how to limit a topic and write a topic sentence. She is not comfortable about asking questions during class. What advice would you give Valery?

Group Activity: Using Prewriting Strategies

Work in pairs or small groups of three or four. Choose questioning, concept mapping, listing, or brainstorming as your prewriting strategy for the following topic: Create a new, healthy drink targeted to college students and give it a name. Consider the important characteristics for selecting a brand name:

- Suggests something about the product's benefits and qualities
- Is easy to pronounce, recognize, and remember
- Is distinctive
- Does not infringe on existing brand names

(Adapted from *Marketing* by Gary Armstrong and Philip Kotler)

Write a paragraph about the steps your group went through to develop and name the new drink.

MyWritingLab™
Complete this activity
at mywritinglab.com

Reading and Writing across the Curriculum: Music

Read the following passage about music and culture from the textbook *Understanding Music*:

It has often been said that music is a universal language, that it goes beyond the limits of nation and race. This is true, but only in a very specific sense. The fact that there is music seems to be universal: Every known human group has music. But for each culture, music has a different meaning. It takes different forms in different cultural groups.

(Adapted from *Understanding Music* by Jeremy Yudkin)

Write a paper about the importance of music to you and your friends or cultural group.

MyWritingLab™
Complete this activity
at mywritinglab.com

Comment on a Contemporary Issue

Using laptops, tablets, and cell phones in the college classroom has caused controversy. Many professors feel that students spend time on their devices rather than paying attention in class. Do you think that students use electronic devices appropriately in class? Choose a prewriting strategy and develop your ideas on the topic. Then write a topic sentence that makes your point.

English Success Tip: First Impressions: Appearance Does Count

Did you ever think that the way your paper looks might affect your grade? Although content, organization, and correctness are most important, instructors may be influenced by your paper's appearance. Just as dressing appropriately for a job interview helps you make a good impression, submitting a neat, legible paper can give your instructor a positive first impression of your writing. Here are tips to improve your papers' appearance:

- Word-process or type all your assignments if possible. If you must write a short assignment by hand, do so neatly.
- Double-space your assignments unless instructed to do otherwise. Double-spaced text allows space for comments or corrections.
- Use a standard 12-point font. A tiny font, such as 10 point, is hard for most to read.
- Don't try to make your paper look longer than it is. Large fonts, large punctuation, triple spacing, and using wider margins are tricks that most instructors recognize.

Handing in a presentable, legible paper doesn't take much effort and shows that you are proud of your work and that you care about your readers.

3 Organizing and Drafting the Paragraph

Learning Objectives

After working through this chapter, you will be able to:

LO 1 Develop and organize the supporting details of a paragraph.

LO 2 Draft a paragraph.

LO 1 Develop and organize the supporting details of a paragraph.

Writing Reminder.
For more information about using examples, see Chapter 6.

Developing and Organizing Supporting Details

Once you have done your prewriting, narrowed your topic, and written your topic sentence, you are ready to organize your ideas and draft your paragraph.

Understand Supporting Details

Supporting details are sentences that contain specific information to back up the main point of the topic sentence. Supporting details are not statements of opinion.

The types of supporting details you use will depend on the purpose of your paragraph. For example, if you are writing about video games that are challenging, your details will be examples of those games. The five types of supporting details are examples, descriptions, steps or procedures, reasons, and facts and statistics.

Examples **Examples** are details that illustrate a main point. Examples can be people, places, things, stories, expert opinions, facts, or statistics. Examples can be written from your own personal observation or knowledge. In the following example, student Sang-Don uses a personal experience to explain his problem understanding prepositions in English:

> For example, during my first English class, the instructor said she was looking for me. I visited her office and asked her, "Why were you looking at me?" The instructor said, "I was not looking at you. I was looking for you, Don." Then she explained the difference between "look for" and "look at."

ACTIVITY 3.1 Writing Examples to Support Topic Sentences

Write three specific examples to support each of the following topic sentences.

1. My professor's office is messy.

_____

_____

2. Some foods sold at fast food restaurants are healthy.

_____

3. My new cell phone has many convenient features.

_____

_____

Descriptions   **Descriptions** are details that explain the characteristics of a person, place, object, or event. Descriptions often use sensory details, such as sight, smell, taste, touch, and hearing, to help the reader visualize the topic. In the following excerpt, Jason describes a few moments during a tense wrestling match:

> As I looked at the scoreboard to notice a tied game, eleven to eleven, the only thing I could hear was the pounding of my heart supporting my exhausted body and the faint sound of my coach and teammates offering me encouragement. As I approached the center of the mat, my eyes met my opponent's with an evil stare of determination and dominance.

ACTIVITY
3.2

Writing Descriptive Details

Write three descriptive details for each of the following topic sentences.

1. The severe thunderstorm damaged several houses on my street.

_____

_____

2. The store was busy with shoppers the week before the holiday.

_____

_____

3. My family's car was in bad condition.

_____

_____

Writing Reminder.
For more information
about using descrip-
tion, see Chapter 8.

Steps **Steps** are details that explain how to do something or how something happens. For example, if your purpose is to tell the reader how to study, your details will be a series of steps to accomplish the process. Allicyn, a massage therapist, explains the steps she follows to massage a client's head:

> Seated at the front of the table, I begin by holding the client's head in the palm of my hand and begin massaging the top of the head. This releases any tension in the tissue, which is the connective tissue that lies directly under the skin. Next, I move to the forehead, gently massaging the soft tissue of the face. By giving continuous pressure to fifteen pressure points on the face, I release any tension the client might have in this area. Then, I take the chin and massage along the jaw line. When I complete the face, I gently pull the ears toward the shoulders.

ACTIVITY **Writing Steps**

3.3   Write three steps for each of the following topic sentences.

1. Students can get a student identification card by following these steps.

   _____

   _____

   _____

2. Using a search engine to find _____ sites is simple.

   _____

   _____

   _____

3. Cooking _____ has several easy steps.

   _____

   _____

   _____

Writing Reminder.
For more information about using steps in a process, see Chapter 9.

Reasons **Reasons** are details that explain the cause for a belief, action, event, or opinion. For example, if you want to explain why you admire a particular person, you would provide reasons to support your opinion. Gabriella has chosen Michelle Obama as a person she admires and has chosen her work in the area of childhood obesity as one reason.

> One reason Michelle Obama is admirable is her campaign against childhood obesity called Let's Move. She has visited schools across the United States to see the changes they are making to serve healthier lunches. Obama also received

commitments from restaurant chains to change their children's menus. In addition, Walmart and Walgreens have agreed to provide fresh produce in places where it is not available.

ACTIVITY 3.4 Writing Reasons

Write three reasons for each of the following topic sentences.

1. Being a full-time worker and full-time student is demanding.

_____

_____

_____

2. Participating in a study group can improve your test grades.

_____

_____

_____

3. Driving while texting is dangerous.

_____

_____

_____

Writing Reminder.
For more information about using reasons, see Chapter 12.

Facts and Statistics **Facts and statistics** are details that can be proved. They can be shown to be true, to exist, or to have happened based on evidence or experience. **Statistics** are facts that consist of numbers.

Here are some examples of facts and statistics:

- Ricardo moved from Colombia to the United States in 2007.
- Shawna has three sisters: Chantal, Keesha, and Tiffany.
- My boyfriend Brian drives a Honda Civic.
- I have completed 24 of the 60 credits required for my associate's degree in criminal justice.

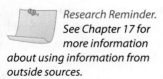
Research Reminder.
See Chapter 17 for more information about using information from outside sources.

Use facts that you know from your own life experience or from talking to people you know. If you want to use information from a source, such as a magazine, book, television or radio news report, or website, either put that information in your own words or quote the information in your paragraph. You must give credit to your source.

ACTIVITY 3.5 Writing Facts

Write three facts about the students in your English class for each of the following topic sentences. You may want to interview your classmates for information.

1. The students in my English class come from different places (or countries).

    _____

    _____

    _____

2. Some students in my English class are studying _____.

    _____

    _____

    _____

3. Many students in my English class have a job.

    _____

    _____

    _____

Avoiding Opinions **Opinions** are statements of beliefs or feelings. You can use an opinion as a main point in a topic sentence, but your supporting details must be examples, descriptions, steps or procedures, reasons, and facts and statistics.

The following sets of sentences show the differences between opinions and specific supporting details.

Opinion	Specific Supporting Details
My friend Tina is a **great** friend.	I left my wallet on my desk at home last Tuesday, so Tina gave me five dollars for lunch at Burger King on College Avenue.
Dupree always looks **tired.**	Dupree works as a forklift operator Mondays through Thursdays from 3 a.m. to 7 a.m.

Quick**Write**

Write your opinion about your college, a friend, a movie you just saw, or something you just bought.

ACTIVITY

3.6

Fact or Opinion?

Identify each sentence below as either a fact or opinion. Write **F** for fact and **O** for opinion in the blank next to each sentence.

_____ 1. There is too much violence on television.

_____ 2. When NBC first aired all its programs in color on February 17, 1961, only 1 percent of American homes had color TV sets.

_____ 3. In the United States, men and women are supposed to be equal—at least that is the stated ideal. (From *Human Communication* by Joseph A. DeVito)

_____ 4. Aaron "T-Bone" Walker is generally credited with being the first blues guitarist to use an electric guitar and his influence on subsequent musicians was tremendous. (From *Crossroads* by Elizabeth F. Barkley)

_____ 5. Attitudes toward gambling in America probably became less negative beginning in the early 1960s when a legal lottery introduced in New Hampshire proved wildly popular. (From *Travel and Tourism* by Paul S. Biederman)

_____ 6. In 1933, Mexican artist David Alfara Siqueiros painted a mural, *America Tropical*, on Olvera Street, the historic center of Chicano and Mexican culture in Los Angeles. (From *A World of Art* by Henry M. Sayre)

_____ 7. The use of fingerprints in identifying offenders was popularized by Sir Francis Galton and was officially adopted by Scotland Yard in 1901. (From *Criminal Justice Today* by Frank Schmalleger)

_____ 8. Designers with a love of computer work and a minimum need for client contact may enjoy becoming specialists in computer-aided design and drafting. (From *Designing Your Future* by Cindy V. Beacham)

Develop Supporting Details

Now that you have learned about the different types of supporting details you can use to prove the point of your topic sentence, you are ready to develop your own. One strategy is to look back at the prewriting notes you made when you narrowed your topic and wrote your topic sentence. For example, Davon's concept map on page 15 included many ideas for supporting details. Another strategy for developing details is to prewrite a second time.

In Chapter 2, you saw Ermilie's prewriting list for money-saving ideas for college students (p. 16). Ermilie reviewed her list, crossing out the weaker points and adding some new supporting details.

Ermilie's Supporting Details

Stop buying expensive drinks	~~Free activities on campus~~
Borrow textbook or buy used	Shop at discount stores
~~Take public transportation~~	~~Get haircuts at cheaper salons~~
~~Get financial aid~~	~~Share music and DVDs~~
~~Don't buy so much makeup~~	No vending machine food
~~Pay bills on time~~	Make shorter calls

Here are the details she added:

Change cell phone plan	Bring snacks from home to school
Buy textbooks online	No eating at expensive restaurants
Get student discounts	Keep same phone longer

Next, Ermilie grouped the items from her list into three major supporting points and explained each point with details from her list:

Ermilie's Supporting Points and Details

1. Books and school supplies

   Buy textbooks online, borrow a textbook, buy a used book, buy school supplies at discount stores

2. Cell phone

   Change to a cheaper plan, make shorter calls to save minutes, keep same phone longer, get student discount

3. Food

   Make healthy snacks and bring them to school, avoid buying expensive coffees and smoothies, avoid buying drinks from vending machines—buy large quantities and bring from home, stay away from expensive restaurants

ACTIVITY **Developing Supporting Details**

3.7 Develop supporting details for the topic you used for the prewriting activities in Chapter 2 or for any topic in this chapter.

Organize Supporting Details

Organizing your paragraph before you write will keep you on track as you write your first draft. Organizing is putting your ideas in logical order. Three methods you can use to organize your ideas are **time order**, **spatial order**, and **order of importance**.

As you read through the explanation and sample paragraph for each method, you will notice that some words are boldfaced. These words are called connectors and transitions. **Connectors and transitions** are words and phrases used to alert the reader that you are beginning a new point. Without these words, the reader may not be able to tell where one point ends and the next one begins. You will find a list of connectors and transitions for each method after the sample paragraph.

Time Order **Time order,** also called chronological order, is the arrangement of details in the order they happened. Time order is most commonly used when writing about the events of a story or a period in history, or when describing how something happens or works.

The paragraph that follows uses time order by describing the process of checking out of a hotel:

The traditional method of guest checkout at hotels involves five stages of customer activities. **First,** the departing guest walks from the room to the front desk in the lobby for checkout. The guest **next** waits in line for desk service. **Then,** upon reaching the front desk, the guest reviews the bill before payment. **At this point,** the guest can question items on the bill or request changes. **When** the bill is approved, the guest makes payment. **Finally,** the guest leaves the front desk to resume activities. Because this checkout method can be time consuming, improved methods are being developed.

(Adapted from *Business Essentials* by Ronald J. Ebert and Ricky W. Griffin)

Common Connector/Transition Words for Time Order		
the first, second, etc.	then, later, soon after	in the meantime, meanwhile
before, previously	at the same time	yesterday, today, tomorrow
after, afterward	immediately	next, eventually, from . . . to

Spatial Order **Spatial order** is the arrangement of details according to their position in physical space. Spatial order is most commonly used when describing a place, an object, or a person. Your details take the readers from one area to another in any number of ways.

- front to back or back to front
- inside to outside or outside to inside
- left to right or right to left
- most outstanding feature to least outstanding feature

The following paragraph uses spatial order.

There are four taste experiences: sour, sweet, bitter, and salty, plus a recently discovered fifth sense, called *umami,* which tastes glutamates. Each of these four taste types is experienced in a specific area of the tongue that contains taste buds with specialized functions. Taste receptors for all tastes are located **in a narrow area surrounding the entire tongue.** Sweet, salty, and sour taste receptors are **in a region just inside the outer edge of the tongue.** Salty and sour receptors are located **in a small region toward the back of the tongue.** Sour-only receptors are located approximately **in the center of the tongue.** There is an area **toward**

the center and front of the tongue where no sensation of taste is experienced. Sweet and sour taste receptors are located just **in front of this region,** with bittersweet and sour tastes being experienced **near the tip of the tongue just inside** the area containing the receptors for all tastes.

(Adapted from *The Pharmacy Technician* by Mike Johnston)

Common Connector/Transition Words for Spatial Order

on/at the left, right	in front of, at the front
on/at the top, bottom, back, front	behind, at the rear
in/at/on the back, front, rear, side	beside, next to, nearby
in the middle, center	beneath, under, underneath, below
inside, on the inside	in the distance, beyond
outside, on the outside	in back of, in front of

Order of Importance **Order of importance** is the arrangement of details according to how interesting, significant, or memorable they are. Order of importance is most commonly used when your supporting details are facts, examples, causes and effects, and comparisons and contrasts.

The following paragraph uses order of importance:

Firefighting is a demanding career that requires very special qualities. **First of all,** candidates should like to work with people and enjoy teamwork. **In addition,** they should be physically fit. They must have strength in muscle groups that are used in firefighting work such as lifting, pushing, pulling, and carrying. **Also,** they should be adept at following instructions under stressful conditions. Firefighters who react without thinking endanger themselves, their fellow firefighters, and the people they are trying to protect. **Most importantly,** they must be able to make quick decisions and be willing to take risks while remaining calm in stressful situations. As a result, fire departments devote great care in choosing their entry-level employees.

(Adapted from *Fire and Emergency Services* by Jason B. Loyd and James D. Richardson)

Common Connector/Transition Words for Order of Importance

the first, second, third, etc.	the most important	of greater importance
first of all, etc.	the least important	one reason, example, etc.
next	equally, less important	another reason, example, etc.

Choose a Plan

After reading about the three methods of organization, you are ready to choose the plan that will work best for your supporting points. Ermilie decided that **order of importance** would work best for her paragraph about ways college students can save money. She decided to put the least important point first and end with the most important because the last point is the one that readers will remember best.

Ermilie's Paragraph Plan

1. Food

   Make healthy snacks and bring them to school, avoid buying expensive coffees and smoothies, avoid buying drinks from vending machines— buy large quantities and bring from home, stay away from expensive restaurants

2. Cell phone

   Change to a cheaper plan, make shorter calls to save minutes, keep same phone longer, get student discount

3. Books and school supplies

   Buy books online, borrow a book, buy a used book, buy school supplies at discount stores

---

ACTIVITY   **Organizing Details**

3.8   Each of the following sets of sentences has supporting details that are not in the correct order. Put the details in order and tell which method of organization you used.

Sentence Group 1

Topic sentence: The cruise industry line faces seasonal variation by demand.

_____ The off-season runs from mid-August through the first week of January and accounts for about 25 percent.

_____ The period between April and mid-August, known as the normal period, also garners 35 to 40 percent of all business, but over a period twice as long as the wave season.

_____ The so-called wave season runs from the second week of January through the end of March and accounts for 35 to 40 percent of annual passengers.

(From *Travel and Tourism* by Paul S. Biederman)

Method of Organization: _____

Sentence Group 2

Topic sentence: Music Television (MTV), which began in 1981, revolutionized television.

_____ In addition, MTV gave bands that were not as well known an opportunity to be seen and heard.

_____ Third, music videos became a new art form.

_____ Most important, MTV became a way for record companies to promote music.

_____ First, it was the only network entirely devoted to music where fans could watch music videos, see interviews with their favorite recording artists, and get music news.

Method of Organization: _____

Sentence Group 3

Topic sentence: Four distinct communities of birds and mammals feed from the top to the bottom of a lowland tropical forest of the Far East.

_____ The zone of tree trunks includes a world of flying mammals, birds, squirrels, and insect-eating bats.

_____ The forest floor is occupied by large herbivores, such as the gaur, tapir, and elephant, which feed on ground vegetation and low hanging leaves.

_____ The group feeding above the treetops is made up mostly of birds, fruit bats, and other species of mammals.

_____ Small ground and undergrowth animals, birds, and small mammals feed at the lower portion of the tree trunks.

(From _Elements of Ecology_ by Robert Leo Smith and Thomas M. Smith)

Method of Organization: _____

ACTIVITY Choosing a Method of Organization

3.9   Using the details for your own paragraph from Activity 3.7, choose a method of organization for your ideas.

Write a Plan

After you have decided how you want to organize your supporting points, your next step is to write a plan for your first draft. Written plans keep you from getting lost or going off the topic while you are writing. Two types of written plans are a scratch outline and a graphic organizer.

Scratch Outline A **scratch outline** is a written plan in which you list each of your supporting points in logical order. Under each of those points, add details to back them up. Here is how a scratch outline might look. This particular outline has three supporting points with one detail for each support, but you may have more.

Scratch Outline

Topic Sentence:

Supporting point 1:

    Detail(s) for supporting point 1

Supporting point 2:

    Detail(s) for supporting point 2

Supporting point 3:

    Details(s) for supporting point 3

Concluding Sentence:

Ermilie put her details into the following scratch outline, which helped her tighten her organization.

Ermilie's Scratch Outline

Topic Sentence: College students can save money by making economical choices.

Supporting Point 1: Food

    Detail: Make healthy snacks and bring them to school instead of using vending machines

    Detail: Bring drinks instead of buying expensive coffees, smoothies, and other drinks

    Detail: Eat out at inexpensive restaurants

Supporting Point 2: Cell phone

    Detail: Change to a cheaper plan

    Detail: Make shorter calls to save minutes usage

    Detail: Keep same phone longer

    Detail: Get student discount

Supporting Point 3: Books and school supplies

    Detail 1: Save on books: buy online, borrow, buy used

    Detail 2: Buy school supplies at discount stores

ACTIVITY

Making a Scratch Outline

3.10   Make a scratch outline based on the following paragraph.

[1]Some people abuse animals by making them fight. [2]For example, dogs are often bred and trained to fight. [3]Dog fighting is getting two dogs to fight until one can no longer fight or has died. [4]Often the owner of the losing dog will kill the dog or abandon it. [5]Although dog fighting is illegal in all states and considered a felony in 48 states, it continues. [6]Hog-dog fighting is portrayed as more acceptable than dog fighting. [7]It allows some protection to a dog as it fights with a wild hog that no longer has tusks. [8]The dog is timed to see how fast it can pin down a hog. [9]Unfortunately, both animals can be seriously injured. Hog-dog fighting violates cruelty laws in some states. [10]Cockfighting is an even older sport than dog fighting. [11]The birds are bred to fight. [12]They are placed in a small area to fight, usually until one is dead. [13]Sometimes owners put artificial spurs on their birds, which are even more dangerous than their normal spurs. [14]Laws against cockfighting make it illegal in most states. [15]One would think that proper feeding, care, housing, and cleanliness are common sense and should be done by anyone who owns or cares for an animal, but that is far from true.

(Adapted from *Introduction to Livestock and Companion Animals* by Jasper S. Lee et al.)

Topic Sentence: _____

Supporting Point 1: _____

Detail: _____

Detail: _____

Detail: _____

Detail: _____

Supporting Point 2: _____

Detail: _____

Detail: _____

Detail: _____

Detail: _____

Supporting Point 3: _____

Detail: _____

Detail: _____

Detail: _____

Detail: _____

Detail: _____

ACTIVITY   **Writing Your Own Scratch Outline**

3.11   Write a scratch outline for the paragraph you have been working on in this chapter.

Graphic Organizer   A graphic organizer is a visual, such as a chart, web, or diagram, used to arrange your thoughts in an organized way. See the next page for a graphic organizer for a standard academic paragraph.

 ACTIVITY   ## Using the Paragraph Graphic Organizer

3.12   Using the paragraph graphic organizer, organize the details of the paragraph you have been working on.

Drafting a Paragraph

LO 2 **Draft a paragraph.**

Once you have a plan for your paragraph, you are ready to draft it. **Drafting** is the process of putting your plan into sentences that explain and support your topic sentence. The purpose of drafting is to get your ideas down in rough form, not to write a perfect paragraph. Ermilie used her scratch outline to guide her as she wrote her rough draft.

> Ermilie's Rough Draft
>
>   College students can save money by making economical choices. Instead of buying that bag of Doritos or Snickers candy bar at vending machine prices, save money by bringing snacks from home. Healthy snacks like home made trail mix, fruit, or cut up vegetables are inexpensive and portable. Cutting down on expensive gourmet coffees or fruit smoothies can save students almost five dollars a day. Most companies offer more than one cell phone plan, students can do research to find the cheapest plan. They can ask about student discounts. In addition, making shorter calls during peak times will help reduce phone bills. Also, students do not have to buy the latest phone every six months. Books are the biggest expense for college students. Buy books online. Some online companies will even ship for free. Buying used books is cheaper than buying new. Students can even make money by selling their used books for less than the bookstore. Avoid the bookstore for supplies; the big discount stores have better prices.

Paragraph Graphic Organizer

Topic Sentence:

Supporting Point 1:

Detail:

Detail:

Supporting Point 2:

Detail:

Detail:

Supporting Point 3:

Detail:

Detail:

Concluding Sentence:

Note that Ermilie's paragraph is not perfect. There are mistakes in it, but she can correct them later. Furthermore, the paragraph just stops; it doesn't come to a satisfying end.

TIPS | **Drafting Your Paragraph**

1. **Follow your plan, but don't be upset about making changes.** If an idea comes to you as you are writing, put it in the margin or in brackets on the computer.

2. **Don't stop writing to correct errors in grammar, punctuation, or spelling.** You will correct these errors later, during the editing and proofreading stages.

3. **Know what to do if you get stuck.** If you get stuck on a word, leave a space and come back to it later. If you get stuck for ideas, use a prewriting strategy.

4. **Don't worry about the length of your paper.** You can always add or remove ideas later.

5. **Take a break when you need one.** Taking a break will help keep you alert and free up your thoughts.

6. **Get an early start on your assignment.** Writing your rough draft in a hurry at the last minute will make more work for you at the revision stage.

 ACTIVITY   Drafting Your Paper

3.13   Draft the paragraph you have been working on in this chapter.

Write the Concluding Sentence

The concluding sentence is the last sentence of the paragraph, the final statement. It shows the reader that the writer has finished supporting the main point and brings the ideas of the paragraph together. The concluding sentences in the following examples make a final comment about the main point.

Topic Sentence	Concluding Sentence
The traditional method of guest checkout at hotels involves five stages of customer activities.	Because this traditional checkout method can be time consuming, improved methods are being developed.
Some people abuse animals by making them fight.	One would think that proper feeding, care, housing, and cleanliness are common sense and should be done by anyone who owns or cares for an animal, but that is far from true.

Here is the concluding sentence that Ermilie wrote for her paragraph about how college students can economize:

> Students who spend economically can avoid money problems and may end up with some money in the bank.

TIPS | **Writing the Concluding Sentence**

1. **Write your concluding sentence to fit the purpose of the paragraph.** For example, if you are contrasting two computers, you could state your preference for one over the other in your concluding sentence. In a paragraph giving a set of instructions on how to plan a party, you could conclude with your opinion about the results of following your instructions. Avoid repeating your topic sentence.

2. **Make sure that your concluding sentence signals the end of the paragraph.** Adding another supporting detail or starting a new topic will make the reader think that you are not done.

3. **State your sentence directly.** You do not need to address your reader with phrases such as these: *As I have said, As you can see, As I have proved,* or *In conclusion.*

 ACTIVITY | Writing a Concluding Sentence

3.14 | Write a concluding sentence for the following paragraph:

 Establishing relationships online has many advantages. For example, online relationships are safe in terms of avoiding the potential for physical violence or sexually transmitted diseases. Another advantage is that Internet communication reveals your inner qualities first rather than your physical appearance. Computer talk is also a benefit for shut-ins and extremely shy people who have trouble meeting others in traditional ways. Finally, online relationships are empowering for those with physical deformities or disabilities.

(Adapted from *Human Communication* by Joseph A. DeVito)

ACTIVITY **Writing Your Own Concluding Sentence**

3.15 Write a concluding sentence for your draft paragraph.

Write the Title

The title is the name you give your paragraph. It gives a brief idea of what the paper is about. The title of a paper can be compared to the title of a book, song, or movie. Because the reader sees the title of your paper first, consider the following TIPS.

TIPS | **Writing the Title**

1. **Catch the reader's interest.** Use your imagination to write a title that will attract the reader. The titles " Descriptive Paragraph" or "Writing Assignment" are uninteresting.

2. **Make it informative.** Your title should give the reader an idea of what your paper is about. Look back over your paper for some key words.

3. **Apply the rules for capitalizing titles.**

   ■ Capitalize the first and last words.
   ■ Capitalize all other words except the following:

   Articles: a, an, the
   Coordinating conjunctions: for, and, nor, but, or, yet, so
   Prepositions: at, on, to, in, after, with, off, by, etc.

 *Grammar Reminder. See Chapter 18 for a longer list of prepositions.*

 ACTIVITY **Writing Your Own Title**

3.16 Write a title for your draft paragraph.

Writing Assignments

Help Desk

Howard was unhappy about the low grade he received on his paragraph about Jamaica. His instructor told him that he did not support his topic sentence. What suggestions would you give him?

> A place people should visit is Jamaica. Through the years, Jamaica has been famous for its beauty. It is also one of the favorite destinations for travelers. I was born in Jamaica, so I can say no one will regret his or her visit to the island. As a Jamaican, I appreciate my country, and I think others will too.

Reading and Writing across the Curriculum: Student Success

College students are expected to have academic integrity. However, many students do not have a clear understanding of what academic integrity is and how to avoid carrying out dishonest acts.

> Academic integrity means following a code of moral values, prizing honesty and fairness in all aspects of academic life—classes, assignments, tests, papers, projects, and relationships with students and faculty. Having academic integrity means valuing education and learning over grades. Unfortunately, the principles of academic integrity are frequently violated on college campuses. Violations of academic integrity—turning in previously submitted work, using unauthorized devices during an exam, providing unethical aid to another student, or downloading passages or whole papers from the Internet—aren't worth the price.
>
> (Adapted from *Keys to Success*, 6th ed., by Carol Carter et al.)

Find out your school's policy for academic integrity. Write a paragraph explaining that policy in your own words. If your school does not have such a policy, look for samples on the Internet and write one for your school.

Comment on a Contemporary Issue

The Internet has had an enormous influence on relationships. For example, many people use the Internet to find friends or romantic partners. They also join communities or discussion groups for a variety of special interests, such as work, child rearing, video games, music, and socializing. The paragraph in Activity 3.14 points out some of the advantages to online relationships. What are some of the disadvantages? Write a paragraph explaining the disadvantages of online relationships in general or of a particular group that you are familiar with such as Facebook.

English Success Tip: Paragraph Length

Many students want to be told the exact number of sentences that a paragraph should have. Requiring a specific number of sentences, a percentage of a page, or a word count does not address the purpose of a paragraph: to make a point and support it fully.

A paragraph of two or three sentences is likely to be too short and does not give enough support. On the other hand, a paragraph can be too long. This can happen when the topic is too broad, when the writer offers too many details, or the writer repeats details.

A successful paragraph will be the right length when it supports a narrowed topic with adequate and relevant details.

Revising, Editing, and Proofreading the Paragraph

4

The purpose of writing a first draft is to put your ideas in rough form. The next important and necessary stages in the writing process are revising, editing, and proofreading.

LO 1 Revise your papers for SOCS: Support, Organization, Connectors and transitions, and Style.

Revising

Revising is the process of taking another careful look at your writing and making changes to improve your topic sentence and supporting details. You may have beliefs about revising that stop you from making valuable changes to your writing. For example, you may feel that you worked hard on your draft and like it the way it is or that you don't have the time to revise your paper. However, even professional writers revise their drafts.

MyWritingLab™
Complete this activity
at mywritinglab.com

QuickWrite

What process do you use to revise your papers?

Checking the Assignment

Before beginning to revise your draft, first make sure that you have fulfilled the requirements of your assignment:

- The paragraph is written about the assigned topic.
- The paragraph has a topic sentence with a narrowed topic and main point.
- The paragraph is written for a college audience.

Checking Requirements of a Paragraph Assignment

4.1   Read the following student paragraph written in response to an assignment about the reasons for staying motivated in college. Then answer the questions about whether or not the student has done the assignment properly.

> [1]Everyone has a reason to go to college. [2]It will be up to you to stay motivated. [3]Before I tell you how I stay motivated, let me tell you my reason for going to college. [4]I won't say that if you wanna be educated, you have to go to school. [5]School is not the only way to make it. [6]Some people choose to go into the Army. [7]Some people won the lotto. [8]Now let's talk about me. [9]Let me tell you how I stay motivated and why. [10]I stay motivated by studying, doing my homework, and staying focused. [11]Believe it or not, if you don't do those things, you won't be able to make it. [12]If you did those but failed, you have to try to find out why you failed and try again. [13]Never give up. [14]I won't stop even if I fail.

1. Is the paragraph written on the assigned topic?

_____

_____

2. Does the paragraph have a topic sentence with a narrowed topic and main point?

_____

_____

3. Is this paragraph written appropriately for a college audience?

_____

_____

_____

 Checking Requirements of Your Paragraph Assignment

4.2   Look over the draft paragraph that you wrote in Chapter 3 to be sure that you have fulfilled the requirements of your assignment:

Have you written about the assigned topic?
Does your paragraph have a narrowed topic and main point?
Is the paragraph written for a college audience?

Revising One Element at a Time: SOCS

Revising can seem like an overwhelming task. To help you revise effectively and use your time efficiently, go over your paper one element at a time. The four elements you need to check when revising are **S**upport, **O**rganization, **C**onnectors and transitions, and **S**tyle. You can easily remember the elements for revising by putting the first letter of each word into the acronym **SOCS.**

Support   The first element in **SOCS** revision is **S**upport. When you revise for support, you look at your details to make sure that they are adequate and relevant. **Adequate** means that your supporting points give enough information to support your points. **Relevant** means that all of your details directly support the main point of the paragraph. They stay on the topic and are not repetitious.

1. **Adequate supporting points give enough information to prove the main point.**

    The student's paragraph below does not give enough information to prove the main point.

    > [1]As an employee of Starbucks Coffee, I encounter some sloppy customers. [2]For example, last Sunday morning, a customer purchased a large coffee and a banana walnut muffin. [3]When he finished, he left his used napkins, spilled coffee and sugar, and muffin crumbs all over the table assuming that it was my job to clean up after him.

    She writes about just one sloppy customer, but additional examples would provide more adequate support and be more convincing to her readers.

 Supporting a Main Point

4.3   Write two more examples to support the main point, "encounter some sloppy customers."

_____

_____

2. **Adequate supporting points are specific.**

    The student who wrote the following paragraph attempts to describe the special qualities of the beach, but she does not give specific details.

    > [1]The beach has many special qualities. [2]If you ask me, they are endless, but I will name a couple. [3]The most obvious is its beauty. [4]I have never seen such a mesmerizing, attractive, gorgeous place in my life. [5]Another special quality is its profound peacefulness. [6]To me it is the ideal example of peace. [7]The sand and water are therapeutic enough to give me peace of mind for the rest of my life. [8]The special quality I hold to my heart is all the priceless memories of me and my friends growing up on the beach.

Note that the writer has not given specific details about the beach. The writer does not specify a particular beach and does not give specific details. For example, she uses opinion words, such as "mesmerizing," "captivating," and "gorgeous" to support "beauty." Another vague quality she mentions is peacefulness/peace.

 ACTIVITY Writing Supporting Points with Specific Details

4.4 Write two supporting points with specific details about the special qualities of the beach or another place in a natural setting.

_____

_____

3. **Adequate supporting points often have details that explain them.**

Sometimes you need to add details to explain your supporting points to help the reader understand them. Read this student paragraph on the reasons people drink alcohol:

> [1]People drink alcohol for several reasons. [2]The first is that they believe that there is no risk in consuming alcohol. [3]The second is that most individuals enjoy the immediate effects. [4]In addition, alcohol, unlike drugs, is accepted. [5]Last, alcohol is available everywhere.

This paragraph has four supporting points, but the writer did not provide any details to help the reader understand each of them.

 ACTIVITY Adding Explaining Details

4.5 Write one explaining detail for sentences 2, 3, 4, and 5.

_____

_____

_____

4. **Relevant details stay on the topic.**

In this paragraph, the student writer goes off his topic, "pumping iron."

> [1]Lifting weights is an activity that helps me improve my health. [2]It helps me to burn fat and to increase the strength of my bones. [3]I can lift weights alone at any time I choose. [4]I mostly lift weights at the gym. [5]My favorite time to go to the gym is early morning or late at night when there is less of a crowd. [6]I enjoy

> the burn of the muscle. ⁷While I work out, I get to do other things, like read a
>
> book between sets, watch television, or listen to music on my iPod. ⁸When I work
>
> out, I enjoy the feeling of doing something to improve my health.

The writer's main point, stated in the first sentence, is that lifting weights helps him improve his health. However, only sentences 2 and 7 are relevant to this main point. The rest of the paragraph is not relevant to the main point.

 Adding Relevant Details

4.6   Provide two additional relevant details that support the topic sentence of the paragraph on lifting weights.

_____

_____

5. **Relevant details are not repetitious. Readers do not want to read the same thing over and over.**

   In the paragraph you read about the beach, the writer repeated herself in sentences 5 and 6:

   > ⁵Another special quality is its profound peacefulness. ⁶To me it is the
   >
   > epitome of peace.

   Here is another example of repetitious details in a section of a student's paragraph on the reasons she likes working at a coffee shop:

   > ¹One of the reasons I like working at the coffee shop is because of the
   >
   > people I meet on a daily basis. ²People from all over town come to the shop on a
   >
   > daily basis. ³Every day I meet different people. ⁴Some are regular customers who
   >
   > come in to visit almost every day.

   The word choices are repetitious and the writer repeats the same point.

 Revising for Repetition and Adding Details

4.7   Revise this part of the student's paragraph on working in a coffee shop, omitting the repetition and adding specific details.

_____

_____

_____

_____

Revising Your Paragraph for Adequate and Relevant Support and Details

4.8 Revise your own draft paragraph to make sure your supporting points and details are adequate and relevant.

Organization The second element in **SOCS** revision is **O**rganization. When you revise for organization, you check to see that your ideas are expressed in a logical order and that each point is equally developed.

1. **Express ideas in a logical order.**

   In Chapter 3, you learned about the three methods of logical order: time order, spatial order, and order of importance. When you wrote the plan for your draft, you chose an order to present your supporting points. During the drafting process, you might have drifted away from the plan. Now you can take another look at your paper to check its organization.

   Read Katie's draft about her jealous friend Alyce, paying attention to logical order.

---

¹My friend Alyce is the most jealous person I know. ²For example, she does not want her boyfriend to talk on the phone when she is with him. ³Last weekend, the three of us were spending time together when his mother called his cell phone. ⁴Alyce's whole mood changed from happy to angry. ⁵She interrupted his conversation by telling him that he should talk to her later. ⁶As a result, he makes his phone calls short to avoid a fight. ⁷Another example of her jealousy is that she cannot stand it when her friends make new friends. ⁸A few weeks ago, I met a girl at work, and I started spending time with her. ⁹Alyce insisted on knowing every detail about my new friend and accused me of not wanting to spend time with her anymore. ¹⁰Alyce called me every day to make plans so I would not have any time for my friend. ¹¹The most obvious example of her jealousy is her negative way of reacting when she thinks other girls have nicer figures than she does. ¹²When Alyce sees a girl whom she believes looks better, she criticizes her. ¹³She says things like "Her nose is so big," "Her shoes do not match," or "Her pants are out of style." ¹⁴It is a good thing jealousy is not a crime because Alyce would definitely be in jail.

Katie uses order of importance to organize her paragraph, but it's difficult to check the order just by reading. Reverse outlining is a technique that will help you check a paper's organization. **Reverse outlining** is the process of outlining your paper after you have written it. You can use the scratch outline covered in Chapter 3 for this process.

Here is a reverse outline of Katie's paragraph.

Topic sentence:	[1]My friend Alyce is the most jealous person I know.
Supporting point 1	Does not want boyfriend to talk on phone when with her.
Detail(s)	Boyfriend's mom called on cell phone; she got angry and interrupted conversation.
Supporting point 2	Does not like it when her friends make new friends.
Detail(s)	Met girl at work. Alyce insisted on knowing every detail; accused me of not wanting to be with her; called every day to make plans.
Supporting point 3	Negative reactions to girls who have better figures.
Detail(s)	Says "Her nose is big," "Her shoes do not match," "Her pants are out of style."
Concluding sentence:	[14]It is a good thing jealousy is not a crime because Alyce would definitely be in jail.

With this reverse outline, you can see that Katie's supports and details all prove the main point of the paragraph. However, sentence 6 is an effect and could be eliminated.

ACTIVITY 4.9   **Preparing a Reverse Outline for Your Draft Paragraph**

Prepare a reverse outline of your draft paragraph and check its organization. Revise the paragraph's organization if necessary.

2. **Develop each point equally.**

When each point is equally developed, your paper will be balanced. Read the following student paragraph about soccer. As you read, check for equal development of supporting points with adequate details. The supporting points are boldfaced.

[1]Now that I am living in the United States and do not have time to play on a soccer team, I enjoy soccer in other ways. [2]**One thing I do is watch soccer games on television.** [3]I bought a special sports package so I can watch games between leagues from all over the world, even the league from my country, Colombia. [4]**Another thing that I do is get together with my friends and play soccer for fun on Sundays.** [5]My group of friends comes from many countries all around the world. [6]Not everyone speaks English, but we communicate with the soccer ball. [7]**I also enjoy soccer by talking about it with my friends and family.** [8]I enjoy soccer now as much as I used to as a young boy in a different country, but in different ways.

There are three supporting points in this paragraph, and the first two give details for their supporting points. The last supporting point, expressed in sentence 7, does not give any details, so the paper is not balanced.

ACTIVITY   Revising Your Paragraph for Equally Developed Points

4.10   Reread your draft paragraph to make sure all of your points are equally developed. If they are not, revise the paragraph by adding details to the points that are not fully developed.

Connectors and Transitions   The third item in a **SOCS** revision is **C**onnectors and transitions. To help the reader follow your ideas in a logical, understandable order, make sure you have used connectors and transitions to join ideas. Also, use synonyms and pronouns to avoid repetition and add variety.

1. **Use connectors and transitions.**

   Connectors and transition words and phrases tell the reader that you are introducing new ideas and adding details as well as showing relationships between them. In Chapter 3, you learned about connectors and transition words for time order, spatial order, and order of importance. Another group of words is used to add details to supporting points.

Common Transition Words for Added Points and Information			
also	first, second, etc.	for instance	last
additionally	finally	furthermore	moreover
another	for example	in addition to	not only . . . but also

The following paragraph about the leading reasons managers waste time shows how addition transitions help you follow the writer's ideas. Notice how they introduce supporting points and add information to the supporting points. The transitions are boldfaced.

To manage time effectively, managers must address four leading causes of wasted time. The **first** cause is paperwork. **For example,** some managers spend too much time deciding what to do with letters and reports. **Another** cause of wasted time is telephone calls. **For instance,** experts estimate that managers get interrupted by the telephone every five minutes. **Also,** the explosive use of cell phones seems to be making this problem even worse for many managers. The **third** cause of wasted time is meetings. Many managers spend up to four hours a day in meetings. Often these meetings are not focused on the agenda and do not end on time. The **last** cause of wasted time is email. Managers are relying heavily on email and other forms of electronic communication. **Moreover,** time is wasted when managers have to sort through spam and a variety of electronic folders, in-boxes, and archives.

(Adapted from *Business Essentials* by Ronald J. Ebert and Ricky W. Griffin)

ACTIVITY   Adding Transitions to a Paragraph

4.11   Revise the following paragraph, adding transitions to help your reader follow the ideas. Remember to change a capital letter to a lowercase letter when it no longer is the first word of a sentence.

[1]Going to college has numerous benefits. [2]Increased income is one clear advantage for degree holders. [3]College graduates get more promotions, are less likely to experience long periods of unemployment, and are regarded more favorably by potential employers. [4]College influences social development. [5]For many students, college is their first opportunity to meet people of ethnic groups and nationalities that are different from theirs. [6]Students, particularly those who live on campus, learn to establish social networks that eventually replace parents as their primary source of emotional support. [7]The longer individuals attend college, even if they don't graduate, the better they can manage problems in their everyday lives, such as balancing family and work schedules. [8]Studies show that these gains happen between the first and later years of college. [9]College attendance is worth the trouble.

(Adapted from *The World of Psychology* by Samuel E. Wood et al.)

ACTIVITY   Revising Your Paragraph for Connectors and Transitions

4.12   Revise your draft paragraph to improve the use of connectors and transitions.

2. **Use synonyms and pronouns.**

   Synonyms and pronouns help to avoid repetition and add variety.

   ■ A **synonym** is a word that means the same as another word. For example, some synonyms for the word *revise* are *change, alter,* or *rethink.*

   > When you **revise** your paragraph, you **alter** its meaning.

   ■ A **pronoun** is a word that replaces a noun. In the following sentence, the pronoun **it** replaces the word **family.**

   > The **family** is the most important consumer buying organization in society, and **it** has been researched extensively.

   The following paragraph shows how synonyms and pronouns add variety.

¹Country music emerged out of the rural American South from the folk traditions of the **British immigrants,** who settled in the New England colonies in the eighteenth century. ²In the nineteenth century, many of the **settlers** moved to the cities, but **others,** especially **those** in the poorer Southeast areas, such as the Appalachian mountains, did not. ³**They** lived in the backwoods without indoor plumbing and other modern conveniences. ⁴Although **they** were poor, **their** lives were rich with music. ⁵**They** kept the old folk music traditions. ⁶Each generation passed down the songs and instrumental music that **they** had learned from the previous generation. ⁷These **poor white folks** with simple country ways were disrespectfully called "hillbillies" when **they** came into town to look for work or buy supplies. ⁸"Billy" is the name for a male goat, and "hill" described the locations of **their** homes deep in the mountains. ⁹"Hillbilly" was also the term used to describe **their** old-time mountain music. ¹⁰It is from **this music** that "country" emerged as type of music in the 1920s.

(Adapted from *Crossroads* by Elizabeth F. Barkley)

- The synonym *settlers* replaces *British immigrants. Poor white folks* replaces *settlers* who did not move to the cities. *This music* refers to the old-time mountain music.
- The pronouns *others, those, they,* and *their* refer to settlers who lived in the backwoods.

ACTIVITY **Revise a Paragraph for Repetitious Words**

4.13   The following sentences were taken from a student's paragraph. Her assignment was to write about tourist attractions in her birthplace. She wrote about her island, the Bahamas. Some words are repeated unnecessarily. Revise the sentences by replacing the repetitious words with synonyms and pronouns.

1. In the Bahamas, people can travel the island in different ways. People can travel the island by taxi, scooter, or jitney bus. People can notice that when traveling in the Bahamas by taxi, scooter, or jitney bus that driving is done on the left side of the road.

_____

_____

2. The straw market in the Bahamas is a famous attraction for tourists to experience. The vendors at the straw market in the Bahamas sell many items. The vendors in the straw markets sell handcrafted straw items like hats, baskets, mats, and bags. The straw market vendors also sell t-shirts, fabric, woodcarvings, and homemade guava jelly.

_____

_____

_____

3. Tourists can enjoy the traditional foods that the people who live in the Bahamas eat. Some of the traditional foods are conch fritters, rice, peas, plantains, curried goat, and oxtail. Tourists can eat the traditional foods cooked in the Bahamian style in many different restaurants. Tourists can eat authentic food from take-out places to five-star restaurants.

_____

_____

ACTIVITY   **Analyzing Your Paragraph for Repetitious Words**

4.14   Analyze your draft paragraph for repetitious words and replace them with synonyms, pronouns, and descriptive words.

Style   The last element of a **SOCS** revision is **S**tyle. **Style** is the way you express yourself in writing, the way you put a sentence or a group of sentences together. Two stylistic elements you can use are tone and sentence variety.

1. **Use a more serious, formal tone.**

   Tone is the writer's choice of words for a particular audience. The choice of a word can change the tone of an entire piece of writing. The tone of a paper can be serious or funny, formal or informal, or sincere or sarcastic, depending on the words you choose and the arrangement of your ideas. College writing is usually serious and formal, not conversational. Choose Standard Written English words that your readers are familiar with.

   Read the following student's paragraph, paying attention to its tone.

> My life as a college student is not easy because I have many things going on. For example, I have temptations. I mean like there are a lot of parties open to me. Then I have the temptation to skip class because most of my instructors don't have an attendance policy. Second, I have a lot of pressure in college. It could be my friend telling me to do the next best thing. My English instructor gets on my back about the grammar of my papers. The last thing I want to touch on is relationships. My relationship with my girlfriend conflicts with school. I'm tempted to hang out with her instead of studying. And when I am not with her she is all I can think about instead of the stuff I'm supposed to be learning in my classes. My life as a college student is a very difficult one.

The writer's tone is too informal and conversational. His informal word choices include *things going on, I mean, parties open to me; skip class, do the next best thing, gets on my back, to touch on, hang out, stuff.* In addition, the writer uses the contractions *don't* and *I'm* and overuses *a lot.*

ACTIVITY

4.15   Revising a Paragraph for Tone

Revise the paragraph about life as a college student, making its tone more serious, formal, and sincere.

ACTIVITY

4.16   Revising Your Draft for Tone

Read over your paragraph for word choice. Replace any words that are informal and conversational with Standard Written English choices.

2. **Use sentence variety.**

Sentence variety is the use of sentences that differ in type and length. Varying your sentences keeps the reader interested. When you use too many short sentences, your writing will sound childish. On the other hand, if you connect three or more sentences with *and, so,* or *but,* your sentences may be so long that the readers will forget what you said at the beginning.

Here is an excerpt of a student paper that illustrates how short sentences can make writing sound elementary:

> [1]I hated my job at Walmart because the managers did not respect the workers. [2]I worked four to eleven every weekday. [3]That was fine for me. [4]Then they had me working from two to eleven on weekends. [5]That was a problem. [6]I went to the manager. [7]I told her that I wanted to talk. [8]She was busy. [9]I waited until she was done. [10]She was helping a customer. [11]She kept ignoring me. [12]She did other things. [13]Those things were not important. [14]She never called me into the office. [15]She did not respect me. [16]I quit.

ACTIVITY

4.17   Revising a Paragraph for Sentence Variety

Revise the paragraph about the student's job at Walmart. You can take some words out and rewrite some of the short, choppy sentences by combining them.

_____

_____

_____

_____

_____

ACTIVITY Revising Your Own Paragraph for Sentence Variety

4.18 Revise your own paragraph for sentence variety.

Peer Review Response Sheet for Revision Stage

Your Name _____ Date _____

Title of Paper Reviewed _____

Directions: Please give careful thought and complete answers to each of these questions. If time permits, do a reverse scratch outline of this paper to see the writer's supporting points and organizational pattern more easily.

1. What is this paper about?

   _____

   _____

2. Do all of the supporting points and details prove the main point of the paper? Which supporting points do not?

   _____

   _____

3. Do any of the supporting points need more details? Which ones?

   _____

   _____

4. Are any points out of order? Where do they belong?

   _____

   _____

5. Does the writer use transitions? Give some examples.

   _____

6. What tone does the writer use? Formal or conversational? Give some examples.

   _____

   _____

   _____

7. Were any sentences hard to understand? Write them here.

   _____

   _____

   _____

| TIPS | **Revising Your Paragraph** |

1. **Give yourself time away from the paper.** Take at least an hour's break. When you return, you will be able to see the paper from a new perspective.
2. **Focus on one element at a time.** Remember **SOCS: S**upport, **O**rganization, **C**onnectors and transitions, and **S**tyle.
3. **If you are using a computer, print your paragraph.** Printing a copy will help you see the entire paper rather than a portion of it. Also, a hard copy is a good backup in case something happens to the electronic file.
4. **Get someone else to read your paragraph. Peer review** is the process of reading another writer's paper and giving practical suggestions to help the writer revise. Peer review can be done in pairs or in a group. Here are some guidelines:

- Choose someone you know you can work with.
- Make a copy of the paper so that both of you have one to read.
- Read the paper out loud while the other person listens closely.
- Offer helpful suggestions without criticizing the writer.
- Focus on the revision strategy of one element at a time: **SOCS: S**upport, **O**rganization, **C**onnectors and transitions, and **S**tyle.

Ermilie's Revised Paragraph

In Chapter 3, page 36, you read Ermilie's draft for the topic Money-Saving Tips for College Students. Following is her revised paragraph.

Ermilie's Revision

One way to save money is to spend less on food. College students can save money by making economical choices. Instead of buying ~~that~~ a bag of Doritos or a Snickers candy bar at vending machine prices, students can save money by bringing healthy snacks from home. ~~Healthy~~ Snacks like homemade trail mix, a piece of fruit, or cut-up vegetables are ~~inexpensive and portable~~ more nutricious than vending machine treats. Cutting down on expensive gourmet coffees or fruit smoothies can save students ~~almost~~ close to five dollars a day. ~~Most companies offer more than one cell phone plan, students can do research to find the cheapest plan.~~ Cell phone costs can also be reduced to save money. Most companies offer discounted rates for students, so its worth the time to research rates and plans to find the cheapest one. Spending less time on the phone with friends at peak times will help reduce phone expenses. Also, ~~students do not have to buy the latest phone every six months.~~ although new phones come out every few months, students can save money by not giving in to the temptation to buy a new one. Books are the biggest expense for college students, so find ways to spend less on books is worth the effort. ~~Buy books online. Some online companies will even ship for~~

> For example, buying   ones.
> ~~free. Buying~~ used books is cheaper than buying new. Students can even make
>   charges. In addition, students can buy books online and spend one-third less.
> money by selling their used books for less than the bookstore. ~~Avoid the~~
>
> ~~bookstore for supplies; the big discount stores have better prices.~~ Students who
>
> make economical choices can avoid money problems and may end up with some
>
> money in the bank.

Editing and Proofreading

LO 2 **Edit and proofread your papers.**

Editing and proofreading are the last steps in the paragraph writing process. **Editing** is the process of reading your paper for errors in grammar, punctuation, and spelling. **Proofreading** is the process of checking your final draft for errors you may have missed.

Editing

Editing involves looking at your paper very closely, sentence by sentence. Look for sentences that may be vague or confusing. In addition, check for errors in grammar, punctuation, and spelling.

TIPS | **Editing Your Paragraph**

1. **Focus on areas of weakness.** If you already know that you tend to make mistakes in a specific area, such as comma placement, you can check for those. Check one type of mistake at a time.

2. **Read your paper out loud.** By using more of your senses, you may be able to hear a part that needs to be revised that you did not notice while reading silently.

3. **Get someone else to read your paper.** You may not be able to find your errors because you do not realize that you have made them or know how to fix them. Find someone in your class or a tutor at your campus writing center who can point out errors that you do not see.

4. **Read your paper backwards.** When you read your paper from beginning to end, you may miss errors because you are caught up in the flow of ideas. Start at the end and read backwards to the beginning.

5. **If you are writing on a computer, use a spell-checker and grammar checker.** The spell-checking feature can automatically correct spelling and typographical errors. However, the program cannot tell whether you have used a word correctly such as *to, two*, or *too* correctly. Also, the program may not recognize some names or technical words. Grammar and style checkers cannot pick up all the errors or variations of meanings in your writing and may make inaccurate suggestions and point out errors that are actually correct.

Ermilie's Edited Paragraph

College students can save money by making economical choices. One way to save money is to spend less on food. Instead of buying a bag of Doritos or a Snickers candy bar at vending machine ~~prices. Students~~ prices, students can save money by bringing healthy snacks from home. Snacks like homemade trail mix, a piece of fruit, or cut-up vegetables are portable and more nutritious than vending machine treats. Also, _{cutting} ~~Cutting~~ down on expensive gourmet coffees or fruit smoothies can save students close to five dollars a day. ^{Another way to save money is to cut cell} ~~Cell~~ phone costs. ~~can also be reduced to save money.~~ Most companies offer discounted rates for students, so, it's worth the time to research rates and plans to find the cheapest one. Spending less time on the phone with friends at peak times ~~and keeping text messaging to a minimum~~ will help reduce phones expenses. Also, although new phones come out every few months, students can save money by not giving in to the temptation to buy a new one. ^{Finally, books} ~~Books~~ are the biggest expense for college students, so _{finding} ~~find~~ ways to spend less on books is worth the effort. For example, buying used textbooks is cheaper than buying new ones. Students can even make money by selling their used books for less than the bookstore charges. In addition, students can buy books online and spend one-third less. Student who make economical choices can avoid money problems and may end up with some money in the bank.

ACTIVITY   Editing a Paragraph

4.19   Practice editing by finding and correcting the errors in the following paragraphs. Each paragraph has two errors.

[1]Hikari Oe was born with his brain extended beyond his skull. [2]Doctors said that the surgery was dangerous. [3]They tell his parents about the possibility of the child's retardation and other nervous system difficulties. [4]Hikaris parents decided to go ahead with the surgery.

[5]When Hikari was about six years old, his parents noticed that he could memorize and sing songs although his ability to speak and understand language was quiet limited. [6]They decided to give him a piano lessons and found a teacher who was willing to take on the challenging student. [7]As the teacher worked with Hikari, it became clear that the child had remarkable musical gifts. [8]Within months, he was playing difficult classical pieces easily; moreover, he began to play his own arrangements of classical forms to create his own pieces.

[9]Though she did not think that the effort would be successful, Hikari's piano teacher decided to try to teach him musical notation so he could write down his compositions. [10]To her surprise, he mastered the difficult skill of writing classical musics in a short time. [11]Today, as a middle-aged man, Hikari Oe is an accomplished and celebrated composer. [12]Of classical music.

(Adapted from *The World of Psychology* by Samuel E. Wood et al.)

Proofreading

Proofreading is your final step before submitting your paper. By reading your paper one last time, you may find a mistake that you missed while editing. Here are some proofreading tips:

> **TIPS** | **Proofreading Your Paragraph**
>
> 1. **Make sure that your paper is neatly written or typed to make it easy for your instructor to read.**
> 2. **If your instructor has given you format guidelines, be sure that you have followed them.** Format guidelines may include the following: positioning of your name, course, and date and title; skipping lines (or double spacing if typing); and writing in ink.
> 3. **Read your paper one last time** for grammar, spelling, and punctuation errors you may have missed while editing.

Ermilie's Final Paragraph

College students can save money by making economical choices. One way to save money is to spend less on food. Instead of buying a bag of Doritos or a Snickers candy bar at vending machine prices, students can save money by bringing healthy snacks from home. Snacks like homemade trail mix, a piece of fruit, or cut-up vegetables are portable and more nutritious than vending machine treats. Also, cutting down on expensive gourmet coffees or fruit smoothies can save students close to five dollars a day. Another way to save money is to cut cell phone costs. Most companies offer discounted rates for students, so it is worth the time to research rates and plans to find the cheapest one. Spending less time on the phone with friends at peak times will help reduce phone expenses. Also, although new phones come out every few months, students can save money by not giving in to the temptation to buy a new one. Finally, textbooks are the biggest expense for college students, so finding ways to spend less on books is worth the effort. For example, buying used textbooks is cheaper than buying new ones. Students can even make money by selling their used books for less than the bookstore charges. In addition, students can buy books online and spend one-third less. Students who make economical choices can avoid money problems and may end up with some money in the bank.

Writing Assignments

Help Desk

Brianna feels that she does not need to revise her papers. She says it takes too much time. Also, she does not like to write and does not want to take the time to revise. For Brianna, writing one draft and copying it over to make it look neat is adequate. In a paragraph, explain to Brianna why revision is important.

Reading and Writing across the Curriculum: Western Civilization

MyWritingLab™
Complete this activity
at mywritinglab.com

 Beginning in 776 B.C.E., wars and conflicts were temporarily suspended every four years where athletes from the whole Greek world met at Olympia to participate in contests in honor of Zeus. Although they were religious events, the contests were highly competitive and violent. Losers were shamed and winners celebrated and rewarded.

The most celebrated hero of the <u>pankration</u>, which combines wrestling and boxing, was Arrichion, who won but died in victory. Although his opponent was slowly strangling him, Arrichion managed to kick in such a way as to horribly dislocate his adversary's ankle. The extreme pain caused the opponent to signal defeat just as Arrichion died, victorious.

(Adapted from *Civilization in the West* by Mark Kishlansky et al.)

A well-known quotation in sports first stated by college football coach Red Saunders is "Winning isn't everything; it's the only thing." Do you think that winning is important? Write a paragraph in which you support your opinion with a specific example.

Comment on a Contemporary Issue

What you do on the Internet tells more about you than you think. Companies track your searches and collect information about you. For example, if you search for information about cars, the websites you visit are tracked and sorted. Soon after, when you go to your favorite websites, you may see an advertisement for one of the cars you researched.

Some consumers feel that the companies doing the tracking are secretly spying on them. Write a paragraph about either the benefits or the disadvantages of tracking people's searching behavior.

English Success Tip: Ewe Can Knot Rely on You're Spell-Checker

Computer spell-checkers search for misspelled words in a sentence. A spell-checking program uses its own dictionary to recommend or correct words it identifies as misspelled.

While spell-checker can catch many errors, they are not 100 percent perfect. Spell-checkers may miss the following errors, as shown by the title of this tip.

Error That Spell-Check Misses	Example
Misspellings of proper names or other words that may not be in the spell-checker's dictionary	*Ewe* should be *You*. An ewe is a female sheep.
Typographical errors that create other words that are correct	*Knot* should be *Not*. Both are correctly spelled words, but *knot* is wrong here.
Wrong use of a correctly spelled word	*You're* should be *Your*. *You're* means you are, but the possessive pronoun *Your* is the correct form in this sentence.
Words that sound the same but differ in meaning	*Can Knot* should be *Cannot*.

5

Writing the College-Level Essay

Learning Objectives

After working through this chapter, you will be able to:

LO 1 Explain the characteristics of a college-level essay and identify its three parts: introduction, body, and conclusion.

LO 2 Write an essay.

LO 1 Explain the characteristics of a college-level essay and identify its three parts: introduction, body, and conclusion.

What Is the College-Level Essay?

The college-level essay is a piece of writing that consists of multiple paragraphs, which prove, discuss, or argue a central idea or thesis. Each of the paragraphs in the essay has a function: to introduce, to support, or to conclude the essay. The length of a college-level essay varies depending on the writing assignment.

In the college-level essay, you may not be asked to write about how you feel, to give "where and when" facts, or to repeat information you learned. Instead, you will be asked to use critical-thinking skills to express your point of view, support it, and present your evidence logically. In addition, you will be expected to use correct grammar and mechanics and to take responsibility for editing and revising on your own.

MyWritingLab™

Complete this activity at mywritinglab.com

QuickWrite

Describe the kinds of papers you were asked to write in school or in the workplace.

Parts of the College-Level Essay

The essay consists of three main parts: the introduction, the body, and the conclusion. The illustration on page 62 shows the purpose and content of each of these types of paragraphs. The number of paragraphs in an essay will vary depending on the topic and purpose.

College-Level Essay Example

Writing Reminder. See Chapter 11 to learn more about using the classification pattern.

The student essay titled "Frequent Flyers" on the next page is an example of the college-level essay. It is based on a narration paragraph that the student wrote about her first parachute jump (see Chapter 7, Narration, page 104). The writer developed this essay using the classification pattern.

Parts of the Essay

Introduction
- **Lead-in:** Gain reader interest
- **Bridge:** Connect the lead-in to the thesis statement
- **Thesis statement:** Present main idea of essay

Body Paragraphs
- **Topic sentence:** Present a point to explain or prove the thesis statement
- **Evidence:** Provide details to support the point

Concluding Paragraph
- **Concluding thoughts:** Provide final comments based on the point you have made in the essay

---

McGee 1

Melinda McGee

Professor Markus

College Preparatory Writing

12 Apr. 2014

Frequent Flyers

The sound of propeller engines accelerating down the runway echoed through the open hanger as I practiced my next skydive move by move. Lying face down, I got onto a board with wheels meant to give me the weightless feeling I would experience once I was in the air. I waited for the list of passengers to be called to board the plane. It was an unusually busy day at this drop zone, the official drop zone for Team USA and home to about twenty teams that compete on the national circuit. It also has the most new jumpers per day than any other drop zone in Florida. Of the two hundred or so jumpers I watched that day, I noticed that they could be classified according to their unique approaches towards jumping, such as the nervous newcomers, the adrenaline junkies, and the freefall flyers.

The most obvious group, the nervous newcomers, approaches jumping with fearful excitement. They are easy to notice because they wear the obviously rented equipment from the drop zone: matching jumpsuits and helmets bearing the Skydive Deland logo. The unmistakable oversized pack on their backs signals a large parachute that is required for student jumpers. The most telling sign, however, is the look on their faces. This is the look that every skydiver has had when jumping for the first time: the nervous stare. Although this look is common when newcomers are strapping on their parachutes or boarding the plane for the first time, it is most evident at 12,500 feet when the airplane door opens. The most memorable were two friends who wanted to make their first jump together. They took their positions at the doorway, each strapped to his instructor in a tandem harness, their toes right to the edge. Suddenly, that nervous look came over their faces. The first friend and his instructor stepped out into the deep blue, but the other froze and refused to go. Then, suddenly, without warning, the second instructor leaned back, and out the door they went.

Unlike the nervous newcomers, the adrenaline junkies are experienced jumpers who approach jumping with an uncontrollable hunger for **white-knuckle** adventure. Their gear consists of the lightest, smallest packs they can buy to be more streamlined while in freefall and to reach higher speeds. Many have made modifications to their jumpsuits, helmets, and parachutes to try to go faster or farther than in previous jumps. Modifying something as complex as a parachute can be dangerous and often the parachute does not open properly. While most skydivers

white-knuckle
causing great fear

are fearful of this possibility, the adrenaline junkies seem to enjoy the extra challenge. Their daring tricks brand them as dangerous because they show off during landings in winds that are unsteady at less than 200 feet. I have seen them doing spirals and hook turns just feet off the ground. Adrenaline junkies try jumping out of hot air balloons, helicopters, and illegally off of buildings and bridges. They are intense skydivers who push the boundaries of the sport.

Neither nervous like the newcomers nor extreme risk takers like the adrenaline junkies, the freefall flyers approach skydiving as a sport. Freefall flyers are the most dedicated group of jumpers; they spend hours practicing to perfect their maneuvers, try new ones, and often enter competitions. These skydivers perform during freefall, the first stage of the jump in which the skydiver exits the plane and falls towards earth before opening the parachute. Dropping at the speed of 160 to 170 miles per hour, the diver has about a minute in which to perform one or more maneuvers. For example, some people fly in on their back, with their head down, on their belly, sitting or standing—any position one can think of. Others enjoy acrobatic maneuvers such as loops, spins, twists, and poses. I have often seen groups jump together to build formations on their bellies, sometimes gripping each other's arms or legs. Freefall flyers take the sport seriously and often compete.

Skydiving has become a popular sport with facilities opening up all over the country. Although it appears dangerous, proper training and modern equipment have made it safe. In addition, almost anyone over eighteen can participate without a concern for physical conditioning. Because skydiving delivers excitement and challenge, as well as the chance to fly like a bird, people continue to come back for more as do the nervous newcomers, the adrenaline junkies, and the freefall flyers.

ACTIVITY
5.1

Analyzing a College-Level Essay

1. What does the writer do to get the reader's attention in the first paragraph?
   _____

2. Underline the main idea sentence of the essay twice. What does the writer intend to explain in her essay?
   _____

3. Underline the topic sentence of each body paragraph. How does the writer connect the main idea sentence with each topic sentence?
   _____
   _____

4. What does the writer talk about in the concluding paragraph?
   _____
   _____

Writing the College-Level Essay

LO 2 **Write an essay.**   To write a successful college-level essay, it is essential to understand the purpose and contents of each part: the introduction, the body, and the conclusion.

The Introduction

The introduction is the first paragraph of the essay. The purpose of the introduction is to get the readers interested in your topic and state the point of your paper. A simple way to build an introductory paragraph is to begin with a lead-in, continue with a bridge sentence or two, and end with the thesis statement. This is not the only way to write the introduction, but it is a helpful model for beginning writers.

The Lead-in: Get the Readers Interested   The introduction begins with a lead-in. The **lead-in** is a technique used to get the readers interested so that they will want to continue reading the rest of your essay.

A lead-in that captures the readers' interest may take some time and creative thinking to develop. You can experiment by trying several of the methods suggested in this section to find one that works best. If you have trouble thinking of an interesting lead-in, try writing the body of the essay first; as you write, an idea for the lead-in is likely to emerge. Techniques can be combined as long as you keep each of them brief.

> **TIP**   Some writers get stuck because they cannot think of an interesting lead-in. Try a prewriting strategy or work on the body paragraphs and return to the introductory paragraph later.

1. **Tell a brief story.** A brief story, also called an anecdote, explains an event that is funny, interesting, or emotional. The story should be related to your topic. It can come from your own or someone else's personal experience. Because most readers enjoy reading a story, this technique is likely to get them involved right away.

Psychology Text Chapter Introduction Using a Brief Story

Jonathan I was a painter who, throughout his successful artistic career, produced abstract canvases with great mixtures of vivid colors. At age 65, he suffered brain damage that left him completely colorblind. When he looked at his own artwork, all he could see was gray, black, and white; where formerly he had seen colors with rich personal associations, now he saw splotches that were "dirty" or "wrong." And it wasn't just his art. In his day-to-day life, for example, he began to limit his diet to black foods and white foods—black olives and white rice still looked right to him, whereas colored foods now appeared disturbingly gray and unpalatable. Over time, as he recovered from his initial sense of confusion, Mr. I began to explore painting in black and white. Despite his loss of color vision, Mr. I's sensory processes still provide him with a version of the world he can appreciate and transform as art. Mr. I's story illustrates how the senses involve a remarkably complicated group of mechanisms. The body and the brain work together to make sense of sensory stimulation.

(Adapted from *Psychology and Life* by Richard J. Gerrig and Philip G. Lombardo)

2. **Give background.** Background consists of facts, history, or other information that helps the reader understand your topic.

Art Appreciation Textbook Chapter Introduction Using Background

Cameras record the world around us, and the history of the camera is a history of technologies that record our world. These technologies are becoming more advanced and skillful. Photography began with images that did not move and then later added motion. To the silent moving image was added sound called a "talkie." To the "talkie" was added color. Film developed in its audience a taste for "live" action, a taste satisfied by live television transmission, video images that allow us to view anything happening in the world as it happens. These technologies are becoming more advanced and skillful. The study of the history of camera arts not only shows how these technologies developed over time but also the way the artists used them to explore time.

(Adapted from *The World of Art* by Henry M. Sayre)

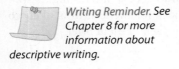

Writing Reminder. See Chapter 8 for more information about descriptive writing.

3. **Use description.** Description can bring actions, places, people, and objects to life. Use subjective description to express your personal impressions through colorful word pictures. Use objective description to give a realistic, unemotional view by using facts that describe without personal opinion.

Student Introduction Using Subjective Description

The sun, clearly above near midday, pierces through the trees of the mountain range like a skilled **archer** shooting target practice. Just as a well conducted orchestra plays its musical arrangement, so does the forest. Water

archer person who shoots with a bow and arrow

bounces off rocks as it trickles down its path, leaves dance their way down to the forest floor, and rocks tumble as they race at the mercy of gravity's will. But they do not play silently. The wind rhythmically whooshes through the trees while the creek bubbles enthusiastically. Twigs snap and pop in a forceful **crescendo.** The music of these mountains creates a lasting impression on those who appreciate nature's splendor. However, observing nature is not the only way to enjoy this area. For people who find pleasure in outdoor activities, the Blue Ridge Mountains are the perfect place for white water rafting, horseback riding, and hiking.

crescendo a gradual increase in loudness

Punctuation Reminder. See Chapter 29 for more information about punctuating quotations.

4. **Use a quotation.** A **quotation** is the words that someone else has said or written. A meaningful quotation can get the readers to think more deeply about your topic. Quotations can come from a variety of sources such as a newspaper, magazine, book, or a song. Slogans, popular sayings, proverbs, and favorite family expressions are other sources.

When using a quotation, be sure to tell the reader the source of the statement. Also, punctuate the statement with quotation marks.

Sociology Textbook Chapter Introduction Using Quotation

In a discussion in a sociology class at Bronx Community College in New York, the instructor explains that people have changed the way they think about race and ethnicity. When he asked students how they would describe themselves, Eva Rodriguez was quick to respond. She said, "This is hard for me to answer. Most people think of race as black and white. But it's not. I have both black and white ancestry in me, but you know what? I don't think of myself in that way. I don't think of myself in terms of race at all. You can call me Puerto Rican or call me Hispanic. I prefer the term 'Latina.' Calling myself Latina says I have mixed racial heritage, and that's what I am. I wish more people understood that race is not clear cut." There are now millions of people in the United States who, like Eva Rodriguez, do not think of themselves in terms of a single category but as having a mix of ancestry. This chapter examines the meaning of race and ethnicity.

(From *Society* by John J. Macionis)

5. **Define a term.** A **definition** is a statement of the meaning of a word or expression. Adding a definition helps the reader understand your own meaning of a word that you use in your paper. Define a word when you have your own personal meaning of a word that is different from one that people usually think of.

In some cases, defining a word is not helpful. Defining words that readers already know will bore them. Also, using a dictionary definition in the first sentence, such as "According to *Webster's College Dictionary* . . . " is an overused, unimaginative method.

Student Introduction Using Definition

> On April 20, 2010, an explosion and fire on the *Deepwater Horizon* offshore oil-drilling rig in the Gulf of Mexico caused the death of eleven workers and the injury of seventeen others. The sea floor oil gusher that resulted from the explosion has been responsible for what is now considered the largest oil spill in U.S. history. British Petroleum (BP) has been blamed for the accident and held accountable for cleanup costs and other damages. An oil spill is an accidental or intentional discharge of oil into the environment. The term is often used when oil is released into the ocean or coastal waters. Many attempts were made to contain and control the oil while millions of gallons of crude oil poured into the Gulf of Mexico. Unfortunately, this disaster has had many negative effects. The Gulf oil spill has resulted in an extensive environmental disaster that has impacted marine and wildlife habitats, human health, and the U.S. economy.

6. **Use the funnel method.** This method is named after an object called a *funnel*, which has a wide opening at the top that slopes into a narrow tube at the bottom. The funnel method starts with a general statement about the topic. Each sentence after that gets more specific, leading the reader to the thesis statement.

   Some general statements are too broad. They are too far from the idea of your thesis statement. Statements that are too broad often begin with phrases like these: "In the United States today," "Throughout human history," or "In our modern world today."

TIP | You do not have to limit yourself to the techniques explained in the previous section. You can develop your own unique lead-in or explore some others such as stating a surprising fact or statistic, asking an intriguing or controversial question, or expressing an opposing point of view.

The Bridge: Connect the Lead-in to the Thesis Statement In order for the readers to see the connection between your lead-in and your thesis statement, you should include a bridge sentence. Avoid directly telling the reader what you are going to do as in this example: Now that I have given some background about my topic, I am going to tell you what I will prove in this paper.

ACTIVITY **Identifying Bridge Sentences**

5.2 Find and underline the bridge sentences in the example introductory paragraphs you read on pages 66–68.

The Thesis Statement The **thesis statement** is a sentence that tells the readers the main point of your essay, that is, what you want them to know, believe, or understand. The main point may explain, analyze, or take a position. The lead-in and bridge of the introduction prepare the readers with information about the subject of the essay, and the thesis tells them specifically what you plan to discuss. Although the thesis statement can be placed anywhere in the introductory paragraph, a good place is at the end of the introductory paragraph.

The thesis statement includes the narrowed topic of the essay and the main point. The thesis statement can be written with or without listing the supporting points of the essay. Thesis statements that include the supporting points, also called a thesis map, can keep you organized as you write.

Thesis with Narrowed Topic and Main Point

Students who take a class in a computer classroom are easily tempted to use the computer for other activities rather than for classwork.

Thesis with Narrowed Topic, Main Point, and Listed Supporting Points (Thesis Map)

Students who take a class in a computer classroom are easily tempted to use the computer for other activities rather than for classwork, such as surfing the Internet, visiting social networking websites, or playing games.

TIPS | **Writing Thesis Statements**

1. **Choose specific words.**

   Not specific: Soccer is a great sport.

   Specific: Soccer promotes healthy development in children for several reasons.

   Specific with listed supporting points: Soccer promotes healthy development in children because it promotes good sportsmanship, develops inner resources, and provides aerobic exercise.

2. **Make a point about your topic rather than state a fact.**

   States a fact: The Mall of America, located in Bloomington, Minnesota, opened in 1992 and has over 500 stores in its four-story building.

   Makes a point: The Mall of America offers a variety of entertainment options under one roof.

   Makes a point with listed supporting points: The Mall of America offers a variety of entertainment options under one roof, such as Nickelodeon Universe, Underwater Adventures Aquarium, and Moose Mountain Golf Adventures.

3. **Make a point that is neither too broad nor too narrow.**

   Too broad: Moving from one country to another is difficult.

   Too narrow: When I came to this country I had trouble understanding the news on television.

Adequate: When I moved from Medellin, Colombia, to Victory Gardens, New Jersey, I had a difficult time.

Adequate with listed supporting points: When I moved from Medellin, Colombia, to Victory Gardens, New Jersey, I had a difficult time learning how to speak English, making new friends, and understanding the laws.

4. **State your point directly.** Avoid announcing what you plan to do or what you think or believe.

   Announcement: In this paper, I plan to discuss the different ways students who take a class in a computer classroom are easily tempted to use the computer for other activities rather than for class work.

   Belief: In my opinion, I believe that students who take a class in a computer classroom are easily tempted to use the computer for other activities than for class work.

   Direct statement: Students who take a class in a computer classroom are easily tempted to use the computer for other activities rather than for classwork.

5. **If you list supporting points in the thesis statement, decide on the most effective order to discuss them and make them grammatically parallel. Parallelism,** also called parallel structure, is the use of the same forms of words, phrases, or clauses when they appear in pairs, in groups, or in lists. Notice the difference between the two pairs of sentences that follow.

   Not Parallel: During my first semester in college, I learned to attend all of my classes, time management, and my study habits improved.

   Parallel: During my first semester in college, I learned to attend all of my classes, manage my time, and improve my study habits.

Style Reminder. See Chapter 32 for more information about parallelism.

TIP If you have trouble writing a thesis statement that lists the supporting points, try writing it in stages.

Narrowed topic: I want to write about _____.

Main point: I want to explain, analyze, or prove that _____
_____.

(Optional) Supporting points: I want to include these supporting points:
_____.

Then, remove the "I want to . . . " and refine the sentence, combining the narrowed topic, main point, and supporting points.

ACTIVITY **Evaluating Thesis Statements**

5.3   Explain what is wrong with each of the following thesis statements.

1. The benefits of having a part-time job while being enrolled in college are gaining work experience, I can make extra money, and to deal with a diverse group of people.

2. I am going to talk about football and how it has affected my life.

3. Auto enthusiasts come in all shapes, sizes, and forms.

4. The restaurants in my area are Italian, Mexican, Hispanic, Greek, French, Japanese, and Chinese.

5. Our economy and our environment can use a lot of help at this point when every bit counts and everything you participate in could make such a difference.

The Body

The **body** of the essay consists of paragraphs that support the thesis statement. Each body paragraph is an academic paragraph. See below for a review of the parts of a paragraph.

Parts of the Body Paragraphs

Topic Sentence
- Connects the point of the paragraph to the thesis statement
- May include words or phrases from the thesis statement

Evidence
- Evidence supports the main point of the topic sentence
- Supporting points are connected with transitions
- Evidence may include reasons, examples, causes, effects, comparisons, contrasts, types or groups, steps, or points of an argument depending on the purpose of the essay
- Supporting points are arranged by time order, spatial order, or order of importance

Concluding Sentence
- Sums up in a new way

Ordering Body Paragraphs Paragraph order will depend on the purpose of the essay or the organizational pattern, such as comparison and contrast, cause and effect, or process. If you have written a thesis statement that lists the supporting points, each body paragraph will discuss one of those points in the order that they appear in the list.

Connecting Body Paragraphs In Chapter 3, you learned that connectors and transitions help readers connect ideas within a paragraph and make the organization easier to follow. Transitions also have an important role in an essay. They connect the main point expressed in your thesis statement with the rest of the paragraphs of the essay.

One strategy you can use to make a transition from one body paragraph to another is to use transition topic sentences. Each topic sentence refers to the main point of the previous paragraph and connects it to the main idea of the new paragraph. This strategy is modeled in the following example. Notice how the transition topic sentences include the main idea from the thesis statement. This thesis statement lists supporting points, but listing them in the thesis is not required.

Thesis statement: Students who take a class in a computer classroom are easily tempted to use the use the computer for other activities rather than for classwork, such as surfing the Internet, visiting social networking sites, or playing games.

Transition Topic Sentence	Example
For body paragraph 1	One activity that tempts students is surfing the Internet.
For body paragraph 2	In addition to surfing the Internet, students visit social networking sites.
For body paragraph 3	Not only do they surf the Internet and visit social networking sites, they also play online games.

The Conclusion

The **conclusion** is the last paragraph of the essay. Its purpose is to remind the readers of the main point of the essay and make final comments. The conclusion is your last chance to connect with the readers and say something that leaves them with a lasting impression. Your goal is to hold the readers' attention to the very end.

The conclusion does not have to be organized in a specific way, nor does it have required parts as the introduction does. However, the conclusion should be as strong as the other paragraphs in the essay.

There are a number of techniques that you can use to create an effective conclusion. Most often, your technique will depend on the purpose of your essay. For example, if you have written a narrative essay, your conclusion will explain how the conflict was resolved and what the narrator learned from the experience. The conclusion for an argument essay will try to convince readers that your position on the issue is the best.

Some of the techniques that are suggested for introductions can also be used for conclusions. For instance, you can end with a thought-provoking question, brief story, or a surprising fact or statistic.

> **TIP** | Make your conclusion interesting by avoiding some of these overused techniques:
>
> 1. Using tag words phrases like these: *In conclusion, In summary, So you can see, Finally,* or *In closing.*
> 2. Listing each of the topic sentences from the body paragraphs.
> 3. Repeating the introduction.
> 4. Announcing to the reader: *In this essay I have tried to show, I have discussed, I have presented.*
> 5. Apologizing for not writing more or for your lack of knowledge of the topic.

Here are several techniques for effective conclusions and examples of each written by students or college textbook authors:

Give Effects: Student Example

"Be all that you can be" has a special meaning for U.S. Army soldiers. The message is simple yet important; the U.S. Army offers a unique opportunity to realize one's potential. Although I exited the service to pursue my education, I credit Army life with transforming me into a mature, responsible individual. Most importantly though, my four-year experience as a soldier blessed me with a sense of bravery to overcome obstacles, the power of determination to succeed, and a newly discovered ability to understand the suffering of all human beings.

Make a Recommendation: Student Example

Becoming a single parent at sixteen quickly transformed me from a carefree adolescent to an adult with more responsibility than I could handle. Rather than enjoying high school, going to parties, and planning my future education, I was changing diapers and losing sleep. I was not prepared for the many challenging changes that took place in my life: working full-time at a low-paying job, not being able to go out with my friends, and being deserted by the baby's father. Through this difficult, life-changing experience, I had to grow up fast. Although I would not change my decision to bring my daughter into the world, I suggest that teenage girls plan for the care and costs of raising a child before getting pregnant.

Project into the Future: Student Example

The many advantages that Facebook offers, such as long distance communication, new friends, and business advertising, will most probably continue to make it a popular site for many years to come. However, because of the potential employer rejection after reading applicants' pages, attacks by sexual predators, and security breaches, users need to be careful about the amount of personal information they share on the site. Even with improvements to privacy settings, security holes are found on a regular basis, and the site is under constant attack by hackers. Facebook users need to understand that their personal information will be accessed and used for purposes that are not always beneficial.

Project into the Future: Textbook Example

The United States has been, and will remain, a land of immigrants. Immigration has brought cultural diversity and stories of hope, struggle, and success told in hundreds of languages. Like those of an earlier generation, today's immigrants try to blend into U.S. society without completely giving up their traditional culture. Some still build racial and ethnic groups in a community, so that in many cities across the country, the little Havanas and Koreatowns of today stand alongside the Little Italys and Chinatowns of the past. In addition, new arrivals still carry the traditional hope that their racial and ethnic diversity can be a source of pride rather than a source of inferiority.

(From *Society* by John J. Macionis)

Call for Action: Student Example

radio frequency energy cell phones give their signals through radio waves, which are comprised of radio-frequency (RF) energy, a form of electromagnetic radiation

Animal and human research studies have given the scientific society a foundation for the possible health hazards of **radio frequency energy** from cell phones. However, scientists who oppose the findings of these studies criticize the research methods that were used. Other researchers have claimed that current studies do not provide absolute proof. More research along with better research methods are needed to prove unquestionably that cell phones present health hazards to humans.

Add to the Significance of the Topic: Student Example

The effects of the Gulf oil spill of 2010 makes it obvious that the United States should move away from its dependence on oil as an energy source. Clean energy fuel technologies must be developed. Automobile manufacturers have responded by producing alternative fuel vehicles that use electricity, hydrogen, fuel cells, and hybrid technology. As more methods to produce alternative fuels are found, the economy and environment will benefit.

Finally, you may include a restatement of your thesis using different words to avoid repeating the same sentence.

The Essay Graphic Organizer

The Essay Graphic Organizer on the following page will help you plan and organize the parts of your essay. Refer to it as you draft and revise, making changes if you add new ideas and deleting ideas that do not work.

Peer Review Reminder. For feedback on your writing, have someone read your paper and make comments on the Peer Review Response Sheet in Chapter 4, page 54.

Writing Assignments

Help Desk

Rose-Marie admits that she has trouble writing introductions. Read her introduction to an essay about her native country, Haiti, and offer her some suggestions to improve it by answering the questions that follow her introduction.

> [1]Haiti is known to be one of the poorest countries in the world. [2]People do not know that although we might be poor, we are very nice people. [3]I would like to teach you about Haiti, the people, their food, and their culture. [4]I hope you are willing to learn about it.

1. Does Rose-Marie's lead-in get your attention? What strategy would you suggest that she use?

   _____

2. Underline the thesis statement. What is the main point? How could she be more specific?

   _____

   _____

3. Circle the numbers of the sentences that make the mistake of directly addressing the reader.

Group Activity: Developing a Thesis Statement and Supporting Points

Many websites are being developed to help college students. One site offers students money to upload their class notes, essays, research papers, and study guides. Every time a file is viewed, the person who posted the information earns money. Another feature of the site is an option to form study groups. Students can communicate with each other anywhere in the world and form networks such as study groups about any topic. The site is also available to teachers.

Along with the benefits of a site such as this one are the potential problems. In small groups of three or four, brainstorm some of the problems that a site like this could have. For example, how would students know if the notes or papers they were downloading

Essay Graphic Organizer

MyWritingLab™
Use the interactive graphic
organizer at mywritinglab.com

Introduction

Lead-in:

Bridge:

Thesis Statement:

Body Paragraph 1

Topic Sentence:

Supporting Point 1:

Supporting Point 2:

Supporting Point 3:

Body Paragraph 2

Topic Sentence:

Supporting Point 1:

Supporting Point 2:

Supporting Point 3:

Body Paragraph 3

Topic Sentence:

Supporting Point 1:

Supporting Point 2:

Supporting Point 3:

Conclusion

Concluding Statement:

were accurate and of good quality? Does a website that provides notes encourage laziness among students? Would students be more likely to skip class and download notes? What would prevent students from copying others' work and using it as their own?

Develop a thesis statement about the possible problems of this type of student information-sharing and networking website. Then, develop three supporting points for each problem you identified using the essay graphic organizer.

Reading and Writing across the Curriculum: Political Science

The Americans with Disabilities Act of 1990 (ADA) requires employers and public facilities to make "**reasonable accommodations**" for people with disabilities. A reasonable accommodation is any change in the workplace that enables a qualified individual with a disability to enjoy equal employment opportunities. It also prohibits discrimination against these individuals in employment. In 1998, the Supreme Court ruled that the ADA offers protection against discrimination to people with AIDS. Unfortunately, Americans with disabilities continue to suffer from discrimination. Stereotypes of the disabled are still common in our culture, especially in the media.

Brainstorm how the media represents the disabled. Choose three ways and support them with examples, using movies, television images, or advertisements.

Comment on a Contemporary Issue

With advances in technology and increased commuting costs, teleworking is quickly becoming popular. **Teleworking** is an arrangement in which companies allow employees to perform their work away from a central office. Teleworkers can work from home, telework centers, or satellite offices.

Telework has both advantages and disadvantages. Some employers report that teleworking actually increases communication and productivity. In addition, more jobs are open to disabled workers as well as single parents. Workers can save money by not having to commute or buy clothing to wear to work. On the other hand, some workers feel the need to be around other people or feel socially and professionally isolated.

Write an essay about the advantages and disadvantages of teleworking. Would you like this arrangement? Why or why not?

Reader Response

In the textbook excerpt on page 74, John J. Macionis points out, "Like those of an earlier generation, today's immigrants try to blend into U.S. society without completely giving up their traditional culture." Write a paper that responds to one or more of these questions:

Text-to-Text	■ Does this reading remind you of something else you have read, heard, or seen (story, book, movie, song, news item, magazine article, website, and so on)?
	■ Are the ideas the same or different? How?
Text-to-Self	■ How do the ideas in the reading relate to your own life, experiences, or ideas?
	■ Do you agree or disagree with what you read?
Text-to-World	■ What does the reading remind you of in the real world?
	■ Does it make you think about something in the past, present, or future? Explain.

Write about an Image

The driver in the photo is getting a ticket. Write an essay explaining the reasons police officers give people tickets.

Style Reminder. See Part 7 for help with improving your writing style.

English Success Tip: The Perils of Padding

Have you ever tried to make an essay longer by adding unnecessary words or material? This may seem like a good way to meet the length requirements of an assignment. However, using this technique, also known as **padding**, makes your writing less effective and does not impress your teacher.

When revising your paper, look for evidence of padding:

- using unnecessary adjectives and adverbs, repetitious words, and wordy expressions which make writing less precise and clear
- adding unnecessary information
- including details that do not prove your main idea or details that repeat the same point

Learning Paragraph and Essay Organization Plans

6 Illustration

Learning Objectives

After working through this chapter, you will be able to:

LO 1 Explain that illustration is a pattern of development that supports a point with examples.

LO 2 Write an illustration paragraph.

LO 3 Write an illustration essay.

What Is Illustration?

Illustration is a pattern of development that supports a point with examples. For instance, if you wanted to write about rude people at your workplace or in college, you would give specific examples of rude behavior to back up your opinion.

MyWritingLab™
Complete this activity
at mywritinglab.com

QuickWrite

Take a few moments to jot down one or more examples of information you learned in a college course.

LO 1 **Explain that illustration is a pattern of development that supports a point with examples.**

Illustration in College Writing

Illustration is used in many college writing assignments where explanations and examples are needed. For example, in a biology class, you may be asked to explain the stages of cellular respiration; in a social science course, you may be asked to give examples to show how the news media influenced an election. Illustration is often used in textbooks to explain difficult concepts. Here is an excerpt explaining a concept in psychology called *observational learning*:

Observational learning is the process of learning new responses by watching the behavior of another. In essence, after observing a model, you may think: If I do exactly what she does, I will get the same reinforcer or avoid the same punishment. A classic example of human observational learning occurred in the laboratory of Albert Bandura. After watching adult models punching, hitting, and kicking a large plastic BoBo doll, the children in the experiment later showed a greater frequency of the same behaviors than did children in control conditions who had not observed the aggressive models. Later studies showed that children imitated such behaviors even when models were cartoon characters.

(From *Psychology and Life* by Richard J. Gerrig and Philip G. Zimbardo)

The main point in an illustration paragraph can be supported with multiple examples or one extended example. The following paragraphs show the two methods.

Multiple Examples

The following illustration paragraph is called "Lessons from the Mat." Jason Duarte, a student, uses several examples to support his main point.

> [1]My participation in high school wrestling taught me valuable lessons. [2]The first lesson I learned was to be responsible. [3]For example, one day, when I was late for practice and I had no good excuse for it, the coach made me run two extra miles and then wrestle the whole team, one person after another for one minute each. [4]There were over twenty people on our team, which meant I had to wrestle over twenty minutes nonstop. [5]I was never late to practice again after that day. [6]Wrestling also taught me to eat foods that promote good health. [7]Many of the foods I enjoyed eating were not nutritious and did not give my body the fuel it needed, but I had a hard time not eating them. [8]One of my worst practices was after a big meal at a fast-food restaurant. [9]I felt slowed down and nauseated. [10]After that experience, I realized that I had to make better food choices to feel energetic at practice. [11]As a result, I added more fruit and vegetables into my diet and ordered healthy items when eating fast food. [12]The most valuable lesson wrestling taught me was to be a good sportsman. [13]Wrestlers must be able to control their aggression once the match is over. [14]At one competition, I saw a wrestler who had just lost a contest start a fight by attacking his opponent. [15]Because of his poor sportsmanship, he was temporarily not allowed to go to school for three days. [16]When I step onto the mat with my opponent, my goal is to win the match, but when the match is over, I shake my opponent's hand, and the intensity of the battle gradually disappears. [17]Even though my wrestling days are long over, the lessons I learned from this sport still remain fresh in my mind.

 ACTIVITY

6.1

Analyzing an Illustration Paragraph with Multiple Examples

Answer the questions about the paragraph you just read, "Lessons from the Mat."

1. Underline the topic sentence.
2. What is the main point of the paragraph?

_____

3. What are the three examples Jason uses to support his main point?

_____

4. Do the examples use factual information or personal experiences?

_____

5. What is the method of organization?

_____

_____

One Extended Example

The following paragraph shows how student writer Jessica Vilca's illustration paragraph called "A Simple Act of Honesty" uses one extended example to support her main point.

> [1]A simple act of honesty can provide personal satisfaction. [2]For example, last semester, at the end of my last class of the day, chemistry, I observed a small canvas bag lying on top of the desk behind me. [3]I waited for almost ten minutes for the owner of the bag to come back for it, but no one showed up. [4]I decided to take the bag home with me and try to find the owner the next time the class met. [5]Curious about what was inside the bag, I opened it and found an iPod, headphones, and a pencil. [6]At the beginning of the next chemistry class, I asked the boy who sat in the same chair where I found the bag if he had left something in class that day. [7]He said he had and listed the three items I had seen in the bag. [8]When I returned his bag, he was surprised and happy, and I felt gratified. [9]Approximately two weeks after that incident, I found one hundred dollars that I thought I had misplaced two months ago. [10]The money was in a shoebox where I had placed it for safekeeping. [11]Perhaps the universe smiled down in favor of my good deed.

ACTIVITY 6.2 **Analyzing an Illustration Paragraph with One Extended Example**

Answer the questions about the paragraph you just read, "A Simple Act of Honesty."

1. Underline the topic sentence.
2. What is the main point of the paragraph?

_____

3. What example does the writer give to support her main point?

_____

4. What are the main events of the narrative example?

_____

_____

_____

_____

> ## ILLUSTRATION   Essentials
>
> The purpose of the illustration pattern of development is to help the reader understand your main point through the use of specific, interesting, accurate examples. Effective illustration has these essential elements:
>
> 1. Illustration makes a point about a general statement or belief.
> 2. The supporting details that illustrate the point are multiple examples or an extended example.
> 3. The supporting details are equally developed and sufficient in number.
> 4. The methods of organization can be order of importance, chronological order, or spatial order, depending on purpose.
> 5. Words are specific and accurate.

The Illustration Paragraph

LO 2 **Write an illustration paragraph.**

Prewriting the Illustration Paragraph

Before you write, you must choose a suitable topic and develop it.

Decide on Your Topic and Purpose   When deciding on your own illustration topic or responding to an assigned topic, consider the following:

1. **Choose a topic that is limited enough to be explained in one paragraph.** A topic like **modern day heroes** might bring to mind many different types of heroes such as people who perform courageous acts, like soldiers, fire fighters, or police officers, or people who are notable in a particular field like medicine or physics. Some people consider celebrities to be heroes. As you can see, it would not be possible to discuss all of those groups in a paragraph. Therefore, you could narrow to one group of heroes or even choose one modern day hero and write about his or her accomplishments.
2. **Choose a topic that can be supported with examples.** A topic such as **how to change a tire** has a different purpose, which is to give the steps in a process.

 ACTIVITY   Evaluating Topics for Illustration Paragraphs

6.3   Explain why each of the following topics would be acceptable or not acceptable for an illustration paragraph.

1. Careers

_____

2. How to design a web page

_____

_____

3. Inaccurate ideas that people who visit or move to the United States have about its culture

_____

4. Economic problems in the United States

_____

5. An admirable quality of an individual

_____

Develop Ideas for Your Topic Prewriting for an illustration paragraph involves developing a strong series of examples or an extended example. Developing ideas by using your preferred prewriting technique will help you discover whether or not you have enough information to support your topic.

Jason chose to write about lessons he learned as a high school wrestler. Here is his concept map:

Jason's Concept Map

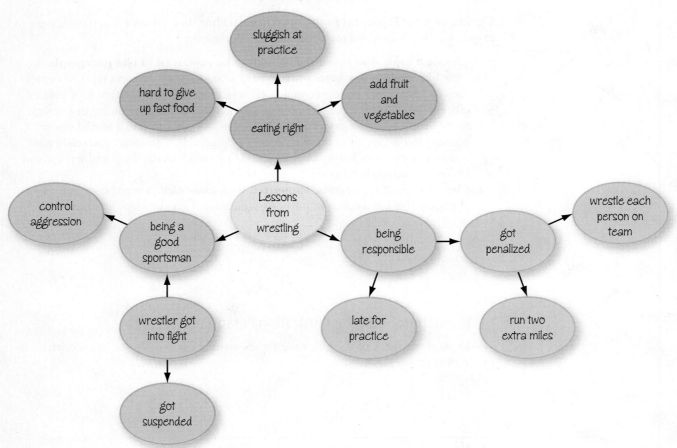

Paragraph Activity: **Prewriting to Develop Ideas**

Using your preferred prewriting technique, develop ideas for one or more of these illustration topics. You can develop a topic with multiple examples or an extended example.

General Topics

advice for new college students
important lessons you have learned
annoying driving behaviors
violent video games
body modifications (i.e., tattoos, piercing)

Writing across the Curriculum Topics

Environmental Science: energy-saving strategies for the home
Film: special effects in movies
Sociology: cultural traditions
Marketing: shopping websites
Travel and Tourism: places for tourists to visit in your city or town

Narrow Your Topic and Write the Topic Sentence The topic sentence of the illustration paragraph includes your **narrowed topic** and your **main point.**

Students taking online courses need to have self-discipline.

My grandfather was the most generous leader of the village in Tai Shang City in China.

Throughout history, **police departments** have adapted to technological advances.

| TIPS | **Writing Illustration Topic Sentences** |

1. **Choose only one topic and one main point.** Only one topic and one main point can be adequately explained in one paragraph. The following chart illustrates incorrect topic sentences and their corrections.

Type of error	Poor topic sentence	Corrected topic sentence
One topic with two main points	Moving out of my parents' home taught me independence and self-discipline.	Moving out of my parents' home taught me self-discipline.
Two topics with one main point	Working out and monitoring food choices have become common practices for people who want to improve their health.	Monitoring food choices has become a common practice for people who want to improve their health.

2. **Choose a specific word or phrase for your topic and main point.** A word that is not specific may be misunderstood. The following topic sentences show the difference between a vague and specific topic and main point.

Vague

Sedona, Arizona, is a wonderful place to visit.

The word *wonderful* in this topic sentence is not specific enough, and your readers may not interpret the word the same way you do.

Specific

Sedona, Arizona, known for its red rock canyons and surrounding forests, offers numerous options for outdoor exploration.

This topic sentence is more specific. Also, a few descriptive words about Sedona provide information for readers unfamiliar with the city.

3. **Avoid using a fact as your main point.** A fact may be used to briefly describe your topic but should not be used as your main point. Facts can be examples that support your main point. Notice how the first topic sentence below is just a fact while the second topic sentence uses a fact to provide just an informative idea as the main point.

Fact as a main point   Pesticides are used to get rid of insects.

Informative idea as a main point   Pesticides have created a wide range of problems.

ACTIVITY   Writing Topic Sentences for an Illustration Paragraph

6.4   Write a main point for each of the following narrowed topics. The resulting topic sentence should be suitable for an illustration paragraph.

1. Joslyn's fear of heights

   _____

2. The food in the college cafeteria

   _____

3. My brother's daring personality

   _____

4. Online shopping

   _____

5. People can save energy

   _____

Paragraph Activity: **Writing a Topic Sentence**

Look over the details you developed for your illustration paragraph (page 85) and write a topic sentence for one of the topics.

Organizing and Drafting the Illustration Paragraph

Develop Supporting Details Supporting details for the illustration paragraph can come from personal experience, personal observation, or discussions in class or with friends and family. Details can also be information that is common knowledge, which is information that most people know. As you develop your details, make sure that they support the main point and are specific. Cross out details that do not support your main point. You may need to do some additional prewriting to develop more details or add information to the ones you have.

 ACTIVITY
6.5   ### Eliminating Details that Do Not Support the Main Point

In each group of sentences, underline the main point in each of the topic sentences. Then circle any details that do not support the main point.

1. Topic sentence: Staying up late is a bad habit I would like to change.
   a. Every night I play games online until 2 a.m.
   b. I know that time should not be wasted.
   c. Instead of turning my cell phone off at night so that I can get some sleep, I cannot resist talking to my friends who call me at 3 or 4 a.m.

2. Topic sentence: My job as a stock clerk keeps me busy.
   a. One of my duties is to put groceries in their proper places on the shelves.
   b. I also help customers find products that they cannot locate on their own.
   c. Last summer I worked in a summer job program in Puerto Rico where I washed patrol cars at a police station.
   d. At the end of the night, my coworkers and I organize the items that have been misplaced and straighten the items on the shelves.

3. Topic sentence: My best friend Jennifer participates in many extracurricular activities.
   a. Jennifer is a senior in high school, and all of her classes are advanced placement (AP).
   b. Jennifer volunteers and teaches a Bible study class at her church.
   c. Three days a week, she has choir practice at school.
   d. She also coaches cheerleaders in her town's Optimist cheerleading program.

Paragraph Activity: **Selecting Details**

Look back at your prewriting for your illustration paragraph (page 85), and evaluate the details to see which ones support your main point. Cross out the details that you do not plan to use. Prewrite to add more details if you need them.

Organize Your Supporting Details After collecting all of the examples and details to support your main point, you are ready to organize them into a plan for your paragraph. An illustration graphic organizer like the one on pages 90 and 91 can help you put your examples and details into a logical order.

Identifying the Example and Explaining Details An illustration paragraph presents each example and explains it. A paragraph that does not explain each example is merely a list of sentences.

The following student paragraph lists examples without explaining them.

> Being a college student can be stressful. One source of stress is the pressure to earn high grades. Another stress is being a student and an employee at the same time. In addition, my friends put pressure on me. Finally, my family gives me more responsibilities than I can handle.

ACTIVITY **Providing Details for Each Example**

6.6 Revise the student's paragraph about college stress by giving an explaining detail for each example.

1. One source of stress is the pressure to earn high grades.

   _____

2. Another stress is being a student and an employee at the same time.

   _____

   _____

3. In addition, my friends put pressure on me.

   _____

4. Finally, my family gives me more responsibilities than I can handle.

   _____

   _____

Using an Illustration Graphic Organizer An illustration graphic organizer can help you organize your examples and explanations. Here is the graphic organizer Jason completed to plan the paragraph you read at the beginning of the chapter, "Lessons from the Mat."

Jason's Illustration Paragraph Graphic Organizer

Topic Sentence: My participation in wrestling taught me valuable lessons.

Example/Evidence 1: To be responsible

Explanation

· Late for practice

· Had to run two extra miles

· Had to wrestle 20 team members, 1 minute each

· Always on time to practice

Example/Evidence 2: To eat healthy foods

Explanation

· Sluggish and nauseated at practice after meal at fast-food restaurant

· Added more fruit and vegetables to diet

· Ordered healthy items when eating at fast-food restaurant

Example/Evidence 3: To be a good sportsman

Explanation

· Wrestler lost a contest and started a fight with opponent

· Student was suspended

· Shake opponent's hand after contest

Paragraph Activity: **Using a Graphic Organizer to Plan**

Choose one of illustration graphic organizers (see pages 90 and 91) and fill it in with your illustration paragraph details. The first one is arranged for a series of examples, which has space for each example and the information that explains, illustrates, or proves the example. Add examples and explanations to extend the organizer as needed. The second organizer is arranged for an extended example, which has space to list the events of the story.

Illustration Graphic Organizer for Multiple Examples

Topic Sentence:

Example/Evidence 1: _____

Explanation

Example/Evidence 2: _____

Explanation

Example/Evidence 3: _____

Explanation

Writing Reminder.
See Chapter 3 for
more information
about methods of paragraph
organization.

Putting Your Ideas into a Logical Order The method you use to organize your examples depends on your purpose. Three methods you can choose from are order of importance, time order, or spatial order.

Illustration Graphic Organizer for an Extended Example

Topic Sentence:

Extended Example (List events or describe)

Paragraph Activity: Organizing the Details

Check the order of details in your illustration graphic organizer to see if you have used a method of organization that fits your purpose. Make changes if necessary.

Write the First Draft

Use your illustration graphic organizer to guide you as you write the first draft. Check off each example as you complete it. In addition, consider the following elements.

*Writing Reminder.
See Chapter 3 for lists
of transition words
used for order of importance, time
order, and spatial order.*

Add Connectors and Transitional Words and Expressions Illustration paragraphs use specific transition words and expressions to give a signal to the reader that you are introducing examples or that you are giving an explanation of the example. Be sure to choose the transition that is appropriate for the type of supporting detail you are presenting. Illustration, order of importance, time order, or spatial order transition words can also be used to introduce examples depending on the purpose of your paragraph.

The following illustration transitions can be used to introduce examples:

An example of this is	Equally important is	The most	The first
An instance of this is	For example,	important	example is
Another example is	For instance,	example is	(the second,
	One example is	To illustrate,	the third)

Paragraph Activity: **Writing the First Draft**

Write a first draft of your illustration paragraph, using the graphic organizer you prepared. Be sure to choose a suitable method of organization and verb tense.

Revising, Editing, and Proofreading

Revise your draft by looking at one element at a time: **S**upport, **O**rganization, **C**onnectors and transitions, and **S**tyle.

REVISION CHECKLIST FOR AN ILLUSTRATION PARAGRAPH

Element	Revision Checkpoints
Topic	☐ The topic is significant and memorable.
	☐ The topic is limited enough to be described in one paragraph.
	☐ The topic can be supported with multiple examples or an extended example.
Topic Sentence	☐ The topic sentence contains the narrowed topic and the main point.
	☐ The narrowed topic is expressed specifically and concisely.
	☐ The main point is a general statement or belief that can be adequately explained in one paragraph.
Support	☐ The support consists of multiple examples or one extended example.
	☐ Each example is introduced and followed by explaining details.
	☐ The examples are adequately explained.
	☐ All examples and details support the main point.
Organization	☐ The paragraph follows order of importance, time order, or spatial order depending on the purpose of the paragraph.
Connectors and Transitions	☐ Appropriate connectors and transitions for illustration, order of importance, time order, or spatial order provide coherence.
Style	☐ Writing is clear, concise Standard Written English.
	☐ Tone is appropriate for a college audience.
	☐ Specific details create reader interest through the use description, narration, and illustration.
	☐ Sentences are varied.

Paragraph Activity: **Revising**

Revise your illustration paragraph draft using the checklist above.

Check Grammar, Punctuation, and Spelling

As you reread your paper to check for grammar, punctuation, and spelling errors, pay special attention for possible errors that may arise in illustration paragraphs:

■ Use present or past tense verb forms consistently throughout the paragraph.
■ Use specific words to explain your examples.
■ Use commas after transition words and phrases where needed.

ACTIVITY 6.7 **Revising, Editing, and Proofreading an Illustration Paragraph**

Read and edit this illustration paragraph written by student Ryan Olkowski, and answer the questions below.

---

[1]At Publix Supermarket, office cashiers have demanding responsibilities that they may be assigned each day. [2]One of these responsibilities is front-end coordinator (FEC). [3]Front-end coordinators supervise the employees who work in the front end of the store, this includes cashiers, office cashiers, and front-end service clerks. [4]The FEC makes sure that the floors and bathrooms get cleaned and that the parking lot is free of carts. [5]At the end of the day, the FEC who closes the store has additional duties. [6]Having employees arrange items on shelves, clean registers, refill bags, empty trash, and sweeping and mopping floors. [7]Another responsibility is working in the back office, known as the money room. [8]Part of this duty is counting and balancing cashier tills as well as making sure cashiers get their breaks or finish their shifts on time. [9]In addition, back office personnel deposit cash and order change for the next day. [10]The most challenging responsibility is working in customer service. [11]On top of the list is handling customer returns and dealing with customer complaints. [12]Other tasks are issuing rain checks, directing phone calls, and processing money orders. [13]Lottery is self-serve now. [14]Although the job as office cashier is rigorous, the benefits are excellent, and there are many opportunities for advancement.

Questions on Revising

1. Underline the topic sentence. What is the narrowed topic and main point?
   Narrowed topic: _____

   Main point: _____

2. Show that the writer has adequate and relevant support by filling in the illustration graphic organizer on the next page.

3. Which sentence is not relevant and can be removed?

   _____

Illustration Graphic Organizer

Topic Sentence:

Example/Evidence 1:

Explanation

Example/Evidence 2:

Explanation

Example/Evidence 3:

Explanation

Questions on Editing and Proofreading

4. Which sentence is a fragment? Find and correct it.

_____

5. Which sentence has a comma splice error? Find and correct it.

_____

Paragraph Activity: **Editing and Proofreading**

Edit and proofread your illustration paragraph. Check that your final draft is complete, accurate, and error-free.

Paragraph Writing Assignments

Help Desk

James was asked to revise the content of his illustration paragraph about the lessons he learned from his grandmother. He thought that his paper had fulfilled the assignment. Read James' paragraph and write him a paragraph suggesting some specific things he can do to improve the content.

> [1]Growing up with my grandmother was a good learning experience for me. [2]I love my grandmother so much. [3]I do not know what I would do without her. [4]My grandmother taught me to appreciate life. [5]She also gave me the faith that I could do whatever I wanted to in my life. [6]She taught me how to love my family. [7]My grandmother showed me how to stand up for myself and be a man. [8]I would not trade this experience for anything in this world.

Group Activity: Learn about Other Cultures

As a college student, you are beginning a new stage of your life. You will meet many new people from this and other countries. Some students' cultures will be unfamiliar to you. This activity will give you an opportunity to learn about other cultures.

In small groups of three or four, identify the different cultures represented by the people in your group. Discuss the customs of the different cultures such as holiday celebrations, raising children, beliefs about health, family relationships, and gender roles.

Write a paragraph with your group or individually, giving examples of the customs you learned about other cultures.

Reading and Writing across the Curriculum: Psychology

You have probably heard the noun *hassle* as an informal term meaning an annoying difficulty or a source of trouble. Psychologist Richard Lazarus uses *hassles* to mean the little stressors that seem to crop up every day:

> Hassles cause more stress than major life events do. Daily hassles include irritating, frustrating experiences such as standing in line, being stuck in traffic, waiting for an appliance or utility repair technician to come to your home, and so on. Relationships are another frequent source of hassles, such as when another person misunderstands us or when coworkers or customers are hard to get along with.
>
> Back in 1981, DeLongis and his colleagues found that the ten hassles most frequently reported by college students they surveyed were as follows:
>
> 1. Troubling thoughts about the future
> 2. Too many things to do
> 3. Not getting enough sleep
> 4. Misplacing or losing things
> 5. Wasting time
> 6. Not enough time to do things you need to do
> 7. Inconsiderate smokers
> 8. Concerns about meeting high standards
> 9. Physical appearance
> 10. Being lonely
>
> (Adapted from *The World of Psychology* by Samuel E. Wood et al.)

Do you think the listed items are still relevant today? Prewrite about the hassles (little stressors) you experience. Choose the most significant hassles in your life and write an illustration paragraph explaining of each of them.

Comment on a Contemporary Issue

U.S. culture places a strong emphasis on body image. The popular media—television, magazines, movies, and the Internet—present images of thin, physically fit women and trim, muscular men. This focus on weight, fitness, and beauty has influenced the way people, especially adolescents, feel about themselves. According to the National Institute on Media and the Family, exposure to soap operas, music videos, fashion magazines, and video games has been associated with a drop in self-esteem in young people.

Write a paragraph giving examples of this emphasis on weight, fitness, and beauty.

Reader Response

The textbook excerpt on page 80 about observational learning explains that people learn by watching others. The author gives an example of a study done where children watched adults hitting and kicking a large plastic doll. Later, the children imitated this behavior.

Have you ever learned something by watching a person, a group of people, or a video? Write a paragraph that responds to one of these questions:

Text-to-Text	■ Does this reading remind you of something else you have read, heard, or seen (story, book, movie, song, news item, magazine article, website, and so on)?
	■ Are the ideas the same or different?
Text-to-Self	■ How do the ideas in the reading relate to your own life, experiences, or ideas?
	■ Do you agree or disagree with what you read?
Text-to-World	■ What does the reading remind you of in the real world?
	■ Does it make you think about something in the past, present, or future?

Write about an Image

Today, t-shirts are a means of personal self-expression. They display designer logos, advertisements, political messages, and humor. You can find just about anything written on a t-shirt, and if it has not been written, you can have your message printed on one.

Write a paragraph giving examples of t-shirt messages that are popular. Describe each of them to give the reader a mental image.

The Illustration Essay

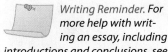

LO 3 **Write an illustration essay.**

Writing Reminder. For more help with writing an essay, including introductions and conclusions, see Chapter 5.

The illustration essay has the same purpose as the illustration paragraph: to support a main point with specific examples. The illustration essay uses the same organizational patterns as the illustration paragraph. Each body paragraph gives either multiple examples or an extended example to support the thesis statement.

The Thesis Statement

The thesis statement for an illustration essay makes a point that can be supported with specific examples. The thesis statement can be expressed in one of two ways:

Thesis with Narrowed Topic **and** Main Point:

Goldie had ongoing problems that were difficult for the family to deal with.

Thesis with Narrowed Topic, Main Point, **and** Listed Supporting Points:

Goldie's ongoing problems that were difficult for the family to deal with were his persistent shedding, his physical problems, and his destructiveness.

The Body Paragraphs

Each of the body paragraphs in the illustration essay can provide multiple examples or an extended example. Each body paragraph can be organized by order of importance, chronological order, or spatial order, depending on the purpose of the paragraph.

Notice how Rebecca uses multiple examples in her illustration graphic organizer to prove her thesis.

Rebecca's Illustration Essay Graphic Organizer

Introduction

Lead-in: Background about the Peres family adopting a Golden Retriever puppy.

Bridge: When the puppy grew up, the family realized he was not a good choice; he had become a nuisance.

Thesis Statement: Goldie's ongoing problems that were difficult for the family to deal with were his persistent shedding, his physical problems, and his destructiveness.

Body Paragraph 1

Topic Sentence: Goldie's persistent shedding was difficult for the family to deal with.

Example 1: Shed hair all over the house.

Example 2: Clogged the family pool and floated on the water.

Example 3: Landed in the food.

Example 4: Clung to the family members' clothing.

Body Paragraph 2

Topic Sentence: Along with Goldie's shedding problem, his persistent physical problems were also difficult for the family.

Example 1: Dry, scaly skin

Example 2: Fur brushing

Example 3: Ear infections

Example 4: Running away

Body Paragraph 3

Topic Sentence: Goldie's destructiveness was the most difficult for the family to handle.

Example 1: Chewed the leather couch.

Example 2: Chewed the table and chair legs.

Example 3: Dug up flower beds and bushes.

Conclusion

They could no longer deal with Goldie's shedding, physical needs, and destructiveness. The Pereses gave Goldie up for adoption.

Illustration Essay Example

The following is Rebecca's essay using multiple examples to explain the problems a family experienced with its Golden Retriever.

Goldie, the Troublesome Dog

by Rebecca Lang

[1]Bringing a dog into the home changes the lives of the people in that home. When the Peres family adopted an eight-week old male Golden Retriever puppy, they were excited. They had selected this breed because they wanted a dog that was playful, loving, and gentle. The children chose the name Goldie because the dog's fur was a light gold color. As a puppy, Goldie enjoyed being with the family, especially when playing with the children. However, cute puppies eventually become adult dogs. When Goldie grew into an eighty-pound adult, the family realized that the dog was not an appropriate choice for them. Goldie had become a nuisance. Goldie's ongoing problems that were difficult for the family to deal with were his persistent shedding, his physical problems, and his destructiveness.

[2]Goldie's persistent shedding was difficult for the family to deal with. His long, golden hair, approximately five inches in length, was a nuisance. His constant shedding left hair everywhere throughout the Pereses' home. Even with the biweekly vacuuming, a fresh carpet of hair covered every surface in the house. The long hair clogged the family's pool filter and floated like a fur blanket on the top of the water. In addition, the lengthy hair would somehow become airborne and land in the Pereses' meals. Not only did the hair land in food, but it clung to the family members' clothing. These hairy clothes had to be shaken and vacuumed before they could be worn, not an enjoyable task. On many mornings, when the children rushed to get ready to go to school and did not shake the fur off of their clothes, they looked as if they had rolled around in a pile of dog hair.

[3]Along with Goldie's shedding problem, his persistent physical problems were also difficult for the family. He had dry, scaly skin, which required constant attention. His skin and coat needed to be washed twice a week with an expensive shampoo recommended by the veterinarian. In addition to the biweekly bathing came the nuisance of fur brushing. This had to be done on a daily basis. Another physical problem was Goldie's frequent ear infections. Because of his floppy ears, he had an ear infection about once every three months. The Pereses had to constantly cleanse the ears with a special solution and apply medication. The worst problem was Goldie's need for exercise,

specifically running free. Although the family provided several daily walks, Goldie needed more vigorous activity. He became an escape artist and ran away whenever he could, whether on a leash or by jumping over the backyard fence. Once Goldie escaped into the neighborhood, it would take hours for the Pereses to finally catch him.

⁴Goldie's destructiveness was the most difficult for the family to handle. He never outgrew his habit of chewing on various household items. Within a year, the inside and outside of the Pereses home was virtually destroyed. The dog's first chewing offense began with the new leather couch, which he had viewed as a huge rawhide bone. Goldie had torn off a three-foot piece of leather from the backside of the leather couch, causing the front of the couch to sag. His second offense included all of the tables and chairs. Goldie had chewed on all of the table and chair legs, leaving them with a splintered look. After this happened, the Pereses decided to keep Goldie in the back yard. However, this led to his final offense, digging up the flowerbeds and bushes and making holes in the grass.

⁵The Pereses concluded that something had to be done. They could no longer deal with Goldie's shedding, physical needs, and destructiveness. They felt that the only solution was to bring Goldie to the Golden Retriever Rescue where he could be adopted by someone who would give him the attention and training that he needed. The Pereses loaded Goldie into the car and tearfully drove him to his new life.

Analyzing an Illustration Essay

ACTIVITY 6.8

Answer the following questions about "Goldie, The Troublesome Dog."

1. Underline the thesis statement in the first paragraph.
2. What technique does the writer use for her lead-in?

_____

3. Underline each of the topic sentences in the body paragraphs.
4. In each body paragraph, does the writer support the thesis by using multiple examples or an extended example?

_____

5. How does the writer conclude the essay?

_____

Illustration Essay Graphic Organizer

Using an illustration graphic organizer will help you place your details in the appropriate pattern. The sample graphic organizer shown on page 102 can be changed to suit your needs by adding paragraphs, examples, and evidence.

Essay Writing Assignments

Write about an Image

Electronic communications help keep people connected and make our lives run more smoothly, but they also create distractions. The constant interruptions keep us from completing our work. Write an essay giving examples of digital distractions that prevent people from getting important things accomplished.

Illustration Essay Graphic Organizer

MyWritingLab™
Use the interactive graphic
organizer at mywritinglab.com

Introduction

Lead-in:

Bridge:

Thesis Statement:

Body Paragraph for Multiple Examples

Topic Sentence:

Example 1 with Evidence/Explanation:

Example 2 with Evidence/Explanation:

Example 3 with Evidence/Explanation:

Body Paragraph for Multiple Examples

Topic Sentence:

Example 1 with Evidence/Explanation:

Example 2 with Evidence/Explanation:

Example 3 with Evidence/Explanation:

Body Paragraph for Multiple Examples

Topic Sentence:

Example 1 with Evidence/Explanation:

Example 2 with Evidence/Explanation:

Example 3 with Evidence/Explanation:

Conclusion

Concluding Statement:

Writing Topics for an Illustration Essay

For your illustration essay, choose one of these options:

- from paragraph to essay: expand the paragraph you wrote in the paragraph section of this chapter
- any of the writing topics in the paragraph section of this chapter
- any topic from the following list:

General Topics

challenges facing college students
responsibilities of a particular job
true heroes
qualities of a public figure whom you admire
values taught by a specific sport, game, or other activity

Writing across the Curriculum Topics

Sociology: products that show the people of United States value convenience
Psychology: examples of observational learning as defined on page 80 of this chapter (the process of learning new responses by watching the behavior of another)
Biology: pet ownership
Business Communications: workplace harassment
Family Studies: alternatives to marriage

English Success Tip: Getting Help with Writing

If you are having problems thinking of or organizing ideas, or noticing and correcting errors, take action and ask for help. Look for free tutoring opportunities or ask a classmate or friend to work with you.

When working with a writing tutor, classmate, or friend, you may want that person to correct every problem for you. In the end, relying on someone else to do your revising, editing, and proofreading will not make you a stronger writer; it will make you weak and dependent. Have the person work with you to help you find, understand, and correct your own errors.

7 Narration

Learning Objectives

After working through this chapter, you will be able to:

LO 1 Explain that narration is a pattern of development that tells a story or gives an account of a significant experience or event.

LO 2 Write a narrative paragraph.

LO 3 Write a narrative essay.

LO 1 **Explain that narration is a pattern of development that tells a story or gives an account of a significant experience or event.**

What Is Narration?

Narration is a pattern of development that tells a story or gives an account of a significant experience or event. Narratives are used in a variety of writing situations. A text message to a friend about something that just happened, a news story recounting the capture of a criminal, and a history book's explanation of a Civil War battle are all narratives. Fiction writers also use the narrative pattern of development to tell their stories.

MyWritingLab™
Complete this activity at mywritinglab.com

QuickWrite

Have you heard a good story in the past few days? Take a moment and write a brief account of the story.

Narration in College Writing

Narratives are frequently used in college writing assignments. For example, you may have an assignment in a history course in which you tell the story of an important event or a discovery someone made. In a business-related course, you might write about the growth of a company, hotel, store, or restaurant. Courses in health care fields often assign medical histories. In the social sciences, narrative writing projects include case studies.

Textbooks frequently explain events through the use of narratives. The following story of the discovery of Ice Age cave paintings in southeastern France is an example.

In 1994, three cave explorers spent the Christmas holiday in the valleys of the Ardèche region in southeastern France where they made a remarkable discovery of a large collection of **Ice Age** art. In the area, explorers had already discovered numerous caves that Ice Age people had

Ice Age a time when ice covered much of the earth, about 10,000 years ago

decorated between about 14,000 and 21,000 years ago. However, nothing already known about the region prepared the team for the breathtaking discovery that awaited them. Sensing a draft from an area of fallen rocks, they dug through the earth and stones to create a gap wide enough for the thinnest of them to crawl through. When she realized that there was a long hallway ahead, she called the others. They shouted into the darkness to get an echo, which would give them a sense of the cave's dimensions. The noise seemed lost in vast emptiness. When they returned with all of their equipment, they found that the hallway led to the biggest cavern ever discovered in this part of France. Yet more astounding was their discovery in an adjoining chamber: a portrait made of in red ochre of a bear, standing over three feet high—preserved for who knew how many thousands of years. It soon became clear that the Chauvet (shaw-VAY) cave, as the explorers named it, after their team leader, was one of the most extensive collections of Ice Age art in the world.

(Adapted from *The Humanities* by Henry Sayre)

The following is an example of a student narrative paragraph called "A House Cleaning Mistake" by Jetty Horta.

[1]The first time I cleaned a house in the United States, I made a big mistake that caused my friend to lose a client. [2]When I came to the United States, I lived with my friend Laura, who was a cleaning lady. [3]One day she asked me if I wanted to clean a house to make some money, and I agreed. [4]When we arrived at the client's house early the next morning, Laura introduced me to the owner of the house. [5]Then, to my surprise, Laura told me that she had to go to clean another house. [6]I did not expect to clean this big house by myself. [7]I was nervous; my hands were sweating. [8]When Laura left, the owner showed me where I could find the cleaning products. [9]A few minutes later, the owner told me she was leaving for work. [10]I was alone in the house, and I started to clean. [11]At around 1:45 p.m., I had only one room left to do, her bedroom. [12]I saw many blankets of different colors and sizes. [13]I also saw five square pillows and a huge, beige round one. [14]I thought that all of these belonged on her bed, so I put all the blankets on the bed and arranged the pillows on top of the blankets. [15]That evening, Laura received a phone call from the lady whose house I cleaned. [16]She told Laura that she never wanted me to clean her house again because I had made her bed with the dog's blankets and pillows. [17]Although I felt bad at the time, now I am able to look back and laugh at this funny experience.

Analyzing a Narrative Paragraph

7.1 Answer the questions about the paragraph you just read, "A House Cleaning Mistake."

1. Underline the topic sentence.
2. When and where does the story take place?

_____

3. Who are the people involved in the events of the story?

_____

4. What is the conflict in the paragraph?

_____

_____

5. How is the conflict resolved?

_____

_____

6. When does the narrative begin and end?

_____

7. Does the story take place in the past or in the present?

_____

NARRATIVE Essentials

The purpose of the narrative pattern of development is to support a main point with a story. The point is the meaning or importance of an event or experience. An effective narration has these essential elements:

1. A narrative tells a story that has a point. The point tells the reader about the meaning or importance of an event or experience.
2. The story happens at a specific time and place in the past.
3. The story has a conflict. The conflict is a problem or struggle in a story. By the end of the story, the conflict is worked out. A conflict can happen between two or more people, between a person and something in his or her environment, or within a person. The conflict makes a narrative interesting to readers. The conflict builds suspense and makes the reader want to find out what happens.
4. The supporting details that help the reader understand the story include the setting, the characters, the conflict, the events, and the resolution (how the conflict is worked out).
5. The events in the story are presented in time order.
6. The story is told using past tense verb forms.

The Narrative Paragraph

LO 2 Write a narrative paragraph.

Prewriting the Narrative Paragraph

Before you write, you must choose a suitable topic and develop it.

Decide on Your Topic and Purpose When deciding on your own narrative topic or responding to an assigned topic, consider the following:

1. **Choose an incident that is significant enough so you can make a point about its meaning or importance.** Writing about an experience with a rude person at work that taught you to control your temper is more meaningful than writing about a smooth day at work when nothing out of the ordinary happened.
2. **Choose an incident that took place in a short period of time.** For example, you can write about your high school graduation ceremony, which took place in a few hours, rather than your entire senior year in high school.
3. **Choose an incident that has only one conflict.** The conflict is the heart of your story and keeps your reader focused and interested in the outcome of your story.

 ACTIVITY   Evaluating Topics for Narrative Paragraphs

7.2   Explain why each of the following topics would be suitable or unsuitable for a narrative paragraph.

1. a fun two-week summer vacation in the city

_____

2. passing the road test for a driver's license

_____

3. shopping at the mall

_____

4. throwing the winning touchdown in the last seconds of a playoff game

_____

Develop Ideas for Your Topic Prewriting for a narrative paragraph involves writing a rough sketch of the story you want to tell. Freewriting or listing works well for narratives. For example, Daniel was asked to write about an event that changed his life. Here is part of his freewrite about an experience in the United States Navy.

> I will never forget how I felt when I saw the news on September 11, 2001. I was in the United States Navy onboard a ship in Norfolk, Virginia. I saw what happened on the news. I was in total shock. One of my cousins worked in one of the towers. I had so many emotions running through me. My time in the navy was coming to an end. I wasn't sure what to do.

 Paragraph Practice: Prewriting

Using your preferred prewriting technique, develop ideas for one or more of these narrative topics.

General Topics

an embarrassing experience
a moment of failure or success
a problem in a relationship
a difficult decision
a misjudgment of someone or something

Writing across the Curriculum Topics

Literature: a favorite childhood story
Psychology: a memorable dream
Education: an experience with a teacher
Environmental Science: a severe weather event
Biology: an encounter with an animal, bird, fish, or snake

Narrow Your Topic and Write the Topic Sentence The topic sentence of the narrative paragraph includes your narrowed topic, which is the event or experience, and the meaning or importance of the event or experience. The student whose paragraph you read about making a mistake while cleaning a house was responding to this topic:

Write about an embarrassing moment

Here is her topic sentence:

> The first time I cleaned a house in the United States, I made a big mistake that caused my friend to lose a client.

TIPS | **Writing Narrative Topic Sentences**

1. **Express your narrowed topic specifically and concisely.**

   Not specific: I made a mistake that taught me to be more responsible.

   Specific: Misplacing a customer's credit card taught me to be more responsible.

2. **Make a point about the meaning or importance of the event or experience.**

   No point: I have always been afraid of lightning and thunder.

   Point: Saving my niece's life during a thunderstorm showed me that I could conquer my fear of thunder and lightning.

3. **Choose a specific word or phrase to describe the meaning or importance of the event or experience.** Avoid general words such as *fun, exiting, wonderful,* and *good.* These words are not concise enough.

   Not specific: Attending cosmetology school instead of college was not good.

   Specific: Attending cosmetology school instead of college made me realize that I should have taken my parents' advice.

 Analyzing Narrative Topic Sentences

7.3   Explain what is wrong with each of the following topic sentences. If a topic sentence is good, write "good."

1. The craziest thing happened to me last Saturday night.

   _____

2. We all make decisions in life; some are positive and some are negative.

   _____

3. It was the morning of June 3, and my mom asked me if I had heard about the eighteen-year-old girl who had been in a car accident.

   _____

4. Being embarrassed by tripping and falling on stage did not ruin my fifth grade graduation.

   _____
   _____

ACTIVITY 7.4   Writing Main Points for Narrative Topics

Each of the following topic sentences has a narrowed topic for a narrative paragraph, but the main point has been left blank. Write a main point, which is the meaning or importance, for each narrowed topic.

EXAMPLE: Getting pulled over for violating a traffic light taught me to drive more carefully.

1. When I almost lost my life in a car accident, I learned

   _____
   _____

2. Being caught in a lie made me realize

   _____
   _____
   _____

3. My parents' divorce taught me

   _____
   _____
   _____

Paragraph Practice: **Writing Topic Sentences**

Write topic sentences for the topic that you prewrote about in Paragraph Practice on pages 107–108.

Organizing and Drafting the Narrative Paragraph

Using your topic sentence as a guide, the next steps are to develop and organize supporting details and write the first draft.

Develop Supporting Details To help your reader to fully understand your narrative, include all the important details of the story:

- **Setting:** the time and place of your story
- **Characters:** the people in the story
- **Conflict:** the problem or struggle in the story (e.g., a disagreement, a choice to be made, an obstacle to overcome, or a person who is difficult to deal with)
- **Events:** the series of actions that happen in the story from beginning to end
- **Resolution:** the solution to the problem, the way found to deal with the situation

Organize Your Supporting Details After collecting all of the information for your story, you are ready to organize the details into a plan for your paragraph.

The pattern used to organize the events in a narrative paragraph is called chronological or time order. **Chronological** or **time order** is the organization of events presented in order from beginning to end.

Jetty's list of events from her paragraph "A House Cleaning Mistake" is shown in her narrative graphic organizer.

Jetty's Narrative Graphic Organizer

Topic Sentence: The first time I cleaned a house in the United States, I made a big mistake that caused my friend to lose a client.

Characters: Name and Description

1. Me (Jetty)

2. My friend, Laura

3. The client (owner of house)

Setting

Location: The client's house

Time: Early morning to evening

Conflict: I was nervous about cleaning the house by myself; I was not sure where to put the blankets and pillows in the client's bedroom.

Events

1. I agreed to clean a house with Laura.

2. We arrived at the client's house in the morning, but Laura left to clean another house.

3. The owner showed me where the cleaning products were located and left for work.

4. I had cleaned all but the bedroom by 1:45 p.m.

5. I saw blankets and pillows of different shapes and sizes and was not sure where they belonged, but I thought they must belong on the client's bed; I arranged them on the bed.

6. The client called Laura complaining that I had placed the dog's blankets and pillows on her bed.

Resolution

The client told Laura that she did not want her to clean her house anymore.

Concluding Sentence: Although I felt bad at the time, now I am able to look back and laugh at this funny experience.

ACTIVITY   Placing Events in Time Order

7.5   The events in the next two paragraphs are out of order. Number the sentences to put the events in their proper time order.

Paragraph 1

_____ 1. Young children's emotions develop according to a biological schedule for a specific age.

_____ 2. Laughter appears somewhere between three and four months.

_____ 3. Somewhere between eighteen months and three years, children begin to show first empathy, envy, and embarrassment, followed by shame, guilt, and pride.

_____ 4. Between the ages of four and six months, the emotions of anger and surprise emerge.

_____ 5. By three months of age, babies can express happiness and sadness.

_____ 6. By about seven months, infants show fear.

(Adapted from _The World of Psychology_ by Samuel E. Wood et al.)

Paragraph 2

_____ 1. John Schnatter, founder of Papa John's, fulfilled his dream to open a pizza chain that delivered superior quality traditional pizza delivered to the customer's door.

_____ 2. To help his father, Schnatter sold his car, used the money to purchase $1,600 of used restaurant equipment, knocked out a broom closet in the back of his father's tavern, and began selling pizzas to the tavern's customers.

_____ 3. Shortly after graduating from Ball State University with a business degree, he faced his first business challenge.

_____ 4. After the success of the pizza in the tavern, Schnattner officially opened the first Papa John's restaurant in 1985 and opened as many stores as the market would bear.

_____ 5. The challenge was that his father's tavern was $64,000 in debt and failing.

_____ 6. Schnatter worked his way through college making pizzas, improving the techniques and tastes that would some day become Papa John's trademark.

_____ 7. Soon the pizza became the tavern's main attraction and helped turn the failing business around.

(Adapted from _Business in Action_ by Courtland Bovee, John V. Thill, and Barbara E. Schatzman)

Paragraph Practice: **Planning the Paragraph**

Choose one of the topics from the prewriting activity on pages 107–108 or your own topic, and using the narrative graphic organizer below, fill in the events and other important information for your narrative paragraph.

Narrative Graphic Organizer

MyWritingLab™
Use the interactive graphic
organizer at mywritinglab.com

Topic Sentence:

Characters: Name and Description   **Setting:**

1.   **Location:**

2.

3.   **Time:**

Conflict:

Events

1.

2.

3.

4.

5.

Resolution

Concluding Sentence:

Paragraph Practice: **Placing Events in Time Order**

Looking back at your graphic organizer, check your list of events. If you have left any events out, add them now.

Write the First Draft As you write your first draft, consider these elements: dialogue, description, transitional words and expressions, and verb tense.

Add Dialogue When telling a story, you may want to include a few lines of dialogue. **Dialogue** is a written conversation. The purpose of using dialogue in your narrative is to give your reader an idea of what your character sounds like. Spoken words need to be punctuated with quotation marks.

Use brief dialogue only at an important moment in your story. Too much dialogue breaks the flow of the narrative and sounds like a conversation, not a story.

Most of the time, you will not need dialogue. However, in the following student paragraph, dialogue is important to the point of the paragraph, which is that the writer did not understand slang expressions.

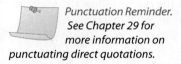

Punctuation Reminder. See Chapter 29 for more information on punctuating direct quotations.

[1]During my first day of high school in the United States, I discovered that the English I had learned in my country did not help me understand slang expressions. [2]As I entered the building that morning, I realized that I did not know where any of my classrooms were. [3]I stopped a student to ask him for directions, and instead, I got my first slang lesson. [4]I said, "Hi." [5]He answered, "What's up, man?" [6]A little confused, I replied, "Nothing. You?" [7]"Chillin" was his response. [8]Without knowing what that word meant, I said, "No, thank you." [9]He gave me a strange look, so I quickly asked him how to get to my class. [10]After he gave me directions, he added, "Got it, dawg?" [11]At that moment, I did a 360-degree spin looking for a dog. [12]After thanking him for his help, he said, "Fa sho," which I spent the rest of the day trying to figure out.

Add Description Use vivid details to create word pictures to help the reader visualize the setting, people, and events. This student paragraph helps the reader visualize the event:

[1]The wind was hitting my Honda Civic a bit harder than usual from the speed I was picking up on the curvy back roads. [2]My favorite song came on the radio, and I sang along and danced to the beat. [3]Looking ahead, I saw a stop sign on a side road. [4]This was the famous Shotgun Road where many of my friends had wrecked their cars. [5]If they had not been such careless drivers, I thought, they would not have had accidents. [6]Pushing on my brakes slowly, I stopped my car. [7]Looking right, I saw a few cars in the distance. [8]On my left, I saw a tall wood telephone post covered with bushes. [9]I could not see the left side of the road.

¹⁰As I looked right again, I could see cars coming closer, so I decided to make a speedy turn and just go for it. ¹¹Making my left turn, not paying attention, I saw an enormous Mack truck about to hit me. ¹²At that moment, I realized that death was right in front of me.

ACTIVITY   Identifying Vivid Details

7.6   Reread the student paragraph and underline parts that help you form a mental image of the event.

Add Connectors and Transitional Words and Expressions Narratives use time order connectors and transition words and expressions to help the reader follow the sequence of events. The following is a list of transitions commonly used for narratives:

after	eventually	once
afterward	finally	one day
after a while	first	previously
after that	immediately	soon
as soon as	in the meantime	the next day
at first	in the past	then
at last	later	today
at that time	last	until
before	meanwhile	when
before this	next	while
during	not long after	yesterday
earlier	now	

Grammar Reminder. See Chapters 22–24 for more information about verb tenses.

TIP   When writing a narrative, be sure to use the appropriate past tense forms and avoid shifting your verbs back and forth from the past tense to the present tense.

Revising, Editing, and Proofreading

Revise your draft by looking at one element at a time: **S**upport, **O**rganization, **C**onnectors and transitions, and **S**tyle. The following Revision Checklist contains the **SOCS** elements as they apply to narrative paragraphs.

REVISION CHECKLIST FOR A NARRATIVE PARAGRAPH

Element	Revision Checkpoints
Topic	☐ The event or experience is significant and memorable.
	☐ The event or experience takes place in a limited period of time.
	☐ The event or experience has a conflict.
Topic Sentence	☐ The topic sentence contains the narrowed topic and the meaning or importance of the event or experience.
	☐ The narrowed topic is expressed specifically and concisely.
	☐ The meaning or importance is described with a specific word or phrase.
Support	☐ The supporting details include the setting, characters, conflict, events, and resolution.
	☐ All supporting details are relevant and adequate.
Organization	☐ The paragraph follows chronological order to show story events from beginning to end.
Connectors and Transitions	☐ Time order connectors and transitions provide coherence.
Style	☐ Writing is clear, concise Standard Written English.
	☐ Tone is appropriate for a college audience.
	☐ Dialogue and vivid details create reader interest.
	☐ Sentences are varied.

Paragraph Practice: **Revising**

Using the revision checklist, revise the first draft of your narrative paragraph.

Peer Review Reminder. For feedback on your writing, have someone read your paper and make comments on the Peer Review Response Sheet in Chapter 4, page 54.

Check Grammar, Punctuation, and Spelling As you reread your paper to check for grammar, punctuation, and spelling errors, pay special attention for possible errors that may arise in narrative paragraphs. Be sure that you have used past tense verb forms. Also, if you used dialogue, check your punctuation and capitalization.

ACTIVITY

7.7 **Revising and Editing a Narrative Paragraph**

Revise and edit Daniel Koffer's paragraph called "Eight More Years." Then answer the questions below.

[1]The September 11, 2001, attacks on the Twin Towers of the World Trade Center in New York City compelled me to reenlist in the United States Navy.

²That day, I was in Norfolk, Virginia, onboard the USS *Porter* DDG-78. ³We had just began a fire fighting drill. ⁴Thirty minutes into the drill, our commanding officer came over the ship's public address system to tell us that a plane had just hit one of the World Trade Center towers. ⁵He wanted everyone to assemble on the mess decks to watch the news. ⁶When I saw that one tower was gone, I was in total shock. ⁷I realized that one of my cousins worked in one of the towers. ⁸Many emotions went through me. ⁹Later that day, when I tried calling my family members to find out if my cousin was okay and to see if anyone else I knew had been injured in the city area, I was unable to reach them. ¹⁰The next day, I was scheduled for my separation physical because my navy contract was almost up. ¹¹As I was waiting to be seen, I realized that getting out of the navy would be the wrong thing to do, so I reenlisted for another eight years to serve my country.

Questions on Revising

1. Underline the topic sentence. What is the narrowed topic and the main point?

   Narrowed topic: _____

   _____

   Main point: _____

2. Show that the writer has adequate and relevant support by filling in the information on setting, characters, conflict, and resolution.

   Setting: _____

   Characters: _____

   Conflict, problem, or struggle: _____

   Resolution: _____

3. What order do the events of the story follow?

   _____

Questions on Editing and Proofreading

4. One sentence in this paragraph has a problem with a verb form. Find the error and write the corrected sentence here.

   _____

5. In sentence 1, the word *navy* is capitalized, but it is not capitalized in sentence 10. Is the use of capitals correct? If yes, tell why. If not, make the correction.

   _____

Paragraph Practice: **Editing and Proofreading**

Edit and proofread your narration paragraph. Check that your final draft is complete, accurate, and error-free.

Paragraph Writing Assignments

Help Desk

Enrico is having a problem keeping the verbs in the past tense in his narrative paragraph. He tends to shift from past verb forms to present verb forms. Circle the verbs that are in the present tense and change them to the appropriate past verb forms.

> [1]One cold winter's day, I cheated death by avoiding a serious accident. [2]I was driving home from college during a snowstorm. [3]I have never driven in the snow before, and I was worried about how my old Nissan Maxima will manage. [4]The snow-covered roads made driving hazardous. [5]One road is especially curvy and slippery. [6]As I approached an especially steep turn, I put my foot on the brake to slow down. [7]Unexpectedly, my tires lock, and the car begins to skid. [8]My hands started to perspire, and my heart was beating rapidly. [9]I thought I was going to crash and die. [10]In a split second, the car suddenly stops. [11]Luckily, there were no other cars on the road. [12]When I realized that I was not hurt and that the car was not damaged, I am happy to be alive.

Group Activity: Working Together to Tell a Story

In this exercise, you will tell a story through photographs. During class time, form groups of two or three, and choose a busy location, such as the library, a lab, advisement/student services, or a place where students get together to socialize on campus, such as the cafeteria, student center, or courtyard. Take a camera, cell phone, or other electronic device that takes pictures and photograph an event that takes place. Then, view the photos and select the ones that best represent the event. If possible, print the photos or upload them to a photo sharing website and arrange them in chronological order. Finally, write a narrative paragraph about the event.

Reading and Writing across the Curriculum: American History

Family stories are memorable stories from our lives and our family's lives. Read the following family story about immigrating to America.

In 1894, Mary Antin, a 13-year-old Jewish girl from Russia, and her mother and sisters made a perilous journey from persecution in tsarist Russia to the ship that would take them from Hamburg, Germany, to join her father in faraway America. Mary and her family were removed from the train at the Russian-German border by Russian police because of improper documents. Once her mother had settled the issue with the help of a local Jewish family, they reboarded the train to Berlin. Outside that city, they were once again removed from the train. Though they did not immediately understand what was happening, German authorities had arranged for a thorough cleansing and health inspection, since a cholera epidemic was raging in Russia. They took their things away, took their clothes off, rubbed them with disinfectant, and forced them to find their clothes thrown in a pile with everyone else's. Then, worried that they would miss the train, they hurried to get back on the train, realizing that they would not be murdered. Finally, Mary and her family boarded a ship for the United States, the place that lay beyond the horizon.

(Adapted from *The American Journey* by David Goldfield et al.)

Write a narrative paragraph about one of your family's stories. The paragraph could be about a holiday celebration, arrival in the United States, a marriage, a vacation, a cherished object, an event that is often recounted, or the funny or strange behavior of a relative.

MyWritingLab™
Complete this activity
at mywritinglab.com

Comment on a Contemporary Issue

We live in a time of rapid advances in technology and product development. While we like these advances, the products we buy today may be **obsolete** (not used anymore) within several years or less. Critics call this technological obsolescence. For example, USB drives have now replaced disks and CDs as storage devices. Cell phone models change so rapidly that a cell phone purchased a year ago is considered an old model, and chargers for it are no longer available.

(Adapted from *Marketing* by Gary Armstrong and Philip Kotler)

Write a paragraph about an experience you had with a product was no longer used or was out-of-date even though it was still working or usable. Consider clothing styles, electronics, kitchen items including appliances, software, cars, grooming products, video games, toys, workout equipment, and so on.

MyWritingLab™
Complete this activity
at mywritinglab.com

Reader Response

On page 105, you read Jetty's paragraph about a mistake she made when cleaning a client's house for the first time. Write a paragraph that responds to one of these questions:

Text-to-Text

■ Does this reading remind you of something else you have read, heard, or seen (story, book, movie, song, news item, magazine article, website, and so on)?

■ Are the ideas the same or different?

Text-to-Self	▪ How do the ideas in the reading relate to your own life, experiences, or ideas?
	▪ Do you agree or disagree with what you read?
Text-to-World	▪ What does the reading remind you of in the real world?
	▪ Does it make you think about something in the past, present, or future?

MyWritingLab™
Complete this activity
at mywritinglab.com

Write about an Image

A photo can tell a story about an object, person, place, or situation. Look at the details in the photo below. In a paragraph, tell the story of what may have happened.

The Narrative Essay

LO 3 **Write a narrative essay.**

 Writing Reminder. For more help with writing an essay, including introductions and conclusions, see Chapter 5.

The narrative essay has the same purpose as the narrative paragraph: to make a point about the meaning or importance of a single, significant experience or event. The narrative essay uses the same organizational pattern, chronological order, as the narrative paragraph. The graphic organizer on page 120 shows how student Myriam Alexandre planned her narrative essay.

Thesis Statement

The thesis statement consists of **an event or experience** and the meaning or importance of the event or experience.

> **The night my family was almost killed,** I learned that the misuse of the simplest words could be dangerous.

Myriam's Narrative Essay Graphic Organizer

Background Information

Characters: Name and Description

1. Me (Myriam)
2. My family
3. Townspeople

Setting

Location: Myriam's house and the forest

Time: Rainy night in January

Conflict: The townspeople came to my house to kill my father; my family members' lives were in danger.v

Introduction

Lead-in: People did not have freedom of speech when I was a child in Haiti.

Bridge: People were arrested for speaking against the government.

Thesis Statement: The night my family was almost killed, I learned that the misuse of the simplest words could be dangerous.

Events (Summarized by Paragraph)

1. My father preached against the government.

2. The people in the town believed my father was a government spy or agent, so they planned to kill him.

3. The townspeople came to our house and threw rocks at the windows, broke into the house, stole our food, and set fire to the sugarcane field.

4. My father took us away from the house, leaving everything behind.

5. We walked thirty minutes into the forest and sat under a tree; we heard the crowd in the distance and saw flames from burning sugarcane.

6. I thought about my father's last sermon in which he said he could say what he wanted and not get hurt for doing it.

Resolution

The family escaped physical harm.

Concluding Statement: That night in the forest, I swore that I would never make the same mistake my father did.

Body Paragraphs

The body paragraphs in the narrative essay are organized by chronological (time) order, the order in which the events happened. Each of the body paragraphs develops the events of the story. A body paragraph can develop one event or several smaller events. Notice how the events are listed in student Myriam's narrative essay organizer. Each event will be developed into a body paragraph.

Narrative Essay Example

Student Myriam Alexandre recounts the events of a frightening night in which she and her family escape persecution.

The Power of Words

1   When I was five years old, freedom of speech in my country, Haiti, was taboo. The government in power was falling, creating chaos and fear. People were afraid for their lives because the government agents reported anyone who spoke against those in power, and with no warning, in the middle of the night, the person was arrested, never to be seen again. The night my family was almost killed, I learned that the misuse of the simplest words could be dangerous.

2   My father, a well-known preacher, teacher, and department director for the board of education, was one of those who criticized the government's actions when he preached and when he spoke with his friends. My mother encouraged him to stop, fearful of what might happen to him. Even though my father had friends in the government who had power, they also told him to stop speaking negatively because they could not protect him from the people who were unhappy with his sermons. However, my father said he would not stop this preaching until the situation in the country changed.

3   The population wrongly believed that my father was one of the government's spies or one of the agents who was giving orders to kill citizens. Therefore, they planned to kill him once the government fell from power. For months, the priest, the governor, and the other teachers of the town made a secret plan to kill my father. They were superstitious and believed that to overcome evil, they had to ask their god for permission to kill an evil, in this case, my dad. Most of the people in our town agreed to kill him. They wanted to decapitate him because they said he was the devil in human form, so if he lost his head, he would not be able to come back from the dead.

4   On a rainy night at the end of January, a countless number of people carrying heavy rocks came to our two-story house, which was on a plantation with a field of sugar cane in front of the house. The crowd wanted to destroy my father completely, so it did not matter if his children got hurt in the process. One group of people threw rocks at every glass window we had. At the time, I was in a deep sleep, and my bed was situated under the window. I never woke up or heard the voices of the crowd until my window and the bricks that surrounded it fell on my bed. It was a miracle that I had rolled over to the only safe spot on my bed and was not hurt. While one group was throwing rocks, another was breaking into the main entrance of the house. At the back of the house, still another group broke into the storage room full of food we had saved for the poor. Others set fire to part of the sugar cane field.

5   While all of this destruction was happening, my father came into the bedroom and grabbed me and my other sisters who had been awakened by the crowd's violent activities. My father decided to get all of us, my sisters, my three brothers, and my mother, out of the house to safety. We could hear the crowd downstairs calling my dad's name, waiting for him to come out so that they could decapitate him.

6   My mother wrapped my two-year-old brother in a white sheet, and we all left by the back door in such a hurry that we forgot our shoes and had no food or objects to help us survive. We walked for approximately thirty minutes into the forest before we stopped under a tree and sat on the wet ground. My siblings and I were shaking; we did not understand what was going on. In the distance, we could hear the crowd singing, cursing, and yelling, and we cold see the flames from the burning sugar cane.

7   Half asleep on the ground, I could hear my mother singing and praying. I began to think about what had happened. I wondered why the crowd hated us until I remembered the last sermon my dad had given the previous week. Suddenly, everything made sense. He said that he could say whatever he wanted because he had the power, so no one could hurt him. That night in the forest, I swore that I would never make the mistake my dad did. I would never speak words that would not have a positive impact on my life or my loved ones.

Analyzing a Narrative Essay

7.8   Answer the following questions about "The Power of Words."

1. Underline the thesis statement. What is the writer's main point?

   _____

2. What technique does the writer use in the lead-in?

   _____

3. What was the conflict of the story?

   _____

   _____

4. What are the main events of the story?

   _____

   _____

   _____

5. In addition to referring to the thesis, what point does the writer make in the conclusion? Underline the sentence.

   _____

   _____

Narrative Essay Graphic Organizer

Using a narrative essay graphic organizer will guide you as you list the important elements of your story: the setting, time, characters, conflict, events, and resolution. The sample graphic organizer on page 124 can be changed to suit your needs by adding body paragraphs to describe events.

Narrative Essay Graphic Organizer

Background Information

Characters: Name and Description

1.
2.
3.
4.

Conflict:

Setting

Location:

Time:

Introduction

Lead-in:

Bridge:

Thesis Statement:

Events (Summarized by Paragraph)

1.

2.

3.

4.

5.

Resolution

Concluding Statement:

Essay Writing Assignments

Write about an Image

 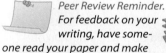

As human beings evolved and transportation and technology improved, people risked going further from original locations, and this natural search for new places and experiences continues to this day. Humankind's seemingly endless series of migrations seems to be an inborn trait of the human species. People travel for a variety of reasons, for example, to visit friends and relatives, to relocate, to do business, to relax, to experience an adventure, and to see places of historical or cultural interest.

(Adapted from *Travel and Tourism* by Paul S. Biederman)

Write a narration essay telling the story of a travel experience that had a significant impact on you or someone you know.

Writing Topics for a Narrative Essay

For your narrative essay, choose one of these options:
- from paragraph to essay: expand the paragraph you wrote in the paragraph section of the chapter
- any of the writing topics in the paragraph section of this chapter
- any topic from the following list:

General Topics

facing a fear
an experience with bullying or peer pressure
standing up for a belief
a conflict over money
a difficulty with a new technology

Writing across the Curriculum Topics

Criminal Justice: an experience involving the legal system
Psychology: a misunderstanding
Family: a family conflict
Anthropology: an experience with a ceremony or activity in your culture
Hospitality: an experience in a restaurant

English Success Tip: Learn from Your Mistakes
with a Writing Improvement Log

Keeping the papers you have written and the tests you have taken in your English course can provide you with valuable information about your progress. Comparing results on papers and tests will show you areas of strength and weakness. Record your problems in a writing improvement log like the one below. Write down grammar, punctuation, and sentence structure errors. Also, list problems with content such as weak supporting details. An example entry has been made to the log to show how to use it.

Writing Improvement Log

Item	Type of Error or Weakness	Correction
In high school, students are tested on small amounts of material. Whereas in college students are tested on much more information.	Fragment	In high school, students are tested on small amounts of material, whereas in college students are tested on much more information.

8 Description

Learning Objectives

After working through this chapter, you will be able to:

LO 1 Explain that description is a pattern of development that presents a person, place, event, or concept in great detail to create a mental picture.

LO 2 Write a descriptive paragraph with a dominant impression.

LO 3 Write a technical descriptive paragraph.

LO 4 Write a descriptive essay.

LO 1 **Explain that description is a pattern of development that presents a person, place, event, or concept in great detail to create a mental picture.**

MyWritingLab™
Complete this activity at mywritinglab.com

What Is Description?

Description is a pattern of development that presents a person, place, object, event, or concept in great detail so that the readers can picture what is described. Description is used in a variety of writing situations. Fiction writers bring characters, scenes, and events to life with description. Technical writers describe objects and mechanisms for instruction manuals, and journalists describe people and events. Menus, catalogs, and travel brochures all use description. Description is often used with other writing patterns, such as narration, illustration, process, and comparison.

QuickWrite

Think about a food that you enjoy eating. Take a moment and write a brief description of it.

Description in College Writing

Description is often used in academic writing. For instance, description enhances many of the essays that you write. In an argument essay, description can make a point more convincing. In addition, in a marketing class, writing a persuasive description can motivate consumers to buy a product or service.

Textbooks often use description. For example, the excerpt on the next page from an art textbook describes a scene in a 1938 painting by artist Thomas Cole titled *The Oxbow*.

The Oxbow captures the Catskill Mountains scene after the storm by presenting themes of light and dark. In the left side of the painting, Cole depicts the wilderness. The two trees at the left have been blasted by lightning. The forest is dense and frightening, and a thunderstorm rolls across the mountainous landscape. This wild scene contrasts dramatically with the civilized valley floor on the right. Here, bathed in serene sunlight, are cultivated fields, hillsides cleared of timber, and farmhouses from whose chimneys rise gentle plumes of smoke. The Connecticut River itself flows in a giant arc that reinforces the tranquility of the scene. Cole's umbrella juts out across the river from the rock at the right. Just below it, to the left, is Cole himself, now at work at his easel. The furious forces of nature have moved on, and the artist captures the scene just as civilization would tame the wild.

(Adapted from *A World of Art* by Henry M. Sayre)

The following is an example of student Daniel Bennett's description of a scene of destruction he witnessed while serving in Iraq.

Picture This

[1]The explosion of a large roadside bomb left behind a devastating scene of destruction. [2]A local Iraqi police chief from a small rural village outside of Fallujah left his station in a small blue and white truck to attend a meeting with other local officials from neighboring communities. [3]A few miles down the heavily traveled road, the chief's life was literally turned upside down while he sat in the passenger side of his truck. [4]Hundreds of pounds of roadside bombs had

been positioned underneath the road in an irrigation tunnel. [5]As the truck drove down the road over the tunnel, the bomb exploded. [6]The force of the explosion from the bomb sent the truck through the air. [7]It rolled over and landed upside down on the roof of a passing vehicle, forcing both vehicles to stop. [8]Barely held together, the chief's truck lay in a crater. [9]The area between the two front tires, which moments before made up the engine compartment, was a mangled heap of metal. [10]No glass remained on either vehicle; all windows were shattered by the blast. [11]Between the two severely dented and crushed vehicles, the drivers' and passengers' personal items were scattered on the road, slightly covered by chunks and piles of dirt. [12]A group of villagers who had witnessed the horrific scene then pushed the police truck off of the roof of the other car. [13]Quickly, several of the witnesses pulled the stunned and wounded drivers and passengers out of the vehicles, careful to avoid the razor-sharp metal frames. [14]Among the confusion, someone called for help, and not long after, ambulances arrived and rushed the bleeding and battered victims to the hospital. [15]Although it seemed impossible at the time, everyone affected by the unprovoked ambush made a complete recovery.

ACTIVITY   Analyzing a Descriptive Paragraph

8.1   Answer the questions about the paragraph you just read, "Picture This."

1. Underline the topic sentence.
2. What is the main point of the paragraph?

_____

3. List three details that support the main point of the topic sentence.

_____

_____

_____

DESCRIPTION   Essentials

The purpose of the descriptive pattern of development is to present a clear picture of a person, place, event, object, or concept. The main point is called the *dominant impression*, which is the one distinctive feature that best describes the topic. All of the details support the dominant impression. An effective description has these essential elements:

1. The description focuses on a dominant impression, which is the one distinctive feature that best describes the topic.

2. The supporting details work together to present a clear picture of the dominant impression.

3. The supporting details include sensory details (touch, smell, taste, sight, hearing).

4. The method of organization is either spatial order or order of importance.

5. Words show instead of tell.

The Descriptive Paragraph

LO 2 **Write a descriptive paragraph with a dominant impression.**

Prewriting the Descriptive Paragraph

Decide Your Topic and Purpose When deciding on your own description topic or responding to an assigned topic, consider the following:

1. **Choose a topic that can be described in one paragraph.** For example, a description of a large shopping mall would require more than one paragraph.
2. **Choose a topic that has one of these purposes:**
   - to make a scene memorable
   - to cause the reader to experience an emotion
   - to create a mood or atmosphere
   - to bring someone or something to life
3. **Choose a topic that has special meaning for you.** You will find it easier to create details that help readers visualize your topic.

ACTIVITY **Evaluating Topics for Descriptive Paragraphs**

8.2 Explain why each of the following topics would be good or not good for a descriptive paragraph.

1. paintings in a large museum

   _____

2. a disorganized workplace

   _____

3. the snowy evening as viewed through a window

   _____

4. a restroom in a service station

   _____

5. a soccer game

   _____

Develop Ideas for Your Topic Prewriting for a descriptive paragraph involves developing factual and sensory details. Factual details are words that explain things such as physical characteristics, names, dates, locations, and numbers. Sensory details are words and phrases that help the reader see, feel, hear, smell, taste, and touch the topic. Both factual and sensory details are necessary in a descriptive paragraph.

Factual Details Factual details provide the framework for the descriptive details.

The following chart contains suggestions for ways to develop the factual descriptions of people, places, and objects:

People	physical features, such as facial features (eyes, hair, mouth, facial hair), coloring, height, build, age, clothing, posture, speech; mannerisms (things that a person does repeatedly with face, hands, or voice that the person may not be aware of)
Places	location, size, weather, scenery, buildings/structures, objects, life forms, design
Objects	color, shape, size, texture, material, amount, pattern/design, ingredients, age, components, or parts

ACTIVITY Developing Factual Details

8.3   Write three factual details for each of the following topics:

1. walking outside on a very hot or very cold day

2. taking a shower or a bath

3. lying in your bed in the dark

Sensory Details Sensory details help the reader experience the person, place, object, or event through the five senses: sight, hearing, taste, smell, and touch. The paragraph describing Thomas Cole's *The Oxbow* that you read on page 128 is filled with sensory details.

Finding Sensory Details

8.4   Reread the paragraph about *The Oxbow* on page 128. List five sensory details from the paragraph.

_____

_____

_____

 Developing Sensory Details

8.5   Use your imagination to think about the following topics. What do you see, hear, smell, taste, and feel? Write three sensory details for each of the topics.

1. walking outside on a very hot or very cold day

_____

2. taking a shower or a bath

_____

3. lying in your bed in the dark

_____

 Paragraph Practice: Prewriting

Using the Description Prewriting Chart on page 133, develop details for one or more of these description topics:

General Topics

an object used in a workplace
a disturbing scene
a worn out object
an angry person
a room at your college or your online classroom

Writing across the Curriculum Topics

Fashion: an article of clothing, accessory, or shoes
Biology: an insect, plant, or animal
Marketing: a print or online advertisement for a product or service
Music: a musical instrument
Art: a work of art (painting, sculpture)

Description Prewriting Chart

Topic:

Factual Details

Sensory Details

Here is Daniel's prewriting chart:

Daniel's Description Prewriting Chart

Topic: A disturbing scene

Factual details

Iraqi police chief, villagers

passengers, drivers

small village outside Fallujah

small blue and white truck

roadside bombs

irrigation tunnel

ambulance

Sensory details

heavily traveled road

trunk sent through the air

mangled heap of metal barely held together

shattered windows

dented and crushed vehicles

items scattered on the road covered with piles of dirt

stunned and wounded drivers and passengers

bleeding and battered victims

Understand the Dominant Impression

The main point in a descriptive paragraph is called the dominant impression. The **dominant impression** is the special quality that best describes your topic. For example, *The Oxbow* painting description at the beginning of the chapter has themes of light and dark as the dominant impression.

You may have many reactions to a topic, but the dominant impression should be the one that is the strongest.

Narrow Your Topic and Write the Topic Sentence The topic sentence of the descriptive paragraph includes the narrowed topic, which is the person, place, object, or event you want to describe, and the dominant impression (the main point).

The student whose descriptive paragraph you read about a roadside bomb explosion on pages 128–129 responded to the topic "a disturbing scene." After looking at his sensory and factual details, he decided to use "devastating scene of destruction" as his dominant impression.

The explosion of a large roadside bomb left behind a devastating scene of destruction.

ACTIVITY   Developing Dominant Impressions

8.6   Think of a dominant impression for each of the following topics:

1. a home that is in poor condition _____

2. a fast-food restaurant at dinnertime _____

3. a car in a junkyard _____

4. a young child who is lost in a large store _____

5. a traffic jam because of road construction _____

TIPS | **Writing Descriptive Topic Sentences**

1. **Choose only one dominant impression.** The dominant impression guides your selection of supporting details. Writing about more than one dominant impression would be confusing to the reader.

   Two dominant impressions: During the dinner hour, the local super-market was full of energetic activity and was crowded.

   One dominant impression: During the dinner hour, the local supermarket was full of energetic activity.

2. **Choose a *specific* dominant impression word or phrase.** Choosing a vague dominant impression will not help the reader picture the topic or share the writer's experience.

   Vague dominant impression: The English classroom in Building 48 was small.

   Specific dominant impression: The English classroom in Building 48 was uncomfortably crowded.

3. **Avoid using a fact as the dominant impression.** A place's location, a person's name or relationship to you, a physical feature, or an object's owner or origin are facts, not distinctive features.

   Fact: On March 18, 1925, the deadliest tornado in United States history killed 689 people and injured 2000.

   Dominant impression: The tornado's destructive force was deadly.

ACTIVITY   Evaluating Descriptive Topic Sentences

8.7   Explain what is wrong with each of the following descriptive topic sentences. If a topic sentence is good, write "Good." The first one has been completed for you.

1. Dr. Martin Cooper is considered the inventor of the first portable handset and the first person to make a call on a portable cell phone in April 1973.

   This topic sentence is a fact and does not contain a dominant impression.

2. Tom O'Brien's abandoned meat packing plant on Federal Street is old.

3. The equipment in Iron Man Gym is rusty and old-fashioned.

4. County Youth Detention Center in Alligator Bay is a demoralizing place.

5. The economy airplane seat was uncomfortable.

Paragraph Practice: **Writing a Topic Sentence**

Look over the details for your descriptive paragraph (see page 133), and write a topic sentence. Be sure your topic is specific and the sentence includes a dominant impression.

Organizing and Drafting the Descriptive Paragraph

Choose Details That Support the Dominant Impression Each of the details must support the dominant impression. For example, if you were describing **a noisy** city street, you would not include details about the delicious cupcakes in the window of a store on that street. Cross out any details that do not support the dominant impression, and if necessary, add new ones.

ACTIVITY   Choosing Details That Support the Dominant Impression

8.8   For each of the topic sentences, circle the dominant impression. Then circle the letters of the detail sentences that support the dominant impression.

1. **Topic sentence:** My child's daycare classroom is a colorful environment
   a. The yellow-green walls are covered with children's paintings hung with masking tape.
   b. On the left side of the room, a big blue plastic bucket holds trucks, wooden puzzles, dolls, and bright-colored boxes of board games.
   c. Cartoon character sheets and pillowcases cover the mattresses and pillows on the three cribs in the back of the room.
   d. The child-care workers are very caring people.
   e. The children put their backpacks in a locker.

2. **Topic sentence:** Ever since my son was born, my bedroom has become a messy scene.

   a. Piles of shoe boxes, some empty and others with missing lids, have accumulated behind the door so that it cannot open all the way.

   b. Squeezed against the left wall is my big king-size bed.

   c. The baby wakes up two to three times a night.

   d. Right next to the bed is the baby's crib filled with stuffed animals and clothes that need to be folded and put away.

   e. The sight of the colorful clothes scattered across the floor looks like the result of a storm.

3. **Topic sentence:** The removal of the grand old oak tree outside my high school brought about a sentimental remembrance of the past

   a. The tree, taller than the three-story school it shaded, had a trunk so thick that a person could hide behind it and never be seen.

   b. To make way for new housing developments, builders have cleared the land of native plants and trees.

   c. In a storm, the branches banged on the walls and windows so loudly that we could hardly hear the teacher.

   d. The fall season was the best time for sitting under that tree, for the leaves would fall into piles on top of our books.

   e. In the spring and summer, during our lunch break, we sat comfortably shaded under that wonderful tree with our shoes off while studying or listening to music.

Paragraph Practice: **Choosing Details That Support Your Dominant Impression**

Looking back at your prewriting chart, evaluate the factual and sensory details. Circle the details that support your dominant impression. Add details if you need them.

Organize Your Supporting Details After collecting all of the supporting details to support your dominant impression, you are ready to organize the details into a plan for your paragraph.

   Choose one of three patterns: spatial order, order of importance, or order by five senses.

Pattern	How to arrange details
Spatial order	Where details are located: front to back, left to right, top to bottom, outside to inside, and so on.
Order of importance	From most important to least important or least important to most important
Order by the five senses	One sense at a time

After you have decided on a plan for organizing your details, use a descriptive paragraph graphic organizer to help guide you as you write your draft. Daniel's details for his paragraph "Picture This" on pages 128–129 are shown in his organizer below.

Daniel's Descriptive Paragraph Graphic Organizer

Topic Sentence: The explosion of a large roadside bomb left behind a devastating scene of destruction.

Dominant Impression: Devastating scene of destruction

Support 1: Roadside bomb explodes under Iraqi police chief's truck

Details:

Hundreds of pounds of roadside bombs put under road in irrigation tunnel

As truck drove over the tunnel, the bombs exploded

Chief's truck sent through the air, rolled over, and landed on roof of a passing vehicle

Support 2: Truck and other vehicle damaged

Details:

Chief's truck lay in a crater barely held together

Engine compartment of chief's truck a mangled heap of metal

No glass on either vehicle

Both vehicles severely dented and crushed

Personal items on road covered by piles of dirt from the explosion

Support 3: Villagers who witness horrific scene take action

Details:

Pulled stunned and wounded drivers and passengers from vehicles

Ambulances called and arrive, rush victims to the hospital

Concluding Sentence: Although it seemed impossible at the time, everyone affected by the unprovoked ambush made a complete recovery.

Paragraph Practice: **Organizing Your Supporting Details**

Organize your details by filling in the Descriptive Details Graphic Organizer. Each point must support the dominant impression. Add more supports and details as needed.

Descriptive Paragraph Graphic Organizer

Topic Sentence:

Dominant Impression:

Support 1:
Details:

Support 2:
Details:

Support 3:
Details:

Concluding Sentence:

Write the First Draft

Use Memorable Images Use words that bring your description to life for the reader: sensory words, active verbs, and comparisons.

Use images that appeal to the senses. Sensory words describe what you hear, smell, taste, see, and feel. They make your writing more realistic.

> **Not sensory:** As the sun came up, the air smelled good.
> **Sensory:** As the sun slowly rose in the clear morning sky, the clean, crisp air smelled of freshly cut grass and tree sap.

Use strong active verbs to show movement. They make it easier for the readers to imagine the action.

> **Not strong:** At the end of the football game, the running back scored a touchdown.
> **Strong:** With only seconds left in the game, the running back leaped from the third yard line and twisted through the air before scoring the winning touchdown.

Make comparisons. Comparisons show how two things that may not seem alike are similar in one way. One kind of comparison is called a **simile.** A simile is a comparison of two things using the words *like* or *as*.

> **The overcooked rice** tasted like blocks of concrete.
> **The newly waxed floor** is as slippery as an ice-covered road.

Add Connectors and Transitions Descriptive paragraphs often use spatial order and order of importance. Spatial connectors and transitions help the readers create a picture in their mind of the position and location of items in your description. The following are some common connectors and transitions to use for spatial order.

Common Connector/Transition Words for Spatial Order	
at/on the left, right	in front of, at the front
at/on the top, bottom, back, front	behind, at the rear
at/in/on the back, front, rear, side	beside, next to, nearby
in the middle/center	beneath, under, underneath, below
inside, on the inside, within	in the distance, beyond
outside, on the outside	in back of, in front of
on one side, on the other side	on top of, on the bottom of
to the left, to the right	across from, over

Writing Reminder.
See Chapter 3 for more information about order of importance transitions.

ACTIVITY   Describing with Spatial Order

8.9   Study the photograph of the butterflies resting on flowers. Then, using transition words for spatial order, write five sentences describing the location of objects in the picture.

EXAMPLE: A butterfly sits on top of the pink flower.

1.
   _____

2.
   _____

3.
   _____

4.
   _____

5.
   _____

Paragraph Practice: **Writing the First Draft**

Using the topic sentence and details you developed, write a first draft of your descriptive paragraph.

Revising, Editing, and Proofreading

Revise your draft by looking at one element at a time: **S**upport, **O**rganization, **C**onnectors and transitions, and **S**tyle. The following Revision Checklist contains the **SOCS** elements as they apply to descriptive paragraphs.

REVISION CHECKLIST FOR A DESCRIPTIVE PARAGRAPH

Element	Revision Checkpoints
Topic	☐ The topic is meaningful and memorable.
	☐ The topic is limited enough to be described in one paragraph.
	☐ The topic achieves one of these purposes: creates a mood, brings someone or something to life, conveys an emotion, or makes the topic memorable.
Topic Sentence	☐ The topic sentence contains the narrowed topic and the dominant impression.
	☐ The narrowed topic is expressed specifically and concisely.
	☐ The dominant impression is described with a specific word or phrase.
Support	☐ All supporting details describe the dominant impression.
Organization	☐ The paragraph follows spatial order or order of importance.
Connectors and Transitions	☐ Appropriate transitions for either spatial order, order of importance, or by five senses provide coherence.
Style	☐ Writing is clear, concise Standard Written English.
	☐ Tone is appropriate for a college audience.
	☐ Specific details create reader interest through the use of sensory images, comparisons, and active verbs.
	☐ Sentences are varied.

Paragraph Practice: **Revising**

Using the Revision Checklist for a Descriptive Paragraph, revise your descriptive paragraph.

Peer Review Reminder. For feedback on your writing, have someone read your paper and make comments on the Peer Review Response Sheet in Chapter 4, page 54.

Check Grammar, Punctuation, and Spelling As you reread your paper to check for grammar, punctuation, and spelling errors, pay special attention to possible errors that may arise in descriptive paragraphs. For example, be sure that you have not shifted verb forms. Another area to look over is word choice. If you have used a thesaurus, be sure that you know the meanings of words and that you have used and spelled these words correctly. Finally, check your use of commas when using two or more adjectives in front of a word to describe it.

ACTIVITY   Revising and Editing a Descriptive Paragraph

8.10   Revise and edit Roslyn's paragraph describing an event. Then answer the questions that follow.

¹My brother's experience of almost dying was a nightmare brought to life. ²In the sunlit kitchen, as I poured freshly squeezed orange juice into a glass. ³I heard my mother scream as if someone had just stab her in the heart and twist the knife. ⁴Dropping the glass and leaving the broken pieces in the orange liquid pooled around it. ⁵I ran into the living room to find my brother, blue-faced with foam coming from his mouth. ⁶His eyes were lifeless. ⁷With tears burning my cheeks like acid, I lie my brother on the floor. ⁸My mother's screaming suddenly sounded far away and mufled compared to the extremely loud drumbeat of my heart. ⁹I stuck my hand down his throat and pulled three marble out. ¹⁰As I raised my hand, I felt his saliva streaming down my hand and dripping off of the marbles. ¹¹I looked at those marbles and realized that I had just beaten death.

Questions on Revising

1. Underline the topic sentence. What is the narrowed topic? What is the dominant impression?

   _____

   _____

2. What method of organization does the writer use?

   _____

3. Show that the writer has used memorable details by giving an example of a sensory image, a comparison, and an active verb.

   _____

   _____

   _____

   _____

4. What verb tense does the writer use?

   _____

Questions on Editing and Proofreading

5. Two sentences in this paragraph have verb tense problems. Find the sentences and write the corrected sentences here.

   _____

   _____

6. Two sentences are fragments. Correct each fragment by adding it to the sentence before or after.

   _____

   _____

   _____

7. One sentence contains a spelling error. Write the corrected word here.

_____

8. One sentence contains an error with plurals. Write the corrected form here.

_____

Paragraph Practice: **Editing and Proofreading**

Edit and proofread your descriptive paragraph. Check that your final draft is complete, accurate, and error-free.

Write a Technical Descriptive Paragraph

LO 3 Write a technical descriptive paragraph.

Technical descriptions are often assigned in college courses. For example, in a chemistry class, you may be asked to write a lab report that describes an experiment you performed. Reports in fields such as engineering, science, and biology also include technical descriptions. A technical description paragraph does not need a dominant impression.

The following paragraph is an example of a technical description. Notice how the student writer uses precise factual details.

> The Bic Matic grip 0.7mm number 2 mechanical pencil is a tool that is used for writing. The pencil consists of two main components: a black plastic outer tube and a black plastic inner tube filled with lead. The pencil measures 8" from the top of the eraser to the pencil opening at the bottom. The 5⅞" shatter-resistant outer tube is a hollow cylinder, open at both ends. A purple plastic 1¼" clip is attached to the outer tube 1" from the top of the pencil. This clip allows the user to clip the pencil to a pocket or notebook. A 1½" thick, contoured, purple rubber grip is placed one half inch above the pencil opening for the writer's comfort. The inner tube, which is also cylindrical and the same length as the outer tube, contains the lead. At the top end is a white eraser that fits snugly into a cup-like holder. At the other end is a claw. When the eraser is pressed, the claw opens to allow the lead to drop through the opening of the outer cylinder. When the eraser is released, the claw closes and keeps the lead from falling out or going back up into the pencil.

Paragraph Writing Assignments

Help Desk

Rodney's description paragraph assignment was to write about a place that he would not like to return to. He chose a detention center.

Some of Rodney's sentences do not clearly support the dominant impression. How could Rodney revise those sentences so that they provide support?

_____

_____

_____

¹The juvenile hall unit is a degrading place for youths facing criminal charges. ²The guard station is in the middle of the room. ³Some cells have as many as three people crowded into them. ⁴The cells are eight feet by ten feet. ⁵In the cells are a toilet, a sink with no running water, and mattresses to sleep on. ⁶On the left and right sides of the room are cells. ⁷Gang symbols have been carved into the walls. ⁸The cells on one side of the room face the cells on the other side of the room. ⁹The cells stink; they smell like sweat, stale food, and urine. ¹⁰The segregation unit is in the back of the room where there are a group of six cells. ¹¹In those cells are youths who are dangerous or that have diseases. ¹²Boredom and anger are common when people are locked up for more than sixteen hours a day.

Group Activity: Writing a Technical Description

In small groups of two or three, choose an object belonging to one person in the group such as a stapler, a cell phone, a lipstick, an item with a zipper, a calculator—any object that has more than one part. For example, a simple ballpoint pen consists of an outer plastic casing, a tube of ink, and a cap to keep the tube in place. Your assignment is to write an objective physical description of the object in one paragraph.

Reading and Writing across the Curriculum: Art

MyWritingLab™
Complete this activity
at mywritinglab.com

Robert Riggs was a successful artist who became well known during the Harlem Renaissance. The Harlem Renaissance was a time in history between 1916 and 1940 when Black American artists used their experiences as a source of inspiration. Riggs was best known for his paintings of prize-fighting and circus scenes. His painting, *The Brown Bomber* (1939), shows the boxing victory of Joe Louis over Max Schmeling. Max Schmeling was a German boxer who was the heavyweight champion of the world before his defeat by Joe Louis.

Write a paragraph that describes what you see in the painting as if you were in the audience watching the fight. Full color versions of this painting can be found online by searching Robert Riggs.

Comment on a Contemporary Issue

Did you ever buy a product that you were excited about buying but soon after disappointed you? Write a paragraph describing the product as you see it now.

Reader Response

In the beginning of this chapter, you read Daniel's paragraph that describes a roadside bomb explosion in Iraq. What was your reaction to his paragraph? Write a paragraph that responds to one of these questions.

Text-to-Text	■ Does this reading remind you of something else you have read, heard, or seen (story, book, movie, song, news item, magazine article, website, and so on)? ■ Are the ideas the same or different?
Text-to-Self	■ How do the ideas in the reading relate to your own life, experiences, or ideas? ■ Do you agree or disagree with what you read?
Text-to-World	■ What does the reading remind you of in the real world? ■ Does it make you think about something in the past, present, or future?

Write about an Image

The people in the photograph express two different emotions. Imagine that you are one of the people in the picture. Write a paragraph describing the situation as if you were the person you selected.

The Descriptive Essay

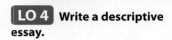

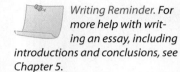

LO 4 **Write a descriptive essay.**

Writing Reminder. For more help with writing an essay, including introductions and conclusions, see Chapter 5.

The descriptive essay has the same purpose as the descriptive paragraph: to create a clear mental picture of a person, place, event, object, or concept. As in the descriptive paragraph, the supporting details are both factual and sensory. The descriptive essay follows the same organization patterns as the descriptive paragraph: spatial order, order of importance, or five senses order.

Thesis Statement

The thesis statement for a descriptive essay expresses a narrowed topic with a main point which is the dominant impression. The following thesis statement example is from the student Amy Kahn's essay "The Aftermath" on pages 149–150 about a hurricane's destruction of a family home.

Thesis with Narrowed Topic **and** Main Point (Dominant Impression):

> The family's home had suffered serious damage.

Thesis with Narrowed Topic **and** Main Point (Dominant Impression) and Supporting Points:

> The family's home had suffered serious damage both inside and outside.

Body Paragraphs

The body paragraphs of the descriptive essay can be organized by using the following patterns:

- **Spatial order:** describing where details are located, such as front to back, left to right, top to bottom, outside to inside, and so on
- **Order of importance:** describing the most important to least important or least important to most important
- **Five senses of order:** describing one sense at a time (sight, hearing, taste, smell, and touch)

Amy developed her details by using a Descriptive Essay Graphic Organizer. Each body paragraph describes an area of the home that was destroyed.

Amy's Descriptive Essay Graphic Organizer

Introduction

Lead-in: Describe the hurricane hitting the house.

Bridge: When the family opened the laundry room door, they were shocked at what they discovered.

Thesis Statement with Dominant Impression: The family's home had suffered serious damage.

Body Paragraphs

Topic Sentence with First Support Point: Inside the house, the master bedroom suffered the worst damage.

Details:

Sliding glass doors shattered
Curtain rod down, curtain bunched on floor
Dented antique lamp, water dripping onto swelling night table
Soaked carpet
Leaves, branches on top of bed
Roof tile on bed
Gash in wall

Topic Sentence with Second Support Point: The other rooms in the house had sustained damage as well.

Details:

Bathroom windows shattered, glass in tub floating in rain water
College student's room with broken window, laptop in water
Posters curling from dampness
Smelly, wet clothing

Topic Sentence with Third Support Point: The storm's fury not only damaged the interior of the house, but also the exterior.

Details:

Cracks, holes, roof imprints on back wall
Tiles blown off roof
Debris around the house
Uprooted tree across driveway
Torn patio screens

Conclusion

Concluding Statement: Although their house had sustained considerable damage, the family felt fortunate to be alive.

Descriptive Essay Example

Student Amy Kahn describes damage to her family's home after Hurricane Wilma.

The Aftermath

1   The outer fringes of the hurricane arrived, bringing with it waves of heavy rain that thrashed against the windows. The wind suddenly increased its speed, lifting and hurling tree limbs and debris into the air. Concrete tiles were torn from neighboring roofs, assaulting the roof and rear of the home with loud thumps as it stood defenselessly. Suddenly, breaking glass and a change in air pressure indicated that the storm entered the house. The family members rushed into the only windowless room, in which a full-size washer and dryer occupied most of the space. They huddled together for the duration of the storm, listening to the storm's progress on their portable radio. After several frightening hours, the winds and rain died down, and the weatherman reported that the worst was over. When the family opened the laundry room door, they were shocked at what they saw. The family's home had suffered serious damage.

2   The master bedroom suffered the worst damage. The glass in the two-panel sliding doors had been shattered into hundreds of tiny pieces and strewn across the large room. The curtain rod dangled from one corner of the window, and the curtains lay bunched together in a tangled, wet lump on the floor. Next to the doors, an antique brass lamp lay on its side, dented and dripping water onto the wood night table, which was swelling from having taken in so much water. Rain had soaked the carpet near the window and was quickly spreading to the dry areas in the room. Leaves, branches, and palm fronds lay across the once-pristine white bedding. In the middle of the king-size bed, a large roof tile rested quietly now after its destructive flight through the window. Across from the bed was a deep gash in the wall.

3   The other rooms in the house had sustained damage as well. Some of the windowpanes in the bathroom had broken, and pieces of glass had fallen into the tub and were now floating in several inches of rainwater. Next to the bathroom, the college student's room did not escape the hurricane's fury either. Rain poured in through yet another broken window. The recently completed research paper lay on the desk in a pool of water next to the laptop, a gift from his grandparents. Torn wall posters hung precariously, curling from the dampness, and clothing that had been left in a huge pile on the floor was wet and covered with debris, creating an unpleasant odor within the room.

4   The storm's fury not only damaged the interior of the house, but also the exterior. The pale yellow stucco exterior had been a target for flying debris. Cracks, gaping holes, and a variety of roof tile imprints were evident on the back wall. The roof itself had lost thirty percent of its tiles; some looked as if they had slid from their original places while others balanced precariously at the edges of the roof. Scattered in disarray round the perimeter of the house was a collection of stones, roofing materials, and other unidentifiable objects. In the front of the house, the large ficus tree, which had once provided shady relief from the sun's intense heat, had been uprooted and had fallen across the driveway, imprisoning the family's car in the garage. The screening from the patio had been torn from its frame and flapped like shredded ribbons in the wind.

5   The hurricane's unusual path had surprised everyone in the town. The storm, which had travelled across the Caribbean Sea into the Gulf of Mexico, made an unexpected turn and moved quickly across the state. The cleanup process was going to take some time, and they would have to do without power for several weeks. Although their house had sustained considerable damage, the family felt fortunate to be alive.

ACTIVITY

8.11

Analyzing a Descriptive Essay

Answer the following questions about "The Aftermath."

1. Underline the thesis statement. What is the dominant impression?

_____

2. What technique does the writer use for the lead-in?

_____

3. Underline the topic sentences for each of the body paragraphs. How does each one connect to the thesis statement?

_____

4. The writer uses sensory details. List examples for sight, smell, and sound.

_____

_____

_____

_____

5. In addition to referring to the thesis, what point does the author make in the conclusion? Underline the sentence.

_____

Descriptive Essay Graphic Organizer

Using a descriptive graphic organizer will help you place your details in the appropriate order. The descriptive essay graphic organizer shown below can be changed to suit your needs by adding body paragraphs and details.

Descriptive Essay Graphic Organizer

MyWritingLab™
Use the interactive graphic organizer at mywritinglab.com

Introduction

Lead-in:

Bridge:

Thesis Statement with Dominant Impression:

Body Paragraphs

Topic Sentence with First Support Point:
Details:

Topic Sentence with Second Support Point:
Details:

Topic Sentence with Third Support Point:
Details:

Conclusion

Concluding Statement:

Essay Writing Assignments

Write about an Image

What do you think happened in the photograph above? What was your first reaction to it? Choose the dominant impression, the one special quality or feature that stands out from all the others, that best describes the photograph. You may have many reactions to this photograph, but the dominant impression is the strongest.

Write an essay as if you were describing the scene for a major news network. Use vivid sensory and factual descriptive details to support your dominant impression.

Writing Topics for a Descriptive Essay

For your descriptive essay, choose one of these options:
- from paragraph to essay: expand the paragraph you wrote in the paragraph section of this chapter
- any of the writing topics in the paragraph section of this chapter
- any topic from the following list:

General Topics

a place where a sporting or entertainment event is held
a home appliance
an electronic communication or gaming device
a piece of equipment
a crowd of people

Writing across the Curriculum Topics

Peer Review Reminder.
For feedback on your
writing, have some-
one read your paper and make
comments on the Peer Review
Response Sheet in Chapter 4,
page 54.

Ecology: plant or animal life in an area you are familiar with
Fashion Design: elements used to show clothing on display at a store, such as tables, wall décor, posters, banners, light effects, and video
Hospitality Management: an unusual vacation spot
Architecture: a building from any period in history
Computer Science: your college or university website or the website of one you would like to attend

English Success Tip: Using a Thesaurus

Descriptive writing creates a clear mental picture of a topic in the reader's mind. Finding the right words to create a mental image or to avoid repeating the same word can be challenging. Using a thesaurus can help. A **thesaurus** is a dictionary of synonyms, words that have the same meanings. *Roget's Thesaurus* is one of the most widely used thesauruses and can be found in print and online at Bartleby.com.

1. Use synonyms that match your writing style. Unusual, long, or impressive-sounding words are not necessarily better choices than simple ones.
2. Choose synonyms that are Standard English, not slang or informal.
3. Be sure to know the meanings of both the original word and the word you want to use to replace it. The synonym may not have the same meaning. Check the definitions in a dictionary.

9 Process

Learning Objectives

After working through this chapter, you will be able to:

LO 1 Describe process as a pattern of development that explains how to do something or how something happens or works.

LO 2 Write a process paragraph.

LO 3 Write a process essay.

LO 1 **Describe process as a pattern of development that explains how to do something or how something happens or works.**

What Is Process?

Process is a pattern of development that explains how to do something or how something happens or works. The two types of process writing are the How-to Process and the How Something Happens or Works Process.

The **How-to Process** paragraph, also called *directional process*, gives step-by-step instructions so that the reader can perform the process. Examples of this type of process writing are how to do a chemistry experiment, how to use a piece of equipment, or how to get to a particular location.

The **How Something Happens or Works Process**, also called *informational process*, explains a process rather than giving step-by-step instructions. The reader does not have to perform it. The purpose is to explain, analyze, or inform the reader about the process. Examples of this type of process writing are explaining how global warming happens or how a U.S. president is elected.

QuickWrite

What is a process you do every day? Brush your teeth? Text a friend? Cook a meal? Take a moment and list the steps in that process.

Process in College Writing

Process is used in many kinds of college writing assignments. For example, a How-to Process paper in nursing may explain the procedure for cleaning a wound. In biology, you may write about how breathing supplies oxygen to our cells. How-to Process is also frequently used in culinary arts, for example, how to remove scales from a fish. How Something Happens or Works Process writing is useful in a criminal justice course, such as explaining how electronic evidence is collected. An assignment in a pharmacy technician course might be to describe how drugs are absorbed in the body.

The two types of process paragraphs, the How-to Process and the How Something Happens or Works Process, are illustrated in the two examples on the same topic that follow.

How-to (Directional) Process Example

[1]A restaurant server should follow these steps to satisfy customers' needs. [2]First, greet the guests. [3]After greeting the guests, introduce and suggestively sell beverages and appetizers. [4]Next, bring the guests their beverages. [5]Give the guests time to make selections from the menu. [6]Then, return to the table to take the entrée orders. [7]Begin at a specific point at the table and take the orders **clockwise.** [8]When the entrées are ready, bring them to the table. [9]After the guests have taken a few bites of their entrées, check to see that everything is to their liking. [10]At this time, ask if the guests would like another drink. [11]As soon as the guests are finished with their entrées, clear the entrée plates.[12]At the same time, suggestively sell desserts. [13]Recommend, describe, or show the desserts. [14]Also, offer after-dinner drinks and coffee. [15]Following these steps will make customers happy and increase the possibility of a generous tip.

(Adapted from *Hospitality Management* by John R. Walker)

clockwise in the direction that the hands of a clock move on an analog clock face

ACTIVITY 9.1 **Analyzing a How-to Process Paragraph**

Answer the following questions about the paragraph you just read.

1. Underline the topic sentence.
2. How does the reader know that the paragraph is a How-to Process?

_____

3. Three of the steps in the paragraph take more than one sentence to explain. Which steps are they?

_____

_____

4. Which sentences command the reader to do something? What are the subjects of those sentences?

_____

_____

5. What method of organization is used for the supporting details?

_____

How Something Happens or Works (Informational) Process Example

[1]Serving guests in a restaurant is a process that is designed to satisfy customers' needs. [2]First, the server introduces himself or herself, offers a variety of beverages and/or specials, or invites guests to select from the menu. [3]This is known as suggestive selling. [4]The server then takes the entrée orders.

⁵Often, when taking orders, the server begins at a designated point at the table and takes the orders clockwise from that point. ⁶In this way, the server will automatically know which person is having a particular dish. ⁷When the entrées are ready, the server brings them to the table. ⁸He or she checks a few minutes later to see if everything is to the guests' liking and perhaps asks if they would like another beverage. ⁹Good servers are also encouraged, when possible, to help clear tables. ¹⁰Busers and servers may clear the entrée plates, while servers suggestively sell desserts by describing, recommending, or showing the desserts. ¹¹Coffee and after-dinner cocktails are also offered.

(Adapted from *Hospitality Management* by John R. Walker)

Analyzing a How Something Works Process Paragraph

9.2 Answer the following questions about the paragraph you just read.

1. Underline the topic sentence.
2. How do you know that the paragraph is a How Something Happens or Works paragraph?

3. What is the difference between the sentences used to explain the processes in the two example paragraphs?

4. What method of organization is used for the supporting details?

5. Which of the two example paragraphs could be used to train a new restaurant server? Why?

PROCESS Essentials

An effective process pattern of development has these elements:

1. Process makes a point about the process to explain how the process is useful, why it is important, or assure readers that they can perform it.
2. The supporting details work together to give all the necessary steps in the process or the appropriate amount of information to understand the process.
3. The process lists any necessary equipment or materials.
4. The process is presented in chronological order or order of importance, depending on the type of process and its purpose.
5. The process gives advice about possible problems and suggests how to resolve them.
6. The process is explained in the present or past tense depending on the type of process and its purpose.

The Process Paragraph

LO 2 **Write a process paragraph.**

Prewriting the Process Paragraph

Choose Your Topic and Purpose When deciding on your own process topic or responding to an assigned topic, consider the following:

1. **Choose a process that you know well.** Having mastered or understood the process, you will be able to explain it, knowing that your instructions work.
2. **Choose a process that can be explained in a single paragraph.** Some topics are too narrow. For example, how to save a file on a computer can be explained in just one or two sentences. On the other hand, some topics require too many steps to be explained completely in one paragraph. Giving a health care worker instructions for bathing an adult sounds like a simple process, but it involves many steps that must be followed carefully.
3. **Choose a process that can be explained easily without being too technical.** You may have the knowledge and ability to perform a process that may seem easy to you but may be too technical for your reader. Installing a home security system, for example, requires knowledge of electrical terminology and circuitry, which a general reader will not have.
4. **Choose a topic that many people do not know how to do.** Writing about a process that most people are familiar with, like how to brush your teeth, may not interest the reader.

ACTIVITY   **Evaluating Topics for a Process Paragraph**

9.3   Explain why each of the following topics would be good or not good for a process paragraph.

1. how to boil water in a microwave

_____

2. how a tornado forms

_____

3. how to pack a suitcase

_____

4. how to play soccer

_____

5. how to rebuild a car engine

Develop Ideas for Your Topic   Prewriting for a process paragraph involves listing the steps in order from start to finish. Kyra decided to write her paragraph on how to do an exercise called a stationary lunge. Here is her prewriting list of steps:

Kyra's Prewriting List of Steps

1. Stand comfortably with the feet slightly apart and the hands on the hips.

2. With one foot, step forward until the knee is over the top of that foot and is in a vertical line with the ankle. When lowering into the lunge, the front knee should not extend past the toe. Only the tip of the toe should be visible. The lower knee gets close to the ground but does not touch. Don't let knee roll inward or outward. Keep the weight on the heel of the extended foot. Keep the back straight and the shoulders back. Don't let the body roll forward. If you can't lower to 90 degrees, lower as much as you can.

3. Put the weight on the heel and use the front leg to push the body up and back to the standing position.

4. Repeat the lunge ten times stepping forward with the same foot and pushing the body up and back.

5. Using the opposite foot, follow the same process of stepping forward into a lunge and pushing the body up and back ten times.

Paragraph Practice: **Developing Ideas**

Practice developing ideas by listing the steps for one or more of these How-to Process paragraph topics.

General Topics

improve a grade in a specific course
operate a simple, useful device found around the home
perform a task at home, school, or work
plan a party or other celebration
impress an instructor

Writing across the Curriculum Topics

Fashion: dress to impress in personal life or at work
Interior Design: decorate a room for a specific person
Communication: convince someone to do something
Fitness: do a particular exercise with or without weights
Finance: save money or spend money carelessly

Narrow Your Topic and Write the Topic Sentence   The topic sentence of the process paragraph states the process and makes a point about it. The point will be one of the following:

- To explain how the process is useful
- To explain why the process is important
- To assure readers that they can perform it

Here are the topic sentences from the two example paragraphs you read at the beginning of the chapter:

How-to Process Topic Sentence

A restaurant server should follow these steps to satisfy customers' needs.

How Something Happens or Works Process Topic Sentence

Serving guests in a restaurant is a process that is designed to satisfy customers' needs.

TIPS | **Writing Process Topic Sentences**

1. **State the process specifically and concisely.**

   | **Process not specifically stated** | Braids are fashionable and very popular today. |
   | **Process stated specifically** | Braiding hair takes practice but can be learned by following these steps. |

2. **Make a point about the process.** The reader needs to know what he or she will be able to do or why the process is important.

   What the reader should be able to do

   No point: Bathing a dog involves six steps.

   With a point: The frustration of bathing an uncooperative dog can be avoided by following these steps.

   Why the process is important

   No point: Follow these simple rules to perform a chemistry lab experiment.

   With a point: Follow these simple rules to guarantee a safe chemistry lab experiment.

ACTIVITY | Evaluating Process Topic Sentences

9.4   Explain what is wrong with each of the following topic sentences. If a topic sentence is good, write "Good." The first one has been completed for you.

1. Follow these steps to find online sources.

   _____

2. These steps must be followed carefully.

   _____

3. To get the most meat from a turkey, follow these simple carving directions.

   _____

4. Here is how to clear a paper jam in a copier.

   _____

Paragraph Practice: **Writing Topic Sentences**

Look over your details for the two topics you worked on in Paragraph Practice: Developing Ideas (page 158) and write a topic sentence for each.

Organizing and Drafting the Process Paragraph

Develop Supporting Details   The reader may not know the process you are writing about; therefore, present all steps or parts of the process clearly and concisely. Keep the following points in mind:

- Include all the steps in order from the beginning of the process to the end.
- Put smaller steps for the same action within a larger step.
- Include any equipment or materials needed.
- Tell the reader about possible difficulties or problems with any of the steps.
- Leave out obvious steps.

Using a Process Graphic Organizer   Using a process graphic organizer can help you list all of the steps in order. Kyra listed her steps for how to do a stationary lunge in the How-to Process Graphic Organizer on page 162. As she filled in the organizer using her prewriting list of steps, she saw that she could group several smaller steps into Step 3.

Paragraph Practice: **Planning**

Choose one of the processes you have been working on in the Paragraph Practice exercises. Using the graphic organizer on page 163, fill in the steps and other information for the process paragraph you will write. Add or subtract steps as needed.

Organize Your Supporting Details   After listing all of the steps for your topic, you are ready to organize them into a plan for your process paragraph. You may want to turn your list into a scratch outline to keep you on track when you write.

Use Chronological Order or Order of Importance   To organize the steps in a process paragraph, you can use either chronological order or order of importance, depending on the process you are explaining. How-to paragraphs require chronological order because the reader must perform the steps in order. In the How Something Happens or Works paragraph, you may use either pattern of organization.

Analyzing a How Something Happens or Works Process Paragraph

9.5   The following How Something Happens or Works paragraph explains a process in stages. Underline each sentence that states a stage in the process. Then circle the number(s) of the sentence(s) that explain each stage.

[1]Fashion styles pass through a four-stage process that occurs over time. [2]The cycle begins with the introduction stage when a style is introduced into the marketplace. [3]At this point there is no way of knowing if the style will be popular with retail buyers and the consumer public. [4]Therefore, due to the cost of materials and production, the styles are usually expensive. [5]The growth stage is next. [6]If the style is generally accepted and successful, copies are marketed at many different prices in the marketplace. [7]During the maturity stage, the style achieves its greatest sales volume. [8]The time of maturity might be one season or many. [9]Not knowing when maturity will happen can leave manufacturers and sellers with merchandise that the public no longer considers fashionable. [10]The final stage is the decline stage. [11]The style has lost its popularity. [12]Left-over pieces are drastically reduced to prices that will sell quickly to get rid of unwanted merchandise. [13]It is urgent to rid the inventory of such items before they are no longer desired at any price.

(Adapted from *Fashion Apparel, Accessories, and Home Furnishings* by Jay Diamond and Ellen Diamond)

Kyra's How-to Process Graphic Organizer

Topic Sentence: The stationary lunge is an effective lower body workout, but it must be performed correctly to avoid injury.

Equipment/Materials: Clothing allowing for movement and flexibility, athletic shoes to support feet

Step 1
- Stand straight with the feet hip-width apart and the hands on the hips.

Step 2
- With the left foot, step forward about one foot..

Step 3
- Lower the body until the left knee is over the top of the left foot.
  - Keep the chest up, shoulders back, and abdominal muscles tight.
  - Do not lean forward on the way down; this puts stress on the back.
  - The front knee should not extend past the toe.
  - The right leg should be bent with the shin almost parallel to but not touching the floor.

Step 4
- Put the weight on the heel of the left foot and push the body up and back to the standing position.

Step 5
- Repeat the lunge ten times, stepping forward with the same foot and pushing the body up and back.

Step 6
- Using the opposite foot, repeat the same process ten times.

Concluding Sentence: Doing stationary lunges on a regular basis will burn calories and strengthen all the major muscle groups in the legs.

How-to Process Graphic Organizer

Topic Sentence:

Equipment/Materials:

Step 1

Step 2

Step 3

Step 4

Step 5

Step 6

Concluding Sentence:

ACTIVITY   Distinguishing between Steps and Details

9.6   The following is a set of directions for putting on a surgical face mask in a health care setting. Some of the sentences are steps and others are details. Put an **S** next to the sentences that are steps and a **D** next to sentences that are details that explain the steps.

1. Locate the top edge of the mask.
2. The mask usually has a narrow metal strip along the edge.
3. Hold the mask by the top two strings or loops.
4. Place the upper edge of the mask over the bridge of the nose, and tie the upper ties at the back of the head or secure the loops around the ears.
5. If glasses are worn, fit the upper edge of the mask under the glasses.
6. With the edge of the mask under the glasses, clouding of the glasses is less likely to occur.
7. Secure the lower edge of the mask under the chin, and tie the lower ties at the back of the neck.
8. To be effective, a mask must cover both the nose and the mouth because air moves in and out of both.
9. A secure fit prevents both the escape and the inhalation of microorganisms around the edges of the mask and the fogging of eyeglasses.
10. Wear the mask only once, and do not wear any mask longer than the manufacturer recommends or after it becomes wet.
11. A mask should be used only once because it becomes ineffective when moist.
12. Do not leave a used face mask hanging around the neck.

(Adapted from *Essentials of Nursing* by Audrey Berman et al.)

Double-Check the Steps and Details Kyra looked at her process graphic organizer to check the accuracy of the steps. She performed the exercise several times to make sure that each step was easy to understand. Kyra also reorganized the details in Step 3.

Write the First Draft As you write the first draft consider these elements: definitions of technical words, verb tense, and transitions and connectors.

Define Words If your process includes technical terms or words that your reader may not know, be sure to define them. Note the two terms and the way the writer defined them in the following process paragraph on how wind makes waves:

> Wind generates waves on large lakes and open seas. The frictional drag of the wind on the surface of smooth water causes it to move in small waves. **Frictional drag is the rubbing of one surface against another.** As the wind continues to blow, it applies more pressure to the steep side of the small wave, and wave size begins to grow. As the wind becomes stronger, short, choppy waves of all sizes appear; and as they absorb more energy, they continue to grow. When the waves reach a point at which the energy supplied by the wind is equal to the energy lost by the breaking waves, they become **whitecaps, waves that are white at the top.** Up to a certain point, the stronger the wind, the higher the waves.
>
> (From *Elements of Ecology* by Robert Leo Smith and Thomas M. Smith)

Choose Commands or Statements The How-to Process uses commands. Commands are used to give orders or make requests. The subject of a command is not stated but is understood to be second person "you." The How Something Happens or Works paragraph uses statements. Statements are used to express facts and opinions.

Commands	Statements
Greet the guests.	First, the server greets the guests.
Return to the table to take entrée orders.	Then the server takes the entrée orders.

TIP Present tense is used for How-to Process paragraphs. Present or past tense is used for How Something Happens or Works Process paragraphs.

Add Connectors: Transitional Words and Expressions How-to Process paragraphs use sequence transitional words and expressions in chronological order to label the steps and connect them.

> **Numerical sequence words:** first, second, third, next, last, the first step, the second step, etc.
> **General sequence words:** after this, as soon as, at the same time, during, finally, last, meanwhile, soon after, then, while

Paragraph Practice: **Writing a First Draft**

Using your topic sentence and paragraph organizer (page 163), write a first draft of your process paragraph.

Revising, Editing, and Proofreading

Revise your draft by looking at one element at a time: **S**upport, **O**rganization, **C**onnectors and transitions, and **S**tyle. The following Revision Checklist contains the **SOCS** elements as they apply to process paragraphs.

- -

REVISION CHECKLIST FOR A PROCESS PARAGRAPH

Element	Revision Checkpoints
Topic	☐ The process is one that you have done before or seen many times.
	☐ The process can be explained in a single paragraph.
	☐ The process can be easily explained without being too technical.
	☐ The process is one that many people do not know how to do.
Topic Sentence	☐ The topic sentence identifies the process and makes a point about it.
	☐ The process is stated specifically and concisely.
	☐ The point explains how the process is useful, why it is important, or assures readers that they can perform it.
Support	☐ All the steps are included from the beginning of the process to the end.
	☐ Any equipment or materials are listed.
	☐ Difficulties or possible problems with any of the steps are explained.
	☐ Obvious steps are left out.
Organization	☐ The How-to Process follows chronological order.
	☐ The How Something Happens or Works Process follows chronological order or order of importance.
	☐ Smaller steps may be grouped into larger steps.
	☐ Some steps may have details to help the reader understand or perform the step.
Connectors and Transitions	☐ Chronological order or order of importance transitions provide coherence.
Style	☐ Writing is clear, concise Standard Written English.
	☐ Tone is appropriate for a college audience.
	☐ Commands or statements are used consistently.

- -

Paragraph Practice: **Revising**

Using the Revision Checklist for a Process Paragraph, revise the first draft of your process paragraph.

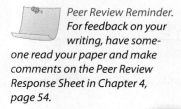

Peer Review Reminder. For feedback on your writing, have someone read your paper and make comments on the Peer Review Response Sheet in Chapter 4, page 54.

Check Grammar, Punctuation, and Spelling As you reread your paper to check for grammar, punctuation, and spelling errors, pay special attention for possible errors that may arise in process paragraphs. For example, be sure that you have not shifted from commands to statements in a How-to Process paragraph.

ACTIVITY   **Revising and Editing a Process Paragraph**

9.7   Revise and edit Kyra's paragraph called "Lunge Fitness." Then answer the questions below.

¹The stationary lunge is an effective lower body workout, but it must be performed correctly to avoid injury. ²Dress comfortably in clothing that allows movement and flexibility and athletic shoes that support the feet. ³First, stand straight with the feet a hip width apart and the hands on the hips, next, with the left foot, step forward about one foot. ⁴Third, lower the body until left knee is over the top of the left foot. ⁵To avoid injury while doing the third step. ⁶Pay attention to form. ⁷Keep the chest up, shoulders back, and abdominal (stomach) muscles tight. ⁸Do not lean forward on the way down, which puts stress on the back. ⁹Be sure that the left knee do not extend past the toe. ¹⁰The right leg should be bent with the shin parallel to but not touching the floor. ¹¹The heel of the right leg will lift so that the weight is on the toe, but the foot should stay in the same position. ¹²In step four, put the weight on heel of left foot and push the body up and back to the standing position. ¹³Last, repeat the lunge ten times stepping forward with the left foot and pushing the body back up. ¹⁴Switch to the opposite foot and repeat the process ten times. ¹⁵Doing stationary lunges on a regular basis will burn calories and strengthen all the major muscle groups in the legs.

Questions on Revising

1. Underline the topic sentence. What are the process and the main point?

   _____

   _____

2. Does the writer uses transitions throughout the paragraph? If not, where are transitions needed and which ones would you use?

   _____

   _____

3. What order does the process follow?

   _____

4. Does the writer use commands or statements?

_____

Questions on Editing and Proofreading

5. One sentence is a fragment and another is a comma splice. Find the sentences and write the corrections here.

_____

_____

6. One sentence has a verb error. Find the error and write the correction here.

_____

7. One sentence is missing the article *the* in two places. Find the sentence and write the correction here.

_____

_____

Paragraph Practice: **Editing and Proofreading**

Edit and proofread your process paragraph. Check that your final draft is complete, accurate, and error-free.

Paragraph Writing Assignments

Help Desk

Mizuki's teacher told her that she left out essential words in her process paragraph, which made the instructions confusing and hard to read. This problem is called **telegraphic writing.** Here is her paragraph. Revise it by filling in words that she has left out.

> [1]Processing patient at Dr. Hernandez's office must be done correctly to avoid errors. [2]First, print out patient appointment schedule for day. [3]Next, when patient comes into doctor's office, ask patient to sign name and time of arrival on patient intake sheet. [4]Confirm patient's name, address, phone number, and insurance coverage to be sure that information is up-to-date and correct. [5]Then, collect patient's co-pay. [6]Finally, put patient's chart in rack and ring bell notifying nurses and doctor that patient's chart is ready.

Group Activity: Planning a Multicultural Event

In a group of three or four students, plan a multicultural three-hour event at your campus. To prepare for this event, complete these writing tasks:

1. Write a set of directions to the location on campus.
2. Write a schedule of events in the order in which they will take place.
3. Write the recipes with instructions for several traditional dishes that you plan to serve.

Reading and Writing across the Curriculum: **Communications**

Presentation aids are used in education and real world situations to clarify ideas and concepts, to reinforce messages, to stimulate the audience, and to be culturally sensitive.

When preparing presentation aids, such as Powerpoint slides, clarity is the most important consideration. You can achieve clarity by following these simple guidelines:

1. Use colors that will make your message instantly clear; light colors on dark backgrounds or dark colors on light backgrounds provide the best contrast. Be cautious about using yellow, which is often difficult to see.
2. Use direct phrases, not complete sentences, and use bullets to highlight your points. Make sure the meaning is clear.
3. Use the aid to highlight a few essential points; don't clutter it with too much information. Four bullets are as much information as you should include.
4. Use typefaces that can be read easily from all parts of the room.
5. Give the slide or chart a title to further guide your listeners' attention and focus.

(From *Human Communications* by Joseph A. DeVito)

Prepare one or more presentation aids for the process paragraph you have written or for another one of the process writing topics on page 158.

Comment on a Contemporary Issue

Campus safety has become a major issue on college campuses across the United States. You can take responsibility for your own safety by knowing what to do and which resources are available. Write a paragraph about the steps students at your school can take to stay safe while driving or walking around campus or to protect personal property.

Reader Response

The textbook excerpt on page 161 explains the four-stage process that fashion styles go through over time: introduction, growth, maturity, and decline. Today, fashion trends do not last very long. Do you follow the trends or buy items that are classic?

Write a paragraph that responds to one of these questions.

Text-to-Text	■ Does this reading remind you of something else you have read, heard, or seen (story, book, movie, song, news item, magazine article, website, and so on)?
	■ Are the ideas the same or different?
Text-to-Self	■ How do the ideas in the reading relate to your own life, experiences, or ideas?
	■ Do you agree or disagree with what you read?
Text-to-World	■ What does the reading remind you of in the real world?
	■ Does it make you think about something in the past, present, or future?

Write about an Image

Take the role of a police officer and write a report about this automobile accident. Write a paragraph explaining how the accident happened.

The Process Essay

LO 3 **Write a process essay.**

The process essay supports its thesis by explaining the steps for performing a process or for understanding a process.

Thesis Statement

📝 *Writing Reminder. For more help with writing an essay, including introductions and conclusions, see Chapter 5.*

The thesis statement for a process essay states the process with a main point. The main point tells readers any of the following:

- How the process is useful
- Why the process is important
- Assures readers that they can perform the process

The following thesis statement example is from the student Allicyn Vaupel's essay "Giving a Therapeutic Back Massage" on pages 173–174.

Thesis with Process and Main Point

> Giving therapeutic back massage will help a client relieve pain if it is done correctly.

Thesis with Process, Main Point, and Steps

Notice that this thesis statement does not list all of the steps because there are too many for the reader to take in at once.

> Giving a therapeutic back massage will help a client relieve pain by beginning with preparing the room and ending with thanking the client.

Body Paragraphs

Each of the body paragraphs supports the thesis by explaining all the necessary steps in the process. Each may discuss one large step or a group of small steps. The body paragraphs guide the reader by accomplishing the following:

- including a topic sentence that indicates which step or group of steps will be explained in the topic sentence.
- following chronological order or order of importance.

Using a process graphic organizer will help you place your steps in order. Here is Allicyn's process graphic organizer for her essay on giving a therapeutic back massage.

Allycin's Process Essay Graphic Organizer

Introduction

Lead-in: Background about how I chose the career of licensed massage therapist

Bridge: This occupation gives me a chance to help people.

Thesis Statement with Point about the Process: Giving a therapeutic back massage will help a client relieve pain if it is done correctly.

Body Paragraphs: Add as many paragraphs as you need.

Step 1: Prepare the room.

Details: Dress the massage table with clean sheets. Prepare massage oil. Play soothing music.

Step 2: Prepare the client.

Details: Introduce yourself. Ask the client about existing medical conditions. Tell the client what to expect. Ask about problem areas. Give client time to get ready. Re-enter the room and dim the lights.

Step 3: Massage the upper back.

Details: Spread massage gel across the client's shoulders. Work upper shoulders, including trapezius muscles. Gradually increase the pressure, avoiding discomfort to the client.

Step 4: Massage from the shoulder blades to the entire back.

Details: Apply pressure from the shoulder blades to the lower back. Massage areas where the client indicates tight muscles. Work the lower back. End with effleurage strokes.

Step 5: Ending the massage session

Details: Give the client final instructions to get feedback. Leave the room so that the client can relax and dress. Re-enter the room and discuss whether the client would like to devise a treatment plan. Give the client a glass of water and advise that he or she drink lots of water to release toxins. Thank the client, clean the room, and wait for the next client to arrive.

Conclusion

Concluding Statement : At the end of the session, you have helped the client feel better by relieving pain and reducing stress.

Process Essay Example

Allicyn Vaupel used her process graphic organizer to write her essay "Giving a Therapeutic Back Massage."

Giving a Therapeutic Back Massage

1   When I was growing up, I always wanted to work in the medical field. However, I knew that attending college for twelve years was not for me. Instead, I decided to become a licensed massage therapist and earned my license after taking the required courses and passing a certification exam. This occupation gives me a chance to help people feel better by working directly with clients in a chiropractor's office. A common problem many people suffer from is back pain, and they often request a massage of this area. Giving a therapeutic back massage in will help a client relieve pain if it is done correctly.

2   Preparing the room is the first step in making a massage enjoyable for the client. Always dress the massage table with a clean set of sheets. Prepare the massage oil by adding some lavender essential oil, which is known for its relaxing effects. To set the mood, play soothing music and light several candles placed on small tables around the room.

3   When the room is ready, welcome and prepare the client for the message. After introducing yourself, ask the client about previous or current medical conditions. Make sure that the client does not have cancer, does not have heart disease, or is in the first trimester of a pregnancy. Then, explain what to expect during the massage and ask the client if there is a particular area that may be painful or that may need more attention. After the preliminary questions have been answered, step out of the room, giving the client sufficient time to get ready and lie on the massage table face down. When the client is ready, I re-enter the room and dim the lights.

4   First, begin by massaging the upper back, isolating and working each muscle group. Take a few pumps of massage gel and spread it across the upper shoulders. The trapezius muscle is in this area. It is a large muscle spanning from the shoulders and partway down the back. Muscle strain or tension can cause these muscles to tighten, causing pain. Gently squeeze the trapezius muscles, following them to the tops of the shoulders. Gradually increase the pressure, avoiding discomfort to the client.

5   Next, move the shoulder blades and work down to the middle and lower back. Placing your fists between the shoulder blades, apply even

pressure down the spine to the lower back. Use your elbows to get deep into the muscle. Use gentle, smooth pressure on both sides of the shoulder blades. If the client indicates a particular area of the back where the muscles are tight or painful, spend most of the time massaging that area. Then, with closed fists, work the lower back. Last do some effleurage stokes, which are long, continuous strokes.

6   When the massage is finished, take the opportunity to give the client final instructions to get feedback about the massage. First, leave the room to give the client a few moments to relax and then to dress. After the client is dressed, re-enter the room. Discuss what was beneficial and whether the client would like to devise a treatment plan. Give the client a glass of water and tell him or her to drink lots of water throughout the day to flush out any toxins that were released from the muscles during the massage. After thanking the client for coming, clean the room and wait for the next client to arrive. At the end of the session, you have helped the client feel better by relieving pain and reducing stress.

ACTIVITY   Analyzing a Process Essay

9.8   Answer the following questions about "Giving a Therapeutic Back Massage."

1. Underline the thesis statement. What process will the writer explain?

   _____

2. What technique does the writer use for the lead-in?

   _____

3. Underline the topic sentences of each of the body paragraphs. What does each topic sentence do?

   _____

4. Circle the transitions in each topic sentence.
5. How many steps does each of the body paragraphs contain?

   a. single step   b. series of steps
6. What point does the writer make in the concluding paragraph?

   _____

Process Essay Graphic Organizer

Using a process graphic organizer will help you place your steps in order. The sample graphic organizer shown on page 175 can be changed to suit your needs by adding body paragraphs. Include any necessary equipment or materials where appropriate.

Process Essay Graphic Organizer

Introduction

Lead-in:

Bridge:

Thesis Statement with Point about the Process:

Body Paragraphs: Add as many paragraphs as you need.

Step 1:

Details:

Step 2:

Details:

Step 3:

Details:

Step 4:

Details:

Conclusion

Concluding Statement:

Essay Writing Assignments

MyWritingLab™
Complete this activity
at mywritinglab.com

Write about an Image

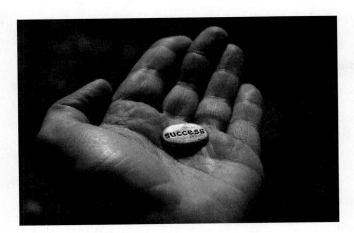

Think about a time when you achieved a desired goal or success in school, in your personal life, or at work. Although you may not have realized it then, you followed a series of steps or strategies to reach your goal. Write an essay in which you describe your process for achieving a specific goal or success.

Writing Topics for a Process Essay

For your process essay, choose one of these options:

- from paragraph to essay: expand the paragraph you wrote in the paragraph section of this chapter
- any of the writing topics in the paragraph section of the chapter
- any topic from the following list:

General Topics

work together as a group on a project in school, at work, or in personal life
find an affordable apartment, house, or condo
maintain a vehicle, home, or equipment
find a reliable source on the Internet for an academic subject
survive a physical or emotional challenge

Writing across the Curriculum Topics

*Peer Review Reminder.
For feedback on your
writing, have some-
one read your paper and make
comments on the Peer Review
Response Sheet in Chapter 4,
page 54.*

Physical Science: prepare for a severe weather event
Health: plan an exercise program for a beginner
Psychology: stop harassment or bullying
Business: get out of debt
Marketing: sell items online

10 Comparison and Contrast

Learning Objectives

After working through this chapter, you will be able to:

LO 1 Define comparison and contrast as a pattern of development that shows how two subjects are similar and/or different.

LO 2 Write a comparison and contrast paragraph.

LO 3 Write a comparison and contrast essay.

LO 1 **Define comparison and contrast as a pattern of development that shows how two subjects are similar and/or different.**

MyWritingLab™
Complete this activity at mywritinglab.com

What Is Comparison and Contrast?

Comparison and contrast is a pattern of development that shows similarities and differences. **Comparison** shows how two subjects are alike, whereas **contrast** shows how two subjects are different. You use comparison and contrast when deciding which course and teacher to sign up for or where to go on a Saturday night. Examples of workplace comparing and contrasting are reports that recommend the purchase of new equipment or suggest alternate ways of doing business.

Comparing and contrasting involve more than developing two different sets of ideas on two different subjects. You will also be analyzing the relationship between them.

QuickWrite

Think about two courses you are taking (or have taken). Write about their similarities and/or differences.

Comparison and Contrast in College Writing

Academic writing assignments often ask you to compare and contrast topics. For instance, in an education course, you may be asked to write about the differences between an online class and a face-to-face class. A writing assignment in a music course may involve comparing and contrasting music of the Renaissance and Baroque periods. Comparing and contrasting men's and women's management styles in a business course is yet another example.

The following paragraphs on probation and parole illustrate the different patterns for organizing comparison and contrast paragraphs. The first paragraph illustrates the point-by-point pattern and the second illustrates the subject-by-subject pattern.

Point-by-Point Paragraph Example

The **point-by-point pattern** of organization compares and/or contrasts both of the subjects one point at a time.

[1]While probation and parole are similar in that they are both offered instead of prison, they work differently. [2]The first difference is when they are offered. [3]Probation is given to offenders instead of sending them straight to jail or prison. [4]On the other hand, parole is given to offenders who have been in prison. [5]Parole is the period of time after the offender is released from prison. [6]Another difference is the purpose of probation and parole. [7]The purpose of probation is to help offenders return to a useful life through community programs. [8]Unlike probation, the purpose of parole is to help offenders gradually get back to living productive lives. [9]For instance, they may have to stay in a halfway house before they are allowed back into the community. [10]The last difference is the way offenders are monitored. [11]Those on probation are monitored by probation officers. [12]They make sure offenders are following the terms and conditions of their probation. [13]If they do not follow the conditions, they will usually receive a jail term. [14]Offenders on parole also must follow terms and conditions of their parole, but they report to a parole officer. [15]If they violate the conditions of their parole, they are sent back to prison for the rest of their original prison term. [16]Although both probation and parole are prison alternatives, probation is used more than parole in the United States because it is considered more effective.

(Adapted from *Criminal Justice Today* by Frank Schmalleger)

ACTIVITY   Analyzing a Point-by-Point Comparison and Contrast Paragraph

10.1   Answer the following questions about the paragraph you just read.

1. Underline the topic sentence in the paragraph above. What is the point of the topic sentence?

_____

2. What do the two subjects have in common?

_____

3. What is the purpose of the paragraph?

_____

4. What are the main points of contrast?

_____

_____

5. Circle the transitional words and expressions used to move readers from point to point.

Subject-by-Subject Paragraph Example

The **subject-by-subject pattern** of organization explains all of the points of comparison and/or contrast for one subject and then explains the same points of comparison and/or contrast for the other subject in the same order. The following paragraph example explains the same information as the previous paragraph but uses the subject-by-subject method.

[1]While probation and parole are similar in that they are both offered instead of prison, they work differently. [2]Probation is given to offenders instead of sending them straight to jail or prison. [3]The purpose of probation is to help offenders return to a useful life through community programs. [4]Offenders on probation are monitored by probation officers. [5]They make sure offenders are following the terms and conditions of their probation. [6]If they do not follow the conditions, they will usually receive a jail term. [7]In contrast, parole is given to offenders who have been in prison. [8]Parole is the period of time after the offender is released from prison. [9]Unlike probation, the purpose of parole is to help offenders gradually get back to living productive lives. [10]For instance, they may have to stay in a halfway house before they are allowed back into the community. [11]Instead of being monitored by probation officers, offenders on parole are monitored by parole officers. [12]If they violate the conditions of their parole, they are sent back to prison for the rest of their original prison term. [13]Although both probation and parole are prison alternatives, probation is used more than parole in the United States because it is considered more effective.

(Adapted from *Criminal Justice Today* by Frank Schmalleger)

ACTIVITY Analyzing a Subject-by-Subject Comparison and Contrast Paragraph

10.2 Answer the following questions about the paragraph you just read.

1. Match the points of contrast for probation with those of parole by filling in the sentence numbers.
   Sentence 2 matches sentence _____
   Sentence 3 matches sentence _____
   Sentence 4, 5, and 6 matches sentences _____
2. Circle the transitions used to show contrast.
3. Why are contrast transitions needed in the second half of the paragraph?
   _____
4. Which of the two paragraphs is more understandable for the reader?
   _____

> ## COMPARISON AND CONTRAST   Essentials
>
> The purpose of the comparison and contrast pattern of development is to identify the similarities and differences of two things and make a point about them. Effective comparison and contrast has these elements:
>
> 1. It makes a point about the similarities and/or differences between two subjects by informing, persuading, or showing understanding.
> 2. The two subjects being compared and/or contrasted must have something in common.
> 3. The supporting details for each subject are relevant and complete. Both subjects are explained equally, and the same points are covered.
> 4. The supporting details are organized either point by point or subject by subject.
> 5. The supporting details in the point-by-point or subject-by-subject patterns are arranged according to their importance or their difficulty.
> 6. Comparison and contrast transitional words or expressions are used to show the movement from one point to another or from one subject to another.

The Comparison and Contrast Paragraph

LO 2 Write a comparison and contrast paragraph.

Prewriting the Comparison and Contrast Paragraph

Before you write, you must choose a suitable topic and develop it.

Choose Your Topic and Purpose When deciding on your own comparison and/or contrast topic or responding to an assigned topic, consider the following:

1. **Choose two subjects that have some characteristics in common.** For example, you might decide to compare or contrast two cars. It would make sense to select two cars from the same group, such as two economy cars, rather than an economy car and a luxury car. While an economy car and a luxury car are both cars, they are in different classes.
2. **Choose two subjects that can be compared and/or contrasted in a single paragraph.** If you decided to compare or contrast two ballpoint pens, you would quickly run out of points to discuss. On the other hand, if you wanted to compare or contrast two colleges, you would need to cover such subjects as programs, fees and tuition, faculty, extra-curricular activities, and entrance requirements. A single paragraph would not give you the chance to cover the features of each subject in any depth.
3. **Choose two subjects that readers do not already know about.** Most readers know the difference between a landline telephone and a cell phone. The similarities and differences are obvious. Therefore, unless you can offer the reader new information or a new way of looking at the subjects, it is best to avoid obvious topics.

ACTIVITY   Evaluating Topics for a Comparison and Contrast Paragraph

10.3   Explain why each of the following topics would be good or not good for a comparison contrast paragraph.

1. two homes where you have lived

_____

2. a fast-food restaurant and a five-star restaurant

_____

3. a manual toothbrush and an electric toothbrush

_____

Develop Ideas for Your Topic Prewriting for a comparison and contrast paragraph involves creating a list of your subjects' similarities and differences in a side-by-side chart. To see how this is done, look at Natasha's side-by-side chart comparing and contrasting her two dogs, Sabra Lee and Butch.

Natasha's Prewriting Chart for Sabra Lee and Butch

Similarities

Sabra Lee and Butch

Five-year old males
Brought up together as puppies
Raised and live in Natasha's house
Eat the same dog food
Given love and attention
Given preventive care

Differences

Sabra Lee	Butch
Responds to commands	Does not respond to commands, just "Food"
Protective watchdog	Passive
Chases monkeys, scares people	Lies around, timid
Affectionate, likes to be hugged, kissed, petted, meet and greet	Does not like affection, runs away and hides
Seeks attention	Does not seek attention
Sleeps on driveway by front door	Sleeps on secluded back patio

Paragraph Activity: **Prewriting**

Choose one of the following topics for a comparison and contrast paragraph, or choose your own topic. Then create a comparison and contrast prewriting chart of their similarities and differences.

General Topics

two jobs (preferably ones you have experienced)
two memorable people (friends, relatives, teachers, bosses, sports fans, athletes, movie or television personalities)
two popular brands of an item
the personalities of two pets that you lived with or knew well
two places where you have lived

Writing across the Curriculum Topics

Music: two musicians, singers, or musical groups
Education: an online class and a traditional face-to-face class
Health: two types of diets (i.e., two types of diets for general health or two types of weight-loss diets)
Marketing: two methods of advertising (ways of persuading people to buy a product or service)
Anthropology: two different cultural views on a topic such as money, treatment of older people, or marriage

Comparison and Contrast Prewriting Chart

MyWritingLab™
Use the interactive graphic
organizer at mywritinglab.com

Similarities

Subject A_____ and Subject B_____

Differences

Subject A _____   **Subject B_____**

Narrow Your Topic and Write the Topic Sentence Narrowing your topic involves looking at your prewriting chart. Decide whether to write about similarities or differences or both. Finally, think about the point you want to make about the two subjects. Then you will be ready to write the topic sentence of your paragraph.

The topic sentence for comparison and contrast includes the following:

1. The **two subjects** that you will compare and/or contrast.
2. The **purpose:** to discuss similarities and/or differences.
3. The point of the comparison and/or contrast.

Natasha wrote this topic sentence contrasting her two dogs:

Although **Sabra Lee and Butch** were brought up in the same home in South Africa, their personalities are vastly different.

Notice how Natasha mentions the similarities briefly and then moves on to the point, the difference between their personalities. She chose to acknowledge the similarities, but her point is to discuss differences.

TIPS | **Writing Comparison and Contrast Topic Sentences**

1. **State your purpose: to compare and/or to contrast.** This tells the reader what to expect from your paragraph.

   > **No purpose:** I took math in high school and in college.

   > **Purpose:** My high school math class differed from my college math class with respect to the demands it placed on students.

   The purpose is to explain the differences between high school and college math classes.

2. **Make a point by giving the reason for the comparison and/or contrast.** Without this, the reader will not know why you are writing.

   > **No point:** The Guatemala City where I grew up is different from the Guatemala City of today.

   > **With a point:** Guatemala City, where I grew up, has been transformed into a modern city since I moved away.

   It is not enough to say that two subjects are different. The point the writer wants to make is that Guatemala City has changed into a modern city.

   > **No point:** Food grown on organic farms is different from food grown on traditional farms.

   > **With a point:** Food grown on organic farms is more nutritious than food grown on traditional farms.

   The point is that organic food is more nutritious. The writer intends to persuade the reader.

Paragraph Activity: **Writing a Topic Sentence**

Write a topic sentence for the topic about which you have been prewriting. Label the two subjects, the purpose, and the point of the comparison and/or contrast.

Your topic sentence: _____

    Subjects: _____

    Purpose: _____

    Point: _____

Organizing and Drafting the Comparison and Contrast Paragraph

Using the topic sentence as a guide, the next steps are to develop and organize supporting details and write the first draft.

Develop Supporting Details Look back at your prewriting chart and choose the details that will support the point you make in your topic sentence. As you choose the details, see if you can group them into categories.

Using a comparison and contrast graphic organizer can help you organize your details by matching details to each category. This tool will help you keep your points organized.

Here is Natasha's contrast graphic organizer. It shows how she grouped her details.

Natasha's Contrast Graphic Organizer

Points of Contrast	Subject A Sabre Lee	Subject B Butch
Obedience	Responds to commands	Does not respond to commands, turns away Responds only to "Food."
Protectiveness	Alert watchdog Sits in front of house and roams on driveway Chases monkeys Scares people passing by Sleeps on driveway by front door	Timid Lies around Scared of everything Sleeps on secluded back patio
Affection	Loves to be hugged, kissed, begs for attention Meet and greet	No desire for affection, runs and hides

Paragraph Activity: Selecting Supporting Details

Choose the details that will support the point you made in the topic sentence you wrote. Then, group your details into categories and fill in the blank graphic organizer below.

Comparison and Contrast Graphic Organizer

MyWritingLab™
Use the interactive graphic
organizer at mywritinglab.com

Point of Comparison and/or Contrast	Subject A	Subject B

Organize Your Supporting Details The two patterns of organization for a comparison/contrast paragraph are point-by-point or subject-by-subject. Once you have selected the pattern, you can arrange your supporting details within the pattern using order of importance.

Point-by-Point The point-by-point pattern is organized by explaining one point of similarity or difference at a time for Subject A and then Subject B.

Point of Similarity or Difference 1
Subject A
Subject B
Point of Similarity or Difference 2
Subject A
Subject B
Point of Similarity or Difference 3
Subject A
Subject B

Subject-by-Subject The subject-by-subject pattern is organized by explaining all of the points of similarities or differences for Subject A and then explaining the same points of similarities or differences for Subject B.

Subject A
Point of Similarity or Difference 1
Point of Similarity or Difference 2
Point of Similarity or Difference 3
Subject B
Point of Similarity or Difference 1
Point of Similarity or Difference 2
Point of Similarity or Difference 3

The subject-by-subject pattern can end up sounding like two separate topics instead topics that are being compared or contrasted. When using this pattern, include reminders of the same point you made for Subject A. Use transition words, mention the point for Subject A, and then give the point for Subject B.

Comparing and Contrasting in the Same Paragraph When comparing and contrasting in the same paragraph, write about the similarities first and then write about the differences.

Similarities
Subject A
Subject B
Differences
Subject A
Subject B

Order of Importance Arranging your points in order of importance—from most to least or least to most—shows the reader how you view them. In the point-by-point pattern, you can choose to put the most important point first or last. In the subject-by-subject pattern, you can arrange the points in order of importance for the first subject and use that same order for the second subject.

Paragraph Activity: **Outlining**

Choose a pattern of organization for your comparison or contrast paragraph. Use the pattern to write a scratch outline.

Write the First Draft As you write your first draft, consider these elements: balance, transitional words and expressions, and verb tense.

Balance Your comparison and contrast paragraph should be balanced in both content and in organization. As you write, follow the same organizational pattern throughout the paragraph.

Add Connectors: Transitional Words and Expressions Following the details of a comparison and contrast paragraph can be confusing to the reader because you are writing about two subjects and explaining matching points about each. To help the reader follow your pattern of organization, you need to add transitional words and expressions.

When using the point-by-point pattern, use transitions to introduce each new point and to connect one explanation to another within each point. When using the subject-by-subject pattern, use transitions to switch from one subject to another in the middle of the paragraph and to move from one point to another within the discussion of each subject.

Following are lists of comparison and contrast connectors and transitions with sentence examples.

Comparison Words	Sentence Examples
Coordinating conjunctions: *and*	Sabra Lee and Butch were raised together, and they are the same age.
Correlative conjunctions: *just as*	Sabra Lee was given love and attention just as Butch was.
Transitions: *similarly, likewise, in comparison*	Sabre Lee and Butch were given love and attention; similarly, they were given preventative care.
Prepositions: *like, similar to*	Similar to Sabra Lee, Butch is five years old.

Contrast Words	Sentence Examples
Coordinating conjunctions: *but, yet*	Sabra Lee obeys commands, but Butch does not.
Subordinating Conjunctions: *although, though, even though, while, whereas, than*	Although Sabra Lee and Butch were raised together as puppies, their personalities are vastly different.
Transitions: *however, on the other hand, in contrast*	In contrast, Butch has no desire to give or to get affection.
Prepositions: *unlike*	Unlike Sabra Lee, Butch is afraid of strangers.

Transition Sentences To keep each of your points and details organized, write a transition sentence each time you begin a new point. Following are some transition sentence beginners you can use.

Purpose	Transition Sentence Beginners
For comparison	One similarity is, Another similarity is, The most important similarity is, The first similarity is, The next similarity is, The last similarity is
	One similarity is that both dogs were raised together.
For contrast	One difference is, Another difference is, The most important difference is
	The first difference is, The next difference is, The last difference is
	Another difference between the dogs is their protectiveness.

Paragraph Activity: **Writing the First Draft**

Using your outline and graphic organizer, write the first draft of your paragraph.

Revising, Editing, and Proofreading

Revision is best done by looking at one element at a time: **S**upport, **O**rganization, **C**onnectors and Transitions, and **S**tyle. The following Revision Checklist contains the SOCS elements as they apply to comparison and contrast paragraphs.

REVISION CHECKLIST FOR A COMPARISON AND CONTRAST PARAGRAPH

Element	Revision Checkpoints
Topic (2 subjects)	☐ The subjects have some characteristics in common.
	☐ The subjects can be fully discussed in a single paragraph.
	☐ The similarities or differences between the two subjects are explained clearly.
Topic Sentence	☐ The topic sentence includes three elements:
	▪ states the two subjects to be compared or contrasted.
	▪ states the purpose, to discuss similarities or differences.
	▪ makes a point about the two subjects.
Support	☐ The supporting details explain points of comparison and/or contrast for each subject.
	☐ All supporting details are relevant and adequate.
Organization	☐ The paragraph follows one of two patterns of organization consistently: point-by-point or subject-by-subject.
	☐ The point-by-point pattern explains both subjects together for each point of comparison or contrast.
	☐ The subject-by-subject pattern explains all the points of comparison or contrast for one subject and then explains the same points for the other subject in the same order.
	☐ Points are arranged in order of importance.
	☐ The paragraph is balanced in both content and in organization.
Connectors and Transitions	☐ Comparison or contrast connectors and transitions provide coherence.
	☐ Connectors and transitions are used to introduce each new point, to connect one explanation to another within each point, and to change subjects.
Style	☐ Writing is clear, concise Standard Written English.
	☐ Tone is appropriate for a college audience.
	☐ Sentences are varied.

Paragraph Activity: **Revising**

Using the Revision Checklist for a Comparison and Contrast Paragraph, revise the first draft of your paragraph.

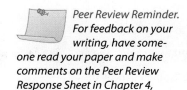

Peer Review Reminder.
For feedback on your
writing, have some-
one read your paper and make
comments on the Peer Review
Response Sheet in Chapter 4,
page 54.

Grammar Reminder.
For more on correcting
sentence fragments,
see Chapter 21.

Check Grammar, Punctuation, and Spelling As you reread your paper to check for grammar, punctuation, and spelling errors, pay special attention for possible errors that may arise in comparison and contrast paragraphs.

1. Avoid using *but* in sentences beginning with *although, even though,* or *while*.

   Incorrect: Although Sabre Lee and Butch were brought up in the same home in South Africa, **but** their personalities are vastly different.

   Correct: Although Sabra Lee and Butch were brought up in the same home, their personalities are vastly different.

2. When using the word *despite*, add the phrase *the fact that*.

   Incorrect: Despite he was raised with affection, as an adult Butch runs away and hides when I try to pet him.

   Correct: Despite the fact that he was raised with affection, as an adult Butch runs away and hides when I try to pet him.

3. Avoid creating a fragment when using *whereas*.

   Incorrect: Whereas Butch turns his back and walks away.

   Correct: Sabra Lee obeys commands, whereas Butch turns his back and walks away.

ACTIVITY **Revising and Editing a Comparison and Contrast Paragraph**

10.4 Revise and edit Natasha's paragraph. Then answer the questions below.

¹Although Sabra Lee and Butch were raised together as puppies in the same home in South Africa, their personalities are vastly different. ²The most notable difference is their obedience. ³Sabra Lee immediately obeys commands given to him. ⁴Butch, on the other hand, just turns his back and walks away when a command is given. ⁵The only statement Butch responds to is "Food!" ⁶Another difference between the dogs is their protectiveness. ⁷Sabra Lee is an alert watchdog, always on the lookout. ⁸When outside, he sits in front of the door to the house or roams around on the driveway, chasing wild monkeys and scaring people passing by on the road. ⁹He even prefers to sleep outside by the front door to protect the house. ¹⁰Unlike Sabra Lee. ¹¹Butch is timid and would rather spend his time lying around rather than chasing intruders. ¹²He sleeps much of the time on his comfortable blanket on the secluded patio in the back of the house. ¹³The dog's personalities also differed in their display of affection toward people. ¹⁴Whenever a family member comes home, Sabra Lee does his "meet and greet," which consists of wagging his tail vigorously while rubbing his body against the individual, begging to

be petted. [15]In contrast, Butch has no desire to give or to get affection. [16]He runs away and hides when anyone tries to pet him. [17]Although Sabra Lee and Butch have different personalities, both dogs are treasured members of the family.

Questions on Revising

1. Underline the topic sentence. What are the two subjects, the focus, and the main point?

_____

2. List the main points of contrast.

_____

3. Does the writer use point by point or subject by subject as her method of organization? Is it effective?

_____

4. How does the writer introduce each major point of contrast?

_____

Questions on Editing and Proofreading

1. The paragraph has one fragment error. Find and correct it.

_____

2. Identify and correct the one verb shift error.

_____

3. The paragraph has one error in apostrophe use. Find and correct it.

_____

Paragraph Activity: **Editing and Proofreading**

Edit and proofread your comparison or contrast paragraph. Check that your final draft is complete, accurate, and error-free.

Paragraph Writing Assignments

Help Desk

Earl has written his rough draft paragraph about the differences between his two friends Diego and Joe. Read Earl's paper and suggest how he can improve its balance.

Diego and Joe have many differences in their lifestyle. To begin, Diego enjoys working out on a regular basis. He runs four to five miles every morning and then goes to the gym where he spends two hours working out. As a result, he is in great physical shape. Joe rarely works out. Another difference is their eating habits. Diego is careful about what he eats. He eats a lean protein, a starchy carbohydrate, and a complex carbohydrate at each meal. In contrast, Joe eats fast food every day. The final difference is their study habits. Diego spends his free time studying because he wants to maintain his 3.5 grade point average. When his friends ask him to go out, even though he is tempted, he tells them that he needs to spend time doing homework or studying. He has joined a math study group for extra help in his college algebra course. Unlike Diego, Joe does not spend much time studying for his courses. If Joe continues with his current lifestyle, he will not be successful like Diego.

_____

_____

_____

MyWritingLab™
Complete this activity
at mywritinglab.com

Reading and Writing across the Curriculum: **Interior Design**

Throughout history, humans have arranged the objects in their environment to meet their needs. Today, interior design is a profession that creates spaces and furnishings to meet the needs of people of all ages and abilities, including the older adults, children, and those who are temporarily or permanently disabled.

Interior designers use **anthropometrics** to determine how much space people need to function in an environment. Anthropometrics is the science of measuring the physical sizes and shapes of the human body in various activities. Designers use this information to plan for the comfort, size, and usefulness of space and furnishings.

(Adapted from _Beginnings of Interior Environments_ by Lynn M. Jones and Phyllis Sloan Allen)

Write a paragraph comparing and/or contrasting how well two restaurants meet the needs of the customer in the way they use their physical space. Choose two restaurants that are similar in the type of food served, the size of the restaurant, and the prices. For example, you could choose two fast-food restaurants.

When developing your details, use these points of comparison and/or contrast:

- Size: Is the restaurant too big, too small, or adequate?
- Furniture: Is the furniture user-friendly? Is it easy to move, rearrange, and clean? Does it fit all sizes? How comfortable is it? Is the furniture arranged for usefulness?

■ Accessibility: Does the restaurant accommodate children, the elderly, and people with disabilities?

■ Ease of use: Is the restaurant easy to enter, exit, order food, and pay?

Comment on a Contemporary Issue: Going Green

"Going green" refers to actions people can take to change their habits as consumers to conserve and improve the natural environment. Many people are becoming aware of their lifestyle's impact on the environment and are making changes. On the other hand, others are resistant to giving up their comfortable lives. Write a paragraph contrasting two people or families, one going green and the other not making lifestyle changes. Some possible categories for your points of contrast could be recycling, pest control, energy use (electricity, water, gasoline), chemical product use (for cleaning, pest control), and vehicle choices.

Reader Response

The textbook excerpt on page 193 explains that interior designers use the sizes and shapes of humans to design rooms and furniture so that people will be comfortable. Which rooms are the most comfortable for your needs? Which rooms are the most uncomfortable?

Write a paragraph that responds to one of these questions.

Text-to-Text	■ Does this reading remind you of something else you have read, heard, or seen (story, book, movie, song, news item, magazine article, website, and so on)? ■ Are the ideas the same or different?
Text-to-Self	■ How do the ideas in the reading relate to your own life, experiences, or ideas? ■ Do you agree or disagree with what you read?
Text-to-World	■ What does the reading remind you of in the real world? ■ Does it make you think about something in the past, present, or future?

Write about an Image: Two Paintings

© Harvard Art Museum/Art Resource, NY, © 2013 Estate of Pablo Picasso/Artists Rights Society (ARS), New York.

Both of these paintings have the same title, *Mother and Child*, but the images the artists use to show a mother and child are very different. Write a paragraph in which you compare and/or contrast these paintings.

The Comparison and Contrast Essay

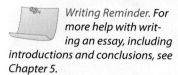 **LO 3** **Write a comparison and contrast essay.**

Writing Reminder. For more help with writing an essay, including introductions and conclusions, see Chapter 5.

The comparison and contrast essay has the same purpose as the comparison and contrast paragraph: to explain how two subjects are alike and/or different. The body paragraphs of the comparison and contrast essay use the same organizational patterns as the comparison and contrast paragraph: point-by-point or subject-by-subject. The comparison and contrast graphic organizers on pages 200 and 201 can also be used to plan your essay. They will help keep you organized as you prewrite, draft, and revise.

Comparison and contrast essays can inform or persuade. For example, in writing a comparison and contrast essay about the differences between two electronic devices, you could provide factual information about the differences in features, storage, and size. On the other hand, if you wanted to persuade the reader that one device was the better choice, you would explain how the features, storage, and size of one are better than those of the other.

Thesis Statement

The thesis statement for a comparison and/or contrast essay includes the following:

1. The **two subjects** that you will compare and/or contrast.
2. The **purpose**: to discuss similarities and/or differences.
3. The point of the comparison and/or contrast.

The following thesis statement example is from Kathryn Butler's essay "Two Coaching Styles" on pages 197 and 198:

Thesis with **two subjects**, purpose, and point of the comparison and/or contrast:
> **Although** Coach L.D. and Coach Slaughter **both coach our softball team,** they differ with respect to their coaching styles.

Thesis with **two subjects**, purpose, and point of the comparison and/or contrast and **listed supporting points of comparison and/or contrast.**
> **Although** Coach L.D. and Coach Slaughter **both coach our softball team,** their coaching styles differ with respect to their attitudes toward the team's performance, techniques for motivating the team, and approaches to winning.

Body Paragraphs

The body paragraphs in the comparison and contrast essay follow one of two patterns: point-by-point or subject-by-subject. The point-by-point pattern explains one point of similarity or difference at a time for Subject A and then Subject B. The subject-by-subject pattern explains all of the points of similarities or differences for Subject A and then explains the same points of similarities or differences for Subject B.

Notice how Kathryn uses a point-by-point compare/contrast essay graphic organizer to develop and organize her points of contrast and details.

Kathryn's Point-by-Point Comparison and Contrast Essay Graphic Organizer

Introduction

Lead-in: Each coach's comments during tense moment followed by team winning the softball game.

Bridge: Coach L.D. congratulates the team for the great play; Coach Slaughter says that the play meets his expectations.

Thesis Statement: Although Coach L.D. and Coach Slaughter both coach our softball team, their coaching styles differ with respect to their attitudes toward the team's performance, techniques for motivating the team, and approaches to winning.

Body Paragraph 1

Topic Sentence: One striking difference between Coach L.D. and Coach Slaughter is their attitude toward our performance.

Subject A: Coach L.D.

Details: Speaks in a calm voice, smiles even after team makes bad plays. Example: Played bad game against Johnson's team; Coach encouraged us.

Subject B: Coach Slaughter

Details: Always yelling, yells in dugout after team makes bad plays. Example: Played an excellent inning against the Devils; Coach gave us lecture about what team was doing wrong.

Body Paragraph 2

Topic Sentence: Another difference between Coach L.D. and Coach Slaughter is their techniques for motivating the team.

Subject A: Coach L.D.

Details: Positive: Expects only average plays and hits, gives rewards for superior plays. Example: Offered $5 for a home run and $10 for a grand slam.

Subject B: Coach Slaughter

Details: Negative: Expects home runs and good plays, gets upset if we do not meet his standards. Example: Mandi hit home run but only heard more batting tips.

Body Paragraph 3

Topic Sentence: The most important difference between Coach L.D. and Coach Slaughter is their approach to winning.

Subject A: Coach L.D.

Details: Wants team to have fun, is understanding and willing to compromise. Example: Changed Melissa's position because she was not happy.

Subject B: Coach Slaughter

Details: Believes winning is life or death. Example: When Kim made bad play because of an injury, Coach Slaughter did not accept her excuse.

Conclusion

Effective Closing Technique: Explain how actions of the two coaches add up to a winning situation.

Concluding Statement: Although Coach L.D. and Coach Slaughter have such different coaching styles, they work well together because they complement one another.

Comparison and Contrast Essay Example

Student Kathryn Butler explains the differences between the styles of two softball coaches.

Two Coaching Styles

1   The score is tied. There are two outs. Coach L.D. says, "Come on girls. You can do it! Make the play at first base." The next batter steps up to the plate. Coach Slaughter screams, "You girls better make the play or you're going to be hearing from me!" The ball leaves the pitcher's hand and floats toward the batter with a slight arch. The ball is hit. The shortstop fields the ball and throws it to first base. The third out is made. The proud softball team hustles into the dugout. Coach L.D. congratulates the team for the great play, while Coach Slaughter tells the team that the play meets his expectations. Coach L.D. and Coach Slaughter have different, but effective attitudes toward our performance, techniques for motivating the team, and approaches to winning.

2   One striking difference between Coach L.D. and Coach Slaughter is their attitudes toward our performance. Coach L.D. always speaks in a calm voice. He never gets upset during the games when the team makes bad plays. He keeps a smiling face waiting for us when the team comes back into the dugout. When our team played the Johnson's team, we could not make a decent play. We were overthrowing the ball, missing easy catches, and hitting ground balls to the pitcher. Coach L.D. encouraged us by saying, "Come on girls. You have what it takes. You just need to concentrate. We can pull out of this slump of bad plays and win this game." His positive attitude and consistent encouragement helped us achieve the positive state of mind we needed to win the game. In every losing situation, Coach L.D. remains calm and cheers us up. On the other hand, Coach Slaughter is always yelling. When our team makes bad plays during a game, he yells that we should be making the outs and winning the game. Every time we return to the dugout after an inning, he lectures us about what we are doing wrong and what we should be doing. When we played the Devils, we were making every play and hitting the ball into the outfield. When we returned to the dugout after an excellent inning for our team, Coach Slaughter said, "This is the type of fielding and hitting I expect from you girls. Don't slack off tonight." His expectations for us help us stay focused on playing well. In every game situation, Coach Slaughter expects perfection and corrects imperfection.

grand slam a home run hit with all three bases occupied by base runners, as a result scoring four home runs

3   Another difference between Coach L.D. and Coach Slaughter is their techniques for motivating the team. Coach L.D.'s technique is to be positive. He only expects average plays and hits from us; anything more is a bonus. Coach L.D. motivates us by giving rewards for superior plays. At our last game, he announced that he would give anyone who hit a home run five dollars and anyone who hit a **grand slam** ten dollars. In contrast, Coach Slaughter's technique is to be negative. He expects home runs and good plays from us. He motivates us by telling us that we will not get a lecture after the game if we play flawlessly. If we do not play perfectly, he is disappointed in us. He wants perfect double plays and home runs, and if we do not meet his standard, he is upset; anything less is a disappointment. When Mandi, our shortstop, hit a home run, she returned to the dugout, only to hear further batting tips from Coach Slaughter. According to him, there is always room for improvement.

4   The most important difference between Coach L.D. and Coach Slaughter is their approach to winning. Coach L.D. just wants us to have fun, and, therefore, he is understanding and willing to compromise. For example, Melissa was not happy playing center field, so she explained her reasons to Coach L.D. He decided that she would also make a good second baseman, so he made the switch, and we have never seen a better second baseman than Melissa. Unlike Coach L.D., Coach Slaughter's believes winning is life or death. For instance, during a game, Kim made a bad play. When Coach Slaughter criticized her, she gave the excuse that her ankle injury was bothering her, but he did not want to hear it. No matter what the excuse, he will not accept it.

5   Although Coach L.D. and Coach Slaughter have such different coaching styles, they work well together because they complement one another. Some of the more sensitive girls on the team need Coach L.D.'s encouragement and lack of criticism in order to feel confident and do their best. However, some of the unmotivated girls need Coach Slaughter's "wake-up calls." When the girls who have been lectured by Coach Slaughter feel that their egos have been bruised, Coach L.D. restores their self-esteem. When the girls who are not trying their best are complimented by Coach L.D., they are brought back to reality by some sharp observations voiced by Coach Slaughter. The combination of these two coaches, who have such opposite philosophies, adds up to a winning situation for all the players on the team.

ACTIVITY
10.5   ## Analyzing a Comparison and Contrast Essay
Answer the following questions about "Two Coaching Styles."

1. Underline the thesis statement. What are the differences the writer will discuss?

   _____

2. What technique does the writer use for the lead-in in the introductory paragraph?

   _____

3. Underline the topic sentences of the body paragraphs. What is the point of each of the topic sentences?

   _____

4. Which organizational pattern does this essay use?

   a. Point-by-point   b. Subject-by-subject

5. In addition to referring to the thesis, underline the point(s) the writer makes in the concluding paragraph.

Comparison and Contrast Essay Graphic Organizers

Using a point-by-point or subject-by-subject graphic organizer will help you place your details in the appropriate pattern. The sample graphic organizers shown on pages 200 and 201 can be changed to suit your needs by adding paragraphs, points, and supporting details.

Point-by-Point Compare/Contrast Essay Organizer

MyWritingLab™
Use the interactive graphic
organizer at mywritinglab.com

Introduction

Lead-in:

Bridge:

Thesis Statement:

Body Paragraph 1

Topic Sentence:

Subject A:

Details:

Subject B:

Details:

Body Paragraph 2

Topic Sentence:

Subject A:

Details:

Subject B:

Details:

Body Paragraph 3

Topic Sentence:

Subject A:

Details:

Subject B:

Details:

Conclusion

Effective Closing Technique:

Concluding Statement:

Subject-by-Subject Compare/Contrast Essay Graphic Organizer

Introduction

Lead-in:

Bridge:

Thesis Statement:

Body Paragraph 1

Topic Sentence: Subject A

First Point:
        Details:

Second Point:
        Details:

Third Point:
        Details:

Body Paragraph 2

Topic Sentence: Subject B

First Point for Subject B:
        Details:

Second Point for Subject B:
        Details:

Third Point for Subject B:
        Details:

Conclusion

Effective Closing Technique:

Concluding Statement:

Essay Writing Assignments

MyWritingLab™
Complete this activity
at mywritinglab.com

Write about an Image: Men, Women, and Shopping

This photograph illustrates a common belief that men and women feel differently about shopping. Write an essay in which you contrast two shoppers of the same or different genders.

Writing Topics for a Comparison and Contrast Essay

For your comparison and contrast essay, choose one of these options:

- from paragraph to essay: expand the paragraph you wrote in the paragraph section of this chapter
- any of the writing topics in the paragraph section of this chapter
- any topic from the following list:

General Topics

two websites on the same subject
beliefs you had when you were young and beliefs you have now
living at home and living away from home
two individuals, one who is positive and the other who is negative
a product you would like to own and the same type of product you own now
    (such as a car, home, electronic equipment, etc.)

Writing across the Curriculum Topics

History: the time period you are living in and the time period that a parent, relative, or other older person grew up in
Education: teaching styles of two college instructors or high school teachers
Communications: face-to-face communication and electronic communication
Business: being self-employed or working for someone else
Cooking: foods of two different cultural groups (two different regions of a country or two different countries)

*Peer Review Reminder.
For feedback on your
writing, have some-
one read your paper and make
comments on the Peer Review
Response Sheet in Chapter 4,
page 54.*

English Success Tip: Keeping a Portfolio of Your Writing

A writing portfolio is a collection of the best examples of your written work over the entire semester. You can save your papers in print or in electronic format.

Some teachers require a writing portfolio as part of the course grade. However, if the portfolio is not a course requirement for you, consider keeping one on your own. Keeping a portfolio is a good way to monitor your progress and showcase your achievements. After the course is over, you will have a record of the writing you have completed.

You can choose the papers you want to include, such as

- papers written in class
- timed writing assignments
- papers written out of class

You can also include prewriting, rough drafts, and final drafts of writing assignments. To keep organized, create a table of contents or list of assignments as shown.

Table of Contents for Portfolio

Date	Type of Writing Assignment	Title

11 Classification

Learning Objectives

After working through this chapter, you will be able to:

LO 1 Define classification as a pattern of development that arranges items into groups based on a single characteristic.

LO 2 Write a classification paragraph.

LO 3 Write a classification essay.

LO 1 **Define classification as a pattern of development that arranges items into groups based on a single characteristic.**

What Is Classification?

Classification is a pattern of development that arranges items within a topic into groups based on a single characteristic. Key words that show how a topic is classified are *types, categories, groups, kinds,* or *components*.

You use classification when you decide to listen to a type of music, such as rap, hip hop, top 40, country, salsa, reggae, and so on, for your own enjoyment. Retail stores use different types of music to influence sales. For example, people spend more money in restaurants that play slow music, while they spend less but leave sooner in restaurants that play fast music. Stores that want to sell to teenagers play loud music because teens like to feel and hear the music.

MyWritingLab™
Complete this activity
at mywritinglab.com

Quick Write

Write about the types of music played in stores and restaurants you are familiar with.

Classification in College Writing

Classification is often used to present material in college courses and in textbooks. In a music appreciation course, the types of instruments in an orchestra or the six main periods in music history are examples of classification. In a criminal justice course, examples of classification are strategies of police work and methods of interrogating a suspect.

There are two types of classification paragraphs that you can write:

- A **formal classification** paragraph explains categories that already exist, such as classifying animals in biology or types of movies.
- An **original classification** paragraph explains categories that the writer makes up, such as types of behaviors among toddlers.

A Classification Paragraph Example

The following paragraph is an example of the formal classification paragraph.

[1]The Filter Theory of Mate Selection suggests that people use a system based on five variables to choose a mate who is the most similar. [2]The first filter is **proximity**, which refers to geographic closeness. [3]It is easier to get to know or interact with someone who is in the same general location. [4]In addition, we tend to marry someone with whom we share things in common. [5]Next is the **homogamy filter**, which refers to forming a relationship with someone who has a similar ethnic and racial background, religious upbringing, age, education level, financial status, and values and beliefs. [6]Another is the **heterogamy filter**, which refers to forming relationships with partners who are of different races, religions, ethnicities, and ages. [7]The **physical attraction filter** suggests that we choose potential mates based on cultural standards of physical attractiveness. [8]People are attracted to those who are at least as or more attractive than they are. [9]Finally, once we have exhausted all of the other filters, we use the **balance sheet filter**, in which we look at what someone can offer us that we cannot find in anyone else. [10]In addition, both individuals want to be committed to the relationship. [11]Applying the Filter Theory can help people understand the rewards and costs of selecting a mate.

(Adapted from *Family Life Now* by Kelly J. Welch)

 ACTIVITY   Analyzing a Classification Paragraph

11.1   Answer the questions about the paragraph you just read about the Filter Theory of Mate Selection.

1. Underline the topic sentence.
2. What is the topic that is being classified?

_____

3. Circle the names of the five filters.
4. What kind of support details are used for each of the filters?

_____

5. Underline the transition words.
6. Why is the balance sheet filter the last one to be covered in the paragraph?

_____

CLASSIFICATION   Essentials

The purpose of classification is to explain a topic by dividing it into groups according to something the groups have in common. Classification may achieve any of the following:

- inform the readers about a topic they are not familiar with
- show knowledge about a course concept to a teacher
- persuade readers by applying a rating system
- give readers a new way of looking at a topic

An effective classification paragraph has these essential elements:

1. The paragraph makes a point about what the items in the topic have in common—the basis of their classification.
2. The groups are complete, fit under the same classification principle, and do not overlap.
3. The supporting details explain each group in a similar way and are developed with the same amount of detail. They can be examples, descriptions, short narratives, and facts.
4. The groups are organized in order of importance.
5. Classification transitional words or expressions help readers see the movement from one point to another or from one subject to another.

The Classification Paragraph

LO 2 **Write a classification paragraph.**

Prewriting the Classification Paragraph

Choose Your Topic and Purpose When deciding on your own classification topic or responding to an assigned topic, consider the following:

1. **Choose a topic that is not too complicated or technical for your readers to understand.** Consider your readers' background knowledge when selecting a topic. For example, many readers do not know about auto engines and might have a hard time understanding a paper classifying them.
2. **Choose a topic that will interest your readers.** For instance, most people know the various types of electronic communication, so the topic would not be interesting. However, you could take a more original approach, such as classifying text messagers.
3. **Choose a topic that can be explained completely in one paragraph.** If your topic is classified into too many groups or categories, you will not be able to include all the information needed to explain each one.

 ACTIVITY   **Evaluating Topics for a Classification Paragraph**

11.2   Explain why each of the following topics would be good or not good for a classification paragraph.

1. types of transportation

_____

2. duties of uniformed police officers

_____

3. types of expenses you have

_____

4. seasons of the year

_____

5. types of poisonous spiders.

_____

Develop Ideas for Your Topic Prewriting for a classification topic involves finding details for your topic, identifying what the details have in common (the basis of classification), and then putting the details into groups based on that common feature.

Understand the Basis for Classification The **basis for classification** is the common feature used to classify or group the details for your topic. For example, each of the items in the following list shows a different basis for classifying chocolate:

- varieties of chocolate
- types of chocolate candies
- health benefits of chocolate
- movies about chocolate
- countries famous for chocolate production

Student Sue chose the topic "college students" for her classification paragraph. She thought of six different ways to classify college students: by gender, major, age, marital status, reasons for attending, and irritating behaviors. She decided to classify students according to their irritating behaviors. As a student who recently returned to college, Sue found the behavior of some students in her environmental science class irritating, and she knew that she could think of several behaviors to write about.

 ACTIVITY 11.3

Developing Classification Principles

Find three different ways to classify each of the following topics.

1. relationships

_____

2. cars

_____

3. games

_____

Paragraph Activity: **Choosing a Basis for Classification**

Prewrite to choose a basis for classification for one of the following topics.

General Topics

clubs, organizations, or teams at your college or in your community
unhealthy weight loss or exercise programs
jobs in your career choice
your personal rating system for video games, movies, websites, or television shows
unpleasant or pleasant chores or responsibilities at home or at work

Writing across the Curriculum Topics

Business: customers or clients
Fashion: clothing, accessories, or shoes for a specific activity or occasion
Environmental Science: endangered species
Culinary Arts: cooking methods or styles
Art Appreciation: web page design

Understand How to Group Ideas When you have chosen your basis for classification for your topic, you are ready to find groups or categories. For example, the topic "Chocolate" can be grouped according to health benefits, one of the bases for classification on page 207.

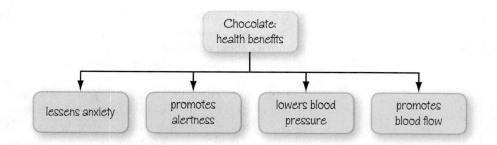

The topic "Chocolate" can also be grouped according to another basis for classification, movies in which chocolate plays a role:

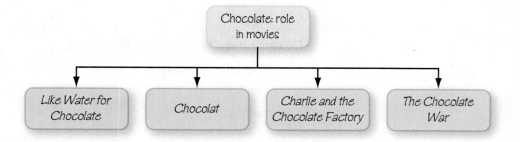

Understand Possible Problems with Groups When choosing your basis for classification and groups for your topic, check for these possible problems:

1. **Group overlap.** Overlap happens when one group fits into more than one category. The next diagram shows some groups for the basis for classification *driver distractions.*

Four of these potential groups overlap.

- The group "text messaging" belongs in "using the cell phone" group. Text messaging is just one way of using a cell phone. Using the cell phone could also include making a call or taking a photo.
- The "putting on makeup" group fits into the "grooming" group. Grooming includes putting on makeup as well as styling hair, shaving, and so on.

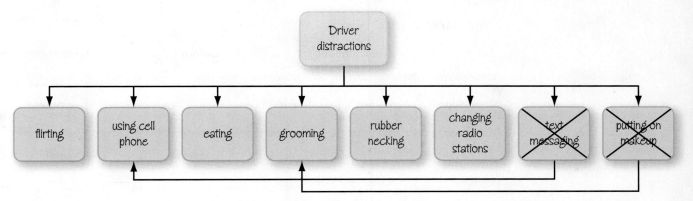

2. **Groups all belong to the same classification principle.** If one or more of the groups do not fit, the classification will not be logical. Look at the groups below for the basis of classification, types of test questions. The group "test-taking strategies" is not a type of test question and does not belong to the basis of classification.

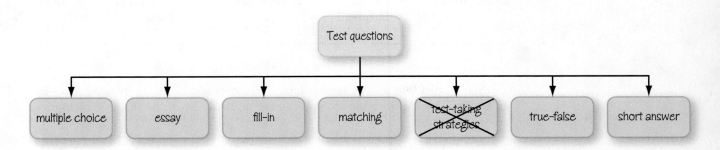

3. **Groups are complete.** All of the groups should be included, particularly when writing about groups that are well known. For example, the Motion Picture Association of America classifies movies according to the suitability of their content for certain audiences. Note how the following list includes all audiences. If you left one of these groups out, your classification would not be complete.

G   General audience; material appropriate for all ages
PG   Parental guidance recommended
PG-13   Parental guidance recommended for children under 13
R   Restricted; children under 17 must be with a parent
NC-17   No one 17 and under will be admitted

Sometimes, you will have more groups than you can discuss in a paragraph. If this happens, you may need to take a different approach to your topic. You may be able to take one of the groups and use it as your topic, then find a new basis for classification, and develop new groups. For example, you could choose PG-13 movies as your topic and then classify the types of movies that are PG-13.

ACTIVITY Identifying Classification Errors

11.4 Find the grouping error for each topic and tell why it is wrong.

O Overlaps with other groups **D** Does not belong with this topic
I Incomplete list of groups

EXAMPLE:

1. sports: a. indoor   b. outdoor   c. competitive

c. competitive, O. Both indoor and outdoor sports can be competitive.
_____

2. sneakers: a. leather   b. vinyl   c. canvas   d. synthetic

_____

3. computers: a. notebook   b. laptop   c. handheld

_____

4. teaching styles: a. good-looking   b. strict   c. not strict

_____

5. natural bodies of water: a. seas   b. oceans   c. dams   d. lakes

_____

6. dog breeds: a. German   b. Chihuahua   c. Doberman   d. Akita
                     Shepherd   Pinscher

_____

Sue created four groups for her topic "college students" using *irritating behaviors* as her basis for classification. As you can see in the figure below she gave each group an original name.

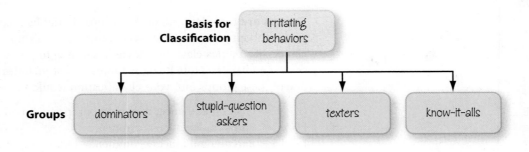

Paragraph Activity: Developing Groups

Using the chart below, develop at least three groups for the basis for classification you selected for one of the topics on page 208. Then check your groups to see that they do not overlap, are clearly different from one another, and are complete.

The chart shown here has four boxes. However, you can add as many boxes as you need.

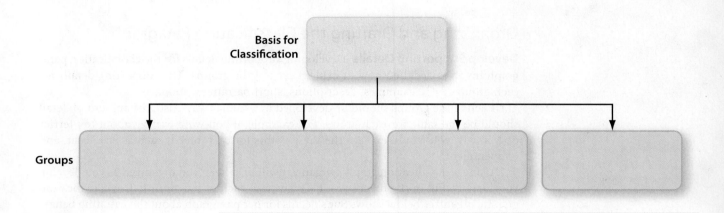

Narrow Your Topic and Write the Topic Sentence At this point, you have chosen a topic, selected a basis for classification, and developed groups. Writing the topic sentence involves putting all of these pieces together.

The topic sentence for the classification paragraph includes the following:

1. The topic that will be classified
2. The purpose, which is **classification**
3. The basis for classification

Here is a topic sentence for a paragraph on the motion picture rating system:

> Movies **can be classified** according to how suitable they are for certain audiences.

Sue wrote this topic sentence classifying students in her class:

> The students in my environmental science class can be classified by their irritating behaviors.

Punctuation Reminder. See Chapter 28 for more information about using colons.

TIPS | **Writing Classification Topic Sentences**

1. **Include all the parts needed to make the point of your paragraph: a topic, the purpose, and the basis for classification.**

    No point: I lived with eighty-seven women for ten weeks during naval training.

    With a point: My roommates in navy boot camp can be classified by their personalities.

2. **Include a specific basis for classification.**

    No basis for classification: I have four kinds of tattoos on my body. It is not enough to give the number of groups.

    With a specific basis for classification: My tattoos can be classified according to their style.

Paragraph Activity: **Writing a Topic Sentence**

Write a topic sentence for the topic and groups you developed in the Paragraph Activity on pages 210–211.

Organizing and Drafting the Classification Paragraph

Develop Supporting Details Developing supporting details for the classification paragraph involves deciding how to explain each of the groups. The supporting details for each group can be examples, descriptions, short narratives, and facts.

Each of the groups should be developed in a similar way. Also, the amount of detail should be the same for each group. For example, if you were writing about toy terrier dog breeds, you would explain the same points for each breed, such as size, coat, and temperament.

Using a classification graphic organizer will help keep you organized as you develop your details. Fill in the names you have given to each of the groups. The classification graphic organizer below shows Sue's details for her paragraph about the irritating behaviors of the students in her environmental science class. First, she describes the behavior of each of the groups and then gives an example.

Sue's Classification Paragraph Graphic Organizer

Topic Sentence: The students in my environmental science class can be classified by their irritating behaviors.

Group 1 dominators	**Group 2** stupid-question askers	**Group 3** texters	**Group 4** know-it-alls
Description Behavior	**Description Behavior**	**Description Behavior**	**Description Behavior**
Take control of class by talking	Ask questions that have already been answered	Text message from cell phones	Know the material, feel and act superior
Details	**Details**	**Details**	**Details**
Ryan made 15-minute speech about problems from coal mining	Laurie asked what to bring the day of the test after teacher had already told class	Jackson texts from phone on lap, never listens, takes notes, or takes part in discussion	Eugene laughs with disrespect when someone cannot answer a question

Concluding Sentence: As an older, returning student, I realize that I have to ignore those who are irritating and focus on learning.

Paragraph Activity: **Developing Details**

Using the classification graphic organizer below or another method, develop details for the topic you have been working on. Add or remove boxes as needed.

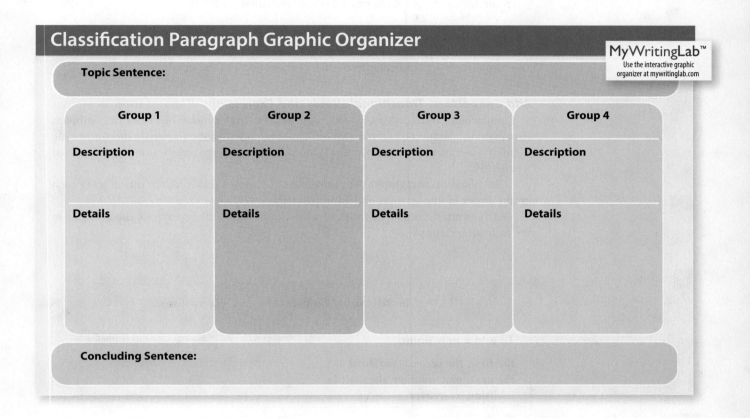

Classification Paragraph Graphic Organizer

MyWritingLab™
Use the interactive graphic organizer at mywritinglab.com

Topic Sentence:

Group 1	**Group 2**	**Group 3**	**Group 4**
Description	Description	Description	Description
Details	Details	Details	Details

Concluding Sentence:

Organize Your Supporting Details

Classification paragraphs are usually organized by order of importance. Depending on your topic, you may also use spatial order or time order. Using your classification graphic organizer, rank your groups from most to least important or least to most important.

Paragraph Activity: **Organizing Supporting Details**

Organize your groups by choosing order of importance, spatial order, or chronological order, and check that you develop each group in the same way with the same amount of detail.

Write the First Draft As you write your first draft, consider balance and transitional words and expressions.

Balance Your classification paragraph should be balanced in both content and in organization. As you write, follow the same organizational pattern throughout the paragraph. Keep the following points in mind to avoid potential problems:

- Develop each group in the same way with the same amount of detail.
- Organize the points for each group in the same order.
- Explain each group completely before moving on to the next one.

Add Connectors: Transitional Words and Expressions Classification is similar to comparison and contrast in that you are writing about more than one subject. However, in classification, you explain the groups without comparing or contrasting them. Transitions for order of importance and for adding information are used most frequently.

Classification paragraphs use connectors and transition words for introducing each group, order of importance, and adding details.

Each group should be introduced with a transition and the name of the group as in the following examples:

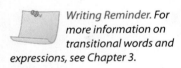

Writing Reminder. For more information on transitional words and expressions, see Chapter 3.

Classification Connectors and Transitions	
To add a new point: *the first, the second, the third, the next, one, another, the last, in addition, moreover*	The first type of test question is multiple choice. Another type of test question is true–false.
To show order of importance: *the most important, the least important, least of all, most of all*	The most important type is the essay question; answering an essay question involves writing skills.

Paragraph Activity: **Writing the First Draft**

Using your graphic organizer and topic sentence, write the first draft of your classification paragraph.

Revising, Editing, and Proofreading

Revise your draft by looking at one element at a time: **S**upport, **O**rganization, **C**onnectors and transitions, and **S**tyle. The following Revision Checklist contains the **SOCS** elements as they apply to classification paragraphs.

REVISION CHECKLIST FOR A CLASSIFICATION PARAGRAPH

Element	Revision Checkpoints
Topic	☐ The topic can be classified.
	☐ The topic can be fully discussed in a single paragraph.
Topic Sentence	☐ The topic sentence includes these elements:
	■ states the subject that you will be classifying.
	■ states the point, which is the basis for classification.
	■ may list the groups.
Support	☐ The groups are complete, fit under the same basis of classification, and do not overlap.
	☐ Supporting details for each group are developed in the same way.
	☐ The supporting details for each group can be examples, descriptions, short narratives, and facts.
	☐ All supporting details are relevant and adequate.
Organization	☐ Each group is discussed completely, one at a time.
	☐ The groups are arranged in order of importance, spatial order, or chronological order.
	☐ The paragraph is balanced in both content and in organization.
Connectors and Transitions	☐ Connectors and transitions provide coherence.
	☐ Transitions are used to introduce each new point and to connect details within each point.
Style	☐ Writing is clear, concise Standard Written English.
	☐ Tone is appropriate for a college audience.
	☐ Sentences are varied.

Peer Review Reminder. For feedback on your writing, have someone read your paper and make comments on the Peer Review Response Sheet in Chapter 4, page 54.

Paragraph Activity: **Revising**

Using the Revision Checklist for a Classification Paragraph, revise your classification paragraph.

Check Grammar, Punctuation, and Spelling As you reread your paper to check for grammar, punctuation, and spelling errors, pay special attention for possible errors that may arise in classification paragraphs. For example, be sure that you do not shift verb tenses or pronouns.

ACTIVITY   Revising and Editing a Classification Paragraph

11.5   Revise and edit Sue's paragraph. Then answer the questions that follow.

¹The students in my environmental science class can be classified by their irritating behaviors: the dominators, the stupid-question askers, the texters, and the know-it-alls. ²The first irritating group is the dominators. ³These students like to be the center of attention, so they take control of the class by monopolizing the discussion. ⁴For example, Ryan, the worst of the dominators, took over the discussion of worldwide cooperation to decrease global warming by giving a fifteen-minute speech expressing his opinion about environmental problems created by coal mining. ⁵Another irritating group is the stupid-question askers. ⁶For some reason, they ask questions that the teacher has already answered. ⁷Last week, for instance, the teacher told the students that they would need to bring a pencil and a scantron for our first major test. ⁸Not ten minutes after this announcement, Laurie, well-known for asking obvious questions, asked the teacher, Do I need to bring a pencil? What else do I need? What happens if I forget them? ⁹The next group, the texters, is a quiet bunch because they are busy using their cell phones to text message instead of paying attention to what is going on in class. ¹⁰Jackson's eyes are never on the teacher. ¹¹He is always looking down at his cell phone hidden in the folds of his baggy t-shirt and typing text messages nonstop from the beginning of class to the end. ¹²The most irritating group, though, is the know-it-alls. ¹³These bright students have read and studied the assigned chapters in the textbook and know all the answers to the teacher's questions, so they feel and act superior. ¹⁴Eugene is the perfect example for the know-it-all group. ¹⁵He has no tolerance for the other students. ¹⁶Slumping back in his chair, he laughs and snickers with disrespect when someone answers a question incorrectly or makes a comment that he thinks is stupid.

Questions on Revising

1. Underline the topic sentence. What are the narrowed topic, the basis for classification, and the groups?

_____

_____

2. The paragraph is missing a concluding sentence. Write an interesting concluding sentence that does not just restate the main idea of the paragraph.

_____

_____

Question on Editing and Proofreading

3. Quotation marks are necessary to show that someone is speaking, but they are missing in this paragraph. Add quotation marks where they are needed.

Paragraph Activity: Editing and Proofreading

Edit and proofread your classification paragraph. Check that your final draft is complete, accurate, and error-free.

Paragraph Writing Assignments

Help Desk

Tyson has written his rough draft paragraph classifying the rules he had to follow in high school. Read Tyson's paper and suggest how he can classify his details into groups.

> Central High School had many frustrating rules that the students had to follow. For example, students had to always wear their picture IDs. In addition, passes were needed to show security guards that we had permission to be in the hallways. If we didn't have an ID and a pass, we would be sent to **internal suspension.** Also, we couldn't wear hats in class because the teachers felt it was disrespectful. We had to be in class by the second bell or we would get a **detention.** There was also a dress code. For example, we couldn't wear gang colors. No shirts with offensive words printed on them. There was also the rule that we could not show our cell phone on school grounds, and it had to be turned off at all times. We couldn't listen to iPods or have them out. No food was allowed in class. Chewing gum, juice, chips, and sunflower seeds are all considered food. Many students did not like the rules, and it's a relief to now be in college where we have more freedom.

internal suspension a form of punishment where students must stay in a room away from other students where they work on school assignments

detention a punishment in which students must stay in school after regular school hours

Group Activity: Working Together to Classify

In small groups, classify the types of entertainment available in the city or town in which you live. Some ideas for the basis of classification could be as follows:

type: sports, music, movies, dancing, car shows, dining, and so on
cost: cheap, moderate, and expensive
age group: children, teens, adults, and so on

Write a classification paragraph for an audience that is not familiar with the area where you live.

Reading and Writing across the Curriculum: **Marketing**

Read this paragraph classifying shopping centers and choose one of the writing assignments that follow.

> Shopping centers can be classified by their size. A regional shopping center, or regional shopping mall, is the largest and most dramatic shopping center. It contains from 40 to 200 stores, including two or more full-line department stories. It is a like a covered mini-downtown and attracts customers from a wide area. A community shopping center is somewhat smaller. It contains 15 to 40 retail stores normally consisting of a branch of a department store or variety store, a supermarket, specialty stores, professional offices, and sometimes a bank. The smallest centers are neighborhood shopping centers or strip malls. They generally contain between 5 and 15 stores, which are close and convenient for consumers. Strip malls usually contain a supermarket, perhaps a discount store, and several service stores— dry cleaner, self-service laundry, drugstore, video-rental outlet, barber or beauty shop, hardware store, or other stores. While these types of shopping centers have dominated the marketplace, changes in consumer preferences and lifestyles will determine the shopping centers of the future.
>
> (Adapted from *Marketing* by Gary Armstrong and Philip Kotler)

Write a classification paragraph about one of the following topics:

- Classify the types of shopping centers in the area where you live or an area that you are familiar with.
- Classify the types of stores in one shopping center in the area where you live or an area that you are familiar with.

Comment on a Contemporary Issue

Do brands matter to you? How important is it for you to have the latest, best cell phone, the most popular sneakers, or a particular clothing line? The following writing activity may give you some insight about how status conscious you are.

Think of three easily recognizable brand-name items that you own or would like to own. Write a paragraph classifying those three items according to what they say about you. For each item, describe it and tell whether or not the brand name is noticeable. Then explain what using or wearing each item says about you. Does it give a positive or negative message?

Reader Response

The textbook excerpt on page 205 explains a theory of selecting a mate. The Filter Theory of Mate Selection states that people use a system that helps them find a mate. The system helps them eliminate people who are not similar to them. Have you ever used any of those "filters" to find a mate? Write a paragraph that responds to one of these questions.

Text-to-Text	■ Does this reading remind you of something else you have read, heard, or seen (story, book, movie, song, news item, magazine article, website, and so on)? ■ Are the ideas the same or different?
Text-to-Self	■ How do the ideas in the reading relate to your own life, experiences, or ideas? ■ Do you agree or disagree with what you read?
Text-to-World	■ What does the reading remind you of in the real world? ■ Does it make you think about something in the past, present, or future?

MyWritingLab™
Complete this activity
at mywritinglab.com

Write about an Image

The Saffir-Simpson Hurricane Scale is a rating of 1 to 5 based on a hurricane's intensity. It gives an estimate of damage to property or flooding expected along the coast. The factor determining the potential damage is wind speed.

    Using the information from the chart below, write a paragraph classifying hurricanes according to their intensity.

SAFFIR/SIMPSON HURRICANE SCALE

CATEGORY 1
Surge: 4–5 feet   Winds and Effects: 74–95 mph *(64–82 kt)*
No real damage to building structures. Damage primarily to unanchored mobile homes, shrubbery, and trees. Also, some coastal flooding and minor pier damage.

CATEGORY 2
Surge: 6–8 feet   Winds and Effects: 96–110 mph *(83–95 kt)*
Some roofing material, door, and window damage. Considerable damage to vegetation, mobile homes, etc. Flooding damages piers and small craft in unprotected moorings may break their moorings.

CATEGORY 3
Surge: 9–12 feet   Winds and Effects: 111–130 mph *(96–113 kt)*
Some structural damage to small residences and utility buildings, with a minor amount of structural failures. Mobile homes are destroyed. Flooding near the coast destroys smaller structures with larger structures damaged by floating debris. Terrain may be flooded well inland.

CATEGORY 4
Surge: 13–18 feet   Winds and Effects: 131–155 mph *(114–135 kt)*
More extensive structural failures with some complete roof failure on small residences. Major erosion of beach areas. Terrain may be flooded well inland.

CATEGORY 5
Surge: 19 feet +   Winds and Effects: 156 mph+ *(135+ kt)*
Complete roof failure on many residences and industrial buildings. Some complete building failures with small utility buildings blown over or away. Flooding causes major damage to lower floors of all structures near the shoreline. Massive evacuation of residential areas may be required.

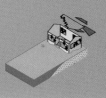

The Classification Essay

LO 3 **Write a classification essay.**

Writing Reminder. For more help with writing an essay, including introductions and conclusions, see Chapter 5.

The classification essay has the same purpose as the classification paragraph: to explain a topic by sorting it into groups according to something the groups have in common. Like the classification paragraph, the classification essay can inform or persuade. For example, in writing an essay classifying your teachers according to their teaching styles, you could explain their choices of activities, classroom policies, and attitudes toward students. On the other hand, if you wanted to persuade, you would develop a rating system for their choices of activities, classroom policies, and attitudes toward students.

Thesis Statement

The thesis statement for a classification essay makes a point about a topic by classifying it into groups according to a common feature called the basis for classification.

The thesis statement for a classification essay includes the following:

1. The topic that will be classified
2. The purpose, which is **classification**
3. The basis for classification

The following thesis statement example is from Nadine Brown's essay "The Misses" on pages 222–223:

Thesis with a **topic**, **purpose**, and basis for classification:

> The babysitters my husband and I employed over a two-year period can be classified according to their unusual character traits.

Thesis with a **topic**, **purpose**, **basis for classification, and list of groups**:

> The babysitters my husband and I employed over a two-year period can be classified according to their unusual character traits **such as Miss Magnetic Fingers, Mrs. Heavenly Bound, and Miss Never Satisfied**.

Body Paragraphs

Each of the body paragraphs in the classification essay explains one of the groups and should follow the same organizational pattern.

- Develop each group in the same way with the same amount of detail.
- Organize the points for each group in the same order.
- Explain each group completely.

Notice how Nadine uses a classification essay graphic organizer to develop and arrange her supporting points and details:

Nadine's Classification Essay Graphic Organizer

Introduction

Lead-in: Brief background about moving to the United States from Jamaica and needing a babysitter for two sons.

Bridge: We thought that finding a babysitter who was right for our family would be a simple process, but our experience proved the opposite to be true.

Thesis Statement: The babysitters my husband and I employed over a two-year period can be classified according to their unusual character traits such as Miss Magnetic Fingers, Mrs. Heavenly Bound, and Miss Never Satisfied.

Body Paragraphs

Body Paragraph 1

Topic Sentence for Group 1: Miss Magnetic Fingers, the first babysitter we employed, created havoc in my life with her deceptive character.

Description: Had two children, spoke excellent English, needed a job
Was told she was honest and hardworking

Details: Deceptive, stole necklaces, earrings, and money; I checked up on her at the local dance club; discovered her wearing my jewelry and dress

Body Paragraph 2

Topic Sentence for Group 2: The next babysitter who replaced Miss Magnetic Fingers was Mrs. Heavenly Bound, who imposed her interpretations of the Bible on the family.

Description: 56-year-old married woman with grandchildren

Details: Overly controlling behavior, brought religious magazines and books and placed them in every room, recommended how to dress, where to go, which occasions to celebrate, insisted we follow her religious beliefs

Body Paragraph 3

Topic Sentence for Group 3: The last babysitter, Miss Never Satisfied, seemed happy at first but later turned out to be a constant complainer.

Description: Recommended by family member, member of our church

Details: Gossiped on phone about low pay, complained about not having enough food in house and was tired of eating food we had, complained about the children, the house temperature, and boring neighborhood

Conclusion

Effective Closing Technique: Discuss the effects of the experiences with the babysitters

Concluding Statement: The experience I had with the babysitters taught me that my family, above all things, came first even if it meant firing someone and quitting my job.

Classification Essay Example

Student Nadine Brown classifies babysitters based on their unusual character traits.

The Misses

1   When my husband, two sons, and I moved to the United States from Jamaica, we both found full-time jobs and needed a babysitter. We thought that finding a babysitter who was right for our family would be a simple process, but our experience proved the opposite to be true. The babysitters my husband and I employed over a two-year period can be classified according to their unusual character traits such as Miss Magnetic Fingers, Mrs. Heavenly Bound, and Miss Never Satisfied.

2   Miss Magnetic Fingers, the first babysitter we employed, created havoc in my life with her deceptive character. I had hired this young woman because she had two children, spoke excellent English, and needed a temporary job. I was told that she was honest and hardworking, so I took her in without reservations. When my world began to turn upside down, I had second thoughts about her. Her sticky magnetic fingers held on to all of my possessions that interested her. My necklaces and earrings disappeared from my jewelry boxes, and my clothing disappeared from my drawers. I had to start counting my money. At first I thought I had just misplaced these items. Then, I started to suspect Miss Magnetic Fingers and decided to do some detective work. If she had stolen my jewelry, she would certainly want to show it off at the local dance club. One Saturday night, I headed to her favorite club, and to my utter amazement, she was swirling on the dance floor wearing my jewelry and my engagement dress. When I confronted her, she admitted her theft and begged for forgiveness, but she was a con artist, and she had to go.

3   The next babysitter who replaced Miss Magnetic Fingers was Mrs. Heavenly Bound, who imposed her interpretations of the Bible on the family. Mrs. Heavenly Bound was highly recommended to us by a family member. This fifty-six-year-old married woman had raised four children and was looking for a babysitting position not merely for monetary gains, but also because, in her words, "All children belong to her." She seemed to be the mother I never had and the grandmother my children needed. Suddenly, our days were filled with messages from the Bible. She brought us religious magazines and books and placed them in every room of the house. Mrs. Heavenly Bound made

recommendations about how I should dress, where I should go, and which occasions I should celebrate. She insisted that we follow her religious beliefs, which differed from ours. Her overly controlling behavior was like a dark cloud nestled over my house. Mrs. Heavenly Bound and I agreed that things were not working out.

⁴   The last babysitter, Miss Never Satisfied, seemed happy at first but later turned out to be a constant complainer. Like Mrs. Heavenly Bound, she had been recommended to us by a family member. She was a devoted member of our church who seemed pleased with the pay and the job itself. The days went by smoothly until I heard Miss Never Satisfied gossiping on the phone about how poorly she was being paid when learning about her friend's salary. She said, "These Jamaicans want you to overwork, but they don't want to pay. I will never work for a Jamaican again." I realized that although she had seemed happy, she really was not. From then on, her personality changed. She complained that we did not have food in the house though I had just shopped two days before. She complained that she was tired of eating chicken and beef, that my children were spoiled and had too many toys, that the house was cold, and that the neighborhood was boring. I had to send her home.

⁵   After having had problems with Miss Magnetic Fingers, Mrs. Heavenly Bound, and Miss Never Satisfied, I had no choice but to quit my job to stay home with my children. This decision turned out to be one of the best decisions of my life. The dark clouds above my home suddenly disappeared. The experience I had with the babysitters taught me that my family, above all things, came first even if it meant firing someone and quitting my job.

ACTIVITY
11.6

Analyzing a Classification Essay

Answer the following questions about "The Misses."

1. Underline the thesis statement. What is the writer's organizing principle?

_____

2. What technique does the writer use in the lead-in?

_____

3. Underline the topic sentences of each of the body paragraphs. What is the point of each body paragraph?

_____

4. Circle the transition words used to introduce each difference in each of the topic sentences.

5. Which patterns of development does the writer use in his body paragraphs?

_____

6. What is the point(s) the writer makes about her experience with babysitters?

_____

Classification Essay Graphic Organizer

Using a classification essay graphic organizer will help you place your details in the appropriate pattern. The sample graphic organizer shown on the following page can be changed to suit your needs.

Classification Essay Graphic Organizer

Introduction

Lead-in:

Bridge:

Thesis Statement:

Body Paragraphs

Body Paragraph 1

Topic Sentence for Group 1:

Description:

Details:

Body Paragraph 2

Topic Sentence for Group 2:

Description:

Details:

Body Paragraph 3

Topic Sentence for Group 3:

Description:

Details:

Conclusion

Effective Closing Technique:

Concluding Statement:

Essay Writing Assignments

Write about an Image

We all have many different roles in our lives. We are workers, teammates, music listeners, students, parents, and so on. We choose clothing styles that match those roles. For example, many workers wear uniforms, and teenagers often dress in the style of celebrities they admire.

Write an essay in which you classify your clothing styles according to the different roles that you play. For example, you wear certain clothes at school, at work, on weekends, and so on.

Writing Topics for a Classification Essay

For your classification essay, choose one of these options:

- from paragraph to essay: expand the paragraph you wrote in the paragraph section of this chapter
- any of the writing topics in the paragraph section of this chapter
- any topic from the following list:

General Topics

computer programs or websites you use for school, work, or entertainment
memory strategies
vehicles
groups of people, such as sports fans, church goers, college students, and so on
living arrangements

Writing across the Curriculum Topics

Biology: insects and bugs found in your area
Family Studies: types of families
Sociology: forms of racism
Pharmacy: nonprescription drugs
Criminal Justice: crimes

*Peer Review Reminder.
For feedback on your
writing, have some-
one read your paper and make
comments on the Peer Review
Response Sheet in Chapter 4,
page 54.*

English Success Tip: Strategies to Reduce Writing Anxiety

Many students experience anxiety when they have a writing assignment. Some worrying is good, but too much writing anxiety can lead to procrastination. You can help yourself gain control of the situation by trying the following strategies:

1. **Pick a place.** Find a comfortable place to write, make it your own space, and use it when you have a writing assignment. Your mind and body will associate that place with the task of writing.

2. **Choose a time.** Set time limits for writing and accomplish what you can in that time frame. If possible, write at the same time every day to establish a routine.

3. **Perform a ritual.** A ritual is a pattern of behavior performed in a set way. Before you start writing, do something that puts you in the mood to write. Here are some ideas: take a walk, have a snack, clear your desk, or listen to relaxing music.

12 Cause and Effect

LO 1 **Define cause as a pattern of development that explains why something happened and effect as a pattern of development that explains the results of something that happened.**

What Is Cause and Effect?

Cause and effect is a pattern of development that explains the reasons for and/or results of a situation. **Cause** explains why something happened. **Effect** explains the results of something that happened. A cause and effect paragraph can explain causes or effects or both.

Some causes and effects are obvious. For example, think about what might cause a student to cheat on a final exam. The most obvious reason is that the student does not know the correct answers. However, other underlying reasons might be that the student did not study or is under pressure to get a good grade. The diagram at the top of page 229 shows possible causes and effects of cheating on a final exam.

Sometimes cause and effect can form a causal chain. One action has an effect, which becomes the cause for another effect, and so on, as shown on page 229.

You use cause and effect to analyze situations in everyday life. For example, you may try to convince a friend to stay in school or to justify why you need to buy an expensive pair of sneakers you have been wanting. At work, a company may have penalties for employees who show up late.

QuickWrite

Write about a situation in which you saw someone cheat in school, at work, or in everyday life. What were the causes and/or effects?

Cause and Effect in College Writing

Cause and effect is often used in college writing. In a college humanities class, for example, you may study why ancient Egypt fell to the Romans or the effects of the introduction of sound on the film industry. In an advertising or business class, you may study the effects of newer media, such as email, the Internet, podcasts, video games, product placement, and video on demand (VOD), on a company's communication about its products.

The main point in a cause and effect paragraph can be developed by giving causes, effects, or both. The paragraphs on pages 229–231 show cause or effect writing.

Causes for Cheating

high grade expectations from parents	
saving face with peers	
too lazy to study	
not enough time to study	cheating on a final exam
everyone else is doing it	
material is too hard	
lack of honor	

Effects of Cheating

will not learn the material needed to know for higher-level classes
if caught, can get into academic trouble: lower grade or fail course
reflects poorly on character
lowers self-concept; student is not smart enough
not getting full value for tuition payment

causal chain → cheating on final exam → getting caught → failing course → lowering GPA → losing financial aid

Effects Paragraph Example

The effects of using a cell phone while driving are explained in this paragraph.

[1]Experiments have shown that cell phone use clearly affects drivers' behavior. [2]One effect is that drivers tend to slow down when talking on the phone. [3]Another effect is that they also have slower reaction times. [4]For example, drivers are slower to hit the brakes and take longer to resume normal speed. [5]A third effect is that they often drift outside the lines of the lane in which they are driving. [6]Using a cell phone also affects drivers' judgment. For

instance, they may stop at green lights. [7]The last effect is that drivers miss stop signs and red lights. [8]Some slam on their brakes when they notice they are part of the way through an intersection at which they were supposed to stop. [9]These effects have been observed just as often in studies using hands-free phones as conventional hand-held models. [10]Thus, experimental studies show definitively that, on average, cell phone use weakens driving ability.

(Adapted from *The World of Psychology* by Samuel E. Wood et al.)

ACTIVITY Analyzing an Effects Paragraph

12.1 Answer the questions about the effects paragraph you just read about cell phone use.

1. Underline the topic sentence. What is the point of the topic sentence?

_____

2. Find and list three effects from the paragraph.

_____

_____

3. Underline the transition words.

Cause Paragraph Example

The following paragraph explains the reasons cell phone studies have been criticized.

[1]Critics have attacked cell phone use studies for many reasons. [2]First, they say other attention-demanding tasks impair driving behaviors just as much as cell phone use does. [3]One study found, for example, that searching for a radio station while driving produced the same kinds of harmful effects on drivers' behavior as cell phone use. [4]Another reason is that the same kinds of effects on driving behavior occurred whether a person was talking on a cell phone or talking to a passenger in the car. [5]Additional criticism involves the nature of the cell phone task itself. [6]In most studies, participants do not have real conversations on their cell phones. [7]Instead of trying to create real-world conversations, experimenters transmitted math problems to drivers that they were supposed to solve in their heads within a limited time

frame. [8]A fourth reason critics attack cell phone use studies is their failure to consider the effects of practice. [9]Critics say that people become more efficient at multi-tasking with practice, a factor that is not thought about in most experiments. [10]Finally, critics note that real-world drivers often take actions to reduce distraction and that they are well aware of the potentially risk-enhancing effects of behavior changes caused by distractions, so they work to manage the number of demands on their attention while driving.

(Adapted from *The World of Psychology* by Samuel E. Wood et al.)

ACTIVITY   Analyzing a Cause Paragraph

12.2   Answer the questions about the reasons paragraph you just read.

1. Underline the topic sentence. What is the point of the paragraph?

2. Underline the transition words and expressions used in the paragraph.
3. How many causes (reasons) are given in the paragraph? List the sentence numbers that introduce each one.

4. Do you think the reasons given in the paragraph are convincing? Why?

CAUSE AND EFFECT   Essentials

Effective cause and effect has these essential elements:

1. It makes a point about the causes and/or effects of a situation.
2. The causes and effects are logical, are complete, and show a clear relationship.
3. The supporting details are organized by order of importance, spatial order, or chronological order.
4. The supporting details are explained with descriptions, examples, short narratives, comparisons, and facts.
5. Cause and effect connectors and transitions help readers see the movement from one cause or effect to another.

The Cause and Effect Paragraph

LO 2 Write a cause and effect paragraph.

Prewriting the Cause or Effect Paragraph

Before you write, you must choose a suitable topic and develop it.

Choose Your Topic and Purpose The purpose of your cause and effect paragraph can be to inform or to persuade. For example, you could inform the reader by giving the reasons your college redesigned the computer lab in the Writing Center. On the other hand, you could persuade the reader that the redesigning of the computer lab was beneficial for students.

When deciding on your own cause or effect topic or writing about an assigned topic, consider the following:

1. **Choose a topic that you know well.** Writing about a topic that you know about or have studied is essential. Cause and effect writing requires that you logically think through the causes and effects of a situation to avoid errors in reasoning. For example, if you do not know the reasons for economic inflation, then you will end up with nothing to say.

2. **Choose a topic that can be explained completely in one paragraph.** Some topics have multiple causes or effects or both and cannot be covered in a single paragraph. Explaining the causes or effects of global warming would be difficult to accomplish in one paragraph because there are many theories about this topic.

3. **Choose a topic that is not too complicated or technical for your readers to understand.** Consider your readers' background knowledge when selecting a topic. For instance, you may know about the potential dangers of genetically modified crops. However, your readers may not have the background to understand the effects that you would supply.

ACTIVITY **Evaluating Topics for a Cause or Effect Paragraph**

12.3 Explain why each of the following topics would be good or not good for a cause or effect paragraph.

1. the effects of the automobile on the U.S. society

_____

2. the reasons someone enlisted in the military

_____

3. a video game that includes numeric relationships causes mathematical challenges

_____

4. the effects of taking _____(a specific college course)

_____

5. the effects of heredity and environment on a person's life

_____

Develop Ideas for Your Topic Prewriting for a cause or effect topic involves exploring both the causes and effects of your topic. Using a cause and effect prewriting chart or your preferred prewriting technique will help you discover whether you have enough causes and/or effects to support your topic.

Student Royce decided to write about the causes and effects of quitting smoking. He had stopped smoking a few months before the semester and was beginning to experience the positive effects. In order to decide whether he wanted to write about causes or effects or both, he filled in a cause and effect prewriting chart as you can see on the following page.

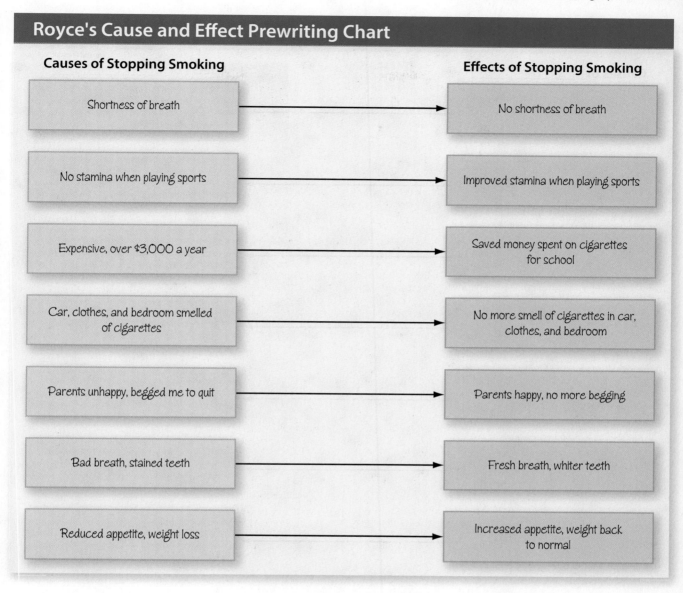

Royce's Cause and Effect Prewriting Chart

Causes of Stopping Smoking

- Shortness of breath
- No stamina when playing sports
- Expensive, over $3,000 a year
- Car, clothes, and bedroom smelled of cigarettes
- Parents unhappy, begged me to quit
- Bad breath, stained teeth
- Reduced appetite, weight loss

Effects of Stopping Smoking

- No shortness of breath
- Improved stamina when playing sports
- Saved money spent on cigarettes for school
- No more smell of cigarettes in car, clothes, and bedroom
- Parents happy, no more begging
- Fresh breath, whiter teeth
- Increased appetite, weight back to normal

Paragraph Activity: **Prewriting**

Using the prewriting chart on page 234 or your preferred prewriting technique, develop causes and/or effects for one of these topics.

General Topics

being a full- or part-time worker while attending college
chatting online with an someone you do not know
making a life-changing decision
moving to another neighborhood, town, city, or country
changing a job or career

Writing across the Curriculum Topics

Foreign language: learning a different language
Sociology: discrimination
Business: using credit cards
Family Studies: a breakup in a relationship
Pharmacy: a medication or abused drug

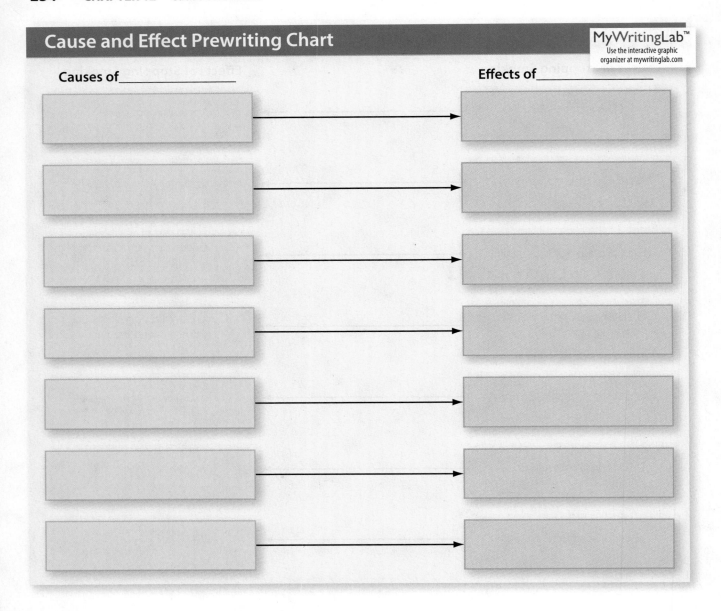

Cause and Effect Prewriting Chart

MyWritingLab™
Use the interactive graphic organizer at mywritinglab.com

Causes of_____

Effects of_____

Narrow Your Topic and Write the Topic Sentence Narrowing your topic involves deciding whether you want to write about causes, effects, or both. You may find it easier to focus your paragraph on causes or effects rather than on both. Look at the causes and effects you listed for one of the topics in the prewriting exercise. Choose the one that has enough details to support in a paragraph.

The topic sentence tells the readers whether you will explain causes and/or effects in your paragraph. The topic sentence for a cause and/or effect paragraph includes the following:

1. The narrowed topic
2. The purpose, which is **cause and/or effect**
3. The point you want to make about the cause and/or effect

Here are examples of topic sentences for cause, effect, and cause and effect.

Cause	My family chose to move to the United States for financial reasons.
Effect	Online social networking has negative effects on the brains of young users.
Cause and Effect	Because hurricanes bring together destructive kinds of weather, they can have devastating effects.

Royce chose to write his topic sentence about the effects of quitting smoking:

Quitting smoking has had many positive effects on my life.

TIPS | **Writing Cause and Effect Topic Sentences**

1. Include your purpose: cause, effect, or cause and effect.

   No purpose: Ben joined the veterans' club this semester.

   With a purpose: Joining the veterans' club has had positive effects on Ben's life.

2. State your point clearly

   Not clear: College students can learn a lot by taking a psychology course.

   Clear: Taking a psychology course affects students by teaching them to understand themselves.

Paragraph Activity: **Writing a Topic Sentence**

Write a topic sentence for the topic about which you have been prewriting. Label the narrowed topic, the purpose, and the point.

Organizing and Drafting the Cause and Effect Paragraph

Develop Supporting Details Developing supporting details for the cause or effect paragraph involves finding relevant, logical causes and/or effects and providing explanations for them.

From your prewriting chart, choose the causes and/or effects that will support the point of your topic sentence. You may need to do some additional prewriting to develop more details.

Find Relevant, Logical Causes and/or Effects Your causes and effects must be based on sound, logical reasoning. One error in logic is called "false cause," which means that just because one thing happened before another does not mean that it caused the other. An example is that a person got a cold because she got caught in the rain. Colds are caused by a person's coming in contact with cold viruses, not by rain.

Writing Reminder.
To learn more about errors in logic for cause and effect, see the English Success Tip at the end of this chapter.

Provide Explanations Support each cause and/or effect with a thorough explanation to help the reader understand the relationship between the causes and effects. You can use facts, examples, short narratives, comparisons, and descriptions.

For example, Royce decided to write about the positive effects he experienced by quitting smoking. One of the effects he listed was that his parents no longer nag him to stop smoking. To further explain this, Royce could tell the reader his relationship with his parents has improved to the point where they enjoy having dinner together every night, discussing their day's activities and their opinions about current events.

Paragraph Activity: **Selecting Supporting Details**

Select the causes and/or effects that you would like to include in your paragraph from your cause and effect chart. Put a checkmark next to each one you select.

Organize Your Supporting Points and Details When organizing your supporting details, first decide on an organizational pattern. Then decide the order in which you present your supporting points and details.

Choosing a Cause and Effect Pattern Cause and effect paragraphs usually follow one of these patterns:

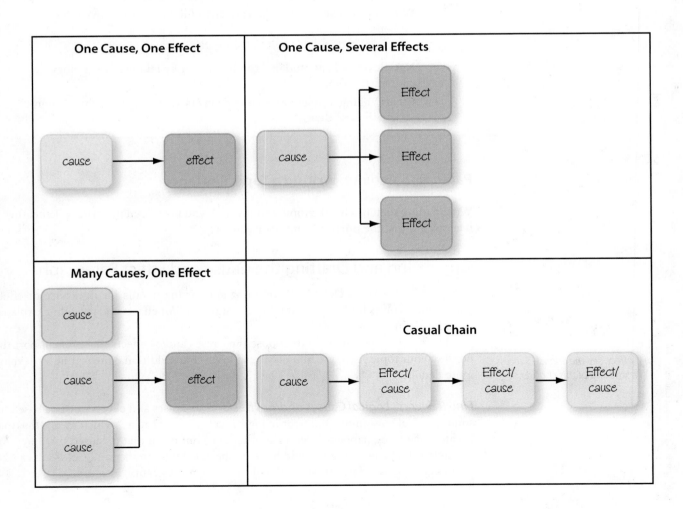

Choosing an Order Choose the most appropriate order to present your details: order of importance, spatial order, or chronological order.

Order of importance	to rank causes or effects, such as the most important to least important reasons for your decision to attend college
Spatial order	to explain causes or effects that occur in a specific location, such as the effects of a tsunami on various parts of an island
Chronological order	to explain causes or effects that occur in a sequence, such as events that led to World War II

Grouping Causes and Effects Grouping causes and/or effects can help you tighten your organization. For instance, Royce grouped his details as health, financial, and emotional effects.

Royce's Effects Grouped	
Group	Effect
Health effects	Stamina has improved, don't get short of breath when doing physical activities No more bad breath; can get teeth whitened and they will stay white Appetite increased, am at a normal weight No frequent colds or bronchitis
Financial effects	Saving the money that I would have spent on cigarettes to pay for school
Emotional effects	Parents happy, no more nagging

After grouping his positive effects, Royce organized the details in a cause and effect paragraph graphic organizer.

Royce's Cause and Effect Paragraph Graphic Organizer

Topic Sentence: Quitting smoking has had many positive effects on my life.

Cause or Effect 1: The first effect was that I was able to save money for college.

Specific Details:

Used to smoke a pack a day, more when out with friends

Spent $45 a week, over $2,000 a year

When stopped smoking, opened money market account to pay for college

Cause or Effect 2: Another effect was that my relationship with my parents improved.

Specific Details:

Parents criticized me for smoking

Complained about smell and secondhand smoke in house and car

When stopped smoking, parents stopped complaining

Developed friendly relationship with parents

Dad rewarded me with tickets to NFL game

Cause or Effect 3: The most important effect of my quitting smoking was that my health improved.

Specific Details:

Could run five miles without chest pains or getting out of breath

Appetite increased, went from underweight to normal weight

Did not get sick, no frequent colds or bronchitis

Concluding Sentence: Quitting smoking was not easy, and I still want a cigarette now and then, but I am proud that I conquered my addiction.

Paragraph Activity: Organizing Supporting Details

Group any causes or effects and choose the pattern and order you want to use for your paragraph. You may find it helpful to use a cause and effect graphic organizer as student Royce did to list the groups and put them in your preferred order. The organizer on page 239 can be changed to suit your needs by adding causes and/or effects and specific details.

Cause and Effect Paragraph Graphic Organizer

Topic Sentence:

Cause or Effect 1:

Specific Details:

Cause or Effect 2:

Specific Details:

Cause or Effect 3:

Specific Details:

Concluding Sentence:

Write the First Draft As you write your first draft, explain each cause and/or effect thoroughly and add connectors and transitional words and expressions.

Balance Your cause and effect paragraph should be balanced in content and organization. As you write, follow one of the organizational patterns on page 236. Explain each cause and/or effect thoroughly so that readers can understand how they are connected.

Add Connectors: Transitional Words and Expressions Connectors and transitions for cause and effect paragraphs can add new points, show order of importance, show causes, and show effects. Study the following chart, which lists connectors and transitions and their use in sentences.

Cause and Effect Connectors and Transitions	
To add a new point: *the first, the second, the third, the next, one, another, the last, in addition, moreover*	One effect is that drivers tend to slow down when talking on the phone.
To give examples: *one example is, another example is, for example, to illustrate, for instance, the first example, the next example*	For instance, they may stop at green lights.
To show order of importance: *the most important, the least important, least of all, most of all*	The most important reason is that using a cell phone while driving affects drivers' judgment.
To show causes: *for, because, since, for this reason, due to, because of*	Drivers using cell phones may stop at green lights because they are not paying attention to the road.
To show effects: *so, so that, as a result, as a consequence, consequently, therefore, thus, that is why*	As a result, they may miss stop signs and red lights.

Revising, Editing, and Proofreading

Revise your draft by looking at one element at a time: **S**upport, **O**rganization, **C**onnectors and transitions, and **S**tyle. The following Revision Checklist contains the **SOCS** elements as they apply to cause or effect paragraphs.

REVISION CHECKLIST FOR A CAUSE AND EFFECT PARAGRAPH

Element	Revision Checkpoints
Topic	☐ The topic addresses causes and/or effects.
	☐ The topic can be fully discussed in a single paragraph.
Topic Sentence	☐ The topic sentence states includes the narrowed topic and the point, which focuses on one of the following: cause, effect, or both.
Support	☐ Supporting details consist of causes and/or effects.
	☐ The causes and effects are based on logical reasoning.
	☐ The explanations for each cause or effect can be examples, descriptions, comparisons, short narratives, and facts.
	☐ All supporting details are relevant and adequate.

Element	Revision Checkpoints
Organization	☐ Each cause and/or effect is discussed completely, one at a time.
	☐ Points are arranged in order of importance, spatial order, or chronological order.
Connectors and Transitions	☐ Cause and effect and addition connectors and transitions provide coherence. Spatial or chronological order transitions are used when appropriate.
	☐ Connectors and transitions are used to introduce each new point and to connect details within each point.
Style	☐ Writing is clear, concise Standard Written English.
	☐ Tone is appropriate for a college audience.
	☐ Sentences are varied.

- -

Paragraph Activity: **Revising**

Using the Revision Checklist for a Cause and Effect Paragraph, revise your cause and effect paragraph.

Peer Review Reminder. For feedback on your writing, have someone read your paper and make comments on the Peer Review Response Sheet in Chapter 4, page 54.

Check Grammar, Punctuation, and Spelling As you reread your paper to check for grammar, punctuation, and spelling errors, pay special attention for possible errors that may arise in cause and effect paragraphs.

Words Easily Confused: Affect and Effect It is easy to confuse these two words because they sound similar. However, they are used differently. **In cause and effect writing, *affect* is a verb meaning to have an influence on, while *effect* is a noun meaning a result.**

| *Affect* as a verb | Moving into my own apartment **affected** my life in many ways. |
| *Effect* as a noun | Moving into my own apartment had many **effects** on my life. |

Repetition When writing a sentence giving a reason, avoid writing **the reason why is because.** This phrase has three reason words when only one is needed. Instead, begin your sentence **the reason is.**

Grammar Reminder. For more information on fragments, comma splices, and run-ons, see Chapter 21.

Sentence Errors Fragments may occur when you begin sentences with words such as ***because*** or ***since***. Comma splice and run-on errors may occur when you use words such as ***for*** (meaning *because*), ***therefore,*** or ***consequently*** to connect two sentences. In addition, check the meanings of these connecting words to ensure that you use them correctly.

ACTIVITY   Revising and Editing an Effect Paragraph

12.4   Revise and edit Royce's paragraph. Then answer the questions that follow.

¹Quitting smoking has had many positive effects on my life. ²The first effect was that I was able to save money for college. ³I used to smoke about a pack a day and more than that when I went out with friends. ⁴I had been spending about forty-five dollars a week on cigarettes. ⁵My yearly expense was two thousand dollars. ⁶When I stopped smoking, I realized that I could save the money I spent on cigarettes by opening a money market account to pay for college. ⁷Another effect was that my relationship with my parents improved. ⁸My parents criticized me every day about my smoking. ⁹They had both quit smoking several years ago. ¹⁰They complained about the secondhand smoke they had to suffer with when I smoked in the house or in their car. ¹¹The lingering odor of cigarette smoke irritated them too. ¹²I felt like an outcast in my own home. ¹³When I stopped smoking, my parents stopped complaining; and we developed a friendly relationship. ¹⁴During dinner, we discussed the events of our day and other issues rather than arguing. ¹⁵My dad was so happy that he rewarded me with tickets to an NFL football game. ¹⁶The most important effect of my quitting smoking was that my health improved, I could now run five miles without getting chest pains or out of breath. ¹⁷In addition, my appetite increased, and I went from being ten pounds underweight to my normal weight. ¹⁸I also noticed that I did not get sick; those frequent colds and bronchitis that I used to suffer from were no longer a problem for me. ¹⁹Quitting smoking was not easy, and I still want a cigarette now and then, but I am proud that I conquered my addiction.

Questions on Revising

1. Underline the topic sentence. What are the narrowed topic and the focus?

   Narrowed topic: _____

   Focus: _____

2. Which sentence is the least relevant to the passage? Circle the number of the sentence.

3. What transitions would be best for sentences 14 and 15?

Sentence 14: _____

Sentence 15: _____

Questions on Editing and Proofreading

4. Which sentence uses the semicolon incorrectly? Write the corrected sentence here.

_____

_____

2. Which sentence has a comma splice error? Write the corrected sentence here.

_____

_____

_____

Paragraph Activity: **Editing and Proofreading**

Edit and proofread your cause or effect paragraph. Check that your final draft is complete, accurate, and error-free.

Paragraph Writing Assignments

Help Desk

Javier has written a cause paragraph on the reasons he enjoys baseball. Read the paragraph and answer the questions below.

> [1]Baseball, which I have been playing ever since I was five years old, is a sport that I enjoy for many reasons. [2]One reason is that baseball keeps me active. [3]If it was not for baseball, I would not be the person I am today. [4]Another reason I enjoy baseball is it is a team sport. [5]I love to cheer on my teammates when they make a good play or get a great hit. [6]I always cheer them on because I want to make them feel good about themselves, which will give them the confidence to make another play or get another hit. [7]The most important reason is that playing baseball can make me some money in the future. [8]In a couple of years, if I am good enough, a major league team will draft me, and I could become very rich just for playing the sport I love.

1. Each reason in a paragraph must be explained with adequate and specific details. Which reason(s) need to be revised by adding more specific details?

_____

_____

2. What details could Javier add to make his supporting points convincing?

_____

_____

Group Activity

You have been asked to develop a list of convincing reasons to solve a problem on your campus or in your community. For example, your college may need additional parking or an improved registration-advisement process. Your community may need a stop light at a specific location or additional law enforcement at a local mall.

In small groups, identify a problem, decide on a solution, and develop a minimum of four strong, logical reasons and explanations for your solution. Then, put these ideas into a paragraph for your school or local newspaper.

MyWritingLab™
Complete this activity
at mywritinglab.com

Reading and Writing across the Curriculum: Health

Noise is one of the common causes of stress and hearing loss in the United States. If you have ever sat close to speakers during a concert, you may have experienced a temporary hearing loss or ringing in your ears hours after the concert was over. Even using headphones or earbuds with the volume up high can cause damage. The following paragraph explains the physical effects of noise:

dilate become wider

> Physically, our bodies respond to noise in a variety of ways. Blood pressure increases, blood vessels in the brain **dilate,** and vessels in other parts of the body constrict. The pupils of the eyes open wider. Cholesterol levels in the blood rise, and some endocrine glands secrete additional stimulating hormones, such as adrenaline, into the bloodstream. Noise-related problems include disturbed sleep patterns, headaches, and tension. Hearing can be damaged by varying lengths of exposure to sound, which is measured in decibels. If the duration of allowable daily exposure to different decibel levels is exceeded, the sensitive hair cells of the inner ear and the hearing nerve become damaged, and hearing loss will result.
>
> (Adapted from *Access to Health* by Rebecca J. Donatelle and ASHA.org, American Speech-Language-Hearing Association)

Write a paragraph about the effects of any type of noise on you in school, at work, or in every day life (including entertainment).

MyWritingLab™
Complete this activity
at mywritinglab.com

Comment on a Contemporary Issue

generalization an idea
based on limited facts that
may be partly true but not
always true

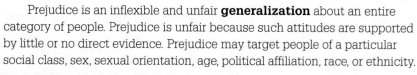

> Prejudice is an inflexible and unfair **generalization** about an entire category of people. Prejudice is unfair because such attitudes are supported by little or no direct evidence. Prejudice may target people of a particular social class, sex, sexual orientation, age, political affiliation, race, or ethnicity.
>
> (Adapted from *Society* by John J. Macionis)

Write a paragraph about the causes and/or effects of prejudice.

Reader Response

At the beginning of this chapter, you read a textbook excerpt about experiments showing that cell phone use affects drivers' behavior. Do you agree? What was your reaction to the excerpt?

Write a paragraph that responds to one of these questions:

Text-to-Text	■ Does the reading remind you of something else you have read, heard, or seen (story, book, movie, song, news item, magazine article, website, and so on)?
	■ Are the ideas the same or different?
Text-to-Self	■ How do the ideas in the reading relate to your own life, experiences, or ideas?
	■ Do you agree or disagree with what you read?
Text-to-World	■ What does the reading remind you of in the real world?
	■ Does it make you think about something in the past, present, or future?

Write about an Image

Prewrite possible causes and effects that this image suggests to you. Then, write a cause and/or effects paragraph using the details from your prewriting activity.

The Cause and Effect Essay

LO 3 **Write a cause and effect essay.**

The cause and effect essay has the same purpose as the cause and effect paragraph: to explain the reasons for and/or results of a situation. **Cause** explains why something happened. **Effect** explains the results of something that happened.

The cause and/or effect essay uses the same organizational patterns as the paragraph. Your essay can focus on causes, effects, or both causes and effects.

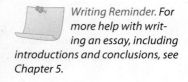

Writing Reminder. For more help with writing an essay, including introductions and conclusions, see Chapter 5.

Cause and effect essays can inform or persuade. For example, in writing a cause and effect essay about a car accident, you could give the reader a factual account of the causes and effects. The drivers of two cars were both attempting to pull into the same parking space when they collided. On the other hand, you could persuade the reader by explaining why one of the drivers was at fault for the crash.

Thesis Statement

The thesis statement for a cause and/or effect essay includes the following:

1. The topic
2. The purpose, which is **cause, effect, or both**
3. The point

The following thesis statement example is from Royce Bonta's essay "Clean Living" on pages 248–249:

Thesis with a **topic**, purpose, and point.

> Quitting smoking had many positive effects on my life.

Thesis with a **topic**, purpose, point, and **list of supporting points**

> Quitting smoking had many positive effects on my life **such as improving my health, saving me money, making my parents happy, and getting the disgusting smell of cigarette smoke out of my car.**

Body Paragraphs

The body paragraphs in the cause and effect essay can consist of causes, effects, or both. Support for causes and effects can consist of facts, examples, short narratives, or descriptions.

The following are possible plans for the essay:

All Causes	All Effects	Cause and Effect Plan A	Cause and Effect Plan B
Paragraph 1: **Cause(s)**	Paragraph 1: **Effect(s)**	Paragraph 1: **Cause, Cause, Cause**	Paragraph 1: **Cause** and **Effect**
Paragraph 2: **Cause(s)**	Paragraph 2: **Effect(s)**		Paragraph 2 **Cause** and **Effect**
Paragraph 3: **Cause(s)**	Paragraph 3: **Effect(s)**	Paragraph 2: **Effect, Effect, Effect**	Paragraph 3 **Cause** and **Effect**

Notice how Royce uses a cause and effect essay graphic organizer to develop and arrange his supporting points and details to prove his thesis:

Royce's Cause and Effect Essay Graphic Organizer

Introduction

Lead-in: Background about becoming a smoker, trying to quit but failing

Bridge: I realized that quitting cold turkey was the best solution and I succeeded.

Thesis Statement: Quitting smoking had many positive effects on my life such as improving my health, saving money, making my parents happy, and getting the disgusting smell of cigarette smoke out of my car.

Body Paragraph 1

Topic Sentence: The most important effect of quitting smoking was that my health improved.

Supporting Details: Can run five miles without getting out of breath; appetite increased, no longer underweight; sense of taste not impaired, enjoy my favorite foods; did not get sick, no more colds and bronchitis; no more smoker's breath, nicotine stains on teeth fading

Body Paragraph 2

Topic Sentence: Quitting smoking not only improved my health, but also saved me money.

Supporting Details: Started putting away money spent on cigarettes to pay for college; during years smoking, cigarettes went from $3 to over $6 a pack; realized could be saving $2,000 a year; cost of health insurance decreased

Body Paragraph 3

Topic Sentence: Another positive effect of quitting smoking besides improving my health and saving me money was that I made my parents happy.

Supporting Details: My mother complained about secondhand smoke; my father did not want me to die from lung cancer from smoking; parents offered money for quitting, but I refused; parents were happy when I quit; family dinner more pleasant, no more arguing about my smoking; no longer rejected in my own home

Body Paragraph 4

Topic Sentence: Getting rid of the disgusting smell of cigarette smoke from my car, while not as significant as other positive effects, was the final benefit of quitting smoking.

Supporting Details: Realize smell is overpowering; realize how difficult to get rid of smell; cleaned car thoroughly; no worry about burning hole in interior

Conclusion

Effective Concluding Technique: other effects

Concluding Statement: Most importantly, I no longer worry about my health, I have been able to save money, my parents are happy, and my car smells fresh and clean.

Cause and Effect Essay Example

Student Royce Bonta had previously written a paragraph about the positive effects he experienced after he quit smoking. He decided to develop his paragraph into an essay. In his introduction, Royce explains his attempts and final success at quitting. Each of the body paragraphs identifies one or more effects on himself or on his family.

Clean Living

1   Several years ago, I took up the bad habit of smoking cigarettes. I never considered myself to be a heavy smoker at one pack a day compared to my friends, who smoked two to three times as many cigarettes a day as I did. At first, I only smoked socially, but slowly I became addicted. I began to realize how smoking affected my life and tried to quit but failed each time. I tried using the nicotine patch, but it gave me nightmares. Nicotine gum tasted awful. I realized that quitting cold turkey was the best solution and the most difficult one, but I succeeded. Quitting smoking had many positive effects on my life such as improving my health, saving me money, making my parents happy, and getting the disgusting smell of cigarette smoke out of my car.

2   The most important effect of quitting smoking was that my health improved. I can now run five miles without getting chest pains or out of breath. In addition, my appetite increased, and I am no longer ten pounds underweight. My sense of taste is no longer impaired by the chemicals from cigarettes, and now I actually enjoy my favorite foods. I also noticed that I did not get sick; those frequent colds and bronchitis that I used to suffer from were no longer a problem for me. As a side benefit, I no longer have smoker's breath, and the nicotine stains on my teeth are fading.

3   Quitting smoking not only improved my health, but also saved me money. I decided not to pay Phillip Morris to kill me any longer. Instead, I opened a savings account, and each week, I deposited the money I would have spent on cigarettes to pay for my education. When I started smoking, a pack of cigarettes was around three dollars, but when I quit, the cost was over six dollars a pack. After calculating what I was spending a year on cigarettes, I figured out that I could save more than two thousand dollars a year. I realized that I could have gone to Home Depot and purchased the materials to construct an elaborate coffin for the price I was paying to slowly dig my grave. Another positive effect was the cost of my health insurance decreased since I was no longer considered high risk.

4   Another positive effect of quitting smoking besides improving my health and saving me money was that I made my parents happy. My mother, a former smoker, has tried repeatedly to get me to stop smoking. She

complained about the secondhand smoke both she and my father had to put up with when I smoked in the house. My father, who lost his mother, sister, and brother-in-law to lung cancer from smoking, did not want me to follow in their footsteps and offered me money to quit, but I had refused. When I finally stopped smoking, my parents were delighted. Family dinners were more pleasant. Instead of arguing about my smoking, we discussed the events of our day. I did not want to take the money my father offered me, but he insisted. I was no longer a person who was rejected in my own home and my relationship with my parents improved.

5   Getting rid of the disgusting smell of cigarette smoke from my car, while not as significant as the other positive effects, was the final benefit of quitting smoking. I realize now how overpowering the smell of cigarette smoke was in the enclosed space of a car and how difficult it is to eliminate the strong, unpleasant smell from the interior after being exposed to it for so long. My car no longer smelled of tobacco smoke, and I did not have to worry about burning a hole in the interior, lowering its resale value.

6   Quitting smoking was not easy, and I still get cravings for a cigarette now and then, but I am proud that I conquered my addiction. I no longer have to feel like an outcast at restaurants, work, and other public places where smoking is not allowed. Most importantly, I no longer worry about my health, I have been able to save money, my parents are happy, and my car smells fresh and clean.

ACTIVITY   **Analyzing a Cause and Effect Essay**

12.5

1. Underline the thesis statement. What is the writer's main point?

2. What technique does the writer use in the lead-in?

3. Underline the topic sentences of each of the body paragraphs. What is the point of each body paragraph?

4. Circle the transition words used to introduce each difference in each of the topic sentences.

5. Which body paragraphs include multiple effects?

6. In addition to referring to the thesis statement, underline the point the writer makes in the conclusion.

Cause and Effect Essay Graphic Organizer

Using a cause and effect graphic organizer will help you place your details in the appropriate pattern: causes, effects, or both. It will also help you see the relationship between the causes and effects. This sample graphic organizer can be changed to suit your needs by adding paragraphs, points, and supporting evidence.

Cause and Effect Essay Graphic Organizer	MyWritingLab™ Use the interactive graphic organizer at mywritinglab.com

Introduction

Lead-in:

Bridge:

Thesis Statement:

Body Paragraph 1: Cause and/or Effect

Topic Sentence:

Supporting Details:

Body Paragraph 2: Cause and/or Effect

Topic Sentence:

Supporting Details:

Body Paragraph 3: Cause and/or Effect

Topic Sentence:

Supporting Details:

Conclusion

Effective Concluding Technique:

Concluding Statement:

Essay Writing Assignments

MyWritingLab™
Complete this activity
at mywritinglab.com

Write about an Image

The message in the fortune cookie in this photograph expresses the outcome that college students expect when they earn their degree. Many students choose a major because it will get them a job that pays well after graduation. Others choose a major that they love even though they may not find a good job right away.

Write an essay explaining the reasons you chose your major. If you have not selected a major yet, write about the reasons for one you are considering.

Writing Topics for a Cause and Effect Essay

For your cause and effect essay, choose one of these options:

- from paragraph to essay: expand the paragraph you wrote in the paragraph section of this chapter to an essay
- any of the writing topics in the paragraph section of this chapter
- any topic from the following list:

General Topics

an accident
participation in an activity or group
a particular college course
popularity of shows about actual crimes
a troublesome habit

Writing across the Curriculum Topics

Anthropology: preserving a particular cultural heritage
Environmental Science: human activity on the environment
Health: a particular illness or disease
Humanities: a particular work or movement in art, music, film, or literature
Psychology: over-concern with weight or physical appearance

Peer Review Reminder.
*For feedback on your
writing, have some-
one read your paper and make
comments on the Peer Review
Response Sheet in Chapter 4,
page 54.*

English Success Tip: Avoiding Common Cause and Effect Errors

Several errors in logic can occur when writing cause and effect papers. Four of the most common errors are explained in the following chart. Be sure to avoid them.

Error in Logic	Example	Explanation
Thinking that one event caused another just because it happened first (mistaking sequence for cause)	Student Manfredo bought a new calculator. As a result, he received an A on his math test.	While Manfredo may have done well on his test when using new calculator, the calculator did not cause the A.
Thinking that because two things happened at the same time that one of those things caused the other.	While Manfredo was taking his math test, it was raining. Therefore, the rain caused him to get a low grade on the test.	Even though it rained at the same time Manfredo was taking his test, the rain was not responsible for his low grade.
Not looking at underlying causes	Manfredo believes that he received an A on his math test because he studied the night before.	Manfredo did much more than study the night before. A week before the test, he joined a math study group where students practiced solving and explaining solutions to problems from class and ones they made up. After every math class, he went over the homework problems and solved them until he could get them right with no difficulty.
Including insignificant causes	Manfredo earned an A on his math test because he turned in all of his homework assignments.	Turning in homework assignments certainly contributed to his good grade, but it was not a significant reason.

13 Definition

Learning Objectives

After working through this chapter, you will be able to:

LO 1 Explain that definition is a pattern of development that discusses what a word, expression, or concept means.

LO 2 Write a definition paragraph.

LO 3 Write a definition essay.

LO 1 **Explain that definition is a pattern of development that discusses what a word, expression, or concept means.**

MyWritingLab™
Complete this activity
at mywritinglab.com

What Is Definition?

Definition is a pattern of development that explains what a word, expression, or concept means. Definitions are used in many writing situations. In the workplace, definition is used in proposals, memos, reports, technical documents, and instructions. In addition, many fields have their own specific terms. For instance, the computer field has hundreds of special words, such as *application, backup, browser, database,* and *software.*

QuickWrite

Write your own definition of a word or expression that you use in college, at work, or in everyday life.

Definition in College Writing

Knowing how to define a word is an important skill to develop in college. Every course you take has specialized terms that you must learn. For example, nursing students must learn the definitions of various diagnoses, called diagnostic labels. There are over 170 labels for clinical use and testing. To show your knowledge of words for your courses, you may be asked to recognize the definitions of specific terms on objective tests or to write a sentence definition or an in-depth explanation of a word.

There are two types of definitions that you may be asked to write: formal and extended.

- A **formal definition** is a concise, brief statement of a word's meaning, usually in a sentence.
- An **extended definition** is a one- to several-paragraph explanation of a word using a variety of writing patterns.

Formal Definition Examples

The following are examples of formal definitions you might find in your college text-books. Each consists of three parts: the word, the group it belongs to, and its features.

binge eating the repeated eating of larger-than-normal amounts of food at one time paired with a sense of lost control over one's eating habits

Bulimia nervosa is an eating disorder that consists of **binge eating** followed by methods to get rid of the extra calories by vomiting or emptying the bowels.

A *business* is an organization that provides goods and services to earn profits.

Greenhouse effect is the buildup of carbon dioxide in the Earth's atmosphere that allows light to enter but prevents heat from getting out.

Culture shock is a feeling of confusion that people experience when they visit or move to a completely different culture.

 ACTIVITY **Identifying the Parts of Formal Definitions**

13.1 For each of the definition examples that you just read, write the group it belongs to and the word's features in the space provided. The first one is done for you.

Word	Group	Features
bulimia nervosa	eating disorder	that consists of binge eating followed by methods to get rid of the extra calories by vomiting or emptying the bowels
business		
greenhouse effect		
culture shock		

Extended Definition Paragraph Example

The following is an example of an extended definition of the term *food contamination* as used in the food service industry.

[1]Food contamination is harmful substances in food that make it unfit for humans to eat. [2]Examples of food contaminants are bacteria, toxic chemicals, dirt, dust, and organisms. [3]When eaten in sufficient quantities, contaminants from food can cause illness or injury, long-lasting disease, or even death. [4]Contamination occurs in two ways: direct contamination and cross contamination. [5]Direct contamination can occur in raw food, such as plants. [6]For instance, bacteria and fungi are present in the air, soil, and water, so food can be easily contaminated by being exposed in the environment. [7]In addition, grains can be contaminated in the field by pesticides sprayed to kill pests, while shellfish can be contaminated when they eat toxic sea plants. [8]The second way is called cross contamination. [9]It can happen when humans, rodents, or insects carry the chemicals and **microorganisms** to foods and food contact surfaces. [10]For example, food handlers can transfer contaminants to food while processing, preparing, cooking, or serving it. [11]Cross contamination also occurs when raw foods come in contact with cooked foods and from smoking, eating, or drinking unless hands are properly washed. [12]Food service workers should store and handle foods in a safe manner to prevent contamination.

(Adapted from *On Cooking* by Sarah R. Labensky and Alan M. Hause)

microorganisms living things, such as bacteria, too small to be seen by the naked eye

ACTIVITY   Analyzing an Extended Definition Paragraph

13.2   Answer the questions about the paragraph you just read about contamination.

1. Underline the topic sentence.
2. Which sentence gives examples of food contamination? List two of the examples.

_____

3. Which sentence explains the effects of eating contaminated food? List two effects.

_____

4. Which sentences explain the ways food can be contaminated? What are they?

_____

DEFINITION Essentials

An effective extended definition paragraph has these essential elements:

1. Makes a point by giving the formal definition of a word.
2. Makes the meaning of the word understandable to the reader.
3. A variety of writing patterns or methods are used as supporting details such as descriptions, examples, causes and effects, comparison and contrast, and process.

4. The supporting details are organized to clearly explain the meaning of the word.

5. Transitional words and expressions connect the different methods used to define the word.

The Definition Paragraph

Prewriting the Extended Definition Paragraph

Choose Your Topic and Purpose The purpose of an extended definition paragraph can be to inform or persuade. You may be asked define a word that is an idea such as *prejudice* or a word that has a standard definition such as *earthquake*. Another type of assignment might be to come up with your own original definition of a word.

When deciding on your own word, expression, or concept to define or writing one that has been assigned, consider the following:

1. **Choose a word that you understand and can explain.** You need to know enough about the word to explain it in several different ways through examples, description, and causes and effects to name a few.

2. **Choose a word that can be defined in a single paragraph.** If you choose a word that is too broad or too general, you will not be able to narrow it down to a single definition. For example, the word *park* is a broad term, which includes a variety of different kinds, such as a water park, a park to walk dogs, a state park, a national park, and so on.

 ACTIVITY

13.3

Evaluating Topics for Definition Paragraphs

Explain why each of the following topics would be good or not good for an extended definition paragraph.

1. volcano
   _____

2. Civil Rights Movement
   _____

3. spider
   _____

4. abuse
   _____

5. geologist
   _____

6. sports
   _____

7. team
   _____

8. philosophy
   _____

Develop Ideas for Your Topic Developing ideas for an extended definition paragraph involves first understanding the methods for defining a word and then prewriting.

Patterns of Development for Writing an Extended Definition An extended definition goes beyond the formal definition sentence. It is a paragraph that expands on the ideas of the formal definition by giving details.

The supporting details do not follow one pattern of development. Instead, you can use several different patterns. For example, the paragraph at the beginning of the chapter that gives the definition for contamination begins with a formal definition and then includes three different patterns of development: cause, effects, classification, and process.

Student writer Josh decided to define *video game* for his extended definition paragraph. He has played video games since he was a child and likes to compete with friends and in online gaming communities.

Your Extended Definition Paragraph: **Prewriting**

Prewriting for an extended definition paragraph involves gathering supporting details to help define your word or expression.

Choose one of the words from this list of topics or a word approved by your instructor.

General Topics

a popular slang term
a specific food
an emotion, such as fear, anger, guilt, happiness, pride, shame
a term from one of your courses
an item of clothing or apparel

Writing across the Curriculum Topics

Music Appreciation: a specific type of music, such as jazz, rock, blues, rap, and so on
Sociology: gang
Biology: a specific plant, fish, bird, reptile, amphibian, or mammal
Criminal Justice: a particular crime, such as robbery, DUI, hate crime, identity theft, child abuse, drug trafficking
Pharmacy: a particular medication or drug

Write the formal definition of your word here. Use italics or underline the word you are defining. Then fill in the definition prewriting chart on page 258.

word _____**verb** _____**is/are** _____

group _____

features _____

Formal definition sentence:

_____

Definition Prewriting Chart

Give one or more examples:

Write a description:

Give a cause and/or effect:

Compare or contrast the word with something else:

Separate the word into groups or kinds:

Tell a brief story to explain the word:

Explain how the word happens or works:

Narrow Your Topic and Write the Topic Sentence After prewriting to develop ideas, you are ready to write your topic sentence.

The topic sentence for an extended definition paragraph is the formal definition of the word or expression you are writing about. On page 254, you learned the parts of a formal definition sentence: the word, **verb**, the group it belongs to, and the features that make it different than others in its group.

A business is an organization that provides goods and services to earn profits.

TIPS | **Writing Definition Topic Sentences**

1. **Write your own definition.** Your paper will express your definition of a word. Avoid copying the dictionary definition. Many dictionary definitions do not provide the group and features of a word.
2. **Write a complete definition.** Do not leave out the group or the features.

3. **Use a word that does not repeat the word or a form of the word you are defining.**

Repeats word	A *waiter* is a person employed to **wait** on people.
Revised	A *waiter* is a person employed to bring food and beverages to people, usually in a restaurant.

4. **Avoid defining your word using "is when" or "is where."**

Is when	A *test* **is when** a person or group answers questions to show a skill or knowledge.
Revised	A *test* is a set of questions or exercises that measures the skill or knowledge of an individual or a group.

Paragraph Activity: **Writing a Topic Sentence**

Write a topic sentence for the word about which you have been prewriting. Remember, the topic sentence is the formal definition.

> Josh wrote this formal definition:
>
> A video game is an electronic, interactive activity that is played by moving images on a video display or computer screen.

Organizing and Drafting the Definition Paragraph

Develop Supporting Details Looking back at your prewriting notes on page 258, choose the details that you want to use in your paragraph.

For his extended definition of *video game*, Josh decided to develop his paragraph by using formal definition, causes, classification (types), and effects.

Paragraph Activity: **Selecting Supporting Details**

Select the information that you would like to include in your paper from your prewriting notes on page 258.

Organize Your Supporting Details As you look at the details you have chosen, organize them in a way that will make the meaning of the word clear and understandable to your readers. You may find it helpful to use an extended definition graphic organizer as student Josh did.

Josh's Extended Definition Paragraph Graphic Organizer

Topic Sentence (Formal Definition): A video game is an electronic, interactive activity that is played by moving images on a video display or computer screen.

Method of Development: Reasons

Support 1: People like to play video games for several reasons.

Details:
Let players do things that are expensive or impossible to do in real life
Help players feel successful; when winning, they feel confident
Help players feel they are in control of their actions, can make choices

Method of Development: Classification

Support 2: Not only do people like to play video games, but also they can choose from many different types of games.

Details:
Action, action-adventure, role-playing, strategy, simulation

Method of Development: Effects

Support 3: Video games have many positive effects on players.

Details:
Teach players how to solve problems, teach how to win and lose
Improve memory and attention
Teach people how to work together
When played on Internet, can connect with people all over the world

Concluding Sentence: Because people enjoy video games so much, educators and game designers should find a way to combine video games and learning.

The following definition graphic organizer can be changed to suit your needs by adding or removing support boxes.

Extended Definition Paragraph Graphic Organizer

Topic Sentence (Formal Definition):

Method of Development:

Support 1:

Details:

Method of Development:

Support 2:

Details:

Method of Development:

Support 3:

Details:

Method of Development:

Support 4:

Details:

Concluding Sentence:

Writing Reminder.
For a complete list of connectors and transitions, see the inside of the back cover.

Write the First Draft As you write the first draft, consider using connectors and transitions.

Add Connectors: Transitional Words and Expressions You will be using several different patterns of development in your extended definition paragraph. The following chart lists connectors and transitions for some of the different patterns of development.

Connectors and Transitions

To add a new point: *the first, the second, the third, the next, one, another, the last, in addition, moreover*	In addition, people can choose from many different types of video games.
To show order of importance: *the most important, the least important, least of all, most of all*	Most important, video games that can be played by more than one person teach people to work together.
To show causes: *for, because, since, for this reason, due to, because of*	People like to play video games because they like to feel that they are successful at something.
To give examples: *one example is, another example is, for example, to illustrate, for instance, the first example, the next example*	For example, video games can teach players how to solve problems.
To show effects: *so, so that, as a result, as a consequence, consequently, therefore, thus, that is why*	As a result, players improve memory and attention.
To compare: *similarly, likewise, in comparison*	Similarly, men and women enjoy playing video games on the computer.
To contrast: *however, on the other hand, in contrast, although, even though, whereas, while*	More males than females play video games; however, the number of females who play is increasing.

Paragraph Activity: **Writing the First Draft**

Using the details you selected from your graphic organizer, write the first draft of your extended definition paragraph.

Revising, Editing, and Proofreading

Revise your draft by looking at one element at a time: **S**upport, **O**rganization, **C**onnectors and transitions, and **S**tyle. The following Revision Checklist contains the **SOCS** elements as they apply to extended definition paragraphs.

REVISION CHECKLIST FOR A DEFINITION PARAGRAPH

Element	Revision Checkpoints
Topic	☐ The topic addresses an extended definition of a word, concept, or expression.
	☐ The topic can be fully discussed in a single paragraph.
Topic Sentence	☐ The topic sentence states the formal definition of the word and consists of the word, the group, and the features.
Support	☐ Supporting details consist of information that makes the meaning of the word understandable to the reader.
	☐ The supporting details are developed using several methods such as descriptions, examples, causes and effects, comparison and contrast, and process.
	☐ All supporting details are relevant and adequate.
Organization	☐ The paragraph is logically organized in a way that makes the definition understandable.
	☐ The paragraph is balanced in both content and in organization.
Connectors and Transitions	☐ Connectors and transitions provide coherence between each pattern of organization used to define the word.
Style	☐ Writing is clear, concise Standard Written English.
	☐ Tone is appropriate for a college audience.
	☐ Sentences are varied.

Peer Review Reminder. For feedback on your writing, have someone read your paper and make comments on the Peer Review Response Sheet in Chapter 4, page 54.

Paragraph Activity: **Revising**

Using the Revision Checklist for a Definition Paragraph, revise the first draft of your extended definition paragraph.

Check Grammar, Punctuation, and Spelling As you reread your paper to check for grammar, punctuation, and spelling errors, pay special attention for possible errors that may arise in definition paragraphs. For example, review the section in this chapter, Tips for Writing Definition Topic Sentences, to avoid grammar errors in your formal definition, such as using *is when* or *is where*.

ACTIVITY

13.4 Revising and Editing an Extended Definition Paragraph

Read and edit Josh's extended definition paragraph and answer the questions that follow.

[1]A *video game* is an electronic, interactive activity that is played by moving images on a video display or computer screen. [2]People like to play video games for several reasons. [3]They let players do a lot of things that are expensive or impossible to do in real life. [4]Also, people like to feel they are successful, so when they win a game or go up a level, they feel competent. [5]In addition, people like to feel that they are in control over their actions, they enjoy the choices that they have when playing video games. [6]Not only do people like to play video games, but also they can choose from many different types of games, for example action, action-adventure, role-playing, strategy, and simulation. [7]Video games have many positive effects on players. [8]For instance: they teach players how to solve problems by figuring out how to do things in different ways. [9]They also teach how to win and lose. [10]Yet another benefit is they improve memory and attention. [11]Games that can be played by more than one person teach people to work together. [12]When these games are played over the Internet, players could connect with people all over the world. [13]Because people enjoy video games so much, educators and game designers should find a way to combine video games and learning.

Questions on Revising

1. Underline the topic sentence. Does the topic sentence contain all the parts of a formal definition? Write the parts here:

   word _____ **verb** _____

   group _____

   features _____

   _____

2. List two of the methods Josh uses for his extended definition supporting details.

   _____

3. What is the purpose of Josh's concluding sentence?

   _____

Questions on Editing and Proofreading

4. One sentence has a comma splice error. Find the error and rewrite the sentence correctly.

   _____

   _____

5. One sentence misuses the colon. Find the error and rewrite the sentence correctly.

   _____

   _____

6. One sentence has a verb shift. Find the error and rewrite the sentence correctly.

   _____

   _____

Paragraph Activity: Editing and Proofreading

Edit and proofread your extended definition paragraph. Check that your final draft is complete, accurate, and error-free.

Paragraph Writing Assignments

Help Desk

Luigi has written an extended definition paragraph on **crowd surfing** at a rock concert. Read Luigi's paragraph and review it by answering the questions below.

> ¹Crowd surfing is where teens are basically carried over the top of a sea of people. ²It is a popular activity at rock concerts. ³However, crowd surfers are susceptible to being dropped. ⁴When crowd surfers are dropped during a show, it is a general rule that the people around them help them up and protect them from being stepped on. ⁵I remember two summers ago during a summertime music festival, where a young female was dropped while crowd surfing. ⁶She landed on her head and was knocked out. ⁷The people around her acted quickly to get her off the ground safe from being trampled. ⁸A **good Samaritan** picked her up and brought her out of the crowd to a waiting medical unit. ⁹Crowd surfing is considered dangerous, but it is really fun to do. ¹⁰Most people only end up with bruises. ¹¹Females need to be careful when crowd surfing because some people may try to touch them in ways that are not appropriate as they are being passed around. ¹²Crowd surfing is illegal in some countries.

good Samaritan a person who helps another in distress

Formal Definition of Crowd Surfing		
Word	Group	Features
Crowd surfing		

1. Underline the formal definition. Fill in the chart above to identify the parts of the formal definition and then advise Luigi how to correct it.
   What is wrong?

   _____

   Rewrite the formal definition, correcting it.

   _____

   _____

2. List the methods Luigi uses to develop his extended definition.

_____

3. Which sentence needs more development?

_____

_____

4. If you could move sentences 9, 10, and 11, where would you place them?

_____

_____

Group Activity

Success is an abstract word. Abstract words refer to concepts or ideas instead of physical things that we can experience with our five senses. Abstract words can mean different things to different people. Some famous people have commented on the meaning of success:

- "Success in life consists of going from one mistake to the next—without losing your enthusiasm."—*Winston Churchill*
- "There are no secrets to success. It is the result of preparation, hard work, and learning from failure."—*Colin Powell*
- "Eighty percent of success is showing up."—*Woody Allen*
- "Always bear in mind that your own resolution to succeed is more important than any other."—*Abraham Lincoln*
- "Success is to be measured not so much by the position that one has reached in life as by the obstacles he has overcome."—*Booker T. Washington*
- "They succeed because they think they can."—*Virgil*

In small groups of three or four, plan and write an extended definition paragraph for the word *success*. You may include one of the quotations listed above in your paragraph.

MyWritingLab™
Complete this activity
at mywritinglab.com

Reader Response

In this chapter, you read Josh's paragraph defining *video game*. Do you spend much time playing video games? Do you think that video games could be developed to teach your coursework?

Write a paragraph that responds to one of these questions:

Text-to-Text	■ Does the reading remind you of something else you have read, heard, or seen (story, book, movie, song, news item, magazine article, website, and so on)? ■ Are the ideas the same or different?
Text-to-Self	■ How do the ideas in the reading relate to your own life, experiences, or ideas? ■ Do you agree or disagree with what you read?
Text-to-World	■ What does the reading remind you of in the real world? ■ Does it make you think about something in the past, present, or future?

Write about an Image

Emblems are body gestures that directly translate into words or phrases. Emblems are culture specific. In other words, hand gestures do not mean the same thing in every culture. Choose one of the gestures pictured below and write an extended definition paragraph explaining what the gesture means in the U.S. culture or another culture that you are familiar with.

Reading and Writing across the Curriculum: Sociology

In society, a *subculture* is a group that has some kind of trait—social, economic, ethnic, or other trait—distinctive enough to make it different from others within the same culture or society. Subcultures consist of people whose experiences have led them to distinctive ways of looking at life or some aspect of it.

The United States society contains tens of thousands of subcultures. Some examples are "chopper" motorcyclists, New England "Yankees," Ohio State football fans, the southern California "beach crowd," and wilderness campers. Some ethnic groups in the United States also form subcultures; their values, foods, religion, language, and clothing may set them apart. Occupational groups formed by police officers or fire fighters are other subculture examples.

(Adapted from *Essentials of Sociology* by James M. Henslin)

Choose a subculture that you are familiar with. Write an extended definition paragraph about that group, explaining their characteristics.

MyWritingLab™
Complete this activity
at mywritinglab.com

Comment on a Contemporary Issue

> Although the form of a family varies from one society to another and even within societies, all societies have families. The U.S. Census Bureau, which collects data about the nation, its people, and the economy, says a *family* "consists of two or more people related by birth, marriage, or adoption residing in the same unit." Thus, according to the federal government, a married couple and their children are considered to be family, while unmarried couples who live together make up a household.
>
> (Adapted from *Family Life Now* by Kelly J. Welch)

Your definition of *family* is may be different from that of the government. How do you define *family*? Write an extended definition paragraph in which you define *family* based on your own unique experiences.

The Definition Essay

LO 3 **Write a definition essay.**

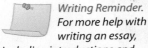

*Writing Reminder.
For more help with writing an essay, including introductions and conclusions, see Chapter 5.*

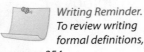

*Writing Reminder.
To review writing formal definitions, see page 254.*

The definition essay has the same purpose as the extended definition paragraph: to explain what a word, expression, or concept means. An extended definition essay can explain the meaning of a word in greater depth than the paragraph version.

An extended definition can inform or persuade. You may want to define a word to show your understanding or to motivate people to accept a point of view. For example, you could inform by defining the word *family* through an explanation of its traditional definition and changes in its meaning over time. On the other hand, through your definition of *family*, you could persuade readers that the definition of family must change as society's needs change.

Like the extended definition paragraph, the essay version uses a variety of patterns of development to support the main idea. The extended definition essay also includes the formal definition of the word, which gives the meaning of a word in a single sentence. The formal definition includes the word, the group the word belongs to, and the features of the word that make it different from others in the group.

Thesis Statement

The thesis statement of the extended definition essay gives the significance or importance of the term being defined. The thesis statement for an extended essay includes the following:

1. The **topic**, which is the word or expression you will define
2. The **purpose**, which is to better understand the word or expression
3. The **point**

The following thesis statement example is from Jones Howard's essay "Moshing" on page 272–273.

Thesis with a **topic, purpose, and point.**

Moshing can be better understood by learning about its features.

Thesis with a **topic, purpose, point, and list of supporting points**

Moshing can be better understood by learning about its features, **including its history and development over time, its dance moves, and preparation for the mosh pit.**

You may want to include the formal definition in the introductory paragraph as part of your lead-in.

Body Paragraphs

The body paragraphs of an extended definition essay use a variety of patterns of organization, such as narration, example, comparison, contrast, cause, effect, description, process, and classification. You can also give the word's history and origin, any misconceptions about it, and a synonym.

Begin each body paragraph with a topic sentence that guides the reader by stating the point of the paragraph. For example, if you are writing about effects, mention it in the topic sentence. Since you may use a different pattern of organization for each body paragraph, organize the supporting details in each of them according to the pattern you used, such as order of importance, chronological order, or spatial order.

Notice how Jones uses an extended definition essay graphic organizer to develop and arrange his supporting points and details to prove his thesis:

Jones' Extended Definition Essay Graphic Organizer

Introduction

Lead-in: Question whether moshing is dancing

Bridge: Formal Definition: Moshing, also known as slam dancing, is an aggressive style of dance with movements that consist of shoving or violently throwing one's body against another dancer.

Thesis Statement: Moshing can be better understood by learning about its features, including its history and development over time, its dance moves, and preparation for the mosh pit.

Body Paragraph 1

Topic Sentence: In both slamming and moshing, participants dance in an area called a pit or mosh pit.

Method of Development: Description

Details:

Open, circular area in front of stage or in middle of crowd

People create them during a concert

Observers stand around edges of pit

Body Paragraph 2

Topic Sentence: Slam dancing developed as a form of self-expression at punk rock concerts.

Method of Development: Description, Effects

Details:

Began in the 1970s and early 1980s as part of the punk rock subculture

Punk rockers did not like popular forms of music

Developed their own that was easy to play, simple guitar cords

Songs were loud and angry to show punk rockers were against society

Lyrics about politics, sex, boredom

Body Paragraph 3

Topic Sentence: Slam dancing is a fast-paced form of dancing that has several moves or steps.

Method of Development: Process

Details:

Pogo, dancers jump up and down in same spot like pogo sticks

Keep legs close together, arms at sides, body stiff

Slam dancers try to bump into other pogo dancers on purpose

Fast arm swinging and kicking to music

(Continued)

Jones' Extended Definition Essay Graphic Organizer *(Continued)*

Body Paragraph 4

Topic Sentence: Moshing developed from slam dancing.

Method of Development: Process, Description, Cause

Details:

1980s and 1990s, grunge rock music became popular; cross between punk and heavy metal music; appealed to people who did not like other music; grunge not popular but moshing still popular in 2000s; moshing a central part of the concert experience

Body Paragraph 5

Topic Sentence: Although slamming moves can still be seen in a mosh pit, moshing moves have become more popular.

Method of Development: Contrast, Description, Effects

Details:

Moshing more violent and aggressive; random bashing into other dancers to get hurt; windmill, dancers swing arms in 360-motion
Stage diving; dancers run off stage into the crowd of moshers in pit; Divers can get trampled or broken bones; females can be groped and grabbed

Body Paragraph 6

Topic Sentence: People who plan to mosh should prepare for the experience.

Method of Development: Instructional Process

Details:

Dress appropriately: wear lightweight, loose clothing; wear sturdy shoes to protect feet; be in shape; drink plenty of water

Conclusion

Effective Concluding Technique: Reasons for slamming

Concluding Statement: These dances can be dangerous, but they are not more devastating than the possible results of a competitive football game.

Definition Essay Example

In the following essay, student Jones Howard writes an extended definition of the term *moshing*.

Moshing

1   If dancing leads to bloodshed, is it still considered dancing? It is hard to imagine that the fans of heavy metal rock music like to dance, but what they call dancing many would call violence. Unlike ballet, salsa, or hip hop, the style of dancing that these rock fans do often results in serious injuries, or, in worst-case situations, death. *Moshing*, also known as *slam dancing*, is an aggressive style of dance with movements that consist of shoving or violently throwing one's body against another dancer. Moshing can be better understood by learning about its features, including its history and development over time, its dance moves, and preparation for the mosh pit.

2   In both slamming and moshing, participants dance in an area called a pit or mosh pit. The pit is an open, circular area in front of the concert stage or in the middle of a crowd. During a concert, people who want to dance create mosh pits. Those who do not want to dance stand around the edges of the pit, leaving an open space for the dancers. Usually, the dancers move in a clockwise motion in the pit.

3   Slam dancing developed as a form of self-expression at punk rock concerts. It began in the 1970s and early 1980s as part of the punk rock subculture. Punk rockers did not like the **commercialism** of the popular forms of music at that time, such as rock, disco, and heavy metal. Therefore, they developed their own music. Punk music was easy to play; the songs used simple guitar chords. Because punk rockers were against society's values, their songs were often loud and angry. Their lyrics were about politics, sex, and boredom.

4   Slam dancing is a fast-paced from of dancing that has several moves or steps. One move is the pogo, in which dancers jump up and down in the same spot, as if they were **pogo sticks**. They keep their legs close together, their arms at their sides, and their body stiff. The slam is similar to pogo, but dancers intentionally try to bump into other pogo dancers. Another move in slam dancing is fast arm swinging and kicking in time to the music.

5   Moshing developed from slam dancing. In the 1980s and 1990s, an alternative form of rock music called grunge became popular. It was a cross between punk and heavy metal music. Grunge appealed to those who did not like those other forms of music. Although the popularity of grunge has long since faded, moshing has not. Its popularity continued into the 2000s, especially with heavy metal rock fans. Moshing has become a central part of the concert experience.

commercialism the activities or attitudes of people who think that making a profit is more important than anything else

pogo stick a pole with a strong spring at the bottom and two footrests on which a person stands and moves along with a series of jumps

6   Although slamming moves can still be seen in a mosh pit, moshing moves have become more popular. Moshing is a more violent and aggressive form of dancing. One kind of move is randomly bashing into other dancers on purpose in order to hurt someone or to get hurt. Another popular move is the windmill where the dancers swing their arms in a 360-degree motion. The motion looks like a spinning windmill. Stage diving is a favorite with daring fans. This move involves dancers sneaking up on stage where the band is playing. If they manage to avoid being asked to leave the stage by security officers, they run quickly from the stage and fling their bodies into the crowd of moshers in the pit. The goal is for the dancers in the pit to catch them and pass them around from one person to another on top of the moshing audience. Stage divers risk getting trampled or suffering broken bones or concussions if the people in the pit do not catch them. In addition, stage divers risk having personal items stolen or removed as they are passed around. Females risk being groped and grabbed.

7   People who plan to mosh should prepare for the experience. First, they should dress appropriately. For example, they should wear loose clothing that is light enough for a workout and lets them move easily. Dancers need sturdy shoes to protect their feet from being stomped on. Because moshing is physical, dancers need to be in shape. The day of the concert, moshers should drink plenty of water because they will sweat a lot while moshing.

8   Those who slam or mosh enjoy it for many reasons. Some find the danger of dancing in a mosh pit exciting. Others enjoy the physical release of pent up energy and emotions or an escape from their everyday identity. These dances can be dangerous, but they are not more devastating than the possible results of a competitive football game.

 ACTIVITY

13.5   Analyzing a Definition Essay

1. Underline the thesis statement. What term does the writer plan to define?

2. What technique does the writer use in the lead-in?

3. Where does the writer state the formal definition? Write the parts here:
    word _____
    verb _____
    group _____
    features _____

4. Which methods of development does the writer use in the body paragraphs?

5. What points does the writer make in the conclusion?

Extended Definition Essay Graphic Organizer

Because your essay will include paragraphs developed by different patterns of organization, you may find it helpful to use an extended definition graphic organizer to plan and arrange your details. The organizer below can be changed to suit your needs by adding or removing paragraphs, supporting points, and details.

| Extended Definition Essay Graphic Organizer | MyWritingLab™ Use the interactive graphic organizer at mywritinglab.com |

Introduction

Lead-in:

Bridge:

Thesis Statement:

Body Paragraph 1

Topic Sentence:

Method of Development:
Details:

Body Paragraph 2

Topic Sentence:

Method of Development:
Details:

(Continued)

Extended Definition Essay Graphic Organizer *(Continued)*

Body Paragraph 3

Topic Sentence:

Method of Development:
Details:

Conclusion

Effective Concluding Technique:

Concluding Statement:

Essay Writing Assignments

Write about an Image: Standards of Beauty

Beauty is the combination of qualities that are pleasing to the senses or mind. Most people view beauty as a pleasing physical appearance. Write an essay defining the standards of beauty for the group or culture you most identify with.

Writing Topics

For your definition essay, choose one of these options:

- from paragraph to essay: expand the paragraph you wrote in the paragraph section of this chapter
- any of the writing topics in the paragraph section of this chapter
- any topic from the following lists:

General Topics

an unexplained phenomenon such as a UFO, ghost, miracle, near death
    experience, crop circles, ESP, intuition
an adjective describing a personal quality, such as compassionate, honest, loyal,
    imaginative, resourceful, patient, jealous
an electronic or computing device
gender
a job, such as administrative assistant, restaurant server, nurse, teacher, social
    worker, psychologist, events planner, fashion stylist

Writing across the Curriculum: Topics

Psychology: a specific mental disorder, such as psychosis, schizophrenia,
    depression, anorexia or bulimia, bipolar disorder
Game Design: a type of video game, such as action, strategy, role playing, sports,
    or vehicle simulation
Hospitality: a form of entertainment (an activity performed for the enjoyment of
    others) such as food service, amusement or theme park, campground, arcade,
    cruise, nightclub
Marketing: advertisement
History: genocide

*Peer Review Reminder.
For feedback on your
writing, have some-
one read your paper and make
comments on the Peer Review
Response Sheet in Chapter 4,
page 54.*

English Success Tip: A New Word Every Day

If you want to improve your vocabulary, try learning one new word every day. Finding new words is as simple as looking in a dictionary; open it to any page and find
a word you do not know. Another way to learn new words is by reading something
that is a bit more difficult than what you are accustomed to. As you come across
a word you do not know, try to figure out what it means, and then look it up to
find out if you were right. To keep track all of those new words you are learning,
create a word list including the correct spelling and the definition; include your
own sentence using the word. Make a commitment to increasing your vocabulary.

14 Argument

Learning Objectives

After working through this chapter, you will be able to:

LO 1 Define argument as a pattern of development that states a point of view on an issue and supports it with evidence in order to persuade readers.

LO 2 Write an argument paragraph.

LO 3 Write an argument essay.

LO 1 **Define argument as a pattern of development that states a point of view on an issue and supports it with evidence in order to persuade readers.**

MyWritingLab™

Complete this activity at mywritinglab.com

What Is Argument?

Argument is a pattern of development that states the writer's point of view on an issue and supports it by giving evidence. The purpose of argument is to persuade readers to agree with the writer's point of view or to take action.

You experience argument in all aspects of life. As a child, you have probably tried to convince a relative or caregiver to let you stay up a little later or to buy you a special toy you felt you could not live without. As you matured, you argued for more important things, such as being allowed to stay out late on weekends or for purchasing a new laptop. In the workplace, you may convince your employer to give you a raise or to try a new way of conducting business.

QuickWrite

Take a few moments to write about a time when you convinced someone to do something or believe something. Explain the situation and the strategy you used to persuade that person.

Argument in College Writing

Much of the information you learn in college has been argued at some point. For example, in the field of psychology, researchers have done studies to prove their hypotheses about the causes of mental problems, the stages of child development, and the process of learning. In the field of environmental science, researchers have presented evidence on both sides of the global warming issue.

Most writing you will do in college is a form of argument. For instance, each of the writing patterns you study in this text asks you to make and support a point, whether you are describing, giving causes and effects, defining, narrating, or comparing and contrasting. In a political science course, for example, you may be asked to write about whether people, especially children, should be forced to repeat the Pledge of Allegiance if it violates their beliefs.

On January 24, 2013, the U.S. Defense Secretary Leon Panetta lifted the 1994 policy that prevented women from participating in the front line of combat. Now, combat arms jobs are open to women. This change was made after recognizing that women were already fighting in combat. The following argument paragraph was written before the policy was lifted, but people still have strong feelings about it.

Argument Paragraph Example

[1]Women should be allowed to serve in military roles that involve fighting. [2] First of all, war combat does not involve the great strength it once did. [3]Computer technology, smaller electronic devices, and other new battle strategies make war less about strength and more about intelligence. [4]Women are not fighting rifle to rifle. [5]Some people insist that women on average have less upper-body strength than men, making them less suited for combat. [6] However, some women surpass some men in upper-body strength. [7]Although opponents feel that forcing women to fight in the military is an attempt to change people's attitudes about women, integrating women into the military is actually a reflection of current society. [8]Gender segregation is not as common today as it once was. [9] In fact, women are waiting longer to wed. [10] Also, it is illegal to discriminate against women in civilian society. [11] Furthermore, recruiters are having more difficulty finding men to fill such jobs as mechanics, analysts, and engineers. [12] Therefore, there is a need for women in these and other roles. [13] Finally, women do not need to be protected from battle as they were in ages past. [14]Tribal women were respected and protected because of their special role in continuing the tribe by having children. [15]Women needed to be fertile and, thus, were protected from battle. [16]Men, with their unending supply of sperm cells, did not have to be protected. [17]Today, however, because of overpopulation, women do not need to have children. [18]Beginning with the first woman who fired a missile in combat in Iraq in 1999, women are here to stay on the front lines and should be allowed to fight if they so desire.
(Adapted from *Family Life Now* by Kelly J. Welch)

ACTIVITY   Analyzing an Argument Paragraph

14.1

1. Underline the topic sentence. What is the issue being argued?

2. How many reasons does the writer give? Briefly list each reason.

_____

_____

_____

_____

3. Circle the transition words and expressions.
4. Which two opposing arguments does the writer acknowledge?

_____

_____

_____

5. Which of the arguments is least convincing to you?

_____

_____

ARGUMENT   Essentials

The purpose of argument is to persuade readers to agree with the writer's point of view or to take action. An effective argument has these essential elements:

1. The argument expresses the writer's point of view on an issue and supports it by giving evidence.
2. The supporting evidence consists of facts, statistics, examples, personal experience, expert testimony, and consequences.
3. The supporting evidence is logical, adequately developed, and convincing.
4. The method of organization is order of importance.
5. Word choices should be neutral and fair-minded.

The Argument Paragraph

LO 2 **Write an argument paragraph.**

Prewriting the Argument Paragraph

Choose Your Topic and Purpose Argument paragraphs are designed to persuade the readers. The paragraph may present a view with no opposition from the audience; persuade an audience to agree with your view; or persuade an audience to take action.

Argument is more complicated than other types of writing. Therefore, you need to choose your topic carefully and analyze how your audience will react to it. Your topic should be an issue that can be argued. An issue is a current subject or problem people are thinking and talking about.

Choosing an Issue for Argument When choosing an issue or responding to an assigned issue for your argument paragraph, consider the following:

1. **Choose an issue that you know well.** In order to write a convincing argument paragraph, you need to know your issue well. Your knowledge can come from personal experience or your own knowledge.

2. **Choose an issue that you care about.** When you have strong feelings about the issue in general or about one side of an issue, you will be more likely to influence the reader to consider your point of view.

3. **Choose an issue for which more than one point of view is possible.** The issue should be one that provokes different opinions. You should be able to identify at least two sides of the issue.

4. **Choose an issue that can be argued.** A fact is not an issue; it cannot be debated because it has already been proven. Some personal opinions cannot be argued with evidence.

5. **Choose an issue that can be argued in a single paragraph.** Some issues are too large to be argued in one paragraph, such as the following: The federal government should provide health care for all citizens who cannot afford their own. While this issue does provoke different opinions, it cannot be adequately argued in one paragraph because there are too many points to argue.

ACTIVITY Evaluating Issues for Argument Paragraphs

14.2 Explain why each of the following issues would be good or not good for a one-paragraph argument.

1. Making English the official language of the United States is ridiculous.

_____

_____

2. High school graduates should take a year off before entering college.

_____

_____

3. Marijuana should be a medical option.

_____

_____

4. The military should be allowed to recruit in high schools.

_____

_____

5. Students should not be allowed to use *Wikipedia.com* as a main source for research papers.

_____

_____

6. The mass media, including television, radio, and the Internet, have a negative influence on the younger generation.

_____

_____

Develop Ideas for Your Issue Prewriting for an argument paragraph involves taking a position on an issue and exploring both sides of it. Sometimes your position on an issue is so strong that you can only see one side. By looking at the other side, you allow yourself to be more open-minded in your thinking. In addition, you will be able to respond to opposing arguments.

Roxanne's For/Against Argument Prewriting Chart

Issue: The Muscovy ducks on our campus should or should not be relocated.

For: Should be relocated	**Against:** Should not be relocated
There are greenish-black, watery droppings all over campus—unhealthy and disgusting. Walking is not pleasant because students have to avoid stepping in duck droppings.	Just walk around the duck droppings.
They interfere with the flow of traffic by standing in the middle of the roads. We have to wait while they waddle from one side of the road to the other.	The ducks don't take so long to cross the street. It's fun to watch them.
They take up parking spaces by sitting in them. Parking spaces near classrooms are hard to enough to find. Even honking won't get them to move.	There are parking spaces on the other side of campus far from the buildings and the ducks. Walking is good for one's health anyway.
They destroy native plants and wildflowers. Newly planted flowers were completely uprooted.	Flowers can be replanted. Ducks help the environment. They eat algae that destroy the lakes. Also, they help control pests by eating mosquitoes, roaches, ants, and spiders.
Because people feed them, they have learned to depend on students and employees for food.	It is enjoyable and gratifying to feed them.
They beg for food. They stand around when we're eating looking up at us and snorting. They jump on people's laps or beg at vending machines. Their aggression is frightening.	The ducks have learned to trust people and are being friendly.

Using a for/against argument prewriting chart will help you explore both sides of your issue and show you whether or not you can support your point of view. To see how this is done, take a look at Roxanne's for/against argument prewriting chart above, which explores both sides of the argument for relocating the Muscovy ducks on her campus.

Paragraph Activity: **Prewriting to Develop Ideas**

Using the for/against argument prewriting chart on page 282, develop ideas for one of the following topics or any other topic mentioned in this chapter.

Argue for OR against any of these topics:

General Topics

requiring military service
allowing females to play on male sports teams
replacing letter grades with pass/fail
texting weakening writing skills
dating in the workplace

Argue for OR against any of these topics:

Writing across the Curriculum Topics

Health: having cosmetic surgery
Education: raising high school standards
Family Life: adopting a child from another country
Communications: pretending to be someone else on a social networking site
Culinary Arts: buying organic food

For/Against Argument Prewriting Chart

MyWritingLab™
Use the interactive graphic
organizer at mywritinglab.com

Issue:

For:	Against:

Narrow Your Topic and Write the Topic Sentence

After you have explored both sides of your topic, decide which side of the issue you want to argue.

The topic sentence for an argument paragraph expresses your stand on an issue. The topic sentence for an argument paragraph consists of **the narrowed topic** and your position on the topic.

Women should be allowed to serve in military roles that involve fighting.

The college should permit smoking only in designated areas.

Roxanne decided to argue for relocation of the Muscovy ducks on her campus.

The Muscovy ducks on our campus should be relocated

TIPS | **Writing Argument Topic Sentences**

1. **Take a strong stand on the issue.**

   Weak: Having designated smoking areas on campus seems like a good idea.
   Weak: Designated smoking areas on campus might or might not work depending on a person's point of view.
   Weak: My campus is considering designated smoking areas.
   Strong: The campus should establish designated smoking areas.

2. **Use verb forms that signal argument such as *should, should not, could, could not, must, must not, needs, requires, must have.***

3. **Avoid using a fact as your topic sentence.** Your topic sentence will state your position, which is your opinion.

   Fact: Secondhand smoke contains over 4,000 chemicals, including over 40 cancer causing agents and 200 known poisons.
   Position: The college should permit smoking only in designated areas.

Paragraph Activity: Writing a Topic Sentence

Look over the details you developed for your argument paragraph in your for/against argument prewriting chart, decide on your position, and write a topic sentence for it.

Organizing and Drafting the Argument Paragraph

Develop Supporting Details After stating your position in your topic sentence, the next step is to understand and develop the kinds of evidence that can be used to support the points of your argument. In addition, you need to think about opposing points of view.

Evidence The types of evidence you can use are facts, statistics, expert authority, example, anecdote, and personal observation. Each of these is defined and explained with examples for the topic "The college should ban smoking anywhere on campus."

Type of Evidence	Example
Facts or Statistics *Facts* are pieces of information that can be shown to be true. *Statistics* are pieces of information that are represented in numbers.	**Reason using facts:** Secondhand smoke has been classified by the Environmental Protection Agency as a known cause of cancer. **Reason using statistics:** According to the American Lung Association, secondhand smoke causes approximately 3,400 lung cancer deaths and 22,700–69,600 heart disease deaths in adult nonsmokers in the United States each year.
Expert authority *Expert authority* is information from someone who has personal experience with the issue or who is an expert in the field. The information is sound and based on facts.	**Reason using expert authority:** Dr. Thomson, president of the college's Center for Health Science, says the college has a responsibility for the health and safety of all students. Recognizing the risks of smoking, the college should impose a smoke-free policy.

Type of Evidence	Example
Example *Examples* illustrate the point you are making. You can use personal examples from your experience or the experience of people you know.	**Reason using example:** Being around secondhand smoke triggers asthma in individuals who have the condition. For example, when my friend Terrell is in an area where people are smoking, his asthma acts up and he coughs and has difficulty breathing.
Anecdote An *anecdote* is a brief story, often a personal experience.	**Reason using an anecdote:** Cigarette smoke residue attaches itself to hair and clothing of anyone around the smoke, not just the smokers. After classes the other day, I picked up my son from the daycare center. I went to give him a big hug and he backed away from me saying, "Mommy, you smell smoky!" As we drove home in the car, the odor irritated his eyes and caused his nose to run.
Personal Observation Descriptive details or examples based on *personal observation*.	**Reason using personal observation:** Restricting smoking will decrease cigarette litter thus making the campus cleaner. Many smokers carelessly drop cigarette butts wherever they want to on campus, creating litter on the walkways and entrances to buildings. Also, workers will not have to spend extra time cleaning up after smokers. The risk of fire started from discarded cigarettes will also be reduced.

 ACTIVITY Developing Convincing Evidence

14.3   Provide one convincing piece of evidence for each of the following arguments. In addition, identify the type of evidence you used.

1. Students should study in groups to learn more effectively.

Your evidence: _____

Type of evidence: _____

2. High schools should do a better job of preparing students for college.

Your evidence: _____

Type of evidence: _____

3. People under 18 should be required to have parental permission to get tattoos and other body modifications.

Your evidence: _____

Type of evidence: _____

4. Playing a game is only fun when you win.

Your evidence: _____

Type of evidence: _____

5. To reduce accidents, all young drivers should complete a safe driver education course before being licensed to drive.

Your evidence: _____

Type of evidence: _____

Paragraph Activity: **Developing Details**

Look back at your for/against argument prewriting chart. Evaluate the points and place a checkmark next to the ones that strongly prove your position. Add new points that may occur to you as you give more thought to your argument.

Organize Your Supporting Details After analyzing your supporting points, you are ready to organize them into a plan for your paragraph. A point-by-point argument graphic organizer will help you identify each of the points of your argument and add supporting evidence both for and against each point.

Roxanne's point-by-point argument graphic organizer is shown below. She used the ideas from her for/against argument prewriting chart and developed the points and support for her argument, choosing only those that were the most convincing.

Roxanne's Argument Paragraph Graphic Organizer

Topic Sentence: The Muscovy ducks on our campus should be relocated.

Point 1 of Argument: Ducks destroy the campus environment.

Details:
Droppings create a health hazard on campus
Ducks have bowel movements on sidewalks—unpleasant to walk on campus
Droppings are wet and slimy; a person could slip, fall, get injured
Destroy native plants and wildflowers
Uprooted all wildflowers that had just been planted by environmental restoration commitee

Point 2 of Argument: The ducks are aggressive toward people.

Details:
Bold unwanted approaches frighten students
When people sit outside on bench to eat a snack or socialize, groups of ducks gather around, push beaks
    against people, beg for food
Have attacked students
One jumped on friend's lap while she was eating chips
Tried to bite her face so she would give the duck food

Concluding Sentence: The Muscovies are an annoyance and a danger; for the benefit of the campus, they should be
    caught and relocated.

Paragraph Activity: **Organizing Supporting Details**

Fill in the point-by-point argument graphic organizer shown on page 287.

Putting Your Ideas into a Logical Order To be effective, your points should be arranged in a way that builds the argument in the most convincing way, which will depend on your purpose. State your points or reasons with supporting evidence. Organize them in order of importance for maximum impact.

Write the First Draft Use your argument graphic organizer to guide you as you write the first draft. In addition, consider these elements: connectors and transitions and argument errors.

Add Connectors: Transitional Words and Expressions Connectors and transitions for argument paragraphs can add new points, show order of importance, and concede points. Study the following chart, which lists connectors and transitions and their use in sentences.

Argumentation Connectors and Transitions	
To add a new point: *the first, the second, the third,* *the next, one, another, the last,* *in addition, moreover*	Another reason the ducks should be relocated is that they are aggressive toward people.
To show order of importance: *the most important, the least* *important, least of all, most* *of all*	The most important reason is that the ducks bite people.
To concede a point (admit that **another point of view exists):** *although, even though,* *whereas, while*	Although some people believe the ducks are being friendly, they do not realize that many people are afraid of the Muscovies.

Argument Errors To make your argument effective, be aware of possible argument errors writers make.

1. **Hasty Generalization.** A **hasty generalization** is an argument based on insufficient evidence or no evidence at all. Using words like *everyone* and *all* can create this error.

Hasty generalization	Everyone knows how to use a computer nowadays, so students should not have to take a computer literacy course.
Improved	Colleges should survey incoming students' computer knowledge to determine whether they should be required to take a computer literacy course.

2. **Circular Reasoning. Circular reasoning** is an attempt to support a statement by repeating it in a different way. In the example, the words *advantageous* and *beneficial* are similar in meaning.

Circular reasoning	College computer literacy classes are beneficial because they are advantageous.
Improved	College computer literacy classes are beneficial because students need to continually upgrade their computer knowledge with rapid advances in technology.

3. **Attack on Character.** Also known as ***ad hominem,*** this error attacks the person rather than his or her arguments.

Ad hominem	The college president wants all students to take a computer literacy course because he is greedy and just wants the college to make money off students.
Improved	The college president believes that students should take a computer literacy course because computer capabilities are essential for success in the business world.

Argument Paragraph Graphic Organizer

Topic Sentence:

Point 1 of Argument:

Details:

Point 2 of Argument:

Details:

Concluding Sentence:

Paragraph Activity: **Writing the First Draft**

Write a first draft of your argument paragraph using the point-by-point argument graphic organizer you prepared.

Writing Reminder.
For more help with
choosing bias-free
words, see Chapter 31.

Revising, Editing, and Proofreading

Revise your draft by looking at one element at a time: **S**upport, **O**rganization, **C**onnectors and transitions, and **S**tyle. The following Revision Checklist contains the **SOCS** elements as they apply to argument paragraphs.

- -

REVISION CHECKLIST FOR AN ARGUMENT PARAGRAPH

Element	Revision Checkpoints
Topic	☐ The issues can be argued.
	☐ The issue provokes differing opinions.
	☐ The issue can be fully discussed in a single paragraph.
	☐ You have strong feelings about the issue.
	☐ You are familiar with the issue.

Element	Revision Checkpoints
Topic Sentence	☐ The topic sentence states includes two elements: the issue and your position on the issue.
	☐ The sentence uses verb forms that signal argument, such as *should, should not, could, could not, must, must not, needs, requires, must have.*
Support	☐ The support consists of the following types of evidence: facts, statistics, expert authority, example, anecdote, and personal observation.
	☐ The support appeals to readers' logic and ethics.
	☐ All supporting details are relevant and adequate.
	☐ Argument errors are avoided.
Organization	☐ Each reason is discussed completely, one at a time.
	☐ The reasons in the argument are arranged in a way that is most convincing: most-to-least or least-to-most important method of organization.
	☐ The paragraph is balanced in both content and in organization.
Connectors and Transitions	☐ Connectors and transitions are used to introduce, add, and argue points.
Style	☐ Writing is clear, concise Standard Written English.
	☐ Tone is appropriate for a college audience.
	☐ Sentences are varied.

Peer Review Reminder. For feedback on your writing, have someone read your paper and make comments on the Peer Review Response Sheet in Chapter 4, page 54.

Paragraph Activity: **Revising**

Revise your argument paragraph draft using the Revision Checklist for an Argument Paragraph.

Check Grammar, Punctuation, and Spelling As you reread your paper to check for grammar, punctuation, and spelling errors, pay special attention for possible errors that may arise in argument paragraphs. If you use an embedded question, be sure to use the correct word order.

Embedded Questions An embedded question is a question within a sentence. Questions written within a sentence should not use question word order.

> **Error:** Some students wonder <u>why do they have to take a computer literacy course?</u>

> **Corrected:** Some students wonder <u>why they have to take a computer literacy course.</u>

ACTIVITY 14.4   Revising, Editing, and Proofreading an Argument Paragraph

Read and edit Roxanne's argument paragraph and answer the questions below:

¹The offensive Muscovy ducks that have taken up residence on our campus should be relocated. ²The first reason is that they destroy the campus environment, for example, the ducks go to the bathroom wherever they please, so the walkways are frequently littered with fresh feces. ³People have to always watch where you are walking to avoid slipping and possibly getting injured. ⁴The Muscovy ducks also destroy the native plants and wildflowers on campus. ⁵To illustrate, last month some of the ducks uproot all of the flowers that had just been planted by the campus environmental restoration committee. ⁶Another reason the ducks should be relocated is that they are aggressive toward people. ⁷Their bold, unwanted approaches annoy and occasionally frighten students, especially when the ducks want food. ⁸For instance, when someone sits outside on a bench to eat a snack or to socialize with other students, groups of snorting ducks gather around that person, pushing their beaks against the individual's legs to beg for a handout. ⁹Specifically, on one occasion, a duck jumped on my friend's lap while she was snacking on some chips; the duck tried to bite her face in an attempt to be fed. ¹⁰The Muscovies are an annoyance and a danger; for the benefit of the campus, they should be caught and relocated.

Questions on Revising

1. Underline the topic sentence. What is the issue? What is the point of view?

_____

2. List the two main reasons that support the topic sentence.

_____

3. Circle the transitions. Which ones introduce reasons or points and which ones introduce examples?

_____

Questions on Editing and Proofreading

4. Find the sentence that contains a comma splice and correct it.

_____

5. Find the sentence that contains a verb shift and correct it.

_____

6. Find the shift in pronoun and correct it.

_____

Paragraph Activity: **Editing and Proofreading**

Edit and proofread your argument paragraph. Check that your final draft is complete, accurate, and error-free.

Paragraph Writing Assignments

Help Desk

Kate was asked to write an argument paper on one of the topics listed in this chapter. She chose the topic "People should/should not drop out of high school." Kate argues that people should not drop out of high school. Read Kate's paper and answer the questions below.

[1]People should not drop out of high school. [2]Dropping out of high school is one of the biggest mistakes many people make. [3]Every day I see my friends experience difficulty. [4]For example, my boyfriend struggles because he is limited to certain jobs. [5]Whether you have an education or not really makes a difference when looking for a job. [6]My boyfriend is limited to certain jobs. [7]Many places do not hire without at least a high school diploma. [8]When he does find a job, there are always negativities like the hours he gets and the amount he gets paid hourly. [9]Most places pay minimum wage if the person lacks an education. [10]He has no future to look forward to because of his lack of education. [11]Not having an education also makes your life pretty boring. [12]It makes someone feel like they are spending much of their life at home. [13]Most people think that not finishing high school and not going to college would not be boring because they think they will have their friends to hang out with during the day. [14]In most cases, though, the reality is that most people work or go to school, so no one is around to hang out with. [15]My boyfriend spends most of his day at home without much to do. [16]He sleeps in late and watches television all day. [17]As the day goes by and there is not much to do, it gets boring for him. [18]People who drop out of high school will never have an easy future.

1. What are Kate's reasons for not dropping out of high school?

_____

2. Is Kate's argument convincing? Explain.

_____

_____

3. List some other reasons for not dropping out of high school.

_____

_____

Group Activity

Many consumer products are either wasteful or difficult to open. For example, in fast-food restaurants, almost every item is wrapped and has a restaurant advertisement or logo on it. Disposable shaving razors use a lot of packaging for such a small product. Some products that are difficult to open include electronic devices, dolls, toothbrushes, and food containers.

In groups of three or four, choose a product whose packaging is either wasteful or impossible to open. Design an improved package that is less wasteful and environmentally friendly. Then write an argument paragraph as a proposal to the company explaining why it should use your new and improved package.

MyWritingLab™
Complete this activity
at mywritinglab.com

Reading and Writing across the Curriculum: **Criminal Justice**

Smart cards are technologically advanced credit card-like devices that can store a considerable amount of unchangeable information about the cardholder. They contain a computer chip and other sources of information used to provide highly secure personal identification.

Smart cards can be used for a variety of purposes. They can store detailed records of a person's medical history or banking transactions. They can enable the holder to purchase goods and services, to enter restricted areas, or to perform other operations. Today, most smart cards are set up for a variety of limited uses. For example, colleges and universities have adopted modified versions for use as student identification cards.

Currently, U.S. government offices have mandated the use of a Personal Identification Verification (PIV) smart card containing chips that store personal information and **biometric data,** including two digitized fingerprints and a photograph. As personal identification technologies continue to develop, some people are concerned that eventually, all citizens will have to carry a national ID smart card.

(Adapted from *Criminal Justice Today* by Frank Schmalleger)

biometric data detailed information about someone's body, such as the patterns of color in their eyes, which can be used to prove who they are

Would requiring all citizens and others living in the United States to carry a national ID smart card provide greater security or invade personal privacy? Write an argument paragraph in which you take a stand on whether or not a national ID smart card should be required.

MyWritingLab™
Complete this activity
at mywritinglab.com

Comment on a Contemporary Issue

Students use computers and other electronic devices for entertainment and social networking, but many do not know how to use online learning classrooms. They must know how to use a variety of search engines and have basic word-processing knowledge. They also need to be familiar with sending and receiving emails and sending and saving files. Should students be expected to have developed these skills on their own or should colleges train students to learn online? Write a paragraph arguing either point:

- Students should have already developed skills for online learning.
- College should train students to learn online.

Write about an Image

This poster was designed to be persuasive. Write an argument paragraph about animals in shelters that makes the same point as the poster does.

The Argument Essay

LO 3 **Write an argument essay.**

Research Reminder. For more information about taking notes and using research, see Chapters 16 and 17.

The argument essay has the same purpose as the argument paragraph: to express the writer's point of view on an issue and support it by giving evidence to persuade readers to agree with the writer's point of view or to take action. The argument essay explores several sides of an issue. In order to be convincing, the arguments and evidence supporting the point of view must be strong.

The argument essay may use the same patterns of development as the paragraph version. However, since the essay discusses the topic in greater depth and includes more evidence and may include opposing viewpoints, other patterns of development are possible.

You may want to do some research on your topic to find out what experts say. To avoid plagiarism, take careful notes by labeling paraphrases, summaries, and direct quotations. Write down all the publication information from the sources you use. When you include material from your sources in your paper, follow the MLA format.

Thesis Statement

The thesis statement for an argument essay includes the **narrowed topic, which is the issue you want to argue,** and your point of view.

The following thesis statement example is from Roxanne Byrd's essay "The Duck Problem" on page 296–297:

Thesis with a **topic** and point of view:

The Muscovy ducks should be relocated.

Thesis with a topic **and** point of view, **and** list of supporting points:

> The Muscovy ducks should be relocated because they spoil the campus environment, they are aggressive toward people, and they cause accidents.

Body Paragraphs

The body paragraphs in an argumentation essay include the reasons for your point of view with evidence. They may also include the arguments against your point of view with your rebuttal of—or answer to—the arguments against. When arranging your reasons and arguments against, you can begin with the strongest and end with the weakest or begin with the weakest and end with the strongest. The figure below shows several organizational plans for an argument essay:

Organization Plans for an Argument Essay

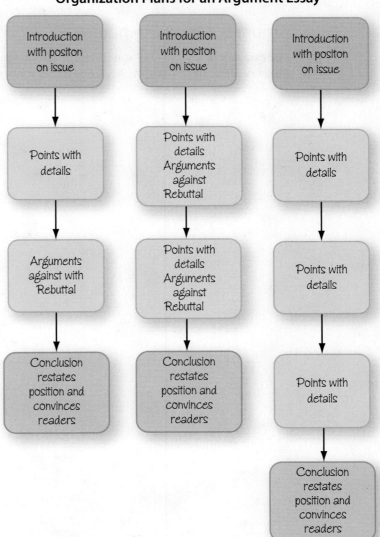

Concluding Paragraph

The concluding paragraph has an important role in your argument essay. Your goal is to convince the reader that your position on the issue is the strongest. After restating your position, you can add any of the following: suggest results or consequences, end with a warning, discuss the future of the subject, or suggest that more research on the subject is needed. No new arguments should be presented in the conclusion.

Argument Graphic Organizer

Using an argument graphic organizer will help you arrange the points and details that support your argument and, if you include them, arguments against (rebuttals). You can change the organizer to suit your needs by adding body paragraphs with points and details.

Notice how Roxanne uses an argument graphic organizer to prove her thesis (see page 295).

Argument Essay Example

The essay on pages 296–297 was developed from a paragraph on the same issue. Student Roxanne Byrd argues that the Muscovy ducks on her campus should be relocated.

Roxanne's Argument Essay Graphic Organizer

Introduction

Lead-in: Description of Muscovy ducks, how they were imported for their meat and eggs; many escaped and are breeding

Bridge: So many ducks have taken up residence on our campus that they have become a nuisance.

Thesis Statement: The Muscovy ducks should be relocated because they spoil the campus environment, they are aggressive toward people, and they cause accidents.

Body Paragraph 1

Topic Sentence: One reason to relocate the Muscovy ducks is that they spoil the campus environment.

Point 1: Droppings create a health hazard.

Details: One duck creates large amount of droppings per day; droppings carry bacteria, can make humans sick; people could slip and fall

Point 2: Destroy native plants and wildflowers

Details: Uprooted wildflowers just planted as part of campus sustainable landscape policy

Argument Against: Benefit environment by controlling pests, eating bugs

Rebuttal: Benefit of sustainable garden is to attract insects that control other pests

Body Paragraph 2

Topic Sentence: Not only do the Muscovy ducks spoil the campus environment, but they are aggressive toward people.

Point 1: Annoy and frighten students, staff, visitors

Details: Ducks gather, push beaks against people, beg for food; have attacked students; one jumped on friend's lap and tried to bite her face

Argument Against: Ducks not afraid due to people's feeding and friendliness

Rebuttal: Fearful of wild creatures or do not want to feel that they are in petting zoo

Body Paragraph 3

Topic Sentence: The most important reason for relocating the Muscovy ducks is that their presence on campus roads and in parking spaces endangers both people and ducks.

Point 1: Roam campus and sit in empty parking spaces

Details: Ducks easily killed by student drivers; interference from ducks crossing roads

Point 2: Accidents occur when ducks cross roads; student stopped short for duck and caused three-car pile up

Argument Against: Need for driver awareness of ducks on campus

Rebuttal: Should not have to worry about running over a duck or having an accident because of one

Conclusion

Effective Concluding Technique: Muscovy ducks are not considered wildlife and are not protected. Law does not stop capture and human killing, but this is not the solution suggested.

Concluding Statement: The Muscovy ducks should be moved to a confined environment where they cannot escape or come into contact with wild birds or people who do not want to interact with them.

Muscovy duck

sustainable landscape policy
one which causes little or no damage
to the environment and therefore able
to continue for a long time

The Duck Problem

¹ Muscovy ducks are a common sight on our college campus, which has a big lake on its border. These ducks are large birds with feathers that can be white, greenish black, blue, brown, or a combination. Their most distinctive characteristics are a crest on the top of their heads and large areas of red, bumpy skin around their eyes and bill. Native to Central and South America, Muscovies were imported to North America and are raised on farms for their eggs and meat. Unfortunately, many have escaped into the wild. As a result, large numbers of wild, breeding Muscovies can be found near local waters. So many of these ducks have taken up residence on our campus that they have become a nuisance. The Muscovy ducks should be relocated because they spoil the campus environment, they are aggressive toward people, and they cause accidents.

² One reason to relocate the Muscovy ducks is that they spoil the campus environment. First of all, their droppings create a health hazard. One Muscovy duck creates a large amount of droppings a day. The droppings carry bacteria that can make humans sick. Since the ducks leave droppings wherever they please, the walkways are frequently soiled with their droppings, making people watch every step while walking across campus. In addition, their greenish-black, watery droppings are slippery when stepped on; therefore, someone could slip, fall, and get injured. Another way they spoil the campus is by destroying native plants and wildflowers. Our campus has a **sustainable landscape policy** where we install native plants to reduce the use of fertilizer and pesticides and conserve water. Both students and faculty have worked to install gardens across campus. However, last month, some of the ducks uprooted all of the rare, native wildflowers that had just been planted by the environmental science classes. Duck lovers argue that the Muscovies benefit the campus environment because they control pests by eating mosquitoes, roaches, ants, and spiders. However, the benefit of creating our sustainable gardens is to attract beneficial insects that control other pests and keep a natural balance.

³ Not only do the Muscovy ducks spoil the campus environment, but also they are aggressive toward people. Their bold, unwanted approaches annoy and occasionally frighten students, staff, and visitors, especially when the ducks want food. For instance, when someone sits outside on a bench to eat a snack or to socialize with other students, groups of hissing, snorting ducks quickly rush toward and gather around that person, pushing their beaks against the individual's legs to beg for a handout. On one occasion,

a duck jumped on my friend's lap while she was snacking on some chips. The duck pecked at her face and in an attempt to get some of her food, bit her on the lip. Duck supporters claim that people are misinterpreting the ducks' intentions. They say that the Muscovies have learned to be unafraid of approaching people because so many students and staff members are friendly toward them and frequently feed them. Nevertheless, the supporters do not realize that many individuals are either fearful of wild creatures or do not want to feel as if they are in a petting zoo.

4 The most important reason for relocating the Muscovy ducks is that their presence on campus roads and in parking spaces endangers both people and ducks. Although the campus is bordered by a lake, the ducks do not limit themselves to that location, roaming the campus grounds for food. For instance, they often sit in empty parking spaces preening their feathers or sleeping. At popular class times, competition for parking spaces is intense, so when a space opens up, students pull in quickly, unaware that a duck may also be occupying it. If a duck is lucky enough to avoid its death in this situation, it may not avoid being run over or causing an accident. Although the campus is small, there are two entrances from the main street with roads leading to student parking areas near classroom buildings. Traffic can get heavy on these roads when students are arriving and leaving. On many occasions, one or more ducks have interfered with the flow of traffic while attempting to cross the road, halting traffic in both directions. The worst problem is that accidents have occurred because of duck crossings. Last semester, one student saw a duck crossing the road, stopped short, and caused a three-car pile up. Those who support the ducks' right to live on campus believe that drivers should be aware that ducks may be in parking spaces and on the roads and should drive accordingly. However, students should not have to worry about running over a duck or having a car accident because of one.

5The Muscovy ducks are a non-native species; they are not considered wildlife. Therefore, they cannot be protected by any state or federal law. In addition, they cannot be relocated to public lands. While the law does not prohibit their capture and humane killing, this is not the solution being suggested. The ducks should be prevented from destroying the campus environment, being aggressive toward people, and causing accidents. Therefore, the Muscovy ducks should be moved to a confined environment where they cannot escape or come into contact with wild birds or people who do not want to interact with them.

ACTIVITY 14.5 Analyzing an Argument Essay

1. Underline the thesis statement. What point does the author plan to argue?

_____

2. What technique does the writer use in the lead-in?

_____

3. Underline the topic sentences of each of the body paragraphs. What is the point of each body paragraph?

_____

4. Circle the transition words used to introduce each difference in each of the topic sentences.
5. Each body paragraph contains an opposing point and answer to that point. Double-underline the point of opposition and answer in each body paragraph.
6. In addition to referring to the thesis statement, underline the additional argument the writer makes in the conclusion.

Writing Reminder. For more help with writing an essay, including introductions and conclusions, see Chapter 5.

Argument Essay Graphic Organizer

This argument essay graphic organizer is based on a plan in which each paragraph presents a point with details that support the argument. If you want to add arguments against and/or rebuttals, you can change the organizer to fit one of the plans on page 299.

Argument Essay Graphic Organizer

MyWritingLab™
Use the interactive graphic organizer at mywritinglab.com

Introduction

Lead-in:

Bridge:

Thesis Statement:

Body Paragraph 1

Topic Sentence:

Point 1 of Argument:

Details:

Body Paragraph 2

Topic Sentence:

Point 2 of Argument:

Details:

Body Paragraph 3

Topic Sentence:

Point 3 of Argument:

Details:

Conclusion

Effective Concluding Technique:

Concluding Statement:

Writing Assignments

Write about an Image: Is a College Degree Necessary?

In the United States, a college degree has been considered the ticket to success. However, Professor Richard Vedder has a different point of view. Dr. Vedder has taught economics at Ohio University for forty-four years and has written extensively about the connection between higher education and the work force. He believes that not everyone has the interest, ability, or need to go to college. In addition, many of the fastest growing jobs do not require a college degree.

What do you think? Write an argument essay for or against getting a college degree.

Writing Topics for an Argument Essay

For your argument essay, choose one of these options:

Peer Review Reminder. For feedback on your writing, have someone read your paper and make comments on the Peer Review Response Sheet in Chapter 4, page 54.

- from paragraph to essay: expand the paragraph you wrote in the paragraph section of this chapter
- any of the writing topics in the paragraph section of this chapter
- any topic from the following list:

General Writing Topics

Argue for OR against any of these topics:

    staying in college
    restricting the use of cell phones in public areas
    taking tests online
    buying dangerous animals as pets
    owning a home

Writing across the Curriculum Topics

Argue for OR against any of these topics:

Education: eliminating developmental courses for college students
Government: electing a female president of the United States
Family Life: parents having access to their children's social network accounts
Business: working for yourself (being self-employed)
Psychology: cheating in a relationship

English Success Tip: Improve Your Writing by Reading

Students often ask how they can improve their writing. Most often, the advice is to study grammar, mechanics, punctuation, and sentence structure. However, reading can help you become a better writer.

Reading stimulates your language development in a number of ways.

- You unconsciously absorb the author's style of writing.
- You learn how different writers express their thoughts.
- You see how writers handle complex ideas.

Reading is especially helpful for English language learners. In addition to the benefits already discussed, by reading in English, you increase your exposure to the language and the way it is used in writing.

Set aside at least fifteen minutes each day to read. Read newspapers, magazine articles, and novels that interest you. You will be amazed at the improvement in your writing skills, and will enjoy the entertainment and stress relief that reading can offer.

Learning Other College Writing Assignments

PART 3

15 Writing under Pressure

Learning Objectives

After working through this chapter, you will be able to:

LO 1 Define timed writing as a writing activity that must be completed within a limited period.

LO 2 Write a timed essay by following the 5 Ps: *Understand the Prompt, Make a Point, Form a Plan, Produce the Essay, and Proofread.*

LO 3 Manage your time for planning, writing, and editing and proofreading an essay.

LO 1 Define timed writing as a writing activity that must be completed within a limited period.

What Is Timed Writing?

Timed writing is a writing activity that must be completed within a limited time period. The purpose of a timed writing activity is to test your ability to think and write under pressure. Learning how to write well in a limited time period will help you handle the pressures of writing in college and in the workplace. For example, writing tasks such as reports, proposals, memoranda, and training materials are done on the spot at work.

Timed Writing in College

In college, a variety of writing activities may be timed. The most common is the essay question or exam. In writing courses, you may be asked to write a paragraph or essay in class to show that you can apply the writing skills you have been practicing and studying. Some colleges have students do a timed-writing sample for placement into certain courses or for exiting from a particular program.

How Is Timed Writing Evaluated?

Timed writing is usually graded differently from traditional writing assignments. First, instructors or other graders understand that writing within a limited time puts enormous pressure on the writer. In addition, they take into consideration that the writer has not had much time to think about, plan, and support the topic. They consider the paper to be a first draft; however, they expect a well-organized essay that follows a method of development appropriate to the topic.

TIMED WRITING   Essentials

Good timed writing has these characteristics:

- The main idea is clearly stated.
- The main idea is supported with specific details.
- A clear pattern of organization is used.
- Ideas are expressed logically.
- Transitional words and expressions show connections between ideas.
- Vocabulary is used effectively.
- Different sentence types give variety to the writing.

How to Approach Timed Writing: The 5 Ps

LO 2 Write a timed essay by following the 5 Ps: *understand the Prompt, make a Point, form a Plan, Produce the essay, and Proofread.*

Although timed writing can be challenging, understanding and applying five basic steps will give you a feeling of control over the process, thus building your confidence. The five steps are as follows: *(1) Understand the Prompt, (2) Make a Point, (3) Form a Plan, (4) Produce the Essay, and (5) Proofread.*

Step 1. Understand the Prompt

What is a prompt? The **prompt** is the topic that you are being asked to write about. Prompts can be written in many ways. Here are some examples.

- **Incomplete sentence:** The most valuable item you own that was not bought in a store
- **Statement:** Sports stars should or should not bear responsibility for being role models.
- **Question:** What childhood experience taught you something about life?
- **Quotation:** "Success is doing ordinary things extraordinarily well."—*Jim Rohn*
- **Scenario:** Many young adults read very little. They get most of their news and information from the Internet, television, and the movies. They would rather read a magazine than a novel. Write an essay in which you explain the reasons for this situation.

Read the Prompt Carefully Take the time to read the prompt carefully to understand what you are being asked to write about. If you do not respond to the prompt or you respond only to part of it, your score could be lowered. Look for key words that may tell you how to develop your essay. For instance, in the scenario example in the previous section, the last sentence tells you that the essay should explain the reasons young adults do not read much. That means you can use the cause and effect pattern of development. The following are some key words that are commonly used in essay prompts:

Key Words in Prompts	What to Do
Argue, take a position	State a point of view on an issue and support it by giving evidence.
Cause, effect, give reasons or results, why	Make a point about the reasons for and/or results of a situation
Classify, categorize, group	Make a point by arranging items within a topic into groups based on a single characteristic.
Compare, contrast, explain similarities or differences	Make a point about how two subjects are similar or different.
Define, explain the meaning	Make a point by explaining what a word, expression, or concept means.
Describe, give details of characteristics or features	Make a point by creating a clear mental picture in the reader's mind.
Illustrate, give examples	Make a point and support it with examples.
Narrate, tell the story of	Make a point by telling a story or giving an account of a significant experience or event.
Process, explain how	Make a point by explaining how to do something or how something happens or works.
Explain, discuss	Make a point by using any of the methods.

If you cannot find key words, you may be able to choose from several different approaches. For example, the topic "A place that people should visit" does not include any key words. Here are some possible approaches:

- Reasons people should visit a particular place
- Examples of what people will see while visiting a historical place of interest
- Description of a location of natural beauty
- Types of things to do or see in a specific place

ACTIVITY   **Choosing a Method of Development for Timed Writing Prompts**

15.1   For the example prompts 1 through 4, choose an appropriate method of development for a paragraph or essay. More than one type may be acceptable.

1. The most valuable item you own that was not bought in a store
   a. argument   b. causes   c. description   d. classification
2. Sports stars should or should not bear responsibility for being role models.
   a. narration   b. process   c. description   d. argument
3. What childhood experience taught you something about life?
   a. narration   b. classification   c. contrast   d. definition
4. "Success is doing ordinary things extraordinarily well."—*Jim Rohn*
   a. narration   b. illustration   c. process   d. cause and effect

---

Step 2. Make a Point

Once you have figured out what the prompt is asking you to do, spend a few minutes prewriting. Your goal is to come up with the main point you want to make—your topic sentence for a paragraph or your thesis statement for an essay.

When developing your topic sentence or thesis statement, include some words from the prompt. Including words from the prompt will show the reader that you are addressing the topic and will keep you on track when you are writing.

Here are some examples of essay exam prompts and thesis statements that respond to them. Note how the thesis statements include words from the prompt and the main point. The supporting points are optional and are in parentheses in the examples.

Prompt: A well-known discount store chain is proposing to build a store in your neighborhood. Do you support or oppose this plan? Give specific reasons for your answer.

Thesis statement: The plan to build a discount store in my neighborhood should be opposed (because the store will cause an increase in traffic, theft, and noise).

Prompt: What are some important qualities of a good manager?

Thesis statement: Some important qualities of a good manager are the ability to communicate, to lead, and to have faith in employees.

ACTIVITY   **Writing Thesis Statements for Timed Writing Prompts**

15.2   After thinking about the following prompts, write a thesis statement for each one. Include some of the words from the prompt.

1. Students who do not want to write their own essays can find dozens of websites on the Internet that sell essays on many different topics. Argue against buying essays on the Internet.

   _____

   _____

2. Discuss the ways you have changed as a result of your experience in college.

   _____

   _____

3. Many schools employ security guards or police officers and have installed security equipment such as video cameras or metal detectors in buildings. Write about security measures that are provided on your college campus or security measures that should be provided on your campus.

   _____

   _____

Step 3. Form a Plan

Once you have written your thesis statement, take a few minutes to jot down some supporting ideas. Write a brief description of the points you want to make. Developing a scratch outline will help to keep you on track as you write. Here is a scratch outline for the thesis statement: "To maintain good health, I eat nutritious foods, exercise five times a week, and meditate every morning."

1. Eat nutritious foods
   —fruits and vegetables
   —low-fat dairy and fish
   —grains and nuts
2. Exercise five times a week
   —lift weights
   —jog
   —cycle
3. Meditate every morning
   —mindfulness meditation practice

Step 4. Produce the Essay

Most of your time should be devoted to writing the essay. Because you are writing within a time limit, you will not be able to support your main ideas with the same amount of detail that you would in a take-home essay. However, you will be expected to complete the essay with enough specific development to prove your main point.

> **TIPS** | **Producing the Essay**
>
> 1. Avoid changing your topic and starting over when you will not have enough time to fully develop another one.
> 2. Avoid focusing on errors in grammar, punctuation, or spelling while you are drafting.
> 3. If you cannot think of an attention-getting introduction, either skip it and return to it later or write an introduction that takes a more general approach.
> 4. Don't spend too much time developing any one supporting paragraph only to discover that you have little time to work on the others.
> 5. If you get stuck, skip to another paragraph. You can always return to it later.
> 6. Don't forget a conclusion, even if you have time to write only one sentence.
> 7. If you are writing your essay by hand, write legibly. If you decide that you want to remove material, neatly draw a line through it.

Step 5. Proofread

In timed writing, proofreading and editing are very important. Save five to ten minutes of your total writing time to read your paper carefully for grammar, punctuation, and spelling errors. If you know that you have a problem with commas, pay specific attention to them as you proofread.

How to Manage Your Time

LO 3 Manage your time for planning, writing, and editing and proofreading an essay.

When writing under pressure, you may forget to keep track of the time and end up with an unfinished paper. To avoid running out of time, budget your time and pay attention to the clock. For example, if you are given 60 minutes, divide your time in the way shown here.

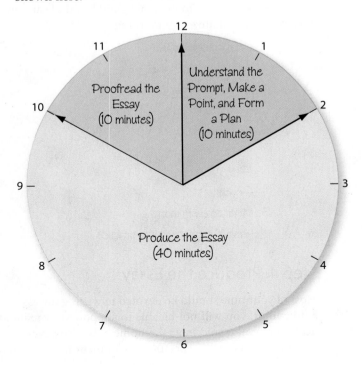

Pay attention to the clock. Sit where you can see it or wear a watch to monitor your time.

Timed Writing Examples

The two student timed-essay examples presented here were written on the same topic: "A business that provides excellent goods or services." Read the essays and answer the questions that follow each one. These examples may contain vocabulary and spelling errors as well as grammar and sentence errors.

ACTIVITY   Evaluating Timed Essay Example 1

15.3   Using the timed writing essentials on page 304, what are the strengths and weaknesses of this essay?

> [1]The Starbucks in Wilton Manors provides excellent services. [2]For example, I am there often sometimes three or four times a week. [3]I like to go there because it is convenient located, comfortable, and they know me by name.
>
> [4]My friends and I live in different neighborhoods, so we decided to choose a place that was conveniently located. [5]This Starbucks is located in a neighborhood that we are familiar with, it was a good choice for us. [6]Starbucks furniture is soft, comfortable, and modern. [7]There is plenty of space to move around. [8]At Starbuck there is wheelchair access from the outside courtyard and from the parking lot. [9]In addition to being conveniently located, and comfortable, they know their customers and they treat them well. [10]Whenever I am there I do not have to wait in line for a long time. [11]Scott, Brian, Dale, Jessica and Bonnie knows me by my name. [11]They know what I like to drink and eat. [12]They also knows how I like my beverage. [13]I get the same drink, a medium mocha frappucino without the whipped cream, and my usual a piece of the Bluberry Crumb coffee cake. [14]One of these days I will try something different just to see their reactions. [15]I like and enjoy going to this Starbucks because they provide excellent customer service. [16]You can tell that just by driving by. [17]The parking lot is always full, and there is a long line of people waiting. [18]This is usually a good sign that it's a good place.

Strengths _____

_____

Weaknesses _____

_____

ACTIVITY | Evaluating Timed Essay Example 2

15.4 Using the timed writing essentials on page 304, what are the strengths and weaknesses of this essay?

---

[1]There are many different types of coffee shops in my neighborhood, but my favorite is Starbuck's coffee. [2]I am a frequent customer there and they always provide excellent customer service, coffee and food.

[3]One noticeable quality of Starbucks is their excellent customer service. [4]The baristas are always dressed well and are smiling. [5]When I walk in they also greet me by name, making the visit a more personal experience. [6]Sometimes they even have my drink ready by the time I get to the front counter. [7]The baristas always make the environment in the store warm and friendly.

[8]Another great thing Starbucks serves is coffee. [9]They import their coffee beans from all over the world and keep them sealed fresh in bags until it is time to grind and brew them. [10]Their coffee is always hot and fresh as they brew a new pot every thirty minutes. [11]I can also add a variety of flavors into my drink such as vanilla, caramel or hazelnut. [12]My drink is always personalized and made exactly how I like it.

[13]Finally, there is their very tasty food. [14]Each morning a bakery delivers fresh pastries to be sold in the store. [15]The pastries come in a large variety from muffins to scones and are very delicious. [16]The baristas also prepare fresh fruit cups and breakfast sandwiches in the morning for customers. [17]The display case for the pastries and food is also kept clean and full of fresh product.

[18]I have loved going to Starbucks since my first initial visit. [19]They always have excellent customer service and goods in nearly every store. [20]I would reccomend for everyone to visit a Starbucks coffee shop at least once.

Strengths _____

_____

Weaknesses _____

_____

Writing Assignments

Reading and Writing across the Curriculum: **Sociology**

Sociologists study how groups influence people, especially those who share a culture and physical location.

> We humans are complex beings. Certainly, we have physical needs of food, shelter, and safety, and satisfying them is important. But this is only part of who we are. We also have a deep need for community, a feeling that we belong—the sense that others care about what happens to us and that we can depend on the people around us.
>
> (From *Essentials of Sociology* by James M. Henslin)

Some people find a sense of community in the city, while others find it in the suburbs (communities located just outside a city), or rural areas. In a timed 60-minute paper, write about why you would prefer to live in a city, a suburb, or a rural area.

Topics for Timed Writing

Set a time limit for writing about one of these topics—45 or 60 minutes.

General Topics

If you had the power to change three things in your community or in the world, what would you change and why?

Giving a gift to a child, such as a pet, a camera, or a bicycle, can contribute to a child's development. What gift would you give to a child and how would it help him or her develop?

What advice would you give to students who are just entering college?

The Dalai Lama, Tibetan spiritual leader, once said, "In the practice of tolerance, one's enemy is the best teacher." Give examples of times when you learned tolerance from people you did not like or did not agree with.

Explain the effect of a particular invention on the family.

Writing across the Curriculum Topics

Environmental Science: Some people believe that human activity is harming the Earth. Others feel that the Earth is a better place to live because of human activity. Which do you believe?

Psychology: Explain the differences between the male and female approaches to solving relationship problems.

Music Appreciation: Many of us like music from our own generation. Convince someone who is not in your generation that your music is worth listening to.

Literature: What book, poem, or story should be required reading for everyone?

Sociology: Many people from other countries come to live in the United States because they believe that it is better than their native country. What features make the United States desirable?

Peer Review Reminder. For feedback on your writing, have someone read your paper and make comments on the Peer Review Response Sheet in Chapter 4, page 54.

English Success Tip: Build Timed Writing Confidence with Practice

Many students experience stress when writing under pressure. Practicing will reduce your anxiety and build your confidence. Here are some things you can to do prepare for timed writing.

1. Make a list of writing prompts that you can use for practice.
2. Expand your knowledge of current events by reading reliable materials or following news reports.
3. Understand the criteria that will be used to grade your paper.
4. Re-create the testing situation. Choose a topic and apply the 5 Ps: **Understand the Prompt, Make a Point, Form a Plan, Produce the Essay, and Proofread**.
5. Make note of the parts of the timed-writing process that were most troublesome for you. Work on these when you practice.
6. Get an objective point of view by asking another student or an assistant in your campus writing center to read your completed paper and evaluate it using the criteria.
7. Practice often.

16

Writing a Summary and Summary-Response Essay

Learning Objectives

After working through this chapter, you will be able to:

LO 1 Describe the summary essay as an essay that restates the main idea and important supporting points of another piece of writing.

LO 2 Prepare to write a summary by reading and taking notes.

LO 3 Write an objective summary essay.

LO 4 Write a summary-response essay.

LO 5 Avoid plagiarism.

LO 1 Describe the summary essay as an essay that restates the main idea and important supporting points of another piece of writing.

What Is a Summary Essay?

As a college writer, you may be asked to write a summary for one or more types of reading material for a course you are taking, such as a chapter or section of a textbook, a newspaper or journal article, a web page, or a whole book.

A summary essay is different from other types of essays you have learned to write. A **summary essay** gives a shortened version of another writer's words and ideas. In your own words, you restate the main idea and the most important supporting points of a reading selection, leaving out minor points and examples. Instead of writing *your* ideas, you write about another writer's ideas. Also, a summary is usually much shorter than an academic essay.

In this chapter, you will learn how to write two kinds of summary essays: an objective summary and a summary-response.

- An **objective summary essay** restates the author's main point and the most important supporting points. An objective summary essay does not include your personal opinions or thoughts on the topic. It leaves out examples and nonessential details.
- A **summary-response essay** is made up of an objective summary of the reading selection and your reaction to the author's ideas.

Preparing to Write a Summary Essay

LO 2 Prepare to write a summary by reading and taking notes.

Before you actually write your summary essay, you need to do some planning:

1. Carefully read the selection you were assigned so that you understand it well.
2. Find the main point and supporting points.
3. Write down the main and supporting points in your own words.

Read to Understand

In order to summarize what you have read, you must understand the author's ideas. If the selection is difficult, you may have to reread it one or more times. Also, if you come across words you do not know, look up their meanings.

Find the Main and Supporting Points

When you are familiar with the selection, the next step is to find the main points and supporting points. To make the process more manageable, divide the material into sections. For example, if your selection is from a textbook, look for headings and subheadings that refer to the point of the section. If the selection does not have headings, divide it by paragraphs.

   When you find the main and supporting points, mark them so that you can find them when you are ready to take notes. For example, you can underline them or make notes in the margins. Cross out points that are not important. This is called annotating.

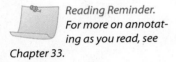

*Reading Reminder.
For more on annotating as you read, see
Chapter 33.*

Take Notes in Your Own Words

The last stage in preparing to write a summary is to take notes from the selection. Starting at the beginning, find the parts that you marked as main and supporting points. Then write each of these points down in your own words. By taking notes in your own words, you will avoid **plagiarizing,** which is stealing someone else's work (see page 320).

   If you are having a hard time writing notes in your own words, read a sentence from the selection and then speak or write it as if you were explaining it to someone else. Your instructor does not expect you to write at the same level as the author of the reading selection; he or she wants to know how well you understand what you have read.

   Using the Summary Notes Graphic Organizer on page 315 will help you keep your notes organized. Begin with the first point and continue in order until you reach the end of the selection. Then go over your notes to be sure that you have written the points in your own writing style.

Summary Notes Graphic Organizer

MyWritingLab™
Use the interactive graphic
organizer at mywritinglab.com

Title of the Reading Section

Author(s):

Main Idea of Reading Section:

Your Summary of Main Idea

Point from Reading:

Your Summary:

Point from Reading:

Your Summary:

Point from Reading:

Your Summary:

Point from Reading:

Your Summary:

Important Words/Definitions:

ACTIVITY Summarize a Short Reading Selection

16.1 Read the following selection about computer technology. Then, write a summary of the passage in no more than fifty words.

¹Although computer technology has helped people in many positive ways, it can be used to violate people's privacy. ²One way people's privacy is violated is through the use of red light cameras. ³These cameras are placed near traffic signals to take pictures of drivers that enter an intersection after the light has turned red. ⁴A computer linked to the camera notes the violation and takes a picture of the drivers and their license plates. ⁵Trained law enforcement officers review the photos to make sure that a traffic violation did happen; then they give out tickets. ⁶Computer hackers also use computer technology to violate people's privacy. ⁷For instance, some hackers try to trick people into giving out their secret bank information. ⁸The hackers send people an email that looks like it comes from their bank. ⁹The email asks them to give their account number or password. ¹⁰The most important violation of people's privacy through computer technology is data mining. ¹¹Data mining uses special software programs to go through information about people and collect it for a specific purpose. ¹²For example, businesses use data mining to learn the buying habits of its customers. ¹³The government uses it to identify terrorists. ¹⁴Although computers benefit society in many ways, privacy is becoming impossible.

_____

_____

_____

_____

Writing an Objective Summary Essay

LO 3 **Write an objective summary essay.**

After you have read and understood the selection and have taken notes from it using your own words and style of writing, you are ready to draft your summary essay.

Many summaries are written for an audience that has not read the selection. Therefore, your goal is to help your readers understand the author's main and supporting points. In other words, your summary takes the place of the reading selection.

Length

The length of an objective summary essay depends on the length of the reading selection. Your essay will be shorter than the selection because it does not include examples and nonessential details. In addition, the objective summary does not include your personal opinions, thoughts, or examples from you own life. Therefore, the summary should be about one-third the length of the original reading.

Word Choice

Use the present tense in the third person. You are writing about what someone else says, so you do not need to refer to yourself or the reader with *I* or *you*.

Even if you mentioned the author in the first paragraph, remind readers that in the body paragraphs of the essay, you are writing about the author's ideas. You do not need to use the author's name with every sentence, however.

Use reporting verbs to show that you are reporting ideas in the reading selection. Choose a verb that shows the author's point of view. Also, avoid using the same verb over and over. Here are a few examples of possible word choices:

The article   **is about, reports, covers, describes**

The author   **explains, states, points out, writes**

Organization

The objective summary consists of an introduction and one or more body paragraphs, depending on the length of the reading. As you write, use your notes. You may also want to go back to the selection.

Research Reminder. To learn more about how to capitalize and punctuate titles of reading selections, see Chapter 17.

The Introduction   The purpose of the introduction is to tell readers who wrote the selection and where it came from, for example, a book, journal, magazine, web page, and so on. The introduction also has a thesis statement, which is the author's main point. If you have information about the author that the reader needs to know, you may include it.

Here is a model of a thesis statement that includes the author's name and title:

In [title of reading], [name of author] **shows/says/explains** [main point].

In "The Power of Peer Pressure: The Asch Experiment," James M. Henslin **shows** that most people go along with the group to fit in even if the group is not correct.

TIP | The first time you mention the author, write out his or her full name. Always spell the author's name correctly. After that, you may refer to the author by last name or full name. Do not refer to the author by first name only.

The Body   The body of the summary essay is the summary itself. It is made up of the author's supporting points. Keep in mind that your summary should be about one-third as long as the original selection.

Using your notes from the Summary Notes Graphic Organizer on page 315, write a sentence for each point. Choose appropriate connectors and transitions between ideas.

ACTIVITY   **Write an Objective Summary Essay**

16.2   Read the following passage "Why Rewards Can Backfire" from a psychology textbook and write an objective summary essay. Take notes on the Summary Notes Graphic Organizer on page 315 to help you plan your essay.

Why Rewards Can Backfire

[1]Money, praise, gold stars, applause, hugs, and thumbs-up signs are all extrinsic reinforcers. **Extrinsic reinforcers** are rewards that are a result of an activity, not rewards from doing the activity. People also work for **intrinsic reinforcers.** Those are rewards people feel from doing the activity, such as enjoyment or satisfaction. Psychologists have found that extrinsic reinforcement sometimes becomes too much of a good thing: If you do something only for the reward, then you may not feel the enjoyment of it.

[2]Consider what happened in a classic study of how praise affects children's intrinsic motivation (Lepper, Greene, & Nesbett, 1973).

[3]Researchers gave nursery-school children the chance to draw with felt-tipped pens during free play and recorded how long each child played with the pens on their own. The children clearly enjoyed this activity. Then the researchers told some of the children that if they could draw with felt-tipped pens they would get a prize, a "Good Player Award" complete with gold seal and red ribbon. After drawing for six minutes, each child got the award as promised. Other children did not expect an award and were not given one. A week later, the researchers again observed the children's free play. Those children who had expected and received an award spent much less time with the pens than they had before the start of the experiment. In contrast, children who had neither expected nor received an award continued to show as much interest in playing with the pens as they had initially.

[4]The researchers who did the felt-tipped pen study suggested that when we are paid for an activity, we interpret it as work. We see our actions as a result of other factors instead of our own interests, skills, and efforts. It is as if we say to ourselves, "Since I am being paid, it must be something I wouldn't do if I didn't have to." Then, when the reward is withdrawn, we refuse to "work" any longer.

[5]Another possibility is that we tend to think of extrinsic rewards as controlling, so they make us feel pressured and make us feel that we do not have any choice ("I guess I have to do what I'm told to do—but *only* what I'm told to do") (Deci et al., 1999).

[6]What is the take-home message about extrinsic rewards? First, they are often useful or necessary: Few people would trudge off to work every morning if they never got paid; and in the classroom, teachers may need to offer students some type of reward to motivate them. Extrinsic rewards should be used carefully and should not be overdone so that intrinsic pleasure in an activity can grow. Educators, employers, and policy makers should recognize that most people do their best when they get real rewards for real achievement *and* when they have interesting, challenging, and different kinds of work to do.

(Adapted from *Psychology* by Carole Wade and Carol Tavris)

Writing a Summary-Response Essay

LO 4 **Write a summary-response essay.**

Instructors often assign a summary-response essay to find out students' reactions to a reading selection. The first part of this type of essay is the objective summary, which you have already practiced in this chapter. The second part is your response or reaction.

Note Your Reactions

In addition to the summary, the summary-response essay includes your reactions to the selection. Your preparation for this essay is the same as for the objective summary essay. However, in addition to reading only for main and supporting points, notice how you feel about the points the author makes. If you feel strongly for or against any ideas, underline or mark them in a way that you will be able to find them later.

As you read, consider the questions in the following Reader Response Notes Organizer. They will help you connect to the selection in three ways: to the reading itself, to yourself, and to the world around you.

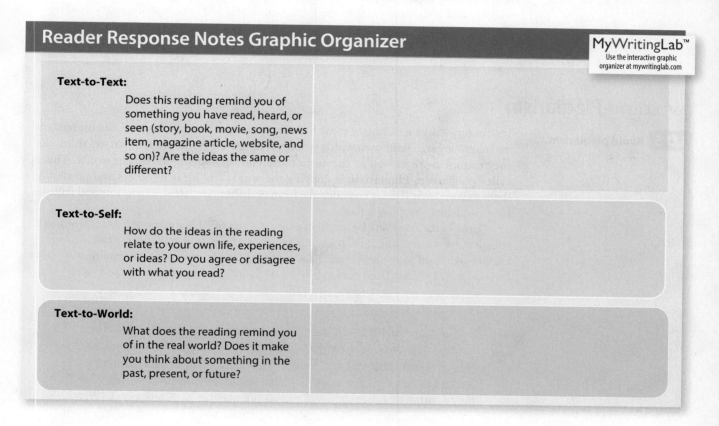

Reader Response Notes Graphic Organizer

MyWritingLab™
Use the interactive graphic
organizer at mywritinglab.com

Text-to-Text:

Does this reading remind you of something you have read, heard, or seen (story, book, movie, song, news item, magazine article, website, and so on)? Are the ideas the same or different?

Text-to-Self:

How do the ideas in the reading relate to your own life, experiences, or ideas? Do you agree or disagree with what you read?

Text-to-World:

What does the reading remind you of in the real world? Does it make you think about something in the past, present, or future?

Organization

The Introduction The introduction of a summary-response essay has these parts:

- Tells readers who wrote the selection and where it came from, for example, a book, journal, magazine, web page, and so on.
- Gives the author's main point.
- States your main point about the reading. Here is an example:

  I agree/disagree with [name of author(s)'s] **point that** [author's point] **based on** [my point].

  I agree with Wade and Tavris's **point that** rewards given as a result of an activity in school should not be done too much **based on** my experience in high school.

The Body The first part of the body is the objective summary, which is about one-third of the length of the original selection.

The second part is your support for your own point about the reading. For your supporting points, you can use your own personal experience, ideas from the reading itself, or information that you already know.

ACTIVITY Write a Summary-Response Essay

16.3 Reread the selection "Why Rewards Can Backfire" on page 318. The, write a summary-response essay on the selection. If you have already written an objective summary on the reading, add your main point to the introduction and add your reaction to the reading after the summary.

Avoiding Plagiarism

LO 5 **Avoid plagiarism.**

Instructors assign a summary essay because they want to know that you can understand and summarize in your own words what you have read. Some student writers think that they cannot write as well as the author and end up copying his or her words. This is called plagiarism. **Plagiarism** is copying the words and ideas of others and presenting them as your own. This is considered a form of dishonesty. Most instructors and colleges have punishments for plagiarism.

Some of the ways student writers plagiarize are by (1) copying the exact words, (2) substituting words, and (3) rearranging words, phrases, and sentences. Read the following passage from page 48 of the college textbook *The Interpersonal Communication Book* by Joseph A. DeVito. Then compare it to the plagiarized examples that follow.

¹A common barrier to intercultural communication occurs when you assume that similarities exist and that differences do not. ²This is especially true of values, attitudes, and beliefs. ³You might easily accept different hairstyles, clothing, and foods. ⁴In basic values and beliefs, however, you may assume that deep down all people are really alike. ⁵They aren't. ⁶When you assume similarities and ignore differences, you'll fail to notice important distinctions and when communicating will convey to others that your ways are the right way and that their ways are not important to you. ⁷Consider this example. ⁸An American invites a Filipino coworker to dinner. ⁹The Filipino politely refuses. ¹⁰The American is hurt and feels that the Filipino does not want to be friendly. ¹¹The Filipino is hurt and concludes that the invitation was not extended sincerely. ¹²Here, it seems, both the American and the Filipino assume that their customs for inviting people to dinner are the same when, in fact, they aren't. ¹³A Filipino expects to be invited several times before accepting a dinner invitation. ¹⁴When an invitation is given only once, it's viewed as insincere.

Plagiarism 1: Copying the Exact Words of the Selection The most common form of plagiarism is copying the exact words of the selection. Parts of the sentences that are copied word for word are highlighted in this example. They come from sentences 1 and 6 in the original passage.

> In *The Interpersonal Communication Book*, Joseph A. DiVito states that **a common barrier to intercultural communication occurs when you assume that similarities exist and that differences do not.** You should not think that all people are alike because they are not. If you do not pay attention to differences, you will communicate **to others that your ways are the right way and that their ways are not** (48).

Plagiarism 2: Substituting Words   Another form of plagiarism is replacing some of the words in the original passage with synonyms, which are words that have the same or similar meanings as another. In this example, the words that were replaced are green.

> In *The Interpersonal Communication Book*, Joseph A. DiVito states that a **usual** barrier **with** intercultural communication **happens** when you **think** that **likenesses have an existence** and that **dissimilarities** do not. When you **presume likenesses** and **ignore** differences, you will be **unable to see** important **differentiations** and will **make known** to others that your **methods** are the **correct** way and their **methods** are not **significant** to you (48).

Plagiarism 3: Rearranging Words, Phrases, and Sentences   Using the same words, phrases, and sentences but placing them in a different order from the original selection is another form of plagiarism. In the following example, the exact words from sentence 1 and part of sentence 6 are rearranged.

> In *The Interpersonal Communication Book*, Joseph A. DiVito states that when you assume that all people are really alike and that differences do not exist, a common barrier to intercultural communication occurs. You will convey that their ways are not important to you and that your ways are the right ways to others (48).

An Acceptable Summary   The following example is an acceptable summary of DiVito's passage.

> In *The Interpersonal Communication Book*, Joseph A. DiVito points out that problems communicating with people of different cultures arise when you mistakenly think they have the same beliefs and values that you do. If you do

not recognize the differences when communicating, you will give others the impression that you do not think their customs are correct or important (48).

Finding Plagiarism

16.4 Working with a partner or on your own, read the following textbook selection about McDonald's and then the sentences that follow. Identify the parts of the sentences that are plagiarized. Also, write the type of error the writer made: copying exact words, substituting words, or rearranging words, phrases, and sentences.

[1]McDonald's has become an international icon of the fast-food industry. [2]With 30,000 restaurants in more than 100 countries, the golden arches have become synonymous with American culture. [3]Yet in recent years, McDonald's seems to have lost its competitive edge both at home and abroad. [4]In the United States, for example, its stores are outdated and its customer service skills seem to be slipping. [5]Moreover, concerns about health have driven many customers away from Big Macs and French fries. [6]McDonald's no longer leads in technology, with rivals inventing new processing and cooking technologies. [7]Profits have dropped, forcing McDonald's to expand aggressively into foreign markets, especially Europe and Asia.

(Adapted from *Business Essentials* by Robert J. Ebert and Ricky W. Griffin)

1. Ebert and Griffin point out that McDonald's does not have its competitive edge both in the United States and abroad.

_____

2. McDonald's has been forced to expand aggressively into foreign markets, especially Europe and Asia, because their profits have dropped.

_____

3. McDonald's used to be in the forefront of food preparation, but now, competitors have improved upon McDonald's older technology.

_____

4. Ebert and Griffin state that McDonald's has become an international icon of the fast-food industry.

_____

Writing Assignment

Reading and Writing across the Curriculum: Marketing

To practice working with longer pieces, write a summary of this passage from the textbook *Marketing* by Gary Armstrong and Philip Kotler. Use the Summary Notes Graphic Organizer on page 315.

[1]About ten years ago, GEICO was a little-known company in the auto insurance industry. Thanks in large part to an industry-changing advertising campaign, GEICO has become a major industry player. GEICO started out as an insurance company that targeted a select customer group of government employees and noncommissioned military officers with exceptional driving records. For nearly 60 years, the company relied mostly on direct-mail advertising and telephone marketing.

[2]In 1996, billionaire Warren Buffet bought the company and told the newly hired Martin Agency, a marketing group, to increase the advertising. In the beginning, the Martin Agency faced a tough task—introducing a little-known company with a funny name to a national audience. Like all good advertising, the GEICO campaign began with a simple but long-lasting theme, one that emphasizes the convenience and savings advantages of GEICO's direct-to-customers system. Every single one of the commercials produced in the campaign so far drives home the now-familiar tagline: "15 minute could save you 15 percent or more on car insurance."

[3]What really set GEICO's advertising apart was the inspired way the company chose to bring its customer benefits to life. At the time, competitors were using serious and emotional appeal advertisements: "You're in good hands with Allstate" or "Like a good neighbor, State Farm is there." To help make its advertising stand out, GEICO decided to deliver its punch line with humor. The creative approach worked and sales began to climb.

[4]As the brand grew, it became apparent that customers had difficulty pronouncing the GEICO name (which stands for Government Employees Insurance Company). Too often, GEICO became "gecko." Enter the charismatic green lizard. In 1999, GEICO ran a 15-second spot in which the now-famous, British-accented gecko calls a press conference and pleads: "I am a gecko, not to be confused with GEICO, which could save you hundreds on car insurance. So stop calling me." The ad was supposed to be a "throwaway." Consumers thought it was funny, and they quickly flooded the company with calls and letters begging to see more of the gecko.

[5]The rest, as they say, is history. Not only has the gecko helped people to pronounce and remember GEICO's name, it's become a pop culture icon. The unlikely lizard has become so well known that it was recently voted one of America's top two favorite icons by attendees of Advertising Week in New York, one of the ad industry's largest and most important gatherings.

[6]Not only has the gecko helped GEICO grow, it has changed the face of the auto insurance industry. Many analysts credit GEICO with changing the way insurance companies market their products in this traditionally boring category. Rising from being unknown only a dozen years ago, the company now serves more than eight million customers, making it the fourth-largest insurance company.

Peer Review Reminder.
For feedback on your writing, have someone read your paper and make comments on the Peer Review Response Sheet in Chapter 4, page 54.

English Success Tip: Summarize to Learn

Summarizing a chapter in a textbook is one of the best ways to learn and understand new material or to study for a test. It also helps you manage long chapters of information more easily.

1. Read the entire chapter to get an idea of what it is about. Notice how the chapter is organized by looking at headings, subheadings, and the topic sentences that follow the headings.
2. Read each section or paragraph and figure out its main idea. Write the main idea in your own words so that it makes sense to you. Leave out minor details.
3. Put all of your sentences together into a summary.

Summarizing textbook material takes practice, but as you become better at it, your reading comprehension will improve as well.

Using Research in College Writing

Learning Objectives

After working through this chapter, you will be able to:

LO 1 Explain how research can be used to strengthen an essay.

LO 2 Find library and Internet sources.

LO 3 Evaluate sources.

LO 4 Take notes from sources to avoid plagiarism.

LO 5 Cite the sources you use in your paper.

LO 6 Prepare a Works Cited list for all of the sources referred to in your paper using Modern Language Association (MLA) style.

LO 1 Explain how research can be used to strengthen an essay.

What Is Research?

Research is the process of finding information about something to learn more about it. In your daily life, for example, you may want to learn about a health issue, find out more about a product or service, or discover career options. Based on your findings, you can make an informed decision or develop a belief.

Research in College Writing

Academic research is done to gather and evaluate information about a subject. This type of research involves reading material in sources that include magazines, newspapers, books, journal articles written by researchers and professionals in a particular field, and websites. Through your reading, you learn what experts in a particular field have learned and written about the subject and then develop your own informed opinion.

One type of college writing assignment is the formal research paper. This paper includes an in-depth study of a topic through reading, taking notes, developing your own idea, and supporting it with evidence from experts.

Not all college writing assignments are formal research papers. For example, you can use research to support points in an argument essay. In this chapter, you will learn basic research skills and how to add research to an essay.

Research in Context

To illustrate how research makes an argument essay more convincing, read the next two paragraphs. The first one is taken from student writer Roxanne Byrd's argument essay in Chapter 14. Her purpose was to persuade college administrators to relocate the annoying Muscovy ducks on campus. In the second example paragraph, Roxanne adds information she found in outside sources through her research on the subject.

Paragraph without Research

> The Muscovy ducks are a non-native species; they are not considered wildlife. Therefore, no state or federal law protects them. In addition, they cannot be relocated to public lands. While the law does not stop people from capturing them and killing them in a humane way, this is not the solution being suggested. In order to prevent the ducks from spoiling the campus environment, being aggressive toward people, and causing accidents, the Muscovy ducks should be moved to a captive environment where they cannot escape or come into contact with wild birds or people who do not want to interact with them.

Paragraph with Research In this paragraph, the information from the two sources Roxanne used is highlighted.

> The Muscovy ducks are a non-native species, **originally imported to the United States from South and Central America to be raised as food. They were also released into lakes and parks by various organizations, businesses, and residents to make those areas more inviting to the public (Schaefer).** Now that the duck population has expanded, they have become a problem. **Since they are not considered native to any state, the Muscovies cannot be protected by any state or federal law, according to the federal Migratory Bird Treaty Act ("Nuisance Muscovy Ducks").** For example, in Florida, they are considered exotic and cannot **be released into the wild because they can transmit disease to native water birds. The only possible solution is to move them to a captive environment where they cannot escape and wander into the wild or public waters (Schaefer).** Although no state or federal law forbids someone from capturing these ducks and humanely killing them ("Nuisance Muscovy Ducks"), this is not the solution being suggested. Therefore, in order to prevent the ducks from spoiling the campus environment, being aggressive toward people, and causing accidents, the Muscovy ducks on campus should be relocated to a place where they can be confined and cared for by individuals interested in raising them for food or keeping them as pets.

There are several styles used for citing and documenting sources in research papers. In this chapter, you will learn how to document your sources and put together a Works Cited list in Modern Language Association (MLA) style.

Finding Sources

With so much information available on the Internet, you may not know where to start looking for good sources. Most students begin with what they are familiar with and know how to use, which is usually an Internet search engine such as Google or Yahoo!. However, the most direct route to academic sources is your college library. Most college libraries have materials that you cannot find on the Internet. College libraries also subscribe to databases that students can use for free. Thus, you must learn how to use both the library and the Internet search engines to locate the best information for your papers.

Internet Research

Internet search engines can provide many sources on a topic. However, not all websites are scholarly, accurate, or reliable. Also, with so many results possible for one search term, sorting through them can be a time-consuming, frustrating process.

To save time and avoid frustration, learn how to use search engines effectively. Here are some tips for using general search engines like Google, Yahoo!, or Bing.

TIPS

Doing Internet Searches

- Be as specific as possible when entering search terms: *ducks* instead of *birds*.
- Put the main subject first. Many search engines first list the matches for the first search word: *ducks pests*.
- Spell the search terms correctly.
- Use a phrase of two or more words in the exact order. Nouns work best: *muscovy ducks*.
- Put quotations marks around words or phrases to find the exact word or phrase on the page: *"Migratory Bird Treaty Act."*
- Use AND between words when you want pages that contain all the words: *ducks AND pests*.
- Use OR between words when you want pages with either of the words: *muscovy ducks OR non-native ducks*.
- If one search term does not get results, try different terms.

Some search engines will give you better results than others. Choose the search engine that will give you the type of information you want. The following chart lists some helpful Internet sites.

Internet Search Engines and Other Useful Sites	
Type of Information	Website Name
Academic Information	Google Scholar
	Infomine
	iSeek
	Directory of Open Access Journals (DOAJ)
	Internet Public Library
	Virtual Learning Resource Center
	Academic Index
	Microsoft Academic Research

Type of Information	Website Name
Magazines and News	Newspapers
	Online Newspapers
	MagPortal
Statistics	Federal Statistics
	U.S. Census Bureau
	Bureau of Labor Statistics
	Zanram Numerical Data Search
General Search Engines	Yahoo!
	Google
	Bing

ACTIVITY   Using Search Engines

17.1   Choose one of the websites from each of the four types in the previous chart and look for one reputable source for the topic "Cyber Abuse" from each. Write down the information about the source such as the author, the title of the article and/or website, the owner or sponsor of the website, and the date of publication; then write the reason you selected it.

Source Information	Reason for Selection
Academic information site	
Magazine and/or news site	
Statistics site	
General Search Engines	

Library Research

Your college library is essential for academic research. While search engines may seem easier and more convenient, the fastest way to find reliable academic resources is through your library's online catalog and databases. Take advantage of the resources your college library offers both online and in the library itself.

Visit the Library Online   Most modern libraries offer electronic catalogs, library networks, and databases. These resources are available from any computer with an Internet connection. Each of them allows you to search for sources by author, title, subject, or key words.

Online Library Resources	
Electronic databases	An **electronic database** is a collection of journals, magazines, and newspapers from many subject areas. Many of these items are not available on the Internet.
	Your library pays to subscribe to databases. As a student, you can use them for free. They will meet most of your academic research needs.
	Examples of databases are *InfoTrac Expanded Academic, LexisNexis Academic, ProQuest Research Library, Wilson Databases,* and *EBSCOhost Academic Search.*
Electronic catalog	The **electronic catalog** lists all the materials the library owns or subscribes to: books, reference works, magazines, newspapers. Your library's electronic catalog may have a special name.
Electronic library network	An **electronic library network** gives you access to the resources of other libraries in your area or state. This service allows you to borrow materials from another library.

ACTIVITY Practice Using Your College Electronic Library

17.2 Using your college electronic library, find a book, magazine, and academic journal article on the topic "Cyber Abuse." For each source, write down the author's name(s), the title of the article or book, the name of the magazine or journal, and the date each source was published. Then, give your reason for choosing it.

Author, Title, and Other Publication
Information   Reason for Selection

Book
_____

_____

Magazine article
_____

_____

Academic journal article
_____

_____

Evaluating Sources

 **Evaluate sources.**

Knowing how to evaluate the quality of the information you have found is another important research skill. You want to be sure that the information is accurate and can be trusted. Articles from scholarly journals, books, and other academic resources in your college library have already been evaluated by other scholars, publishers, or librarians.

On the other hand, newspaper and magazine articles have not been evaluated in the same way as scholarly resources. Some articles do not include an author or references. In this case, you will need to evaluate them carefully. Does the article show that the subject has been researched? Is the information fact or opinion? Is the author trying to persuade you to his or her point of view? Can the facts presented be found in another source?

The Internet offers information from all over the world. Much of that information has not been evaluated or checked for accuracy. Anyone can publish on the Internet or copy someone else's work and put it on his or her website. Also, the person or organization that set up the site may not be qualified to give information on the topic or may try to influence your beliefs. Some sites can be hateful or harmful or give incorrect information about such topics as health, science, and business; or imitate someone or something in a humorous way. Therefore, it is important for you to evaluate the information you find on websites before considering it as a source for a paper and citing it in your writing.

To help you evaluate the sites you find on the Internet, use the Q&A Checklist for Evaluating Online Sources. This involves asking six questions about each site: Who, What, Where, When, Why, and How.

- -

Q&A CHECKLIST FOR EVALUATING ONLINE SOURCES

The Question	What to Look For
Credibility: Who published the site?	☐ Find the part of the Web address (URL) that tells who is responsible for the site. Often, it is at the end of the URL: **.edu** = educational institutions **.gov** = government agencies **.mil** = military **.org** = organizations **.com** = commercial business **.net** = network **.mobi** = sites for mobile device use **.biz** = small businesses **.tv** = multimedia sites **.name** = personal pages **Countries other than the U.S. will always include their own URL codes.** ☐ A symbol called a tilde (~) in the URL can mean that you are looking at information that is someone's personal opinion. ☐ *About Us, Mission Statement,* or *Contact Us* can give you information about the publishers.
Authority: What are the author's credentials?	☐ Check for information about the author, such as experience, education, or training. ☐ Use a database or search engine to find out what else the author has written or what has been written about the author.
Accuracy: Where is the information from?	☐ Check for list of sources. ☐ Look for errors in spelling or grammar.
Currency: When was the site published?	☐ Find the date the page was first published. ☐ Find the most recent update. ☐ Look for other clues to help identify the date, such as copyright notice.

Purpose: Why was the site developed?	☐ Decide whether the purpose is to inform, teach, persuade, sell, or entertain.
	☐ Look for ways the site may try to influence the reader.
	☐ Check facts on a fact-checking site.
	☐ Look up the author or group in a search engine.
Presentation: How is the information presented?	☐ Look for a format that is easy to read.
	☐ Check for how well pages are organized.
	☐ Decide if advertisements interfere with the page's purpose.
	☐ See if graphics are not distracting.

Here is an evaluation of the Federal Bureau of Investigation's Cyber Crimes website using the Q&A checklist:

Credibility: Who published the site? This is a U.S. government website. The FBI is a government branch.

Authority: What are the author's credentials? No author is indicated. If no author is mentioned, assume that the content is written by FBI staff writers with appropriate credentials. From the home page, link to "Reports and Publications."

Accuracy: Where is the information from? From the Cyber Crimes department and other FBI departments. No errors in spelling or grammar.

Currency: When was the site published? No specific date is listed. News updates and press releases are updated daily. Link to "News" from the FBI's main site. All links work and are up to date.

Purpose: Why was the site developed? The site was developed to inform and educate the public about the cyber crimes arm of the FBI. All of the categories of information provided can be viewed from the home page, for example, Cyber Threats and Scams, Cases and Takedowns, Wanted by the FBI, and Protections.

Presentation: How is the information presented? The format is easy to read. Pages and links are well organized. There are no advertisements to interfere with the content. Graphics are purposeful, not distracting.

ACTIVITY   **Evaluating Websites**

17.3   Evaluate a website that you found for Activity 17.1 on cyber abuse using the Q&A Checklist.

Research Reminder. For more information on using summaries, see Chapter 16.

Roxanne's Source Evaluation Roxanne found information on several websites and articles through her college's online databases. After evaluating her sources using the Q&A Checklist, she realized that some of her websites did not have the credibility or authority she needed. For example, one site consisted of a duck lover's pictures and personal notes about the Muscovy ducks and their hatchlings in her neighborhood. After discarding the sources that were not credible, she had four strong sources that she could use in her paper.

Saving Information

When you find information you would like to use, create a system to keep the materials organized. One method is to download all the information to your computer or storage device. Create a specific folder where you can easily find the materials when you need them. Also, always make a backup copy on a device of your choice or an online storage site. If you prefer to work from print or photocopies, keep a separate folder for them.

Taking Notes from Sources

LO 4 Take notes from sources to avoid plagiarism.

When you have selected information from your sources to use in your paper, you are ready to take notes. Note-taking is an important step in the process of adding research to an essay. After you have taken accurate notes from your sources, you will not have to go back to the sources to find the information. You will be able to easily insert each note where it belongs.

Choose a system for taking notes that will help you stay organized. You can write your notes in electronic files, on paper, or on index cards (note cards). Whichever method you use, be sure to write down the author, title, and page number of your source with each note.

Roxanne's Note-Taking Roxanne used note cards to write her paraphrases, summaries, and direct quotations from her sources that she wanted to use in her paper. Here is an example of one of her note cards.

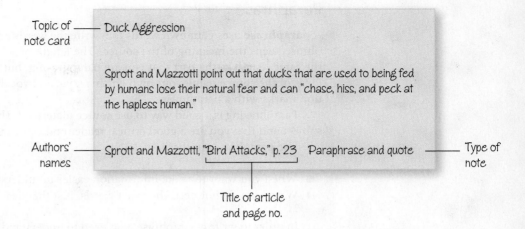

Topic of note card — Duck Aggression

Sprott and Mazzotti point out that ducks that are used to being fed by humans lose their natural fear and can "chase, hiss, and peck at the hapless human."

Authors' names — Sprott and Mazzotti, "Bird Attacks," p. 23   Paraphrase and quote — Type of note

Title of article and page no.

Copying information from your sources directly into your paper is considered **plagiarism.** To avoid plagiarism, use these acceptable forms: direct quotation, paraphrase, and summary.

The examples for direct quotations, paraphrases, and summaries come from this excerpt from the textbook *Game Design and Development* by Ernest Adams and Andrew Rollings, pages 120–121.

[1]Video game designers create a game's system of right and wrong behavior. [2]They tell a player which actions should be performed to win the game; those actions are considered good or desirable. [3]Likewise, they tell the player to avoid certain actions; these are considered bad or undesirable. [4]The players who come into the world must adopt the game standards, or they will lose the game. [5]Game designers are strongly discouraged from creating games that reward or even allow the player to do truly hateful things. [6]Games that expect a player to participate in sexual assault, torture, or child abuse spoil the reputation of the game industry as a whole.

(Adapted from *Game Design and Development* by Ernest Adams and Andrew Rollings)

Direct Quotation

A **direct quotation** uses the exact words of a source. The direct quotation matches the original source word for word. Place quotation marks at the beginning and end of the information that you have quoted.

"Games that expect a player to participate in sexual assault, torture, or child abuse spoil the reputation of the game industry as a whole."

Some writers think that using lots of direct quotations is a good way to add sources to a research paper. However, quoting the words of others does not show readers that you took the time to understand your sources and connect others' ideas to your own. Also, adding a large number of direct quotations to make a paper long enough is a technique that will not fool your instructor. Here are some instances when direct quotations are appropriate:

- To give evidence that supports a point
- To give a definition, a theory, or a law
- To give an example
- To emphasize someone's opinion
- To add the ideas of an expert

Paraphrase

A **paraphrase** uses your own words to rewrite the words or ideas of your source. A paraphrase keeps the meaning of the source. The length of the paraphrase should be about the same length as the part that you are paraphrasing, but the paraphrase expresses the ideas of the source using your own writing style and vocabulary. You do not use quotation marks with a paraphrase.

Paraphrasing is a good way to use source material. It shows that you understand the subject and that you are a good critical reader and thinker.

Use paraphrases in these instances:

- When you want to make information easier to understand
- When you do not need the exact words, just the idea

In order to write a paraphrase, you need to understand the source and be able to put it in your own words. To write an effective paraphrase, follow these steps:

- Read the passage as many times as necessary until you understand it.
- Set the passage aside and write your paraphrase.
- Check your version with the original passage to make sure that the selection is in your words and writing style. Follow the same order of details as the original.
- Be sure that you have not added your own ideas or opinions.

Summary

A **summary** uses your own words to write the main point of a source. It leaves out examples and explanations. A summary is about one-third as long as your source.

Summarizing is another good way to use source material. It shows that you are a critical reader and thinker. Use summaries when you want to give the main point(s) of a selection.

In order to write a summary, you need to understand the source, find the main points, and put them in your own words. To write an effective summary, follow these steps:

- Read the passage as many times as necessary until you understand it.
- Find the main points.
- Write the main points in your own words.
- Check your version with the original passage to make sure that the selection is in your words and writing style.
- Be sure that you have not added your own ideas or opinions.

Writing Reminder.
To learn more about the process of writing summaries, see Chapter 16.

ACTIVITY Practice Paraphrasing, Summarizing, and Quoting

17.4   With a partner or on your own, read the following passage, which was taken from the textbook *Crossroads* by Elizabeth F. Barkley, a multicultural study of America's popular music, page 280. Then answer the questions that follow.

---

turntable a piece of equipment used in record players and having a flat, round surface that turns the record around while it is being played

[1]Hip hop was originally used to refer to the background music for rap. [2]Several techniques developed to make this background music more interesting. [3]For example, an early technique called "scratching" involved playing a record on a **turntable** but changing the direction of rotation back

and forth rapidly to create a rhythmic beat. [4]A variation was to use a second turntable to play the same record straight through while one scratched the record in a different rhythm on the first turntable. [5]In addition to "scratching," another technique used multiple turntables to insert sections from one recording into another called "cutting." [6]A related technique was to move between recordings. [7]If the recordings had different tempos or speeds, the player used a mechanism that controlled the speed to keep a constant beat pattern to blend the different songs. [8]These are just some of the techniques that evolved to create the background music.

(Adapted from *Crossroads* by Elizabeth F. Barkley)

1. Write a summary of the passage.

   _____

   _____

2. Make sentence 5 a direct quotation.

   _____

   _____

3. Paraphrase sentence 3.

   _____

   _____

   _____

Adding Source Information and Giving Credit

LO 5 **Cite the sources you use in your paper.**

Now that you have taken notes in the appropriate forms of direct quotations, paraphrases, and summaries, you are ready to add them to your paper. When you add your notes, you need to give credit to the authors to show that you have borrowed their ideas.

The Modern Language Association (MLA) requires you to record your sources in two ways: within the paper and at the end of the paper. In this section you will learn how to document your sources within the paper.

TIPS | **Identifying Common Knowledge**

Some information that is generally known and accepted by most people, not just experts, does not need to be cited. This information is considered **common knowledge.** Examples of common knowledge are dates of holidays, names of presidents, and capitals of states or countries. When in doubt, document the source.

Giving Credit to Your Sources

When you use a source in your paper, you must give a brief citation for it to show that you have borrowed the idea. This is called an **in-text citation.** You use an in-text citation each time you quote, paraphrase, or summarize any source.

An in-text citation usually includes the name of the author(s) and the page number of the source where the original information is located. Some sources do not have authors or pages, so an alternative must be used.

Using a Signal Phrase A good way to introduce a source is to use a signal phrase. A **signal phrase** is a phrase, clause, or sentence that leads into your source material. It lets readers know that the idea that is presented is not yours. A signal phrase includes the name of the author(s) and indicates where the source comes from followed by a verb. You may also include the author's credentials to show that he or she is an expert. Here is an example of a signal phrase that introduces a paraphrase:

AUTHOR	AUTHOR'S CREDENTIALS	VERB

Dr. Robin M. Kowalski, a psychology professor at Clemson University, explains that cyberbullying and schoolyard bullying are not the same and that the people who participate in each type are not the same group.

Using the same verb in your signal phrase, such as *states*, is repetitious and uninteresting. Instead, choose a verb that shows the author's point of view. The following chart gives some examples of verbs that match different points of view:

Neutral	Shows Opposition	Agrees	Suggests or Implies	Questions
comments	argues	admits	concludes	asks
describes	complains	agrees	implies	inquires
explains	disagrees		predicts	questions
illustrates	insists		speculates	
observes			suggests	
points out				
reports				
says				
shows				
thinks				
writes				

MLA Format for In-Text Citations

An in-text citation includes the name of the author(s) and the page(s) of the source. If the source does not have an author or page, other information is used. The following are just a few examples.

MLA Format for In-Text Citations	
Author's name in sentence	Carmen Gentile reported that high school senior Katherine Evans was suspended for writing negative statements about her English teacher on Facebook (A20).
	*A20 refers to section A, page 20 of a print newspaper.
Author's name in parentheses	Evans fought her suspension for cyberbullying by suing the principal of her school (Gentile A20).

Source with no author	When adults are involved in cyberbullying, it is called cyberstalking or cyberharassment ("What Is Cyberbullying?").
Source with no page numbers Many Internet sources do not have page numbers.	"Cyberbullying refers to the new, and growing, practice of using technology to harass, or bully, someone else" (McDowell).

More examples can be found in the most recent *MLA Handbook for Writers of Research Papers* or on reputable websites.

ACTIVITY   Practicing Giving Credit to Sources

17.5   With a partner or on your own, use your answers for Activity 17.4 and add in-text citations for the summary, direct quotation, and paraphrase. The passage was on page 280 of Barkley's book.

1. _____

_____

_____

2. _____

_____

3. _____

_____

Roxanne's Adding and Documenting Sources in the Text of Her Paper Using her note cards, Roxanne added her paraphrases, summaries, and direct quotations into her paper. She made sure that her source information was not plagiarized and that it was accurate. As she added the information, she followed the MLA in-text citations guidelines.

Listing Sources: MLA Works Cited

LO 6 **Prepare a Works Cited list for all of the sources referred to in your paper using Modern Language Association (MLA) style.**

Placed at the end of your paper, the **Works Cited** is a list of all of the sources you referred to in your paper. The in-text citations in your paper give readers a small amount of information about each of the sources, but the Works Cited list gives them the full publication information for each source. If readers want to find the publication information about a source you used in your paper, they can turn to the Works Cited list, which is the last page of your paper.

You may have read other sources while doing your research but later decided not to use them. You do not need to list any of the sources that you did not refer to in your paper.

The Modern Language Association (MLA) has specific guidelines for where to put the Works Cited, how to order the sources on the Works Cited list, and how to format the information for each source.

Placement of the Works Cited

The list of the works you have cited is the last page of your paper. If possible, make your list before you add your in-text citations so you will know what information to put in them. Roxanne's Works Cited list is shown on page 347.

- Begin the Works Cited list on a new page.
- Number the page as the next page of your paper. For example, if the paper ends on page 3, then the Works Cited list will begin on page 4.
- Center the title, Works Cited, one inch from the top of the page. Capitalize only the first letter of each word: Works Cited. Use the same size font as the rest of the paper. Do not underline, boldface, or use quotation marks for the Works Cited title.

Order of the Sources in the Works Cited

- List the sources in alphabetical order by the author's last name. Do not number the sources.
- If the source does not have an author, alphabetize by the first major word in the title. Ignore *A, An,* or *The,* if any of those are the first word of the title. For example, for the article, "The Danger of Cyberbullies," alphabetize by "Danger."
- Type the first line of each source beginning at the left-hand margin. If you need more than one line for all of the information about the source, indent the second and all other additional lines five spaces (½ inch).
- The publication information for each source consists of various parts. Each part has a punctuation mark. Put one space after each punctuation mark.
- Double-space the entire list. Do not double-space twice between entries.

Common Works Cited Formats

MLA style for the most common sources and their Works Cited forms is explained in this section. These types are grouped into categories: print sources, electronic sources, and other sources. No matter what type of source you use, there are common rules for listing authors' names and for capitalizing titles.

Listing Authors in Any Source The name of the author is always the first piece of information you give for the source unless the source does not have an author. Below are models for one author, two or three authors, or four or more authors.

One author	Last name, First name.	Willard, Nancy E.
Two or three authors	Last name, First name, and First name Last name.	Hinduja, Sameer, and Justin W. Patchin.
Four or more authors	Last name, First name, et al.	Corbett, Patrick E., et al.

If the author has a middle initial, place it after the first name. A suffix like *Jr.* or a roman numeral appears after the first name and middle initial if there is one (e.g., Martin, John D., III.)

Capitalizing Titles in Any Source   The MLA has specific rules for capitalizing titles. To simplify the rules, here are the words that are NOT capitalized when they are in the middle of a title:

- Articles: *a, an, the*
- Prepositions: e.g., *in, of, to, on, between*
- Coordinating conjunctions: *and, but, or, nor, for, so, yet*
- The "to" in infinitives: *How to Stop Cyberbullying*

Print Sources

Print sources include books, magazines, newspapers, and journals that are not online.

Books (Print)

Author Name(s). *Title of Book.* Place of publication: Publisher, year of publication. Medium of publication.

Example

Hinduja, Sameer, and Justin W. Patchin. *Bullying beyond the School Yard.* Thousand Oaks: Corwin, 2009. Print.

If the book does not have an author, begin with the title of the book. Write the title in italics. Include the subtitle if the book has one. Leave out *A, An,* or *The* before the publisher's name. If the publisher has more than one name, list the first name only. Leave out *Inc., Press, Publishers, Books,* etc.

Essay, Short Story, or Other Work in an Anthology (Print)

A work in an anthology gives information about the work being cited, the editor of the anthology, and the publication information of the anthology.

Author Name(s). "Title of part of book being cited." *Title of Book.* Ed. Editor's name. Place of publication: Publisher, year. Page numbers. Medium of Publication.

Example

Hoff, Diane, and S. N. Mitchell. "Gender and Cyberbullying: How Do We Know What We Know?" *Truths and Myths of Cyber-bullying: International Perspectives on Stakeholder Responsibility and Children's Safety.* Eds. Andrew Churchill and Shaheen Shariff. New York: Lang, 2009. 76–188. Print.

For more than one editor, write Eds.

Encyclopedia or Dictionary

Author name(s). "Title of entry." *Title of Encyclopedia or Dictionary.* Edition. Year of publication. Medium of publication.

If no author is provided, begin with the title of the entry. The edition may not be stated. If the reference is specialized, such as *Encyclopedia of Criminology*, give full publication information.

Example

Humphreys, R. A. Laud. "Crime and Criminology." *Encyclopedia Americana.* 2009 ed. Print.

Magazine Articles

Author Name(s). "Title of Article." *Name of Magazine* Day Month Year: Page number(s). Medium of publication.

Example

Groc, Isabelle. "Taunting with Tech: Cyberbullying Is on the Rise in America's Schools." *PC Magazine* 4 Sept. 2007: 20. Print.

Newspaper Articles

Author Name(s). "Title of Article." *Name of Newspaper* Day Month Year, ed.: page number(s). Medium of publication.

Example

Gentile, Carmen. "Student Fights Record of Cyberbullying." *New York Times* 8 Feb. 2009, late ed.: A20. Print.

- Leave out *The* in the title of the newspaper. If the city is not included in the name of a local newspaper, add the city in brackets.
- Abbreviate all months except for May, June, and July. If the edition is listed, place a comma after the year and then provide the edition. If no edition is listed, leave it out.
- Include all of the page numbers of the article. If the article is not printed on consecutive pages, write only the first page number and a + sign and follow it with a period. Sometimes the article is in a section of the newspaper that has its own page numbers. Write the section and page number like this: B1.

Scholarly Journal Articles

Author Name(s). "Title of Article." *Name of Journal.* Volume Number.Issue Number (year of publication): Page number(s). Medium of publication.

Example

Kowalski, Robin M. "Cyber Bullying: Recognizing and Treating Victim and Aggressor." *Psychiatric Times* 25.11 (2008): 45. Print.

- Some journals have volume and issue numbers, and some have only volume numbers. Write the year of publication in parentheses followed by a colon.
- Include all of the page numbers of the article. If the article is not printed on consecutive pages, write only the first page and a + sign followed by a period.

Electronic Sources

Electronic sources include information published on the Internet. These sources might be websites or online databases.

Basic Website Sources Web publications can be challenging to document. Web pages often have many links, making it hard to figure out where one ends and another begins.

Author Name(s). "Title of Web Page." *Title of Website.* Publisher or sponsor of site, Date of publication, revision, or update. Medium of publication. **Date of access.**

Example

"Cyberbullying." *StopBullying.gov.* U. S. Department of Health Resources and Services Administration, n.d. Web. 20 Nov. 2013.

- Give the name of the author, compiler, editor, narrator, etc., if available. If no author is given, begin with the title.
- Sometimes the title of the web page is the same as the title of the overall website. If they are the same, put quotation marks around the name of the page and omit the name of the website.
- The publisher or sponsor could be an educational institution, a company, or a nonprofit organization. You can usually find it at the bottom of the home page. If not available, write N.p.
- Write the day, month, and year or the most recent update of the publication. The date is often listed at the bottom of the web page. If there is only a copyright date or year, write that. If nothing is available, write n.d.
- Date of access is the date you found it on the web. Write the day, month, and year (31 Dec. 2013).

Online Databases If your source came from a library database or subscription service, follow the guidelines for the print source (book, magazine, newspaper, journal), and after that, give information about the database you used.

Example

Mishna, Faye, Alan McLuckie, and Michael Saini. "Real-world Dangers in an Online Reality: A Qualitative Study Examining Online Relationships and Cyber Abuse." *Social Work Research* 33.2 (2009): 107+. *Academic One File.* Web. **16 Nov. 2013.**

After giving the information for the print source, add the name of the database in italics, medium of publication (Web.), and date of access.

Additional Common Sources

Other sources you may cite include television or radio shows, films, videos, interviews, or podcasts.

Television or Radio Show

"Title of the episode or segment." *Title of the Program Series.* **Name of network (if any). Call letters, city of the local station (if any), date of broadcast. Medium of reception.**

Example

"Cyberbullying." *The Tyra Banks Show.* **CW. WTVX, West Palm Beach, 4 Feb. 2008. Television.**

Film, Video, DVD

Title. Director. **Distributor. Year of release. Medium.**

Example

Playing It Safe Online. Dir. Anson W. Schloat. **Human Relations Media. 2008. DVD.**

Online Podcast

Speaker(s) if available. "Title of Podcast Episode." *Title of Podcast.* **Publisher or Sponsor, Date of publication or posting. Title of larger site. Medium. Date of access.**

Example

Reynolds, Matthew, Dr. Corrine Fendon, and Marci Hertz. "Electronic Aggression." *Podcasts at CDC*. National Center for Injury Prevention and Control, Division of Violence Prevention. 28 Nov. 2007. Center for Disease Control and Prevention. Web. **6 July 2013.**

Personal Interview

A personal interview is one that you, the researcher, conducted, either in person, on the telephone, or online.

Name of person interviewed. Kind of interview (Personal or Telephone). **Date of interview.**

Example

Williams, Marya. Personal interview. **19 Nov. 2013.**

Roxanne's Works Cited List Roxanne referred to the guidelines and examples in this chapter to provide the publication information for each source that she used in her paper. Her Works Cited on page 347 lists the sources in alphabetical order, double-spaced according to MLA style.

 ACTIVITY Practicing with Works Cited Entries

17.6 The following sources were selected for use in a research paper on cyberbullying. Use the MLA guidelines explained in this section to arrange the publication information for each source in a Works Cited list. Then put the sources in alphabetical order. Write your list in the space provided or on your own paper.

Source: A scholarly journal article in print
The title is "Sticks and Stones Can Break My Bones, but How Can Pixels Hurt Me?" The article was written by Wanda Cassidy, Margaret Jackson, and Karen N. Brown. It was published in 2009 in *School Psychology International*, volume 30, pages 383–402.

Source: A newspaper article on an electronic database
The article was written by Jon Boone in the April 11, 2007, page 2 of the *Financial Times*. The title is "Google Urged to Join Team Tackling Cyber-bullying." The article was retrieved from the *Academic OneFile* database on November 21, 2013.

Source: A book in print.
The book was published in 2007 by Research Press in Champaign, Ill. The author is Nancy E. Willard. The title of the book is *Cyberbullying and Cyber Threats.*

Source: A website.
The article appeared on the CNET News website on August 19, 2009. The title is "Missouri Woman Charged with Cyberbullying" and was written by Lance Whitney. The article was found on the web on November 22, 2013. The sponsor of the site is CBS Interactive, Inc.

Works Cited

_____

_____

_____

_____

_____

_____

_____

_____

MLA Model Research Essay

The following is Roxanne's research essay using the MLA style.

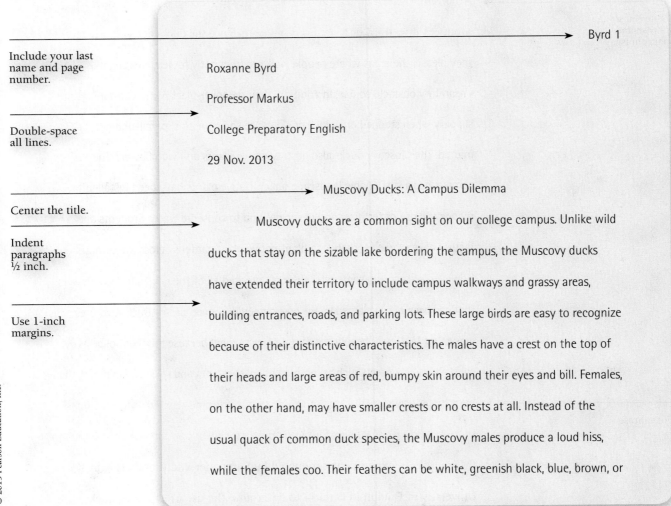

Byrd 1

Include your last name and page number.

Double-space all lines.

Center the title.

Indent paragraphs ½ inch.

Use 1-inch margins.

Roxanne Byrd

Professor Markus

College Preparatory English

29 Nov. 2013

Muscovy Ducks: A Campus Dilemma

Muscovy ducks are a common sight on our college campus. Unlike wild ducks that stay on the sizable lake bordering the campus, the Muscovy ducks have extended their territory to include campus walkways and grassy areas, building entrances, roads, and parking lots. These large birds are easy to recognize because of their distinctive characteristics. The males have a crest on the top of their heads and large areas of red, bumpy skin around their eyes and bill. Females, on the other hand, may have smaller crests or no crests at all. Instead of the usual quack of common duck species, the Muscovy males produce a loud hiss, while the females coo. Their feathers can be white, greenish black, blue, brown, or

Byrd 2

a combination of these colors. Because of the female's ability to lay eight to ten

eggs three times a year, their population has increased to the point that the

ducks have become a nuisance to students, staff, and visitors. The Muscovy ducks

should be relocated because they spoil the campus environment, are aggressive

toward people, and get in the way of cars, causing accidents.

The college takes pride in keeping the campus clean and green; however,

the Muscovy ducks have spoiled the campus environment. First of all, the daily

manure production of the freely roaming ducks creates a hazardous mess.

Note the signal phrase and paraphrase.

According to Joe Schaefer of the University of Florida, one adult duck

produces one-third of a pound of manure. Since the ducks defecate wherever

they please, the areas where people walk are frequently fouled, creating an

unsanitary obstacle course. In addition, their greenish-black, watery droppings are

slippery when stepped on, which could cause someone to slip, fall, and get

injured. The Muscovy ducks also destroy native plants and wild flowers. The

campus has a sustainable landscape policy. Native plants have been installed to

reduce the use of fertilizer and pesticides and to conserve water. Students and

faculty have worked together to plant native plant gardens across the campus.

However, last month, some of the ducks uprooted all of the rare, native wildflowers

that had been newly planted by the environmental science classes. Duck advocates

argue that Muscovies benefit the campus environment because they control pests by

eating bugs and insects such as mosquitoes, roaches, ants, and spiders, eliminating the

Paraphrase

need for pesticide use. In fact, Muscovies were originally called "Musco Ducks"

because they were known for controlling mosquito populations on farms

(Maynard). An experiment conducted by Surgeoner and Glofcheskie at the

University of Guelph in Ontario to determine the use of Muscovy ducks

to control flies on farms showed that "ducks are better than flypaper"

Paraphrase with quotation

("Waiter, There's a Duck"). However, the campus is not a farm, and insect control

is less of a problem than the destruction of the beauty and cleanliness of the

campus.

Not only do the Muscovy ducks spoil the campus environment, but also

Paraphrase

they are aggressive toward people. When people feed them on a regular basis,

ducks come to expect being fed and can become aggressive (Johnson and

Paraphrase and quotation

Hawk). **Sprott and Mazzotti point out that the ducks who are used to being**

fed by humans lose their natural fears and can "chase, hiss, and peck at the

hapless human." Because some duck-loving students and staff regularly feed the

ducks, they think all people will do the same. As a result, they boldly beg for food in a

way which frightens students, staff, and visitors. For instance, when someone sits

outside on a bench to eat a snack or to socialize with other students, groups of

hissing, snorting ducks rush toward and gather around that person, pushing their

beaks against the individual's legs to beg for a handout. On one occasion, a duck

jumped on my friend's lap while she was snacking on some chips. The duck pecked at

her face, and in an attempt to get a chip, bit her on the lip. Duck supporters claim

that Muscovy ducks are friendly birds and that people misinterpret the ducks'

intentions. Those who have been attacked by a Muscovy duck would heartily disagree.

The most important reason for relocating the Muscovy ducks is that they

get in the way of cars and cause accidents. Unaware of the danger, the ducks tend

to roost wherever they please, which include campus roads and parking spaces. For

instance, they frequently sit in empty or occupied parking spaces, preening their

feathers or sleeping. When students arrive for class, they are focused on hunting

for available parking spaces, not for ducks that may be in those spaces. If a duck is

lucky enough to avoid its demise in this situation, it may not be able to avoid being

run over on the roads. During peak class times, traffic builds on the two narrow roads used as entrances and exits to the campus. The Muscovies also use these roads to waddle from the lake to the campus. On a good day for the ducks, kind-hearted drivers stop to ensure that the ducks get across safely; however, the wait for them to complete their slow journey across the road causes a huge backup of impatient student drivers. Not all duck crossings end successfully, unfortunately. For example, last semester, a student driver stopped short to avoid hitting a duck while exiting the campus and caused a multiple car collision. Those who support the ducks' right to live on campus believe that drivers should watch out for ducks in parking spaces and on the roads. If the ducks were relocated to a safe place, they would have a better chance of survival, and drivers would not have to be concerned about harming them while driving.

Paraphrase

Paraphrase

Paraphrase

The Muscovy ducks are a non-native species, originally imported to the United States from South and Central America to be raised as a source of food. They were also released into canals and lakes by various organizations, businesses, and residents for ornamental purposes (Schaefer). Because they are not native to any state, Muscovies cannot be protected by any state or federal law, according to the federal Migratory Bird Treaty Act ("Nuisance Muscovy Ducks"). For example, in Florida, they cannot be released into the wild because they can transmit disease to native water birds. The only possible solution is to move them to a captive environment where they cannot escape and wander into the wild or public waters (Schaefer). Therefore, in order to prevent the ducks from spoiling the campus environment, being aggressive toward people, and causing accidents, the Muscovy ducks on campus should be relocated to a place where they can be confined and cared for by individuals interested in either raising them for food or as pets.

Byrd 5

Works Cited

Johnson, Steven Albert, and Michelle Hawk. "Florida's Introduced Birds: Muscovy Duck."

EDIS. University of Florida IFAS Extension, 12 Mar. 2009. Web. 29 Aug. 2013.

Maynard, Pam. "Raising Chickens and Poultry for Home Pest Control." *Grit.com.*

Ogden Publications, May/June 2009. Web. 21 Nov. 2013.

"Nuisance Muscovy Ducks." *MyFWC.com.* Florida Fish and Wildlife Conservation

Commission, 2009. Web. 21 Nov. 2013.

Schaefer, Joe. "Domestic Duck Problems in Urban Areas." *EDIS.* University of Florida

IFAS Extension, Mar. 1999. Web. 29 Oct. 2013.

Sprott, Patricia, and Frank J. Mazzotti. "Bird Attacks." *Florida Animal Control*

Association. Florida Animal Control Association, June 1991. Web. 15 Aug. 2013.

"Waiter, There's a Duck in My Soup." *Economist* Nov. 1989: 101. *Academic One File.*

Web. 29 Oct. 2013.

Begin Works Cited on a new page, and center the title.

Indent each line after the first line ½ inch.

Double-space the entire list.

Writing Assignments

Add Research to an Essay

Enhance a paper you have already written by adding research. Choose a paper that you have written this term that has a topic that can be researched. Read through the paper to find places where you could add details from outside sources. Think about adding statistics, expert opinions, facts, and examples. Add the sources to your paper using the MLA format and include a Works Cited list.

Reading and Writing across the Curriculum: Criminal Justice

Cybercrime, sometimes called *computer crime* or *information-technology crime,* uses computers and computing technology as tools in crime commission. Computer criminals manipulate the information stored in computer systems in ways that violate the law.

(From *Criminal Justice Today* by Frank Schmalleger)

Research and write a paragraph or an essay giving examples of *one* type of cybercrime. Find three (or more) reliable sources, take notes, add the information to your paper, and create a Works Cited list. Some examples of cybercrime are credit card fraud, identity theft, child pornography, indecent chat-room behavior, software and media piracy, website vandalism, release of viruses and worms, spam marketing, invasion of privacy, cyber-spying, and most forms of hacking.

Writing Topics for Researching

For further practice with research and creating a Works Cited list, choose one of the following topics:

General Topics

aviation and airport security
paranormal phenomena
impact of social networking sites
alternative energy
racism

Writing across the Curriculum Topics

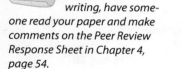

Peer Review Reminder. For feedback on your writing, have someone read your paper and make comments on the Peer Review Response Sheet in Chapter 4, page 54.

Biology: endangered species
Journalism: the future of print media, such as newspapers
Education: standardized testing
Pharmacy: performance-enhancing drugs in sports
Psychology: mass shootings

English Success Tip: Signaling the Author

When you are introducing the author and title of someone's work, avoid the following common errors:

1. Drop the "in" and the "it."

Incorrect: In the passage by Elizabeth F. Barkley, it explains how country music came from the folk music of the rural American South and over the years was shaped by the commercial entertainment industry.

Correct: The passage by Elizabeth F. Barkley explains how country music came from the folk music of the rural American South and over the years was shaped by the commercial entertainment industry.

2. Avoid repetition.

Repetitious: In the passage "Country Music in a Historical and Social Context" by Elizabeth F. Barkley, the author explains how country music came from the folk music of the rural American South and over the years was shaped by the commercial entertainment industry.

Correct: In the passage "Country Music in a Historical and Social Context," Elizabeth F. Barkley explains how country music came from the folk music of the rural American South and over the years was shaped by the commercial entertainment industry.

Building Powerful Sentences

18 Simple Sentences

Theme: *Business*

LO 1 Define a simple sentence.

What Is a Simple Sentence?

A **simple sentence** is a group of words that has at least one subject and one verb; together they express a thought that has a clear beginning and ending. The words are arranged in a pattern that makes a statement, asks a question, or gives an instruction.

In grammar, the word *simple* gives the idea that the sentence is short and at a low academic level. However, simple sentences can be long or short and can have many details.

Simple is a grammar term used to describe a sentence with at least one subject and verb. The subjects are orange and the verbs are blue.

The manager plans.

The manager and the employees plan.

The manager plans and organizes.

The manager and the employees plan and organize.

Yesterday, during the weekly meeting, the manager and the employees developed a new strategy for the sales staff and divided the staff into teams.

Subjects and Verbs in Context

In the following passage about workplace design, the subjects are orange and the verbs are blue.

Some **workplaces have** a large number of workers in a very large space. Human factors **psychologists,** those who combine psychology and product design, **call** the large space an open design. Sometimes there **are partitions** or other **kinds** of barriers between workers. With this kind of arrangement, **organizations can use** large spaces flexibly. **Individual workspaces can be rearranged**. Further, **open designs are** cheaper.

> They **have** few walls and doors. However, many **workers do** not **like** open designs. For one thing, these **workplaces are** noisier than those with individual workspaces. **Workers** sometimes **complain** about interruptions and lack of privacy. Moreover, a private **office is perceived** as a status symbol. **Employees** in management positions **expect** to have rooms with doors. **They want** privacy for meetings with employees. Consequently, most **open designs include** at least a few private spaces, usually managers' offices and conference rooms.
>
> (Adapted from *The World of Psychology* by Samuel E. Wood et al.)

Finding the Subject

LO 2 Identify the subject(s) of a sentence.

The **subject** tells who or what the sentence is about. The subject is usually a noun or pronoun.

Noun Subjects

Singular or Plural Subjects can be **singular,** meaning one, or **plural,** meaning more than one.

> **Singular subject:** An employee is happier in a healthy work environment.
> **Plural subject:** Employees are happier in a healthy work environment.

Grammar Reminder.
A **noun** *is the name of a person, place, thing, idea, or activity. For more information about nouns, see Chapter 26.*

Compound Subjects Subjects can be compound. A compound subject consists of two nouns connected with any of these words: ***and, or, either . . . or, neither . . . nor,*** or ***not only . . . but also.***

> Work responsibilities ***and*** child-care duties often cause stress.
> ***Either*** my health ***or*** my job performance can be affected.
> ***Neither*** my boss ***nor*** my teachers understand my child-care problems.

Noun Subjects Ending in *-ing* Some subjects end in *-ing* and look like verbs. They are called **gerunds,** which act as nouns.

> Working in a large company gives me good experience.

Numbers, Fractions, Percentages, and Money Amounts Amounts can be the subject of a sentence.

> Ninety-five percent of workplace desks and chairs can be adjusted for comfort.
> Forty dollars was deducted from my paycheck for health care.

PRACTICE Identifying Noun Subjects

18.1   Identify the noun subjects in each of the following sentences. To find the noun subject, ask who or what is or does something.

EXAMPLE: Interstate banking is a fairly new development.
1. The government passed a law for interstate banking in 1994.
2. Interstate banking is the operation of banks or branches across state lines.

Grammar Reminder.
*A **pronoun** is a word that is used in place of a noun. For more information about pronouns, see Chapter 25.*

3. Government agencies regulate these banks.
4. Thirty percent is the most business an interstate bank can control per state.
5. Deposits and credit services must be offered to meet the needs of the community.

Pronoun Subjects

Personal Pronouns Personal pronouns refer to a specific noun.

I	you	he	she	it	we	they

He has his own computer workstation.

Possessive Pronouns Possessive pronouns show ownership.

mine	yours	his	hers	its	ours	theirs

Mine is the last workstation in the row.
Hers is the office on the left with the large window.

Indefinite Pronouns **Indefinite pronouns** refer to nouns that are not named or specific.

all	each, each one	more	one
another	either	most	other, others
any	everybody	much	several
anybody	everyone	neither	somebody
anyone	everything	nobody	someone
anything	few	no one	something
both	many	nothing	such

Everyone in the office stayed late today.
Most of the workers earned overtime pay.

Compound Pronouns A compound pronoun subject consists of two pronouns connected with any of these words: ***and, or, either . . . or, neither . . . nor, or not only . . . but also.***

He ***and*** I always prepare the meeting agenda.

PRACTICE **Identifying Pronoun Subjects**

18.2   Identify the pronoun subjects in each of the following sentences. To find the pronoun subject, ask who or what is or does something.

EXAMPLE: Everyone can benefit from electronic banking.
1. You and others should know about changes to payment by check.
2. Eventually, most will be replaced in banks by electronic images.
3. They will use a substitute check for payment.
4. All of us should appreciate the amount of time and energy saved by the process.
5. No one will have much time to put money in an account to cover a check.

Identifying Prepositions and Prepositional Phrases

LO 3 **Identify prepositional phrases.**

Knowing how to recognize prepositions and prepositional phrases makes finding the subject of a sentence easier because the subject is never in a prepositional phrase.

Prepositions

A **preposition** is a word that shows time, place, or direction. The following is a list of the most commonly used prepositions.

Commonly Used Prepositions				
aboard	at	down	off	toward
about	before	during	on	under
above	behind	except	onto	underneath
across	below	for	out	up
after	beneath	from	outside	upon
against	beside	in	over	with
along	besides	inside	past	within
amid	between	into	since	without
among	beyond	like	through	
around	by	near	throughout	
as	concerning	of	to	

Prepositional Phrases

Prepositions most often appear in prepositional phrases. Prepositional phrases add information to a noun or a verb. A **prepositional phrase** is a group of words that begins with a preposition and ends with a noun or a pronoun. It does not have a subject or a verb. The noun or pronoun at the end of the prepositional phrase may have words in front of it such as articles (*a, an, the*) or adjectives.

A sentence can have more than one prepositional phrase. You can find a prepositional phrase anywhere in a sentence. Sometimes one prepositional phrase comes right after another.

> Five employees walked **into the manager's office.**
> They brought their reports **with them.**
> They wrote their reports **about recycling.**

Prepositional Phrase or Infinitive. The word **to** is sometimes used with the simple form of a verb. This is called an **infinitive**. The infinitive is not a prepositional phrase.

Infinitive: Employees are not permitted **to make** personal phone calls during business hours.

The infinitive is not a verb, so it will not have a verb ending (*–s, –es, –ed, –ing*).

> Employees are not permitted to ~~makes~~ make personal phone calls.

The preposition *for* is not used before the infinitive:

> Employees are not permitted ~~for~~ to make personal phone calls during business hours.

PRACTICE   Identifying Prepositional Phrases

18.3   Identify the prepositional phrases in the following sentences.

EXAMPLE: McDonald's has become an icon ⌐of the fast food industry.⌐

1. McDonald's has lost its competitive edge at home and in other countries.

2. Many of its stores are outdated.

3. Concerns about health have driven customers away from Big Macs and French fries.

4. McDonald's has had to expand into foreign markets, especially in Europe and Asia.

5. To appeal to consumers in foreign countries, McDonald's serves popular local foods like salmon sandwiches in Scandinavia and beer in Germany.

PRACTICE   Writing Sentences with Prepositional Phrases

18.4   Write ten sentences that describe the office workers in the photograph shown here. Use at least one prepositional phrase in each sentence. Underline all of your prepositional phrases.

Finding the Verb

LO 4 **Identify the verb(s) of a sentence.**

A **verb** gives information about the subject by expressing what the subject does (the action) or what the subject is (a state of being). The three kinds of verbs are action, linking, and helping.

Grammar Reminder.
A **verb** *is a word or word group that expresses action, movement, or mental condition or state. See Chapters 22, 23, and 24 for more on verbs.*

Action Verbs

An **action verb** expresses what the subject of the sentence does or did. The action can be a physical or mental activity. Most verbs in English are action verbs.

> Franz decorated his office with family photos and his college diploma.
>
> Jen arranges her files in alphabetical order.
>
> The manager makes the schedule for the week on Fridays.

PRACTICE **Identifying Action Verbs**

18.5 Identify the action verbs in the following sentences.

EXAMPLE: A modern cruise ship |carries| an average of 2,000 passengers and 1,000 crew members.

1. Three thousand people create a lot of waste.
2. On a typical day, a ship of this size produces seven tons of solid garbage.
3. The ship dumps fifteen gallons of highly toxic chemical waste and 30,000 gallons of sewage.
4. Cruise ships also collect ballast water while on the ocean.
5. Later they discharge the water, with living things and pollution, in other parts of the world.

(Adapted from *Business Essentials* by Ronald J. Ebert and Ricky W. Griffin)

ballast lo keep a ship stable when it is on the ocean, ships fill a huge tank with water

Linking Verbs

A **linking verb** connects or "links" the subject with a word that describes or renames the subject. The linked information can be a noun, a pronoun, or an adjective. A linking verb does not show action.

> The company is a strong competitor in the automotive industry.
>
> The company is his.
>
> The company became successful.

Learn the linking verbs so that you can recognize them.

am	were	become	look	sound
is	being	feel	remain	taste
are	been	get	seem	turn
was	appear	grow	smell	

TIP | **Some Verbs Have More Than One Job**

Here are some linking verbs that can also do the job of action verbs depending on how they are used in a sentence:

appear	get	look	smell	taste
feel	grow	remain	sound	turn

Linking verb: The computer technician looks tired.
Action verb: The computer technician looks for the problem on the hard drive.

> **PRACTICE**   **Identifying Linking Verbs**
>
> **18.6**   Identify the linking verbs in the following sentences.

1. Attitudes are our beliefs and feelings about ideas, situations, and people.
2. Job satisfaction is an important attitude in the workplace.
3. A satisfied employee seems happy about performing his or her job.
4. Dissatisfied employees appear more stressed out.
5. Job security and fair treatment remain important to employee satisfaction.

Helping Verbs

A **helping verb,** also called an auxiliary verb, is a verb form used with a main verb to express a specific time in a sentence. A helping verb is placed in front of the main action or linking verb. One or more helping verbs may be needed depending on the verb tense being expressed. Together these verbs make a **verb phrase.**

Helping Verbs *Be, Have,* **and** *Do*   *Be,* **have,** and **do** are irregular verbs that have different forms:

Forms of the verb *be:*	am, is, are, was, were, be, being, been
Forms of the verb *have:*	has, have, had
Forms of the verb *do:*	do, does, did

No two companies are organized exactly the same way.

Most businesses have developed organization charts of a company's jobs and structure.

The organization chart does not show the two new jobs in the finance department.

> **TIP**   *Be, do,* and **have** can also function as helping verbs and as main verbs:
> *Have* **as main verb:** Many managers have a large number of employees.
> *Have* **as helping verb:** Many managers have had meetings with their employees this week.

Other Helping Verbs   Other helping verbs are called **modals.** They do not change their forms. They are always placed first in front of other helping verbs and the main verb. Modal helping verbs express necessity, possibility, permission, or ability.

can	may	shall	will
could	might	should	would
must	ought to		

A manager can delegate work to others.

Managers should recognize the benefits of effective delegation.

PRACTICE   Identifying Helping Verbs

18.7   Identify all of the helping verbs in the following sentences.

1. For years now, Southwest Airlines has been flying high in the short-trip, low-fare market.
2. Southwest's emphasis on reliability and customer service had kept the airline virtually unchallenged.
3. Most airlines have not managed to copy the operational success of Southwest.
4. Thanks to David Neeleman, JetBlue has become one of the most profitable new airlines in the United States.
5. David Neeleman had been working at Southwest for a short time, but he was fired.
6. Neeleman had had extensive experience in the airline industry before his job at Southwest.
7. He did copy some of Southwest's strategies and lessons for JetBlue.
8. JetBlue has been filling planes to capacity.

(Adapted from *Business Essentials* by Ronald J. Ebert and Ricky W. Griffin)

Adverbs between Main and Helping Verbs   Adverbs are sometimes placed between a helping verb and action or linking verb. The adverb is not part of the verb. Examples of these adverbs are as follows:

almost	not	only	seldom	usually
always	now	rarely	sometimes	first
never	often	recently	soon	

Gossip in companies can **often** distort information.

Informal groups in the workplace should **not** interfere with employees' work responsibilities.

Office gossip is **not** permitted in our company.

PRACTICE   Identifying Verbs and Adverbs

18.8   Underline the verbs and circle any adverbs that come between the main and helping verbs.

1. The euro was first introduced in 2002.
2. It has now replaced other currencies, such as the German deutsche mark and the French franc.
3. The euro will soon become as important as the dollar and the Japanese yen in international commerce.
4. Companies with international operations must always watch exchange-rate changes.
5. These changes can sometimes affect overseas demand for their products.

Compound Verbs

A compound verb consists of two separate verbs connected by **and** or **or**.

> Agreeable workers have a high level of understanding **and** cooperate well with others.

> A worker with a low level of agreeableness becomes irritable easily **and** is often uncooperative.

PRACTICE **Identifying Compound Verbs**

18.9 Identify the compound verbs in the following sentences.

1. On-the-job training occurs at the work site and happens informally.
2. For example, an employee may explain and demonstrate the use of the photocopier.
3. Off-the-job training is done away from the work site and gives workers a place to study.
4. Educational improvement will give workers more skills and will motivate them to work toward higher-level jobs.
5. Vestibule training is held in a pretend work environment and makes the off-the-job training more realistic.

(Adapted from *Business Essentials* by Ronald J. Ebert and Ricky W. Griffin)

PRACTICE **Identifying Subjects and Verbs**

18.10 Circle the subjects and underline the verbs in the following sentences.

1. Most consumers have participated in a variety of sales promotions.
2. Free samples allow customers to try products without risk.
3. A coupon promotion gives a person savings off regular prices.
4. Premiums are free or reduced-price items, such as pencils or coffee mugs.
5. Low-interest credit cards can be given to consumers in return for buying a product.
6. In addition, consumers may win prizes by entering contests.
7. Displays near checkout counters will often grab customers' attention.

Simple Sentences with Harder-to-Find Subjects and Verbs

Some subjects and verbs may be harder to find, as in sentences with inverted word order, prepositional phrases, commands, and appositives.

Sentences with Inverted Word Order

Not all sentences begin with a subject followed by a verb. Sometimes the subject and verb are inverted; in other words, the subject comes after the verb.

Questions In a question, the subject usually follows the verb or is between a helping verb and a main verb.

> Will you copy these files for me?
>
> Where is the key to the supply room?
>
> Can John unlock the door to the supply room?
>
> Where should we meet?

Sentences Starting with *Here/There* In a sentence starting with *here* or *there*, the subject usually follows the verb. Neither **here** nor **there** can be subjects.

> **There** are two forms of flexible scheduling in the workplace.

TIP	To help find the subject and verb, cross out *here* or *there*. Look for the subject after the verb.
	~~Here~~ is the schedule for the flextime program.

Sentences with Prepositional Phrases

Sentences can begin with one or more prepositional phrases.

> **In the workplace**, work sharing allows two people to share a single full-time job.

One or more prepositional phrases can also be placed between the subject and the verb.

> An increased sense **of freedom and control in flexible schedules** reduces stress.

TIP	To avoid confusing the noun in a prepositional phrase with the subject of the sentence, circle or cross out the prepositional phrases to set them apart from the subject.
	A growing number ~~of United States workers~~ do a large portion of their work by telecommuting.

Commands

A command expresses a direction or instruction. The subject, *you*, is not stated.

> (You) Press the Enter key after inputting the data.

Sentences with Appositives

An **appositive** is a noun or a noun with its modifiers. An appositive explains or identifies the word in front of it.

> **Noun as appositive:** Lowell Karo, **an accountant**, has many clients.
>
> **Noun with modifiers as appositive:** Lowell Karo, **an accountant with many clients**, is very busy during tax season.

> **TIP** To avoid confusing the noun in the appositive with the subject of the sentence, circle or cross it out to set it apart from the subject.
>
> Tania Chen, ~~consultant to a large telecommunications company~~, can choose her own schedule.

PRACTICE Identifying Subjects and Verbs

18.11   Circle the subjects and underline the verbs in the following sentences.

1. Have you ever shopped online?
2. Electronic retailing, also called e-retailing, has become very popular.
3. There are millions of small businesses with their own websites.
4. Through e-retailing, consumers can buy many different kinds of products.
5. In place of traditional mail catalogs, electronic displays give millions of users pages of product information.
6. How does e-retail help the seller?
7. There are no costs for printing and mailing catalogs or advertisements.
8. Use a chat room to talk securely about a product with a service operator.
9. For answers to specific questions, an online shopper can have a one-on-one chat.
10. Also, cybermalls, a collection of business websites, represent a variety of products and stores for online shopping in one place.

MyWritingLab™
Complete this activity
at mywritinglab.com

Review: The Simple Sentence

The following paragraphs contain all simple sentences. Circle the subjects, underline the verbs, and bracket the prepositional phrases in each sentence.

[1]Radio Frequency Identification (RFID) is a powerful new technology. [2]This technology can be used in nearly every civilian industry . [3]One way to use RFID is to track store inventory. [4]An RFID code number is assigned to each item at the time of manufacturing . [5]The code contains information about the item such as the time and place of manufacture and the product's location. [6]The code is stored on an RFID label . [7]The label has a microchip and tiny antenna. [8]That label is attached to a piece of tape and placed on a product . [9]It communicates by radio signals with RFID scanners . [10]The scanner gets the product's information, such as its current location and price. [11]A computer updates the information about the product from stage to stage .

[12]RFID is much faster than barcode scanning. [13]Radio waves from RFID scanners can communicate with many tags at the same time . [14]Barcodes can

only scan one at a time   with laser beams . [15] Imagine a loaded grocery cart under an overhead scanner . [16] That scanner would read all items at the same time . [17] Then, at the checkout stand, an itemized total would be ready for you . [18] The RFID information instantly reorders the items for replacement   in the store .

(Adapted from *Business Essentials* by Ronald J. Ebert and Ricky W. Griffin)

Writing Assignment

Write a paragraph describing a place where you have worked or where business is conducted. Circle the subjects, underline the verbs, and bracket the prepositional phrases.

Joining Ideas Using Compound Sentences

Theme: *Communication*

Learning Objectives

After working through this chapter, you will be able to:

LO 1 Explain what a compound sentence is.

LO 2 Combine two independent clauses to make a compound sentence.

LO 1 Explain what a compound sentence is.

What Is a Compound Sentence?

A **compound sentence** consists of two or more independent clauses that are connected with appropriate connecting words and punctuation. An **independent clause** is a group of words with at least one subject and verb and makes sense on its own. A simple sentence, which you studied in Chapter 18, has one independent clause. In this chapter, you will learn three ways to combine independent clauses to build compound sentences:

COMMA + COORDINATING CONJUNCTION:

I want to improve my verbal skills, so I am taking a human communications course.

SEMICOLON:

I want to improve my verbal skills; I am taking a human communications course.

SEMICOLON + TRANSITION WORD OR PHRASE + COMMA:

I want to improve my verbal skills; therefore, I am taking a human communications course.

Compound Sentences in Context

In the following passage about how the media influences people, the compound sentences are blue. Notice how the compound sentences are connected in three different ways.

[1]Media messages have effects on readers, listeners, and viewers. **[2]Some messages seek to influence people in obvious ways; for example, there are advertisements on television or on the Internet and editorials in the newspaper**. [3]Other media messages use indirect ways through dramas and sitcoms.

[4]Researchers have proposed three theories of media influence. [5]An early theory is called the one-step theory. [6]**The media influences people in one step, for it is direct and immediate**. [7]This theory sees people as passive and easily influenced. [8]Another theory views media influence as a two-step process. [9]**First, the media influences opinion leaders; then, these opinion leaders influence the rest of the people**. [10]The multistep theory is a more current one. [11]The media may influence an individual on a specific issue. [12]**The individual then interacts with others; as a result, they influence the individual to change his or her opinion**.

(Adapted from *Human Communication* by Joseph A. DeVito)

Building Compound Sentences

LO 2 **Combine two independent clauses to make a compound sentence.**

Two or more independent clauses can be connected in three ways: with a comma and coordinating conjunction; with a semicolon; or with a semicolon, a transitional expression, and a comma.

Connect Independent Clauses Using a Comma and a Coordinating Conjunction

Two independent clauses can be connected with **a comma and a coordinating conjunction.**

INDEPENDENT CLAUSE + **,** COORDINATING CONJUNCTION + INDEPENDENT CLAUSE.

Emotions are often heard or seen through words, but a large part of the emotional experience is nonverbal.

A **coordinating conjunction** is a word used to connect two or more words, phrases, or clauses. Here are the seven coordinating conjunctions:

but   or   yet   for   and   nor   so

| TIP | To remember these words, use an acronym like BOYFANS or FANBOYS. These acronyms are made from the first letter of each of the coordinating conjunctions. |

Each of the coordinating conjunctions has a specific meaning. Choose the coordinating conjunction that best expresses the meaning you want to convey.

	Coordinating Conjunctions and Their Uses	
Coordinating Conjunction	Use	Example
for	to give a reason	A person's home decorations are a form of nonverbal communication, for they tell something about that person.
and	to add ideas or to show similarities	Expensive furniture may give the idea of wealth, and the way they match communicates a sense of style.
nor	to show a negative choice	Many teenagers do not choose their own decorations, nor do they choose their own furniture.
but	to show the difference between ideas	Bookcases lining the walls show the importance of reading, but the absence of books may communicate the opposite.
or	to show a choice or alternative	Office furnishings can communicate high status with a mahogany desk and oriental rugs, or they can show lower status with a metal desk and bare floor.
yet	to show an unexpected difference between ideas	People may know nothing about you, yet they will form opinions about you on the basis of room decorations.
so	to show the result	Watching television is important to some people, so they arrange their chairs around their television.

(Sentences adapted from *The Interpersonal Communication Book* by Joseph A. DeVito)

TIP   Place a comma before the coordinating conjunction, not after it.

Incorrect: Bookcases filled with books reveal the importance of reading but, the absence of books may communicate the opposite.

Correct: Bookcases filled with books reveal the importance of reading, but the absence of books may communicate the opposite.

> ### PRACTICE   Identifying Simple and Compound Sentences
>
> **19.1**   For each sentence below, write **S** for any simple sentences and **C** for any compound sentences.

EXAMPLE: Colors can influence our perceptions and behaviors. S

1. Color communication takes place on many levels, and the English language is filled with color symbolism.

2. In the presence of red light, a person's breathing increases, and in the presence of blue light, it decreases.

3. People blink their eyes more with exposure to red light but do not blink more with exposure to blue light.

4. Being "in the red" means a person is in debt, but "being in the black" means a person is making a profit.

5. People described coffee from a yellow can as weak, yet they identified coffee from a brown can as strong and from a red can as rich.

(Adapted from *The Interpersonal Communication Book* by Joseph A. DeVito)

> ### PRACTICE   Using Coordinating Conjunctions in Compound Sentences
>
> **19.2**   For each of the following sentences, give a coordinating conjunction that best expresses the meaning of the sentence. Each conjunction is used one time: *but, or, yet, for, and, nor, so.*

1. Clothing protects people from the weather and from injury in sports, _____ it conceals parts of your body.

2. Clothing also serves as a form of cultural display, _____ it communicates your ethnic group.

3. Jewelry communicates messages about people, _____ men with earrings will be judged differently from men without earrings.

4. People wearing piercings jewelry may wish to communicate their own messages, _____ these messages infer an unwillingness to conform.

5. In a study on attraction, male and female models without glasses were rated positively, _____ the same models with glasses were rated more negatively.

6. Tattoos can communicate the name of a loved one or a symbol of affiliation, _____ they can communicate to the wearers themselves a more adventurous and creative image.

7. Nose-pierced job applicants did not receive high scores on character and trust, _____ were they given high scores on sociability and hirability.

(Adapted from *The Interpersonal Communication Book* by Joseph A. DeVito)

PRACTICE Writing Your Own Compound Sentences

19.3 Study the following photograph of two men applying for a job. Write five compound sentences about what each man communicates by the way he dresses.

Use the coordinating conjunctions *and, but, or, so*, and *yet* one time. Remember to place a comma in front of the coordinating conjunction.

EXAMPLE: One man is wearing baggy jeans, and the other man is wearing suit pants.

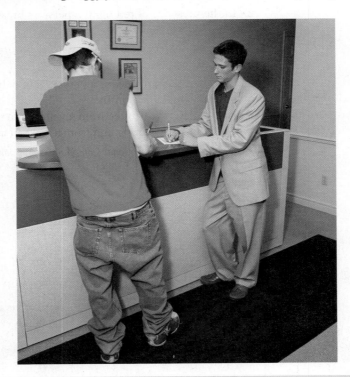

Connect Independent Clauses Using a Semicolon

Another way to connect two independent clauses is to place a semicolon (;) between them.

INDEPENDENT CLAUSE + ; + INDEPENDENT CLAUSE.

At times, a person may say the wrong thing; the most common way to explain it is with an excuse.

TIP A coordinating conjunction should not be placed after the semicolon.

Incorrect: The main reason for making an excuse is to project a positive image; and it also represents an effort to reduce stress.

Correct: The main reason for making an excuse is to project a positive image; it also represents an effort to reduce stress.

PRACTICE Using a Semicolon in Compound Sentences

19.4   Insert the semicolon between each pair of simple sentences.

EXAMPLE: A good excuse can be accepted; it will reduce the negative reaction.

1. Good excuse makers use excuses in moderation bad excuse makers rely on excuses too often.
2. Good excuse makers avoid blaming others blaming is characteristic of bad excuse makers.
3. Accepting responsibility for an excuse will make a person seem more believable those denying responsibility seem less believable.
4. Denial is the worst of all excuses these excuses do not accept responsibility.
5. Effective excuses vary from one culture to another they depend on a culture's values and beliefs.

(Adapted from *The Interpersonal Communication Book* by Joseph A. DeVito)

 PRACTICE Writing Your Own Compound Sentences with Semicolons

19.5   Write five compound sentences about the couple in the following photograph. Use a semicolon to connect each of your two related simple sentences.

EXAMPLE: Marlon wants to apologize; Kara does not want to listen.

Connect Independent Clauses Using a Semicolon and a Transitional Word or Phrase

A semicolon and a transitional word or phrase can also be used to connect two independent clauses.

INDEPENDENT CLAUSE + ; TRANSITION WORD OR PHRASE, + INDEPENDENT CLAUSE.

Physical space is an important factor in interpersonal communication; however, people rarely think about it.

Like coordinating conjunctions, transitional words and phrases have specific meanings. In the sentence above, the transitional word **_however_** shows a contrast between the two independent clauses. Always choose the transition that best expresses the relationship between two independent clauses.

The following chart lists the most commonly used transitional words and phrases according to the relationship they show. If you are not sure of the meaning of the word, look it up in a dictionary and see how it is used in a sentence.

Transitional Words and Phrases and Their Uses

Word or Phrase	Use	Sentence Example
also, in addition, moreover, furthermore, equally important	to add information (meaning *and*)	Some people need personal space; moreover, they do not like people standing too close.
for example, for instance, to illustrate	to give an example	The need for personal spaces varies from culture to culture; for example, people from Latin countries are comfortable standing closer to others.
however, in contrast, on the other hand, otherwise	to make a contrast or give an alternative (meaning *but*)	Older adults need greater personal space; however, younger adults do not.
as a result, consequently, therefore, thus	to express an effect or result (meaning *so*)	The need for personal space changes; therefore, it grows or shrinks depending on the situation.
in fact, in other words	to clarify a point	As children age, their personal space increases; in fact, the older the child, the larger the personal space.
in the same way, likewise, similarly, in comparison	to make a comparison	A doctor keeps a certain distance from a patient; similarly, an instructor keeps a certain distance from students in a classroom.
afterward, in the meantime, later, subsequently	to express time	Edward T. Hall was the first person to study personal space; later, he named this field *proxemics*.

PRACTICE Using Transitional Words and Phrases in Compound Sentences

19.6 Write the transitional word or phrase that best expresses the relationship between each of the following compound sentences. Use each one of these transitions one time: *in fact, for example, in contrast, moreover, therefore*.

EXAMPLE: Throughout your life, you will meet many people ; however, you will develop few friendships.

1. Friendships develop over time _____ they develop in stages.
2. New acquaintances are at one end of the friendship progression _____ intimate friends are at the other.

3. Communications increase as people progress from the initial contact stage to intimate friendship _____ they talk about issues that are closer and closer to their inner self.

4. In a developing friendship, people are torn between revealing and not revealing personal information _____ friendships do not always follow a straight path.

5. Friendships become stable at a comfortable level for each person _____ some will remain casual while others will remain close.

(Adapted from *The Interpersonal Communication Book* by Joseph A. DeVito)

PRACTICE　Punctuating Compound Sentences

19.7　Insert the proper punctuation in each of the following sentences.

networking
meeting people who
might be useful to
know, especially in
your job

EXAMPLE: All forms of communication take place at work; in addition, all forms of relationships may be seen.

1. **Networking** is often viewed as a technique for getting a job however it actually has other uses.

2. Informal networking is sharing information with someone at work or school for example a new student might ask about the best places to eat or about the best English teachers.

3. Formal networking is organized and planned for example formal networks may include professional associations that people join.

4. Networks provide information in fact people can learn about new developments in their field.

5. Many jobs are not advertised therefore people can learn about job openings through networks.

PRACTICE　Combining Independent Clauses

19.8　Combine each pair of sentences below. First, figure out the relationship between the first and second independent clause. Next, choose a transition that best expresses that relationship. Then join the two independent clauses. Remember to punctuate your sentence with a semicolon before the transition and a comma after it.

EXAMPLE:

a. In television shows, workers move in and out of romantic relationships with little difficulty.

b. Real-life office romance can be complicated.

Contrast transition: In television shows, workers move in and out of romantic relationships with little

difficulty; on the other hand, real-life office romance can be complicated.

1a. Some organizations have rules against workplace romantic relationships.
1b. Members can be fired for such relationships.

_____

_____

2a. On the positive side, the work environment seems a perfect place to meet a romantic partner.

2b. Employees work in the same office, have similar training, and spend a great deal of time together.

_____

_____

3a. Office relationships can be tempting.

3b. Most of them fail.

_____

4a. An office relationship may be good for the two individuals.

4b. It may not be good for other workers.

_____

_____

5a. Other workers may be jealous of the romance.

5b. They may make up destructive office gossip.

_____

_____

(Adapted from *The Interpersonal Communication Book* by Joseph A. DeVito)

PRACTICE   **Writing Your Own Compound Sentences**

19.9   Write five compound sentences about the photograph. Use a different transitional expression in each sentence. Be sure to punctuate sentences correctly.

e-card a digital greeting card

EXAMPLE: Someone at Tanya's workplace likes her; furthermore, he emails her romantic **e-cards** every day.

Review: Identifying and Punctuating Compound Sentences

In the following paragraph about communicating with people from other cultures, some of the sentences are simple, and some are compound. The compound sentences are not punctuated correctly.

- Underline the compound sentences.
- Add the correct punctuation.

The first compound sentence has been corrected for you.

¹Learning about other cultures is the best way to prepare for intercultural communication. ²You can see a movie or documentary with a realistic view of the culture, or you can read material about the culture. ³Another way to learn is to read magazines and websites from a particular culture. ⁴Talking with members of the culture will also help; furthermore you can chat in an international chat room. ⁵Being aware of cultural differences will build your cultural sensitivity; in fact cultural sensitivity is important for interpersonal communication. ⁶Without it, there can be no communication between people of different gender, race, or nationality so you need to be mindful of cultural differences.

(Adapted from *The Interpersonal Communication Book* by Joseph A. DeVito)

Writing Assignment

Write a paragraph about the advantages or disadvantages of dating someone with whom you work. Include three compound sentences in your paragraph. Use each of the three methods you learned in this chapter:

- Two independent clauses joined with a comma and coordinating conjunction.
- Two independent clauses joined with a semicolon.
- Two independent clauses joined with a semicolon, a transition word or phrase, and a comma.

20 Joining Ideas Using Complex Sentences

Theme: *Health and Wellness*

Learning Objectives

After working through this chapter, you will be able to:

LO 1 Identify the parts of a complex sentence: the independent clause and dependent clause.

LO 2 Write complex sentences using subordinating conjunctions to begin dependent clauses.

LO 3 Write complex sentences using relative pronouns to begin dependent clauses.

LO 1 **Identify the parts of a complex sentence: the independent clause and dependent clause.**

What Is a Complex Sentence?

A **complex sentence** includes an independent clause and a dependent clause. The independent clause expresses a complete idea, but the dependent clause does not. The dependent clause "depends" on the independent clause for its meaning and is not a complete sentence by itself. Dependent clauses can begin with two types of dependent words: subordinating conjunctions or relative pronouns. These dependent words show the relationship between the independent and dependent clause.

People have become conscious of their lifestyles because the media focuses on health problems.

People who want to make healthy lifestyle choices need to be informed consumers.

Complex Sentences in Context

In the following textbook passage about vegetarianism, the dependent clauses are in green.

The term *vegetarianism* means different things to different people. Strict vegetarians, or *vegans*, avoid all foods of animal origin, including dairy products and eggs. Far more common are *lacto-vegetarians*, **who eat dairy products but avoid flesh foods**. Their diet can be low in fat and cholesterol **if they consume skim milk and other low-fat or non-fat products**. *Ovo-vegetarians* add eggs to their diet, **while *lacto-ovo-vegetarians* eat both dairy products and eggs**. *Pesco-vegetarians* eat fish, diary products, and egg, **whereas *semi-vegetarians* eat chicken, fish, dairy products, and eggs**. Some people **who are in the semi-vegetarian category** prefer to call themselves "non-red meat eaters."

(Adapted from *Access to Health* by Rebecca J. Donatelle)

Building Complex Sentences with Subordinating Conjunctions

LO 2 Write complex sentences using subordinating conjunctions to begin dependent clauses.

One way to build a complex sentence is by starting one of the independent clauses with a subordinating conjunction. Adding the subordinating conjunction changes the independent clause to a dependent clause.

> Our bodies cannot produce certain essential nutrients. We must get them from the foods we eat.

> Because our bodies cannot produce certain essential nutrients, we must get them from the food we eat.

Understanding Subordinating Conjunctions

Subordinating conjunctions are connecting words that you can use to start a dependent clause. They show cause and effect, time, contrast, condition, or location. The following chart explains each of the types of subordinating conjunctions.

Subordinating Conjunctions		
Subordinating Conjunctions	Purpose	Sentence Examples
because, now that, since	**Cause and Effect** gives reasons or results.	Because you are hungry, the brain tells the stomach to churn. You feel hunger pangs since the stomach muscles have nothing to churn.
after, as, as long as, as soon as, before, by the time, every time, once, since, until, when, whenever, while	**Time** tells when.	As you think about food, you begin to produce saliva. Digestion begins when you chew your food.
although, even though, though, while, whereas	**Contrast** shows one idea is in contrast to another.	Although you have just eaten a meal, your stomach takes two to six hours to empty. Some chemical digestion starts in the stomach, whereas most of it occurs in the small intestine.
even if, if, in case, in the event that, only if, so that, unless, whether or not	**Condition** explains that an action can only take place if a certain condition is fulfilled.	Stomach acid will not be released unless you see, smell, or taste food. If some stomach acid flows back up into the esophagus, you may experience heartburn.
where, wherever	**Location** tells where.	Food passes from the stomach to the small intestine where nutrients are absorbed.

PRACTICE   Identifying Subordinating Conjunctions and Dependent Clauses

20.1   Circle the subordinating conjunctions and underline the dependent clauses in each of the following sentences.

EXAMPLE: [Although] *serving size* and *portion* are often used interchangeably, they actually mean very different things.

1. A serving is the recommended amount a person should consume, while a portion is the amount a person chooses to eat at any one time.
2. When most people select a portion, it is usually much bigger than a serving.
3. A serving size of meat, poultry, or fish is three ounces, whereas a serving size of cheese is one ounce.
4. Experts have developed some tips so that people can judge how big a serving size should be.
5. Since most people have trouble visualizing a true serving size, experts suggest relating it to an everyday item.
6. For example, a small baked potato is considered a serving if it is the size of a computer mouse.
7. Imagine a deck of cards to determine a serving of meat, poultry, or fish even though the serving appears to be small.

PRACTICE   Analyzing Complex Sentences

20.2   In each of the sentences, identify the dependent clause and write the kind of relationship between the two clauses:

cause and effect   condition   contrast   time   location

EXAMPLE: When someone eats too quickly or does not chew food thoroughly, he or she may choke. time

1. Unless breathing is restored within minutes, brain damage or death may result. _____

2. In 1974, American surgeon Henry J. Heimlich devised a new method to help choking victims because slapping a person's back did not unblock the airway. _____

3. The Heimlich Maneuver can be performed as long as the victim is conscious. _____

4. A person can perform the Heimlich Maneuver wherever the choking incident occurs. _____

5. The process is carried out so that the foreign object can be removed from the throat to get air flowing. _____

6. Although the procedure is usually used for choking victims, it can also be performed on drowning victims. _____

7. When no one is around to help, you can use the Heimlich Maneuver on yourself. _____

Using Subordinating Conjunctions to Write Complex Sentences

A dependent clause that begins with a subordinating conjunction can often be placed at the beginning or end of the complex sentence as long as the intended meaning of the sentence does not change.

Begin with the independent clause and add the dependent clause.

> The amount of sugar in one's diet can be hard to control because it can be hidden in certain foods.

Begin with the dependent clause and add the independent clause.

> Because it can be hidden in certain foods, the amount of sugar in one's diet can be hard to control.

Punctuating Dependent Word Groups with Subordinating Conjunctions

Apply the following rules for using commas with dependent clauses.

INDEPENDENT CLAUSE + NO COMMA + DEPENDENT CLAUSE.

> Experts recommend eating whole fruit and avoiding fruit products with corn syrup since they are often high in added sugar.

DEPENDENT CLAUSE + , + INDEPENDENT CLAUSE.

> Since they are often high in sugar, experts recommend eating whole fruit and avoiding fruit products with corn syrup.

A comma is not needed after a subordinating conjunction.

Incorrect: Although, proteins in the body are certainly important, carbohydrates give people energy to sustain normal daily activity.

Correct: Although proteins in the body are certainly important, carbohydrates give people energy to sustain normal daily activity.

TIP | Always use a comma before a dependent clause that begins with *while* or *whereas*.
> Simple sugars provide short-term energy, whereas complex carbohydrates provide sustained energy.

 PRACTICE Punctuating Complex Sentences

20.3 Identify the subordinating conjunctions in the following complex sentences. Add commas where they are needed. Some of the sentences are correct.

EXAMPLE: The feeling of anxiety before a test can be useful <u>because</u> it can make you more careful or alert. Correct.

1. When a person's anxiety does not go away and gets worse over time he or she has an anxiety disorder.

2. With an anxiety disorder, the body triggers the person's alarm system even though there is no danger.

3. Although feelings of anxiety are scary they do not hurt the person.

4. Some people have a general feeling of worry whereas others have a sudden attack of panicky feelings.

5. If a person feels worried over personal finances this worry does not mean that the person has an anxiety disorder.

6. Whenever people worry about something for hours every day and cannot sleep or perform usual tasks they are suffering from more than normal anxiety.

7. Men and women are both affected by general anxiety disorder though women are twice as likely to be affected.

PRACTICE   Using Subordinating Conjunctions

20.4   In the following sentences, choose the subordinating conjunction that best expresses the relationship between the two word groups. Use each of the following subordinating conjunctions once.

since	whereas	while	now that
if	when	because	even though

EXAMPLE: <u>Now that</u> the United States is considered one of the fattest nations on Earth, the health of the population is at risk.

1. Obesity is a label used to refer to individuals _____ their body fat is beyond normal for a person based on age, sex, and body type.

2. One way to measure overweight and obesity is a standard height-weight chart, _____ another measurement is the body mass index (BMI) formula, which is based on the relationship of weight to height.

3. Some people, such as lean, muscular athletes, would be considered overweight according to BMI charts _____ these individuals do not have excess body fat.

4. Men's bodies should contain between 11 and 15 percent total body fat, _____ women's bodies should be within a range of 18 to 22 percent body fat.

5. Generally, _____ men exceed 20 percent body fat and women exceed 30 percent body fat, they have slipped into obesity.

6. _____ men's and women's body structures and sex hormones differ, their desirable body fat ranges differ.

7. Too much fat and too little fat are both potentially harmful _____ a certain amount of fat is needed to insulate the body, cushion body parts, and maintain good body functions.

(Adapted from *Access to Health* by Rebecca J. Donatelle)

PRACTICE   Writing Complex Sentences

20.5   The obesity problem in this country has made some people concerned about their weight. Write five complex sentences about the photo shown here. Use a different subordinating conjunction in each sentence. Be sure to write a subject after the subordinating conjunction.

EXAMPLE:

Health professionals are concerned about high rates of obesity because obesity can have a negative effect on health.

Building Complex Sentences with Relative Pronouns

LO 3 Write complex sentences using relative pronouns to begin dependent clauses.

Another way to build a complex sentence is by starting one of the independent clauses with a relative pronoun. Adding the relative pronoun changes the independent clause to a dependent clause. The dependent clause describes the noun or makes it more specific. The relative pronoun shows the reader that the dependent clause refers to the noun it describes.

Athletes must train to increase stamina and muscle strength. Athletes compete in physically strenuous sports.

Athletes who compete in physically strenuous sports **must train to increase stamina and strength.**

Understanding Relative Pronouns

A **relative pronoun** is a word that refers to a noun. When a relative pronoun begins a dependent clause, the clause adds information to the word it refers to.

Relative Pronouns		
Relative Pronoun	Use	Sentence Example
who **whom**	Use **who** or **whom** to refer to people. **Who** is sometimes used to refer to animals possessing special intelligence.	The average adult who does not sweat profusely requires only about one-fourth of a teaspoon of salt per day. People for whom high blood pressure is a problem should cut back on sodium.
that	Use **that** to refer to places, things, ideas, activities, and animals. **That** gives specific information that is necessary to the meaning of the sentence.	The majority of sodium in our diet comes from highly processed foods that contain added sodium to enhance flavor and preserve food.
which	Use **which** to refer to places, things, ideas, activities, and animals. Use **which** for information that is not necessary to the meaning of the sentence.	Examples of high sodium foods which contain several hundred milligrams of sodium per serving are pickles, fast foods, salty snack foods, processed cheeses, smoked meats and sausages, and breads and bakery products.
whose	Use **whose** to show ownership for people, places, things, ideas, activities, animals.	People whose goal is to reduce sodium intake can choose low-sodium or salt-free products.

PRACTICE **Identifying Relative Pronouns and Dependent Clauses**

20.6   In each of the following sentences, circle the relative pronoun and underline the dependent clause. Then draw an arrow to the word that the dependent clause is describing.

EXAMPLE: As of 2002, any food (that) is sold as organic has to meet the criteria set by the U.S. Department of Agriculture under the National Organic Rule.

1. Farmers who label their food 100 percent organic must grow and manufacture their products without the use of added hormones, pesticides, and synthetic fertilizers.

2. Also, a crop that can be called organic cannot have been treated with synthetic products for three years.

3. Organic products appeal to people who are concerned about food safety.

4. They want to avoid non-organic food grown with chemicals that cause cancer, immune system problems, and many other ailments.

5. The market for organics has been increasing by over 20 percent per year, which is five times faster than food sales in general.

6. It is difficult to determine if people who eat only organic food are healthier.

7. Many farmers are choosing organic farming, which is better for the environment.

(Adapted from *Access to Health* by Rebecca J. Donatelle)

Using Relative Pronouns to Write Complex Sentences

Writing complex sentences with a dependent clause that begins with a relative pronoun involves two steps: (1) forming the dependent clause and (2) placing it next to the word it describes in the independent clause.

The dependent clause with relative pronouns follows one of two patterns:

Dependent Clause Pattern	Example Sentence
Pattern 1 RELATIVE PRONOUN + SUBJECT + VERB	Recreational physical activities that you enjoy provide health benefits.
Pattern 2 RELATIVE PRONOUN AS SUBJECT + VERB	Adding more physical movement to your day, which might include parking farther from your destination, can contribute to overall health.

TIP

When forming a dependent clause using pattern 2, remember to take out the subject the pronoun is replacing.

Some **people** can still be physically active and benefit from physical exercise. Some **people** have physical limitations.

Some **people** who ~~**people**~~ have physical limitations can still be physically active and benefit from exercise.

PRACTICE Combining Simple Sentences to Create Complex Sentences

20.7   Combine each pair of sentences into a complex sentence. Use a relative pronoun to change the second sentence into a dependent clause. Underline the dependent clause. Use *who, which, that,* or *whose.*

EXAMPLE: The term *aerobic* describes any type of exercise. The exercise increases heart rate.

The term *aerobic* describes any type of exercise <u>that increases heart rate.</u>

1. A person is described as being in good shape. The person has an above-average aerobic capacity.

_____

2. Aerobic capacity is a term. The term is used to describe the function of the heart, lungs, and blood vessels.

_____

3. The most beneficial aerobic exercises are total body activities. These activities involve all the large muscle groups of the body.

_____

_____

4. There are three main components of an aerobic exercise program. The three components are frequency, intensity, and duration.

_____

_____

5. People will need to vigorously exercise at least three times a week. People want to improve their cardiovascular endurance.

_____

_____

6. A person can make improvements by doing less intense exercise more days a week. A person is a newcomer to exercise.

_____

_____

7. A person should begin at a low intensity and progress slowly. A person's lifestyle has not involved physical activity.

_____

_____

(Adapted from *Access to Health* by Rebecca J. Donatelle)

Using *Who* and *Whom* to Start Dependent Clauses Follow these rules to use *who* and *whom*.

Rule	Sentence Example
whom When the dependent clause has a subject, use *whom*. **WHOM + SUBJECT + VERB**	Dr. Murray E. Jarvik, **whom scientists admired for his contributions to smoking cessation,** helped invent the nicotine patch.
who When the dependent clause does not have a subject, use *who*. **WHO + VERB**	Dr. Murray E. Jarvik, **who helped invent the nicotine patch,** was admired for his contributions to smoking cessation.

PRACTICE **Using *Who* and *Whom***

20.8   In each of the following complex sentences, fill in the blank with **who** or **whom**.

EXAMPLE: Dr. Murray Jarvik, ___who___ was a professor at the University of California, was a leader in the study of how drugs affect human behavior.

1. Jarvik, _____ always wondered why people smoked, discovered that nicotine was the key addictive component in tobacco.
2. Tobacco harvesters, _____ Jarvik and his colleague Jed Rose studied, became sick with green tobacco sickness.
3. The workers _____ became ill were absorbing nicotine from the tobacco through their skin.
4. Their discovery led Jarvik and Rose, _____ realized that small doses of nicotine might help people stop smoking, to invent the nicotine patch.
5. They could not get permission to try the nicotine patch on people _____ they had chosen as testers.
6. Jarvik and Rose, _____ were nonsmokers, decided to try the patch on themselves.
7. The patch gave them the same effects that people _____ smoke experience.
8. Smokers, for _____ the patch was invented, were able to get nicotine patches by prescription in 1992 and over the counter in 1996.

Punctuating Dependent Clauses with Relative Pronouns

To decide whether to use commas or not, you must decide if the dependent clause is essential or nonessential to the meaning of the sentence. Then follow the rules explained in the chart below.

- **Essential** means that the information in the dependent clause is needed to make the noun specific. *That* is generally used to introduce essential dependent clauses although *which* can also be used.
- **Nonessential** means that the information in the dependent clause is not needed because the noun it describes is already specific. The dependent clause adds extra information that could be omitted. *Which* is used to introduce nonessential information.

Dependent Word Group	Comma Rule	Sentence Example
Essential	**No commas** before or after the dependent clause	An echocardiogram is a test that uses sound waves to create a moving picture of the heart.
Nonessential	**Commas** before and after the dependent clause	An echocardiogram, which causes no discomfort, allows doctors to see the heart beating and to see the structures of the heart.

PRACTICE   **Punctuating Essential and Nonessential Word Groups**

20.9   Identify the dependent clause in each sentence. Add commas to the nonessential dependent clauses.

EXAMPLE: Techniques <u>that allow physicians to see the organs and organ systems without surgery</u> are constantly improving. Essential, no commas

1. Computed tomography (CT) which is a noninvasive X-ray produces a three-dimensional image of the organ or structure.
2. A CT scan is a procedure that identifies minor differences in the density of tissues.
3. The CT scans produce high-resolution images of cross-sections of the body which can be studied.
4. Magnetic resonance imaging (MRI) which is also a noninvasive technique is commonly used to make images of the brain, spine, limbs, joints, heart, blood vessels, abdomen, and pelvis.
5. During an MRI, the patient lies very still on a platform that moves into a scanner.
6. The platform can move into either a narrow, closed, high-magnet scanner which may cause people to feel closed in or into an open, low-magnet scanner.
7. Earplugs are offered to the client to reduce the discomfort from the loud noises that occur during the test.

(Adapted from *Fundamentals of Nursing* by Barbara Kozier and Glenora Erb)

PRACTICE   **Writing Complex Sentences**

20.10   Write five complex sentences about the picture below. Use a different relative pronoun for the dependent clause in each sentence. You can write about your own personal experience with X-rays or other imaging technologies. You can also write about people you know who work in the field or about any medical procedure.

EXAMPLE: The X-ray that was taken after the accident showed a fracture in my leg.

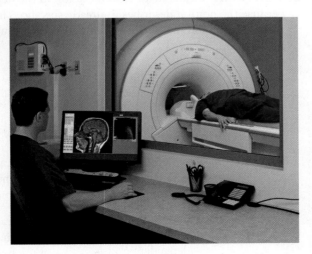

Review: Complex Sentences

In small groups or on your own, combine each pair of sentences using the dependent word in the parentheses. Answers may vary.

EXAMPLE: *(which)* An herb is a plant. The herb can be used for its health benefits.
An herb is a plant, which can be used for its health benefits.

1. *(before)* Plants were used as medicine. Pharmaceutical drugs were invented.

_____

2. *(although)* Herbs as medicines have been in use for almost 4,000 years. They have become popular recently.

_____

3. *(which)* At least one-fourth of all drugs contain ingredients derived from plants. Doctors prescribe them.

_____

4. *(that)* Ginger is an herb. Ginger is effective against nausea.

_____

5. *(because)* Herbs are not regulated by the Food and Drug Administration. They are considered dietary supplements.

_____

6. *(who)* People can find herbal products in grocery stores, on the web, and in natural food markets. People want to buy herbal products.

_____

7. *(if)* Some herbal products can be harmful. A person does not take the right amount.

_____

8. *(so that)* Consumers must become informed. They can choose the proper herb and correct dosage.

_____

Writing Assignment

Write a paragraph about activities you or people you know participate in that are not healthy. In your paragraph, include four complex sentences. Underline each complex sentence.

- Include two sentences, each with a dependent clause that begins with a subordinating conjunction.
- Include two sentences, each with a dependent clause that begins with a relative pronoun.

Correcting Fragments, Comma Splices, and Run-ons

21

Theme: *Astronomy*

LO 1 **Identify fragments, comma splices, and run-on sentences.**

What Are Fragments, Comma Splices, and Run-ons?

An important English sentence writing skill is using the correct punctuation to show where a sentence begins and ends. Some student writers have problems dividing up their ideas into separate sentences. As a result, they may make three common sentence errors: fragments, comma splices, and run-ons. These errors confuse readers because they cannot tell where one idea ends and the next idea begins.

Study the following examples of fragments, comma splices, and run-ons.

A **fragment** is an incomplete sentence. It may be missing a subject, verb, or both.	Which is called Earth.
A **comma splice** happens when two independent clauses are connected with a comma.	We live on a rocky planet, it is called Earth.
A **run-on** happens when two independent clauses are combined into one sentence without any punctuation between them.	We live on a rocky planet it is called Earth.

In this chapter, you will learn how to correct these three types of sentence errors.

Fragments, Comma Splices, and Run-ons in Context

In the following passage about the Moon, you will see one of each type of sentence error: a fragment, a comma splice, and a run-on.

¹The Moon is our nearest neighbor in space. ²Apart from the Sun, it is the brightest object in the sky. ³**The Moon revolves around the Earth in one month the Moon completes one revolution and returns to its starting point.**

⁴**The Moon's appearance undergoes a regular cycle of changes, these changes take about 29.5 days to complete.** ⁵The cycle starts with the new Moon. ⁶**Which is barely visible.** ⁷Then, each night it grows a little. ⁸One week after the new Moon, half of the Moon can be seen. ⁹Two weeks after the new Moon, the full Moon is visible. ¹⁰During the next two weeks, the moon becomes less and less visible until it becomes new again.

(Adapted from *Astronomy Today* by Eric Chaisson and Steve McMillan)

PRACTICE Identifying Fragments, Comma Splices, and Run-ons

21.1   Identify the three sentence errors in the passage you just read as a fragment, comma splice, or run-on.

Sentence 3: _____

Sentence 4: _____

Sentence 6: _____

PRACTICE Identifying Fragments, Comma Splices, and Run-ons

21.2   Identify the errors in each of the following word groups as a fragment, comma splice, or run-on.

EXAMPLE: The Sun is our star, it is the closest star to our planet.
Comma splice
_____

1. The Sun is a glowing ball of gas. That contains no solid material.

_____

2. It is the main source of energy. Affecting weather, climate, and life on Earth.

_____

3. Without the Sun, it would be so cold that no living thing would survive the Earth would be frozen.

_____

4. The Sun does not rise or set, it just looks like it does because the Earth is moving.

_____

5. On its surface, the Sun's average temperature is 10,000 degrees Fahrenheit. Also, more than 28,000 million degrees at its core.

_____

6. The Sun is not a quiet place it releases energy suddenly.

_____

7. Sometimes the Sun releases large amounts of gases, these are known as solar flares.

_____

8. Scientists are studying the different kinds of solar activity. To learn more about it.

_____

Correcting Fragments

LO 2 **Correct fragments.**

In Chapter 18, you learned that a sentence is a group of words that has at least one subject and one complete verb. Together they express a thought that has a clear beginning and ending.

In grammar, when a word group is missing one or more of those important parts, it is called a **fragment**. A fragment is not a complete sentence and is considered an error. The types of fragments you will learn about in this section are dependent clause fragments, incomplete verb fragments, and phrase fragments.

Dependent Clause Fragments

A dependent clause is a word group that begins with a dependent word and has a subject and a verb. Because it has a subject and a verb, you might think that it is an independent clause, but it is not. In grammar, when you add a dependent word at the beginning of a sentence, the independent clause becomes a dependent clause. It cannot be punctuated as a sentence.

> **Two independent clauses:** Asteroids are not planets. They are too small.
>
> **Dependent clause fragment:** Because they are too small.
>
> **Correct:** Asteroids are not planets because they are too small.

The following dependent words are used to begin dependent clauses. Learn to recognize these words when you see them.

> **Subordinating conjunctions:** _although, as, as long as, as soon as, because, before, even if, even though, if, once, since, so that, unless, until, when, whenever, where, whereas, wherever, while_
>
> **Relative pronouns:** _who, whom, which, that, whose_

To correct a dependent clause fragment, either attach it to an independent clause or rewrite it as an independent clause.

> **Dependent clause fragment:** Since asteroids are not planets.
>
> **Attached to an independent clause:** Since asteroids are not planets, astronomers call them _planetoids_.
>
> **Rewritten as an independent clause:** ~~Since~~ Asteroids are not planets.

Grammar Reminder. **To learn more about how dependent clauses are used in sentences, see Chapter 20.**

TIP Be careful not to confuse dependent words with transition words. Transition words like *however, therefore, consequently,* and *also* do not make dependent clauses.

Asteroids are not planets; therefore, astronomers call them planetoids.

PRACTICE Correcting Dependent Clause Fragments

21.3   Each pair of items has one dependent clause fragment and one independent clause. First, identify the dependent clause fragment. Then correct it by adding it to the independent clause or by changing it to an independent clause.

observatory a building from which scientists can watch the planets, the stars, the weather, etc.

EXAMPLE: In 1801, the night was clear and bright with stars. <u>When astronomer Giuseppe Piazzi was at work in his **observatory** in Sicily.</u>

In 1801, the night was clear and bright with stars when astronomer Guiseppe Piazzi was at work in his

observatory.

1. Piazzi had been looking for a new planet. Which other astronomers were also trying to find.

2. While he was looking at a group of stars. He saw a tiny point of light.

3. He thought it was a dim star. That was not on his chart.

4. When he looked for the star the next night. It had moved.

5. The object did not act like a star. Because it moved each night.

6. He reported his discovery to another astronomer. Whose name was Johann Bode.

7. Piazzi thought the object was a comet. Whereas Bode thought it was the new planet.

8. Piazzi gave the object a name. Which was Ceres.

9. Before other astronomers would believe his discovery. Piazzi had to show the object's path in the sky.

10. Piazzi could not figure out Ceres's path. Even though he watched it for six weeks.

11. Ceres seemed to be lost. Until other astronomers found it a year later.

Incomplete Verb Fragments

When part of a verb is left out, a fragment is created. Often, the verb that is left out is a helping verb. To correct an incomplete verb fragment, add an appropriate helping verb.

> **Incomplete –*ing* verb fragment:** In the 1800s, most women taking care of their homes and families.
>
> **Correct:** In the 1800s, most women **were taking** care of their homes and families.
>
> **Incomplete –*ed/–en* verb fragment:** They not allowed to vote.
>
> **Correct:** They **were** not **allowed** to vote.

PRACTICE   **Correcting Incomplete Verb Fragments**

21.4   Correct each of the following incomplete verb fragments by adding an appropriate helping verb.

Grammar Reminder.
To learn more about
helping verbs, see
Chapters 18 and 24.

EXAMPLE: In 1839, astronomers learning new information quickly because of better telescopes and photographs.
were learning
_____

1. Astronomers begun to collect information on hundreds of thousands of stars.

   _____

2. The director of the Harvard College Observatory looking for workers to help.

   _____

3. He known that women could do the work, so he hired a group of women as assistants.

   _____

4. Although the women paid as unskilled workers, their work was accurate.

   _____

5. These women paving the way for future generations of women astronomers.

   _____

Phrase Fragments

A phrase is a group of words that is missing a subject or a verb or both. Phrases add information by explaining or describing a word or idea. To correct a phrase fragment, attach it to an appropriate independent clause.

Prepositional Phrase Fragment A prepositional phrase is a group of words that begins with a preposition and ends with a noun or a pronoun. It describes a word in the sentence.

Grammar Reminder.
To learn more about
prepositional phrases
see Chapters 18.

> **Prepositional phrase fragment:** Of rock, ice, and gas.
>
> **Attached to an independent clause:** Comets are pieces of rock, ice and gas.

Explaining Phrase Fragment An explaining phrase gives examples or lists. This type of fragment can be corrected by attaching it to an independent clause or by rewriting it as an independent clause.

> **Example phrase fragment:**
>
> Such as Halley's Comet named after Edmund Halley.
>
> > **Corrected by attaching fragment to an independent clause:**
> >
> > A comet is usually named by the person who discovered it, such as Halley's Comet named after Edmund Halley.
> >
> > **Corrected by rewriting fragment as an independent clause:**
> >
> > Halley's Comet was named after Edmund Halley.
>
> **List phrase fragment:**
>
> Halley, Shoemaker-Levy 9, Hale-Bopp, Swift-Tuttle, and Hyakutake.
>
> > **Corrected by attaching fragment to an independent clause:**
> >
> > Five comets have been discovered, **for example,** Halley, Shoemaker-Levy 9, Hale-Bopp, Swift-Tuttle, and Hyakutake.
> >
> > **Corrected by rewriting fragment as an independent clause:**
> >
> > These comets are Halley, Shoemaker-Levy 9, Hale-Bopp, Swift-Tuttle, and Hyakutake.

Appositive Phrase Fragment An appositive phrase explains or identifies a noun or a pronoun. The phrase can be placed before or after the noun or pronoun.

> **Appositive phrase fragment:**
>
> A region beyond the planet Neptune.
>
> > **Corrected by attaching fragment to an independent clause:**
> >
> > Most comets come from the Kuiper Belt, a region beyond the planet Neptune.
> >
> > **Corrected by rewriting fragment as an independent clause:**
> >
> > The Kuiper Belt is a region beyond the planet Neptune.

PRACTICE   Correcting Phrase Fragments

21.5   Correct each of the following phrase fragments by adding it to the independent clause or rewriting it as an independent clause.

EXAMPLE: When it is far from the Sun, a comet is a dark, cold object. With an icy center.

When it is far from the Sun, a comet is a dark, cold object with an icy center.

1. A comet is made up of several elements. Gas, water, chunks of metal, and rocks.

_____

2. Comets orbit the Sun in two distant places. The Kuiper Belt and the Oort cloud.

_____

3. These are places very far away. At the very edge of the solar system.

_____

4. A comet spends many years in the Kuiper Belt or the Oort cloud moving quickly. Through space in all directions.

_____

5. Sometimes something happens to make a comet change direction. Such as crashing into another comet or coming very close to another comet.

_____

_____

6. The new path could bring the comet into the inner solar system. Near the hot Sun.

_____

7. As it passes the Sun, it begins to melt and leaves behind bright tails. One in front of it and one behind it.

_____

_____

8. Each tail can be very long. For instance, several million miles in length.

_____

9. Some comets cross Earth's orbit every year. Like Comet Swift-Tuttle.

_____

solar system the Sun and the group of planets that move around it, or a similar system somewhere else in the universe

10. As of 2010. Astronomers have discovered about 4,000 comets in our **solar system.**

_____

Correcting Comma Splices and Run-ons

LO 3 **Correct comma splices and run-on sentences.**

Comma splices and run-ons are punctuation errors. These errors happen when the writer joins two independent clauses without the correct punctuation. As a result, readers cannot tell where one sentence ends and the next one begins.

A **comma splice** happens when two independent clauses are connected with a comma.

The Hubble telescope was invented, astronomers wanted a clear view of the stars.

A **run-on** happens when two independent clauses are combined without any punctuation between them.

The Hubble telescope was invented astronomers wanted a clear view of the stars.

Comma splices and run-on errors can be corrected in several ways:

Grammar Reminder.
To learn more about joining ideas to build compound sentences, see Chapter 19, and to build complex sentences, see Chapter 20.

Method to Correct	Example
Add a period.	The Hubble telescope was invented**.** Astronomers wanted a clear view of the stars.
Add a comma and a coordinating conjunction.	The Hubble telescope was invented**, for** astronomers wanted a clear view of the stars.
Add a semicolon.	The Hubble telescope was invented**;** astronomers wanted a clear view of the stars.
Add a semicolon, a transition, and a comma.	Astronomers wanted a clear view of the stars**; therefore,** the Hubble telescope was invented.
Change one independent clause to a dependent clause.	The Hubble telescope was invented **because astronomers wanted a clear view of the stars.**

PRACTICE Correcting Comma Splices and Run-ons

21.6   The following sentences are comma splices or run-ons. Correct each of the sentences using the method in the parentheses. Remember to add the correct punctuation.

- Choose from these coordinating conjunctions: *and, but, for, so*
- Choose from these transitions: *as a result, then, instead, therefore, in addition*
- Choose from these subordinating conjunctions: *since, when, because*

EXAMPLE: The Hubble telescope was named after Dr. Edwin P. Hubble he was a famous astronomer. (Use a semicolon.)

The Hubble telescope was named after Dr. Edwin P. Hubble; he was a famous astronomer.

1. On April 24, 1990, the U.S. space shuttle *Discovery* carried the Hubble to outer space the crew put it into orbit on April 25. (Use a transition word)

2. Large telescopes on Earth can see as far as the Hubble, they cannot see objects as clearly. (Use a transition word)

3. Earth telescopes stay in one place, the Hubble goes around the Earth every ninety-seven minutes at about five miles per second. (Use a coordinating conjunction)

4. The Hubble telescope gets its energy from two solar panels it does not need a rocket motor. (Use a coordinating conjunction)

5. The telescope is located 353 miles above the Earth the rain, clouds, and lights do not interfere with its view. (Use a transition word)

_____

_____

6. Engineers use satellites to communicate with the telescope, they give it directions. (Use a period)

_____

7. Astronauts visit the Hubble every few years they need to make repairs and replace old equipment. (Use a subordinating conjunction)

_____

8. Eventually, the Hubble's time will end the parts will stop working. (Use a coordinating conjunction)

_____

9. The Hubble cannot orbit around the Earth any longer, it will fall through Earth's atmosphere and into the ocean. (Use a subordinating conjunction)

_____

_____

10. The Hubble's discoveries have made a huge impact on astronomy our view of the universe has changed. (Use a transition)

_____

_____

_____

PRACTICE   Correcting Comma Splices and Run-ons

21.7   Proofread the following passage for comma splices and run-ons. Correct the seven errors by rewriting each of the sentences.

[1]Astronomer Jill Tarter devoted her entire career to looking for signs of intelligent life elsewhere. [2]Her interest in outer space started as a young girl, she and her father used to walk on the beach at night and look up at the stars. [3]He taught her about the constellations. [4]She always wondered if there were other beings living elsewhere she never felt that humans were alone in the universe.

[5]Tarter was the director of the Center for SETI, SETI stands for search for extraterrestrial intelligence. [6]The SETI Institute is looking for evidence. [7]SETI uses giant radio telescopes pointed at the stars to scan space for signals from alien species. [8]The SETI Institute has been searching the universe for an intelligent signal for more than twenty-five years.

⁹In 2009, Dr. Tarter received a special award it gave her the chance to set up the website setiQuest.org. ¹⁰This website gives everyone a chance to help search for signals from the SETI telescopes. ¹¹A community was created at setilive.org; therefore, people people from all over the world can get involved.

¹²Anyone can participate help is needed. ¹³Many different kinds of signals are coming in at the same time twenty-four hours a day. ¹⁴There are so many signals that the computers cannot sort all of them. ¹⁵Also, quite a few of these signals are made by humans. ¹⁶They come from radio, televisions, and cell phones. ¹⁷The computers have trouble identifying signals from extraterrestrials (ETs). ¹⁸From their personal computers, volunteers can help by looking for signals that are not human-made.

¹⁹Science fiction movies show aliens as angry, destructive beings.

²⁰Tarter does not agree she thinks that other beings would come to Earth to explore. ²¹To date, no signals have been found, Tarter is hopeful.

Review: Sentence Errors

Proofread the following passage for fragment, comma splice, and run-on errors. Then, correct the errors using the methods you learned in this chapter. There are a total of eight errors, and the first one has been corrected for you.

air, which

¹The atmosphere is the air. ²Which is wrapped around a planet. ³The Earth's atmosphere is made up of a variety of gases. ⁴Mostly oxygen, nitrogen, and argon. ⁵Small particles float in the atmosphere. ⁶For example, dust, pollen, and water.

⁷On Earth, gravity keeps the air around us and everything else from drifting off into space. ⁸Gravity acts like a magnet and pulls objects together. ⁹People not actually feel gravity.

¹⁰On Earth, the atmosphere exerts pressure. ¹¹In outer space the pressure is nearly zero it is a **vacuum** with no atmosphere.

¹²Without a protective suit. ¹³An astronaut would not survive very long. ¹⁴The human body could only survive for a few seconds at the most. ¹⁵The blood and body fluids would boil, then they would freeze. ¹⁶There would be swelling and tissue damage. ¹⁷The person would become unconscious in less than 15 seconds. ¹⁸Because the brain would not have any oxygen.

vacuum a space from which most or all of the air, gas, or other material has been removed or is not present

Writing Assignment

MyWritingLab™
Complete this activity
at mywritinglab.com

Write about an Image

Almost 9,000 asteroids are located near the Earth, and nearly 1,000 more are discovered every year. These asteroids contain valuable and useful materials such as nickel, iron, water, and metals.

In April 2012, a group of billionaires and scientists formed a company called Planetary Resources. They plan to develop and use low-cost robotic spacecraft to explore the near-Earth asteroids. They want to figure out ways to bring the materials from the asteroids to use on Earth and to help the economy.

What do you think of this plan? Do you think that it will be helpful or harmful?

- Write ten sentences expressing your thoughts about this project.
- Then, proofread and edit your sentences for fragments, run-ons, and comma splices.

Building Grammar Skills

22 Subject-Verb Agreement

Theme: *Sociology*

Learning Objectives

After working through this chapter, you will learn to:

LO 1 Identify singular and plural subjects and verbs.

LO 2 Understand present tense.

LO 3 Make present tense verbs agree with singular subjects.

LO 4 Make present tense verbs agree with plural subjects.

LO 5 Make present tense verbs agree with indefinite pronoun, collective noun, and inverted subjects.

LO 6 Make helping verbs agree with singular and plural subjects.

LO 1 **Identify singular and plural subjects and verbs.**

What is Subject-Verb Agreement?

Subject-verb agreement is a grammar rule that states that a subject and verb must agree in number. The subject and the verb must both be either singular or plural.

The subject of the sentence decides whether the verb is singular or plural.

■ If the subject of a sentence is **singular,** the verb must have a **singular ending.**
■ If the subject is **plural,** the verb must have a **plural ending.**

A **singular subject** is one person, place, thing, idea, or activity. A **plural subject** is more than one of those items. In each of the following sentences, the subjects are written in blue and the verbs are written in green. Notice how singular subjects take singular verbs and plural subjects take plural verbs.

Singular and Plural Subjects and Verbs	
Singular subject and singular verb form	Plural subject and plural verb form
A **sociologist studies** society and human behavior.	**Sociologists study** society and human behavior.
A **person learns** acceptable behavior from his or her experiences in society.	**People learn** acceptable behavior from their experiences in society.
I learn about society by watching television.	**We learn** about society by watching television.

Subject-Verb Agreement In Context

In the following passage from a sociology text, the subjects are blue and the verbs green.

¹In society, **males** and **females are sorted** into different roles. ²**This is called** gender socialization. ³Different **attitudes** and **behaviors are expected** from males and females. ⁴**We get** these gender messages from our family and from the mass media.

⁵**We** first **learn** our gender role from our family or caretakers. ⁶The **lessons begin** in infancy and **continue** throughout childhood. ⁷**Parents let** their preschool sons roam farther from home than their preschool daughters. ⁸**They encourage** rough-and-tumble play in boys. ⁹**They** also **urge** them to get dirtier and be more defiant.

¹⁰Other **influences come** from the mass media, especially television. ¹¹**Television reinforces** stereotypes of the sexes. ¹²For example, there **are** more male **characters** than female characters. ¹³Male **characters have** higher-status positions. ¹⁴Sports **news** also **maintains** traditional stereotypes. ¹⁵Women **athletes receive** little coverage. ¹⁶Also, male **newscasters give** women's achievements less importance.

(Adapted from *Essentials of Sociology* by James M. Henslin)

Present Tense Verbs

LO 2 **Understand present tense.**

Tense is the form of the verb that shows when an action or state happens.

Present tense is a verb form used to write about an action or state that is happening now, happens all the time, or is a fact. Present tense verbs change their endings to match the subject in number and person. **Number** refers to whether the subject is singular (one) or plural (more than one). **Person** applies to who the subject is: the writer (**I, we**), the person written to (**you**), or someone or something being written about (**he, she, it, they,** or a noun).

The present tense has two forms: the base form and the **–s** or **–es** form. In the following chart, you can see that an **–s** or **–es** is added only to singular noun subjects and some pronoun subjects:

No –s or –es	Add –s or –es
I eat breakfast every morning.	**He eats** breakfast every morning
You eat breakfast every morning.	**She eats** breakfast every morning.
We eat breakfast every morning.	**It eats** breakfast every morning.
They eat breakfast every morning.	**My brother eats** breakfast every morning
The people eat breakfast every morning.	**Jeremiah eats** breakfast every morning.

Subject-Verb Agreement with Singular Subjects

LO 3 Make present tense verbs agree with singular subjects.

If the subject is singular, the verb form in the present tense ends in **–s** or **–es**.

The sociology class meets in the auditorium.

Heather sits in the front of the room. She attends every class.

The professor teaches the class on Mondays and Wednesdays.

> PRACTICE   Making Subjects and Present Tense Verbs Agree
>
> 22.1   Write the correct present tense form of each verb in the parentheses.

EXAMPLE: Video games ___expose___ players to action. (expose)

1. They also _____ players powerful ideas and images about gender. (give)
2. Some video games _____ gender stereotypes. (show)
3. Many video games _____ females passive or background characters. (make)
4. Lara Croft _____ the stereotypical gender role. (break)
5. Digital fantasy girl Lara Croft _____ in *Tomb Raiders* and its many sequels. (star)
6. With both guns blazing, Lara _____ her enemies with intelligence and strength. (conquer)
7. Lara Croft _____ women's changing role in society. (reflect)

Singular Subjects That Seem Plural

Some subjects do not seem to be singular, but they are singular. Study the following chart to learn about them.

Singular Subjects THAT May Not Seem Singular	
Singular subject	**Example**
–*ing* subjects: writing, studying, teaching	**Teaching** has many rewards.
Companies and organizations: ■ Honda, Nintendo, Starbucks, Walgreens ■ Environmental Protection Agency, Disabled American Veterans, Mothers Against Drunk Driving	**Mothers Against Drunk Driving** (MADD) **has** a mission to stop drunk driving and to help victims of this violent crime.
Singular nouns ending in **–s**: ■ athletics, economics, politics, mathematics ■ measles, AIDS, news ■ United States, Paris, Buenos Aires	**Mathematics is** Pat's best subject.
Titles: *The Joy Luck Club, The Kite Runner, Fundamentals of Nursing,* "The Star-Spangled Banner"	*The Kite Runner* **tells** the story of a young boy from Kabul who betrays his best friend and lives his life regretting it.

Singular subject	Example
Hours, minutes when considered units of time: three hours, ten minutes	**Sixty minutes is** not enough time to write a polished essay.
Two subjects that express a single idea: spaghetti and meatballs, peanut butter and jelly, red beans and rice	**Spaghetti and meatballs makes** a delicious meal.

PRACTICE Identifying Correct Verb Forms for Singular Subjects

22.2   Identify the correct form of the verb that agrees with the subject in each of the following sentences. You may want to eliminate prepositional phrases to help you find the subjects.

EXAMPLE: Self-knowledge (help, helps) a person make choices.

Grammar Reminder.
For more help with finding subjects and verbs, see Chapter 18.

1. Self-knowledge about your areas of ability (help, helps) you explore majors and choose careers.
2. Howard Gardner (is, are) the person responsible for the theory of multiple intelligences.
3. *Frames of Mind* (is, are) Gardner's first book on multiple intelligences.
4. Gardner (report, reports) ten years of research in this first book.
5. *Multiple Intelligences* (is, are) his latest book, which includes the most recent developments and research.
6. Gardner's definition of intelligence (take, takes) the concept of intelligence beyond what a standard IQ test can measure.
7. His theory (state, states) that people have a different range of intelligences for solving different kinds of problems.

Irregular Present Tense Verbs: *Be, Have, Do*

Be, have, and **do** are irregular verbs and have special present tense forms.

Be	*Have*	*Do*
I am a student.	**I have** a good schedule.	**I do** the assignments.
He/she/it is a student.	**He/she/it has** a good schedule.	**He/she/it does** the assignments.
We/you/they are students.	**We/you/they have** a good schedule.	**We/you/they do** the assignments.

PRACTICE   Writing the Correct Present Tense Form of *Be, Have,* and *Do*

22.3   Write the correct present tense form of *be, have,* or *do* as indicated in the parentheses for each sentence.

EXAMPLE: Gender ____is____ the behaviors and attitudes for males and females. (be)

1. Each human group _____ its ideas of "maleness" and "femaleness." (have)
2. A person's sex _____ inherited, but his or her gender _____ learned. (be)
3. Society _____ a role in teaching people about gender. (have)
4. Ideas of gender _____ different from one culture to another. (be)
5. Each gender group _____ what is expected. (do)
6. They _____ also given different privileges in their society. (be)
7. Society's gender rules _____ responsible for opening or closing doors to property and power. (be)

Subject-Verb Agreement with Plural Subjects

LO 4 **Make present tense verbs agree with plural subjects.**

If the subject is plural, the verb ***does not*** end in *–s* or *–es.*

The sociology classes meet in the auditorium.

Heather and Jose sit in the front of the room. They attend every class.

The professors teach classes on Mondays and Wednesdays.

Compound Subjects

Some sentences have more than one subject, called a **compound subject.** A compound subject is joined by any of these words: ***and, or, nor, either/or, neither/nor,*** and ***not only/but also.***

Compound Subjects Joined by *And*

Compound subjects joined by ***and*** take plural verbs.

| **Two singular compound subjects** | A high school diploma **and** a college degree open doors of opportunity. |
| **Two plural compound subjects** | In high school, ability groupings **and** educational tracks affect students' educational opportunities. |

PRACTICE   Choosing the Correct Verbs for Plural and Compound Subjects

22.4   Identify the correct verbs in the following sentences.

EXAMPLE: Some U.S. high schools (place, places) students into one of three tracks.

1. General, college prep, and honors (is, are) the three tracks.
2. Students on the lowest track (tends, tend) to go to work after high school.
3. Sometimes, these high school graduates (takes, take) vocational courses.

4. The honors groups usually (attends, attend) well-respected colleges.

5. Local colleges and regional universities (attracts, attract) students in the middle track.

6. Schools now (assigns, assign) students to ability groups.

7. Researchers (disagrees, disagree) on the benefits of ability grouping.

8. Labeling and segregation (creates, create) problems for students' self-esteem.

9. Emphasis on cooperation and sharing in the classroom (contributes, contribute) to learning and (is, are) a better alternative to ability grouping.

(Adapted from *Essentials of Sociology* by James M. Henslin)

Compound Subjects Joined with *Or, Nor, Either/or, Neither/nor, Not only/but also*

When two subjects are joined with *or, nor, either/or, neither/nor,* or *not only/but also,* the verb agrees with the subject after the *or, nor,* or *but also.*

Either/or	**Either** Professor Young **or** Professor Martin plans to teach sociology next semester.
Neither/nor	**Neither** the professor **nor** the students come to the college on Fridays.

Intervening Phrases

Prepositional phrases and phrases like **along with, as well as, together with, and in addition to** usually do not affect subject-verb agreement.

Each student in my English class at the college wants to succeed.

The professors as well as the counselors and advisors care about student success.

Plural Subjects That Seem Singular

Some single-word subjects seem like one thing but are considered plural.

Plural Subject	Example
Single things with parts: binoculars, glasses, scissors, tweezers, shorts, jeans, pants	Jeans are a popular wardrobe item.
Sports teams: New York Giants, Miami Heat, Utah Jazz, Philadelphia Phillies	The **Boston Celtics** are a professional basketball league in the United States.
Decades: 1930s, 1960s	The **1960s** are known in popular culture as the decade of social revolution.

Identifying Correct Verb Forms

22.5   Identify the correct verb in each of the following sentences.

EXAMPLE: Over one million children (is, [are]) currently being home schooled.

1. Home schooling parents (is, are) unhappy with public and private schools.
2. Two of every 100 students across the United States (is, are) being taught at home.
3. Home schoolers (receives, receive) an intense, one-on-one education.
4. Mothers (teaches, teach) 90 percent of the students.
5. Most fathers of home-schooled students (is, are) in the labor force.
6. Neither behavior issues nor isolation (is, are) a problem for home schoolers.
7. Sports programs or physical education through the public schools (is, are) available to home-schooled children.
8. **Peer pressure**, bullies, and competition (does, do) not harm a home schooler's self-esteem.
9. Neither teenage trends nor dangerous experimentation (influences, influence) their lives.
10. Mothers and fathers (has, have) to sacrifice a loss in income because one parent must stay home, but they feel that the sacrifice is worth it in the long run.

(Adapted from *Essentials of Sociology* by James M. Henslin)

peer pressure social pressure on somebody to adopt a type of behavior, dress, or attitude in order to be accepted as part of a group

Subject-Verb Agreement with Other Subjects

Indefinite Pronoun Subjects

LO 5 Make present tense verbs agree with indefinite pronoun, collective noun, and inverted subjects.

Indefinite pronouns are words that refer to nonspecific people or things. Some indefinite pronoun subjects are always singular or always plural, while others can be singular or plural.

Singular Indefinite Pronouns as Subjects When used as subjects, the following indefinite pronouns are singular and take a singular verb form. In the present tense, the verb ends in an **–s** or **–es.**

Singular Indefinite Pronouns as Subjects			
anyone	someone	no one	everyone
anybody	somebody	nobody	everybody
anything	something	nothing	everything
another	one	other	each
either	neither		

Everyone wants to be a part of a group.

One meets that need by being a member of a group.

One of the sociologists says that the group we choose influences our behavior.

Anyone gets messages about conformity and deviance from his or her group.

Plural Indefinite Pronouns as Subjects When used as subjects, the following indefinite pronouns are plural and take a plural verb form. In the present tense, the verb *does not* end in an *–s* or *–es*. The plural indefinite pronouns are ***both, few, many, others,*** and ***several.***

Many of the researchers say that family is important for teaching values.

Others point out that delinquents often come from families that get in trouble with the law.

Singular or Plural Indefinite Pronoun Subjects Some indefinite pronouns can be singular or plural: ***all, any, most, none,*** and ***some.***

To decide if the indefinite pronoun subject is singular or plural, look at the noun or pronoun in the phrase that follows it. If the word in the phrase is singular, then the verb is singular; if the word in the phrase is plural, then the verb is plural. This rule also applies to fractions and percentages.

Most of us have strong inner desires to do things that get us in trouble.

Most of this desire is stopped.

All of our behavior is a result of our self-control.

Some of our inner controls include conscience and ideas of right and wrong.

Ninety percent of teenagers use social media.

TIP | A helpful way to remember the indefinite pronouns that can be singular or plural is by the acronym **SANAM**, **s**ome, **a**ny, **n**one, **a**ll, **m**ost.

Collective Noun Subjects

Some words refer to a group of people or things. They are called **group** or **collective nouns.** They can describe the group as a whole (only one) or the individuals in the group (more than one).

Common Collective Nouns				
army	class	crowd	group	senate
audience	club	family	jury	society
band	committee	gang	public	team

When the word describes the group as a whole, then it is singular. All members of the group are acting as one, all doing the same thing or thinking the same way. The verb is singular.

The international student club meets on Monday afternoons.

When the word describes the individuals in the group, then it is plural. The members of the group are acting individually. The verb is plural.

The international student club disagree on the way to raise money.

PRACTICE   Editing for Subject-Verb Agreement with Indefinite Pronouns and Group Words

22.6   Identify any verbs that do not agree with their subjects and write the correct verb. Write **C** if the sentence is correct.

deviant different from what is acceptable in society

EXAMPLE: One of the best examples of **deviant** groups ~~are~~ motorcycle gangs. is

1. One of the studies are the result of sociologist Mark Watson's living with and observing outlaw bikers.
2. Each of the outlaw bikers see the world as hostile and weak.
3. Everyone prides himself on looking dirty and mean.
4. No one get in their way.
5. Many treat women as lesser beings.
6. The gang **devalue** women.
7. Few thinks of themselves as winners in life.
8. Ninety-five percent of the bikers believes they are losers.
9. All of them takes pleasure in shocking people with their appearance.
10. The police has been having more trouble going undercover in the biker gangs.

devalue treat someone as if he or she is unimportant

(Adapted from *Essentials of Sociology* by James M. Henslin)

Inverted Subjects

In some sentences, the subject does not come first. Notice the position of the subjects and verbs in the following sentences.

Sentences Beginning with *Here/There*   In most sentences that begin with **here** or **there,** the subject comes after the verb. Neither **here** nor **there** is the subject of the sentence.

> **There** are many groups that make up our society.

Sentences Beginning with Prepositional Phrases   In some sentences that begin with one or more prepositional phrases, the subject may follow the verb.

> **Among the important groups in our lives** is our family.

Questions   In questions that begin with verbs, the subject follows the verb or comes between the helping verb and the main verb.

> Are friendship groups important to our well-being?

> Can friendships offer a sense of belonging?

Sentences with Dependent Clauses Beginning with *Who, Whom, Whose, Which,* or *That*   **Who, whom, whose, which,** and **that** are relative pronouns that take the place of subjects when they begin dependent clauses. The verb in the dependent clause should agree with the word that the relative pronoun refers to.

> As humans, we have an intense need for face-to-face interaction that gives us feelings of self-esteem.

Identifying Subjects and Correct Verbs When Subjects Do Not Come First

22.7   Underline the subjects and identify the correct verbs in the following sentences.

EXAMPLE: There (is, are) six types of groups that make up society.

1. A social group consists of two or more people who (interact, interacts) with one another.
2. (Is, Are) you a member of a group?
3. A primary group, which (offers, offer) people a feeling of belonging, consists of family and friends.
4. The second type is the secondary group; this group consists of people who (lacks, lack) strong emotional ties to one another.
5. There (is, are) another group called a peer group.
6. In peer groups (is, are) individuals of equal age or status.
7. Online groups, which (differs, differ) from traditional social groups, are the newest type of social group.
8. In addition to online gaming and dating groups, there (is, are) many other online groups.

Subject-Verb Agreement with Helping Verbs

LO 6 **Make helping verbs agree with singular and plural subjects.**

Helping verbs are used with main verbs to form verb tenses. *Be, do,* and *have* and modal helping verbs have special rules for subject-verb agreement.

Be, Do, Have

When **be, do,** and **have** are used as the only helping verb before the main verb, they should agree with their subjects. Study the use of helping verbs in the following sentences.

Helping Verb	Sentence Examples
BE: *am, is, are, was, were*	I **am working** on my sociology project right now.
	Farah **is working** on her sociology project right now.
	The **students are working** on their projects now.
	Sara **was writing** her sociology paper late last night.
	The **students were writing** their sociology papers last night.
HAVE: *has, have, had*	Sara **has learned** about social groups in her class.
	Sociologists have developed ideas about social groups.
DO: *does, do, did*	Sara **does enjoy** her sociology class.
	Many **students do** not **know** much about sociology.

Modals

Agreement rules do not apply with modals: *can, could, shall, should, will, would, may, might, must.* They also do not apply when *has* or *have* is the second of two helping verbs.

Sara may decide to major in sociology.

She must have enjoyed her sociology class.

PRACTICE **Choosing the Correct Helping Verbs**

22.8   Underline the correct forms of the helping verbs in the next selection. The first one has been done for you as an example.

¹United States families (is, <u>are</u>) changing. ²Single-parent families (has, have) been increasing due to divorce. ³At this time, fewer children (is, are) living with two parents—only 65 percent. ⁴After a divorce, most children (is, are) being raised by one parent. ⁵Women (is, are) heading most single-parent families.

⁶Divorce (do, does present difficulties for children. ⁷Adjustment problems (is, are) known to continue into adulthood. ⁸Many divorced fathers (does, do) not maintain ongoing relationships with their children. ⁹Also, financial difficulties (is, are) known to be greater for the former wives. ¹⁰Usually, single female parents (is, are) not able to earn as much as their former husbands. ¹¹For single mothers, poverty (have, has) become the primary strain.

(Adapted from *Essentials of Sociology* by James M. Henslin)

MyWritingLab™
Complete this activity
at mywritinglab.com

Review: Subject-Verb Agreement

Correct the nine subject-verb agreement errors in the following passage. The first one has been done for you.

                                            [have]
¹Why do people in poverty-stricken countries <u>has</u> so many children?

²To understand this, we must understand why Celia and Angel are so

happy about having their thirteenth child. ³We must take the role of the

other to understand how they see it. ⁴Celia and Angel's culture tell them

that twelve children is not enough for three reasons.

⁵The first reason is the status of parenthood. ⁶In the least industrialized

nations, motherhood is the most prized status a woman achieve. ⁷The more

children a woman give birth to, the more she is thought to have achieved the purpose for which she was born. [8]Similarly, a man prove his manhood by fathering children. [9]The more children he fathers, especially sons, the better because through them, his name live on.

[10]Second, the community support this view. [11]The last reason is that for poor people, children are economic assets. [12]They begin contributing to the family income at a young age. [13]Their government do not provide social security or medical and unemployment insurance. [14]This motivate people to bear more children so that the children can take care of them when they become too old to work or when no work is to be found.

(Adapted from *Essentials of Sociology* by James M. Henslin)

Writing Assignment

Write about an Image

The photograph shows groups of dried fruit and nuts that are alike. Most of us have belonged to groups at some point in our lives. Practice subject-verb agreement by writing five sentences about one or several of the groups you have belonged to in your lifetime. If you prefer, write your sentences about the food groups in the photo below.

Sentence 1: Use a compound subject.
Sentence 2: Use a group word subject.
Sentence 3: Use an indefinite pronoun subject.
Sentence 4: Use a dependent clause starting with who, which, or that.
Sentence 5: Write a yes/no question.

23 Past Tense

Theme: *Humanities*

Learning Objectives

After working through this chapter, you will be able to:

LO 1 Define past tense.

LO 2 Form the past tense for regular and irregular verbs.

LO 3 Form questions and negative statements in the past tense.

LO 1 Define past tense.

What Is the Past Tense?

The **past tense** is a verb form that expresses an action or state that began and ended at one specific time in the past. The diagram shows when a past tense action or state happened.

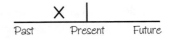

Thomas Edison and W. K. Laurie Dickson **invented** the Kinetoscope in 1889. The kinetoscope **was** the first continuous-film motion-picture viewing machine.

Past Tense in Context

In the following passage about silent movies, the past tense verb forms are green.

Before movies **had** sound, movies **were** by no means "silent." Every theater **had** a piano or organ to provide musical accompaniment to the films it **projected.** This **made** cinema a multimedia event. A live musician or orchestra **reacted** to and **participated** in the presentation of the film.

The introduction of sound radically **changed** the motion-picture industry. For one thing, theaters everywhere **had** to be wired, a process that **took** several years to accomplish. For another, filmmakers **added** sound to the film itself. This **changed** the culture of film. In the 1920s, the cinema **was** the world's largest employer of musicians. Then, just as the Great Depression **hit** in 1929, thousands of cinema musicians **found** themselves out of work.

Sound also **changed** the nature of acting in the cinema. Before sound, communication with the audience **depended** on facial expression and physical gesture, often exaggerated. Now actors **had** to rely on speech to communicate, and many silent-era stars simply **lacked** a powerful voice. Dialogue writing **became** important, so **playwrights gained** influence. Finally, sound **brought** foreign languages into the theaters.

(Adapted from *The Humanities*, Book 6, by Henry M. Sayre)

playwright someone who writes plays

Past Tense Forms

LO 2 Form the past tense for regular and irregular verbs.

Past tense verb forms can be regular or irregular. Regular verbs form the past tense by adding a *–d* or *–ed* to the end, while irregular verbs do not follow this pattern.

Regular Past Tense: My friends and I enjoyed the movie.

Irregular Past Tense: We saw the movie a second time.

TIP | *Was* or *were* is not added to the verb to form the past tense.

                  went
He ~~was go~~ home last night.

Regular Past Tense Verb Forms

Regular verbs are so named because they always form the past tense by adding a *–d* or *–ed* to the end of the base form of the verb. The base form is the verb without any endings added to it.

watch + *–ed*: Reginald watched an action movie.

like + *–d*: He liked the special effects.

Spelling of Regular Past Tense Verbs Some verbs change their spellings when adding *–d* or *–ed* endings. The spelling rules are explained in the following chart:

Spelling Rules for Regular Past Tense Verbs		
If the verb ends in	**Make the past tense**	**Example**
–e	Add *–d*	change	changed
consonant + *y*	Change *–y* to *–i* and add *–ed*	apply	applied
one vowel + one consonant (not *w* or *y*)	Double the consonant and add *–ed*	clap	clapped
–c	Add *–ked*	panic	panicked
all other endings	Add *–ed*	react	reacted

PRACTICE

Writing Correct Regular Past Tense Verbs

23.1 Write the past form of the each verb in parentheses. Don't forget to check the spelling.

EXAMPLE: In 1888, George Eastman (invent) __invented__ celluloid film for a new camera called the Kodak.

1. W. K. Laurie Dickson (devise) _____ a wheel with teeth to move the roll of film.

2. Thomas Edison (decide) _____ on a 35-millimeter width for the film strip of his new motion-picture camera.

3. Only one person at a time (watch) _____ the film through a small hole.
4. Each film (stop) _____ after about twenty seconds.
5. People (enjoy) _____ these short movies in viewing parlors.
6. The movies shown to a large audience (occur) _____ on December 28, 1895.
7. That night, August and Louis Lumière (show) _____ the audience ten films that lasted for about twenty minutes.
8. Another famous Lumière brothers' film (depict) _____ a single train arriving at a station.
9. The audience (panic) _____ as the train got closer to the camera because it seemed so real to them.

(Adapted from *The Humanities* by Henry Sayre)

Irregular Past Tense Verb Forms

Irregular verbs do not form the past tense by adding **–d** or **–ed.** There are over 400 irregular verbs in English. The following chart lists the most commonly used irregular verbs in the past tense. The base form is given first, and next to it is the past tense form.

Irregular Past Tense Verbs

Base Verb	Past Form	Base Verb	Past Form	Base Verb	Past Form
arise	arose	drink	drank	have	had
awake	awoke	drive	drove	hear	heard
be	was, were	eat	ate	hide	hid
beat	beat	fall	fell	hit	hit
become	became	feed	fed	hold	held
begin	began	feel	felt	hurt	hurt
blow	blew	fight	fought	keep	kept
break	broke	find	found	know	knew
bring	brought	fit	fit	lay	laid
build	built	fly	flew	lead	led
burst	burst	forbid	forbade	leave	left
buy	bought	forget	forgot	let	let
catch	caught	forgive	forgave	lie	lay
choose	chose	freeze	froze	lose	lost
come	came	get	got	make	made
cut	cut	give	gave	meet	met
deal	dealt	go	went	pay	paid
do	did	grow	grew	quit	quit

Base Verb	Past Form		Base Verb	Past Form		Base Verb	Past Form
read	read		shine	shone		teach	taught
ride	rode		sing	sang		tear	tore
ring	rang		sit	sat		tell	told
rise	rose		sleep	slept		think	thought
run	ran		speak	spoke		throw	threw
say	said		spend	spent		understand	understood
see	saw		spring	sprang		wake	woke
seek	sought		stand	stood		wear	wore
sell	sold		steal	stole		win	won
send	sent		swim	swam		write	wrote
set	set		swing	swung			
shake	shook		take	took			

PRACTICE   **Writing Irregular Past Tense Verbs**

23.2   Fill in the correct past tense form of each irregular verb in the parentheses. The first one has been done for you.

[1]At the end of the 1800s, motion pictures (be) _____ were merely an interesting novelty.

[2]That changed when businessmen (understand) _____ their real motion picture audience. [3]At that time, thousands of immigrants (come) _____ to the United States mostly from southern and central Europe. [4]They lived in overcrowded apartment houses in city slums and (do) _____ not have much money to pay for entertainment. [5]However, they (have) _____ a nickel (approximately $1 in today's money) to pay for a movie.

[6]In 1905, the nickelodeon theater (bring) _____ motion pictures to the masses. [7]By 1910, the number of nickelodeon theaters (grow) _____ to 10,000 in the United States. [8]The nickelodeon (begin) _____ to offer a variety of films. [9]Most films (run) _____ for ten to fifteen minutes.

[10]Vitagraph, an early movie producer, (give) _____ viewers a military film, a drama, a Western, a comedy, and a special feature each week. [11]Working-class immigrants who did not know much English (feel) _____ comfortable watching these silent films because language was not an obstacle.

(Adapted from *The Humanities* by Henry Sayre)

Easily Confused Past Tense Forms

The Irregular Verb *Be*   Past tense verbs usually have one form with the exception of the past tense of the irregular verb *be*, which has two forms: **was** and **were**. Therefore, when using *be* in the past tense, be sure that the subject and form of *be* agree.

Subject	Singular Form of *Be*	Plural Form of *Be*
First person pronoun	I **was** at the film debut.	We **were** at the film debut.
Second person pronoun	You **were** at the film debut.	You **were** at the film debut.
Third person pronoun	He (She, It) **was** at the film debut.	They **were** at the film debut.
Third person noun(s)	Farah **was** at the film debut.	Farah and Jean **were** at the film debut.

PRACTICE   **Using the Past Tense of** *Be*

23.3   For each of the following sentences, write **was** or **were.** The first one has been done for you.

[1]The early nickelodeon films __were__ short. [2]Most _____ on one reel; they held 1,000 feet of film and ran ten to fifteen minutes. [3]Audiences wanted to see movies that _____ longer. [4]D. W. Griffith _____ the person who met the demand.

[5]He _____ the foremost single-reel director at that time. [6]His film *The Birth of a Nation* had its public showing in 1915, and it _____ a big success. [7]*The Birth of a Nation* _____ about the Civil War and Reconstruction, a period in United States history; the film _____ controversial because of its racist elements. [8]The film's box office receipts _____ the largest in film history.

[9]An important aspect of *The Birth of a Nation* _____ the number of camera shots Griffith invented to create visual variety in film. [10]Some of these _____ the full shot, the medium shot, the close up, and the long shot. [11]Griffith's film techniques _____ responsible for influencing every film since then; however, the film is a painful record of racist views in America in 1915.

(Adapted from *The Humanities* by Henry Sayre)

Questions and Negative Sentences

LO 3 **Form questions and negative statements in the past tense.**

To write a question or a negative sentence in the past tense, add the helping verb **did**. Do not add a **–d** or **–ed** to the base verb. The helping verb shows the verb tense of the sentence.

Past	Question	Negative Sentence
The students **took** a humanities course.	**Did** the students **take** a humanities course?	The students **did not take** a humanities course.
They **learned** about art, history, and philosophy.	**Did** they **learn** about art, history, and philosophy?	They **did not learn** about art, history, or philosophy.

When the main verb is **was** or **were**, no helping verb is needed to form a question or a negative sentence in the past tense.

Past	Question	Negative Sentence
The course **was** enjoyable.	**Was** the course enjoyable?	The course **was not** enjoyable.

PRACTICE 23.4 Forming Questions and Negative Sentences

Part A Forming Questions

Change the sentence into a question:

EXAMPLE: Leonardo da Vinci was a famous artist.

Was Leonardo da Vinci a famous artist?

1. Da Vinci lived from 1452 to 1519.

_____

2. Da Vinci liked to show the personality of the people he painted.

_____

3. He was famous for his painting the *Mona Lisa*.

_____

mysterious referring to something that has not yet been explained or understood

4. The woman in the painting had a **mysterious** smile.

_____

5. For many years, people wanted to know the reason for her smile.

_____

Part B Forming Negative Sentences

Make each of the sentences in Part A untrue by changing them to negative sentences.

EXAMPLE: Leonardo da Vinci was not a famous artist. _____

1. _____
2. _____
3. _____
4. _____
5. _____

MyWritingLab™
Complete this activity at mywritinglab.com

Review: Past Tense

Write the correct past tense form for each of the verbs in the parentheses. The first past tense form has been done for you.

boll weevil infestation the spread of a beetle pest in the cotton crop

[1]In 1914, nearly 90 percent of all African Americans (live) __lived__ in the South. [2]As millions of men in the North (go) _____ to fight in Europe during the World War, a huge demand for labor followed. [3]Because of the demand for labor, Southern blacks (begin) _____ to move north—between 200,000 and 350,000 in the years 1915 to 1918 alone. [4]Also, in the 1920s, a **boll weevil infestation** (hurt) _____ the cotton crop industry, causing more people to move North. [5]Many others (leave) _____ to escape racial discrimination and segregation.

[6]The African-American population (grow) _____ 40 percent in the Northern states, mostly in the largest cities like Detroit, Chicago, and New York City. [7]Many educated and socially conscious African Americans (choose) _____ to settle in Harlem, a neighborhood in New York

City. [8]Harlem (become) _____ a center for culture and politics for black America.

[9]A movement called the Harlem Renaissance (arise) _____. [10]This movement (bring) _____ up major issues that affected the lives of African Americans at that time. [11]People (give) _____ expression to the issues of racism and social inequality. [12]Through art, literature, music, drama, painting, sculpture, movies, and protests, people (communicate) _____ the most essential part of the African-American experience.

[13]The Harlem Renaissance affirmed that African Americans (have)_____ a unique cultural heritage. [14]The movement (be) _____ a celebration of heritage and racial pride. [15]The influence of the Harlem Renaissance (spread) _____ throughout the nation.

(Adapted from *The Humanities* by Henry M. Sayre)

Writing Assignment

MyWritingLab™
Complete this activity
at mywritinglab.com

Write about an Image

Find a photograph of yourself when you were younger. If you do not have a picture, imagine how you looked at a time in your past or write about one of the children in the photo. Practice using the past tense verb forms you learned about in this chapter by writing at least five original sentences describing yourself at the time the photo was taken. You can write about your height, weight, hair and eye color, clothing style, hairstyle, jewelry, tattoos, and so on.

EXAMPLE: I wore a blue jacket and a baseball cap.

24 Past Participles

Theme: *Criminal Justice*

Learning Objectives

After working through this chapter, you will be able to:

LO 1 List the uses of past participles.

LO 2 Form regular and irregular past participles.

LO 3 Use the present perfect tense.

LO 4 Use the past perfect tense.

LO 5 Use passive voice.

LO 6 Use past participles as adjectives.

What Is a Past Participle?

A **past participle** is a verb form that is used to make the present perfect and past perfect tenses, to form passive voice, and to describe nouns.

LO 1 **List the uses of past participles.**

Present perfect tense *HAS/HAVE* + PAST PARTICIPLE	The number of students studying criminal justice **has grown**.
Past perfect tense *HAD* + PAST PARTICIPLE	Police departments **had increased** their recruiting efforts before the county cut taxes.
Passive voice FORM OF *BE* + PAST PARTICIPLE	People who speak a foreign language **are given** bonuses by police recruiters.
To describe nouns (as adjectives)	Many police departments have job openings for **interested** candidates.

Past Participles in Context

In the following passage about the history of treating criminals, the past participles and their helping verbs, if any, are in green.

¹A mere 200 years ago, before people **were imprisoned, convicted** law breakers **were** routinely **subjected** to physical punishment that often resulted in death. ²Physical punishment fit the belief of *lex talionis*, the law of retaliation. ³Under *lex talionis*, the **convicted** offender **was sentenced** to a punishment that was close to the original injury. ⁴This rule of "an eye

for an eye, a tooth for a tooth" generally copied the offense. [5]If a person **had blinded** another, he **was blinded** in return. [6]Murderers **were executed**, sometimes by the same method they **had used** in committing the crime. [7]In an important historical development, around the year 1800, the purpose for imprisonment changed. [8]Prisoners **were** no longer **imprisoned** to be physically punished; instead they **were imprisoned** as punishment.

[9]Since that time, the effort **has been** to humanize the treatment of offenders. [10]However, previous attempts at rehabilitation **had failed** because large numbers of offenders returned to crime and to prison. [11]By 1995, the prison system **had focused** completely on the concept of just deserts. [12]This concept bases the amount of punishment on how bad the crime is. [13]"Get tough" actions **have resulted** in longer required sentences, an increase in the use of life without parole, and more maximum-security prisons. [14]Many states **have** also **adopted** "three strikes, you're out" laws, which mandate long prison terms for criminal offenders convicted of a third violent crime or felony.

(Adapted from *Criminal Justice Today* by Frank Schmalleger)

Regular and Irregular Past Participles

LO 2 **Form regular and irregular past participles.**

The past participles of most verbs are formed by adding a *–d* or an *–ed* to the end of the base verb.

The Internet has chang<u>ed</u> the way people break the law.

Some verbs form their past participles in different ways.

Law enforcement teams have found it difficult to keep up with Internet crime, but they have made progress.

The following chart lists the base verb and the past participle forms for irregular verbs. The base verb form is given first, then the past participle verb form. Review the past participle tense forms and study the ones you do not know.

Irregular Past Participles			
Base Verb	**Past Participle** *HAS/HAVE* OR *HAD* + PAST PARTICIPLE	**Base Verb**	**Past Participle** *HAS/HAVE* OR *HAD* + PAST PARTICIPLE
Verbs with the Same Base Verb and Past Participle Forms			
become	become	fit	fit
burst	burst	hit	hit
come	come	hurt	hurt
cut	cut	let	let

Base Verb	Past Participle *HAS/HAVE* OR *HAD* + PAST PARTICIPLE	Base Verb	Past Participle *HAS/HAVE* OR *HAD* + PAST PARTICIPLE
quit	quit	run	run
read	read	set	set

Verbs with Different Base Verbs and Past Participle Forms

arise	arisen	go	gone
awake	awoken	grow	grown
be	been	have	had
beat	beaten	hear	heard
begin	begun	hide	hidden
blow	blown	hold	held
break	broken	keep	kept
bring	brought	know	known
build	built	lay	laid
buy	bought	lead	led
catch	caught	leave	left
choose	chosen	lie	lain
deal	dealt	lose	lost
do	done	make	made
drink	drunk	meet	met
drive	driven	pay	paid
eat	eaten	ride	ridden
fall	fallen	ring	rung
feed	fed	rise	risen
fight	fought	say	said
find	found	see	seen
fly	flown	seek	sought
forbid	forbidden	sell	sold
forgot	forgotten	send	sent
forgive	forgiven	shake	shook
freeze	frozen	sing	sung
get	got/gotten	sit	sat
give	given	sleep	slept

Base Verb	Past Participle	Base Verb	Past Participle
	HAS/HAVE OR *HAD* + **PAST PARTICIPLE**		*HAS/HAVE* OR *HAD* + **PAST PARTICIPLE**
Verbs with Different Base Verbs and Past Participle Forms			
speak	**spoken**	tear	**torn**
spend	**spent**	tell	**told**
spring	**sprung**	think	**thought**
stand	**stood**	try	**tried**
steal	**stolen**	understand	**understood**
swim	**swum**	wake	**woken**
swing	**swung**	wear	**worn**
take	**taken**	win	**won**
teach	**taught**	write	**written**

Grammar Reminder.
For a list of irregular past tense verbs, see Chapter 23.

TIP	The past participle must have a helping verb in front of it, but the past tense does not.

He could have ~~went~~ gone to the police academy for training.

He ~~done~~ did well on his entrance test.

PRACTICE Using Past Participles

24.1 Write past participle forms of the base verb in the parentheses. The first one has been done for you.

pandemic a dangerous disease that infects many people at one time

[1]In 2005, the World Health Organization (WHO) discovered that Meridian Bioscience of Cleveland, Ohio, had ___lost___ (lose) some samples of a potentially dangerous flu virus.
[2]The company had _____ (send) samples to over four thousand laboratories in eighteen countries. [3]The Bio-kits contained the influenza A (H2N2) virus, which had _____ (cause) the flu **pandemic** of 1957–1958.
[4]These kits were _____ on behalf of several U.S. organizations that had _____ (set) testing standards for laboratories.
[5]The organizations had _____ (want) to test the labs' ability to identify flu viruses. [6]Most of the laboratories were in the United States with some in South America, but the few that were sent to the Arab world had

_____ (raise) fears. [7]The WHO feared that Islamic terrorists had _____ (get) hold of the viral material and had _____ (plan) to use it to spread the disease, creating a worldwide epidemic. [8]On May 2, 2005, the scare had _____ (end). [9]The CDC announced that it had _____ (find) the last remaining sample of the virus at the American University of Beirut in Lebanon. [10]A local delivery service had _____ (misplace) the sample. [11]Someone had _____ (discover) it in a warehouse at the Beirut airport. [12]Although the incident had _____ (come) to a successful conclusion, it had _____ (increase) concerns about the spread of contagious flu viruses and possible crimes committed through the use of these substances.

(Adapted from *Criminal Justice Today* by Frank Schmalleger)

PRACTICE   **Editing Past Participles**

24.2   The past participles are underlined in each of the following sentences. Circle any incorrect past participles and write the correction above them. The first one has been done for you.

    [1]Research in the area of nutrition has led⟨lead⟩to the development of biocriminology, a field of study that links violent or disruptive behavior to eating habits, vitamin deficiencies, and other conditions that affect body tissues.

    [2]In one early study in 1943, researchers had <u>tryed</u> to find out if chemical imbalances could be a cause of crime. [3]Authors of the study had <u>linked</u> murder to hypoglycemia (low blood sugar), which is caused by too much insulin in the blood or by poor nutrition.

    [4]A number of studies have <u>report</u> that allergic reactions to common foods have <u>cause</u> violence and homicide; for example, people who have <u>ate</u> foods that they are allergic to can have swelling of the brain and brain stem. [5]Other studies have <u>prove</u> that food additives, such as monosodium glutamate, dyes, and artificial flavorings, have <u>produce</u> criminal behavior. [6]The amount of coffee and sugar prisoners have <u>drank</u> is greater than that of the outside population, leading researchers to connect excessive coffee and sugar intake to crime.

    [7]Hormones have also <u>came</u> under investigation as having a role in criminal behavior. [8]Some studies of the levels of the male sex hormone,

testosterone, have <u>showed</u> a link to aggressive behavior. [9]Sex offenders with high levels of testosterone have <u>became</u> more violent with their victims. [10]In 2007, researchers at the University of Michigan proved young men with higher blood levels of testosterone had <u>enjoy</u> making others angry.

The Present Perfect Tense

LO 3 Use the present perfect tense.

The **present perfect tense** is used to show that something happened at some time before now and continues now. The present perfect tense consists of **has** or **have** and the past participle. The helping verb must agree with the subject. The following chart shows how to use the present perfect tense.

How to Use the Present Perfect Tense	
Use	**Example**
An action started in the past and is continuing now.	Steve **has worked** as a prison officer since last January.
	Steve **has had** his job for six months.
	Use **for** with an amount of time. Use **since** to refer to a time in the past.
An action repeats in the past and is continuing now. More repetition may occur.	He **has found** a dozen illegal cell phones in inmates' cells this week.
	Cell phone smuggling into prisons **has become** a serious problem in the past several years.
	Use words like **this week, today, so far, already.**
An action happened at some nonspecific time in the past.	Steve **has witnessed** violence among inmates several times.
	Use words like **many, once, several times, recently.**

Comparing Present Perfect to the Past and Present Tenses

The present perfect tense is sometimes confused with the past tense or with the present tense. The following chart explains the differences.

Present *The action is at this moment.*	Steve **works** as a prison officer.
Past *The action is completed.*	Steve **worked** as a prison officer a year ago.
Present Perfect *The action began in the past and continues to the present.*	Steve **has worked** as a prison officer since last January.

24.3   Use the correct form of the past or present perfect tense of the verb in the parentheses to complete this student's paragraph.

¹Today, my college friends think that I am a well-behaved, respectful person. ²However, in high school, I _____ (be) the opposite. ³I never _____ (obey) my teachers, I _____ (curse) at people, and I _____ (write) on desks. ⁴I _____ (do) not respect anyone. ⁵About five years ago, my math teacher _____ (give) me advice. ⁶He _____ (teach) me that respecting others would help me succeed in life. ⁷Since then, I _____ (change) my behavior. ⁸I _____ (learn) to be quiet when my classmates take tests. ⁹Instead of being disrespectful, I _____ (become) polite when greeting people. ¹⁰In addition, instead of being rude to my teachers, I _____ (be) courteous. ¹¹I am proud to say that I _____ (grow) into a righteous man.

The Past Perfect Tense

LO 4 **Use the past perfect tense.**

The past perfect tense is used to write about two actions that happened in the past; one action finished before the other. The past perfect tense is formed by combining **had** and the past participle.

The past perfect tense and the past tense are often used together. The past perfect tense shows the first action in the past, and the past tense shows second action in the past.

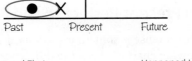

Happened First   Happened Later

Steve **had worked** as an interrogator in the army before he **became** an officer at the state prison.

After he **had taken** a few criminal justice courses, he **chose** law enforcement as his career.

Comparing Past Perfect to Past Tense

Past Perfect	Past
Two actions happened in the past. One happened before the other in the past.	The action is completed. Only one event happened in the past.
After the prison guards **had found** an illegal cell phone under a prisoner's mattress, they **seized** it.	The prison guards **found** an illegal cell phone under a prisoner's mattress.

PRACTICE   Using Past and Past Perfect Tenses

24.4   Identify the correct past or past perfect verb form in each of the following sentences.

EXAMPLE: In 2002, a jury (convicted, had convicted) Andrea Pia Yates for the drowning murders of her five young children.

1. The judge (ordered, had ordered) Yates to serve life in prison.
2. She (wanted, had wanted) to save her children from the devil, so she killed them one at a time.
3. Before she killed her children, Yates (attempted, had attempted) suicide twice.
4. After she (gave, had given) birth to her last child, she suffered from postpartum depression.
5. At the trial, both the prosecution and the defense (agreed, had agreed) that she was severely mentally ill.
6. Yates' attorneys did not convince the jury that their client (killed, had killed) her children by reason of insanity.
7. The legal definition of insanity asks what a person (knew, had known) at the time of the crime.
8. Jurors (learned, had learned) of her history of mental illness, but they reasoned that she knew that what she was doing was wrong.
9. They believed this because she (called, had called) the police immediately after she had killed the children.
10. In a new trial in 2006, the jury (found, had found) Yates not guilty by reason of insanity.

(Adapted from *Criminal Justice Today* by Frank Schmalleger)

Passive Voice

LO 5 **Use passive voice.**

Past participles are also used to make passive voice. **Voice** is a grammar category for verbs. English verbs have two voices: active and passive. When writing, if you want to focus on the subject of the sentence, use the active voice. If the goal is more important than the subject, then use passive voice.

The passive voice consists of a form of the verb **be** and the past participle. Notice the difference between active and passive voice and their verb forms in the following examples:

Active Voice	Performer	Action	Goal
The active voice focuses on the subject that performs the action.	The police officer	caught	the car thief.
Passive Voice	Goal	Action	Performer
Be + past participle			
The passive voice focuses on the receiver of the action. The subject of the sentence is not the performer.	The car thief	was caught	by the police officer.

Passive voice can be used with many verb tenses. Here are examples of how **be** is used with the past participle to form both active and passive voice:

Verb Tense	Active	Passive be + past participle
Simple present	Criminal justice agencies **use** computer-based training.	Computer-based training **is used** by criminal justice agencies.
Present progressive	Criminal justice agencies **are using** computer-based training.	Computer-based training **is being used** by criminal justice agencies.
Future	Criminal justice agencies **will use** computer-based training.	Computer-based training **will be used** by criminal justice agencies.
Simple past	Criminal justice agencies **used** computer-based training.	Computer-based training **was used** by criminal justice agencies.
Present perfect	Criminal justice agencies **have used** computer-based training.	Computer-based training **has been used** by criminal justice agencies.
Other helping verbs: **can, could, would, should, might, must**	Criminal justice agencies **can use** computer-based training.	Computer-based training **can be used** by criminal justice agencies.

TIP The *by* phrase can be omitted when the doer of the action is understood.

Police-pursuit driving **simulators** are widely used in training programs ~~by police training divisions~~.

simulator a computerized system that imitates real conditions

Identifying Active and Passive Voice

24.5   Read the following sentences and decide if the underlined verb is active or passive. Write **A** for active and **P** for passive.

DNA profiling the process used to help police identify someone suspected of committing a crime, which involves testing human bodily fluids, bones, hair, and teeth found at the scene of a crime and comparing it with the DNA of the accused person

EXAMPLE: **DNA profiling** <u>uses</u> human DNA for identification.   A

1. DNA <u>is</u> a nucleic acid found in the center of cells.
2. A large role <u>is played</u> by DNA in criminal cases throughout the country.
3. DNA <u>can convict</u> or <u>can clear</u> a suspect.
4. DNA <u>is considered</u> highly reliable by the U.S. Department of Justice.
5. Originally, DNA <u>was used</u> by laboratories as a test to determine paternity.
6. The first use of DNA in criminal cases <u>began</u> in 1986 in England.
7. DNA testing <u>has been called</u> one of the most important technological breakthroughs in criminology.
8. DNA profiling <u>requires</u> only a few human cells for comparison.
9. Sufficient genetic material <u>is provided</u> by one drop of blood, a few hairs, a small amount of skin, or a trace of body fluid.
10. Because DNA does not change, genetic tests <u>can be conducted</u> on evidence taken from crime scenes for a long time after fingerprints have disappeared.

(Adapted from *Criminal Justice Today* by Frank Schmalleger)

Using Active and Passive Voice

24.6

Part A

Change the underlined verb from the active to passive form in each of the sentences, and rewrite each sentence in the space provided. The first sentence is done for you.

EXAMPLE: A defendant <u>offers</u> some type of defense.

Some type of defense is offered by a defendant.

1. The defendant <u>gives</u> evidence and arguments.

_____

2. The U.S. legal system <u>recognizes</u> four categories of defense.

_____

3. The alibi defense <u>claims</u> that the defendant is innocent.

_____

alibi an excuse used to show that a person could not have committed a crime

4. Witnesses and documentation <u>supports</u> an **alibi**.

_____

Part B

Change the underlined verb from the passive to active form in each of the sentences below.

self-defense justification when the person claims that it was necessary to harm an attacker for his or her own safety from injury or death

5. The **self-defense justification** <u>can be used</u> by a person who harms an attacker.

_____

6. This defense <u>should be used</u> by a person only when cornered with no path of escape.

_____

outweigh is more important than something else

7. The protection of property <u>is **outweighed**</u> by the protection of human life.

_____

8. Reasonable, non-deadly force <u>can be applied</u> by a property owner to prevent others from unlawfully taking or damaging it.

_____

Past Participles as Adjectives

LO 6 **Use past participles as adjectives.**

Past participles can be used as adjectives. When past participles are used as adjectives, they describe how someone feels or felt.

Participle before a noun	He is a **frightened** man.
Participle after a linking verb	The man seemed **frightened** by the thief.

TIP A past participle cannot be used to describe the subject after a linking verb. The **–ing** verb form must be used.

The movie was frightening. **Not:** The movie was frightened.

PRACTICE Identifying Participles as Adjectives or Verbs

24.7 For each of the following sentences, indicate whether the underlined word is a past participle adjective or past participle verb form.

EXAMPLE: On April 20, 1999, twelve Columbine High School students and a teacher were <u>killed</u> by two students.   Verb

outcasts people not accepted by the others

1. Eric Harris and Dylan Klebold were <u>seen</u> as **outcasts** at Columbine.
2. The community was <u>horrified</u>.
3. A year before the murders, Harris and Klebold were <u>caught</u> with stolen tools by Littleton, Colorado, police.
4. In the months before the attacks, two 9 millimeter firearms and two 12-gauge shotguns were <u>bought</u> for them by a friend, Robyn Anderson.

5. On the day of the attacks, their plan to set off bombs in the cafeteria was <u>spoiled</u> when the bombs failed to explode.

6. Harris and Klebold were <u>disappointed</u> that the bombs did not explode.

7. They were <u>armed</u> with guns, knives, and bombs as they entered the school's cafeteria at around 11:20 a.m.

8. They walked through the hallways, into classrooms, and into the library shooting at students and teachers, many who were <u>hurt</u> or <u>killed</u>.

9. All students and employees were <u>terrified</u>.

10. Shortly after 12 p.m., Harris and Klebold were <u>finished</u> shooting others and committed suicide.

MyWritingLab™
Complete this activity at mywritinglab.com

Review: Past Participles

Decide whether each of the underlined items in the following passage is correct or has an error in the use of past participles or perfect tenses. Write the correction above the error. If the item is correct, write a *C* above it. The first one has been corrected for you.

Miranda warnings You have the right to remain silent. Anything you say can be used against you in a court of law. You have the right to speak to an attorney and to have an attorney present while you are being questioned. If you cannot afford to hire an attorney, one will be appointed to represent you at government expense.

[1]The famous *Miranda v. Arizona case* of 1966 <u>has established</u> the well-known **Miranda warnings.**

^established

[2]The case involved Ernesto Miranda, whom police <u>have arrested</u> in Phoenix, Arizona. [3]Miranda was accused of having kidnapped and raped a young woman. [4]At police headquarters, the victim <u>identified</u> him. [5]After police <u>had question</u> him for two hours, Miranda signed a confession that formed the basis of his later conviction on the charges.

[6]His conviction <u>was overturn</u> on appeal. [7]The U.S. Supreme Court ruled that Miranda's conviction <u>had been</u> unconstitutional. [8]Interrogators <u>have not warned</u> him of his rights during questioning. [9]Therefore, evidence police <u>had receive</u> as a result of questioning could not be used against him. [10]Later, Miranda was convicted after the court <u>had gave</u> him a fair trial. [11]As a result of *Miranda v. Arizona*, suspects eighteen years or older who are in custody <u>are advise</u> of their Miranda rights before any questioning begins.

(Adapted from *Criminal Justice Today* by Frank Schmalleger)

Writing Assignment

Write about an Image

Write five sentences about some things that have changed since you became a college student. Use the present perfect tense.

EXAMPLE: I **have learned** some good test-taking strategies.

25 Pronouns

Theme: *Music*

Learning Objectives

After working through this chapter, you will be able to:

LO 1 Define and identify the different types of pronouns.

LO 2 Correctly use subject, object, and possessive pronouns.

LO 3 Make pronouns agree with their antecedents.

LO 4 Make pronouns refer to one specific antecedent.

LO 1 Define and identify the different types of pronouns.

What Is a Pronoun?

A **pronoun** is a word that is used to refer to another noun or pronoun or to replace a noun or pronoun. Writers use pronouns so that they do not have to keep repeating the same noun:

Repetitious: Workers around the world have found ways of singing together to help workers work, lighten workers' loads, and give workers a feeling of togetherness.

Improved: Workers around the world have found ways of singing together to help them work, lighten their loads, and give them a feeling of togetherness.

Pronouns have other uses as well. They can be used as adjectives and to form questions. The following chart shows how pronouns can be used in sentences.

How Pronouns Are Used	
To refer to another noun or pronoun	Almost all **people** sing whether **they** can carry a tune or not.
To replace a noun or pronoun	Some **people** sing in the shower, while **others** sing in the car. **Others** replaces *people.*
To modify a noun	**Their voices** sound better in enclosed spaces. My brother sings **that song** every day.
To ask a question	**Who** likes to sing in the car?

Pronouns in Context

In the following passage about the influences of rock and roll music, the pronouns are blue.

The early influences on rock and roll were **many** and varied. First and most important was the mixture of slow blues singing with a harder, more rhythmic background sound **that** became known as rhythm and blues (R&B). Early R&B artists included singers such as Muddy Waters, **who** grew up on a Mississippi plantation and moved to Chicago. **Most** were black. Rhythm and blues mixed two sounds. **One** was the rural sound of the blues, and the **other** was the rhythms of the city streets. The personal sound of one man with a guitar was expanded in R&B to include a group of musicians.

Also important to the early growth of rock and roll were the hard-driving sounds of Little Richard and Chuck Berry. Little Richard was from the South, and **he** pounded the piano and screamed **his** lyrics like a wild man. **He** and **his** group were responsible for **some** of the early hits of rock and roll, such as "Tutti Frutti" and "Rip **It** Up." Chuck Berry wrote **all** of **his** own music. **His** songs spoke directly to teens **who** were sitting in class but ready to party.

Another of the early influences on rock and roll was country music. Before the term "rock and roll" was widely used, the early sound was known as "rockabilly" ("rock" + "hillbilly"). **It** combined the drive of rhythm and blues with the elements of country and western, a style popular in the rural South for **its** fiddle playing, guitar picking, and warm vocal harmonies. Rockabilly stars **who** scored big hits at this time were Jerry Lee Lewis and Johnny Cash. **All** of these artists were white, poor, and from the rural South.

(Adapted from *Understanding Music* by Jeremy Yudkin)

Pronoun Case

LO 2 **Correctly use subject, object, and possessive pronouns.**

Case is the form personal pronouns take to show how they function in a sentence: as a subject, as an object, or as a possessive.

Pronouns as Subjects

The following pronouns are used as subjects: *I, you, he, she, it, we, they, who, whoever*.

Subject pronouns are used as subjects of verbs and after linking verbs.

Subject Pronouns	
Subject of a verb	**She** likes to sing the latest pop hit song.
Compound subject of a verb	**She** and **I** like to sing together.
Pronoun combined with a noun as subject	**We** singers plan to form a group.
After a linking verb	The singer is **she**.

TIP	To be sure that you are using the correct pronoun(s) in a compound subject, use this process: omit one half of the compound and check it.

Example: Him and me had a band.
Him ~~and me~~ had a band. ~~Him and~~ me had a band.

Correction: He and I had a band.

Pronouns as Objects

The following pronouns are used as objects: *me, him, her, it, us, you, them, whom, whomever.* Object pronouns are used as objects of verbs and objects of prepositions.

Object Pronouns	
Object of a verb	The panel of judges **heard me** sing.
Compound object of a verb	The panel of judges **heard her** and me sing.
Pronoun and noun as object	The panel of judges **heard us singers** perform.
Object of a preposition	The judges had a good opinion **of me.**

TIP	To be sure that you are using the correct pronoun(s) in a compound object, use this process: omit one half of the compound and check it.

Example: The panel of judges heard he and I sing.
The panel of judges heard he ~~and I~~ sing. The panel of judges heard ~~he and~~ I sing.

Correction: The panel of judges heard him and me sing.

PRACTICE   Using Subject and Object Pronouns

25.1   Circle the correct pronoun in each of the following sentences. The first one has been done for you.

¹My friend Jenna and (I, me) had to attend an orchestral concert for our music appreciation class. ²We asked two of our friends from our class to go with (we, us). ³Neither (them, they) nor (us, we) knew what to expect. ⁴Our professor gave (we, us) students some advice. ⁵Since most people get dressed more formally

for the concert, my friends and (me, I) could not wear tee shirts and jeans. [6](They, Them) are not appropriate clothes for an orchestral concert. [7]My teacher told (us, we) to arrive at the concert hall early.

[8]To become more familiar with the songs on the program, Jenna and (me, I) watched videos of those songs on YouTube. [9]Jenna, (me, I), and our friends also looked for information about the composers on the Internet. [10]While the musicians were warming up, Darvins and (me, I) named the instruments that (us, we) had learned about in class. [11]None of (we, us) students thought that the concert would be so inspiring and memorable.

Pronouns as Possessives

Pronouns showing ownership are called possessive pronouns. The following are possessive pronouns: ***my, mine, his, hers, its, our, ours, your, yours, their, theirs, whose.***
Some possessive pronouns are used as adjectives and others are used in place of nouns.

As an adjective: Jazz singers use their voices in special ways.

In place of a noun: Theirs are used in special ways. (their voices)

Apostrophes with Pronouns Possessive pronouns do not need apostrophes.

Word Reminder. For more information about confusing word pairs, see Chapter 31.

Ellie brought ~~her's~~ hers to practice.

Malcolm brought ~~his'~~ his to practice.

Possessive pronouns and contractions are sometimes confused.

Possessive Pronoun	Contraction
its	it's = it is
their	they're = they are
your	you're = you are

A small group of pronouns, called indefinite pronouns, can be changed into possessive pronouns by adding an *'s*: ***anybody's, anyone's, everybody's, everyone's, nobody's, no one's, one's, somebody's, someone's.***

Everyone's performance was excellent.

Possessive pronouns *do not* have plural forms such as *everybodies, somebodies,* or *nobodies.*

PRACTICE **Using Possessive Pronouns**
25.2 Circle the correct possessive pronoun or possessive adjective.

EXAMPLE: That mp3 player is (my, mine).

1. Jack did not bring his music; he listened to (her, hers).
2. Saika is one of (his, his') best friends.
3. Some friends of (our, ours) plan to share (their, they're, there) music with us.
4. We are going to download some songs onto (your, you're) phone.
5. My favorite group just released (its, it's) latest song.
6. That new song is going to be (everyones, everyone's) favorite.

Reflexive and Intensive Pronouns

Reflexive pronouns and **intensive pronouns** look the same, but they are used differently. They are formed by adding *–self* or *–selves* to the end of a personal pronoun. They have singular and plural forms:

> **Singular forms:** *myself, yourself, himself, herself, itself, oneself*
>
> **Plural forms:** *yourselves, ourselves, themselves*

Hisself, ourself, theirself, and *theirselves* are not standard English forms.

Reflexive Pronouns Reflexive pronouns refer to the subject. They work as objects of verbs or prepositions.

Object of a verb	He watched **himself** in the video.
Object of a preposition	He made a video of **himself**.

Intensive Pronouns Intensive pronouns add emphasis to the noun they refer to.

The performers **themselves** are responsible for their own actions.

They will take responsibility **themselves**.

Reflexive pronouns should not be used as subjects:

Bryan and ~~myself~~ I are members of the marching band.

PRACTICE   Using Reflexive and Intensive Pronouns

25.3   Fill in the correct reflexive or intensive pronoun. Choose from the following singular and plural forms: *myself, yourself, himself, herself, itself, ourselves, yourselves,* or *themselves.*

EXAMPLE: In the nineteenth century, members of the middle class bought ___themselves___ sheet music.

1. After dinner, a woman would give a piano performance by _____

2. During that time, many composers made a good income for _____ from their music.

3. Before this, the church _____ dictated the style or content composers had to use.

4. Pianos became much cheaper, so you could own one _____

5. The Romantic era brought with it a new sound from larger orchestras, which I _____ enjoy listening to.

Pronouns in Sentences That Compare

In sentences that compare, the part of the sentence that compares is a dependent clause that begins with the subordinating conjunction *than* or *as*. Sometimes the comparison dependent clause ends with a pronoun. When you read the sentence, it will seem as if the rest of the clause is missing. The pronoun is the subject of the dependent clause, so use a subject pronoun after *than:*

> Jamal plays piano better than she.
> Jamal plays the piano better than she plays the piano.

Who and *Whom*

Who and **whom** are called relative pronouns. They appear in questions and in dependent word groups. **Who** is a subject pronoun and is used as the subject in a question or a dependent clause. **Whom** is an object pronoun and is used as an object of a verb or object of a preposition in a dependent word group. The following chart shows how to use **who** and **whom.**

Who and Whom in Questions

Who as subject: **Who** is the most famous musician of all time?

Whom as object:

  Object of a verb: **Whom** should I choose?
  Object of a preposition: About **whom** are you speaking?

Who and Whom in Dependent Clauses

Who as subject of the dependent clause:

  The composer **who** started to write music at age six was Mozart.

Whom as object in a dependent clause:

  Object of a verb: The composer **whom** I admire is Mozart.
  Object of a preposition: Mozart is the composer about **whom** I wrote my paper.

TIP | If you have trouble figuring out whether to use **who** or **whom**, substitute a personal pronoun for **who** or **whom** to help you decide which one to use:

  he or *she* = *who*   *him* or *her* = *whom*

 Using Pronouns Correctly

25.4

Part A

Circle the correct pronoun in the following comparisons.

EXAMPLE: Andrew practices as hard as (me, I).

  1. She is a better performer than (he, him).
  2. We have been writing songs longer than (them, they).
  3. Tamika sings in the choir more often than (she, her).
  4. Andrew practices playing his guitar longer than (me, I).
  5. They are less talented than (us, we).

Part B

Circle the correct form (*who* or *whom*).

EXAMPLE: Michael Jackson, (who, whom) was called the "King of Pop," died on June 25, 2009.

6. (Who, Whom) became famous for his spins, kicks, anti-gravity lean, and moonwalk?

7. Jackson was one of the few artists (who, whom) was inducted into the Rock and Roll Hall of Fame twice.

8. Jackson, to (who, whom) many awards had been given, had a great impact on world music and culture.

9. Quincy Jones, (who, whom) made the elaborate video *Thriller* with Jackson, said that Jackson changed the music business.

10. Jackson, with (who, whom) Jones shared a Grammy award for Album of the Year, also won a Grammy for "Billy Jean," a hit from that album.

Pronoun-Antecedent Agreement

LO 3 **Make pronouns agree with their antecedents.**

An **antecedent** is a word or phrase that a pronoun refers to.

ANTECEDENT   PRONOUN   PRONOUN

Jimi Hendrix used **his** guitar to play **his** highly original music.

The basic rule for pronoun-antecedent agreement is that a **pronoun** must agree with its antecedent.

■ A singular pronoun must have a singular antecedent:

ANTECEDENT   PRONOUN

Hendrix, who was left-handed, had to make changes to **his** Stratocaster guitar to play it.

■ A plural pronoun must have a plural antecedent:

ANTECEDENT   PRONOUN

His special effects were creative, and they made him famous.

PRACTICE   Identifying Pronouns and Antecedents

25.5   Circle the antecedent of each underlined pronoun. Then draw an arrow from the pronoun to the antecedent.

EXAMPLE: Jimi Hendrix was fascinated with guitars when he was a child.

1. Jimi's father bought Jimi **his** first real guitar; however, **it** was made for a right-handed player.

2. Jimi was left-handed, so by reversing the strings on the guitar, Jimi could play **it**.

3. Hendrix never learned to read music, but **he** trained his ear by listening to other guitarists and observing **their** style.

4. He had to watch other guitarists play a song and then figure out how to play **it** left-handed.

5. In the 1960s, Hendrix went to London where he introduced many new guitar techniques, and <u>they</u> impressed audiences and guitarists.

6. Electronics whiz Roger Mayer worked with Hendrix, and <u>they</u> created effects that helped Hendrix create <u>his</u> heavy psychedelic sound.

7. Hendrix's musical sounds are as fresh today as <u>they</u> were when <u>he</u> first played <u>them</u>.

Compound Subject Antecedents

Special rules apply with compound subjects.

1. When the antecedent is a compound subject joined by **and**, the pronoun that refers to them is always plural. It does not matter if one or both of the antecedents is plural.

   Customers and fans want quick, easy ways to get their music.

2. When the compound subject antecedents are joined by **or, neither . . . nor, either . . . or,** or **not only . . . but also,** the pronoun agrees with the second antecedent.

   Either Aiden **or** Brian will record original music on his laptop.

   Either Aiden **or** the band members will record original music on their laptop.

TIP | To decide which pronoun to use with **or, neither . . . nor, either . . . or,** or **not only . . . but also,** cross out the part of the compound subject before the **or, nor,** or **but also.**

A teenager or his **parents** often have **their** own music preferences.

PRACTICE Using Correct Pronoun–Compound Antecedent Agreement

25.6 Circle the connecting words *and, or, either/or,* or *neither/nor.* Then underline the compound antecedent and circle the correct pronoun.

EXAMPLE: Denmark, South America, and Asia had (its, their) version of flutes dating from the Stone Age.

1. Open-holed instruments or beaked instruments go by (its, their) generic term "flute."

2. Both a flute and a whistle produce (its, their) sound when a player blows an air stream into the open hole of the instrument.

3. Either cymbals or a drum makes (its, their) sounds by striking (it, them).

4. Sticks or tubes are played by banging (it, them) on a hard surface.

5. Both the harp and the lute were used in ancient customs and have kept (its, their) popularity.

6. Either the piano or the violin is played when (its, their) strings are plucked, bowed, or struck.

Collective Noun Antecedents

A **collective noun** is a word that refers to a group of people or things. It can describe the group as a whole (only one) or the individuals in the group (more than one). The following are common collective nouns:

army	class	crowd	group	senate
audience	club	family	jury	society
band	committee	gang	public	team

A collective noun can be singular or plural depending on the meaning.

■ If the members of the group are acting as a unit, doing the same thing or thinking the same way, the pronoun that refers to the noun is singular.

The **group** agreed to perform **its** hit songs at the concert.

■ If the members of the group are acting as individuals, doing different things or thinking differently, the pronoun that refers to the noun is plural.

The **group** gave **their** individual opinions about which songs to play.

PRACTICE 25.7 Using Correct Pronoun–Collective Noun Antecedent Agreement

Underline the antecedents and circle the correct pronoun.

EXAMPLE: The <u>orchestra</u> will rehearse (ⓘits, their) musical pieces several days a week.

1. An orchestra spends more time rehearsing (its, their) music before a concert than playing (it, them) at a concert.

2. The audience expressed (its, their) appreciation of the performance with a **standing ovation.**

3. The audience showed (its, their) disappointment by walking out or talking.

4. The Alvin Ailey dance troupe will begin (its, their) international tour in July.

5. The American Ballet Company temporarily disbanded in 1938 because (it, they) disagreed on the dance arrangements.

6. The group broke up to develop (its, their) own solo careers.

standing ovation an action where an audience stands up and claps for a long time to show appreciation

Indefinite Pronoun Antecedents

Indefinite pronouns do not refer to a specific person, thing, or idea. Some indefinite pronouns are always singular or always plural. Others can be singular or plural depending on the meaning of the sentence.

acronym a word formed from the first letter or first few letters of each word

Singular Indefinite Pronouns Use a singular pronoun to refer to singular indefinite pronouns.

The following list of indefinite pronouns is singular. Even pronouns that refer to many people or things, such as ***everyone, everybody,*** and ***everything,*** are considered singular. An easy way to remember this list of pronouns is with the **acronym** *A NOSE.*

A	N	O	S	E
anyone	no one	one	someone	everyone
anybody	nobody	other	somebody	everybody
anything	nothing		something	everything
another	neither			each
				either

Anyone can improve his or her enjoyment of music by becoming an experienced listener.

Everyone has his or her music preference.

TIP | A singular indefinite pronoun may have an of the prepositional phrase placed after it.

PREP PHRASE

One of the drummers won an award for his performance at the football game.

Even if the noun at the end of the of the prepositional phrase is plural, the antecedent must agree with the subject of the sentence.

Plural Indefinite Pronouns Use a plural pronoun to refer to plural indefinite pronouns.

both   few   many   others   several

Many like to listen to their favorite music while studying.

Others keep their radio playing in the background at home all the time.

Singular or Plural Indefinite Pronouns A few indefinite pronouns can be singular or plural depending on the noun that the pronoun refers to. These pronouns have special rules for agreement.

An easy way to remember them is with the acronym *SANAM*.

S	A	N	A	M
some	any	none	all	most

To decide which pronoun to use, look for the word that the pronoun refers to. The antecedent may be in the prepositional phrase that follows it as in these examples:

- If the noun that the pronoun refers to is singular, then the pronoun is singular.

  Most **of the** class practiced its songs for the concert.

- If the noun that the pronoun refers to is plural, then the pronoun is plural.

  Most **of the** students practiced their songs for the concert.

PRACTICE   Using Correct Pronoun-Antecedent Agreement

25.8   Underline the indefinite pronoun antecedent and circle the correct pronoun that refers to it.

EXAMPLE: <u>Some</u> of the folk music passed down through the generations had (its, their) words changed.

1. No one may know the age of (his or her, their) folk song.
2. Each of the folk singers gives (his or her, their) personal interpretation of a song.
3. Anyone can change the tempo or melody of (his or her, their) song.
4. One does not have to train (his or her, their) voice to be a folk singer.
5. All of the Native American cultures have used music to teach (its, their) oral history.
6. Most of the tribe's music reflects (its, their) use of drums, rattles, and other percussion instruments.
7. None of the singers try to match (his or her, their) notes with the other singers.

Plural Antecedents with Singular Meaning

Some antecedents have plural forms, but they are considered singular.

Plural Antecedent	Example
Titles of single entities: books, organizations, countries	The textbook *Musical Encounters* gives **its** readers a multicultural approach to music study.
Singular nouns ending in –s: news, mathematics, economics, measles, athletics	The **news** directs **its** delivery to gain viewers.

Correcting Pronoun Shifts

A pronoun shift is an error that happens when the writer switches from one pronoun to another pronoun to refer to the same antecedent.

Shift: If a person works hard, you can be successful.

Correct: If a person works hard, he or she can be successful.

Shift: Learning about music helps us develop the skills you need to evaluate it.

Correct: Learning about music helps us develop the skills we need to evaluate it.

PRACTICE **Correcting Pronoun Shift Errors**

25.9 Underline the pronoun that is shifted and write your correction above it.

EXAMPLE: When people hear Tejano, <u>you</u> *they* may remember the pop star of the 1990s, Selena Quintanilla-Perez.

1. She brought Tejano to the U.S. culture, and they brought attention to Mexican musical traditions.
2. Mexican-American farm workers took Mexican music, and he blended it with music of other immigrant groups that lived in the community.
3. Selena spoke English, but her father insisted that you needed to learn to speak Spanish to be successful in both the United States and Mexico.
4. Abraham, Selena's father, believed that you should stay true to her Mexican roots.
5. Selena gave Mexican-Americans ethnic pride while they also highlighted Mexican language, music, and culture.

Pronoun Reference

LO 4 Make pronouns refer to one specific antecedent.

A pronoun should refer to a specific antecedent.

No antecedent: Shauna's singing was so loud that she did not need a microphone.

With antecedent: Shauna sang so loudly that she did not need a microphone.

No antecedent: It says in the newspaper that the concert was rescheduled for tomorrow night.

Clear: The newspaper reporter said that the concert was rescheduled for tomorrow night.

A pronoun should refer to only one antecedent:

Unclear antecedent: The drummer told the guitarist that he should practice more often.

Clear antecedent: The drummer told the guitarist to practice more often.

Pronouns such as *this* and *which* should refer to a specific noun, not a group of words that explain an idea or situation.

Refers to a group of words:	Christa did not go to rehearsal, which was not considerate of her.
Clear:	Christa was inconsiderate by not going to rehearsal.
Refers to a group of words:	Christa called Sam late last night to explain why she missed rehearsal. This made Sam angry.
Clear:	Christa called Sam last night to explain why she missed rehearsal. Her late night call made Sam angry.

PRACTICE **Correcting Pronoun Use**

25.10   Underline the vague pronoun in each sentence and correct it. You may need to rewrite the sentence.

Chante
EXAMPLE: Shireen took Chante to the college's multicultural festival so <u>she</u> could enjoy dance, music, and food from different cultures.

1. They say that the festival attracts many students each year.
2. Chante took her student ID and her ticket out of her wallet and showed it to the security guard at the entrance to the festival.
3. Shireen explained to Chante that she would enjoy the Jamaican booth.
4. On the center stage, they heard a reggae band playing and saw students dancing to the music. This was fun to watch.
5. Someone stepped right in front of Chante and blocked her view. It upset her.
6. Shireen and Chante listened to the music for a half hour before she decided to try some jerk chicken, rice, and peas.
7. While Shireen was holding her plate of food and her cell phone, she dropped it.
8. They had run out of food, but Shirleen had a good time anyway.

MyWritingLab™
Complete this activity
at mywritinglab.com

Review: Pronoun Use

Read the following excerpt for errors in pronouns. Find the errors and correct them. The first error has been corrected for you. One sentence in the excerpt is correct.

[1]Robert Schumann ~~he~~ was an early Romantic composer whose music was inspired by literature. [2]His father was a bookseller, so he had unlimited access to the popular writings of the day. [3]As a young man Schumann hisself wrote poems and novels. [4]He studied law but was not interested in it; instead he drank heavily

and spent their money on having a good time. [5]Schumann met Friedrich Wieck, a famous piano teacher, and Schumann took lessons from he.

[6]When Schumann heard Paganini, whom was a famous Italian violinist, play a concert, he was impressed and decided to become a master of the piano. [7]Schumann took a room in Wieck's house so Wieck and him could devote all they time to practice. [8]Clara, Wieck's daughter, was half Schumann's age, but she could play piano better than him. [9]Schumann practiced constantly and permanently damaged his hand. [10]This ended his piano playing career.

[11]He turned from performing to composing and fell in love with Clara, who was fifteen years old at the time. [12]Wieck saw that Schumann barely made a living, and he did not want his daughter with someone as poor as him. [13]Wieck took his daughter away on long tours and would not let the two of them be in each others' company. [14]While apart, Schumann and Clara they wrote secret letters to each other. [15]Finally, Clara and him had to go to court to get freedom to marry.

Writing Assignment

MyWritingLab™
Complete this activity
at mywritinglab.com

Write about an Image

Using the different types of pronouns you learned about in this chapter, write five to ten sentences describing the performers in the photo. Then underline the pronoun(s) in each sentence and write the type of pronoun it is.

EXAMPLE: <u>One</u> of the performers holds an orange trash can.   Indefinite pronoun

Nouns and Noun Markers

Theme: *Travel and Tourism*

Learning Objectives

After working through this chapter, you will be able to:

LO 1 Identify nouns.

LO 2 Identify and use common, proper, compound, and collective nouns.

LO 3 Use singular and plural nouns.

LO 4 Choose appropriate noun markers.

LO 1 **Identify nouns.**

What Is a Noun?

Nouns are words used to name people, things, activities, and ideas. There are more nouns than other kinds of words in the English language. Along with verbs, nouns are the chief building blocks of a sentence.

Nouns in Context

In the following passage about museums, the nouns are blue.

Museums provide many **options** for **people** to learn about cultural **activity**. Among art **museums**, the most prominent **museums** hold original **collections** that concentrate on a special **category**. The **Museum of Modern Art** in **New York City** features **hundreds** of twentieth-century **paintings** by **artists** such as **Pablo Picasso, Andy Warhol, Jackson Pollock,** and **Jasper Johns. Museums** that focus on historic **houses** are **birthplaces** of American **presidents**, including that of **Abraham Lincoln** in **Hodgenville, Kentucky, Franklin D. Roosevelt** in **Hyde Park, New York,** and **Harry Truman** in **Independence, Missouri.** The famous **Andersonville Prison** in **Georgia**, where captured Union **soldiers** were imprisoned during the **American Civil War,** also fits into this **group. Museums** devoted to **science** like the **Smithsonian National Air and Space Museum** in **Washington, DC**, provide a **history** of the **discovery** and **development** of **aviation** and space **exploration** during the twentieth **century.** This **museum** has actual or rebuilt **models** of original **aircraft** and space **rockets** and **modules.** Natural history **museums** display **items** from the **world** of **nature,** such as human **evolution, biodiversity,** and environmental **issues,** among other **topics.** The **Museum National d'Histoire Naturelle** in **Paris** and the **Natural History Museum** in **London** are leading **examples** of this **type** of **museum.**

(Adapted from *Travel and Tourism* by Paul S. Biederman)

Types of Nouns

LO 2 Identify and use common, proper, compound, and collective nouns.

Nouns can be grouped to make them easy to understand and identify: common and proper nouns, compound nouns, and collective nouns.

Common and Proper Nouns

A **common noun** is a word that refers to a general person, place, thing, activity, or idea. A common noun begins with a lowercase letter unless it is the first word in a sentence. A **proper noun** is a word that refers to a specific person, place, thing, activity, or idea and begins with an uppercase letter no matter where it is placed in a sentence.

Common Nouns	Proper Nouns	Examples
pilot	Charles Lindbergh	Charles Lindbergh was the first pilot to make a nonstop flight alone across the Atlantic Ocean in May 1927.
hotelier	Cesar Ritz	Cesar Ritz was a famous Swiss hotelier.
city	Las Vegas	Gambling was legalized in the city of Las Vegas in 1931.
airplane	Cessna	Cessna is the world's largest manufacturer of private airplanes.

PRACTICE **Writing Common Nouns**

26.1   List ten common nouns that are items that can be placed in a large suitcase.

_____

_____

PRACTICE **Using Proper Nouns in Sentences**

26.2   Answer the following questions using proper nouns. Write your answers in complete sentences and underline each proper noun. In each sentence, use the name of the person who answered the question.

EXAMPLE: Which country would you like to visit?

Alcee would like to visit Egypt.

1. What is the name of the city or town you live in now?
2. What is the name of a tourist site you have visited?
3. What countries are your relatives or your ancestors from?
4. What is the name of your favorite park, theater, or museum?
5. What is the name of a hotel or motel that you have heard about or stayed in?

Compound Nouns

A **compound noun** consists of more than one word: for example, two nouns (*tour package*); a preposition and noun (*underground*); an adjective and a noun (*monthly rates*); or an –*ing* verb and a noun (*swimming pool*).

Compound nouns have three forms.

Compound Noun Form	Examples
one word	keyboard, flashlight, bedroom, database
two words	police officer, seat belt, swimming pool, real estate
hyphenated	sister-in-law, editor-in-chief, passer-by

> **TIP** | Consult a good dictionary to check the spelling of compound nouns.

PRACTICE Writing Compound Nouns

26.3 List five compound nouns for each of the following words. Use a dictionary if needed.

EXAMPLE: paper <u>paperback, paperwork, paper towel, paper clip, newspaper</u>

1. air _____

2. fire _____

3. rain _____

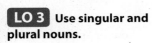

Grammar Reminder. For more information about subject-verb agreement with collective nouns, see Chapter 22.

Collective Nouns

Collective nouns refer to a group of people or things. They can describe the group as a whole or the individuals in the group. Collective nouns are singular if the members in the group are acting as a unit, but they are plural if the members are acting as individuals.

Here are some common collective nouns:

army	class	crowd	group	senate
audience	club	family	jury	society
band	committee	gang	public	team

Singular and Plural Nouns

LO 3 Use singular and plural nouns.

A **singular noun** refers to one person, place, thing, activity, or idea. A **plural noun** refers to more than one.

Regular Plural Nouns

Most singular nouns form their plurals by adding –s to the end of the noun.

Singular nouns: railroad, customer, island

Plural nouns: railroads, customers, islands

Some nouns form their plurals using different rules as explained in the following chart.

Forming Noun Plurals		
Noun	Add for Plural	Examples
Most nouns ending in **–s, –ss, –sh, –ch, –x,** or **–z**, including names that end in **–s**	**–es**	bus, buses Jones, Joneses church, churches kiss, kisses fox, foxes wish, wishes buzz, buzzes
Most nouns ending in a **vowel + –o**	**–s**	stereo, stereos patio, patios tattoo, tattoos radio, radios video, videos
Most nouns ending in a **consonant + –o**	**–es**	echo, echoes tomato, tomatoes hero, heroes veto, vetoes potato, potatoes volcano, volcanoes *Exceptions*: auto, autos piano, pianos Latino, Latinos solo, solos memo, memos soprano, sopranos
Most nouns ending in a **vowel + –y**, including names of people	**–s**	boy, boys key, keys day, days Riley, Rileys holiday, holidays turkey, turkeys
Most nouns ending in a **consonant + –y**	Change **y** to **i** and add **–es**	baby, babies country, countries berry, berries salary, salaries company, companies spy, spies *Exception*: With proper nouns, add **–s** the Kellys, the O'Gradys
Most nouns ending in **–f, –fe,** or **–lf**	Change the **f** to **v** and add **–s** or **–es**	elf, elves loaf, loaves half, halves self, selves knife, knives wife, wives *Exceptions*: belief, beliefs staff, staffs chief, chiefs
Compound nouns: one word two words hyphenated nouns	**–s** **–s** to last word Check the dictionary.	keyboard, keyboards police officer, police officers sister-in-law, sisters-in-law grown-up, grown-ups

PRACTICE Forming Plural Nouns

26.4   Spell the plural form of each of the following nouns. The first one has been done for you.

1. emergency ___emergencies___
2. journey _____
3. Marotta _____
4. passer-by _____
5. stepmother _____

6. family _____
7. tomato _____
8. calf _____
9. veto _____
10. yourself _____

Irregular Plural Nouns

Irregular nouns do not form plurals by adding *–s* or *–es*. The following chart explains the rules and exceptions.

Forming Irregular Noun Plurals	
Irregular Plural Nouns	**Examples**
Nouns with different plural forms	child, children mouse, mice foot, feet ox, oxen man, men woman, women
Nouns that have the same singular and plural forms	deer, sheep, equipment *Names of fish:* cod, halibut, perch, salmon
Nouns that end in *–s* with no singular form	*Tools/instruments:* scissors, tweezers, pliers, tongs *Clothes:* pants, jeans, pajamas, shorts *Eyewear:* binoculars, glasses, goggles
Nouns that end in *–s* but are singular	economics, gymnastics, mathematics, measles, news, mumps
Plural nouns that do not end in *–s*	people, police, cattle
Nouns that are both singular and plural	headquarters, species, crossroads

TIP The words *persons* and *people* are both used to refer to more than one individual; however, the preferred usage is *people*. *Persons* is preferred in legal contexts: Vehicles with fewer than three **persons** may not use the restricted highway lane.

PRACTICE   Changing Plural Nouns to Singular Nouns

26.5   Write the singular form for each of the plural nouns. If the form does not change, write **NC** for "no change." The first one has been done for you.

1. economics __NC____
2. feet _____
3. children _____
4. pants _____
5. sheep _____
6. jeans _____
7. teeth _____
8. ladies _____

PRACTICE   Editing for Plural Noun Errors

26.6   Proofread the following paragraph for eight errors in plural nouns.

ecolodge a special type of hotel, usually located in or near a protected area and managed in a way that conserves the environment

[1]Traveler who want to visit natural areas that conserve the environment and help the local people will enjoy going to the Sukau Rainforest in Malaysia. [2]The Sukau Rainforest Lodge is a twenty-room **ecolodge.** [3]It is located on the Kinabatangan River, which is Malaysia's second-longest river. [4]The nearby Kinabatangan Wildlife Sanctuary is famous for its wildlife, including elephants, monkeys, and orangutans. [5]Visitor can observe wildlife from the comfort of riverboats or hike along jungle walkways. [6]The area is also known for the Gomantong Caves, home to an estimated two million bats. [7]Many other animal specie can be observed. [8]Hoofed mammals, which are active at night, include deers, cattles, and pig. [9]Birds are plentiful, with over 200 different type in the region.

(Adapted from *Travel and Tourism* by Paul S. Biederman)

Mass Nouns

Mass nouns name things that cannot be counted. They are also called uncountable nouns. Mass nouns have only singular forms.

> **No plural form:** Renaldo bought new furniture for the living room.
>
> **Not:** Renaldo bought new ~~furnitures~~ for the living room.
>
> **No plural form:** The airline lost our luggage.
>
> **Not:** The airline lost our ~~luggages~~.

Here are some common mass nouns:

Category	Examples
idea words	advice, love, happiness, freedom, intelligence, work, education
liquids	juice, water, oil, soup, gasoline, coffee, milk
things made up of small pieces	rice, corn, salt, sand, sugar, hair, oatmeal, dirt
whole groups of similar items	mail, luggage, money, fruit, jewelry, furniture, traffic, equipment, information, vocabulary, music

Category	Examples
materials and metals	cloth, plastic, wool, gold, silver, steel
languages	French, Chinese, Russian, English, Spanish
recreation	tennis, soccer, football, chess, checkers
natural phenomena	fog, rain, lightning, snow, cold, darkness
diseases, medical conditions	measles, arthritis, flu, diabetes
fields of study	economics, history, psychology, marketing, computer science
activities (*–ing* words)	sleeping, studying, writing, driving
solids	ice, butter, bread, cheese

Expressing Quantity with Mass Nouns To express how much or how many with mass nouns, use quantity or container words before them.

> **Quantity words:** several pieces of furniture, some furniture; a piece of advice, more advice; a slice of bread, a loaf of bread; a great deal of rain, some rain

> **Container words:** a gallon of milk, a teaspoon of salt, a bottle of water, a glass of juice, a bowl of soup

PRACTICE Editing Singular and Plural Nouns

26.7 There are seven mistakes in the use of plural nouns in this paragraph. Find and correct the errors. The first mistake is corrected for you.

¹In the United States, Coney Island was the birthplace of the
amusement
~~amusements~~ park, the roller coaster, and the hot dog. ²Long before
Disneyland, Six Flags, and Universal Studios, many ~~American~~ went to Coney
Island and its amusement park. ³Coney Island is located on the south
shore of Brooklyn, New York, facing the Atlantic Ocean. ⁴It started out as
an upscale seaside resort after the Civil War in the mid-1800s with ~~hotel~~,
restaurants, and bathing facilities. ⁵In the 1920s, Coney Island became the
nation's first mass tourism amusement park. ⁶Visitors could ride a choice of
thrilling roller coasters, ferris wheels, and carousels, buy ~~souvenir~~, and eat
fast food. ⁷They could also go for a swim in the ocean or sit in the ~~sands~~ on
the beach. ⁸During the summer, especially on ~~weekend~~, a million ~~visitor~~ a
day were not uncommon. ⁹Today, the crowds are not as massive. ¹⁰However,

> Coney Island still reflects the same mixing of Brooklyn's diverse population
> and languages as it did in the last century.
>
> (Adapted from *Travel and Tourism* by Paul S. Biederman)

Noun Markers

LO 4 **Choose appropriate noun markers.**

Noun markers are words that signal that a noun will follow. They sometimes tell if a noun is singular or plural.

> **Many** billions of dollars are spent **every** year on conventions and meetings. Cities compete vigorously for **this** business because of **its** economic impact.

This chart lists the types of noun markers with examples of their use in a sentence.

Noun Markers	
Type	**Markers**
Articles	***a, an, the*** Conventions and meetings are **a** significant part of **the** travel and tourism sector.
Demonstrative pronouns	***this, that, these, those*** **These** conventions and meetings are held by many different groups such as professional and trade organizations.
Indefinite pronouns	***all, any, both, each, either, enough, every, few, fewer, less, little, many, more, most, much, neither, no, several, some*** **Some** meetings are held for training employees. Government agencies stage meetings of **all** kinds.
Numbers	***one, two, three, four,*** etc.; ***first, second, third,*** etc. Paris is **one** city that has become a popular host for international meetings.
Possessive nouns	***the teacher's, Javier's, a manager's*** A **planner's** job is to arrange and carry out all the details related to a variety of meeting formats.
Possessive adjectives	***my, your, his, her, it, our, their, whose*** A trade show gives suppliers of goods and services an opportunity to show **their** latest products.

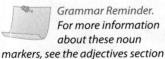

Grammar Reminder. For more information about these noun markers, see the adjectives section of Chapter 27.

Frequently Confused Noun Markers

Some noun markers have specific uses and are frequently confused.

Articles: *A, An, The* **Articles** are words used to make nouns general or specific. Articles are used in front of nouns.

■ **A** and **an** refer to people, places, or things that are general. **A** and **an** can also show membership in a group.

A trip to a foreign country can be educational.

Peter bought an airline ticket for a trip to Bali.

■ **The** refers to people, places, or things that are specific. **The** is used in front of nouns that have already been mentioned or when the reader knows what the writer is talking about. **The** can also refer to one of a kind.

The flight time from Atlanta, Georgia, to Bali is about twenty-five hours.

No article is used in these situations:

■ With mass nouns that refer to general terms such as **life** or **water**

A/An/The Poverty affects people all over the world.

■ With nouns that are languages, sports, and academic subjects

A/An/The English is spoken in many countries.

TIP	Use **a** when the next word starts with a consonant sound. Use **an** when the next word starts with a vowel sound.

PRACTICE Using *A, An,* or *The*

26.8   In the space provided, write *a, an,* or *the* before each noun. If no noun marker is needed, write an **X**.

EXAMPLE: **X** People travel to experience other cultures and meet new people.

¹Tourism can have a positive social and cultural impact on communities. ²First of all, tourism has made _____ significant contribution to international understanding. ³World tourism organizations recognize that tourism is a way to enhance respect for human rights without distinction as to race, sex, language, or religion. ⁴In addition, tourism gives people _____ opportunity to see how others live. ⁵Also, _____ tourists can interact socially with people in _____ host community. ⁶A London pub or a New York café are good places for _____ social interaction. ⁷Even a visit to another part of _____ United States would be socially and culturally stimulating. ⁸For example, New Orleans has _____ very diverse social and cultural heritage. ⁹Over the years, _____ Spanish, French, British, and Americans have lived in New Orleans. ¹⁰The food, music, dance, and social norms are unique to the area.

(Adapted from *Introduction to Hospitality Management* by John R. Walker)

Many, Much/Few, Less, Little **Many** and **few** are used with plural nouns.

People like to travel for **many** reasons.

Few people would refuse a chance to travel.

Much, less, and **little** are used with mass nouns.

Some people do not have **much** time to travel.

Soft adventure travelers like controlled trips with **less** risk.

Hard adventure travelers have **little** fear of being exposed to risk.

This, These/That, Those **This, these/that,** and **those** refer to things that are either near or far in distance or time.

This, These	*That, Those*
Use *this* and *these* to refer to things that are near in distance or time.	**Use *that* and *those* to refer to things that are far in distance or time.**
Before singular nouns, use *this*.	**Before singular nouns, use *that*.**
Distance: **This** museum is only a few miles away.	Distance: **That** island is one hundred miles from my city.
Time: I am going to visit the museum **this** week.	Time: Many people visit a ski resort during **that** time of the year.
Before plural nouns, use *these*.	**Before plural nouns, use *those*.**
Distance: **These** tourists want to explore the rain forests.	Distance: **Those** trips to the rain forests in the Amazon are for families.
Time: **These** boat trips take travelers from the city to the jungle in three days.	Time: **Those** canoe trips down the river last for four hours.

PRACTICE   Find Noun Markers

26.9   Choose the appropriate noun marker in the parentheses. If no noun marker is needed, choose the **X**.

EXAMPLE: (The, X̄) Early humankind first imagined traveling to the moon, planets, and stars by viewing the night sky.

1. The first tourist trips into (X, the) space involved (a, the) flight that circled the Earth.
2. (These, X) Two or three travelers and an experienced pilot were launched from (a, an) aircraft at nine miles above the Earth.
3. They rocketed to (a, an) altitude of 60 miles, considered the end of the Earth's atmo-sphere, and then they turned around.
4. (This, these) trip took about an hour.

5. Passengers saw a (few, little) spectacular views of Earth as well as experiencing several minutes of weightlessness.

6. As technology improved, spaceships were able to fly higher and reach (the, X) orbiting altitude.

7. (Those, this) orbiting vehicles were small and uncomfortable and had (few, little) amenities.

8. In the first decade of 2000, orbital travel cost $500,000 for a two-day journey and $1 million for (a, X) five days.

(Adapted from *Travel and Tourism* by Paul S. Biederman)

TIP	A quick way to identify a noun is to test it by answering one of these questions:

Can the word follow *a, an,* or *the*?

The _____ is here.
It is on **a** _____ .

Can you put a possessive pronoun in front of it?

My _____ is wonderful.
Where are **their** _____ ?

Can you put a quantity word in front of it?

Three _____ are in the box.
Give me **some** _____ .

MyWritingLab™
Complete this activity
at mywritinglab.com

Review: Nouns

The following passage has errors in singular nouns, plural nouns, and noun markers. Find and correct them. The first one has been done for you.

¹To understand the way people eat now, we have to look back about 500 years ago when plants, animals and microbes were transferred among the Americas, Europe, Asia, and Africa. ²The plants and animals survived

journeys
deadly journies and successfully adapted to new climates. ³Seeds traveled in the pants cuffs or pleats of the clothing of persons. ⁴They also were caught in the fabric of cloth bundles and sacks.

⁵From Eurasia to the Western and Southern hemispheres went wheat, sugars, rices, and fruit such as banana, coconuts, apples, pears, apricot, peachs, plums, cherrys, and olives. ⁶Animals that provided meat and dairy were also transported. ⁷Yams, okra, and collard greens were among the much vegetables that made the crossing from Africa.

⁸Quinine, a medicinal plant from Peru, had enormous long-term importances because it could control the effects of malaria. ⁹Native Americans provided tobacco, which was thought to aid digestion. ¹⁰Most important gifts from New World were corn and white and sweet potatos.

¹¹These informations about the transfer of plants and animals was considered largest ever made on Earth.

(Adapted from *The World* by Felipe Fernandez-Armesto)

Writing Assignment

MyWritingLab™
Complete this activity
at mywritinglab.com

Write about an Image

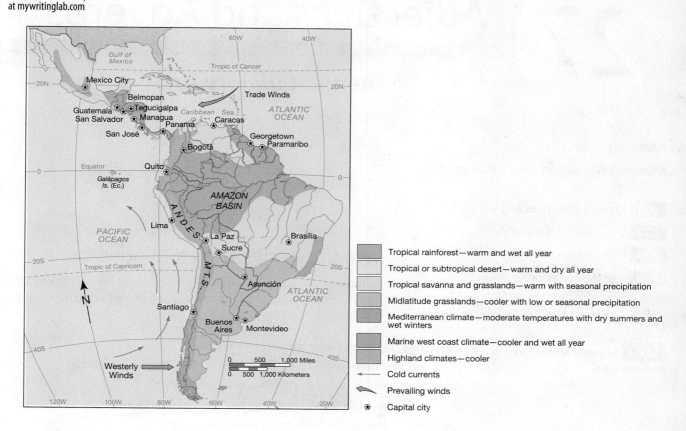

The large size of South America makes its climate varied. Each region has its own characteristic weather conditions.

Study the map of Latin America. Notice that the legend is color coded to match the region on the map. The legend describes the region and its climate. Write a sentence describing the climate of each of the seven regions (for a total of seven sentences). Underline the common and proper nouns and noun markers in each sentence.

EXAMPLE: <u>The</u> tropical <u>rainforest</u> in <u>the</u> <u>Amazon</u> <u>basin</u> has <u>warm</u> and <u>wet</u> <u>weather</u> <u>all</u> <u>year</u>.

27 Adjectives and Adverbs

Theme: *Culinary Arts*

Learning Objectives

After working through this chapter, you will be able to:

LO 1 Identify adjectives and adverbs.

LO 2 Use adjectives correctly.

LO 3 Use adverbs correctly.

LO 4 Use the comparative forms of adjectives and adverbs.

LO 1 Identify adjectives and adverbs.

What Are Adjectives and Adverbs?

Adjectives and adverbs are modifiers. They make the words they modify more specific. However, adjectives and adverbs are used differently.

Adjectives describe or limit **nouns** or **pronouns**:

Food **preparers** should have a basic **understanding** of nutrition.

Adverbs describe a verb, an adjective, or another adverb:

The human body only survives a short time without water.

Many dishes can be made more nutritious.

Chefs are very often asked to modify dishes served to guests with health concerns.

Adjectives and Adverbs in Context

In the following passage about food and health, the adjectives are blue and the adverbs are green.

> Since the days of **prehistoric** hunters and gatherers, people have understood that **some** animals and plants are **good** to eat and others are **not.** For thousands of years, cultures across the world have attributed **medicinal** and **beneficial** effects to **certain** foods, **particularly** plants. They have recognized that food that might be **fine** to eat may be **unhealthy** if it is prepared or stored **improperly.**
>
> **Not** until the **past** few decades have people become **increasingly** concerned about the way foods affect **their** health and the **specific** foods that promote **good** health and longevity. **These consumer** concerns have had an impact on the **food service** industry. As a result, **culinary** students **now** study nutrition as part of **their** training. The relationship of the way people eat to the prevention of **chronic weakening** diseases such as obesity, diabetes, and heart disease will **greatly** influence what is served in restaurants and sold in stores.
>
> (Adapted from *On Cooking* by Sarah R. Labensky and Alan M. Hause)

Adjectives

Adjectives give information about nouns by describing or limiting them. In grammar, we say that adjectives *modify* nouns.

Adjectives That Describe Nouns

Adjectives that describe nouns give information such as opinion, size, age, shape, color, material, purpose, taste, touch, smell, sound, and place of origin.

People want to eat delicious, low-fat, fresh **meals** in restaurants.

The crisp, green, Granny Smith **apple** tasted sour.

Adjectives That Limit Nouns

Adjectives that limit nouns make the nouns more specific or general.

Each **fruit** and **vegetable** contains many **nutrients**.

Iman eats five **servings** of fruit every **day**, but she does not eat enough **vegetables**.

The following chart shows some examples of words that limit nouns:

Articles	Pronouns	Number Words	Possessive Pronouns
a, an, the	this, that, these, those; all, any, both, each, either, enough, every, few, fewer, less, little, many, more, most, much, neither, no, several, some	one, two, three, four, etc.; first, second, third, etc.	my, your, his, her, its, our, their

Adjectives do not have singular or plural forms. Do not add an **–s** to an adjective.

My professor gives ~~difficults~~ difficult assignments.

I have a ~~five-years-old~~ five-year-old sister.

Placement of Adjectives

Adjectives are placed before nouns and after linking verbs. Several adjectives may modify a single noun.

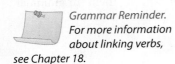

*Grammar Reminder.
For more information
about linking verbs,
see Chapter 18.*

Before nouns	Herbs refer to the **large group** of sweet-smelling **plants.**
After linking verbs	Sweet basil is **flavorful.**
In pairs or a list	Sweet basil is an herb with **green, tender leaves** and a **strong, warm, peppery flavor.**

> **TIP** | Some common linking verbs are *am, is, are, was, were, being, been, appear, become, remain, feel, seem,* and *look.*

PRACTICE   **Identifying Adjectives**

27.1   Identify the adjectives in the following sentences. A sentence may have more than one adjective.

EXAMPLE: The menu is the soul of <u>every</u> restaurant.

1. Most menus offer consumers enough selections to build an entire meal.
2. Food service operations may have separate menus for breakfast, lunch, and dinner.
3. If brand names are used, those brands must be served.
4. A typical North American meal consists of three courses.
5. The first course may be a hot or cold appetizer, soup, or salad.
6. The second course is the entrée or main dish, usually meat, poultry, fish, or shell-fish along with a vegetable and starch.
7. A sweet preparation or fruit and cheese is offered for dessert, the third course.
8. For a meal served in the European tradition, the salad would be presented as a **palate cleanser** after the main dish and before the dessert.

(Adapted from *On Cooking* by Sarah R. Labensky and Alan M. Hause)

palate cleanser
a food offered in the
middle of a meal to
remove lingering flavors
so that the next course
may be enjoyed

Participles as Adjectives

Present and past participles of verbs are often used as adjectives.

Present Participles as Adjectives   Present participles are formed by adding *–ing* to the base verb: **mix + ing = mixing.**

Cooking oils are refined from various seeds, plants, and vegetables. To sauté foods properly, put a small amount of fat into the **frying pan** and pay attention to **heating time.**

Past Participles as Adjectives   Regular past participles are formed by adding *–ed* to the base verb: **mix + ed = mixed.**

*Grammar Reminder.
For more information
on participles, see
Chapter 24.*

Many food service operations use **prepared condiments** and flavorings. Old Bay seasoning is widely used in making **boiled shrimp** or **crab.**

¶ Using Commas with Adjectives

Sometimes you will use several adjectives together to describe or limit a noun. To decide when to use commas between adjectives, note the following rules.

Use commas to separate adjectives that equally modify the same noun.

These adjectives can change places without changing their meaning.

> Five-spice powder includes sweet, sour, bitter, salty, and hot **flavors.**
> Five-spice powder includes bitter, salty, sour, sweet, and hot **flavors.**

Do not use commas in these situations:

■ **When the first adjective modifies the next one:**

> The chef made spicy Italian salad dressing.

■ **Before or after _and_ between two adjectives:**

> Spices are an inexpensive **and** tasty way to add flavor to food.

■ **Between the last adjective and the noun:**

> Dried herbs and spices should be stored in a cool, dry **place.**

TIP | To decide whether or not to use commas, use the following tests:
The _And_ Test: Place **and** between the adjectives. If the sentence still makes sense, then place a comma between the adjectives.
The Reversing Test: Reverse the order of the adjectives. If the sentence makes sense, then place a comma between the adjectives.

PRACTICE Using Commas with Adjectives

27.2 Insert commas where they are needed between adjectives. Some sentences are correct. The commas and semicolons already placed in the sentences are correct.

EXAMPLE: Aleppo pepper has a sharp, sweet, fruity flavor.

1. The spice anise is used in pastry fish shellfish and vegetable dishes.
2. Annatto seeds give a bright yellow-orange color to foods, and they are often used in cheeses and margarine.
3. Fresh capers are not used; the salty and sour flavor develops after they are soaked in strongly salted white vinegar.

4. Caraway, the world's oldest spice, is used for its fragrant spicy taste.
5. Mustard seeds are small hard spheres with a bitter flavor.
6. Black white and green peppercorns come from the same plant but are picked at different times.
7. Wasabi is a pale green root that is similar but unrelated to horseradish.
8. Sesame seeds are native to India; they are small flat ovals and have a nutty earthy taste when roasted or ground.

Adverbs

LO 3 Use adverbs correctly.

Adverbs describe verbs, adjectives, or other adverbs.

What Adverbs Do	Examples
Describe a verb	Owners should **carefully inspect** their restaurants for pests.
Describe an adjective	Flies can be **very hard** to control.
Describe an adverb	Rats and mice can **very easily** find their way into restaurants.

Adverbs describe how, when, where, or to what extent. Many adverbs end in **–ly** but not all of them do.

Questions	Adverb Examples	In a Sentence
How	angrily, badly, carefully, easily, expertly, fast, quickly, quietly, slowly, suddenly, well	Insects and rodents can quickly spoil food.
When	afterwards, always, constantly, early, first, later, never, next, now, immediately, often, sometimes, then, today, tomorrow, usually, yesterday	Insects or rodents should be removed from the kitchen immediately.
Where	anywhere, away, around, behind, down, everywhere, here, inside, over, somewhere	The chefs found ants everywhere in the kitchen.
To What Extent	almost, completely, entirely, extremely, not, only, perfectly, really, somewhat, too, very	Some bugs can be very hard to get rid of completely.

Conjunctive Adverbs

Conjunctive adverbs are used as transitions between ideas to connect two independent clauses or within a sentence to show addition, time, contrast, effect, and summary. Examples are *however, therefore, consequently, moreover, otherwise, furthermore.*

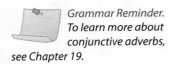

Grammar Reminder. To learn more about conjunctive adverbs, see Chapter 19.

Competitive cooking television shows are popular; moreover, they have caused enrollment in culinary schools to increase.

Placement of Adverbs

Adverbs can be moved around

Modifying a verb	At the beginning, in the middle, or at the end of a sentence	**Soon** the chef **will prepare** the meal.
		The chef **will soon prepare** the meal.
		The chef **will prepare** the meal **soon**.
Modifying an adjective or adverb	Usually in front of the word it modifies	Some meals are **very delicious**.
		The chef cooks **quite often**.

TIP   Some adverbs can change their meaning depending on where they are placed in a sentence. A few of them are ***almost, ever, hardly, nearly, only,*** and ***quite.*** Notice the difference in the meaning of *only* in the following sentences.

> Only my boss asked to taste the food.
>
> My boss only asked to taste the food.
>
> My boss asked to taste only the food.

Using Commas with Adverbs

Do use a comma after an adverb that introduces a sentence.

> Tomorrow, I have to work a double shift.

Do use commas before and after conjunctive adverbs that interrupt a sentence.

> The restaurant, however, will be closed for renovations next week.

PRACTICE   Identifying Adverbs

27.3   Identify the adverbs.

EXAMPLE: Wine making began 5,000 years ago in ancient Mesopotamia (today's Iraq).

1. Containers with traces of wine that once filled them have been found in tombs of Egyptian pharaohs.
2. Images and written records about grapes and wine suggest that the upper classes of Egypt enjoyed wine that was mostly sweet.
3. Wine was equally prized by the upper classes of ancient Greece.
4. When the Romans dominated Greece, wine became available to the lower classes because of its unusually low prices.
5. By the 1700s, France quickly became the greatest of the European wine-making nations.

6. Now, wine from many countries commands respect throughout the world.

7. Modern technologies have given wine makers control over almost every aspect of the process.

(Adapted from *On Cooking by* Sarah R. Labensky and Alan M. Hause)

Using Adjectives and Adverbs Correctly

Some writers make mistakes when they use adjectives and adverbs. Two common problems are the following:

■ Using an adjective to modify another adjective:

Perfectly prepared food is ~~real~~ really important to diners in a restaurant.

■ Using an adjective to modify a verb:

Restaurants can lose customers when food is prepared ~~bad~~ badly.

Remember that adjectives modify nouns and adverbs modify verbs, adjectives, and other adverbs. Study the examples in the chart below:

Adjective	Adverb
good	**well**
The food tasted **good.** The restaurant served **good** food.	The food was prepared **well.**
Use **well** when referring to health: Eating chicken soup may help a person with a cold feel **well.**	
bad	**badly**
The meal tasted **bad.** The chef cooked a **bad** meal.	The chef cooked **badly.**
real	**really**
The chef used **real** sugar in the dessert, not an artificial sweetener.	The dessert was **really** sweet.

PRACTICE   Using Adjectives and Adverbs Correctly

27.4   Identify the correct adjective or adverb.

EXAMPLE: Fish and shellfish have become (increasingly, increasing) popular in recent years.

1. Good-quality fish and shellfish are now (easily, easy) available to almost every food-service operation.

2. Many fish and shellfish are (real, really) expensive and go bad (quick, quickly).

3. Fish can be hard to identify because many fish look (similarly, similar).

4. The FDA publishes a (regular, regularly) updated list of approved names for food fish.

5. Fish must be cooked (good, well) enough so that it is firm, not mushy and soft.

6. If the fish smells (bad, badly), throw it out.

7. Fish and shellfish inspections are performed (voluntary, voluntarily).

8. Grade A fish must look (good, well) with no physical marks or defects.

(Adapted from *On Cooking* by Sarah R. Labensky and Alan M. Hause)

Comparatives and Superlatives

LO 4 **Use the comparative forms of adjectives and adverbs.**

Adjectives and adverbs have special forms for comparing two or more people or things. The **comparative** form is used when comparing two people or things.

Apples have more pesticide residue than cucumbers.

Some people believe that organic food is better than conventional food.

The **superlative** form is used when comparing three or more people or things.

Some people believe that eating organic food is the best way to avoid pesticides.

Of all fruit, apples have the most pesticide residue.

Forming Adjective and Adverb Comparatives and Superlatives

syllable one or more letters used to make a single sound

Comparatives and superlatives are formed according to the number of **syllables** in the adjective or adverb.

Forming Comparative and Superlative Adjectives and Adverbs		
Adjective or Adverb Form	Comparative	Superlative
One syllable ending in a consonant	add **–er**	add **–est**
fast	**faster**	**fastest**
soon	**sooner**	**soonest**
One syllable ending in **–e**	add **–r**	add **–st**
large	**larger**	**largest**
late	**later**	**latest**
One syllable ending in a vowel and consonant	double the consonant and add **–er**	double the consonant and add **–est**
big	**bigger**	**biggest**
Two or more syllables	add **more** + word	add **most** + word
thoughtful	**more thoughtful**	**most thoughtful**
convenient	**more convenient**	**most convenient**

Adjective or Adverb Form	Comparative	Superlative
Two syllables ending in **–y**	change the **–y** to an **–i** and add **–er**	change the **–y** to an **–i** and add **–est**
pretty	**prettier**	**prettiest**
Adverbs ending in **–ly**	use **more** + adverb	use **most** + adverb
carefully	**more carefully**	**most carefully**

Some adjectives can follow either rule:

Two-syllable Adjective	Comparative	Superlative
clever	cleverer, more clever	cleverest, most clever
gentle	gentler, more gentle	gentlest, most gentle
friendly	friendlier, more friendly	friendliest, most friendly
quiet	quieter, more quiet	quietest, most quiet
simple	simpler, more simple	simplest, most simple

TIP   Be sure to use the correct word order for comparative and superlative forms.
–er form: use **than** before the second item being compared

At my house, chocolate ice cream is more popular **than** vanilla ice cream.

–est form: use **the** because one thing is compared to the rest of the group.

At my house, chocolate ice cream is the most popular flavor.

PRACTICE   Using Comparative and Superlative Adjectives and Adverbs

27.5   Correct any errors in the use of comparative or superlative adjectives and adverbs. Remember, the comparative compares two people or things, and the superlative compares three or more people or things. One sentence is correct.

EXAMPLE: A cold food product has a ~~more dull~~ [duller] flavor than a warm product.

1. Because they are served cold, some ice creams and custards have to be made more sweeter.

2. Frozen custard contains a highest percent of egg yolks and cream than standard ice cream.

3. Gelato is an Italian style ice cream with a more low milk fat content than American products.

4. Today, low-fat ice cream is richer, creamier, and more smooth than it used to be.

5. New stirring methods most thoroughly separate the tiny milk fat globules than the older method.

6. Frozen yogurt uses yogurt as a base, which makes it easiest to digest than ice cream.

7. Frozen yogurt is not more healthy than regular yogurt if it has large amounts of sugar and fat.

8. Gelato is more thicker than ice cream because it does not have much air in it from churning or stirring.

9. The top four more popular flavors of ice cream are vanilla, chocolate, butter pecan, and strawberry.

10. Recently, candy and ice cream companies have been partnering to produce more tasty ice creams.

Irregular Comparatives and Superlatives

The comparative and superlative forms of **good** and **well** and **bad** and **badly** are irregular. Study the chart below to learn more about them.

Adjective or Adverb	Comparative	Superlative
good or well	better	best
The winning chef prepared a **good** meal. The winning chef cooked **well**	The winning chef cooked a better meal than the other finalist.	The winning chef cooked the **best** meal of all.
bad or badly	worse	worst
The chef who lost cooked a **bad** meal. The losing chef cooked **badly**.	The chef who lost cooked worse than the other finalist.	The chef who lost cooked the worst meal.

TIP | These forms of *better, best, worse,* and *worst* are not correct: *more better, most better, bestest, more worse, worser, most worst, worstest.*

Here are some other irregular comparative and superlative forms:

	Comparative	Superlative
much, many	more	most
little (amount)	less	least
far (distance)	farther	farthest

> **PRACTICE** Using Irregular Comparative and Superlative Forms
>
> **27.6** Choose the correct irregular comparative or superlative form.

EXAMPLE: Is buying organic food really ([better], best) for you?

1. Few studies have been conducted to prove that organic food is (more, the most) nutritious than non-organic food.
2. Higher prices for organic food are due to (more, the most) expensive farming and tighter government regulations.
3. Organic farms yield (less, the least) produce than non-organic farms do.
4. Organic food is (more, the most) expensive of all foods.
5. Some experts say that organic farming has (less, the least) impact on the environment than other types of farming.
6. Non-organic strawberries, apples, carrots, and grapes are foods that have the (more, most) pesticide and insecticide residues remaining on them.
7. Non-organic vegetables that have (less, the least) amount of pesticide and insecticide residues are asparagus, avocados, and cabbage.
8. Some people will travel (farther, the farthest) to buy organic food than to buy non-organic food.
9. It is (better, best) to buy organic or non-organic produce from local farmers than from supermarkets because it is fresher and the nutrients are at their peak.
10. Eating more fruit and vegetables and eliminating junk food is the (better, best) thing people can do for their health.

Review: Adjectives and Adverbs

Circle and correct the errors in adjectives and adverbs. Two sentences are correct. The first error has been corrected for you.

¹America has become a service-oriented economy, and people are traveling and dining out offener *(more often)* than ever before. ²The demand for hospitality managers has never been greatest than now. ³However, the hospitality field is the worse choice for people looking for a regular five-day 40-hour workweek with weekends off. ⁴Hospitality professionals get paid to work when other people are enjoying themselves. ⁵Recently, companies have come to realize that to keep their managers, they cannot expect managers to work endless hours with least time off. ⁶Much companies now limit the number of hours managers work.

⁷Not every person matches good with every hospitality position. ⁸Some positions require high energy and excellent people skills. ⁹Others call for people

who can work quiet and pay attention to details. [10]If managers do not choose employees good, they may hire the wrong people. [11]The positions will not be filled successful, and managers will be stuck with poor employees.

[12]After graduating from college, people may take any available management position that pays good. [13]Once they get used to making adequate money, they may find least satisfaction with the job. [14]The mismatch becomes obvious, and they may change jobs more soon than they would like. [15]People who work at a job that is not a good match will find it more hard to be effective managers. [16]College students should think about what is real important to them before taking a job in the hospitality field. [17]They need to figure out who they are and what they like to avoid making a worse choice.

(Adapted from *Introduction to Hospitality Management* by John R. Walker)

Writing Assignment

Write about an Image

Compare the nutritional information shown here for two snack chips. Write five sentences about their differences using comparatives and superlatives.

EXAMPLE: Cheddar and sour cream chips are **higher** in fat than tortilla chips.

Cheddar and Sour Cream Chips	
Serving Size: 1 Big Grab bag • 1.5 oz • 42.5g	
Amount Per Serving	
Calories 240	Calories from Fat 140
	% DV
Total Fat 15g	**23%**
Saturated Fat 4g	**20%**
Trans Fat 0g	
Cholesterol 0mg	**0%**
Sodium 350mg	**15%**
Total Carbohydrate 21g	**7%**
Dietary Fiber 2g	**8%**
Sugars <1g	
Protein 3g	**6%**
Vitamin A 0%	Vitamin C 15%
Calcium 2%	Iron 2%
Vitamin E 10%	Thiamine 6%
Niacin 10%	Vitamin B6 6%
Phosphorus 0%	Zinc 2%
Unofficial Pts: 6	**©DietFacts.com**

Percent of Calories from:
Fat-58.3%   Carb-35%   Protein-5%
(Total may not equate 100% due to rounding.)

Tortilla Chips	
Serving Size: 1 bag • 1.125 oz • 31.8g	
Amount Per Serving	
Calories 140	Calories from Fat 35
	% DV
Total Fat 4g	**6%**
Saturated Fat 1g	**5%**
Trans Fat 0g	
Cholesterol 0mg	**0%**
Sodium 240mg	**10%**
Total Carbohydrate 24g	**8%**
Dietary Fiber 2g	**8%**
Sugars 3g	
Protein 2g	**4%**
Vitamin A 0%	Vitamin C 2%
Calcium 2%	Iron 2%
Thiamine 2%	Riboflavin 2%
Niacin 6%	Vitamin B6 10%
Phosphorus 8%	
Unofficial Pts: 3	**©DietFacts.com**

Percent of Calories from:
Fat-25%   Carb-68.6%   Protein-5.7%
(Total may not equate 100% due to rounding.)

Using Correct Punctuation, Mechanics, and Spelling

28

Commas, Semicolons, and Colons

Theme: *Business and Marketing*

Learning Objectives

After working through this chapter, you will be able to:

LO 1 Identify commas, semicolons, and colons.

LO 2 Use commas to separate words in a series, introductory words and word groups, interrupter words and phrases, sentences, dates and addresses, and quotations.

LO 3 Use semicolons to connect two related sentences and to simplify a series.

LO 4 Use colons to signal a series or a long quotation, to separate titles and subtitles, and hours and minutes.

What Are Commas, Semicolons, and Colons?

Commas, semicolons, and colons are three important punctuation marks used within sentences to separate words or groups of words. They help readers understand which words go together. Each mark looks different:

comma   **,**   semicolon   colon

LO 1 Identify commas, semicolons, and colons.

Commas, Semicolons, and Colons in Context

Notice the use of commas, semicolons, and colons in the following passage about psychological pricing in marketing.

Most consumers don't have all the time, ability, or information they need to figure out whether they are paying a good price for an item, which includes the following: researching the different brands or stores, comparing prices, and getting the best deals. Instead, they may rely on certain information that signals whether a price is high or low. For example, the fact that a product is sold in a respected and admired department store might signal that it is worth a higher price.

As a result, many sellers consider the psychology of prices. For example, many consumers use price to judge quality. Consumers perceive higher-priced products as having higher quality. A $100 bottle of perfume may contain only $3 worth of scent, but some people are willing to pay the $100 because this price indicates something special.

A retailer might show a higher manufacturer's suggested price next to the marked price, which would indicate that the product was originally priced much higher. Another approach is displaying a less expensive product next to a more expensive one; as a result, the shopper would think that the less expensive product was in the same class.

(Adapted from *Marketing* by Gary Armstrong and Philip Kotler)

 # Commas

LO 2 Use commas to separate words in a series, introductory words and word groups, interrupter words and phrases, sentences, dates and addresses, and quotations.

Commas are used more frequently than other punctuation marks. This section explains seven ways to use commas.

In a Series

Use a comma after each word in a series and right before the *and* or *or*. A series is a list of three or more words, phrases, or clauses.

Series of words	In the 1960s, people did not know about **personal computers, cell phones, iPods,** or the Internet.
Series of phrases	Companies need to **keep up with new technologies, update their products,** and **take advantage of new opportunities.**
Series of clauses	Every new technology replaces an older technology, and as a result, **CDs hurt phonograph records, digital photography hurt the film business,** and **mp3 players hurt the compact disc player industry.**

Do not use commas if each of the items in the series is connected with ***and*** or ***or***.

Technology has released such wonders as **antibiotics <u>and</u> robotic surgery <u>and</u> credit cards.**

 PRACTICE Using Commas with Items in a Series

28.1 Underline each series of three or more items and add commas to separate the items.

EXAMPLE: Companies collect information about <u>consumers, competitors,</u> and <u>developments in the marketplace.</u>

1. They use techniques such as observing consumers going to **trade shows** and monitoring consumer reviews on the Internet.

trade show an event at which goods and services in a specific industry are shown and demonstrated

2. Companies monitor blogs and Internet sites to find out what people are saying about their products their performance and their reputation.

3. They also monitor their competitors' new strategies product launches or techniques.

4. Suppliers resellers and key customers can offer important information about other companies.

5. Competitors can learn about other companies by reading their annual reports visiting trade show exhibits and checking their web pages.

6. Spies from other companies could pose as company drivers internal security guards or executives.

7. For a fee, companies can subscribe to over 3,000 online databases and search services such as ProQuest LexisNexis and Dow Jones News Retrieval.

8. Most companies are now training employees to protect information from competitors to collect information and to avoid using illegal means to get secret company information.

(Adapted from *Marketing* by Gary Armstrong and Philip Kotler)

Introductory Words and Word Groups

Use a comma after introductory expressions, phrases, and clauses.

Introductory transitional words and phrases	**First,** all products go through several phases and complete their life cycles.
	As a result, newer, better products come along.
Introductory prepositional phrase	**Through research and development,** a company can create an original product.
Introductory verbal phrase *Exception:* when followed by a verb	**Testing the new product,** the company found that consumers would buy it.
	Finding a new product to develop *can be* expensive.

PRACTICE   Using Commas with Introductory Words and Phrases

28.2   Identify the introductory words or phrases and place a comma after them. If the sentence is correct without a comma, write **C**. The first one has been done for you.

[1]In fact**,** studies indicate that up to 90 percent of all new consumer products fail. [2]For example of the new food, beverage, and beauty products each year, at least 70 percent fail within that year. [3]First the product may be poorly designed. [4]Despite poor research results a high-level executive might push a favorite idea. [5]Priced too high a product will not sell.

⁶On the other hand sometimes competitors fight back with a cheaper or better product.

⁷Behind each failed product are wasted money and hopes.   ⁸Failing to bring value to customers smokeless cigarettes never sold well. ⁹Therefore to create successful new products, companies must take a customer-based, systematic approach.

(Adapted from *Marketing* by Gary Armstrong and Philip Kotler)

Interrupter Words and Phrases

Use commas around interrupter words and phrases. An interrupter can be removed without changing the sentence's meaning.

Words or phrases that add information	People born between 1977 and 2000, **called Millennials or Generation Y,** are a diverse group.
	Millennials, **who grew up with computers and the Internet,** are consumers of all means of communication.
	Kim, **an international student,** uses her cell phone to stay in touch with friends and family throughout the day.
Transitions	Reaching the Millennials, **therefore,** requires creative marketing approaches.

PRACTICE   Using Commas with Interrupters

28.3   Identify the interrupters and place commas to set them off from the rest of the sentence.

EXAMPLE: In 1955, Ray Kroc**,** a 52-year-old salesman of milk-shake-mixing machines**,** discovered a number of seven similar restaurants owned by Richard and Maurice McDonald.

1. Kroc saw the McDonald brothers' fast-food concept as a perfect fit therefore for America's on-the-go lifestyles.
2. Kroc bought the small chain for $2.7 million, and of course the rest is history.
3. McDonald's quickly grew as a matter of fact to become the world's largest fast-feeder.
4. The Golden Arches are I believe one of the world's most familiar symbols.
5. Just as the marketplace provided opportunities for McDonald's however it has also presented challenges.

6. The company has struggled after all to address changing consumer lifestyles.

7. Fast-casual restaurants those offering imaginative meals in fashionable surroundings were attracting customers.

8. Americans were in addition looking for healthier eating options.

9. McDonald's has made major efforts with its plan to improve business Plan to Win.

10. Even McDonald's character the clown Ronald McDonald is trimmer and fitter.

(Adapted from *Marketing* by Gary Armstrong and Philip Kotler)

Compound Sentences

Use a comma before the coordinating conjunction (*and, but, for, nor, so, yet*) that connects two independent clauses in a compound sentence.

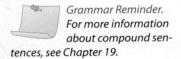

*Grammar Reminder.
For more information
about compound sen-
tences, see Chapter 19.*

In the past, most catalogs were printed**,** **but** today, more catalogs are online.

Companies have not given up their printed catalogs**,** **for** they convince shoppers to use the online versions.

PRACTICE   Using Commas in Compound Sentences

28.4   Edit the following passage by adding commas to the compound sentences.

mass-media advertising
selling through television, radio,
newspapers

direct marketing selling directly
to the consumer by sending catalogs,
and email and by calling people

[1]Direct marketing is a selling approach**,** and technology has helped to transform it. [2]Many companies still use **mass-media advertising** but they supplement with **direct marketing.** [3]Other companies use direct marketing as the only approach for it is convenient, easy, and private. [4]Direct marketers never close their doors and customers do not have to battle traffic. [5]Good catalogs and websites give a great deal of information so shoppers do not have to depend on a retail salesperson who may not know as much about a product. [6]Shoppers can learn about products and services on their own yet they can interact with sellers by phone or on the seller's website if necessary.

Complex Sentences

A complex sentence can have a dependent clause that begins with a subordinating conjunction or a dependent clause that begins with a relative pronoun. There are special comma rules for each of these kinds of clauses.

Dependent Clauses That Begin with Subordinating Conjunctions Place a comma at the end of the dependent clause when it is at the beginning of the sentence but not when it is at the end of the sentence.

If a company wants to compete in today's market, it should have a website.

A company should have a website if it wants to compete in today's market.

Grammar Reminder. For more information about commas in complex sentences, see Chapter 20.

Dependent Clauses That Begin with Relative Pronouns Place a comma before and after a dependent clause that is non-essential. A non-essential dependent clause can be taken out of the sentence without changing the meaning of the sentence. No commas are needed before or after a dependent clause that is essential.

Non-essential: A brand website, **which is the most basic type,** is designed only to inform people about a company's products.

A company needs a good website **that will get customers to visit it many times.**

PRACTICE Using Commas in Complex Sentences

28.5   Edit the passage by adding commas to complex sentences. The first one is done for you.

post to make information available online

No comma

¹Many people prefer online shopping because it offers shoppers many advantages. ²People who do not like fighting traffic or looking for parking spaces enjoy shopping online. ³As long as they can connect to the Internet they can shop. ⁴Time is not a problem either because online stores never close.

⁵Also, when people want to find out more about a product they can do their own independent research. ⁶They can visit company websites for information although the company may not sell the product. ⁷To find out what others think customers can visit product websites that invite customers to review products. ⁸The reviews are **posted** whether they are good or bad. ⁹Although customer reviews are helpful shoppers may prefer to visit websites with reviews written by experts.

¹⁰People can also compare prices online so that they can find the most reasonable price for a product. ¹¹The cost to have the product sent does not have to be a concern since many companies offer free or discounted shipping. ¹²Another benefit of online shopping is product availability. ¹³A desired product can be found online whereas it may not be available locally. ¹⁴A greater variety of products and items that are hard to find can be found online anywhere in the world. ¹⁵Finally, shoppers do not have to worry about receiving an item with missing parts or mangled boxes.

Dates and Addresses

Use commas for dates and addresses according to these rules:

Commas for Dates	Examples
Between the date and the year	October 31, 2001
	The first iPod was released on October 23, 2001.
Between the day and the date	Tuesday, October 31, 2001
	The first iPod was released on Tuesday, October 23, 2001.
After the year	The first iPod was released on October 23, 2001, and the rest is history.
Note: no comma between the month and the day or the month and the year	The first iPod was released on October 31.
	The first iPod was released in October 2001.
Commas for Addresses	**Examples**
Between the street, city or town, and state	The college bookstore is located at 123 Main Street, Phoenix, Arizona.
After the state or country within a sentence	The college bookstore is located at 123 Main Street, Phoenix, Arizona, right next to the student center.
	The U.S. Toyota sales president travels to Toyota City, Japan, at least once a year.
Note: no comma before a zip code	His mailing address is 123 Main Street, Phoenix, AZ 85003.

PRACTICE Using Commas with Dates and Addresses

28.6   Add commas to the following passage. The first one is done for you.

[1]Bill Gates was born on Friday, October 28, 1955. [2]Gates grew up in Seattle Washington with his parents and two sisters. [3]In 1973 Gates enrolled as a freshman at Harvard University in Cambridge Massachusetts. [4]When he was a junior, Gates took a leave of absence from Harvard to work with his friend Paul Allen at a microcomputer company in Albuquerque New Mexico in November 1975. [5]Gates and Allen developed a partnership called "Micro-Soft," and on November 26 1976 the trade name "Microsoft" was registered in New Mexico. [6]The first retail version of Microsoft Windows was launched on November 20 1985 and the company struck a deal with IBM in August to develop a system called OS/2. [7]Gates took a management and executive role in Microsoft from 1975 to 2006. [8]He decided to dedicate more time to **philanthropy** on June 15 2006 and his last full-time day at Microsoft was Friday June 27 2008. [9]The Microsoft Corporation is located at One Microsoft Way Redmond WA 98052.

philanthropy helping the poor, especially by giving money

Direct Quotations

Direct quotations often include a signal phrase. A signal phrase identifies the person making the statement using words such as "she states" or "he writes." Use commas to separate the signal phrase from the direct quotation according to the following rules:

Signal phrase at the beginning	He said, "The aim of marketing is to affect customers' buying behavior."
Signal phrase in the middle	"The aim of marketing," he said, "is to affect customers' buying behavior."
Signal phrase at the end	"The aim of marketing is to affect customers' buying behavior," he said.

Do not use a comma when the quotation is integrated with the sentence:

Kolter emphasizes that "the aim of marketing is to affect customers' buying behavior."

PRACTICE Using Commas with Quotations

28.7 Insert commas within the following quotations.

rumble to make a continuous low sound

EXAMPLE: Armstrong and Kolter said, "Harley-Davidson has **rumbled** its way to the top of the heavy-weight motorcycle market."

1. One sports T-shirt said "I'd rather push a Harley than drive a Honda."
2. "You take off the leather jacket and pants and the helmet, and you'll never know who you'll find " said one Harley fan.
3. "Independence, freedom, and power " stated a Harley-Davidson executive "were the universal Harley appeals."
4. One analyst remarked "It's much more than a machine. It is part of their own self-expression and lifestyle."
5. "We sell a dream here " points out a Harley-Davidson dealer.
6. According to Armstrong and Kolter "The average Harley customer is a 47-year-old male with an average household income of $82,000."
7. "Harley-Davidson's marketers spend a great deal of time " they said "thinking about customers and their buying behavior."

(Adapted from *Marketing* by Gary Armstrong and Philip Kotler)

Semicolons

LO 3 Use semicolons to connect two related sentences and to simplify a series.

Use semicolons to connect two related sentences and simplify a series of items.

■ **Connect two related sentences**

Money is a medium of exchange; we use it as a way of buying and selling things.

Money keeps its value; therefore, it can be used for future purchases.

■ **Simplify a series of items**

The most spendable forms of money are **cash, paper money and metal coins;** a check, an order instructing a bank to pay a payee; and a checking account, bank account funds owned by the depositor.

(Adapted from *Business Essentials* by Ronald J. Ebert and Ricky W. Griffin)

PRACTICE Using Semicolons

28.8 Add semicolons to the following sentences.

EXAMPLE: There is a saying that money makes the world go round; however, the cultures of the world have different attitudes towards it.

1. In some countries, money is exchanged with respect Japan is a good example.
2. Money is rarely passed from hand to hand in Japan instead, people pick up money from little trays and dishes placed next to cash registers.
3. Also, it is not good form to talk about how much you make or have in the bank these are private matters.
4. This is also true in the United Kingdom it is often considered bad manners to talk about money.
5. In some places, people have a more relaxed attitude toward money the United States is one of them.
6. People in the United States freely discuss how much they make how much they paid for their houses and how much they have.
7. Notes and coins are exchanged with little formality in the United States people put bills on a counter or slap them into someone's hand.
8. In some countries, money helps set apart a country from its neighbors people often feel a sense of pride toward their national currencies.
9. In 2002, the euro replaced the currencies of twelve European nations officials worried that many Europeans would not want to give up their currencies.
10. However, people made the switch easily old currencies disappeared quickly.

(Adapted from *Business Essentials* by Ronald J. Ebert and Ricky W. Griffin)

 Colons

LO 4 Use colons to signal a series or a long quotation, to separate titles and subtitles, and hours and minutes.

mutual funds amounts of money that are managed by an investment company

Use a colon in the following ways:

■ **To introduce a list of items at the end of a complete sentence**

Securities include the following: stocks, bonds, and mutual funds.

■ **To introduce a quotation**

Ebert and Griffin caution students about the securities markets: "**Mutual funds** trading is a risky industry featuring rapid buying and selling in the financial marketplace."

■ **To introduce a second sentence that explains or adds details to the first**

Sachi decided to take the company's offer: the company will pay for her college courses as long as she maintains a B average.

■ **To separate titles and subtitles**

The required textbook for our class is *Marketing: An Introduction*.

■ **To separate hours and minutes**

Our class begins at 10:30 a.m.

Do not use a colon after a verb:

Three ways financial professionals manage mutual funds are✗creating, buying, and selling.

PRACTICE Using Colons

28.9   Add colons to the following sentences.

EXAMPLE: Many brand names have become identified with the product category: Kleenex, Levi's, Jell-O, Scotch Tape, and Ziploc.

1. The following brand names became generic aspirin, nylon, escalator, thermos, and shredded wheat.
2. According to Armstrong and Kolter, a brand name should have these qualities "(1)It should suggest something about the product's benefits and qualities. (2) It should be easy to pronounce, recognize, and remember. (3) The brand name should be distinctive. (4) It should be **extendable.** (5) The name should translate easily into foreign languages. (6) It should be capable of registration and legal protection."
3. A brand name should be extendable Amazon.com began as an online bookseller but chose a name that would allow expansion into other categories.
4. To learn about marketing to improve people's well-being, read the book *Social Marketing Improving the Quality of Life.*
5. The Super Bowl, which usually begins around 6 30 p.m. Eastern Standard Time, has a lot to offer advertisers because it is the most-watched television event of the year.

(Sentences 1–4 adapted from *Marketing* by Gary Armstrong and Philip Kotler)

extendable using the brand name in one category that people know well to market a new product in another category, for example Sun-Maid raisins and Sun-Maid raisin muffins

---

MyWritingLab™
Complete this activity at mywritinglab.com

Review: Commas, Semicolons, and Colons

Add commas, semicolons, and colons as needed to the following passage.

[1]When most people think of athletic footwear, global brands such as Nike and Adidas come to mind. [2]However,a small, new company called And1 quickly made a name for itself. [3]The company began as a graduate school research project for Jay Coen Gilbert Seth Berger and Tom Austin. [4]The idea for the name And1 came from a phrase that basketball broad casters use.

[5]The company started out with "trash talk" tee shirts,which became a huge success. [6]Trash talk is a form of **boasting** or insulting another player. [7]For example one slogan said "Call 911. I'm on fire." [8]Soon after And1 added shoes and shorts to its product line. [9]The clothing and shoes were designed to appeal to eleven- to seventeen-year-olds who were hard core "ballers " the street name for basketball players. [10]And1 became very

boasting talking proudly about one's abilities

popular among children teenagers and young adults. [11]The clothing was meant for those who love basketball but it was not meant for those who wanted to make a fashion statement.

[12]At the core of its business was a growing line of tapes that highlighted the skills of **playground legends** showing their incredible moves. [13]One successful promotional activity was "mixtapes" created by talented streetball players these mixtapes showed the players doing tricks with the basketball.

[14]In 2009, Ebert and Griffin said And1 is successful because it knows, hires and promotes to its target market." [15]To help keep itself fresh, And1 hires mostly younger staffers and pays close attention to their advice. [16]In addition And1 knows that most high school basketball players do not go on to play in college or professionally;therefore And1 donates money to projects that emphasize and contribute to education.

(Adapted from *Business Essentials* by Ronald J. Ebert and Ricky W. Griffin and http://wep .wharton.upenn.edu/newsletter/spring07/allstar.html)

playground legend a person who is well known for playing basketball at neighborhood basketball courts

Writing Assignment

MyWritingLab™

Complete this activity at mywritinglab.com

Write about an Image

Study the photograph showing a young woman who has just bought her first car. Write ten sentences about the photograph applying the rules you learned in this chapter about commas, semicolons, and colons.

EXAMPLE: Jessica saved her money, and she finally had enough for a down payment on a car.

29

Other Marks of Punctuation

Theme: *Fashion*

Learning Objectives

After working through this chapter, you will be able to:

LO 1 Use the apostrophe to form contractions and show ownership.

LO 2 Use quotation marks to set off exactly quoted words, titles of short works, and parts of whole works.

LO 3 Use hyphens, dashes, and parentheses correctly.

What Are Other Marks of Punctuation?

Apostrophes, quotation marks, hyphens, dashes, ellipses, and parentheses are punctuation marks. Each of these marks is used for specific reasons according to special rules.

apostrophes **,**   quotation marks **" " "**   hyphen **‐**

dash **▬**   parentheses **( )**

Other Punctuation Marks in Context

In the following passage about the environmental effect of the clothing we wear, the punctuation marks you will learn about in this chapter are in bold.

> Clothes do more than protect our bodies from the weather. Our clothes make symbolic statements about our wealth, status, lifestyle, sex role, personality, and taste. Therefore, fashion is influenced by consumers**'** personal preferences for the kind of statement they want to make**—**whether simple and unnoticeable, businesslike, sensual, or attention-grabbing.
>
> Recently, a new consideration has entered the world of high fashion: the environmental effect of the clothing that we wear. The cultivation of cotton, a globally used natural fiber, requires a great amount of water**—**approximately 5,000 gallons for enough fiber to make a T-shirt and a pair of jeans**—**and typically uses more pesticides than any other crop. The manufacture of synthetic fibers may involve chemicals that contaminate the environment, and such clothes are not biodegradable when discarded. Dyes can be toxic when discharged into the environment.

Efforts are being made to develop "eco-correct" textiles that are less environmentally harmful. The list of "eco-correct" textiles includes synthetics that can be continuously recycled. One example is "leather" made from the discarded skins of food fish who are not endangered species. Also included are plant fibers such hemp and bamboo (which grow like weeds with little care), organically grown cotton, and fibers made from seaweed. These fibers should not be grown to take the place of food crops and should not require pesticides.

(Adapted from *The Art of Seeing* by Paul Zelanski and Mary Pat Fisher)

Apostrophes

LO 1 **Use the apostrophe to form contractions and show ownership.**

An **apostrophe** is a mark of punctuation that is used to show ownership and in some abbreviations.

Apostrophes to Show Ownership

Apostrophes are used with nouns and some indefinite pronouns to show ownership. Words that show ownership are called **possessives**.

Hernando's girlfriend designs and sews her own clothes.

She wants to design women's clothing and become famous.

Apostrohes with Singular Nouns To make singular nouns or indefinite pronouns possessive, add an apostrophe and an **–s.**

Singular nouns not ending in –s	Antoinette's jeans were expensive. A designer creates a product with the customer's needs in mind.
Singular nouns ending in –s *Note:* If the added –s makes the word hard to pronounce, it can be omitted.	College students are the business's best customers. Delores's clothing is fashionable. Or Delores' clothing is fashionable.
Family names ending in –s	Mr. Rodrigues's company is in Honduras.
Indefinite pronouns ending in –body or –one (*anybody, anyone, somebody, someone, everybody, everyone, nobody, no one, one*)	Everyone's shirt had long sleeves. Someone's hat was left in the classroom.
Singular compound nouns	My father-in-law's factory makes zippers.

Apostrophes with Plural Nouns Regular plural nouns usually end in **–s.** To make plural nouns possessive, add an apostrophe. Notice the possessive form of irregular plural nouns.

Plural nouns ending in –s	Magazine editors' preferences appear in their monthly fashion magazines. Designers' ideas come from many different sources.
Plural nouns not ending in –s	Children's clothing started to be produced early in the twentieth century. International trends and styles have influenced men's clothing.
Plural family names	The Rodrigueses' home is in San Antonio, Texas.
Plural compound nouns	My brothers-in-law's store sells clothing for large men.

Grammar Reminder. See Chapter 26 for more information about regular and irregular noun plurals.

Apostrophes with Individual and Joint Ownership To show that two people own one thing, add an apostrophe and **–s** to the second name.

Sheree and Vanessa's clothing store is called SherVan.

To show that two people each own something separately, add an apostrophe and **–s** to both names.

Sheree's and Vanessa's stores were originally in different towns.

TIP | The possessive form is correct if you can turn it into an "of" expression.

Hernando's girlfriend   girlfriend of Hernando
women's clothing   clothing of the women

PRACTICE Adding Apostrophes to Make Singular and Plural Possessives

29.1 Rewrite the phrases by putting the noun or indefinite pronoun that comes after the "of the" into the possessive form.

EXAMPLE: the uniform of the player   the player's uniform
the uniforms of the players   the players' uniforms

1. the shoes of the child
2. the glasses of Chris
3. the clothes of Lee and Wei, joint ownership
4. the hat of Mr. Gonzales
5. the hat of the Gonzaleses
6. the jacket of someone
7. the stores of Santos and Alexis, individual ownership
8. the jackets of the men
9. the employee of the brother-in-law
10. the dresses of the sisters-in-law

Apostrophes with Abbreviations and Numbers

No apostrophes are needed for capital letters and abbreviations.	The students received As and Bs on their projects. The college awarded 250 BAs last winter.
Use apostrophes for lowercase letters so they will not be mistaken for words	The word *choose* has two o's.
No apostrophes are needed for decades: 1990s, 2000s, 2010s	Tattoos started to become a popular fad in the 1990s.
No apostrophes are needed for numbers: 5s, 10s, 20s	Her cell phone number ends with two 5s.

Apostrophes with Time and Quantity Words

Words such as *minute, hour, day, week, month, year,* and *summer* express time. Words such as *dollar, pound,* and *mile* express quantity. Add an apostrophe and *–s* to show ownership.

Singular	Plural
He paid one month's rent for his studio.	He paid two months' rent for his studio.
She had one year's experience working as a buyer.	She had three years' experience working as a buyer.
It is hard to survive on one dollar's worth of food a day.	It is easier to survive on twenty-five dollars' worth of food a day.

PRACTICE **Adding Apostrophes to Show Ownership**

29.2 Add apostrophes to words that show ownership in the following sentences.

                          Today's children's
EXAMPLE: Todays childrens clothing is far different from the products that were available in the early twentieth century.

1. Boys and girls clothes in the early 1900s were not fashionable.
2. Many outfits children wore were cut down and remade from their parents old clothes.
3. Yesterdays children did not get to decide what they wanted to wear.
4. They had to wear a parents selection for them.
5. Their clothes were small versions of adults clothing styles.

6. Today, successful television programming has influenced this generations styles and fashions.

7. Peer groups also play a part in young consumers preferences.

8. When an adults style is popular, it is often copied for children.

(Adapted from *Fashion Apparel, Accessories, and Home Furnishings* by Jay Diamond and Ellen Diamond)

Avoid Problems with Apostrophes

Contractions and possessive pronouns are sometimes confused.

Contraction		Possessive Pronoun	
it's (it is)	**It's** on sale.	its	The store has **its** sale on Saturday.
you're (you are)	**You're** going to buy a new pair of jeans.	your	**Your** new jeans cost $100.
they're (they are)	**They're** buying the latest fashions.	their	**Their** new outfits are fashionable.
who's (who is)	**Who's** the best dressed at school?	whose	**Whose** sweater is this?

Singular possessive nouns are also often confused with plural nouns.

Singular	Singular Possessive	Plural	Plural Possessive
lady	lady's	ladies	ladies'
The **lady** shopped for a new pair of shoes.	The **lady's** shoe size was a 12.	Some **ladies** have large feet.	The store did not have any **ladies'** shoes in size 12.
employee	employee's	employees	employees'
The **employee** brought his lunch to work.	The **employee's** wife prepared his lunch.	Many **employees** prefer to buy their lunch at the company cafeteria.	the **employees'** cafeteria has a large selection of food.

TIP	Do not use an apostrophe before an **–s** verb ending.
	starts
	The class ~~start's~~ in ten minutes.

PRACTICE   **Edit for Apostrophes**

29.3   Add apostrophes where needed or correct incorrectly used apostrophes. The first one is done for you.

Handbags
[1]~~Handbag's~~ are an extremely important part of the fashion business. [2]Not long ago, handbag makers designed their handbags to go with clothing and shoe manufacturer's styles. [3]A designers' signature appeared on a label inside the bag. [4]During the ~~1970's~~, designer signatures started to appear on the bags themselve's.[5]The designer handbag popularity began when a famous LV logo was displayed on an expensive vinyl handbag collection, and a large number of customers' immediately bought them.

[6]In todays' environment, the designer bag market continue's to expand. [7]Prada, for example, one of the worlds upscale names, markets a collection of handbags that sells for over $1,000. [8]The publics' acceptance of these designer label handbags has become important in the retail market. [9]Many fashion retailers have set aside separate departments in their stores to feature individual designers names. [10]Still, comparatively inexpensive handbags produced outside of the United States account for much of the industrys' sales. [11]Copies of designer bags can be found at flea markets and street vendor's stands around the world.

(Adapted from *Fashion Apparel, Accessories, and Home Furnishings* by Jay Diamond and Ellen Diamond)

" " Quotation Marks

LO 2 **Use quotation marks to set off exactly quoted words, titles of short works, and parts of whole works.**

Quotation marks have many uses. They mark the beginning and end of a direct quotation. They are also used with certain words, phrases, and titles. Quotation marks are used in pairs.

In academic writing, direct quotations are used in research papers to give statistics and ideas from experts. Direct quotations are also used when writing a conversation.

Quotation marks can be double or single. Each has a specific use.

Double quotation marks: " " Single quotation marks: ' '

Quotation Marks with Direct Quotations

A **direct quotation** reports the exact wording of a speaker or writer. A sentence with a direct quotation includes a signal phrase, a reporting verb, and the quotation. A signal phrase identifies the name of the person. The reporting verb consists of words such as *states* or *writes*. The direct quotation begins and ends with double quotation marks. Note how direct quotations are written in the following examples:

Writing Reminder. For more information on using signal phrases with quotations in documented papers, see Chapter 17.

Signal Phrase and Direct Quotation

Famous twentieth-century French designer Coco Chanel said, "Fashion is made to become unfashionable."

Signal Phrase Interrupting a Direct Quotation

"Fashion," said Coco Chanel, "is made to become unfashionable."

Signal Phrase at the End of a Direct Quotation

"Fashion is made to become unfashionable," said Coco Chanel.

Complete Sentence Introducing a Direct Quotation

Coco Chanel explains her attitude toward fashion: "Fashion is made to become unfashionable."

Two Quoted Sentences with a Signal Phrase

"I don't design clothes," comments designer Ralph Lauren. "I design dreams."

Quotation Marks with a Question as the Direct Quotation

J. Esther once asked, "What do nudists wear on casual Fridays?"

Quotation Marks with a Question about a Direct Quotation

Who said, "I base most of my fashion sense on what doesn't itch"?

PRACTICE Using Quotation Marks

29.4 Underline the signal phrase and punctuate the quotation. Remember to capitalize the first word of a quoted sentence.

EXAMPLE: "^Ffashion is never in crisis because clothes are always necessary," says Achille Maramotti, founder of Max Mara.

1. clothes don't make a man states Herbert Harold Vreeland, but clothes have got many a man a good job

2. Comedian Gilda Radner offered her humorous point of view about fashion   i base my fashion taste on what doesn't itch

3. I knew exactly what I wanted to do explains designer Tommy Hilfiger I wanted to build a brand of clothing around my own attitude and my own lifestyle

4. According to writer Henry David Thoreau every generation laughs at the old fashions, but follows religiously the new

5. I don't know who invented the high heel but all men owe him a lot said Marilyn Monroe

6. Woolfgang Joop comments   I think that fashion is about surprise and fantasy. It's not about rules

7. if men can run the world, why can't they stop wearing neckties? asks journalist Linda Ellerbee how intelligent is it to start the day by tying a little noose around your neck?

Using Single Quotation Marks Use single quotation marks for a quotation that is inside another quotation.

chapeaus the French word for hats

According to Jay Diamond and Ellen Diamond, "French designers have always designed 'chapeaus' that brought excitement to fashion events."

(Adapted from *Fashion Apparel, Accessories, and Home Furnishings* by Jay Diamond and Ellen Diamond)

Double Quotation Marks or Italics with Titles

Use quotation marks for titles of short works and parts of whole works. Use *italics* for titles of whole or long works. The following chart gives examples.

Quotation Marks versus Italics for Titles	
Quotation Marks for Short Works and Parts of Whole Works	Italics for Whole Works or Long Works
Short Story or Chapter in a Book: "The Necklace"	**Book:** *The Complete Short Stories of Guy de Maupassant*
Short Poem: "The Men Who Wear My Clothes"	**Long Poem:** *The Odyssey*
One Show in a Television Series: "We Expect Fashion"	**Television Series as a Whole:** *Project Runway*
Song: "Suit and Tie"	**Record Album:** *20/20 Experience*
Encyclopedia Article: "History of Fashion"	**Encyclopedia:** *Britannica Online Encyclopedia*
Website Article: "Vera Wang: Medieval Modern"	**Website:** *fashionwiredaily.com*
Magazine or Newspaper Article or Essay: "Street Style"	**Magazine or Newspaper:** *Essence Magazine*
Skit, Monologue, or Short Commercial: "Hurt You" (Geico Caveman commercial)	**Play or Movie:** *The Devil Wears Prada*

Writing Reminder. Titles must also be capitalized correctly. For information about how to capitalize titles, see Chapter 30.

PRACTICE **Using Quotation Marks or Italics with Titles**

29.5   Add quotation marks or italics to the titles.

Aesop a Greek who lived from 620 to 560 BC and was known for his stories with lessons

EXAMPLE: The lesson of **Aesop's** story "A Wolf in Sheep's Clothing" is that appearances can make you believe something that is not true.

1. Chapter 2 of the textbook in Inside Fashion Design is called What Does a Designer Do?
2. The short story Clothes, written by Chitra Banerjee Divakaruni, is about a woman from India who is caught between two worlds, India and the United States.
3. On the Job, an episode of a cable television program, The Fashion Show, had contestants work for a top designer.
4. Blue Suede Shoes is considered the first rock and roll song, written and first recorded by Carl Perkins in 1955.
5. Apparel News, a weekly newspaper that covers California manufacturers and fashion trends, had an article entitled Night and Day.

Problems with Quotation Marks

Follow these guidelines to avoid mistakes with quotation marks.

Do not put quotation marks around the title of your own essay, unless you refer to it in a sentence.

Shiva's essay title is "Peer Pressure and Fashion."

Do not put quotation marks around indirect quotations. An **indirect quotation** reports what someone else says.

Direct quotation: Carmella told me, "My favorite store is having a sale."
Indirect quotation: Carmella told me that her favorite store was having a sale.

Add quotation marks to direct questions.

Incorrect: He asked do I want to pay cash or pay with a credit card?
Correct: He asked, "Do I want to pay cash or pay with a credit card?"

PRACTICE Avoiding Problems with Quotation Marks

29.6 Add or remove the quotation marks. Remember to use a capital letter for the first word of a quoted sentence.

EXAMPLE: The title of my essay was "How to Create a Design Portfolio."

1. Davon asked me, why do you get dressed up to come to school?
2. Natasha told me that "her mother taught her how to sew."
3. She had to read a chapter called Retailing Strategies for Success.
4. Sara got the best grade in the class for her essay   Dressing for the Workplace.
5. The production manager asked, how much is each garment going to cost us to manufacture?

Hyphens, Dashes, and Parentheses

LO 3 Use hyphens, dashes, and parentheses correctly.

 Hyphens

Hyphens are short horizontal lines used to divide a word or form a compound word. There is no space between the hyphen and the word or letters in front of it or after it.

> **Compound words:** Spanish-speaking employees, attorney-at-law.
>
> **Spelled out numbers and fractions:** one-tenth, twenty-two years old, twenty-five-year-old cousin

In general, avoid dividing words at the end of a line. If necessary, divide words between syllables. Check a dictionary if you are not sure how to divide a word.

 Dashes

Dashes look like two hyphens next to each other and are used to add nonessential information to a sentence. There is no space between the word in front of the dash and the word after the dash. Dashes are used primarily in informal writing.

> Showroom models have the body proportions used in fashion drawings—**broad shoulders, narrow hips, and long legs**—so they can show samples effectively.

( ) Parentheses

Parentheses are curved punctuation marks that appear in pairs, one at the beginning of the word, phrase, or sentence, and one at the end. Parentheses are used to include nonessential information or give an acronym.

> **Nonessential information:** Most manufacturers *knock off* (copy identically or slightly change) clothes that sell well.
>
> **Acronym:** Many apparel manufacturers use computer-aided design (CAD).

PRACTICE   Using Hyphens, Dashes, and Parentheses

29.7   Add hyphens, dashes, and parentheses.

EXAMPLE: The first man—made fiber was called rayon.

1. First developed by a French chemist in 1850, rayon was made from cellulose a plant fiber .

2. Rayon was first produced in the United States in 1910 at a fiber factory in Pennsyl vania.

3. Spandex is a synthetic fiber known as elastane in Europe and other parts of the world that has become a very popular fabric.

4. Spandex is made of at least eighty five percent polymer polyurethane, a toxic chemical.

5. Flax is a gold colored plant whose stems are used for fiber to make linen.

   (Some information adapted from *Fashion Apparel, Accessories, and Home Furnishings* by Jay Diamond and Ellen Diamond)

Review: Punctuation

Correct the errors in using apostrophes, quotation marks, hyphens, and parentheses. The first error has been corrected for you.

> "Leather."
> [1]Chapter 3 in our textbook is titled 'Leather.' [2]Two thirds of the chapter explains the properties of leather and how leather is produced. [3]The professor asked the class, "why is leather so popular?" [4]According to statistics from the Leather Apparel Industry, leather sales are three billion dollars a year.
>
> [5]Leather is the general term for all hides pelts of the large animals or skins pelts from smaller animals . [6]Leather s physical properties make the final products functional as well as fashionable. [7]When compared with fabrics, leather is far superior in terms of it's ability to resist tearing. [8]Ladies and men s leather shoes absorb moisture, retain their shape, and adjust to outside temperatures.
>
> (Adapted from *Fashion Apparel, Accessories, and Home Furnishings* by Jay Diamond and Ellen Diamond)

Read the following paragraph about the history of jeans. Then, follow the instructions that follow the paragraph.

> [1]Denim jeans have become a basic apparel item worn by almost all consumers. [2]Jeans were first made by Levi Strauss, a German tailor who emigrated to California in the mid-nineteenth century to mine for gold. [3]He was unsuccessful as a miner and began to manufacture sturdy work pants out of heavy canvas twill, imported from France, called *serge de Nimes*. [4]This was shortened to *denim*. [5]Denim was dyed with indigo dye made from plants imported from India. [6]This dye was duplicated chemically in the twentieth century. [7]The dye bleeds, and denim apparel gradually become softer blue after being washed many times. [8]Later, famous designers from Europe and the United States stepped in to establish the jean as status fashion.
>
> (Adapted from *Inside Fashion Design* by Sharon Lee Tate)

Add signal phrases and quotation marks to the following sentences as directed.

EXAMPLE: Add a signal phrase at the beginning of sentence 1 and quotation marks to the sentence.

Signal phrase
According to Sharon Lee Tate, "Denim jeans have become a basic apparel item worn by almost all consumers."

1. Add quotation marks to sentence 2 and a signal phrase at the end of the sentence.

_____

_____

2. Add a signal phrase in the middle of sentence 7. Then add quotation marks where needed.

_____

_____

3. Add a complete sentence to introduce the author and quotation for sentence 3. Follow the introductory sentence with the direct quotation.

_____

_____

4. Add a signal phrase at the beginning of sentence 5 and quotation marks to the direct quotation.

_____

_____

Writing Assignment

Write about an Image

Some people are interested and fashion and follow the current trends, while others do not feel fashion is important. How important is being fashionable to you? What kind of clothing do you like to wear? What influences you to choose the clothes you wear?

Practice the forms of punctuation you learned about in this chapter by writing ten sentences about fashion. You can answer the questions above or choose your own ideas about the topic of fashion. Use each of these punctuation marks at least once: apostrophes, quotation marks, hyphens, dashes, and parentheses.

30 Spelling and Capitalization

Theme: *World Geography*

Learning Objectives

After working through this chapter, you will be able to:

LO 1 Apply spelling rules for words with *ei* and *ie*, prefixes, and suffixes.

LO 2 Capitalize first words of sentences, proper nouns, proper adjectives, and titles.

What Are Spelling and Capitalization?

Spelling is the forming of words with letters in the correct order. **Capitalization** is the practice of using capital letters at the beginning of certain words. Spelling and capitalization are essential to good writing. Each of these skills has specific rules.

Spelling and Capitalization in Context

In the following passage about how geography connects people, places, and regions of the world, capitalized nouns are blue and words frequently misspelled are green.

The study of **geography** helps us understand how the people, places, and regions of the world are **dependent** on one another. It also shows how the lives of people in **different** parts of the world have become **closely** connected. For example, networks of labor and production cross **countries** and continents into one global **assembly** line. The raw materials are made in one place, **processed** in another place, and sent somewhere else to be **assembled.** Then they are finished in yet another location.

A pair of **Lee Cooper** jeans, for instance, was assembled in many places. First, the cotton was grown and picked in **Benin,** a country in **West Africa.** The denim fabric was made and **dyed** in **Milan, Italy.** Then, the denim was colored with a **synthetic** dark blue dye from **Germany.** Next, the denim was stonewashed using **pumice,** a stone used to give the jeans a worn **appearance.** The pumice came from a volcano in **Turkey.** Then, the jeans were assembled. The thread to sew the jeans was from **Lisnaskea, Northern Ireland.** Teeth for the **zippers** were made in **Japan,** while the brass **rivets** were made out of copper from **Namibia** in southern **Africa,** and zinc from **Australia.** The sewing took place in **Jebel, Tunisia.** Finally, they were sold in a store in the **United Kingdom.**

(Adapted from *World Regions in Global Context* by Sallie A. Marston et al.)

Spelling

LO 1 Apply spelling rules for words with *ei* and *ie*, prefixes, and suffixes.

Spelling correctly is an important part of good writing. An incorrectly spelled word may confuse readers or give them a bad impression of your writing. Although spell-checking programs are helpful, they cannot tell the difference in meaning between words such as **two, too,** or **to** and **hear** or **here.**

Spelling in English can be difficult. For one, words are not always spelled the way they sound. Also, many words were brought into English from other languages. The best way to improve your spelling is to learn the rules and when in doubt, look in a dictionary.

Consonants, Vowels, and Syllables

Words are made up of vowels, consonants, and syllables. Knowing what these terms mean will help you understand spelling rules.

The letters of the English alphabet are divided into consonants and vowels.

Consonants: *b, c, d, f, g, h, j, k, l, m, n. p, q, r, s, t, v, w, x, y, z*

Vowels: *a, e, i, o, u,* and sometimes *y*

Syllables are single units of sound. Every word has one or more syllables. Most syllables have at least one vowel or vowel sound.

1	2	3		1	2	3		1	2
syl-	la-	ble		con-	so-	nant		vow-	el

Spelling Rules for *ei* and *ie*

A well-known memory aid for *ei* and *ie* is this: *i* before *e* except after *c* or when the *ei* is pronounced *ay.* However, there are some exceptions.

i before *e*	achieve, believe, field, friend, piece
except after *c*	ceiling, conceive, deceive, perceive, receipt
or when *ei* is pronounced *ay*	eight, beige, freight, rein, veil
	Exceptions: ancient, caffeine, conscience, foreign, forfeit, height, leisure, neither, protein, science, society

---

TIP As a spelling memory aid, find a word inside the word:

Have a **pie**ce of **pie**.

A fri**end** is always there until the **end**.

Never be**lie**ve a **lie**.

Applying the *ei* and *ie* Rule

30.1   Insert ***ei*** or ***ie*** in the following words.

EXAMPLE: rel ___ie___ ve

1. rec_____ve   6. h_____ght
2. n_____ghbor   7. n_____ce
3. pr_____st   8. gr_____f
4. ch_____f   9. hyg_____ne
5. y_____ld   10. sl_____gh

Spelling Rules for Prefixes

A **prefix** is a letter or group of letters added to the beginning of a word to change the meaning and make a new word. When adding a prefix to the word, the spelling of the original word does not change. When the prefix ends with the same letter that begins the word, you have a double letter:

mis (meaning *wrong*) + spell = misspell

Here are some common prefixes: ***anti–, bene–, bi–, con–, de–, dis, ex–, in–, mis–, non–, pre–, pro–, re–,*** and ***un–.***

Adding Prefixes

30.2   Correct any words that are not spelled correctly. Write **C** if the word is correct.

EXAMPLE: unecessary ___unnecessary___

1. disappear _____   6. ennvision _____
2. overeact _____   7. substitute _____
3. consider _____   8. fullfill _____
4. ilegal _____   9. unoticed _____
5. comunicate _____   10. adress _____

Spelling Rules for Suffixes

A **suffix** is a letter or group of letters added to the end of a word to change the meaning and make a new word. The spelling of a word can change when a suffix is added.

For example, the suffix ***–er*** means a person who does an action. When ***–er*** is added to the end of ***geography,*** the new word is ***geographer,*** which means a scientist who studies the Earth's physical features and the people, plants, and animals that live in different areas.

geography + ***er*** = ***geographer***

Here are some common suffixes: ***–able, –ence, –er, –ful, –ion, –ist, –ity, –ize, –less, –ly, –ment, –ness,*** and ***–ous.***

English has special spelling rules for adding suffixes to words. Read and study the rules for adding suffixes to words ending in **–e**, words ending in a consonant and **–y**, doubling the final consonants.

Rules for Adding Suffixes to Words Ending in –e

■ If the suffix begins with a consonant, keep the **–e** and add the suffix.

care + ful = careful   announce + ment = announcement

Exceptions: Drop the **–e** when the suffix has a vowel in front of it.

argue + ment = argument   true + ly = truly   nine + th = ninth

■ If the suffix begins with a vowel, drop the **–e** and add the suffix.

move + able = movable   admire + ation = admiration

Exceptions: Keep the **–e** when the word has a soft **–ce** or **–ge** sound

courage + ous = courageous   notice + able = noticeable

 PRACTICE   Adding Suffixes to Words Ending in –e

30.3   Apply the rules to add the suggested suffix to each word.

EXAMPLE: place + ment __placement__

1. care + less _____
2. use + age _____
3. continue + ous _____
4. announce + ment _____
5. value + able _____
6. battle + ing _____
7. nine + th _____
8. sue + ing _____
9. advise + able _____
10. manage + able _____

Rules for Adding Suffixes to Words Ending with a Consonant and –y

If the word ends with a consonant + **–y**, change the **–y** to an **–i** and add the suffix.

worry + ed = worried   eighty + eth = eightieth

Exceptions: If the suffix begins with an **–i** or if it ends a proper name, keep the **–y.**

cry + ing = crying   Stravinsky + s = Stravinskys

Adding Suffixes to a Word That Ends with a Vowel and –y

If the word ends with a vowel + **–y,** keep the **–y** and add the suffix.

pay + ment = payment   delay + ing = delaying

Exceptions:

pay + ed = paid   day + ly = daily   say + ed = said

PRACTICE Adding Suffixes to Words Ending with –y

30.4   Apply the rules to add the suggested suffix to each word.

EXAMPLE: terrify + ing ________

1. beauty + ful _____
2. satisfy + ed _____
3. rely + able _____
4. joy + ful _____
5. happy + er _____
6. delay + ing _____
7. O'Reilly + s _____
8. fly + ing _____
9. messy + ier _____
10. day + s _____

Adding Suffixes to Words Ending in a Consonant When adding suffixes to words ending in a consonant, sometimes the consonant should be repeated. Another way to say this is the consonant is doubled.

The rules for doubling consonants are based on syllables. The best way to tell how many syllables are in a word is to sound the word out. The rules also refer to which syllable in a word is stressed. **Stress** is the loudness given to a particular syllable in a word when speaking it. In spoken English, some syllables in a word are stressed and some are not.

First syllable stressed: happen, enter

Second syllable stressed: begin, commit, equip

TIP | Dictionaries show which syllable is stressed with a stress mark ('). The mark is placed before the syllable that is stressed:

'hap py   be'gin

Here are the rules for doubling the consonant when adding a suffix.

Rules for Doubling the Final Consonants for One-Syllable Words

■ If the word ending in a consonant + vowel + consonant has one syllable, double the final consonant.

hop + ing = hopping   drip + ing = dripping

Exceptions: Do not double the last consonant when the words end in –w, –x, or –y.

sew + ing = sewing   fix + ing = fixing

■ If the word ends with two or more consonants, do not double the final consonant.

debt + or = debtor   wish + ed = wished

■ If the word ends with two or more vowels and a consonant, do not double the final consonant.

tear + ing = tearing   sweet + est = sweetest

Rules for Doubling the Final Consonants for Words with Two or More Syllables

■ If the first syllable is stressed, do not double the final consonant.

happen + ed = happened   enter + ing = entering   accept + ed = accepted

■ If a word has more than one syllable, and the last syllable is stressed, double the final consonant.

begin + ing = beginning   commit + ed = committed   equip + ed = equipped

PRACTICE   **Doubling Final Consonants before Adding Suffixes**

30.5   Apply the rules to add the suggested suffix to each word.

EXAMPLE: submit + ed ___submitted___

1. occur + ed _____
2. benefit + ing _____
3. prefer + ed _____
4. excel + ed _____
5. thin + est _____
6. plan + ing _____
7. big + est _____
8. show + ing _____

Spelling Out Certain Words

Some words should be spelled out in academic writing.

numbers that begin sentences	**Fifty** percent of Southeast Asia's people live in cities. **Sixteen hundred** different languages are spoken in India.
numbers under 100	**ten**, not 10 **twenty-four**, not 24
units of measurement	**feet** not ft. **miles per hour**, not mph
days, months, and holidays	**Monday**, not Mon. **August 6**, not Aug. 6
people's first names	**William**, not Wm.
courses in general	**English**, not Eng.

PRACTICE   Spelling Out Words

30.6   Correct any numbers or abbreviations that should be spelled out.

EXAMPLE: Native people of Amer. domesticated the wild tobacco plant more than 5,000 years ago.

1. They grew 2 main types of tobacco.
2. One type was grown in the northeastern U.S. and Can.
3. Another type of tobacco was grown in Central and S. America.
4. Native people in these countries developed all of the ways to use tobacco, such as smoking, inhaling, and chewing, before people from Eur. came to the Americas.
5. In 1620, 40,000 lbs. of tobacco were exported from Virginia to England.
6. 1770 was the year that the oldest tobacco shop in the United States opened in Lancaster, PA.
7. 46 million residents of the United States smoke cigarettes.

   (Adapted from *World Regions in Global Context* by Sallie A. Marston et al.)

Avoiding Clipped Words

Avoid using clipped words in college writing. A clipped word is the shortened form of a word. Study the following examples of clipped words and their complete forms:

ad = advertisement	photo = photograph
burger = hamburger	teen = teenager
exam = examination	typo = typographical error

Capitalization

Capitalization is the practice of using capital letters at the beginning of certain words.

Capitalize First Words of Sentences

Always capitalize the first word of a sentence.

> As a world region, Europe is located between the Americas, Africa, and the Middle East.

> "Overall, Europe accounts for almost two-fifths of world trade," states Marston.

Capitalize Proper Nouns and Proper Adjectives

Proper nouns and proper adjectives are capitalized according to these rules.

Names of People	
First, middle, and last names and middle initials	George Herbert Bush
	Simone de Beauvoir
	Thomas A. Edison
	Shamu
Names with more than one part	Tom MacGregor
	Maureen O'Hara
	Oscar de la Hoya
	Rocco De Luca
Initials and abbreviations that come before or after names	Jonas Salk, M.D.
	Mr. Peter T. Roth
	Sr. Perez
	J. K. Rowling
	James Carter, Jr.
Titles before names	Senator Reed
Names of relationships when they replace proper names	Aunt Yolanda
	But: My **aunt** will visit next week.
	Please ask **Father** for the car keys.
	But: My **father** has the car keys.

Other Proper Nouns and Adjectives

Names of groups: organizations, teams, government bodies, institutions	National Audubon Society, New York Giants, Central High School, United Nations, Pennsylvania State University
National and ethnic groups and their languages	Chinese, Haitian, Navaho, African American, Hispanic
	Note: In current practice, the terms *black* and *white* are not capitalized when referring to a group of people.
Specific places: cities, counties, states, countries, continents, islands, streets, regions, bodies of water	Rio de Janeiro, Atlantic Ocean, Broward County, Main Street, New Mexico, Houston, Texas, South America, Lake Erie, Korea, the West
Historical events, periods, movements	World War II, the Romantic Period, the Space Age, the Civil Rights Movement
Days of the week, months, holidays	Friday, December, Independence Day, New Year's Day, Ramadan
Religions, their followers, sacred writings, deities	the Bible, the Koran (or Qur'an), the Torah, the Vedas, Christianity, Christians, Islam, Muslims, Judaism, Jews, Buddhism, Buddhists, Jehovah, God, Allah, Buddha
Planets, stars, constellations, heavenly bodies	Mars, Sirius, Andromeda, the Milky Way
Businesses and brand names	Amazon.com, Dell, Taco Bell, Kodak, Levi's, Colgate, Kleenex, Gatorade
Internet terminology	Internet, World Wide Web, RAM, Wi-Fi
	But: website, web page

PRACTICE Capitalizing Proper Nouns and Adjectives

30.7 Capitalize proper nouns and proper adjectives.

EXAMPLE: The most populated region of the world is east asia. _East Asia_____

1. This region consists of china, japan, mongolia, north and south korea, and taiwan. _____

2. The philosophy of confucianism is the most widely recognized belief system in china. _____

3. Formalized religions include taoism, tibetan buddhism, and islam. _____

_____

4. The official language of china is mandarin. _____

5. Other languages spoken on a regular basis are cantonese, xiang, minn, and hakka; fifty-three ethnic minorities have their own languages. _____

(Adapted from *World Regions in Global Context* by Sallie A. Marston et al.)

Capitalize Titles

Capitalize the first and last words of a title.

> **World** *Regions in Global* **Context**

Capitalize a word that comes after a colon or semicolon.

> *World Regions in Global Context:* **Peoples,** *Places, and Environments*

Do not capitalize these words unless they appear at the beginning or end of the title or after a colon or semicolon.

Articles: *a, an, the*
Prepositions: *at, by, down, in, into, of, off, on, up, to,* and so on
Conjunctions of fewer than five letters: *and, but, for, nor, or, so, yet*

Article title: "**S**cientists **C**apture **H**aiti **D**isaster with **H**igh-**T**ech **I**maging **S**ystem"
Book title: *The* **D**iscoverers: **A** *History of* **M**an's *Search to* **K**now **H**is **W**orld *and* **Himself**

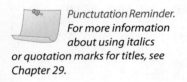 *Punctutation Reminder. For more information about using italics or quotation marks for titles, see Chapter 29.*

PRACTICE Capitalizing Titles

30.8 Add capital letters to the titles.

EXAMPLE: *a dictionary of geography* <u>A Dictionary of Geography</u>

1. "inspiring tomorrow's geographers" _____

2. *antarctica: the blue continent* _____

3. "a history and overview of earth day" _____

4. "tsunamis: how safe is the united states?" _____

5. *maps: finding our place in the world* _____

Avoiding Capitalization Errors

The following words do not need to be capitalized:

names of seasons	Our class will take a field trip to Bear Mountain this **spring.**
subjects in general	Ricardo is taking a **geography** class this semester.
directions	To get to the mall, go **east** on Main Street.
titles not attached to names	Our geography **professor** is well known in the field.
	My **mother** is proud of my good grades in geography.

PRACTICE 30.9 Correcting Errors in Capitalization

Correct any capitalization errors.

EXAMPLE: John Pennekamp Coral Reef State Park is located North of Key Largo, Florida. ___north___

1. Last year, my Geography class took a two-day field trip there, which turned out to be better than I expected. _____

2. Our Professor planned the trip so that we could learn about the unique coral reef formations and mangrove swamps. _____

3. The last thing that I wanted to do was to spend two nights in the florida Keys' heat and humidity. _____

4. I had never been to Key Largo before, but my Dad, who used to go on fishing trips there before he married my Mother, told me that I would enjoy it. _____

5. I would have preferred an air-conditioned hotel room instead of in a tent on the campgrounds, but I made sure to bring my Off! brand Insect Repellent and plenty of Sunscreen. _____

6. While driving North to get home, we talked about how awful Professor Tarpon's cooking was and about what we learned about the geography of the area. _____

7. I wrote an article about Pennekamp Coral Reef State Park for the College newspaper. _____

Review: Spelling and Capitalization

Correct any spelling and capitalization errors in the following passage. The first sentence has been corrected for you.

Antarctica   South Pole

¹The continent of antarctica is located over the south pole.²During the six-month Winter, the Sun does not rise above the horizon, so the continent stays in twilight. ³The temperature averages minus sixty deg., and by sept. each year, half of the surrounding Ocean is frozen. ⁴The frozen area creates a large ice pack that has an area of 32 mil. mi. and a thickness of 6.6 ft.

⁵Glaciers and snowfields cover most of the continent; the largest glaciers, such as the lambert and the beardmore, are so large that they force huge amounts of ice into the seas. ⁶The landscapes of antarctica are almost completely silent because nothing grows in the region, and the Sea is quiet because it is frozen for most of the year. ⁷The most active and noisy residents are the millions of Seals and Penguins and the occasional giant blue whale coming to the surface offshore.

⁸Although few people live there, many are interested in antarctica for scientific research and for using its natural resources such as Iron Ore, Coal, Gas, and Oil that may lie beneath it.

⁹In 1958, the antarctic treaty was created and signed by 45 countries. ¹⁰The Treaty baned nuclear tests and the disposal of radioactive waste. ¹¹It also ensured that the continent can only be used for peacefull purposes, mainly for scientific research.

(Adapted from *World Regions in Global Context* by Sallie A. Marston et al.)

Writing Assignment

MyWritingLab™
Complete this activity
at mywritinglab.com

Write about an Image

Imagine that you are a geographer who has just discovered the island in the photograph. On a sheet of paper, write down the features of the island. Include details such as location, names of bodies of water, the island's physical appearance, weather, plants and trees, insects, birds, and wildlife. Give names to these items.

Write five to eight sentences describing your observations and thoughts the day you arrived on the island. Check for spelling and capitalization errors.

Improving Your Writing

PART 7

31 Concise and Appropriate Words

Theme: *Business Communications*

Learning Objectives

After working through this chapter, you will be able to:

LO 1 Choose concise words to make writing precise, understandable, original, and accurate.

LO 2 Choose bias-free words when writing about gender, age, disability, ethnicity, and race.

LO 3 Use commonly confused words correctly.

What Are Concise and Appropriate Words?

Writers' word choices reveal a great deal about them and give readers a positive or negative impression. Concise and appropriate words are important features of good academic and workplace writing.

Words that are **concise** express what needs to be written without unnecessary words. Words that are **appropriate** are suitable for a particular situation or occasion. They are essential when writing about gender, age, disability, ethnicity, and race.

Concise and Appropriate Words in Context

The following two letters were written by **Medicare** employees. Medicare is a U.S. government health insurance plan for people over 65. Medicare receives many false claims from health care providers every year. To reach these providers more effectively, they changed their original letter to make it easier to understand.

Medicare Fraud Letter: Wordy

Investigators at the contractor will review the facts in your case and decide the most appropriate course of action. The first step taken with most Medicare health care providers is to reeducate them about Medicare regulations and policies. If the practice continues, the contractor may conduct special audits of the providers' medical records. Often, the contractor recovers overpayments to health care providers this way. If there is sufficient evidence to show that the provider is consistently violating Medicare policies, the contractor will document the violations and ask the Office of the Inspector General to prosecute the case. This can lead to expulsion from the Medicare program, civil monetary penalties, and imprisonment. (111 words)

Medicare Fraud Letter: Concise

We will take two steps to look at this matter: We will find out if it was an error or fraud. We will let you know the result. (28 words)

Choose Concise Words

LO 1 **Choose concise words to make writing precise, understandable, original, and accurate.**

Writing that is concise does not use unnecessary words.

Avoid Wordy Expressions

Wordy expressions contain more words than are necessary. The following chart lists some wordy expressions and gives precise words to replace them.

Wordy	Precise
as a result of, due to the fact that, for the reason that	because
at that time	then
at the present time	now
despite the fact that, in spite of the fact that	although
for the purpose of	for, to
in the event that	if
in the near future	soon
last but not least	last

TIP Some college writers add unnecessary words to make their paper longer to meet assignment requirements. Adding unnecessary words makes writing wordy and less effective.

PRACTICE Replacing Wordy Expressions

31.1 Replace wordy expressions with precise words that you learned in the list above, and rewrite each sentence.

EXAMPLE: At this point in time, the committee needs to meet for the purpose of planning the community outreach projects.

Now, the committee needs to meet to plan the community outreach projects.

1. In this day and age, with so many people out of work, we need to hold a Thanksgiving food drive in the near future.

2. Due to the fact that the holidays are approaching at a rapid rate, we will place boxes for food donations at the local supermarkets.

3. We hope to collect enough food to fill the homeless shelter's pantry despite the fact that many people are struggling financially.

4. The company also plans to collect a great number of holiday gifts for the children in the domestic abuse shelter for the reason that they may not receive any presents.

_____

5. Last but not least, during the holidays, we plan to volunteer along with shelter officials to prepare and serve meals in the event that there are large crowds.

_____

Avoid Redundant Expressions

A **redundant expression** uses two or more words that mean the same thing. The chart below gives examples of redundant expressions and explains why they are redundant.

Redundant Expression	Why is the Expression redundant?
and also	*And* and *also* mean the same thing.
three in number	*Three* is a number.
combine into one	*Combine* means to join together to make a single thing or group.
consensus of opinion	*Consensus* is a generally accepted opinion.
each and every	*Each* means every person or thing in a group, and *every* means all members of a group.
first and foremost	*First* and *foremost* mean the same thing.
month of June	*June* is the name of a month.
new innovation	*Innovation* means something new.
past experience	*Experience* is something that happened in the past.
past history	*History* consists of past events.
red in color	*Red* is a color.
same identical	*Identical* means exactly the same.
small in size	*Small* is a size.
the reason why is because	*Reason, why,* and *because* all mean the same thing.
true fact	A *fact* is something that is true.
3 p.m. in the afternoon	The abbreviation *p.m.* means afternoon (or evening).
unexpected surprise	A *surprise* is something unexpected.

PRACTICE   Replacing Redundant Words and Phrases

31.2   Replace the redundant words and phrases in this letter. Refer to the chart on page 508 if necessary.

Dear Mr. Nelson,

¹Thank you for your recent application for a position at D.B. Marketing. ²We are reviewing applications and also expect to schedule interviews in the month of October.

³We have received fifty-five in number applications, which was an unexpected surprise. ⁴Each candidate is well qualified with excellent past experience. ⁵Therefore, it will take a while for the hiring committee to reach a consensus of opinion about the candidates we would like to interview. ⁵If you are selected, first and foremost you will receive a call from a Human Resources staff member some time after 1 p.m. in the afternoon. ⁶The reason why is because staff members are available at that time.

⁷Thank you again for your interest in D.B. Marketing.

Sincerely,

Elana Figueuroa

Avoid General Words

Specific words help the reader create a mental picture and make writing more accurate and interesting. In contrast, **general words** are less specific and can mean different things to different readers.

> **General:** job   **Specific:** senior accountant for Softbyte Press
>
> **General:** person   **Specific:** Sarah Jones, production manager
>
> **General:** One of our workers was injured by a piece of equipment recently.
>
> **Specific:** Alan Hill suffered a broken thumb while working on a lathe yesterday.
>
> (From *Technical Communication* by John Lannon)

Examples of general adjectives are *good, a lot, awful, awesome, bad, beautiful, big, cute, difficult, exciting, expensive, fantastic, fine, funny, glamorous, interesting, many, nice, pretty, several, some, ugly,* and *unusual.*

PRACTICE   Choosing Specific Words

31.3   Revise the following sentences changing vague words to specific ones.

EXAMPLE: The office worker keyboarded the report.

The administrative assistant keyboarded the quarterly earnings report.

1. Spencer is a very lazy worker.

_____

2. The patient was not feeling too well.

_____

3. We need this information as soon as possible.

_____

4. The kitchen staff prepared the food.

_____

5. We had a good meeting.

_____

6. Bad weather in our area damaged the computer systems.

_____

7. At our auto shop, we can fix anything.

_____

Choose Appropriate Words

LO 2 **Choose bias-free words when writing about gender, age, disability, ethnicity, and race.**

Choosing appropriate words is essential when writing about gender, age, disability, ethnicity, race, and sexual orientation. If you have any biases, they may show up in your writing without your realizing it. A **bias** is a personal opinion that influences your judgment, usually in an unfair way. Bias in writing gives a negative image about a person or group and disrespects readers. Bias-free writing treats people fairly.

Bias-free Language for Gender

Gender-biased words and expressions give incorrect ideas about men and women. Use *he or she* or the plural form *they* to refer to nouns when the gender is not known.

> **Biased:**   A good lawyer will make sure that his clients are aware of their rights.

> **Unbiased:** A good lawyer will make sure that his or her clients are aware of their rights.

Replace words such as job titles and qualities that stereotype men and women. A **stereotype** is an idea that people have about what someone or something is like, especially an idea that is wrong. For example, many people assume that nurses and teachers are females, while doctors and company presidents are males.

Words that stereotype men	Replacements
businessman, fireman, policeman, salesmen	business person, fire fighter, police officer, sales associate
Words that stereotype women	Replacements
female doctor, maid, waitress, housewife, working mother	doctor, house cleaner, server, homemaker, worker

Bias-free Language for Age

The use of negative stereotypes and language aimed at specific age groups is considered **ageism.** In the U.S. culture, ageism is directed toward older adults; aging is viewed in a negative way in language and in the media.

Avoid words like ***senior citizen, old folks, seniors, golden agers, grandmotherly, elderly,*** and ***80-years-young.*** Avoid reference to a person's age when it is not relevant.

Ageist: Representative Brown, an elderly politician, has decided to run for another term in office.

Not ageist: Representative Brown has decided to run for another term in office.

Ageist: Maria Ramirez, 59, has just joined our finance department.

Not ageist: Maria Ramirez has just joined our finance department.

Bias-free Language for Disability

A **disability** is an illness, injury, or condition that makes it difficult for someone to do the things that other people do.

Avoid words like ***handicapped*** or ***crippled;*** instead, use ***disabled*** or ***differently abled.*** In general, avoid referring to a person's disability. If the reference is necessary, use words that treat disabilities or illness in a neutral way.

Biased: The AIDS victim received a promising new treatment.

Unbiased: The AIDS patient received a promising new treatment.

Biased: Ford Smith, a blind employee, had the highest number of sales this month.

Unbiased: Ford Smith had the highest number of sales this month. (Do not mention disability unless necessary or relevant.)

Bias-free Language for Ethnic and Racial Groups

An **ethnic group** refers to people of the same race or nationality who share a distinctive culture. A **racial group** is a set of individuals who share physical characteristics or biological descent.

Avoid identifying people by their ethnic or racial group, but if a label is necessary, be sure to use an acceptable word for that label. Words that are insulting to any ethnic or racial group should be avoided.

> **TIP** Whether to use African American or black, Pacific Islander or Asian, or Hispanic American or Latino, for example, depends on many things such as group or individual preference.

Bias-free Language for Sexual Orientation

Sexual orientation is a person's emotional, romantic, and/or sexual attraction to the same, opposite, or both sexes. Identify people by what they do rather than by their sexual orientation.

PRACTICE Using Bias-Free Language
31.4 Revise words, phrases, or sentences that use biased language.

EXAMPLE: The committee wants to hire the right man for the job.
Replace man with person. _____

1. Candidate Rocio Perez, married and the mother of a ten-year-old, will attend the debate. _____ _____

2. Senior citizen Paul Ormand is still an active, successful sales representative.

   _____

3. I will have my girl make the appointment. _____

4. The president of the company, a woman, met with her sales staff. _____

5. An **epileptic,** Lisa does an excellent job. _____

6. Our department has completed a man-sized job. _____

7. The male nurse won the patient's confidence. _____

8. The team consisted of two female astronauts, one male navigator, and three male technicians. _____

9. Rudolph Giuliani, Italian-American lawyer and politician, served as mayor of New York from 1994 to 2001. _____

10. Every teacher should prepare and submit her lesson plans by Friday. _____

epileptic someone who has epilepsy, a condition of the brain, which causes a person to become unconscious for short periods or to move in a violent and uncontrolled way

Commonly Confused Words

LO 3 **Use commonly confused words correctly.**

Some words can be confused because they sound alike or look alike. Writers cannot depend on spell-checkers to find errors when words sound alike but have different spellings and meanings. Look over the lists of commonly confused words to review those you are not familiar with.

Commonly Confused Word Pairs A through C

Word Pairs	Meaning	Examples
accept	to receive, admit, or believe	The company **accepted** Gerry's application.
except	not including	All of the candidates **except** Gerry were called in for interviews.
a lot	a large number, very much	**A lot** of employees bring their children to the company daycare center.
alot	an incorrect spelling of **a lot**	
already	before the present time	Our team had **already** done the research, so the report was easy to write.
all ready	prepared for what one is about to do	Our team was **all ready** to write the report.
been	the past participle of **be**	Charlene has **been** an administrative assistant for two years.
being	the **–ing** form of **be**	Charlene was **being** helpful when she offered to work late to finish the paperwork.
break	to damage something, to interrupt, to stop, an opportunity	The copier **breaks** frequently.
brake	a device that slows or stops a vehicle	Juan quickly pressed down on the **brake** to stop the truck.
breath	air taken in or out of lungs	Selma took a deep **breath** before speaking.
breathe	to take air into the lungs and let it out again	Selma learned to **breathe** deeply when stressed.
complement	to help make someone or something more complete	Alan **complemented** his résumé with letters of recommendation.
compliment	Giving praise or admiration	The interviewer **complimented** Alan on his resume.
conscience	knowledge of right and wrong and a feeling one should do what is right	He had a guilty **conscience** after he lied about being too sick to go to work.
conscious	aware of what is happening	The boss became **conscious** of the employee's poor work.

PRACTICE Choosing the Correct Word

31.5 Some of the boldfaced words in the following sentences are not correct. If the word is not correct, write the correct word above it. If the word is correct, write a **C** above it.

EXAMPLE: ~~Alot~~ A lot of frustrated consumers go online to complain about problems with products.

1. Consumers who write product reviews seem to **complement** products less and complain more.

2. For example, when a product **brakes,** the online consumer may not know where to look for help.

3. When they write to companies for help, they are **all ready** frustrated.

4. To add to the problem, these consumers are **effected** by poor online service.

5. Some companies are **conscious** of the problem and have **been** setting up consumer social networks where consumers' questions and comments are **excepted.**

6. Employees representing companies that sell the products are **already** with answers to consumers' questions.

7. Customers can **breath** a sigh of relief knowing that the company cares about them and is **being** helpful.

Commonly Confused Word Pairs D through P

Word Pairs	Meaning	Examples
decent	socially acceptable, appropriate	He always wears decent clothes to work.
descent	a movement downward or ancestral background	The airplane's descent was not smooth due to the storm.
elicit	to get a response or information from someone	Many companies elicit online reviews from customers.
illicit	illegal or not morally acceptable	Workers should not download illicit software or music at work.
everyday	commonplace	Buying a cup of coffee on the way to work was an everyday routine for Marie.
every day	happening or done each day	Marie buys a cup of coffee every day on her way to work.
imply	to suggest something without saying it directly	Though he did not say it, the manager implied that some people would be laid off.
infer	to reach a conclusion based on known facts	We inferred from the manager's remarks that we would not be laid off.
it's	a contraction of *it is*	It's going to be a difficult work day because several employees are sick.
its	possessive form of *it*	The company displayed its new logo at the entrance to the building.

Word Pairs	Meaning	Examples
knew	the past tense of **know,** which means to have information or to understand something	Jessie knew how to write a good memo.
new	recently created, not previously used or owned	Jessie was promoted to a new position because of her writing skills.
lose	become unable to find, not make a profit, to be defeated	The store did not lose money this month.
loose	not attached, not tight	Chris likes to wear loose clothing to work to be comfortable while sitting at a desk all day.
passed	the past tense of **pass,** which means to go or move forward, to succeed aware of	Vanessa passed her nursing certification exam. Alex passed me in the hallway without saying hello.
past	the time before and until now	Vanessa spent the past two years studying to be an accountant.

PRACTICE   Choosing the Correct Word

31.6   Some of the boldfaced words in the following sentences are not correct. If the word is not correct, write the correct word above it. If the word is correct, write a **C** above it.

EXAMPLE: Employees who observe ~~elicit~~ *illicit* or unethical behavior in their companies may not **know** *C* how to deal with it.

1. Talking to a supervisor about an action that the employee has observed **everyday** may not be an option.

2. The supervisor may **infer** that the employee is not loyal to the company even if the supervisor does not say it.

3. On the other hand, the supervisor may be upset that the employee **new** about the behavior and wants to take action.

4. When the employee has no options, he or she may report the individual to **illicit** help from the company ethics hot line or the news media.

5. Sometimes, **it's** the only way to bring a problem to management's attention.

6. As a result, the employee who made a **descent** decision to expose the problem may **loose** his or her job.

7. From **passed** experience, companies have set up formal ways to report problems such as rule breaking, criminal activity, and cover-ups.

Commonly Confused Word Pairs P through T

Word Pairs	Meaning	Examples
piece	a part of something or a single thing	The people attending the conference were asked to sign their names on a **piece** of paper.
peace	calm and quiet or a time when there is no war	Miranda enjoyed the **peace** and quiet in the office after the employees went home for the day.
principle	a rule of behavior or a basic truth	We buy recycled paper for the copier as a matter of **principle**.
principal	most important or a person in charge of a school	A good way to remember **principal** is this sentence: The principal is your pal. The **principal** reason for the budget crisis is overspending.
quiet	making little or no noise or without much activity	The construction work outside the building disturbed our **quiet** office.
quite	very or really	The workers were **quite** disturbed by the noise.
quit	to leave or to stop doing an action	James **quit** his job because he found a better position.
rise	to move up from a lower to higher position or to increase	As we started the corporate race Saturday morning, the sun began to **rise**.
raise	an increase in salary or to cause to rise, to increase in size, value, or amount	The corporate race **raised** $10,000 for charity.
site	a place where something is, was, or will be	The new **site** for the company is downtown next to the bank.
cite	to mention something as proof or to repeat a passage from	In his proposal, James **cited** evidence from two specialists in the field.
sight	the ability to see, range of vision	Pat's **sight** got worse from working at the computer every day.
stationary	not moving, still	The subway remained **stationary** while passengers got off.
stationery	paper on which one writes	**Stationery** includes envelopes and will help people remember the *e* when spelling the word.
suppose	to expect or believe, make a suggestion	The attorney **supposes** that the jury will not take long to reach a verdict.
supposed	past and past participle of ***suppose***	Employees are not **supposed** to smoke in the rest rooms.
taught	the past tense and past participle of ***teach***	The trainer **taught** us how to operate the new equipment.
thought	the past tense and past participle of ***think***	We **thought** the new equipment would be easy to operate.

Word Pairs	Meaning	Examples
their	belonging to certain people, animals, or things	Their meetings are always at 4 p.m.
they're	contraction meaning **they are**	They're meeting at 4 p.m.
there	a location other than here	The conference room is over there, next to the main entrance.

PRACTICE **Choosing the Correct Word**

31.7   Some of the boldfaced words in the following sentences are not correct. If the word is not correct, write the correct word. If the word is correct, write a **C**.

quite
EXAMPLE: The teachers of Sun County are **quiet** upset.

1. They have not had a **raise** in three years, and **their** thinking of going on strike.

2. The **principle,** who had always supported them, **taught** that he should stay neutral.

3. He has to remain **quiet** and keep the **piece** between the teachers and the school board.

4. The teachers threatened to **raise** up and organize a strike at the **cite** of the main administrative center.

5. They listed **they're** complaints in a letter typed on a **piece** of school **stationary** and sent it to the local newspaper.

6. The teachers **suppose** that the school board would reconsider its decision.

7. The school board said it would give them more money if the city would **raise** taxes.

Commonly Confused Word Pairs and Examples T through Y

Word Pairs	Meaning	Examples
then	at that time, next, or after that	Jamal made sure his schedule for Friday was clear, and **then** he made several appointments.
than	used to join two items in comparison	Jamal is busier on Thursday **than** he is on Friday.
threw	past tense of **throw,** to send through the air	She **threw** the old copy of the report in the trash.
though	although	**Though** Clarisse spent several hours on her presentation, she was not happy with it.

Word Pairs	Meaning	Examples
through	from one end or side to the other, or having finished	Tony looked **through** the files, but he could not find the document.
thru	slang for **through,** not appropriate for use in academic English	
to	in the direction of, for the purpose of	Sara went **to** the meeting in the conference room.
too	in addition or very	Chet took **too** many days off last month.
two	the number which is the sum of one and one	Hank had to give **two** speeches, one to the clients and one to the bosses.
use	to do something with an item or person to accomplish a task	I always **use** grammar check when I write.
used	past tense and past participle of **use** or previously owned	I **used** grammar check after writing my email to the employees.
we're	the contracted form of **we are**	**We're** meeting at the attorney's office.
where	to, at, or in what place	**Where** will the meeting take place?
were	past tense of **be** for pronouns **you, we,** and **they** and plural nouns	The employees **were** in New York for a conference.
whether	if, used when writing about one or more possibilities	Keith did not know **whether** the boss had read his report.
weather	the temperature and other outside conditions	The stormy **weather** caused many employees to be late.
who's	contracted form of **who is**	**Who's** writing the manual for the new equipment?
whose	used to talk about the person or thing something belongs to	The employee **whose** cell phone was stolen was very upset.
write	to put words, letters, numbers, or symbols on paper or an electronic device	Most employees **write** many emails.
right	correct or true, suitable	Employees should make sure that their English usage is **right.**
your	the person or people being referred to	The boss was impressed with **your** work.
you're	contraction for **you are**	**You're** hired.

PRACTICE   Choosing the Correct Word

31.8   Some of the boldfaced words in the following sentences are not correct. If the word is not correct, write the correct word above it. If the word is correct, write a *C* above it.

through
EXAMPLE: Written communication can be enhanced ~~thru~~ visual elements, such as charts or pictures.

1. Sometimes, visuals can convey message points more effectively **then** words.

2. They can provide more information **too** while holding the reader's attention.

3. Busy readers **who's** time is limited often skip **threw** the written words and look at the visuals to get the central meaning of the message.

4. The designer must be careful that the **right** images are **use** because they can mean different things in different cultures.

5. Also, a poorly designed visual can confuse **you're** readers.

6. Today people can make higher quality videos **then** they **use** to.

7. People can understand visuals **weather** they have high or low reading skills.

MyWritingLab™

Complete this activity
at mywritinglab.com

Review: Commonly Confused Words

Edit the following passage for nine errors with commonly confused words.

¹Fast as it is, email may be to slow for today's fast-paced workplace. ²As a result, instant messaging (IM) might replace email in the workplace. ³The use of instant messaging has all ready increased.

⁴Although instant messaging makes everyday communication faster, it can lead to knew problems. ⁵First of all, employees may send personal messages to co-workers when their suppose to be working. ⁶Also, a brief conversation can turn into a long one, causing workers to loose hours of productive work time. ⁷Another problem is that people forget about been polite and are less professional when instant messaging then they should be. Finally, a co-worker whose bored can distract others with unimportant chats.

(Adapted from *Workplace Writing* by Sharon J. Gerson and Steven M. Gerson)

Writing Assignment

MyWritingLab™
Complete this activity
at mywritinglab.com

Write about an Image

In the photograph, one employee is gossiping to another while the third tries to hear what they are saying. **Gossip** is conversation or reports about other people's private lives that might be unkind, disapproving, or not true.

In many instances gossiping would be considered unethical; for example, when you use it to unfairly hurt another person, when you know it's not true, when no one has the right to such personal information, or when you are breaking a promise of secrecy.

(From *Human Communication* by Joseph A. DeVito)

Write eight sentences that tell about an experience you had or heard about that involved gossip. As an alternative, you can write sentences about what you think is happening in the photograph. Make sure that your word choices are concise and appropriate.

EXAMPLE: The man is listening to the ladies' conversation.

32 Parallelism

Theme: *Nursing*

Learning Objectives

After working through this chapter, you will be able to:

LO 1 Maintain parallelism with words, phrases, or clauses in pairs.

LO 2 Maintain parallelism with words or phrases in a series, list, or outline.

What Is Parallelism?

Parallelism is the use of the same forms of words, phrases, or clauses when they appear in pairs, in groups, or in lists.

| Parallelism | Clara Barton was an American **teacher, nurse, and humanitarian**. During the U.S. Civil War, she established an agency to **obtain** and **deliver** supplies to wounded soldiers. |

Parallelism in Context

In the following passage about the importance of critical thinking for nurses, examples of parallel structure are green.

[1]Critical thinking is essential to **safe, competent, skillful** nursing practice. [2]Every day, nurses have to make vital decisions that may determine the well-being **of their clients and even of their survival**. [3]Often, nurses have **to think and act** in situations where there are **neither clear answers nor standard procedures**. [4]In order to make decisions, nurses must **use and learn** a large amount of knowledge. [5]They cannot function if they limit themselves to the information they learned **in school or in books**. [6]**Treatments, medications, and technology** change constantly. [7]Also, a client's condition may change **from minute to minute**. [8]Therefore, nurses need to master critical thinking skills **to process and to evaluate information they previously learned and new information they have and will continue to learn**.

(Adapted from *Fundamentals of Nursing* by Audrey Berman et al.)

Words, Phrases, or Clauses in Pairs

LO 1 Maintain parallelism with words, phrases, or clauses in pairs.

When words, phrases, or clauses appear in pairs, they should be in the same form.

Words	A health assessment differs with children and adults.
Phrases	With children, the nurse should proceed from the least uncomfortable to the most uncomfortable.
Dependent clauses	The nurse should explain when the examination will take place and what will happen during the exam.
Independent clauses	The examination room should be well lighted, and the equipment should be efficiently organized.

Not consistent	A nurse can wear *either* a disposable water-resistant gown *or* an apron that is made out of plastic during procedures when the uniform is likely to become soiled.
Consistent	A nurse can wear *either* a disposable water-resistant gown or a plastic apron during procedures when the uniform is likely to become soiled.

PRACTICE **Consistency through Parallel Words, Phrases, or Clauses in Pairs**

32.1 Rewrite the following sentences so that the pairs of words, phrases, or clauses are parallel.

EXAMPLE: A physical examination can be organized using either a head-to-toe approach or one that uses a body systems approach.

A physical examination can be organized using either a head-to-toe approach or a

body systems approach.

1. Usually, the nurse records a general impression about the client's overall appearance and status of health.

2. The head-to-toe approach begins the examination at the head, and the toes are last.

3. The nurse assesses all body parts and comparing findings on each side of the body.

4. The nurse can either give a complete examination or focus on what the problem area is.

5. Nurses use a written format or a format that is on a computer that organizes the information from the examination.

6. The information gathered during the assessment must be complete, and accuracy is also important.

7. The information from the nursing interview should agree with the physical examination information.

8. Nurses need to be able to separate facts from giving an opinion to avoid making a mistake.

Words or Phrases in a Series, List, or Outline

LO 2 **Maintain parallelism with words or phrases in a series, list, or outline.**

Each word or phrase that is in a series, list, or outline must be parallel.

Series of Items or Numbered List within a Sentence

A series of items	The nursing process consists of assessing, diagnosing, planning, implementing, and evaluating.
A numbered list of items within a sentence	The nursing process consists of (1) assessing, (2) diagnosing, (3) planning, (4) implementing, and (5) evaluating.

Not consistent	Assessing the patient includes collecting, organizing, validating, and a record of the information.
Consistent	Assessing the patient includes collecting, organizing, validating, and recording the information.

Bulleted or Outlined Items

Bulleted items	A nurse asks the patient for the following information about his or her health history:

- childhood illnesses
- childhood immunizations
- allergies
- accidents and injuries
- hospitalization for serious illnesses
- medications

Outlined items

I. Social Data

   A. Family relationships/friendships

   B. Ethnic affiliation

   C. Educational history

   D. Occupational history

   E. Economic status

   F. Home and neighborhood conditions

(Adapted from *Fundamentals of Nursing* by Audrey Berman et al.)

Compare the bulleted lists below. Items that are not consistent are red; items that are consistent are green.

Not Consistent	Consistent
Important Times for Medication Check	Important Times for Medication Check
■ On admission ■ During shift reports ■ During transfers ■ New medication orders ■ When the patient is discharged	■ On admission ■ During shift reports ■ During transfers ■ During new medication orders ■ Upon patient discharge

PRACTICE Consistency through Parallel Series, Bulleted Lists, and Outlines

32.2   Revise the sentences, lists, or outlines that have series, bulleted lists, or outlines that are not consistent.

EXAMPLE: An infection can be transmitted through any of the following mechanisms: (1) direct transmission, (2) that which is indirect, and (3) airborne transmission.

An infection can be transmitted through any of the following mechanisms: (1) direct transmission, (2) indirect transmission, and (3) airborne transmission.

1. An infection can be directly transmitted from one person to another through touching, biting, or a kiss.

2. The droplet sprays from the infected person into healthy person's mucous membranes of the eye, nose, or the person's mouth when the individuals are within three feet of one another.

3. Uninjured skin is the body's first line of defense against infection by these actions:
   - Creates a barrier
   - Sheds bacteria
   - It produces oils that wash away germs.

4. I. Steps for hand cleaning with alcohol-based antiseptic hand rub:

A. Apply palm full of product into cupped hand.

B. Next, you should rub palms against palms.

C. **Interlace** fingers palm to palm.

D. Rub palms to back of hands.

E. Don't forget to rub each finger individually on all sides.

F. It is important to continue until product is dry.

A. _____

B. _____

C. _____

D. _____

E. _____

F. _____

(Adapted from *Fundamentals of Nursing* by Audrey Berman et al.)

interlace cross one finger over and under another, as if woven together

MyWritingLab™
Complete this activity
at mywritinglab.com

Review: Parallelism

Edit the following paragraph for six errors in parallelism.

[1]Nurses and nursing students need to think about the values they have about life, death, health, and values about illness. [2]In their daily work, nurses deal with basic human events such as babies being born, death, and suffering.

[3]The nurse has a special relationship with the client. [4]Also, nurses are the ones who support and to speak for clients. [5]They have to support the clients and families who face difficult choices.

[6]Nurses have to decide what they think is right and wrong. [7]Making difficult decisions is stressful for nurses. [8]They want to do what is best for the client. [9]However, they also want to consider the client's family and the person who is the employer of the client.

[10]If a client asks for an opinion, nurses do not give it. [11]The choices that nurses might think are right may not apply to the client's situation. [12]The client, members of the family, spiritual counselors, and the health care team decide together. [13]Communicating and to work together are important skills for nurses.

(Adapted from *Fundamentals of Nursing* by Audrey Berman et al.)

Writing Assignment

Write about an Image

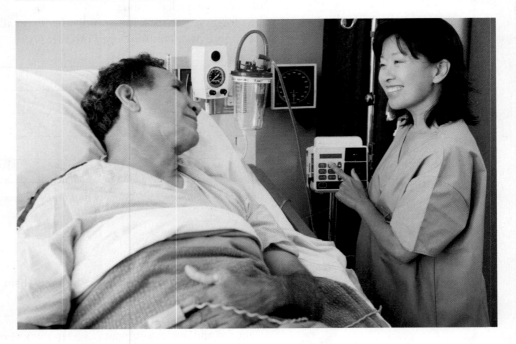

Write five sentences about an experience you or someone you know had with a nurse or other health care worker or write about the photograph. Check your sentences for parallelism. Reread several times to catch any errors.

EXAMPLE: When Tim had surgery, his nurses took his blood pressure, his temperature, and his pulse.

PART 8

Reading

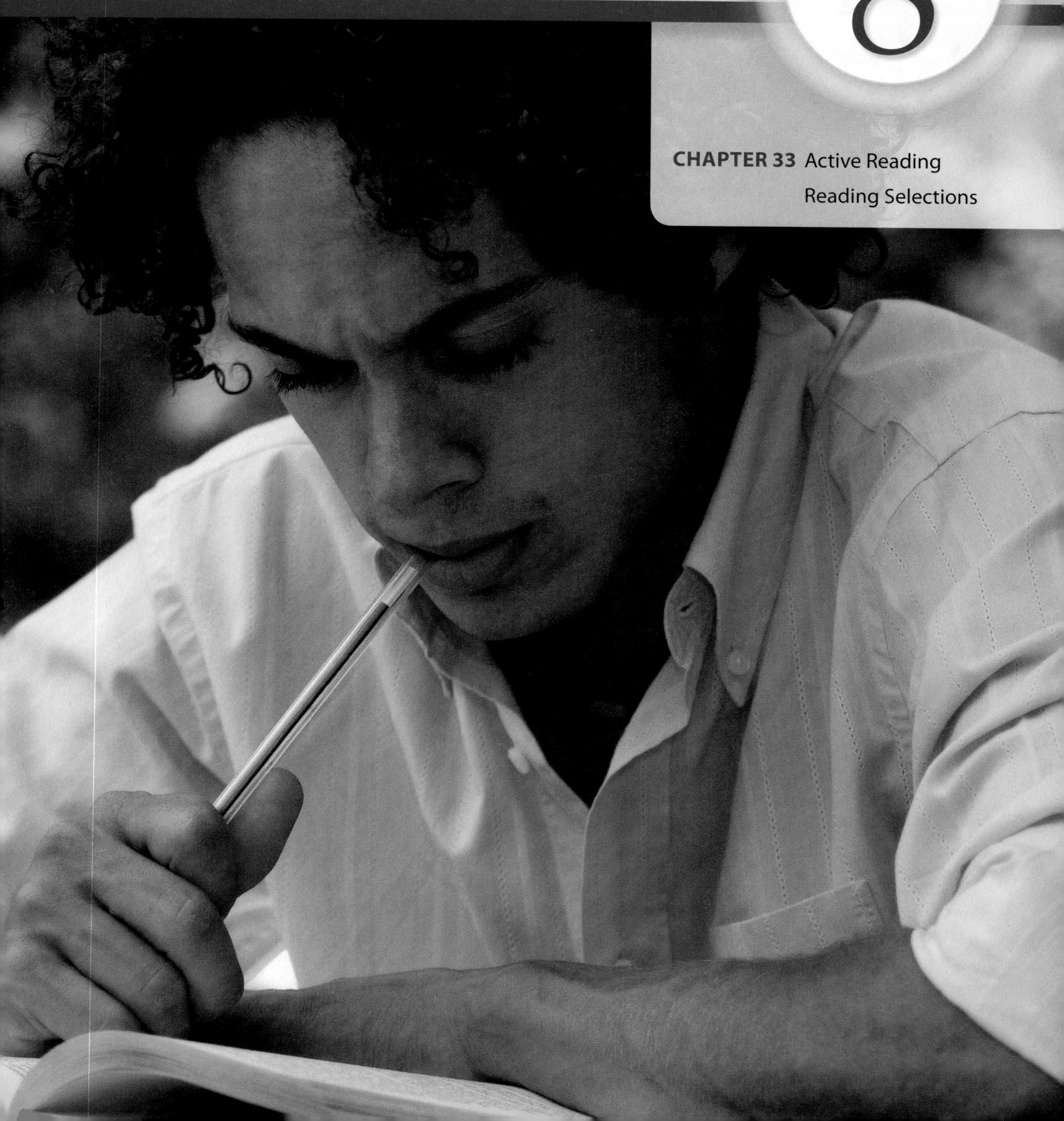

33 Active Reading

Learning Objectives

After working through this chapter, you will be able to:

LO 1 Describe the stages of the active reading process.

LO 2 Use prereading strategies to prepare for reading.

LO 3 Use reading strategies to improve your comprehension.

LO 4 Reflect upon and interpret what you have read.

As a college student, you will be doing quite a bit of reading. Many of your tests, papers, and class discussions will be based on reading assignments. The types of reading materials for college assignments will vary. These include textbooks, academic journals, and magazine and newspaper articles. In English courses like the one you are taking now, you may also read professional and student essays and fiction.

Textbooks, academic journals, and magazine and newspaper articles have different features. When you know how a reading is organized, you can choose the best reading strategy to use. The chart below describes the features of each type of reading:

academic journal a publication in which researchers publish articles on their work. Before an article is published, it has to be reviewed by researchers working in the same field to guarantee the quality of the research.

Examples of College Reading Materials	
Type of Reading	**Features**
Textbooks	Textbooks usually include these elements: ■ Units, chapters, and sections ■ Headings and subheadings ■ Chapter summaries ■ Chapter study questions
Academic Journal Articles	Journal articles follow a standard format: ■ Short summary (also called an abstract) ■ Introduction to the subject of the article ■ Review of research that has already been done on the subject ■ Methods of research ■ Discussion of the results
Newspaper and Magazine Articles	Newspaper and magazine articles follow a similar format, but a magazine article may have more pictures and may be longer: ■ A lead paragraph gets the readers attention and briefly tells who, what, where, when, why, and how. ■ The story begins with essential information and ends with less important information. ■ Body paragraphs are short. ■ The article ends with a final thought on the subject.

PRACTICE Getting to Know College Reading Materials

33.1   Choose a textbook, an academic journal article, a newspaper article, or a magazine article. Looking at the chart on page 528, find the features that are listed in the material you have selected.

What Is Active Reading?

LO 1 Describe the stages of the active reading process.

When your professors assign reading materials, they expect you to learn, think about, and respond to those materials. Learning how to be an active reader will help you get the most out of your reading assignments.

Active reading is the use of a variety of strategies before, during, and after you read to help you understand, learn, and study what you have read. Active reading takes time and effort, but you will get more from your reading than if you simply read and highlight.

The active reading process has three stages: (1) get ready to read, (2) understand the reading, and (3) remember and think about the reading.

Stage 1. Get Ready to Read

LO 2 Use prereading strategies to prepare for reading.

In this stage, you prepare to read by looking over the material to find out what it is about, what you already know about the topic, what your purpose for reading is, and how difficult the reading is. Answer the following questions while you look over the reading material:

- -

GET READY TO READ CHECKLIST

What is the reading about? The reading material offers clues about its content.

- Look at the title to get an idea of the subject of the reading.
- Look through the reading itself.

  ☐ Check the length of the reading.

  ☐ Look at the key parts of the reading. Use the chart on page 528 as a guide.

  ☐ Look at images, charts, or graphs.

What do you already know about the subject? Having some knowledge about the subject makes reading easier.

  ☐ Think about your background knowledge of the topic.

  ☐ Search online for more information.

What is your purpose for reading? Having a purpose helps you focus on getting the information you need.

  ☐ To learn information for a test

  ☐ To write a summary

  ☐ To make an outline

  ☐ To get ready to talk about the main ideas

  ☐ To write a paper about the reading

  ☐ Other _____

How difficult is the reading? A more difficult reading will take more time and effort.

☐ Vocabulary words are new to me.

☐ The writing is at a higher level than I am used to.

☐ The explanations are hard to understand.

- -

Take Prereading Notes

Taking prereading notes is an active reading strategy. This strategy involves looking through the reading for certain features to get an overall idea of what it is about and then writing them down in a prereading graphic organizer.

Prereading Graphic Organizer

Title	
Author	
Type of reading (textbook selection, magazine article, news article, website, and so on)	
Topic of reading (look for clues in title, headings, and graphics)	
Purpose for reading	
List any words or phrases that are in bold print or italics.	
List any headings.	
Describe any graphics (photos, drawings, charts, maps, and so on)	
Write number of paragraphs or pages.	
Explain prior knowledge of subject.	
Find unfamiliar words and/or concepts.	

Tori was assigned to read a section of her textbook *Essentials of Sociology* by James M. Henslin on pages 547–548. She prepared to read by filling in the Get Ready to Read Checklist on page 529.

After reading the selection, Tori filled in the Prereading Graphic Organizer:

Tori's Prereading Graphic Organizer

Title	"Beauty May Be Only Skin Deep, but Its Effects Go on Forever: Stereotypes in Everyday Life"
Author	James M. Henslin
Type of reading (textbook selection, magazine article, news article, website, and so on)	Textbook excerpt from <u>Essentials of Sociology</u>
Topic of reading (look for clues in title, headings, and graphics)	Title gives the idea that the excerpt will be about how beauty affects our everyday life
Purpose for reading	Homework assignment
List any words or phrases that are in bold print or italics.	"Stereotypes" is in bold and defined
List any headings.	How Self-Fulfilling Stereotypes Work
Describe any graphics (photos, drawings, charts, maps, and so on).	Chart under heading How Self-Fulfilling Stereotypes Work
Write number of paragraphs or pages.	4 paragraphs
Explain prior knowledge of subject.	I have heard the expression "beauty is only skin deep." According to what the dictionary says, the quote means that physical beauty is only on the outside and is not as important as a person's intellectual, emotional, and spiritual qualities—but I think our culture and the media focuses on how important physical beauty is. Women have a lot of pressure on them to look beautiful so they go on extreme diets and want to get plastic surgery.

Find unfamiliar words and/or concepts.	Word/Concept	Definition
	self-fulfilling stereotype	the idea that a person will behave in the way others think he or she will behave
	stereotype	qualities given or judgments made about groups of people without knowing them, related to their race, nationality, or sexual orientation to name a few
	ingenious	very clever and skillful
	homely	not good-looking
	reserved	tending to keep your feelings or thoughts private rather than showing them
	permeate	to spread through something; to be present in every part of it
	revenues	income

PRACTICE | Taking Prereading Notes

33.2 Choose a selection from a textbook for one of your courses or from one of the reading selections in this textbook and fill in the Prereading Graphic Organizer on page 530.

Stage 2. Understand the Reading

LO 3 **Use reading strategies to improve your comprehension.**

After you have prepared to read by looking over the material and taking prereading notes, you are ready for the next stage: read to understand. As an active reader, check frequently to see if you understand what you have read. Instead of silently reading and highlighting, use strategies that help you understand and learn the material. Three of these strategies are annotating, taking notes, and RAP.

Annotating

Annotating is the process of writing comments and notes directly on the reading materials. Annotating keeps you involved in your reading. Also, writing notes and comments are helpful for paragraph summaries, questions about the material, important vocabulary words and definitions, and your thoughts or opinions. When you annotate, your notes will stand out so that you can find important information later.

Writing Reminder. For more information on concept maps, see Chapter 2.

Before annotating, read the section or passage to get a sense of what it is about. You can write notes and comments, use symbols, or draw concept maps. If you prefer to use symbols, it is a good idea to make a set of symbols that you plan to use every time you annotate. For example, you can use circles for words you need to look up or learn or put boxes around important ideas. Another way to annotate is to draw concept maps in the margins.

Here is Tori's annotated version of the textbook excerpt "Beauty May Be Only Skin Deep, but Its Effects Go on Forever: Stereotypes in Everyday Life."

Purpose of experiment—are stereotypes self-fulfilling?

Description of experiment

?? Look up

Beauty May Be Only Skin Deep, but Its Effects Go on Forever: Stereotypes in Everyday Life

1   Mark Snyder, a psychologist, wondered whether **stereotypes**— our assumptions of what people are like—might be self-fulfilling. He came up with an <u>ingenious</u> way to test this idea. He (1993) gave college men a Polaroid snapshot of a woman (supposedly taken just moments before) and told them that he would introduce them to her after they talked with her on the telephone. Actually, the photographs—showing either a pretty or a homely woman—had been prepared before the experiment began. The photo was not of the woman the men would talk to.

2   <u>Stereotypes came into play immediately.</u> As Synder gave each man the photograph, he asked him what he thought the woman would be like. The men

Men reacted more positively to photo of pretty woman

Main idea

Summary

who saw the photograph of the attractive woman said that they expected to meet a poised, humorous, outgoing woman. The men who had been given a photo of the unattractive woman described her as awkward, serious, and unsociable.

3   The men's stereotypes influenced the way they spoke on the telephone to the women, who did not know about the photographs. The men who had seen the photograph of a pretty woman were warm, friendly, and humorous. This, in turn, affected the women they spoke to, for they responded in a warm, friendly, outgoing manner. And the men who had seen the photograph of the homely woman? On the phone, they were cold, reserved, and humorless, and the women they spoke to became cool, reserved, and humorless. Keep in mind that the women did not know that their looks had been evaluated—and that the photographs were not even of them. In short, stereotypes tend to produce behaviors that match the stereotype. This principle is illustrated in this figure:

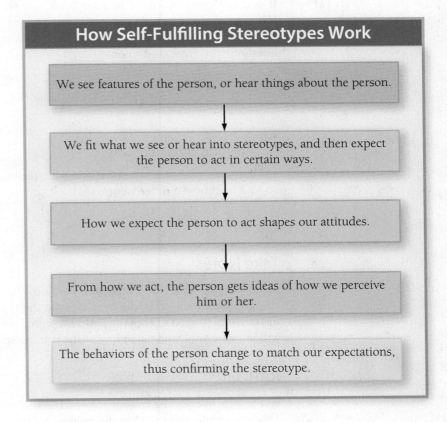

How Self-Fulfilling Stereotypes Work

We see features of the person, or hear things about the person.

↓

We fit what we see or hear into stereotypes, and then expect the person to act in certain ways.

↓

How we expect the person to act shapes our attitudes.

↓

From how we act, the person gets ideas of how we perceive him or her.

↓

The behaviors of the person change to match our expectations, thus confirming the stereotype.

4   Although beauty might be only skin deep, its consequences permeate our lives (Katz 2005). Beauty bestows an[1] advantage in everyday interaction, but it also has other effects. For one, if you are physically

Effects of being
attractive

attractive, you are[2]likely to make more money. Researchers in both Holland and the United States found that advertising firms with better looking executives have[3]higher revenues (Bosman et al. 1997; Pfann et al. 2000). The reason? The researchers suggest that people are more willing to associate with individuals whom they perceive as good-looking.

Men	Women
■ Shown photos of women	■ Did not see photos of men and didn't know about photos
■ Were warm and friendly to pretty woman, cold to homely woman	■ Responded the same way that men talked to them

TIP | If you don't want to write in your book, use sticky notes. Write down important ideas, words, summaries, and questions. You can use different colored sticky notes: one color for main ideas, another color for vocabulary words to learn, another for questions you have, and so on.

PRACTICE | Annotating a Reading

33.3 Annotate a reading selection. Use the selection you worked with in Practice 33.1 or 33.2 or choose a different one.

Take Notes

Some students find that taking notes on a reading helps them to understand it better. Using paper or an electronic device, write the main ideas and supporting points from the reading. Instead of copying word for word, put the ideas in your own words, which will increase your understanding of the reading selection.

RAP

RAP is an active reading strategy to use while you are reading to check your understanding. This is especially helpful when the material is difficult or when your mind starts to wander. RAP can be done silently or out loud. It consists of three parts: Read, Ask, and Paraphrase.

- **R**ead a paragraph or section.
- **A**sk yourself what the main ideas are.
- **P**ut the main ideas in your own words.

Click and Clunk

Click and Clunk is another strategy for checking reading comprehension or figuring out words you do not know. Say "click" to yourself when you understand and "clunk" when you come across something that is confusing. Clunks are things that you should pay more attention to.

Responding to Clunks	
When you don't understand part of the reading	■ Reread the passage. ■ Reread a few sentences after it for further explanation.
When you don't understand a word	■ Reread the sentence for clues. ■ Reread the sentences before and after. ■ Look for smaller words within the word. ■ Look it up in a dictionary.

Stage 3. Remember and React to the Reading

LO 4 **Reflect upon and interpret what you have read.**

The active reading process does not end when you have read the very last word of the material.

Remember the Reading

To remember what you have read, use your annotations and notes to make a reading map. A reading map includes the main idea, the supporting evidence and explanations, and the conclusion. Add rows for more main ideas and supporting evidence as needed.

Reading Map Graphic Organizer

MyWritingLab™
Use the interactive graphic
organizer at mywritinglab.com

Main Idea:

Supporting Evidence/Explanation:

Supporting Point	Explanation

Conclusion:

After annotating the selection, Tori made a Reading Map of it (see page 537). To map the supporting evidence and explanation, she used the chart from the reading and added the information about the experiment to it.

Tori's Reading Map Graphic Organizer

Main Idea: People tend to believe stereotypes, which affects their actions. As a result, the people who are stereotyped behave the way others think they should behave.

Supporting Evidence/Explanation: Psychologist Mark Snyder did an experiment to find out whether stereotypes affect a person's attitude and whether a person acts the way we expect him or her to act.

Supporting Point	Explanation
1. "We see features of the person, or hear things about the person."	College men were shown a photo of pretty or homely women.
2. "We fit what we see or hear into stereotypes, and then expect the person to act in certain ways."	The men described how they thought the women would act. They gave positive behaviors for pretty women and negative behaviors for homely women.
3. "How we expect the person to act shapes our attitudes."	On the phone, the men were warm and friendly to the pretty women and cold and formal with the homely women.
4. "From how we act, the person gets ideas of how we perceive him or her."	The women got an idea of what the men thought of them from the way the men talked to them.
5. "The behaviors of the person change to match our expectations thus confirming the stereotype."	The way the men spoke to the women affected the way they spoke to the men. The women spoke to the men in the same way they were spoken to.

Conclusion:
Researchers suggest that people are more willing to spend time with individuals that they think are good-looking.

PRACTICE   Mapping a Reading

33.4   Map a reading selection. Use a selection you worked with in the other practices in this chapter or choose a different one. Use the Reading Map Graphic Organizer on page 536.

React to the Reading: Reader Response

While you were reading, you probably had thoughts and opinions about the material. Reacting to the reading involves thinking about what you have read and linking your thoughts something else you have read, to your own life experiences, or to something in the real world. *Text* means the reading selection.

Text-to-Text	■ Does this reading remind you of something else you have read, heard, or seen (story, book, movie, song, news item, magazine article, website, and so on)?
	■ Are the ideas the same or different?
Text-to-Self	■ How do the ideas in the reading relate to your own life, experiences, or ideas?
	■ Do you agree or disagree with what you read?
Text-to-World	■ What does the reading remind you of in the real world?
	■ Does it make you think about something in the past, present, or future?

PRACTICE   Reader Response

33.5   Respond to a reading selection by answering the questions for text-to-text, text-to-self, or text-to-world. Use the selection you worked with in the other practices in this chapter or choose a different one.

READING SELECTIONS

FAMILY STUDIES
Theme: *Singlehood*

■ Kelly J. Welch, excerpt from *Family Life Now*, "Being Single"
■ Eleanore Wells, excerpt from *The Spinsterlicious Life: 20 Life Lessons for Living Happily Single and Child-free*

SOCIOLOGY
Theme: *Peer Pressure*

■ James M. Henslin, excerpt from *Essentials of Sociology*, "The Power of Peer Pressure: The Asch Experiment"
■ Julia Alvarez, "Names/Nombres"

HISTORY
Theme: *The Holocaust*

■ Robert A. Devine et al., excerpt from *America Past and Present*, "The Face of the Holocaust"
■ Elie Wiesel, excerpt from *Night*

HOSPITALITY
Theme: *Guest Service*

■ John R. Walker, excerpt from *Introduction to Hospitality Management*, "The Disney Approach to Guest Services"
■ Jane Engle, "Server Tips: How to Get More Out of Customers"

BIOLOGY
Theme: *The Science of Attraction*

■ Teresa Audesirk, Gerald Audesirk, and Bruce E. Byers, excerpt from *Biology*, "Sex and Symmetry"
■ David Perrett, "Why Women Fall for Men Who Look like Their Father . . . and Other Astonishing Secrets of the Science of Attraction"

HEALTH AND WELLNESS
Theme: *Mind-Body Connection*

■ B. E. Pruitt, John P. Allegrante, and Deborah Prothrow-Stith, excerpt from *Health*, "Stages of Stress"
■ Daniel G. Amen, M.D., "Kill the Ants That Invade Your Brain"

ANTHROPOLOGY

Theme: *Race*

- Carol R. Ember, Melvin Ember, and Peter N. Peregrine, excerpt from *Anthropology*, "Race: A Meaningless Idea"
- Charisse Jones, "Light Skin versus Dark"

EDUCATION

Theme: *Classroom Courtesy*

- Don Kauchak and Paul Eggen, excerpt from *Introduction to Teaching*, "What Role Should Punishment Play in Classroom Management?"
- Alan Bloom, "Making Cell Phones in the Class a Community Builder"

FAMILY STUDIES   Theme: *Singlehood*

Being Single Individuals experience singlehood in a variety of ways. As you read the following textbook excerpt from *Family Life Now*, think of people you know who fit each of sociologist Peter Stein's categories of singles.

Get Ready to Read: Preview the reading and then fill in a Prereading Graphic Organizer like the one on page 530.

Excerpt from *Family Life Now*
Being Single
Kelly J. Welch

1   In U.S. culture, and in cultures around the world, marriage is assumed to be the next stage in a person's life following adolescence and early adulthood. But not everyone who dates has marriage on his or her mind. To be certain, U.S. culture today is seeing increasing numbers of singles, and singlehood is becoming a popular trend among the young and old as well.

2   Historically, American culture viewed singlehood as a transitional stage that preceded marriage and parenting; being single was not viewed as a lifestyle that adults purposely chose, but as a stepping stone to the eventual, expected adult roles of spouse and parent. This is changing, however. In 1970, the number of unmarried adults was less than 28 percent; in contrast, in 2005, 44 percent of households nationwide were maintained by unmarried men or women.

3   Singles are a complex and diverse group, and there are differences in how people experience singlehood. People may be single because they have never married, because they are divorced, because they are widowed, or because they are lesbians or gay men who are not legally allowed to wed.

4   Sociologist Peter Stein developed a system for grouping singlehood into four categories. It takes into account that some people are single by choice, while others are single for the time being, or are unintentionally single.

- *Voluntary temporary singles*: Singles in this category include those who have never married, as well as those who were previously married and are now divorced or widowed. Voluntary singles are not opposed to marriage; rather, they are not currently looking for a mate because it is not a priority. Voluntary temporary singles may delay marriage for a number of reasons, including the desire to pursue their education or career goals.
- *Voluntary permanent singles*: This category of singles includes those who chose deliberately to remain unmarried. The choice to remain single is stable and permanent over time. Voluntary permanent singles

involuntary not done by choice

include never-marrieds, those who have divorced and have no intention of remarrying, cohabiting individuals, gay and lesbian couples, and certain members of the clergy, such as priests and nuns.

- **_Involuntary_** _temporary singles:_ Among this category are singles who want to be married and who are actively seeking a marriage mate. This group of singles includes people who have never married, as well as those who were previously married and are now divorced or widowed. It also includes single parents who have never been married.

- _Involuntary permanent singles:_ In this category are those singles who wanted to marry but did not find a marriage mate. These singles may be never married, divorced, or widowed. Over time, they come to accept their unmarried status.

5   As Stein's groups illustrate, singlehood can be a transitional stepping stone, it can be an unexpected phase in the life course because of divorce or the death of a spouse, or it can be a deliberate choice. It shows us that being single is a fluid, changeable state. In other words, there will always be people who are single for a certain period of time, and there will always be people who remain single throughout their lives—either by choice or circumstance.

Understand the Reading

1. What is the main idea of the reading selection?

_____

2. What are the four categories of singles?

_____

3. How has the view of singlehood changed in the United States culture?

_____

Vocabulary in Context. The following words appear in the reading selection. Write a definition for each of the following words as they are used in the reading selection. If you are not sure of the meaning, try to figure it out from the other words and sentences around it.

Word	Para	Definition
stepping stone	2	_____
cohabit	4	_____
widowed	3, 4	_____

Remember the Reading. Map the reading selection. Fill in a Reading Map like the one on page 536. Then, using your own words, summarize the reading.

React to the Reading

1. **Reader Response:** Think about the reading and link it to something else you have read, to your own life experiences, or to something in the real world.

Text-to-Text	■ Does this reading remind you of something else you have read, heard, or seen (story, book, movie, song, news item, magazine article, website, and so on)?
	■ Are the ideas the same or different?
Text-to-Self	■ How do the ideas in the reading relate to your own life, experiences, or ideas?
	■ Do you agree or disagree with what you read?
Text-to-World	■ What does the reading remind you of in the real world?
	■ Does it make you think about something in the past, present, or future?

2. **QuickWrite:** Choose one of Stein's groups of singles and give examples of two people who fit that group.
3. **QuickWrite Jump Off:** Write a paper giving one or more examples for each group of singles.

Happily Single In the previous reading selection, Stein groups singles into categories. One group is the voluntary permanent group. People in this group have decided to remain single. As you read the following selection from *The Spinsterlicious Life,* notice how author Eleanore Wells gives examples of words used to describe single women in United States culture.

Get Ready to Read: Preview the reading, and then fill in a Prereading Graphic Organizer like the one on page 530.

The Spinsterlicious Life: 20 Life Lessons for Living Happily Single and Child-free
Lesson 1
Eleanore Wells

1   Marriage. Kids. They're not for everybody.

2   Recently, Lauren—my best friend for more than 25 years—called me an "old maid." It began innocently enough (though few of Lauren's comments are innocent, given her wicked sense of humor). Practicing my Spanish, I had left her a phone message playfully identifying myself as Señorita Wells, and Lauren was kind enough to point out to me that I was too old to be a señorita. She went on to explain that *señorita* (like *mademoiselle* and even, to a somewhat lesser extent, *miss*) is used to refer to a young

unmarried woman, NOT an old unmarried woman. It seems there is no word for that. The concept of a delightful middle-aged woman who has never had a husband (or children) is too far outside what is expected in society for there to be a word to describe it. So that's when Lauren cheerfully volunteered the "old maid" option. So I stand corrected: There *is* a word for this poor woman . . . just not one that I like so much.

3   I began a halfhearted search for a word that aptly describes this life-stage of mine. I couldn't be bothered to pick up a hard-copy dictionary, so I just went online. I Googled the definition of "old maid," and the *Collins Essential English Dictionary* said this:

4   old maid, n. 1. A woman regarded as unlikely ever to marry.

5   Okay, that certainly is me . . . by my own definition and that of most people who know me. I'm often amused by the calls I get from past suitors to ask me out again when they're between relationships of their own. I have this vision of them, newly single, thumbing through their phone contacts and wondering who they can find to help fill some time. And then they remember me. When they call, they are usually kind enough to ask if I'm seeing anyone, but I don't think even one has ever asked if I was now married. They just kind of know.

6   I kept looking. Answers.com added more color to the definition:

1. Old maid, n. *Offensive*. A woman who has remained single beyond the conventional age for marrying.

7   This definition also fits me, technically, though I don't think I want to adopt it if it's going to offend (although I guess the offense is actually to me). Plus, I can't help but think of the **withered old crone** in the Old Maid card deck. When I was growing up, we would play the game whose goal was not to be the player who ended up the Old Maid. Ending up an Old Maid was obviously bad. Plus, the Old Maid was ugly, with scraggly hair, a big nose, and warts. I don't look quite like that, so I guess I don't want her representing me. And, fittingly, there was only ONE lonely, 7, Old Maid card in the deck. All the other cards had a mate—because, clearly, that's the way things should be.

withered old crone an unattractive, old woman

8   At the opposite end of the spectrum is *bachelorette*. It sounds light-hearted and fun. I think of my youth, and cocktails, short dresses, high heels, and unencumbered weekend mornings. That still feels like me, although my gut knows there's a problem—without my actually having to look it up. *Webster's New World College Dictionary* says:

Jane Austen British author (1775–1817) who chose to remain single. Famous for novels such as *Pride and Prejudice*

spinster an unmarried woman who is past the usual age for marrying and is considered unlikely to marry —now often considered an insulting word

blue collar people who do work needing strength or physical skill rather than office work

9

bach·elor·ette, noun *Informal.* An unmarried, usually young woman.

This definition confirms my suspicions that I passed that a decade or two ago. But there's always spinster. I think of **Jane Austen.** I'm pretty sure this doesn't quite fit me, either, but it's a thought.

spinster. *Archaic*: An unmarried woman of gentle family.

10

While I'm not exactly sure what "gentle family" means, I doubt that it describes mine though I have a great family. The Encarta Dictionary says it means "upper class, relating to high social status." I grew up in a **blue-collar** family in Washington, D.C. We're good people, but good, solid, working-class people, so I'd be taking a few liberties with *spinster,* too—but there's something about it that I like. It's archaic, and I think I like the idea of resurrecting a word that's past its prime. It sounds sturdy and not completely pathetic.

11

So *spinster* it is, at least for now. But why am I not, instead, a wife and/or mother? Lord knows I've been asked that question a gazillion times. My most honest answer, really, is that I think I was absent the day those genes were being given out. I don't have a memory of ever aspiring to be either of those things (let's just assume "aspiring" is the right word). When I played "house" with Renée, Jackie, and Carla as a kid, everyone wanted to be the mother (who was also a wife) . . . except me. I often agreed to be the man/husband/father . . . not that I wanted to be a man (I'm straight), but we were playing make-believe and I didn't see what the fuss was about, so I was happy to accept this role so we could get the game moving along. What difference did it really make? If I remember correctly, I was the only one who felt that way. I was the only one not vying to play Mama.

12

It's always remarkable to me when I come across a grown woman who brightly declares, "I've known since I was a kid exactly what kind of wedding I wanted." I'm thinking to myself, "What is wrong with her?" In all these years, I can honestly say that I've never fantasized about my wedding or what I would name my kids. (Yeah, I've met women who picked their firstborn's name long before they even knew who the father would be.) I don't think I ever actually thought that marriage and kids were necessarily bad things, but they never seemed to be for me . . . and I really was and remain puzzled why just about everybody else in the whole wide world felt that it was for them.

on the fence informal expression meaning undecided

square-peg-round-hole informal expression meaning trying to combine two things that do not belong or fit together

13   Most of the spinsters I know are kind of spinsters-by-default in that they didn't actively choose it. Some definitely wanted to be married, but just weren't able to make it happen. Others were kind of **on the fence:** wanting it, but not willing to work too hard at it. As far as I know, I'm the only one I know who went out of her way to make sure that marriage didn't happen. This used to make me feel kind of weird sometimes—that whole **square-peg-round-hole** thing. I often get the raised-eyebrow look when I say I actually chose this. People don't know what to make of it. Now it's their turn to think "What's wrong with her?" (meaning me).

14   I still chuckle, though, at the advice I was given, when I was just a spinster-in-training, from an older woman I knew who had also managed never to have a husband or child. She told me that I should just "find someone and marry him." Even if I didn't like him very much, I should do it; I had to stay only a little while. Then I could divorce him, because, you see, "It's better to be a has-been than a never-was"! I'm not sure I buy that, but I know that a lot of people do.

15   I have been fortunate (fortunate?) enough to have had a few boy-friends who wanted to marry me, so it's not like I didn't get a chance. It just never felt right. And marriage seems really hard. Consistently, whenever I have tried to entertain the notion of marriage for even a nanosecond, it has been impossible to look 15 years down the road and still see that same guy's face. No matter how much I loved him. That image just didn't work for me. How in the world was I supposed to pick someone and stay there? I don't even plan most of my vacations too far into the future, because I might change my mind.

Don't Fence Me In

16   Amelia Earhart—aviator, brave soul, free spirit, and the first person to fly solo over both the Atlantic and the Pacific oceans—has come closest to describing my feelings about my own marriage. In a letter to her then-fiancé in 1931 she wrote, "I cannot guarantee to endure at all the confine-ments of even an attractive cage." I totally get that.

17   And kids? All I know is that they can be great . . . for a few minutes. When I'm around them, I spend most of my time pretending that they're cuter and more interesting than I actually think they are. When their parents aren't looking, I pinch them. (Not really.)

18   And here's something I'm finding rather interesting: Lately there's been a rash of studies and articles about how some people are finding that raising kids can be really hard and rather unfulfilling. Maureen Dowd wrote in a *New York Times* column and quoted a researcher who found that "the one thing in life that will make you less happy is having children."

19   And I think the title of an article in *New York* magazine, "All Joy and No Fun: Why Parents Hate Parenting," pretty much says it all. Should this stuff really be a newsflash, though? Kids are cute, wonderful, and delightful, but they're also expensive, time-consuming, irritating, anxiety-producing, and a lot of work. And sometimes, when they grow up, they lose the "cute." (Both articles go on to talk about how unwilling people are to admit they wish they hadn't had kids or that their kids were helping destroy their happiness, so I won't belabor this point.) Honestly, sometimes I wonder if parents who are "concerned" that I don't have kids are really members of the **misery-loves-company** club. Just a thought . . .

20   So, here I am: 56 years old, still single, still with no children. (Lauren has been married to Albert for more than 25 years, most of them happy.) And while I've never second-guessed the "no kids" thing (well, almost never), I do sometimes wish there was such a thing as Rent-a-Husband. I can see times when one might come in handy.

21   When I meet a guy these days, I'm not necessarily seeking marriage, but I am no longer repelled by the thought of something seriously long-lasting. At this age, "till death do us part" isn't that long, so it's not so daunting, and I am finally ready to spend some Saturday nights sprawled on the couch rather than on a date. Fortunately, I'm too old to have to even think about kids.

misery loves company
a proverb meaning that people who are sad like to be with others that are sad

Understand the Reading

1. What is the main idea of the reading selection?

_____

2. The author gives examples of three words used in the United States culture to describe single women. What are they and what do they mean?

_____

3. Why does the author call her life *spinsterlicious*?

_____

Vocabulary in Context. The following words appear in the reading selection. Write a definition for each of the following words as they are used in the reading selection. If you are not sure of the meaning, try to figure it out from the other words and sentences around it.

Word	Para	Definition
halfhearted	3	_____
aptly	3	_____
suitor	5	_____
scraggly	7	_____
unencumbered	8	_____
pathetic	7, 10	_____
resurrecting	10	_____
repelled	21	_____

Remember the Reading. Map the reading selection. Fill in a Reading Map like the one on page 536. Then, using your own words, summarize the reading.

React to the Reading

1. **Reader Response:** Think about the reading and link it to something else you have read, to your own life experiences, or to something in the real world.

Text-to-Text	■ Does this reading remind you of something else you have read, heard, or seen (story, book, movie, song, news item, magazine article, website, and so on)?
	■ Are the ideas the same or different?
Text-to-Self	■ How do the ideas in the reading relate to your own life, experiences, or ideas?
	■ Do you agree or disagree with what you read?
Text-to-World	■ What does the reading remind you of in the real world?
	■ Does it make you think about something in the past, present, or future?

2. **QuickWrite:** If you are or were once single, write about either the positive or negative aspects of being single.
3. **QuickWrite Jump Off:** Write a paper giving examples of people who are happily married *or* happily single.

Connect the Illustration Readings

1. Being single has become more acceptable in the United States. However, not all religious or cultural groups agree. What are your feelings about singlehood?
2. One example of voluntary permanent singles in Stein's groups is people who are cohabiting (living together). Do you think society has become more accepting of cohabiting?

SOCIOLOGY   Theme: *Peer Pressure*

The Asch Experiment The pressure to conform is motivated by the human need to be liked, to be correct, or to fit a social role. Changing your thinking or behavior to fit into a group can have positive or negative effects. As you read this textbook excerpt, think about how you would have reacted as a student in Dr. Asch's experiment.

Get Ready to Read: Preview the reading, and then fill in a Prereading Graphic Organizer like the one on page 530.

Excerpt from *Essentials of Sociology*
The Power of Peer Pressure: The Asch Experiment
James M. Henslin

1   How influential are groups in our lives? To answer this, let's look first at *conformity* in the sense of going along with our peers. Our peers have no authority over us, only the influence we allow.

2   Imagine that you are taking a course in **social psychology** with Dr. Solomon Asch and you have agreed to participate in an experiment. As you enter his laboratory, you see seven chairs, five of them already filled by other students. You are given the sixth. Soon the seventh person arrives. Dr. Asch stands at the front of the room next to a covered easel. He explains that he will first show a large card with a vertical line on it, then another card with three vertical lines. Each of you is to tell him which of the three lines matches the line on the first card.

3   Dr. Asch then uncovers the first card with the single line and the comparison card with three lines. The correct answer is easy, for two of the lines are obviously wrong, and one is exactly right. Each person, in order, states his or her answer aloud. You all answer correctly. The second trial is just as easy, and you begin to wonder why you are there.

4   Then on the third trial, something unexpected happens. Just as before, it is easy to tell which lines match. The first student, however, gives the wrong answer. The second gives the same incorrect answer. So do the third and the fourth. By now, you are wondering what is wrong. How will the person next to you answer? You can hardly believe it when he, too, gives the same wrong answer. Then it is your turn, and you give what you know is the right answer. The seventh person also gives the same wrong answer.

5   On the next trial, the same thing happens. You know that the choice of the other six is wrong. They are giving what to you are obviously wrong answers. You don't know what to think. Why aren't they seeing things the

social psychology the branch of psychology that studies persons and their relationships with others, with groups, and with society as a whole

same way you are? Sometimes they do, but in twelve trials they don't. Something is wrong, and you are no longer sure what to do.

6   When the eighteenth trial is finished, you heave a sigh of relief. The experiment is finally over, and you are ready to bolt for the door. Dr. Asch walks over to you with a big smile on his face and thanks you for participating in the experiment. He explains that you were the only real subject of the experiment! "The other six were stooges. I paid them to give those answers," he says. Now you feel real relief. Your eyes weren't playing tricks on you after all.

7   What were the results? Asch tested fifty people. One-third (33 percent) gave in to the group half the time, giving what they knew to be wrong answers. Another two out of five (40 percent) gave wrong answers but not as often. One out of four (25 percent) stuck to their guns and always gave the right answer. I don't know how I would do on this test (if I knew nothing about it in advance), but I like to think that I would be part of the 25 percent. You probably feel the same way about yourself. But why should we feel that we wouldn't be like *most* people?

8   The results are disturbing, and more researchers have replicated Asch's experiment than any other study. In our land of individualism, the group is so powerful that most people are willing to say things that they know are not true. And this was a group of strangers! How much more conformity can we expect when our group consists of friends, people we value highly and depend on for getting along in life?

Understand the Reading

1. What is the main idea of the textbook excerpt?

_____

2. Summarize the Asch experiment.

_____

3. What were the results of the Asch experiment and why were they disturbing?

_____

Vocabulary in Context.   The following words appear in the reading selection. Write a definition for each of the following words as they are used in the reading selection. If you are not sure of the meaning, try to figure it out from the other words and sentences around it.

Word	Para	Definition
conformity	1	_____
		_____
trial	3	_____
		_____
heave a sigh of relief	6	_____
		_____

bolt for	6	_____
stooges	6	_____
stuck to their guns	7	_____ _____
replicate	8	_____
individualism	8	_____ _____

Remember the Reading. Map the reading selection. Fill in a Reading Map like the one on page 536. Then, using your own words, summarize the reading.

React to the Reading

1. **Reader Response:** Think about the reading and link it to something else you have read, to your own life experiences, or to something in the real world.

Text-to-Text	■ Does this reading remind you of something else you have read, heard, or seen (story, book, movie, song, news item, magazine article, website, and so on)?
	■ Are the ideas the same or different?
Text-to-Self	■ How do the ideas in the reading relate to your own life, experiences, or ideas?
	■ Do you agree or disagree with what you read?
Text-to-World	■ What does the reading remind you of in the real world?
	■ Does it make you think about something in the past, present, or future?

2. **QuickWrite:** Conformity is defined as behavior that follows the usual standards expected by a group or society. Write about a time when you or someone you know conformed to the standards of a group or society. The situation could have been positive or negative.

3. **QuickWrite Jump Off:** Develop your QuickWrite story into a narrative paper. Make a point about the meaning or importance of the experience or event in your main idea sentence.

The Power of Names Has anyone ever mispronounced your name? Imagine the frustration many immigrants experience when English speakers have difficulty with their names. To avoid this, some people translate their names to English equivalents or replace them with American names. While reading this personal essay, notice how names play an important role in the author's struggle for identity in a new culture.

Get Ready to Read: Preview the reading, and then fill in a Prereading Graphic Organizer like the one on page 530.

Names/Nombres
Julia Alvarez

1   When we arrived in New York City, our names changed almost immediately. At immigration, the officer asked my father, *Mister Elbures*, if we had anything to declare. My father shook his head, "No," and we were waved through. I was too afraid we wouldn't be let in if I corrected the man's pronunciation, but I said our name to myself, opening my mouth wide for the organ blast of the *a*, trilling my tongue for the drum-roll of the *r*. *All-vah-rrr-es!* How could anyone get *Elbures* out of that orchestra of sound?

2   When we moved into our new apartment building, the **super** called my father *Mister Alberase*, and the neighbors who became mother's friends pronounced her name *Jew-lee-ah* instead of *Hoo-lee-ah*. I, her namesake, was known as *Hoo-lee-tah* at home. But at school, I was *Judy* or *Judith*, and once an English teacher mistook me for *Juliet*.

super superintendent; the person who manages an apartment building

3   It took awhile to get used to my new names. I wondered if I shouldn't correct my teachers and new friends. But my mother argued that it didn't matter. "You know what your friend Shakespeare said, *'A rose by any other name would smell as sweet.'*" My father had gotten into the habit of calling any famous author "my friend" because I had begun to write poems and stories in English class.

4   By the time I was in high school, I was a popular kid, and it showed in my name. Friends called me *Jules* or *Hey Jude*, and once a group of trouble-making friends my mother forbade me to hang out with called me *Alcatraz*. I was *Hoo-lee-tah* only to Mami and Papi and uncles and aunts who came over to eat **sancocho** on Sunday afternoons—old world folk whom I would just as soon go back to where they came from and leave me to pursue whatever mischief I wanted to in America. JUDY ALCATRAZ: the name on the Wanted Poster would read. Who would ever trace her to me?

sancocho a stew of beef, chicken, or fish with vegetables, plantains, and yucca

5   My older sister had the hardest time getting an American name for herself because *Mauricia* did not translate into English. Ironically, although she had the most foreign-sounding name, she and I were the Americans in the family. We had been born in New York City when our parents had first tried immigration and then gone back "home," too homesick to stay. My mother often told the story of how she had almost changed my sister's name in the hospital.

6   After the delivery, Mami and some other new mothers were cooing over their new baby sons and daughters and exchanging names and weights and delivery stories. My mother was embarrassed among the Sallys and Hanes and Georges and Johns to reveal the rich, noisy name of *Mauri-cia,* so when her turn came to brag, she gave her baby's name as *Maureen.*

7   "Why'd ya give her an Irish name with so many pretty Spanish names to choose from?" one woman asked.

8   My mother blushed and admitted her baby's real name to the group. Her mother-in-law had recently died, she apologized, and her husband had insisted that the first daughter be named after his mother, *Mauran.* My mother thought it the ugliest name she had ever heard, and she talked my father into what she believed was an improvement, a combination of *Mau-ran* and her own mother's name, *Felicia.*

9   "Her name is *Mau-ree-shee-ah,*" my mother said to the group of women.

10   "Why that's a beautiful name," the new mothers cried. *"Moor-ee-sha, Moor-ee-sha,"* they cooed into the pink blanket. Moor-ee-sha it was when we returned to the States eleven years later. Sometimes, American tongues found even that mispronunciation too tough to say and called her *Maria* or *Marsha* or *Maudy* from her nickname *Maury.* I pitied her. What an awful name to have to transport across borders!

11   My little sister, Ana, had the easiest time of all. She was plain *Anne*—that is, only her name was plain, for she turned out to be the pale, blond "American beauty" in the family. The only Hispanic thing about her was the affectionate nicknames her boyfriends sometimes gave her. *Anita,* or as one goofy guy used to sing to her to the tune of the banana advertisement, *Anita Banana.*

12   Later, during her college years in the late '60s, there was a push to pronounce Third World names correctly. I remember calling her long distance at her group house and a roommate answering.

13   "Can I speak to Ana?" I asked, pronouncing her name the American way.

14   "Ana?" The man's voice hesitated. "Oh! You must mean *Ah-nah!*"

15   Our first few years in the States, though, ethnicity was not yet "in." Those were the blond, blue-eyed, **bobby sock years** of junior high school before the '60s ushered in peasant blouses, hoop earrings, **serapes.** My initial desire to be known by my correct Dominican name faded. I just wanted to be Judy and merge with the Sallys and Janes in my class. But inevitably, my accent and coloring gave me away. "So where are you from, Judy?"

bobby sock years refers to a time when bobby socks were popular in the 1950s. Bobby socks have thick uppers that were turned down into a cuff at the ankles.

serapes colorful shawls

16 "New York," I told my classmates. After all, I had been born blocks away at Columbia Presbyterian Hospital.

17 "I mean, *originally*."

18 "From the Caribbean," I answered vaguely, for if I specified, no one was quite sure on what continent our island was located.

19 "Really? I've been to Bermuda. We went last April for spring vacation. I got the worst sunburn! So, are you from Portoriko?"

20 "No," I sighed. "From the Dominican Republic."

21 "Where's that?"

22 "South of Bermuda."

23 They were just being curious, I knew, but I burned with shame whenever they singled me out as a "foreigner," a rare, exotic friend.

24 "Say your name in Spanish, oh please say it!" I had made mouths drop one day by rattling off my full name, which according to Dominican custom, included my middle names, Mother's and Father's surnames for four generations back.

25 "Julia Altagracia Maria Teresa Alvarez Tavares Perello Espaillat Julia Pérez Rochet González," I pronounced it slowly, a name as chaotic with sounds as a Middle Eastern bazaar or market day in a South American village.

26 My Dominican heritage was never more apparent than when my extended family attended school occasions. For my graduation, they all came, the whole lot of aunts and uncles and the many little cousins who snuck in without tickets. They sat in the first row in order to better understand the Americans' fast-spoken English. But how could they listen when they were constantly speaking among themselves in florid-sounding phrases, **rococo** consonants, rich, rhyming vowels?

rococo fancy, ornate style of art of the early eighteenth century

27 Introducing them to my friends was a further trial to me. These relatives had such complicated names and there were so many of them, and their relationships to myself were so convoluted. There was my Tia Josefina, who was not really my aunt but a much older cousin. And her daughter: Aida Margarita, who was adopted, una hija de crianza. My uncle of affection, Tio Jose, brought my **madrina** Tia Amelia and her *comadre* Tia Pilar. My friends rarely had more than a "Mom and Dad" to introduce.

madrina godmother

28 After the commencement ceremony my family waited outside in the parking lot while my friends and I signed yearbooks with nicknames which

recalled our high school good times: "Beans" and "Pepperoni" and "Alcatraz." We hugged and cried and promised to keep in touch.

Vamanos let's go

29   Our goodbyes went on too long. I heard my father's voice calling out across the parking lot. *"Hoo-lee-tah!* **Vamonos!"**

tios **and** *tias* **and** *primas*
uncles, aunts, and female cousins

30   Back home, my *tios* **and** *tias* **and** *primas,* Mami and Papi, and *mis hermanas* had a party for me with *sancocho* and a store-bought *pudin,* inscribed with Happy Graduation, Julie. There were many gifts—that was a plus to a large family! I got several wallets and a suitcase with my initials and a graduation charm from my godmother and money from my uncles. The biggest gift was a portable typewriter from my parents for writing my stories and poems.

mis hermanas my sisters

31   Someday, the family predicted, my name would be well-known throughout the United States. I laughed to myself, wondering which one I would go by.

Understand the Reading

1. What is the main idea of the narrative essay?

_____

2. How does the title of the narrative "Names/Nombres" suggest the writer's conflict?

_____

3. Why does the writer spell out different pronunciations of names?

_____

Vocabulary in Context.   The following words appear in the reading selection. Write a definition for each of the following words as they are used in the reading selection. If you are not sure of the meaning, try to figure it out from the other words and sentences around it.

Word	Para	Definition
declare	1	
trilling	1	
namesake	2	

ironically	5	_____
		_____
cooing	6	_____
ushered in	15	_____
chaotic	25	_____
florid-sounding	26	_____

Remember the Reading. Map the reading selection. Fill in a Reading Map like the one on page 536. Then, using your own words, summarize the reading.

React to Reading

1. **Reader Response:** Think about the reading and link it to something else you have read, to your own life experiences, or to something in the real world.

Text-to-Text	■ Does this reading remind you of something else you have read, heard, or seen (story, book, movie, song, news item, magazine article, website, and so on)?
	■ Are the ideas the same or different?
Text-to-Self	■ How do the ideas in the reading relate to your own life, experiences, or ideas?
	■ Do you agree or disagree with what you read?
Text-to-World	■ What does the reading remind you of in the real world?
	■ Does it make you think about something in the past, present, or future?

2. **QuickWrite:** Being accepted into a group is important to children, especially when they go to a new school. Write about a time when you or someone else was not accepted into a group at school.
3. **QuickWrite Jump Off:** Write a narrative paper about an incident that shows how names can affect a person's self-image and identity.

Connect the Narrative Readings

1. What are the similarities between "The Power of Peer Pressure: The Asch Experiment" and the essay "Names/Nombres"?

_____

2. What do both readings conclude about the people's need to conform?

_____

HISTORY

Liberating the Camps When the U.S. generals and soldiers opened the doors of the Nazi concentration camps to free the people imprisoned, they were not prepared for what they found. Even those who had experience in fighting and had seen death and destruction were sickened by the unspeakable conditions. As you read this textbook excerpt, imaging what it must have been like for the liberators and the prisoners.

Get Ready to Read: Preview the reading, and then fill in a Prereading Graphic Organizer like the one on page 530.

Excerpt from *America Past and Present*
The Face of the Holocaust
Robert A. Divine et al.

Nazi death camps camps built by Nazi Germany during the Second World War (1939–1945) to systematically kill millions of people by gassing and extreme work under starvation conditions; while there were victims from many groups, Jews were the main targets

1   The liberation of the **Nazi death camps** near the end of World War II was not considered an important goal to be achieved; nor was it a planned operation. Since 1942, the U.S. government had known that the Nazis were murdering Jews in groups, but officials of the Roosevelt administration were divided on what to do about it. Some argued for air raids on the death camps, even if such raids were likely to kill large numbers of the Jewish inmates. Others strongly stated that the air raids alone would not stop the killing, that they would divert resources from the broader attack against Germany, and that military victory was the surest path to the liberation of the camps. In part because no one in the United States comprehended the full extent of the evil of **Hitler's "final solution,"** Roosevelt sided with the latter group, and no special action was taken against the death camps. As a result, it was by chance that **Allied forces** first stumbled upon the camps, and the GIs who threw open the gates to that living hell were totally unprepared for what they found.

Hitler's "final solution" Hitler's plan and execution of killing European Jews

Allied forces soldiers from countries that were against Germany and Italy

2   *Inside the Vicious Heart,* Robert Abzug's study of the liberation of the concentration camps, discusses the phenomenon of the inability to see the obvious because the truth is so horrible. He calls it "double vision." Faced with a revelation so terrible, witnesses could not fully comprehend the evidence of the systematic murder of more than six million men, women, and children. But as the Allied armies advanced into Germany, the shocking evidence increased. On April 4, 1945, the Fourth Armored Division of the Third Army unexpectedly discovered Ohrdruf, a relatively small concentration camp. Ohrdruf's liberation had a tremendous impact on American forces. It was the first camp discovered in its original state with its shocking display of the dead and dying. Inside the compound, corpses were piled in heaps in the barracks. An infantryman recalled, "I guess the most vivid recollection of the whole camp is the pyre that was located on the edge of the camp. It was a big pit, where they stacked bodies—stacked bodies and wood and burned them."

3   On April 12, generals Eisenhower, Bradley, and Patton toured Ohrdruf. The generals, professional soldiers familiar with the damage and destruction of

battle, had never seen anything like it. Years later, Bradley recalled, "The smell of death overwhelmed us even before we passed through the stockade." More than 3200 naked, extremely thin bodies had been flung into shallow graves. Others lay in the street where they had fallen.

4　　　　Eisenhower ordered every available armed forces unit in the area to visit Ohrdruf. "We are told that the American soldier does not know what he is fighting for," said Eisenhower. "Now at least he will know what he is fighting against." He urged government officials and journalists to visit the camps and tell the world. In an official message Eisenhower summed it up:

> We are constantly finding German camps in which they have placed political prisoners where unspeakable conditions exist. From my own personal observation, I can state unequivocally that all written statements up to now do not paint the full horrors.

5　　　　On April 11, the Timberwolf Division of the Third Army uncovered Nord-hausen. They found three thousand dead and only seven hundred survivors. The scene sickened battle-hardened veterans:

> The odors, well there is no way to describe the odors. . . . Many of the boys I am talking about now—these were tough soldiers, there were combat men who had been all the way through the invasion—were ill and vomiting, throwing up, just at the sight of this.

6　　　　For some, the liberation of Nordhausen changed the meaning of the war.

I must also say that my fellow GIs, most thought that any stories they had read in the paper . . . were either not true or at least exaggerated. And it did not sink in, what this was all about, until we got into Nordhausen.

7   If the experience at Norhausen gave many GIs a new sense of mission in battle, it also forced them to distance themselves from the realities of the camps. Only by closing off their emotions could they go about the shockingly horrible task of sorting out the living from the dead and taking care of survivors. Margaret Bourke-White, whose *Life* magazine photographs brought the horrors of the death camps to millions on the home front, recalled working "with a veil over my mind."

People often ask me how it is possible to photograph such atrocities. In photographing the murder camps, the protective veil was so tightly drawn that I hardly knew what I had taken until I saw prints of my own photographs.

8   By the end of 1945, most of the liberators had come home and returned to nonmilitary life. Once home, their experiences produced no common moral responses. No particular pattern developed in their occupational, political, and religious behavior, beyond a fear of the rise of postwar totalitarianism shared by most Americans. Few spoke publicly about their role in the liberation of the camps; most found that after a short period of grim fascination, their friends and families preferred to forget. Some had nightmares, but few reported being tormented by memories. For the liberators, the ordeal was over. For the survivors of the Holocaust, liberation was but the first step in the difficult, painful process of rebuilding broken bodies and destroyed lives.

Understand the Reading

1. What is the main idea of the reading?

_____

2. The U.S. government knew that the Nazis were murdering large numbers of Jews, but the officials of President Roosevelt's administration had different opinions about what to do about it. What were the opinions?

_____

3. Describe what the troops found at Ohrdruf and Nordhausen.

_____

Vocabulary in Context.   The following words appear in the reading selection. Write a definition for each of the following words as they are used in the reading selection. If you are not sure of the meaning, try to figure it out from the other words and sentences around it.

Word	Para	Definition
air raids	1	_____
divert	1	_____
phenomenon	2	_____
systematic	2	_____
infantryman	2	_____
pyre	2	_____
stockade	3	_____
unspeakable	4	_____
unequivocally	4	_____
atrocities	7	_____
veil	7	_____
grim	8	_____

Remember the Reading. Map the reading selection. Fill in a Reading Map like the one on page 536. Then, using your own words, summarize the reading.

React to the Reading

1. **Reader Response:** Think about the reading and link it to something else you have read, to your own life experiences, or to something in the real world.

Text-to-Text	■ Does this reading remind you of something else you have read, heard, or seen (story, book, movie, song, news item, magazine article, website, and so on)? ■ Are the ideas the same or different?
Text-to-Self	■ How do the ideas in the reading relate to your own life, experiences, or ideas? ■ Do you agree or disagree with what you read?
Text-to-World	■ What does the reading remind you of in the real world? ■ Does it make you think about something in the past, present, or future?

2. **QuickWrite:** Throughout history, people failed to understand and accept the others who were different. As a result, many individuals and whole groups of people have been treated badly and often killed. Describe a situation in which a person or people were not accepted because they were different.

3. **QuickWrite Jump Off:** Write a paper describing a war scene from any period in the history of the world. You may choose a scene in a photograph or one from a personal experience. To find war photographs, look in history textbooks, magazine or newspaper articles, or search on the Internet.

First Night in a Concentration Camp Elie Wiesel was fifteen years old when he and his family were deported by the Nazis from Romania to the Auschwitz concentration camp in Poland. After the American army freed the camps, Wiesel was hospitalized. While there, he wrote the outline for the book *Night*, describing his experiences during the Holocaust. However, he was not ready to publicize his experiences and waited ten years to write the book. Wiesel has continued writing novels and has won many awards for his humanitarian work. As you read this excerpt, imagine what it must have been like for a teen-aged boy to arrive at a concentration camp.

Get Ready to Read: Preview the reading, and then fill in a Prereading Graphic Organizer like the one on page 530.

Excerpt from *Night*
Elie Wiesel

1   Never shall I forget that night, the first night in camp, that turned my life into one long night, seven times sealed.

2   Never shall I forget that smoke.

3   Never shall I forget the little faces of the children, whose bodies I saw transformed into smoke under a silent sky.

4   Never shall I forget those flames that consumed my faith forever.

5   Never shall I forget that nocturnal silence which deprived me for all eternity of the desire to live.

6   Never shall I forget those moments that murdered my God and my soul and turned my dreams to ashes.

7   Never shall I forget those things, even were I condemned to live as long as God Himself.

8   Never.

9   The barrack we had been assigned to was very long. In the roof some blueish skylights. This is what the antechamber of Hell must look like. So many crazed men, so much shouting, so much brutality!

10   Dozens of inmates were there to receive us, sticks in hands, striking anywhere, anyone, without reason. The orders came:

11   "Strip! Hurry up! *Raus!* hold on only to your belt and shoes. . . . "

12   Our clothes were to be thrown on the floor at the back of the barrack. There was a pile there already. New suits, old ones, torn overcoats, rags. For us it meant true equality: nakedness. We trembled in the cold.

13   A few **SS** officers wandered through the room, looking for strong men. If vigor was that appreciated, perhaps one should try to appear sturdy? My

Raus get out

SS a major organization under Adolph Hitler and the Nazi Party; responsible for the majority of war crimes

crematoria a building in which dead people's bodies are burned

Birkenau the extermination camp in the Auschwitz complex; site of the crematories

father thought the opposite. Better not to draw attention. (We later found out that he had been right. Those who were selected that day were incorporated into the Sonder-Kommando, the Kommando working in the **crematoria.** Bela Katz—son of an important merchant of my town—had arrived in **Birkenau** with the first transport, one week ahead of us. When he found out we were there, he managed to get word to us that, having been chosen because of his strength, he had been forced to put his own father's body into the furnace.

14   The blows continued to rain on us:

15   "To the barber!"

16   Belt and shoes in hand, I let myself be dragged along to the barbers. They took our hair off with clippers and shaved all the hair on our bodies. My head was buzzing; the same thought over and over: not to be separated from my father.

17   Freed from the barber's clutches, we began to wander about the crowd, finding friends, acquaintances. Every encounter filled us with joy—yes, joy: "Thank God! You are still alive!"

18   Some were crying. They used whatever strength they had left to cry. Why had they let themselves be brought here? Why didn't they die in their beds? Their words were interspersed with sobs.

19   Suddenly, someone threw his arms round me in a hug: Yechiel, the Sighetel rabbi's brother. He was weeping bitterly. I thought he was crying with joy at still being alive.

20   "Don't cry, Yechiel," I said. "Don't waste your tears. . . . "

21   "Not cry? We're on the threshold of death. . . . Soon we shall be inside. . . . Do you understand? Inside. How could I not cry?"

22   I watched darkness fade through the blueish skylights in the roof. I no longer was afraid. I was overcome by fatigue.

23   The absent no longer entered our thoughts. One spoke of them—who knows what happened to them?—but their fate was not on our minds. We were incapable of thinking. Our senses were numbed, everything was fading into a fog. We no longer clung to anything. The instincts of self-preservation, of self-defense, of pride, had all deserted us. In one terrifying moment of lucidity, I thought of us as damned souls wandering through the void, souls condemned to wander through space until the end of time, seeking redemption, seeking oblivion, without hope of finding it.

Understand the Reading

1. What is the author describing in this excerpt?

    _____

2. What is the dominant impression of the excerpt?

    _____

3. In paragraph 23, the author writes, "Our senses were numbed, everything was fading into a fog. We no longer cling to anything." What does he mean?

    _____

Vocabulary in Context.   The following words appear in the reading selection. Write a definition for each of the following words as they are used in the reading selection. If you are not sure of the meaning, try to figure it out from the other words and sentences around it.

Word	Para	Definition
nocturnal	5	_____
antechamber	9	_____
brutality	9	_____
barrack	12	_____
vigor	13	_____
sturdy	13	_____
blows	14	_____
rain	14	_____
threshold	21	_____
lucidity	23	_____
void	23	_____
redemption	23	_____
oblivion	23	_____

Remember the Reading.   Map the reading selection. Fill in a Reading Map like the one on page 536. Then, using your own words, summarize the reading.

React to the Reading

1. **Reader Response:** Think about the reading and link it to something else you have read, to your own life experiences, or to something in the real world.

Text-to-Text	■ Does this reading remind you of something else you have read, heard, or seen (story, book, movie, song, news item, magazine article, website, and so on)?
	■ Are the ideas the same or different?
Text-to-Self	■ How do the ideas in the reading relate to your own life, experiences, or ideas?
	■ Do you agree or disagree with what you read?
Text-to-World	■ What does the reading remind you of in the real world?
	■ Does it make you think about something in the past, present, or future?

2. **QuickWrite:** What does it mean to feel hopeless? Write about a time when someone felt hopeless.

3. **QuickWrite Jump Off:** The first seven paragraphs of the excerpt from *Night* begin with the words, "Never shall I forget. . . ." These paragraphs describe the narrator's reactions to his experience during his first night at the concentration camp. Using the same style as the writer, describe your reactions to a terrible experience.

Connect the Description Readings

1. "The Face of the Holocaust" and the excerpt from *Night* present two different views of the Holocaust. Explain the differences.

2. The Holocaust is one of many examples throughout history of intolerance—of people's refusal to accept ideas, beliefs, or people who are different. Describe a situation of intolerance that happened in the recent past or that is occurring now.

HOSPITALITY   Theme: *Guest Service*

The Disney Approach Walt Disney theme parks are popular travel destinations around the world: California, Florida, Hong Kong, Tokyo, and Paris. The success of Disney's theme park business is a result of its commitment to exceptional customer service. As you read this textbook excerpt, note how Disney expects employees to serve and care for guests during their visit to the parks.

Get Ready to Read: Preview the reading, and then fill in a Prereading Graphic Organizer like the one on page 530.

Excerpt from *Introduction to Hospitality Management*
The Disney Approach to Guest Services
John R. Walker

To all who come to this happy place: Welcome! Disneyland is your land; here, age relives fond memories of the past, and here youth may savor the challenge and promise of the future.

Disneyland is dedicated to the hard facts that have created America, with the hope that it will be a source of joy and inspiration to all the world.

—Disneyland Dedication Plaque, July 17, 1955

1   When Walt Disney conceived the idea to build Disneyland, he established a simple philosophical approach to his theme park business, based on the tenets of quality, service, and show. Walt Disney was committed to service. Disney's mission statement is simple: "We create Happiness." To reinforce the service concept, Disney has guests, not customers, and cast members, not employees. Disney's ability to create a special brand of magic requires the talents of thousands of people fulfilling many different roles. However, the heart of it is the frontline cast members. Through the processes of hiring and training, cast members learn how Disney expects them to serve and care for guests during their visit to the park or resort.

2   Disney uses a 45-minute team approach to interviewing called *peer interviews*. In one interview there may be four candidates and one interviewer. The candidates may include a housewife returning to the work force, a teacher looking for summer work, a retiree looking for a little extra income, or a teenager looking for a first job. All four candidates are interviewed in the same session. The interviewer looks for how they individually answer questions and how well they interact with each other—a good indicator of their future onstage treatment of guests. The most successful technique used during the 45 minutes is to *smile*. The interviewer smiles at the people being interviewed to see if they *return the smiles*. If they don't, it doesn't matter how well they interview. They won't get the job.

3   On the first day at work, every new Disney cast member participates in a one-day orientation program at the Disney University, "Welcome to Show Business." The main goal of this experience is to learn the Disney approach to helpful, caring, and friendly guest service. The cast member training follows the Disney service model.

- *Smile.* This is the universal language of hospitality and service. Guests recognize and appreciate the cast members' warmth and sincerity.

- *Make eye contact and use body language.* This means stance, approach, and gestures. For instance, cast members are trained to use *open* gestures for directions, not pointed fingers, because open palms are friendlier and less directive.

- *Respect and welcome all guests.* This means being friendly, helpful, and going out of the way to exceed guests' expectations.

- *Value the magic.* When stage cast members are on stage, they are totally focused on creating the magic of Disneyland. They don't talk about personal problems or world affairs, and they don't mention that you can find Mickey in more than one place.

- *Initiate guest contact.* Cast members are reminded to actively initiate guest contact. Disney calls this being aggressively friendly. It is not enough to be responsive when approached. Cast members are encouraged to take the first step with guests. They have lots of little tricks for doing this, such as noticing a guest's name on a hat and then using the name in conversation or kneeling to ask a child a question.

- *Use creative service solutions.* For example, one Disneyland Hotel cast member recently became aware of a little boy who had come from the

Midwest with his parents to enjoy the park and then left early because he was ill. The cast member approached the supervisor with an idea to send the child chicken soup, a character plush toy, and a get-well card from Mickey. The supervisor loved the idea, and all cast members are now allowed to set up these arrangements in similar situations without a supervisor's approval.

■ *End with a "thank you."* The phrases cast members use are important in creating a service environment. They do not have a book of accepted phrases; rather, through training and coaching, cast members are encouraged to use their own personality and style to welcome and approach guests, answer questions, anticipate their needs, thank them, and express with sincerity their desire to make the guest's experience exceptional.

4 How does this training translate into action? When a guest stops a street sweeper to ask where to pick up a parade schedule and the sweeper not only answers the question but recites the parade times from memory, suggests the best viewing spots on the parade route, offers advice on where to get a quick meal before parade time, *and* ends the interaction with a pleasant smile and warm send-off, people can't help but be impressed. It also makes the sweepers feel their jobs are interesting and important, which they are.

5 Once the initial cast member training is completed, these concepts must be applied and are continually reinforced by leaders who possess strong coaching skills.

Understand the Reading

1. What is the main idea of the reading?

_____

2. Explain two of the approaches of the Disney service model that cast members learn when they go through the training process.

_____

3. Give an example of how the training translates into action.

_____

Vocabulary in Context. The following words appear in the reading selection. Write a definition for each of the following words as they are used in the reading selection. If you are not sure of the meaning, try to figure it out from the other words and sentences around it.

Word	Para	Definition
conceive	1	
tenets	1	
front line	1	
indicator	2	
stance	3	
responsive	3	

Remember the Reading.   Map the reading selection. Fill in a Reading Map like the one on page 536. Then, using your own words, summarize the reading.

React to the Reading

1. **Reader Response:** Think about the reading and link it to something else you have read, to your own life experiences, or to something in the real world.

Text-to-Text	■ Does this reading remind you of something else you have read, heard, or seen (story, book, movie, song, news item, magazine article, website, and so on)?
	■ Are the ideas the same or different?
Text-to-Self	■ How do the ideas in the reading relate to your own life, experiences, or ideas?
	■ Do you agree or disagree with what you read?
Text-to-World	■ What does the reading remind you of in the real world?
	■ Does it make you think about something in the past, present, or future?

2. **QuickWrite:** Write about a training process you experienced in school, work, or volunteer service, or write about the process you used to train someone.
3. **QuickWrite Jump Off:** Develop your QuickWrite into an instructional or informational process paper.

Increasing a Server's Tips Service is important to a restaurant's success from the time customers enter a restaurant to the time they leave. This newspaper article reports the results of researcher Michael Lynn's study "Mega Tips: Scientifically Tested Techniques to Increase Your Tips." As you read, think about your own experiences with servers and the techniques they used that influenced the amount you left for a tip.

Get Ready to Read: Preview the reading, and then fill in a Prereading Graphic Organizer like the one on page 530.

Server Tips: How to Get More Out of Customers
Jane Engle

1   Your waitress tells jokes, touches you on the shoulder and draws pictures on the check. Does she have a thing for you? Think again. She may be angling for a bigger tip, using a list of 14 suggestions from a researcher's new booklet.

2   "Mega Tips: Scientifically Tested Techniques to Increase Your Tips," by Michael Lynn, an associate professor at the Cornell University School of Hotel Administration in Ithaca, N.Y., is based on more than 25 years of studies by Lynn and others.

3   Among other tactics Lynn suggests to servers is to recommend higher-priced entrées, wear unusual clothing, introduce themselves, call customers by name, and even offer sunny weather forecasts.

4   You may be wondering where service fits in. It doesn't. Which is the most surprising conclusion in Lynn's work. If you thought you were, at most, mildly confused about how much to leave servers, read on. It turns out that we don't know our own minds, much less the mores of tipping.

5   People typically say they tip to reward good service, Lynn said, which seems logical, "but it's obviously not true."

6   In his studies, he asked diners to rate their server's performance based on attentiveness, knowledge, promptness, and other measures. Then he tallied the tips. The two numbers had little correlation. Service quality accounted for only 4 percent of the differences in diners' tips, he found.

7   What does boost tips, he said, are higher meal tabs and servers' actions that help them connect with their patrons.

8   Research shows the bill's total accounts for about 70 percent of the differences in tips—hardly a shock, given that most people tip on a percentage of the check; the usual recommendation is 15 to 20 percent. That's one reason savvy servers prompt diners to choose pricier entrées and extras such as appetizers, after-dinner drinks, and desserts.

9   Such suggestive selling works well during slow times. During busy times, the best strategy is "get 'em their entrées, get 'em out," said Lynn, who worked his way through college as a bartender, busboy, and waiter. Better to have a table of four wolfing down $20 rib-eye steaks than dawdling over $2 coffees and $5 slices of cake. No wonder some diners feel they're being rushed out the door on Saturday nights. They are.

10   But it's the customer–server rapport that's really revealing. What we're buying with restaurant tips is not service, Lynn contended, but social approval from our server and tablemates. The motive: "I don't want them to think I'm a cheapskate and a bad guy." If we feel a personal connection with a server, we care more about what she or he thinks of us. We're willing to pay more for that approval, so we tip more, Lynn said.

11   Many of Lynn's tactics will sound familiar to frequent diners. His advice to servers:

- Wear something unusual. "This will help customers perceive you as an individual rather than a faceless member of the staff." In one study, waitresses who wore flowers in their hair earned 17 percent more in tips than those who didn't.

- Introduce yourself by name. This can "make you seem friendly and polite and make the customer feel more empathy for you." In a study at a Charlie Brown's restaurant in Southern California, taking this step increased average tips from $3.49 to $5.44.

- Squat next to the table. This makes you more equal to the customer, brings your face closer and improves eye contact. In one study, this action earned about $1 more per table in tips.

- Touch your customers, preferably on the shoulder (which feels less private than other zones) for a second or two. Effect on tips: As much as 17 percent was left, up from 12 percent. Diners may flinch at this idea, but that's because "people don't know what they like," Lynn said. They may not even notice they're being touched, but no matter, they'll still tip more.

- Repeat customers' orders, word for word. This increases others'"liking for and interpersonal closeness to the imitator." In a Netherlands study, it also doubled tips.

- Call customers by name. It's flattering—and profitable, earning 10 percent more in tips at several Kansas restaurants studied.

- Draw on the check. A "smiley face" personalizes the transaction and improves customers' mood. In a study at a Philadelphia restaurant, this increased waitresses' tips by nearly 18 percent but, oddly, had no significant effect on waiters' tips.

- Smile. At a Seattle cocktail lounge, a waitress earned 140 percent more in tips when she sported a "large, open-mouthed smile."

- Write "thank you" on checks. This may make diners "feel obligated to earn that gratitude by leaving larger tips." In one study, the average tip went up from 16 to 18 percent on a "thank you."

- Give customers candy. "People generally feel obligated to reciprocate when they receive gifts from others." Effect on tips in one study: 23 percent instead of 19 percent.

12 My favorite suggestion is to write a favorable weather forecast on the check.

13 "Sunny weather puts people in a good mood, and people in a good mood leave bigger tips than those in a bad mood," Lynn's booklet says. The payoff in one study: 19 percent more in tips.

14   Manipulative?

15   "Of course," Lynn said.

16   He acknowledged that there are insincere servers "who hate a customer's guts, and yet they smile, write 'thank you' on the check and 'come again.'" But more common, he said, are servers who like their customers and want to please them but aren't sure how. That's where his pointers come in.

17   Diners who don't care to become best friends with their server or who cringe at being touched by a stranger may find Lynn's work dispiriting because it looks as though "Hi, I'm Mike, I'll be your waiter" isn't going away soon—at least not at the middle-brow eateries that Lynn's studies focus on.

18   Lynn, by the way, takes his own advice. He tips 15 to 20 percent or even 40 percent if he's at a regular lunch spot, he said.

"It really depends," he added, "on how much I like the server."

Understand the Reading

1. What is the main idea of the article?

_____

_____

2. List four of the tactics Lynn suggests to get bigger tips.

_____

_____

3. What does research show that customers are buying with their tips?

_____

_____

Vocabulary in Context. The following words appear in the reading selection. Write a definition for each of the following words as they are used in the reading selection. If you are not sure of the meaning, try to figure it out from the other words and sentences around it.

Word	Para	Definition
angling	1	_____
tactics	3	_____
tally	6	_____
correlation	6	_____
savvy	8	_____

rapport	10	_____
cheapskate	10	_____
empathy	11	_____
reciprocate	11	_____
manipulative	14	_____
dispiriting	17	_____

Remember the Reading. Map the reading selection. Fill in a Reading Map like the one on page 536. Then, using your own words, summarize the reading.

React to the Reading

1. **Reader Response:** Think about the reading and link it to something else you have read, to your own life experiences, or to something in the real world.

Text-to-Text	■ Does this reading remind you of something else you have read, heard, or seen (story, book, movie, song, news item, magazine article, website, and so on)? ■ Are the ideas the same or different?
Text-to-Self	■ How do the ideas in the reading relate to your own life, experiences, or ideas? ■ Do you agree or disagree with what you read?
Text-to-World	■ What does the reading remind you of in the real world? ■ Does it make you think about something in the past, present, or future?

2. **QuickWrite:** Write about a time when you had poor service at a restaurant that provided tables where you could sit down and eat. If you have never eaten at a sit-down restaurant, write about poor service at a fast-food restaurant.
3. **QuickWrite Jump Off:** Write about the steps you would take to improve service at the restaurant you wrote about in your QuickWrite.

Connect the Process Readings

1. What advice for dealing with customers is similar in both reading selections?
2. Which advice will be useful to you now or in future employment?

Symmetry Both humans and animals are selective when choosing mates. What do they look for? Scientists tell us it is symmetry. **Symmetry** means being the same, or even, on each side. Notice the results of researchers' experiments as you read the text-book excerpt "Sex and Symmetry."

Get Ready to Read: Preview the reading and then fill in a Prereading Organizer like the one on page 530.

Excerpt from *Biology*
Sex and Symmetry
Teresa Audesirk, Gerald Audesirk, and Bruce E. Byers

1   What makes a man sexy? According to a growing body of research, it's his symmetry. Female sexual preference for symmetrical males was first documented in insects. For example, biologist Randy Thornhill found that symmetry accurately predicts the mating success of male Japanese scorpion-flies. In Thornhill's experiments and observations, the most successful males were those whose left and right wings were equal or nearly equal in length. Males with one wing longer than the other were less likely to mate; the great-er the difference between two wings, the lower the likelihood of success.

2   Thornhill's work with scorpionflies led him to wonder if the effects of male symmetry also extend to humans. To test the hypothesis that female humans find symmetrical males more attractive, Thornhill and colleagues began by measuring symmetry in some young adult males. Each man's degree of symmetry was calculated by measurements of his ear length and

the width of his foot, ankle, hand, wrist, elbow, and ear. From these measurements, the researchers developed an index that summarized how much the size of these features differed between the right and the left sides of the body.

3   The researchers next gathered a panel of heterosexual female observers who were unaware of what the study was about and showed them photos of the faces of the males who had been measured. As predicted by the researchers' hypothesis, the panel judged the most symmetrical men to be most attractive. Apparently, a man's attractiveness to women is correlated with his body symmetry.

4   How did the women know which males were most symmetrical? After all, the researchers' measurement of male symmetry was based on small differences in the sizes of body parts that the female judges did not even see during the test.

5   Perhaps male body symmetry is reflected in facial symmetry, and females prefer symmetrical faces. To test this hypothesis, a group of researchers used computers to alter photos of male faces, either increasing or decreasing their symmetry. Then heterosexual female observers rated each face for attractiveness. The observers had a strong preference for more symmetrical faces.

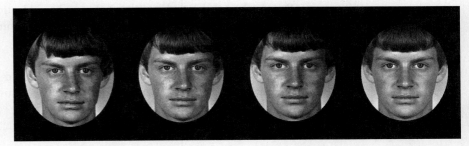

Faces of varying symmetry Researchers used sophisticated software to modify facial symmetry. From left a face modified to be less symmetrical; the orginal, unmodified face; a face modified to be more symmetrical; a perfectly symmetrical face.

6   Why would females prefer to mate with symmetrical males? The most likely explanation is that symmetry indicates good physical condition. Something that interferes with the normal development of an embryo can cause bodies to be asymmetrical, so a highly symmetrical body indicates healthy, normal development. Females that mate with individuals whose health and vitality are shown by their symmetrical bodies might have offspring that are similarly healthy and vital.

Understand the Reading

1. What is the main idea of the reading?

_____

2. Explain the researchers' experiment to test the hypothesis that female humans find symmetrical males more attractive.

_____

_____

3. Look at the pictures of the young man's face. The second photograph was not modified. Which picture do you prefer and why?

_____

Vocabulary in Context. The following words appear in the reading selection. Write a definition for each of the following words as they are used in the reading selection. If you are not sure of the meaning, try to figure it out from the other words and sentences around it.

Word	Para	Definition
hypothesis	2, 3, 5	_____
		_____
correlated	3	_____
asymmetrical	6	_____
embryo	6	_____
vitality	6	_____
offspring	6	_____

Remember the Reading. Map the reading selection. Fill in a Reading Map like the one on page 536. Then, using your own words, summarize the reading.

React to the Reading

1. **Reader Response:** Think about the reading and link it to something else you have read, to your own life experiences, or to something in the real world.

Text-to-Text	■ Does this reading remind you of something else you have read, heard, or seen (story, book, movie, song, news item, magazine article, website, and so on)?
	■ Are the ideas the same or different?
Text-to-Self	■ How do the ideas in the reading relate to your own life, experiences, or ideas?
	■ Do you agree or disagree with what you read?
Text-to-World	■ What does the reading remind you of in the real world?
	■ Does it make you think about something in the past, present, or future?

2. **QuickWrite:** Which physical qualities do you find attractive in a romantic partner? Which physical qualities do you find unattractive?
3. **QuickWrite Jump Off:** Write a paper comparing your preferred body type in a romantic partner to the body type preferred in advertising, movies, television, and videos.

Choosing a Partner The authors of "Sex and Symmetry" point to research that shows people prefer symmetry. However, symmetry is not as important to some people. Psychologist David Perrett discusses other factors that influence our choice of partners.

Get Ready to Read: Preview the reading and then fill in a Prereading Graphic Organizer like the one on page 530.

Why Women Fall for Men Who Look like Their Father . . . and Other Astonishing Secrets of the Science of Attraction
David Perrett

Why are some women considered beauties? Can you tell if someone is "the one" by their face? And why ARE we attracted to men who look like our fathers? In a new book, a leading expert on attractiveness, Professor David Perrett, of the University of St. Andrews, answers these compelling questions.

Like Father Like Husband

1   It has long been speculated that women tend to choose partners who look like their fathers—and men will pick wives who resemble their mothers in some way. But isn't it just an old wives' tale?

2   Well, it's certainly true that the characteristics of our parents are imprinted in our minds as children, so that we remember and recognize our parents from a very early age.

3   This is a result of observing our families at close quarters and is seen in other mammals.

4   But it seems these "remembered" characteristics do go on to influence who we find attractive in later life.

5   We conducted a large-scale survey, asking 300 men and 400 women (all of whom were in a relationship and who had been brought up by two parents) to tell us their hair and eye color, as well as that of their partner and their parents.

Family ties: Angelina Jolie's partner Brad Pitt (left) resembles her father Jon Voight

6   From this information, we found that the main predictor for the choice of a partner's eye and hair color—for men and women—was the eye and hair color of the parent of the opposite sex.

7   Your own hair and eye color, or those of the parent of the same sex, were far less important. In other words, if a man has a blonde, blue-eyed mother, he is quite likely to choose a blonde, blue-eyed partner.

8   If a woman's father has dark hair and dark eyes, her partner is likely to have a similar appearance.

9   But it's not just our parents' coloring that affects the partners we choose in later life—it's their facial features as well. Researchers at the University of Pecs, Hungary, compared individual photographs of young, married couples with individual photographs of their parents at a similar age to them.

10   Participants in the study were asked to match up the newlyweds, and then pick out the couples' parents.

11   The first point of note is that the participants identified a distinct facial resemblance between the young newlyweds.

12   We've often found that people pick out someone of a similar level of attractiveness to themselves when offered a series of faces to pick from. This appeared to be one of the subconscious "rules" people used when matching up the couples in this study.

13   Then there were similarities in face shape; people paired up couples with matching features. Of most interest, however, was the similarity between a young man's partner and his mother.

14   Again, observers found it surprisingly easy to match up the pictures of a man's mother with the pictures of the man's wife.

15   Equally, in a separate study, it was found that young women's fathers looked very similar to the men they married.

16   However, the participants of the study could not match the men's fathers to the men's partners—which proves that we don't like faces simply because they resemble familiar family members.

17   We tend to be attracted to people who resemble our opposite sex parent. This is particularly the case when people have had a good relationship with the parent in question—it seems we want to replicate that good experience in our romantic relationships.

Pretty Women

Drawing attention to her best features: Scarlett Johansson has big eyes and lips, deemed attractive in a woman, and uses makeup to highlight them.

18   An important factor in facial attractiveness is how "female" or "male" we look.

19   As we pass through puberty, our bone structure is influenced by sex hormones.

20   Thanks to a flood of **testosterone**, as boys turn into men their eyebrow ridges grow more prominent, and their jawbones enlarge rapidly.

21   In women, the sex hormone **estrogen** prevents the bone growth we see in men's faces. The result is that while a man's head shape changes a lot as he goes through puberty, a woman's head shape stays as it is and retains childlike proportions—less prominent brows and jaws, thicker lips, a smaller nose, a smaller head size, and large eyes.

22   In our laboratory, we gave people the ability to choose the female head shape they found most attractive by allowing them to control face shape interactively using a computer. Moving the computer mouse in one direction made the female face on the screen look progressively more masculine.

23   An astonishing 95 per cent of men and women decided that feminization of women's faces (jawline softer and eyes and lips more pronounced)

testosterone sex hormone that affects the production of sperm and signals certain physical changes at puberty, such as the growth of facial hair

estrogen the female sex hormone that activates physical changes at puberty, such as the growth of breasts

made them more attractive. This is reflected in the use of makeup. Women apply lipstick and eye makeup to enhance their features.

24   And face makeup gives the appearance of a clear complexion—indicating good health, which is seen as attractive. In our studies, we subtly manipulated facial skin color and texture in photographs of faces, creating identical faces that were either high or low in skin health.

25   Sure enough, the faces with high skin health—(even skin color and tone, fewer spots, small pores, and less fine lines and wrinkles)—were judged the most attractive. Skin condition, attractiveness, and health are intimately linked because many of the things we do that cause us to age prematurely (smoking, poor diet, drinking too much, stress, a lack of sleep, fresh air, and exercise) show their effects on our faces.

26   If our skin looks old for our age, then it suggests that our bodies may have aged too—and we may be a less than desirable mate and long-term partner.

Age before Beauty

27   What is it that gives our age away? You would think we could judge someone's face by doing some mental math like this: "Face shape looks 50. Skin is pretty good, say 40. Hair—more like 60. All told, I'd guess 50."

28   But we don't. Instead, when it comes to weighing up someone's age, we simply take the easy route and focus just on the oldest looking part of the face. We proved this by airbrushing images so that an old woman's face was given younger hair and vice versa.

29   In our research, putting younger hair on an older face did not shift the person's perceived age from what people guessed the woman to be when they looked at pictures of her with age-appropriate hair.

30   But an "older" hairdo on a younger face did shift the perceptions of age of the woman concerned. Most people guessed her to be significantly older than the picture of her with her age-appropriate hair.

31   So the bad news is that to look young, all your facial features must be youthful. If any one part looks older than the rest, we pick up on it and ignore the parts that are wearing well.

How to Be More Attractive

32   First impressions can change: How attractive we think someone is can depend on how long we've known them.

33   Whether or not someone is traditionally good-looking, their attractiveness changes the more we get to know them.

34   When we asked people to rate old school friends, for example, they judged those they like admired as having been the most attractive.

35   But when strangers then rated the same individuals, the results were very different.

36   Similarly, the ratings that people gave each other at the beginning of a team exercise compared with the ratings at the end showed the same thing.

37   By the end of the exercise, people had changed their assessments according to how helpful, cooperative, and hardworking the other person had been.

38   The changes in attraction were more marked in women than men. Women's assessments of appearances strongly reflected what they have found out about personalities and deeds.

39   Men's judgments were more resilient; although swayed by deeds, they continued to reflect physical appearance. Yes, sadly, men are a little more shallow.

cliché d unoriginal   40   So, despite being **clichéd,** it really does seem that inner beauty is what matters most. Our consideration of another person's inner beauty, as expressed through their personality, actually translates into an assessment of their outward physical attractiveness.

41   Perhaps the best beauty tip, therefore, is to aim to be a kind and helpful person.

42   Unlike the claims made for so many overpriced face creams, this one really has been "scientifically proven" to work.

Understand the Reading

1. What is the main idea of the reading selection?

_____

2. What factors contribute to a person's attractiveness?

_____

3. Several studies were reported in the reading selection. Describe one of the studies and include the results.

_____

_____

Vocabulary in Context.   The following words appear in the reading selection. Write a definition for each of the following words as they are used in the reading selection. If you are not sure of the meaning, try to figure it out from the other words and sentences around it.

Word	Para	Definition
speculate	1	_____
imprint	2	_____
prominent	20, 21	_____
progressively	22	_____
feminization	23	_____
pronounced	23	_____
prematurely	25	_____
airbrushing	28	_____
resilient	39	_____
shallow	39	_____

Remember the Reading.   Map the reading selection. Fill in a Reading Map like the one on page 536. Then, using your own words, summarize the reading.

React to the Reading

1. **Reader Response:** Think about the reading and link it to something else you have read, to your own life experiences, or to something in the real world.

Text-to-Text	■ Does this reading remind you of something else you have read, heard, or seen (story, book, movie, song, news item, magazine article, website, and so on)?
	■ Are the ideas the same or different?
Text-to-Self	■ How do the ideas in the reading relate to your own life, experiences, or ideas?
	■ Do you agree or disagree with what you read?
Text-to-World	■ What does the reading remind you of in the real world?
	■ Does it make you think about something in the past, present, or future?

2. **QuickWrite:** Choose someone you have known for a while. Write a paper comparing your opinion of the person's attractiveness before and after you got to know him or her.

3. **QuickWrite Jump Off:** At the end of the reading selection, the author states, "Inner beauty is what matters most." Write a paper comparing inner beauty with outer beauty.

Connect the Comparison and Contrast Readings

1. The U.S. culture has a certain idea of what is attractive. However, cultural and ethnic groups within the U.S. culture have their own ideas of attractiveness. Compare two groups that view beauty differently.

2. The reading from *Biology* tells us that symmetry is the basis for attraction. On the other hand, the other selection by David Perrett tells us about other qualities that make people attractive. Compare the ideas in the two readings.

HEALTH AND WELLNESS   Theme: *Mind-Body Connection*

Stress Stress happens when something causes the body to act as if it is under attack. Some sources of stress are physical, such as an injury. Other sources of stress can be mental, like problems at work or with finances. As you read the textbook excerpt from *Health*, notice the stages that the body goes through when stressed.

   Get Ready to Read: Preview the reading and then fill in a Prereading Graphic Organizer like the one on page 530.

Excerpt from *Health*
Stages of Stress
B. E. Pruitt, John P. Allegrante, and Deborah Prothrow-Stith

1   You are walking in a park. Suddenly, you see a large dog that isn't on a leash. The dog is growling. How do you react? Instantly, your mind sizes up the situation. You recognize the dog could be a threat to your safety. When you perceive something to be a threat, your body springs into action. Your body's response isn't under your control—it's automatic.

2   All stressors trigger the same stress response. However, the intensity of the response will vary. The body's response to stress occurs in three stages—the alarm stage, the resistance stage, and the exhaustion stage.

3   **Alarm Stage**   During the alarm stage, your body releases a substance called **adrenaline** (uh DREN uh lin) into your blood. Adrenaline causes many immediate changes in your body, as shown in the figure below. Extra sugar released into your blood combines with oxygen in body cells to give you a burst of energy. Your heart beats faster, your breathing speeds up, and your muscles tense. Your attention narrows as you focus on the stressor.

4   These changes prepare you to either "fight" the stressor or "take flight" and escape. Thus, this initial reaction of the body to stress is called the **fight-or-flight response.** This response probably helped early humans

adrenaline a substance released in the body of a person who is feeling a strong emotion (such as excitement, fear, or anger) and that causes the heart to beat faster and gives the person more energy

Fight-or-Flight Response

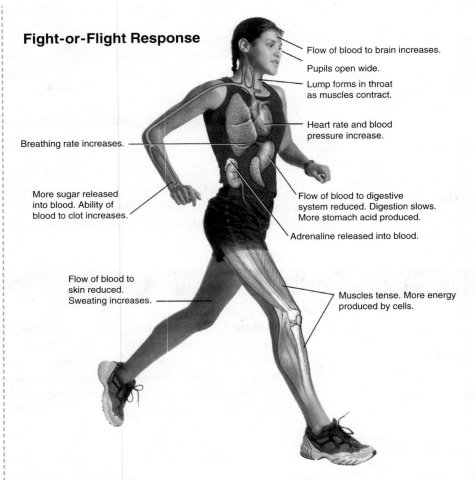

Flow of blood to brain increases.

Pupils open wide.

Lump forms in throat as muscles contract.

Heart rate and blood pressure increase.

Breathing rate increases.

More sugar released into blood. Ability of blood to clot increases.

Flow of blood to digestive system reduced. Digestion slows. More stomach acid produced.

Adrenaline released into blood.

Flow of blood to skin reduced. Sweating increases.

Muscles tense. More energy produced by cells.

survive. Today, your body still reacts to any stressor with the same set of changes even when fight-or-flight is not a useful response.

5   **Resistance Stage**   Sometimes you can deal with a stressor quickly. You find the keys you thought were lost or you know the answers to the questions on a quiz. If, however, you are unable to successfully respond to a stressor during the alarm stage, your body moves into the resistance stage. During this stage, your body adapts to the continued presence of the stressor. You may think you are no longer stressed because the symptoms from the alarm stage disappear. However, the work that your body does during the resistance stage uses up a lot of energy. As a result, you may become tired, irritable, and less able to handle any added stress.

6   **Exhaustion Stage**   The third stage of the stress response is the exhaustion stage. Your body can no longer keep up with the demands placed on it. Your physical and emotional resources are depleted.

7   The exhaustion stage does not occur with each stress response. If it did, your body would wear out. Exhaustion occurs only if a stressor continues for a long time—usually weeks, months, or even years. People may reach the exhaustion stage when they experience extreme stress that is beyond their control—such as the death of a family member.

Understand the Reading

1. What is the main idea of the reading selection?

   _____

2. Briefly explain the three stages of the body's response to stress.

   _____

   _____

3. Explain the fight-or-flight response.

   _____

   _____

Vocabulary in Context.   The following words appear in the reading selection. Write a definition for each of the following words as they are used in the reading selection. If you are not sure of the meaning, try to figure it out from the other words and sentences around it.

Word	Para	Definition
perceive	1	_____
spring into action	1	_____
trigger	2	_____
stressor	3	_____
		_____
depleted	6	_____

Remember the Reading.   Map the reading selection. Fill in a Reading Map like the one on page 536. Then, using your own words, summarize the reading.

React to the Reading

1. **Reader Response:** Think about the reading and link it to something else you have read, to your own life experiences, or to something in the real world.

Text-to-Text	■ Does this reading remind you of something else you have read, heard, or seen (story, book, movie, song, news item, magazine article, website, and so on)?
	■ Are the ideas the same or different?
Text-to-Self	■ How do the ideas in the reading relate to your own life, experiences, or ideas?
	■ Do you agree or disagree with what you read?
Text-to-World	■ What does the reading remind you of in the real world?
	■ Does it make you think about something in the past, present, or future?

2. **QuickWrite:** List the stresses in your life and then put them into groups. For example, one group might be stress associated with school. Another might be work-related stress.

3. **QuickWrite Jump Off:** Using three of the groups that you developed in the QuickWrite, write a paper in which you explain the stress in each of your groups.

Changing the Brain Dr. Amen is an assistant clinical professor of psychiatry and human behavior at the University of California, Irvine School of Medicine. He teaches medical students and psychiatric residents about using brain imaging. Dr. Amen believes that people can change their brains. As you read this excerpt from a website, note how your beliefs affect your thoughts.

Get Ready to Read: Preview the reading and then fill in a Prereading Graphic Organizer like the one on page 530.

Kill the Ants That Invade Your Brain
Daniel G. Amen, M.D.

1   The brain is a three-pound supercomputer. It is the command and control center running your life. It is involved in absolutely everything you do. Your brain determines how you think, how you feel, how you act, and how well you get along with other people. Your brain even determines the kind of person you are. It determines how thoughtful you are; how polite or how rude you are. It determines how well you think on your feet, and it is involved with how well you do at work and with your family. Your brain also influences your emotional well-being and how well you do with the opposite sex.

2   Your brain is more complicated than any computer we can imagine. Did you know that you have one hundred billion nerve cells in your brain, and every nerve cell has many connections to other nerve cells? In fact, your brain has more connections in it than there are stars in the universe! Optimizing your brain's function is essential to being the best you can be, whether at work, in leisure, or in your relationships.

3   The thoughts that go through your mind, moment by moment, have a significant impact on how your brain works. Research by Mark George, MD, and colleagues at the National Institutes of Health demonstrated that happy, hopeful thoughts had an overall calming effect on the brain, while negative thoughts inflamed brain areas often involved with depression and anxiety. Your thoughts matter.

4   I often teach my patients how to metaphorically kill the ANTs that invade their minds. ANTs stand for Automatic Negative Thoughts. The ANTs

are automatic. They just happen. But they can ruin your whole day, maybe even your life. For example, I once treated a college student who was ready to drop out of school. He thought he was stupid because he didn't do well on tests. When his IQ (intelligence level) was tested, however, we discovered that he had an IQ of 135 (in the superior range). He just wasn't a good test taker. I have identified nine different kinds of ANT species, or ways your thoughts can distort incoming information to make you feel bad. Here are four ANT species:

Mind reading—predicting you know that another person is thinking something negative about you without them telling you. I often tell my patients that, "A negative look from someone else may mean nothing more than he or she is constipated. You don't know. You can't read minds. I have 25 years of training in human behavior and I still can't read anyone's mind."

Fortune telling—predicting a bad outcome to a situation before it has occurred. Your mind makes happen what it sees. Unconsciously, predicting failure will often cause failure. For example, if you say, "I know I will fail the test," then you will likely not study hard enough and fail the test.

Always or never thinking—this is where you think in words like always, never, every time, or everyone. These thoughts are over-generalizations which can alter behavior. For example, I have a friend who asked out an attractive woman. She turned him down. He told himself that no one will ever go out with him again. This ANT prevented him from asking out anyone else for over nine months.

Guilt beatings—being overrun by thoughts of "I should have done . . . I'm bad because . . . I must do better at . . . I have to." Guilt is powerful at making us feel bad. It is a lousy motivator of behavior.

5   You do not have to believe every thought that goes through your head. It's important to think about your thoughts to see if they help you or they hurt you. Unfortunately, if you never challenge your thoughts you just "believe them" as if they were true. ANTs can take over and infest your brain. Develop an internal anteater to hunt down and devour the negative thoughts that are ruining your life.

6   Once you learn about your thoughts, you can chose to think good thoughts and feel good or you can choose to think bad thoughts and feel lousy. You can train your thoughts to be positive and hopeful or you can just allow them to be negative and upset you. That's right, it's up to you! You can learn how to change your thoughts and optimize your brain. One way to learn how to change your thoughts is to notice them when they are negative and talk back to them. If you can correct negative thoughts, you take away their power over you. When you think a negative thought without challenging it, your mind believes it and your brain reacts to it.

Understand the Reading

1. What is the main idea of the reading?

_____

_____

2. What are Automatic Negative Thoughts (ANTs)?

_____

_____

3. Describe two of the Automatic Negative Thought species.

_____

_____

Vocabulary in Context.   The following words appear in the reading selection. Write a definition for each of the following words as they are used in the reading selection. If you are not sure of the meaning, try to figure it out from the other words and sentences around it.

Word	Para	Definition
optimizing	2	_____
inflame	3	_____
metaphorically	4	_____
distort	4	_____
overgeneralizations	4	_____

Remember the Reading.   Map the reading selection. Fill in a Reading Map like the one on page 536. Then, using your own words, summarize the reading.

React to the Reading

1. **Reader Response:** Think about the reading and link it to something else you have read, to your own life experiences, or to something in the real world.

Text-to-Text	■ Does this reading remind you of something else you have read, heard, or seen (story, book, movie, song, news item, magazine article, website, and so on)?
	■ Are the ideas the same or different?
Text-to-Self	■ How do the ideas in the reading relate to your own life, experiences, or ideas?
	■ Do you agree or disagree with what you read?
Text-to-World	■ What does the reading remind you of in the real world?
	■ Does it make you think about something in the past, present, or future?

2. **QuickWrite:** Write about an Automatic Negative Thought you have had.
3. **QuickWrite Jump Off:** Using Amen's types of Automatic Negative Thoughts, write a classification paper describing each one with details that apply to you or people you know.

Connect the Classification Readings

1. How can Dr. Amen's strategies for killing the ANTS (Automatic Negative Thoughts) help a person avoid or help deal with the stress response?
2. Our thoughts are often responsible for stress. Many people have three patterns of thinking that make us feel stress: negative self-talk about ourselves; negative self-talk about other people or situations; and worried or fearful thoughts about the future. Write a paper explaining each of the three types of patterns of thinking.

ANTHROPOLOGY   Theme: *Race*

Race and Culture Races are invented by cultures, not biology. Ideas about race are learned through exposure to the beliefs of family, peers, culture, and social groups. In different societies around the world, race has been used to separate people and to treat them unequally. As you read this excerpt adapted from a textbook, notice how anthropologists view race and how their view differs from that of society.

    Get Ready to Read: Preview the reading and then fill in a Prereading Graphic Organizer like the one on page 530.

Excerpt from *Anthropology*
Race: A Meaningless Idea
Carol R. Ember, Melvin Ember, and Peter N. Peregrine

1   In some societies, such as the United States, the idea that humans are divided into "races" is accepted as truth. People are asked for their "race" on the census. Most Americans probably believe that "races" are real, meaningful categories based on differences in skin color and other physical characteristics. However, this is not necessarily the case. You may have noticed that we put "races" in quotes. We have done so on purpose because most **anthropologists** believe that "race" is a meaningless idea when applied to humans. To understand why we say that, we first need to consider what the concept of race means in biology.

anthropologist someone who scientifically studies humans, their customs, beliefs, and relationships

biologist a scientist who studies
life science

2   Biologists classify all forms of life into groups. Just as with animals, plants, and insects, biologists classify humans. They found that people living in different geographical locations in the world had different physical characteristics, such as skin color, hair texture, and facial features. **Biologists** classified these groups into *varieties,* or **races.** If people understood that the term *race* was just a system that biologists use to describe differences within a species from one population to the next, the concept of race would probably not be controversial. But, as applied to humans, racial groupings have often been thought to imply that some "races" are inferior to others.

3   Many anthropologists and others believe that the concept of race interferes with the search to explain how physical differences developed in humans. They have two reasons for this belief. One is the misuse and misunderstanding of the term *race.* The other is that race has been connected to racist thinking. In any case, classifying people by race is not scientifically useful in that search. Populations cannot be grouped according to certain characteristics because these characteristics vary from region to region.

4   How can groups be clearly divided into "races" if most people from one region show small differences from those in a neighboring region? Skin color is a good example. Groups of people who originally came from places close to the equator where the sun is strongest tend to have darker skin. Darker skin appears to protect the body from damaging ultraviolet radiation. For example, in the area around Egypt, there is a change of skin color as you move from north to south in the Nile Valley. Populations originating in places farther north developed lighter skin colors because the sunlight was not as strong.

5   Some of our physical differences make us think that it is possible to divide humans into races. However, when these physical characteristics are studied in detail, that cannot be concluded at all. It is an illusion that there are races. The diversity of human beings is so great and so complicated that it is impossible to classify the 5.8 billions of individuals into separate "races." Human populations do vary biologically in some ways, but it is important to understand that few of these ways are connected with each other. All humans are nearly alike genetically under the skin.

Understand the Reading

1. What is the main idea of the excerpt?

_____

_____

_____

2. According to the authors of the reading, how do biologists define race?

_____

_____

_____

3. Why is the term *race* controversial?

_____

_____

_____

Vocabulary in Context. The following words appear in the reading selection. Write a definition for each of the following words as they are used in the reading selection. If you are not sure of the meaning, try to figure it out from the other words and sentences around it.

Word	Para	Definition
census	1	_____
species	2	_____
		_____
		_____
racist	3	_____
		_____
ultraviolet radiation	4	_____
originating	4	_____
illusion	5	_____
diversity	5	_____

Remember the Reading. Map the reading selection. Fill in a Reading Map like the one on page 536. Then, using your own words, summarize the reading.

React to the Reading

1. **Reader Response:** Think about the reading and link it to something else you have read, to your own life experiences, or to something in the real world.

Text-to-Text	■ Does this reading remind you of something else you have read, heard, or seen (story, book, movie, song, news item, magazine article, website, and so on)? ■ Are the ideas the same or different?
Text-to-Self	■ How do the ideas in the reading relate to your own life, experiences, or ideas? ■ Do you agree or disagree with what you read?
Text-to-World	■ What does the reading remind you of in the real world? ■ Does it make you think about something in the past, present, or future?

2. **QuickWrite:** We are not born with any beliefs about racial differences. What we think about race is learned. What messages have you received about race throughout your life? Where did they come from?

3. **QuickWrite Jump Off:** The authors of the excerpt on race present the anthropologists' view that people can't be separated into races because human diversity is so great and complicated. However, throughout history, people have used race as a basis for discrimination. Write a paper defining discrimination.

Colorism Colorism is a form or discrimination within racial groups in which there is skin tone variation. Members of the same race with lighter skin are treated more favorably than those with darker skin. As you read Clarisse Jones's magazine article "Light Skin versus Dark," think about how colorism influences the culture in the United States and other parts of the world.

Get Ready to Read: Preview the reading and then fill in a Prereading Graphic Organizer like the one on page 530.

Light Skin versus Dark

Charisse Jones

1   I'll never forget the day I was supposed to meet him. We had only spoken on the phone. But we got along so well, we couldn't wait to meet face-to-face. I took the bus from my high school to his for our blind date. While I nervously waited for him outside the school, one of his buddies came along, looked me over, and remarked that I was going to be a problem, because his friend didn't like dating anybody darker than himself.

2   When my mystery man—who was not especially good-looking—finally saw me, he took one look, uttered a hurried hello, then disappeared with his smirking friends. I had apparently been pronounced ugly on arrival and dismissed.

3   That happened nearly fifteen years ago. I'm thirty now, and the hurt and humiliation have long since faded. But the memory still lingers, reinforced in later years by other situations in which my skin color was judged by other African Americans—for example, at a cocktail party or a nightclub where light-skinned black women got all the attention.

4   A racist encounter hurts badly. But it does not equal the pain of "colorism"—being rejected by your own people because your skin is colored cocoa and not cream, ebony and not olive. On our scale of beauty, it is often the high yellows—in the lexicon of black America, those with light skin—whose looks reap the most attention. Traditionally, if someone was described that way, there was no need to say that person was good-looking. It was a given that light was lovely. It was those of us with plain brown eyes and darker skin hues who had to prove ourselves.

5   I was twelve, and in my first year of junior high school in San Francisco, when I discovered dark brown was not supposed to be beautiful. At that age, boys suddenly became important, and so did your looks. But by that time—the late 1970s—black kids no longer believed in that sixties mantra,

"Black is beautiful." Light skin, green eyes, and long, wavy hair were once again synonymous with beauty.

6   Colorism—and its subtext of self-hatred—began during slavery on plantations where white masters often favored the lighter-skinned blacks, many of whom were their own children. But though it began with whites, black people have kept colorism alive. In the past, many black sororities, fraternities, and other social organizations have been notorious for accepting only light-skinned members. Yes, some blacks have criticized their lighter-skinned peers. But most often in our history, a light complexion had been a passport to special treatment by both whites *and* blacks.

7   Some social circles are still defined by hue. Some African Americans, dark and light, prefer light-skinned mates so they can have a "pretty baby." And skin-lightening creams still sell, though they are now advertised as good for making blemishes fade rather than for lightening whole complexions.

8   In my family, color was never discussed, even though our spectrum was broad—my brother was very light; my sister and I, much darker. But in junior high, I learned in a matter of weeks what had apparently been **drummed into the heads** of my black peers for most of their lives.

9   Realizing how crazy it all was, I became defiant, challenging friends when they made silly remarks. Still, there was no escaping the distinctions of color.

10   In my life, I have received a litany of twisted compliments from fellow blacks. "You're the prettiest dark-skinned girl I have ever seen" is one; "You're pretty for a dark girl" is another.

11   A light-complexioned girlfriend once remarked to me that dark-skinned people often don't take the time to groom themselves. As a journalist, I once interviewed a prominent black lawmaker who was light-skinned. He drew me into the shade of a tree while we talked because, he said, "I'm sure you don't want to get any darker."

12   Though some black people—like film-maker Spike Lee in his movie *School Daze*—have tried to provoke debate about colorism, it remains a painful topic many blacks would rather not confront. Yet there has been progress. In this age of **Afrocentrism,** many blacks revel in the nuances of the African American rainbow. Natural hairstyles and dreadlocks are in, and Theresa Randle, star of the hit film *Bad Boys,* is only one of several darker-skinned actresses noted for their beauty.

---

drummed into the heads
to teach something to someone by repeating it a lot

Afrocentrism emphasizing the importance of African people in culture, philosophy, and history

13   That gives me hope. People have told me that color biases among blacks run too deep ever to be eradicated. But I tell them that is the kind of attitude that allows colorism to persist. Meanwhile, I do what I can. When I notice that a friend dates only light-skinned women, I comment on it. If I hear that a movie follows the tired old scenario in which a light-skinned beauty is the love interest while a darker-skinned woman is the comic foil, the butt of "ugly" jokes, I don't go see it. Others can do the same.

Understand the Reading

1. What is the main idea of the article?

_____

_____

_____

2. How does Charisse Jones define "colorism"?

_____

_____

3. What is the history of "colorism"?

_____

_____

_____

Vocabulary in Context.   The following words appear in the reading selection. Write a definition for each of the following words as they are used in the reading selection. If you are not sure of the meaning, try to figure it out from the other words and sentences around it.

Word	Para	Definition
smirking	2	_____ _____
high yellows	4	_____
lexicon	4	_____
mantra	5	_____
subtext	6	_____
notorious	6	_____
hue	7	_____
spectrum	8	_____
defiant	9	_____

Word	Para	Definition
litany	10	_____
provoke	12	_____
revel	12	_____
nuance	12	_____
bias	13	_____

Remember the Reading.   Map the reading selection. Fill in a Reading Map like the one on page 536. Then, using your own words, summarize the reading.

React to the Reading

1. **Reader Response:** Think about the reading and link it to something else you have read, to your own life experiences, or to something in the real world.

Text-to-Text	■ Does this reading remind you of something else you have read, heard, or seen (story, book, movie, song, news item, magazine article, website, and so on)?
	■ Are the ideas the same or different?
Text-to-Self	■ How do the ideas in the reading relate to your own life, experiences, or ideas?
	■ Do you agree or disagree with what you read?
Text-to-World	■ What does the reading remind you of in the real world?
	■ Does it make you think about something in the past, present, or future?

2. **QuickWrite:** Write about an experience with one or both of these:
   - Not wanting to have someone as a friend because of his or her appearance, beliefs, or residence, and so on
   - Being rejected or left out

3. **QuickWrite Jump Off: Discrimination** is defined as the unfair treatment of a person or particular group of people because of religion, race, sex, sexual preference, color, disability, or other personal features. Using this definition as a starting point, write a paper giving examples of this definition. You may include the example you wrote about in your QuickWrite.

Connect the Definition Readings

1. What is the difference between the view of skin color in "Race" and in "Light Skin versus Dark"?
2. Is classifying people according to race a good or a bad idea? Why?

Punishment in the Classroom When you were in high school, you may have had classes where students were disruptive and prevented others from learning. In some schools, this behavior was tolerated, while in others consequences or punishments were given. Unfortunately, students may bring that same type of disruptive behavior to college classrooms. Examples are tardiness, texting in class, constant talking, interrupting the instructor, and lack of preparation for class. As you read the following textbook excerpt, think about whether or not you believe that punishment is necessary in the classroom.

Get Ready to Read: Preview the reading and then fill in a Prereading Graphic Organizer like the one on page 530.

Excerpt from *Introduction to Teaching*
What Role Should Punishment Play in Classroom Management?
Don Kauchak and Paul Eggen

1   Did you ever get a speeding ticket? What happened to your behavior after you received the ticket—at least for a while? Most of us can agree with the idea that punishment works—temporarily. But then what?

2   Teachers in general, and especially beginning teachers, worry about whether they will be able to maintain order in their classrooms. Many turn to punishment, but punishment as a major management tool is controversial. People who support punishment say it's effective and necessary, but critics say it's ineffective and harmful. The role of punishment in classroom management, as well as in child raising in general, has been debated for centuries, and this controversy continues today.

3   Punishment is the process of decreasing or eliminating undesired behavior through some unpleasant consequence. Punishment can range from a teacher action as simple as saying, "Andrew, stop whispering," to *corporal punishment,* the use of physical actions to punish, such as paddling students, to eliminate undesirable behavior. Most punishment in the classroom is not corporal, and usually occurs in the form of simple desists, time-out, or detention. **Desists** are verbal or nonverbal communications teachers use to stop a behavior (Kounin, 1970) such as telling a student to stop whispering, or putting fingers to the lips to signal "Shhh." **Time-out** involves removing a student from the class and physically isolating him or her in an area away from classmates. **Detention,** most commonly used with older students, is similar to time-out, and involves taking away some of the students' free time by keeping them in school either before or after school hours.

The Issue

4   Punishment can be effective in reducing or getting rid of unwanted behaviors (How did your driving change after receiving a speeding ticket?). Some critics suggest, however, that punishment should never be used in classrooms (e.g., Kohn, 1996), and research indicates that methods based on rewarding positive behavior are more effective than those using punishment (Alberto & Troutman, 2006). Critics also argue that the use of punishments to keep an orderly classroom overemphasizes control and obedience

instead of emphasizing that students are responsible for their actions—which contributes to personal development (Frieberg, 1999b). Critics further contend that punishing students for simple acts, such as talking without permission, fails to examine possible causes for the behavior, such as poor teaching or a student's not understanding why it's important to give everyone a chance to speak. In addition, punishment can have unplanned consequences, such as resentment and hostility, and can damage teachers' efforts to create a positive classroom climate.

5   On the other hand, research indicates that desists, when given immediately, briefly, and unemotionally, can be effective (Emmer et al., 2009; Evertson et al., 2009). Further, research indicates that time-out is effective for a variety of disruptive behaviors (Alberto & Troutman, 2006), and although somewhat controversial, detention is widely used and generally viewed as effective (L. Johnson, 2004).

6   Some forms of punishment are used in almost all classrooms; experienced teachers believe punishment is acceptable when the severity of the punishment matches the severity of the misbehavior (Cowan & Sheridan, 2003). Additional research suggests that punishment is sometimes necessary; when all punishments are removed, some students become more disruptive (Pfiffner, Rosen & O'Leary, 1985; Rosen, O'Leary, Joyce, Conway, & Pfiffner, 1984). Punishment for unacceptable behavior can actually be helpful because it helps unruly students learn new, more acceptable behaviors quickly (Lerman & Vondran, 2002).

You Take a Stand

7   Now it's your turn to take a position on the issue. What role should punishment play in classroom management?

Understand the Reading

1. What are three kinds of punishments used in the classroom that do not use physical actions?

_____

2. What is the argument in favor of punishment in the classroom?

_____

3. What is the argument against punishment?

_____

Vocabulary in Context.   The following words appear in the reading selection. Write a definition for each of the following words as they are used in the reading selection. If you are not sure of the meaning, try to figure it out from the other words and sentences around it.

Word	Para	Definition
punishment	2	_____ _____
corporal punishment	3	_____ _____
desists	3	_____ _____
time-out	3	_____ _____ _____
detention	3	_____ _____
overemphasize	4	_____
resentment	4	_____ _____
contend	4	_____
severity	6	_____

Remember the Reading.   In a small group or on your own, map the reading selection. Fill in a Reading Map like the one on page 536. Then, using your own words, summarize the reading.

React to the Reading

1. **Reader Response:** Think about the reading and link it to something else you have read, to your own life experiences, or to something in the real world.

Text-to-Text	■ Does this reading remind you of something else you have read, heard, or seen (story, book, movie, song, news item, magazine article, website, and so on)? ■ Are the ideas the same or different?
Text-to-Self	■ How do the ideas in the reading relate to your own life, experiences, or ideas? ■ Do you agree or disagree with what you read?
Text-to-World	■ What does the reading remind you of in the real world? ■ Does it make you think about something in the past, present, or future?

2. **QuickWrite:** Classroom management can be challenging for instructors. Write about a time when one or more students created problems in a classroom.

3. **QuickWrite Jump Off:** Using the situation that you described in the QuickWrite, write a paper arguing that the way the teacher handled the situation was right or wrong. As an alternative assignment, argue for or against punishment in the classroom.

Cell Phones in the Classroom The use of electronic devices especially cell phones in college classrooms has brought about debate among college professors who have mixed opinions. Some feel that the lure of these devices can distract students from learning. In this article, cell phone use in the classroom. As you read, think about whether you agree with Professor Bloom's cell phone policy.

Get Ready to Read: Preview the reading and then fill in a Prereading Graphic Organizer like the one on page 530.

Making Cell Phones in the Class a Community Builder
Alan Bloom

Cell Phones Do Not Distract in Class

1 The first time a student's cell phone rang in my class, I was angry and frustrated. With their musical ringers, cell phones that go *off* in class are rude and distracting. But how to respond? I've never been very good at playing the heavy. Was there any way I could take this annoying occurrence and twist it so that it would contribute to a more positive classroom environment?

2 I've devised a "cell phone protocol" that has enabled me to make peace with the problem. As it appears in the syllabus, the protocol reads: **"Please turn off your cell phone ringer while in class. Mind you, violation of this protocol will demand punishment—though one that clearly does not infringe on your eighth amendment rights."** I then ask someone to identify the eighth amendment, and as a history professor, I'm happy to report that someone can always explain the constitutional limits on cruel and unusual punishment. I advise students to turn off their ringers in class, and I note that if someone's phone rings, he or she will have to provide the class with food. It doesn't have to be an extravagant meal (remember the eighth amendment!), but there must be enough for everyone. In the beginning, I offered the possibility of a subsidy to economically unable students. However, I abandoned it once I realized that if students could afford a cell-phone package, they could provide treats to about 30 classmates.

3

The community-building process develops in earnest when a phone actually rings in class. During an episode that otherwise involves an unpleasant exchange, there is now occasion for celebration, as students cheer at the possibility of their upcoming snack. The cell phone protocol, much like a kangaroo court in baseball, which exacts minor fines for small indiscretions, helps to build an **esprit de corps** and I push this outcome even further. When it is difficult to figure out whether the cell phone rang or was in vibration mode, I encourage the students to vote as to whether or not a violation has occurred.

esprit de corps a feeling of loyalty among members of a group

4

So what are the drawbacks of this policy? There are few. The biggest is that even with my policy, cell phones still ring in class and they are just as rude and distracting. I see no way around this problem. In my class, students are distracted, but we grow closer as a result of it. The other potential problem is that an instructor might not want food in the classroom, fair enough, just have the punishment be something like telling a joke or sharing a poem.

5

The policy has also produced some wonderful surprises that make me proud of my students. Once a student decided to skip the standard fare of candy and brought in dried fruit. Although most of her peers (and her teacher) were disappointed with the healthy alternative, this student took the opportunity to encourage people to eat a more healthy diet. And at the end of this past semester, one of my quietest students informed the class that she was disappointed in a classmate who still hadn't brought in food for his transgression. The chastened student, who apparently had extra money on his meal card, brought in a buffet for his dumbfounded classmates.

6

Ultimately, though, the greatest advantage of the cell phone protocol occurs when someone's phone rings in class and the other students start hooting joyously. It doesn't make the phone ringing less distracting; but on the other hand, how often do you hear students cheering in the classroom?

Understanding the Reading

1. What is the main idea of the article?

    _____

    _____

2. Explain how the professor of the first article deals with cell phone use in his class and how the students react to the policy.

    _____

    _____

3. What surprised Professor Bloom about his students?

    _____

    _____

Vocabulary in Context.   The following words appear in the reading selection. Write a definition for each of the following words as they are used in the reading selection. If you are not sure of the meaning, try to figure it out from the other words and sentences around it.

Word	Para	Definition
protocol	2	_____
extravagant	2	_____
subsidy	2	_____
indiscretion	3	_____
dumbfounded	5	_____
transgression	5	_____
chastened	5	_____

Remember the Reading.   Map the reading selection. Fill in a Reading Map like the one on page 536. Then, using your own words, summarize the reading.

React to the Reading

1. **Reader Response:** Think about the reading and link it to something else you have read, to your own life experiences, or to something in the real world.

Text-to-Text	■ Does this reading remind you of something else you have read, heard, or seen (story, book, movie, song, news item, magazine article, website, and so on)?
	■ Are the ideas the same or different?
Text-to-Self	■ How do the ideas in the reading relate to your own life, experiences, or ideas?
	■ Do you agree or disagree with what you read?
Text-to-World	■ What does the reading remind you of in the real world?
	■ Does it make you think about something in the past, present, or future?

2. **QuickWrite:** Do any of your instructors have policies about the use of cell phones or other electronic devices in class? Write about these policies and explain whether or not they have been effective.

3. **QuickWrite Jump Off:** Write a paper arguing for or against penalties for using cell phones (or electronic devices).

Connect the Argument Readings

1. Both readings in this section, "What Role Should Punishment Play in Classroom Management?" and "Making Cell Phones in the Class a Community Builder," discuss whether or not punishment should be used in the classroom. Which information presented in the first article can be helpful to college teachers?

2. Do you think that disruptive behavior such as cell phone use, repeated tardiness, lack of preparation, sleeping, and arguing would stop if students had a voice in determining their class rules and consequences?

Credits

Photo Credits

p. 1: © Jupiter Images/Stockbyte/Getty Images; **p. 78:** © Michael Newman/PhotoEdit, Inc.; **p. 79:** © PNC/Stockbyte/Getty Images; **p. 96:** © Mark Wilson/Boston Globe/Getty Images; **p. 101:** © Alphaspirit/Fotolia; **p. 119:** © Nikada/iStockphoto; **p. 125:** © Larry Lilac/Alamy; **p. 128:** © Francis G. Mayer/Corbis; **p. 141:** © Lilkar/Shutterstock; **p. 145:** © Bettmann/Corbis; **p. 146:** © R.Ashrafov/Shutterstock; **p. 152:** © Steven Day/AP Images; **p. 164 (bottom left):** © Yaniev/Fotolia; **p. 164 (bottom right):** © Yaniev/Fotolia; **p. 170:** © iStockphoto/Thinkstock; **p. 176:** © Enigma/Alamy; **p. 194 (bottom left):** © Megan Duncanson, DBA MADART, Inc.; **p. 194 (bottom right):** © Harvard Art Museum/Art Resource, NY, © 2013 Estate of Pablo Picasso/Artists Rights Society (ARS), New York **p. 202:** © Image Source/Getty Images; **p. 226:** © Daniel Laflor/iStockphoto; **p. 245:** © John Richardson/Alamy; **p. 251:** © Douglas Pulsipher/Alamy; **p. 267 (middle top):** © Andresr/Shutterstock; **p. 267 (middle left):** © Tad Denson/Shutterstock; **p. 267 (middle right):** © Yuri Arcurs/Shutterstock; **p. 275:** © Jack Hollingsworth/Photodisc/Getty Images; **p. 292:** © Capital Humane Society, Lincoln, NE; **p. 296:** © Tracy tucker/iStockphoto; **p. 300:** © Abbas Momani/Agence France Presse/Getty Images; **p. 303:** © Phase4photography/Fotolia; **p. 349:** © Rachel Watson/Getty Images; **p. 354:** © Jacob Wackerhausen/iStockphoto; **p. 366:** © Iliene MacDonald/Alamy; **p. 367:** © Jason Stitt/Shutterstock; **p. 370:** © Mike Kemp/Getty Images; **p. 377:** © Simone van den Berg/Shutterstock; **p. 382:** © James Steidl/Shutterstock; **p. 394:** © Juan Gaertner/Shutterstock; **p. 395:** Intellistudies/Fotolia; **p. 407:** © Valentyn Volkov/Shutterstock; **p. 415:** © Mandy Godbehear/Shutterstock; **p. 428:** © Roger Jegg/Shutterstock; **p. 443:** © Fernando Alvarado/Corbis; **p. 469:** © Tina Chang/Corbis; **p. 480:** © Mandy Godbehear/Shutterstock; **p. 492:** © Tiyi99/Fotolia; **p. 504:** © Leoks/Shutterstock; **p. 505:** © Intellistudies/Fotolia; **p. 520:** © Alamy; **p. 526:** © Catherine Yeulet/iStockphoto; **p. 527:** © Diego Cervo/Shutterstock; **p. 556:** © Roger-Viollet/The Image Works; **p. 570:** © Bruce MacQueen/Fotolia; **p. 571:** © by Prentice-Hall. Used by permission of Pearson Education, Inc. **p. 573 (left):** © Joel Ryan/AP Images; **p. 573 (right):** © Evan Agostini/AP Images; **p. 575:** © JM11/Wennphotos/Newscom.

Text Credits

Chapter 1

Ember, Carol R., Ember, Melvin, and Peregrine, Peter N., Adapted from *Anthropology*. Copyright © and used by permission of Pearson Education, Inc.

Ember, Carol R., Ember, Melvin, and Peregrine, Peter N., From *Anthropology*. Copyright © and used by permission of Pearson Education, Inc.

Chapter 2

Armstrong, Gary and Kotler, Phillip, "Characteristics for Selecting a Brand Name," from *Marketing: An Introduction*. Copyright © 2009 by Pearson Education, Inc. Used by permission of Pearson Education, Inc.

Weixel, Suzanne and Wempen, Faithe, From *Food and Nutrition for You*. Copyright © and used by permission of Pearson Education, Inc.

Yudkin, Jeremy, From *Understanding Music*, 5/e. Copyright © 2008 by Pearson Education, Inc. Used by permission of Pearson Education, Inc.

Chapter 3

Biederman, Paul S., Adapted from *Travel and Tourism: An Industry Primer*, 1/e. Copyright © 2008 by Pearson Education, Inc. Used by permission of Pearson Education, Inc.

Carter, Carol, Bishop, Joyce, and Kravits, Sarah Lyman, From *Keys to Success*, 6/e. Copyright © and used by permission of Pearson Education, Inc.

DeVito, Joseph A., From *Human Communication*, pp. 17, 203, 268, 308. Copyright © 2006 by Pearson Education, Inc. Used by permission of Pearson Education, Inc.

Lee, Jasper S., Hutter, Jim, and Rudd, Rick, From *Introduction to Livestock and Companion Animals*. Copyright © and used by permission of Pearson Education, Inc.

Nichols, David C., "Existence of MTV Since 1981," from *Musical Encounters*. Copyright © and used by permission of Pearson Education, Inc.

Smith, Robert L. and Smith, Thomas M., From *Elements of Ecology*. Copyright © and used by permission of Pearson Education, Inc.

Chapter 4

Barkley, Elizabeth F., Adapted from *Crossroads*. Copyright © and used by permission of Pearson Education, Inc.

Ebert, Ronald J., Griffin, Ricky W., and Van Sykle, Barbara, From *Business Essentials*, 6/e. Copyright © 2007 by Pearson Education, Inc. Used by permission of Pearson Education, Inc.

Kishlansky, Mark, From *Civilization in the West*. Copyright © and used by permission of Pearson Education, Inc.

Wood, Samuel E., From *The World of Psychology*, pp. 116–117, 230, 330–331, 371, 597. Copyright © 2008 by Pearson Education, Inc. Used by permission of Pearson Education, Inc.

Chapter 5

Gerrig, Richard J. and Zimbardo, Phillip G., From *Psychology and Life: Discovering Psychology*, pp. 571–575. Copyright © 2009 by Pearson Education, Inc. Used by permission of Pearson Education, Inc.

Sayre, Henry M., From *The World of Art*. Copyright © and used by permission of Pearson Education, Inc.

Macionis, John J., From *Society*. Copyright © and used by permission of Pearson Education, Inc.

Chapter 6

Gerrig, Richard J. and Zimbardo, Philip G., From *Psychology and Life: Discovering Psychology*, pp. 571–575. Copyright © 2009 by Pearson Education, Inc. Used by permission of Pearson Education, Inc.

Wood, Samuel E., From *The World of Psychology*, pp. 116–117, 230, 330–331, 371, 597. Copyright © 2008 by Pearson Education, Inc. Used by permission of Pearson Education, Inc.

Chapter 7

Armstrong, Gary and Kotler, Phillip, From *Marketing: An Introduction*, 9/e. Copyright © 2009 by Pearson Education, Inc. Used by permission of Pearson Education, Inc.

Biederman, Paul S., Adapted from *Travel and Tourism: An Industry Primer*, 1/e. Copyright © 2008 by Pearson Education, Inc. Used by permission of Pearson Education, Inc.

Bovee, Courtland L., Thill, John V., and Schatzman, Barbara E., From *Business in Action*. Copyright © and used by permission of Pearson Education, Inc.

Goldfield, David, Adapted from *The American Journey*. Copyright © and used by permission of Pearson Education, Inc.

Horta, Jetty (Student). "A House Cleaning Mistake."

Wood, Samuel E., "Placing Events in Time Order," from *The World of Psychology*, pp. 116–117, 230, 330–331, 371, 597.

Copyright © 2008 by Pearson Education, Inc. Used by permission of Pearson Education, Inc.

Chapter 8

Bennett, Daniel (Student). "Scene of Destruction."

Sayre, Henry M., Adapted from *The World of Art.* Copyright © and used by permission of Pearson Education, Inc.

Chapter 9

DeVito, John, From *Human Communication,* pp. 17, 203, 268, 308. Copyright © 2006 by Pearson Education, Inc. Used by permission of Pearson Education, Inc.

Diamond, Jay and Diamond, Ellen, From *Fashion Apparel and Accessories and Home Furnishings,* 1/e. Copyright © 2007 by Pearson Education, Inc. Used by permission of Pearson Education, Inc.

Smith, Robert L. and Smith, Thomas M., From *Elements of Ecology.* Copyright © and used by permission of Pearson Education, Inc.

Walker, John R., From *Introduction to Hospitality Management,* 1/e. Copyright © 2004 by Pearson Education, Inc. Used by permission of Pearson Education, Inc.

Chapter 10

Jones, Lynn M. and Allen, Phyllis S., From *Beginnings of Interior Environments.* Copyright © and used by permission of Pearson Education, Inc.

Schmalleger, Frank J., From *Criminal Justice Today: An Introductory Text for the 21st Century,* 10/e. Copyright © 2009 by Pearson Education, Inc. Used by permission of Pearson Education, Inc.

Chapter 11

Armstrong, Gary and Kotler, Phillip, From *Marketing: An Introduction,* 9/e. Copyright © 2009 by Pearson Education, Inc. Used by permission of Pearson Education, Inc.

Welch, Kelly J., From *Family Life Now: Conversations about Marriages, Families and Relationships,* pp. 7, 252, 506, 523. Copyright © 2007 by Pearson Education, Inc. Used by permission of Pearson Education, Inc.

Chapter 12

Macionis, John J., Adapted from *Society.* Copyright © and used by permission of Pearson Education, Inc.

Wood, Samuel E., From *The World of Psychology,* pp. 116–117, 230, 330–331, 371, 597. Copyright ©

2008 by Pearson Education, Inc. Used by permission of Pearson Education, Inc.

Chapter 13

Henslin, James M., From *Essentials of Sociology: Down to Earth Approach,* pp. 98–99, 115, 119, 147, 351, 359–360, 390, 1331–1334. Copyright © 2007 by Pearson Education, Inc. Used by permission of Pearson Education, Inc.

Labensky, Sarah R. and Hause, Alan M., From *On Cooking.* Copyright © and used by permission of Pearson Education, Inc.

Welch, Kelly J., From *Family Life Now: Conversations about Marriages, Families and Relationships,* pp. 7, 252, 506, 523. Copyright © 2007 by Pearson Education, Inc. Used by permission of Pearson Education, Inc.

Chapter 14

Schmalleger, Frank J., From *Criminal Justice Today: An Introductory Text for the 21st Century,* 10/e. Copyright © 2009 by Pearson Education, Inc. Used by permission of Pearson Education, Inc.

Welch, Kelly J., From *Family Life Now: Conversations about Marriages, Families and Relationships,* pp. 7, 252, 506, 523. Copyright © 2007 by Pearson Education, Inc. Used by permission of Pearson Education, Inc.

Chapter 15

Henslin, James M., Adapted from *Essentials of Sociology: Down to Earth Approach,* pp. 98–99, 115, 119, 147, 351, 359–360, 390, 1331–1334. Copyright © 2007 by Pearson Education, Inc. Used by permission of Pearson Education, Inc.

Chapter 16

Armstrong, Gary and Kotler, Phillip, From *Marketing: An Introduction,* 9/e. Copyright © 2009 by Pearson Education, Inc. Used by permission of Pearson Education, Inc.

Chapter 17

Barkley, Elizabeth F., Adapted from *Crossroads.* Copyright © and used by permission of Pearson Education, Inc.

DeVito, Joseph A., Adapted from *The Interpersonal Communication Book,* pp. 48, 51–52, 141, 142, 179, 181–183, 201–211, 281–282. Copyright © 2007 by Pearson Education, Inc. Used by permission of Pearson Education, Inc.

Ebert, Ronald J., Griffin, Ricky W., and Van Sykle, Barbara, From *Business Essentials,* 6/e. Copyright © 2007 by Pearson Education, Inc. Used by permission of Pearson Education, Inc.

Ebert, Ronald J., Griffin, Ricky W., and Van Sykle, Barbara, From *Business Essentials*, 6/e. Copyright © 2007 by Pearson Education, Inc. Used by permission of Pearson Education, Inc.

Chapter 29

Diamond, Jay and Diamond, Ellen, From *Fashion Apparel and Accessories and Home Furnishings*, 1/e. Copyright © 2007 by Pearson Education, Inc. Used by permission of Pearson Education, Inc.

Tate, Sharon L., Adapted from *Inside Fashion Design*. Copyright © and used by permission of Pearson Education, Inc.

Zelalnski, Paul and Fisher, Mary P., From *The Art of Seeing*. Copyright © 2005 by Prentice-Hall, Inc. Used by permission of Pearson Education, Inc.

Chapter 30

Marston, Sallie A., Knox, Paul L., Liverman, Diana M., Adapted from *World Regions in Global Context: People, Places and Environments*, 3/e. Copyright © 2008 by Pearson Education, Inc. Used by permission of Pearson Education, Inc.

Chapter 31

Bovee, Courtland L. and Thill, John V., From *Business Communication Today*. Copyright © and used by permission of Pearson Education, Inc.

DeVito, Joseph A., From *Human Communication*, pp. 17, 203, 268, 308. Copyright © 2006 by Pearson Education, Inc. Used by permission of Pearson Education, Inc.

Lannon, John, From *Technical Communication*. Copyright © and used by permission of Pearson Education, Inc.

Zinsser, William and Harty, Kevin J., Adapted from *Strategies for Business and Technical Writing*. Copyright © and used by permission of Pearson Education, Inc.

Chapter 32

Berman, Audrey J., Snyder, Shirlee, Kozier, Barbara J. and Erb, Glenora, From *Kozier and Erb's Fundamentals of Nursing*, 8/e. Copyright © 2008 by Pearson Education, Inc. Used by permission of Pearson Education, Inc.

Chapter 33

Amen, Daniel G., From *Change Your Brain, Change Your Life*. Copyright © by Daniel G. Amen. Used by permission of Daniel G. Amen.

Audesirk, Teresa, Audesirk, Gerald, Byers, Bruce E., From *Biology*. Copyright © by Prentice-Hall. Used by permission of Pearson Education, Inc.

Bloom, Alan, "Making Cell Phones in the Classroom a Community Builder," from *The Teaching Professor* by Alan Bloom. Copyright © 2007 by Alan Bloom. Used by permission of Magna Publications.

Ember, Carol R., Ember, Melvin, and Peregrine, Peter N., Adapted from *Anthropology*. Copyright © and used by permission of Pearson Education, Inc.

Jones, Charisse, "Light Skin Versus Dark," from *Glamour*, September 1995. Copyright © 1995 by Charisse Jones. Used by permission of Charisse Jones.

Kauchak, Don and Eggen, Paul, From *Introduction to Teaching*. Copyright © and used by permission of Pearson Education, Inc.

Pruitt, B. E., Allegrante, John P., and Prothrow, Deborah Stith, From *Health*. Copyright © by Prentice-Hall. Used by permission of Pearson Education, Inc.

Walker, John R., From *Introduction to Hospitality Management*, 1/e. Copyright © 2004 by Pearson Education, Inc. Used by permission of Pearson Education, Inc.

Wiesel, Elie, From *Night* by Elie Wiesel, translated by Marion Wiesel. Translation copyright © 2006 by Marion Wiesel. Used by permission of Hill and Wang, a division of Farrar, Straus and Giroux, LLC.

Index